GEORGE LUCAS

Also by Brian Jay Jones

Jim Henson: The Biography

Washington Irving: An American Original

GEORGE LUCAS

A LIFE

BRIAN JAY JONES

Little, Brown and Company

New York Boston London

Little, Brown and Company
Hachette Book Group
1290 Avenue of the Americas, New York, NY 10104
littlebrown.com

First Edition: December 2016

Little, Brown and Company is a division of Hachette Book Group, Inc. The Little, Brown name and logo are trademarks of Hachette Book Group, Inc.

The publisher is not responsible for websites (or their content) that are not owned by the publisher.

The Hachette Speakers Bureau provides a wide range of authors for speaking events. To find out more, go to hachettespeakersbureau.com or call (866) 376-6591.

ISBN 978-0-316-25744-2
LCCN 2016941644

10 9 8 7 6 5 4 3 2 1

LSC-C

Printed in the United States of America

For Barb

(The Force is strong with this one.)

Contents

GEORGE LUCAS

Prologue

Out of Control

March 1976

R2-D2 refused to work.

It wasn't stubbornness on the part of the droid—a trait that would endear the character to millions of *Star Wars* fans around the world. Rather, as the first day of filming began on *Star Wars* in the Tunisian desert on the morning of March 22, 1976, R2-D2 *wouldn't* work. His batteries were already dead.

The little droid wasn't the only one with a problem. Several other robots, operated via remote control by crew members standing just out of sight of the movie camera, were also malfunctioning. Some fell over, others never moved at all, while still others had their signals scrambled by Arabic radio broadcasts bouncing off the desert floor, sending them careening wildly out of control across the sand or crashing into one another. "The robots would go bananas, bumping into each other, falling down, breaking," said Mark Hamill, the sun-washed twenty-four-year-old actor playing hero Luke Skywalker. "It took hours to get them set up again."[1]

The movie's director, a brooding, bearded thirty-one-year-old Californian named George Lucas, simply waited. If a robot worked properly, even for a moment, Lucas would shoot as much footage of it as he possibly could until the droid sputtered to a stop. Other times, he'd have a malfunctioning unit pulled along by invisible wire, until the wire broke or the droid fell over. It didn't matter anyhow; Lucas planned to fix everything in the editing room. It was where he preferred to be anyway, as opposed to squinting through a film camera in the middle of the desert.

It was the first of what would be eighty-four long, excruciating days filming *Star Wars*—twenty days severely over-schedule. And the shoot was a disaster almost from the beginning. "I was very depressed about the whole thing," Lucas said.[2]

Lucas's misery was due partly to the fact that he felt he had already lost control of his own film. He laid the blame at the feet of parsimonious executives at 20th Century Fox, who had nickel-and-dimed him every step of the way, denying him the money he needed to ensure that everything worked. But the suits at Fox were skeptical; science fiction, they insisted, was a dead genre, and the necessary props, costumes, and special effects were expensive. As far as the studio was concerned, Lucas could get by on a shoestring budget, and simply fix his robot problems as he went along. "It was purely a case of Fox not putting up the money until it was too late," seethed Lucas. "Every day we would lose an hour or so due to those robots, and we wouldn't have lost that time if we'd had another six weeks to finish them and test them and have them working before we started."[3]

It wasn't just the remote-control robots that were giving him trouble. Anthony Daniels, a classically trained, very British actor who'd been cast in the role of the protocol droid C-3PO, was miserable inside his ill-fitting, gleaming gold plastic costume, and unable to see or hear much of anything. With every movement he was poked or cut—"covered in scars and scratches," he sighed—and when he fell over, as he often did, he could only wait for someone on the crew to notice and help him to his feet.[4] Within the first week of filming, Daniels despaired that he would ever complete the movie in one piece. "It was very, very difficult getting things to work," Lucas said later. "The truth is that the robots didn't work at all. Threepio works very painfully.... I couldn't get Artoo to go more than a few feet without running into something.... Everything was a prototype...like, 'Gee, we're going to build this—we have no money, but have to try to make this work. But nothing really worked."[5] Lucas vowed he'd never cede control over his films to executives at the studios again. What did they know about filmmaking? "They tell people what to do without reason," Lucas complained. "Sooner or later, they decided they know more about making movies than directors. Studio heads. You can't fight them because they've got the money."[6]

If *Star Wars* worked out, one thing would have to change for sure: *he'd* control the money.

Still, there were some things he'd never control, no matter how much he might wish otherwise. The wildly unpredictable weather in Tunisia, for example, wasn't making production any easier. During the first week of filming, it began raining in Tunisia's Nefta Valley for the first time in seven years and didn't stop for four days. Equipment and vehicles bogged down in the mud, requiring assistance from the Tunisian army to pull everything out of the muck. It was often cold in the morning and blazing hot by afternoon, and Lucas would begin most days in his brown coat, hands shoved deep in the pockets as he peered through the eyepiece of the camera; as the sun rose higher in the sky, he would shrug off his coat, put on his sunglasses, and direct his actors in a checked work shirt, with a baseball cap pulled low over his eyes. When it wasn't raining, high winds tore up the sets, ripping apart the sandcrawler and blowing one set, as a crew member put it, "halfway to Algeria."[7]

And sand, it seemed, got into everything, stinging eyes, abrading skin, and getting into nearly every crack and crevice. Though Lucas kept his Panavision cameras wrapped in plastic sheeting to prevent any damage from wind and sand, a lens from one camera was still nearly ruined. He was plagued by equipment problems as well as just plain bad luck. A truck caught fire, damaging several robots. When trucks failed, Lucas would move equipment on the backs of donkeys.

By the end of the first two weeks of filming, Lucas was exhausted. With the constant setbacks caused by bad weather, malfunctioning droids, and ill-fitting costumes, he felt he'd gotten only about two-thirds of what he'd wanted on film—and what he had, he wasn't happy with. "It kept getting cut down because of all the drama," said Lucas, "and I didn't think it'd turned out very well." He was so upset he even skipped a party he hosted himself to mark the end of the Tunisian shoot, shutting himself into his hotel room to wallow in his own misery. "I was seriously, seriously depressed at that point, because nothing had gone right," he sighed. "Everything was screwed up. I was desperately unhappy."[8]

A little more than a year before it was scheduled to hit theaters, if it ever did, the *Star Wars* project was a mess, and the movie was going to be terrible.

Lucas was certain of it.

PART I

HOPE

1944–1973

1

Scrawny Little Devil

1944–1962

The victorious underdog—and the more brilliant and unappreciated the better—was a narrative George Lucas would always love. Lucas liked to think there was a triumphant dark horse involved with his ancestors somewhere along their journey, "some criminal or somebody who got thrown out of England or France," he told an interviewer. But it's no secret that Lucas enjoys being enigmatic; it's practically in his blood. "My family came from nowhere," he once explained. "Nobody knows where we originally came from."[1]

As a fourth-generation northern Californian, Lucas could already trace his ancestry back further than most Americans, with the roots of his family tree burrowing down deep into the soil of Modesto, California, after winding through Arkansas and Illinois and Virginia nearly a century before the American Revolution. But "that's it," Lucas insisted, going no further. Whether he came from a line of colonial farmers or cobblers or brick masons didn't matter, and looking back wasn't his way. "I'm always sort of living for tomorrow, for better or for worse," he said. "It's just a personality quirk."[2] There was one thing, however, of which he was certain. "It's great not to have been born a prince," Lucas once noted. "I appreciate that. I truly believe in this country, that you can do anything if you apply yourself."[3]

Apply yourself. It was the kind of admonition that George Lucas Sr.—Lucas's small-town Methodist father—could have made. And, waving a finger stridently in his only son's face, probably *had*.

George Lucas Sr., as his son later described him, "was a very old-fashioned kind of guy...kind of a classic small-town businessman who you'd see in a movie."[4] As the owner of Modesto's most successful stationery store—and president of the local Retail Merchants Bureau, no less—George Lucas Sr. was smart, conservative, a pillar of the Modesto community. And he had been working hard—*applying himself*—practically all his life.

George Walton Lucas Sr. was born in 1913 in Laton, California—then as now little more than a dot on the map just south of Fresno—the only son among the bevy of daughters of Walton and Maud Lucas. Walton, an oil field worker, was also a diabetic, and in 1928, when George Sr. was fifteen, Walton died of complications from the disease—a condition that would leapfrog one generation on its way through to Walton's famous grandson. Within a year of Walton's passing, Maud had moved George Sr. and his older sister Eileen twice, first to nearby Fresno, and then more than ninety miles up the San Joaquin Valley to Modesto, where George Sr. would live the rest of his life.

Founded in 1870 among the wheat fields lining the Tuolumne River, Modesto was established as one of the final stops on the Central Pacific Railroad as it wound its way northward from Los Angeles toward the capital at Sacramento. The town forefathers, in fact, had deferentially insisted on naming the new settlement Ralston, after William Ralston, the director of the Central Pacific. Ralston, however, declined to have the town named for him, a touch of humility that allegedly inspired the town's new designation: Modesto, the Spanish word for *modesty*.

Despite its name, the little town of Modesto had big ambitions, reflecting California's can-do attitude as well as its tendency toward immediate gratification. By the time it was formally established in 1884, there were twenty-five buildings on the site, most of them housing businesses whose owners—sensing the ample opportunity that came with living near the railroad—had simply picked up their homes and office buildings and relocated to Modesto from nearby Paradise City or Tuolumne City.

Modesto took its time to become a metropolis—it wouldn't hit 100,000 residents until the 1980s—but as the town grew, it took its civic pride seriously, and by the early 1900s was boasting of its residents' well-manicured lawns and colorful rosebushes, as well as its commitment to education and culture. In 1912 its proud residents erected an enormous arch to welcome visitors as they bounced down Ninth Street in their automobiles—a new and exotic invention that no one was quite sure was going to catch on—and passed under the city's motto in blazing incandescent lights: WATER, WEALTH, CONTENTMENT, HEALTH.[5] It was a motto as straightforward as its residents.

By the time George Lucas Sr. arrived in Modesto with his mother and sister in 1929, its population had grown to just slightly under fourteen thousand, sprawled out across a well-organized series of flat grids typical of western towns. As the United States began its slump into the Great Depression, George Sr. split his time between classes at Modesto High School and a job as an apprentice to a mechanic in a typewriter repair shop, already plying a trade at the age of sixteen. In the 1930 census, both Maud and Eileen listed their occupation as "none," making George the lone and much-needed source of support for his sister and widowed mother.[6] Earning a living, then, was a responsibility George Sr. took seriously. There would be no frittering away his time, no goofing off, no daydreaming. George Sr. decided he'd study law and become a lawyer, and applied himself in high school to getting good grades. And yet, at Modesto High School, the serious young man—stiff-backed, with a head of dark, wavy hair and a rail-thin body made for buttoned-up suits—fell in love at first sight with a girl in his history class and immediately informed his mother that he was going to marry her—even if he didn't actually know her name yet.[7]

After a bit of prying, George Sr. learned he'd been smitten by Dorothy Bomberger, a young woman who belonged to one of Modesto's oldest and most prominent families. That their famous son could later declare himself a fourth-generation Californian was due entirely to his pedigree as a Bomberger, a family whose roots in America predated the Declaration of Independence. For generations the Bombergers had been quietly making the investments in real estate that would give their family both wealth and reputation. By the 1900s, various branches of Bombergers owned and managed property across the San Joaquin Valley—and Dorothy's father, Paul, had additional interests in seed companies and car dealerships—making them one of the valley's best-known and most prosperous families. The comings and goings of Bombergers would be a regular topic on the society pages of the *Modesto Bee and News-Herald.*

Dorothy was a dark-eyed and dark-haired beauty, wispy and some-what fragile, but a good catch—and she and George Sr. were a good-looking, popular, and utterly devoted couple. In their senior year, they were co-starring in the class play, a three-act comedy called *Nothing but the Truth,*[8] and George would serve as class president with Dorothy as his vice president. After graduation, they briefly attended Modesto Business College together, where George joined the Delta Sigma fraternity, while Dorothy continued to be active with the Phi Gamma Girls' Club.[9] Soon, George took a job with Lee Brothers, one of Modesto's newer but smaller stationery stores, serving customers out of a cramped shop on Tenth Street. To his surprise, he found he actually liked the stationery business. "It was pure dumb luck," he said later. "I wasn't even sure what 'stationery' meant."[10] His plans for studying law were abandoned.[11]

On August 3, 1933, George Sr. and Dorothy were married at the local Methodist Episcopal Church. Given the Bomberger connection, it was hailed as a "wedding of widespread interest" by the local news-paper, which dutifully reported on the planning and mailing of invitations to the ceremony.[12] George was twenty, Dorothy eighteen—and the young couple set off on their way with the nation officially in the midst of the Depression. But while Dorothy was educated and well connected, George, with his stiff back up and conservative Methodist hackles raised, refused to permit his wife to work. Working—*applying oneself*—and supporting a family were a man's obligation. George would work, then, while Dorothy would stay home and look after the children George was certain were all but inevitable.

Shortly after the wedding the Lucases moved to Fresno, where George had landed a job with H. S. Crocker Co., Inc., one of California's largest stationery stores. The job paid $75 per week, a respectable sum at a time when a new refrigerator could be had for a hundred dollars.[13] But Dorothy missed her family—so in early 1934, after only five months in Fresno, back they went to Modesto, where George found work at Modesto's chief stationery outfit, the L. M. Morris Company.[14]

L. M. Morris, initially established by a group of brothers in 1904, was one of the oldest stationery stores in the region. LeRoy Morris had bought the business from his brothers in 1918, renamed it the L. M. Morris Company, and made the store a cornerstone of downtown Modesto, where it would remain at its same I Street address for nearly sixty years. By the time George Sr. began his employment there in 1934, the company was proudly celebrating its thirtieth anniversary.[15]

Morris specialized in office furniture, typewriters, and adding machines, but over the years it had begun to diversify, adding motion picture cameras and projectors, children's books and toys, and a gift department its owner boasted was "full of the latest novelties." As usual, George Sr. applied himself with gusto—"I liked the kind of customer I got to serve," he explained later—and quickly distinguished himself among Morris's twelve employees.[16] Sure enough, when LeRoy Morris placed a gigantic ad in the *Modesto Bee* in late 1934, there, just below Morris's own photo, was a picture of George Sr., staring back at readers with just a hint of a smile.[17]

George was more than just hardworking; he was ambitious and savvy, and he knew how to read people. And it didn't hurt that he and LeRoy Morris hit it off immediately, both perhaps knowing that they needed each other. While the fifty-year-old Morris had two grown married daughters, he had no son, no successor to whom he could pass on the business.[18] Meanwhile, George Sr.—who had lost Walton Lucas to diabetes less than a decade earlier—had no father, no paternal figure, no family legacy to inherit. Each filled a role for the other. It was a subtle, complex mentor-apprentice relationship, exactly the kind that George Sr.'s own son would covet—and explore on the movie screen—decades later.

Things were going well enough that only a little more than a year into his employment with Morris, George Sr. somewhat brazenly mentioned to his employer that he hoped to have a store of his own, "or at least part of one," by the time he was twenty-five.[19] In 1937—when George Sr. was twenty-four—Morris offered his industrious protégé 10 percent of the business, with an eye toward an eventual full partnership. George protested that he had no money to invest in the firm, but Morris wouldn't hear of it. "You'll sign a note you owe me so much," Morris told the young man. "This business is no good if it won't pay out."[20] With an official share in the company, George Sr. began working six days a week, determined to vindicate Morris's professional and paternal devotion.

While George Sr. was concentrating on business at L. M. Morris, Dorothy was attending to their home life with an equal dedication. In late 1934 she gave birth to their first child, a daughter named Ann, followed two years later by a second daughter they christened Katherine, but whom everyone would always call Katy or Kate. With his family growing and business succeeding, George bought a lot at 530 Ramona Avenue out on the edge of Modesto and, using $5,000 borrowed from Dorothy's parents, built a respectable single-story stuccoed house he was certain he and Dorothy would fill with more children.

But two pregnancies in three years had taken a toll on Dorothy's health. Delicate from the start, and likely suffering from pancreatitis, Dorothy found each pregnancy harder than the last, compelling her to take long periods of bed rest—and after Kate's birth, doctors advised her to stop having children.[21] Yet she and George would continue to try to conceive over the next eight years, suffering through at least two miscarriages.

Finally, in late 1943, Dorothy became pregnant again, this time with a baby she carried to term. At 5:30 a.m. on Sunday, May 14, 1944—a pleasant, clear Mother's Day morning—Dorothy gave birth to a son. Perhaps recognizing that with Dorothy's frail health, this might be his only chance for a namesake, George abandoned the name Jeffrey, which had earlier been considered for the newborn, in favor of a name much more appropriate for an heir apparent: George Walton Lucas Jr. The baby was very small—only five pounds, fourteen ounces—but healthy, squirming so much when the attending doctor put the infant on Dorothy's stomach that she nearly dropped him. "Don't let him fall off," she warned. "This is the only son I've got!"[22]

Like his parents, George Jr. had dark hair and dark eyes, as well as another distinguishing feature that ran through the Lucas line: ears that had a tendency to stick out. George Jr.'s, in fact, were more prominent than most, and one was even a bit floppy—a defect that George Sr. was quick to remedy by taping it up. George Sr. would eventually proclaim it "a good ear,"[23] but George Jr.'s ears, which leaned upward and stuck out, would always be one of his defining features. "[He] was a scrawny little guy with big ears," recalled sister Kate warmly.[24]

Scrawny. It was one of the many diminutive adjectives Lucas would hear for decades. As a toddler "[he] was quite small," said his mother. "Really a peanut then."[25] At age six, Lucas weighed thirty-five pounds; by high school he would reach his full height of five-foot-six and barely tip the scales at a hundred pounds. "A scrawny little devil," said George Sr.[26]

Lucas's youngest sister, Wendy, would be born three years later, the last child Dorothy would have. Perhaps predictably, the two pregnancies had severely taxed her strength, and for most of George Jr.'s childhood, Dorothy would spend much of her time in and out of hospitals or confined to bed. "Her health kind of went downhill," remembered Kate. The care of the children was left largely to an outgoing housekeeper named Mildred Shelley, whom everyone called Till. Till could be strict and quick with the back of her hand, but she was also loud and funny, telling stories in a southern drawl, and the Lucas children adored her. Because of Till, said Kate, "we were never without a mother figure."[27] But it was George, she thought, who had a special place in Till's heart. "He was the only boy in the family, so he was sort of the apple of everybody's eye," said Kate.[28] For his part, Lucas would always speak fondly of the lively Till. "I have very warm feelings about that time," he said—a positively glowing remembrance from the famously tight-lipped Lucas.[29]

In 1949, when George Jr. was five years old, LeRoy Morris—making good on his promise of a decade earlier—sold George Lucas Sr. the L. M. Morris Company. Morris and Lucas announced their transaction on January 26 in the pages of the *Modesto Bee,* after which Morris retired—and unexpectedly died seven days later.[30] "He was one of God's gentlemen," George Sr. said of his partner, surrogate father, and benefactor. "He prepared me to little by little take over his business.[31] Now George Sr. planned to do the same for his own son. If all went as intended, George Jr. would work hard—*apply himself*—join the company, and, little by little, take over the family business. It was an ambitious goal—and it would also prove to be a major point of contention between father and son.

For George Lucas Jr., growing up in Modesto as the son of the town's most prosperous stationer was never a bad life. But Lucas would always remain ambivalent, and slightly conflicted, about his childhood. "I had my share of traumas and problems," he said later, "but at the same time I enjoyed it quite a bit."[32] At times his father irritated him; each summer George Sr. would force his son to shave his head down to a tight crew cut, a ritual Lucas hated. "My father was strict," Lucas noted later, though even that memory became somewhat muddled. "I mean, he wasn't *overly* strict," Lucas added. "I mean, he was reasonable. And he was fair. My father was extremely fair."[33] Fair or not, when it came down to it, Lucas remembered being "very angry" with his father for most of his childhood.

While Lucas's most devoted boyhood companion was probably his younger sister, Wendy, he did have a stable group of friends, including best friend John Plummer, whom Lucas met when he was four and would remain a lifelong friend, and the slightly older George Frankenstein. The three of them would regularly play together at Lucas's house on Ramona Avenue, where even Plummer and Frankenstein gave George Sr. a wide berth. "My memory is, you never crossed him," said Frankenstein of Lucas's father. "I mean, if you ever did something to tick him off...he was like a one-strike kind of person."[34] As John Plummer put it, "Every time Mr. Lucas came around, you just kind of hid."[35]

Still, there were advantages to hanging out with the son of a stationer: George Jr. could get the latest toys and gadgets right off the shelves of his father's store. "He had all the goodies," said Frankenstein, "and he was very willing to share."[36] George was particularly proud of sharing a gigantic three-engine Lionel train, which, he admitted, "took up most of my bedroom," winding through elaborate miniature sets George had made using army men, toy cars, and weeds and small plants pulled from the yard.[37] At one point he even managed to lay his hands on concrete from a local lumberyard, which he and his friends poured into handmade molds to form small buildings for the train to whiz past. Later he would build small dioramas—which he always called "environments"—that he would display in a wooden case with a glass top and side. "I was always interested in building things," said Lucas, "so I had a little shed out back where I had a lot of tools, and I would build chess sets and dollhouses and cars—lots and lots of race cars that we would push around and run down hills and things."[38]

One of his most memorable projects—built with the help of the always willing Plummer—was an elaborately constructed kid-sized roller coaster that used a winding coil of phone cable to pull a cart up to the top of a steep incline—at which point the cart would be released to go clattering down another series of ramps to the ground. "How we didn't kill people, I don't know," confessed Plummer.[39] "It was probably only four feet tall, but we did it. It was fun, it was a great event; all the neighborhood kids came over. And we kind of got known for doing stuff like that. George was creative. He wasn't a leader, but he was much more imaginative....He always came up with a lot of the ideas."[40]

"When I was very young, I loved make-believe," said Lucas. "But it was the kind of make-believe that used all the technological toys I could come by, like model airplanes and cars. I suppose that an extension of that interest led to what later occupied my mind, the *Star Wars* stories."[41] Still, "there wasn't much as a kid that inspired me in what I did as an adult."[42] Or so he would always claim.

Unlike a later friend and collaborator, Steven Spielberg, who made magical childhoods a centerpiece of many of his films, Lucas never had a romantic or idealized view of childhood. "I was very much aware that growing up wasn't pleasant, it was just...frightening," Lucas said later. "I remember that I was unhappy a lot of the time. Not really unhappy—I enjoyed my childhood. But I guess all kids, from their point of view, feel depressed and intimidated. Although I had a great time, my strongest impression was that I was always on the lookout for the evil monster that lurked around the corner."[43]

Sometimes the monsters were the other kids on his own block, who bullied and intimidated the small George Jr., holding him down while taking his shoes off his feet and throwing them into the lawn sprinklers. George wouldn't even fight back, leaving his sister Wendy to chase away the aggressors and retrieve his wet shoes.[44]

It makes sense, then, that throughout much of his life, the diminutive Lucas would seek out big brother figures to serve as mentors and protectors. One of the first was the fiancé of George's oldest sister, Ann; Lucas was absolutely devoted to him. "That's one of the ways of learning," Lucas acknowledged later. "You attach yourself to somebody older and wiser than you, learn everything they have to teach, and move on to your own accomplishments." When the young man was killed in Korea, Lucas was devastated. It was little wonder Lucas always looked back on his childhood with slightly jumbled emotions. It was a "normal, tough, repressed childhood filled with fear and trepidation all over the place," said Lucas. "But generally I enjoyed it. It was good."[45]

He was equally ambivalent about Modesto. For years, a slight embarrassment would tinge the way he talked about his hometown. While he would eventually come to embrace his status as a son of Modesto with pride — and his film *American Graffiti* would practically make it a destination — Lucas was, for the first several decades of his life, always slightly self-conscious about his Modesto roots. When asked where he was from, Lucas would respond with an ambiguous and unhelpful "California." If pressed, he would admit to coming from "northern California," or sometimes the slightly more specific "south of San Francisco," before finally muttering, "Modesto."[46] Still, he knew his hometown had its charms. "Modesto was really Norman Rockwell, *Boys' Life* magazine...raking leaves on Saturday afternoons and having bonfires," Lucas put it later. "Just very classic Americana."[47]

And for a boy growing up in the 1950s, that Americana also involved regular attendance at Sunday school — an obligation Lucas quickly grew to loathe. "When I got to be old enough — twelve or thirteen — I rebelled against it," he said.[48] In fact, even as a child, Lucas already had a complicated relationship with God; at six — an age when most children see God as simply a benevolent bearded man in the sky — Lucas had a "very profound" mystical experience that would shape the way he looked at spirituality in his life and work. "It centered around God," he recalled. He found himself wondering "'What is God?' But more than that, 'What is reality? What is this?' It's as if you reach a point and suddenly you say, 'Wait a second — What is the world? What are we? What am I? How do I function in this, and what's going on here?'"[49] They were questions Lucas would struggle with, explore, and, with the creation of the Force in *Star Wars*, attempt to answer in his films.

"I have strong feelings about God and the nature of life, but I'm not devoted to one particular faith," Lucas said later.[50] While Lucas was raised a Methodist, he was more intrigued by the services at Till's German Lutheran church, where worshippers still wore broad hats and bonnets and spoke in sharply accented, reverential tones. Lucas was fascinated by the formality of their rituals, which were much like an elaborate, well-scripted play in which everyone knew their roles. "The ceremony provides something essential for people," Lucas acknowledged.[51] He would always remain "curious, academically, about organized religion," and his views on God and religion would continue to evolve over time.[52] He would eventually describe his religion as a melding of Methodist and Buddhist. ("It's Marin County," he said in 2002, noting the area's famously left-leaning ways. "We're *all* Buddhists up here.")[53] For now, however, he would remain a devoted, albeit frustrated, Methodist. George Lucas Sr. would have it no other way.

As bad as Sunday school could be, for Lucas it had nothing on the regular classroom. He remembered being terrified his first day of classes at John Muir Elementary School—"a feeling of total panic," he called it—and things would never get much better: "I was never very good in school, so I was never very enthusiastic about it."[54] In the beginning, he seemed to show promise. "He did well. He was bright," noted Dorothy Elliot, his second-grade teacher. "[But] George was... quiet as a little mouse. He never spoke unless you spoke to him first."[55] To Lucas, however, there just wasn't much in school worth talking about. "One of the big problems I had, more than anything else, was that I always wanted to learn something other than what was being taught," he said. "I was *bored*."[56] While he enjoyed his art classes and diligently performed in the third-grade play—where he received last billing—Lucas hated math, his spelling was terrible, and writing would always be a painfully slow process. Even in high school, he had to rely on his sister Wendy, three years younger, to read through his assignments, looking for errors.

Lucas may have struggled with spelling and writing, but he enjoyed reading, a pursuit likely encouraged by his mother, who spent long stretches recuperating with a book in and out of hospital beds. His mother had often read him Grimm's fairy tales as a toddler; but when he was left on his own, Lucas's tastes ran toward adventure stories like *Kidnapped*, *Treasure Island*, and *Swiss Family Robinson*. He also amassed an enormous collection of Landmark books, a series of histories and biographies written for younger readers. "I was addicted to [them]," said Lucas. "I used to love to read those books. It started me on a lifelong love of history.... As a kid I spent a lot of time trying to relate the past to the present."[57]

Still, Lucas would admit later, "I wasn't that much of a reader."[58] And yet, that wasn't entirely true either. Besides the Landmark books, there was something else Lucas collected and read ravenously: comic books. "I was never ashamed that I read a lot of comic books," he said.[59] Lucas discovered comics at a moment when they were selling in the millions in nearly every genre imaginable, from romance and western, to crime and horror, to superheroes and science fiction. John Plummer, whose father had a connection with the operator of the local newsstand, would bring home armloads of comics every week, their front covers missing and filed as unsold. "George used to sit out on my front porch all the time just reading them," Plummer remembered.[60] Even long after Plummer had been called inside for dinner, George would stay on the porch by himself, hunched over his pile of comics, reading intently.

Eventually, George and his sister Wendy would pool their allowances to buy comics of their own, ten for a dollar, and soon had a collection large enough that their father built a shed in the backyard with a space devoted solely to them. George and Wendy would throw quilts on the ground inside the shed and sit for hours, poring over comic books.[61] It was no wonder Lucas was attracted to comics; given his struggles with spelling and writing, his learning style was clearly more visual than verbal. Comics were "storytelling through pictures,"[62] he said, and pointed out that it was in comic books where he first learned "strange facts" and exotic vocabulary, words like *scone*.[63] At Lucas's best, his own storytelling style would mimic the colorful rat-a-tat bravura of the comic book page: words and images working together to propel the action forward, with little time for speeches or soliloquies.

Perhaps predictably, Lucas preferred science fiction comics to superheroes. "I liked adventures in outer space," he admitted.[64] While

Lucas may have swooned over the sumptuous Wally Wood art and science fiction stories-with-a-twist in EC's hugely popular *Weird Science* comics, he preferred DC's more colorful intergalactic policeman, Tommy Tomorrow, who had taken up regular residency in the back pages of Superman's *Action Comics*. Plummer thought he understood his friend's preferences. "One of the things that came out of them... was the values that were so important to us," Plummer said. "There were the good guys and the bad guys. I think that put a pretty strong [im]print on him."[65]

If Lucas had to choose a favorite character, however, it wasn't to be found in the pages of a science fiction comic at all. Rather, it was Scrooge McDuck, the money-hoarding, globe-trotting uncle of Donald Duck, who starred in his very own comic book, *Walt Disney's Uncle Scrooge*, published monthly by Dell. As written and drawn by Carl Barks, Uncle Scrooge's stories were smart, funny, and genuinely sophisticated, with Barks sending Scrooge and an elaborate cast of colorful characters on adventures in South American gold mines, atop Far Eastern mountains, under the oceans, back in time, or in outer space.

Lucas loved it—there would be a bit of Uncle Scrooge's continent-hopping adventuring in Indiana Jones's DNA—and was fascinated not only by Scrooge's exploits but also by his conniving four-color capitalist ways. "Work smarter, not harder," was Scrooge's motto, and his stories were full of inventive schemes that, more often than not, made him even richer and more successful. In Scrooge's world, hard work paid off, yes—but so did cleverness and a desire to do something in a way no one had ever thought of before. Scrooge's ethic reflected those of writer-artist Carl Barks, who hailed "honor, honesty, [and] allowing other people to believe in their own ideas, not trying to force everyone into one form."[66]

Lucas found it all exciting and inspiring. "To me, Uncle Scrooge... is a perfect indicator of the American psyche," he observed later. "There's so much that is precisely the essence of America about him that it's staggering."[67] The lessons Lucas learned from Uncle Scrooge would, to some extent, shape the kind of artist and businessman he would become in the future: conservative and driven, believing strongly in his own vision and pursuing it aggressively, while at the same time nursing just a tinge of nostalgia for better times that may or may not ever have existed. Years later, when he was just on his way to amassing a fortune that would rival Scrooge's own, one of the first artworks Lucas would buy was a page of Carl Barks's original art for an *Uncle Scrooge* comic — a coy tip of the hat to his four-color forefather.

Besides Carl Barks, there was another artist Lucas adored who did the same kind of "storytelling in pictures" that Lucas admired in Barks, albeit in a slightly different format. Whenever he had the chance, Lucas would track down copies of the *Saturday Evening Post* just so he could stare at the gorgeously painted photorealistic front covers by illustrator Norman Rockwell. Rockwell's work for the *Post* was intentionally sentimental, with boys and girls cheerfully swimming, ice-skating, raking leaves, playing ball, climbing trees, or celebrating Christmas or the Fourth of July. Even if they were getting into mischief, they were rarely in trouble, and instead were looked on kindly by understanding parents and authority figures. Lucas got a kick out of the detail in Rockwell's work; it was like a comic strip compressed into one panel, and trying to figure out the entire story Rockwell was telling in a painting became something of a parlor game for Lucas. "Every picture [shows] either the middle or the end of the story, and you can already see the beginning even though it's not there," Lucas said. "You can see all the missing parts…because that one frame tells everything you need to know."[68]

Rockwell, Lucas said, offered "a sense of what America was thinking, what [Americans'] ideals were, and what was in their hearts."[69] It didn't matter that Lucas had never splashed in a swimmin' hole or seen a sparkling white Christmas, or that he could barely play baseball; Rockwell's paintings were snapshots of Life as It Ought to Be. Lucas would never be mawkish about his own childhood, but he could be very sentimental about the one that he *might* have had in a Rockwell painting. Decades later, as with the work of Carl Barks, Lucas would also collect the art of Norman Rockwell. To Lucas, it was something rare and valuable: art that actually spoke to him.

In May 1954, George Lucas Jr. turned ten—and that summer came a new addition to the Lucas home that would change his life forever: television.

For his first ten years, George—like millions of Americans at the time—would sit on the floor in front of the radio, mesmerized by radio dramas, many of which used incredibly elaborate and convincing sound effects. "I've always been fascinated by the fantasy of radio," Lucas said later. "I loved to listen and imagine what the images would look like."[70] He was particularly fond of suspenseful thrillers like *Inner Sanctum* and *The Whistler*, as well as adventures like *The Lone Ranger*. Radio, he said, "played an important part in my life." But it would be nothing compared to television.[71]

John Plummer had actually gotten a television set first. In 1949, Plummer's father brought home a little Champion TV set, which he put in the garage, then constructed a small set of bleachers so neighbors could crowd around to watch boxing. George's own father was intrigued but skeptical; he would wait a few years for the technology to improve before he made an investment in such an expensive device. While George Jr. would watch as much television as he could over at the Plummer house, he would have to wait five more years for a TV of his own.

Once he had one, however, he wasn't quite sure what to do with it. The problem, as Lucas remembered it, was that "there wasn't much to watch on television."[72] Still, the *Modesto Bee* dutifully reported the television schedules each day, listing the fare shown on channels like KJEO from Fresno and KOVR from Sacramento, both of which had signals too weak to be picked up clearly in Modesto. It took patience and a bit of finesse to tune in the few stations with stronger signals— mainly KRON from San Francisco and KTVU from Stockton—but once Lucas had tuned them in, he didn't want to tune out. Ever.

Like generations of kids, Lucas would get up on Saturday morning to watch cartoons, sitting cross-legged in front of the set with his cat Dinky.[73] The set could be on all day, rolling through game shows and newscasts, baseball games and comedies—and George Sr. had very carefully installed it on a rotating stand so the family could turn the TV toward the dining room to watch as they ate dinner. In the evenings, it was tuned to more serious fare like the courtroom drama *Perry Mason* or westerns like *Have Gun, Will Travel,* which Lucas never missed.[74]

But the TV shows that Lucas remembered the most fondly were those thirty-minute blocks of local programming in the late afternoon and early evening that broadcasters, looking for content, simply filled with installments of old movie serials.[75] There were westerns and jungle adventures, cops and Canadian Mounties, spies and space operas, all in thirty-minute installments practically made for television—and ending on cliff-hangers, guaranteeing that viewers would tune in the next afternoon. "Movie serials were the real stand-out event," said Lucas. "I especially loved the Flash Gordon serials."[76]

Produced by Universal in the 1930s, the three Flash Gordon serials—based on Alex Raymond's beloved comic strip—were quickly and cheaply made, with props, sets, and costumes borrowed from other Universal horror and science fiction films. And they were straight-ahead pulp-fiction fun, eye-rolling and over the top but earnest, with Flash battling Ming the Merciless and saving the galaxy in the process. "Thinking back on what I really enjoyed as a kid, it was those serials, that bizarre way of looking at things," said Lucas. "I don't think I ever grew out of it. Those serials will always be something I remember, even though they were pretty awful technically."[77]

Lucas was part of the first generation raised in front of the TV set—a pop culture phenomenon that would forever change the way audiences related and responded to their entertainment. TV shows were quick, convenient, and disposable, there with the click of an ON button and a twist of the dial. With only thirty- or sixty-minute blocks in which to tell a story—and commercials breaking up the narrative— TV plots had to move rapidly, propelling the plot forward, often at the expense of character development. Attention spans were demanding, and any lag in the action would send viewers spinning the TV dial to another channel, looking for something better. As television grew louder and faster, subtlety became passé—or, at the very least, challenging. It would fundamentally change the way Lucas—and other filmmakers of his generation—would tell stories with the movie camera.

For the first time, too, one didn't have to go to a movie theater to watch movies; instead, George could watch them in his own living room, spinning the TV around toward the dining room to ensure he never missed a moment. Lucas remembered watching "a whole run of westerns on television, John Wayne films, directed by John Ford, before I knew who John Ford was," adding, "I think those were very influential in my enjoyment of movies."[78]

As for seeing movies in the theater...well, Lucas rarely went. "We had a couple of theaters in Modesto. They'd show *The Blob* and *Lawrence of Arabia* and things like that."[79] But he was unimpressed. Even as a teenager, Lucas was more interested in what was going on inside the theater than up on the screen. "I would mostly go to the movies...to chase girls," he admitted.[80] While Lucas recalled seeing a few memorable films either on TV or in the Modesto movie theaters—*Forbidden Planet, Metropolis, The Bridge on the River Kwai*—for the most part, movies were simply a pleasant diversion, not an inspiration.

The young Lucas may have been ambivalent about movies, but there was one entertainment, in fact one place, he was *very* passionate about. "I loved Disneyland," Lucas said—and so, it seemed, did George Lucas Sr., who flew the entire family to southern California to be there for the park's opening day in July 1955.[81] The Lucases remained in Anaheim for a week, staying at the Disneyland Hotel and diving into the park daily—a practice they would make a regular tradition. With its themed, immersive locations and rides, the place made an immediate impression on eleven-year-old George. "I wandered around. I'd go on the rides and the bumper cars, the steam boats, the shooting galleries, the jungle rides," he said. "I was in heaven."[82]

Disneyland in the 1950s was a far cry from the thrill-ride-and-roller-coaster-centric park it is today—but no one, then or now, designed attractions quite like Disney's famous Imagineers. One of the cleverest rides was Rocket to the Moon, luring in visitors with the promise of a virtual trip to the moon and back. The mechanics were simple but convincing: riders sat in a small, round theater with enormous windows—actually video screens—set into the floor and ceiling, giving them the sense they were seeing the open sky and the moon through the window above, and the diminishing earth through the window below, as they rocketed through space. Decades later, when Lucas was given the opportunity to develop a *Star Wars*–themed ride for the Disney parks, he would use a setup similar to Rocket to the Moon—video screens acting as windows in a spaceship—then synchronize those on-screen images with state-of-the-art motion technology to give riders an even more convincing, and exhilarating, space travel experience. For now, however, Disney's rocket ride was thrilling enough—and back in Modesto, the boy who hated writing set to work excitedly reporting his adventures at Disneyland for a new local newspaper.

The newspaper was the *Daily Bugle*, and it was one that Lucas had helped start that summer with a ten-year-old friend, Melvin Cellini. After watching a TV show in which several characters tried to come up with a name for a newspaper, Cellini had been inspired to create a paper of his own and sought out Lucas as a willing collaborator. Their first issue, which Lucas and Cellini distributed for free at Muir Elementary School on August 4, announced itself with a banner headline declaring, "MELVIN CELLINI OPENS NEWSPAPER—APPOINTS GEORGE LUCAS STAR REPORTER."[83]

The boys were enthusiastic, but producing a daily newspaper—including printing a hundred copies of each issue—was a lot of work. "Paper will be given out Monday to Friday," they reported. "But this Friday it won't be out because the press broke down." Lucas, whose do-it-all-yourself instincts were already kicking in, quickly talked his father into letting them use the printing presses down at L. M. Morris for the *Bugle*, promising to repay any expenses. But in less than a week, the novelty had worn off. "The *Daily Bugle* stops," they reported to their readers. "The *Weekly Bugle* will be put out on Wednesday only. There is the same news." And, they stressed, they weren't hiring. "We need no reporters, printers or newsboys. No subscriptions taken."[84]

Despite its struggles, a kid-run newspaper was enough of a novelty that it made the pages of the *Modesto Bee*, complete with a posed photo of George and Cellini leaning over an issue of the *Weekly Bugle*, deep in conversation. Lucas, his hair in a close crew cut and wearing a breezy tropical-print shirt, already knew the prop needed to sell his image as the *Bugle*'s star reporter, and had tucked a newly sharpened pencil smartly behind his right ear.[85]

The *Bugle* soon folded—but if Cellini was disappointed by the lost revenues he had predicted from selling "about 200 copies a week" at a penny per issue, Lucas never gave it another thought. He wasn't in it for the money, he told the *Bee*. Anything he earned from the *Bugle* he planned to put right back into the newspaper, paying any delivery boys and reimbursing L. M. Morris for the costs of paper, ink, and stencils.[86] While Lucas may not have realized or appreciated it, his father—and Scrooge McDuck—had taught him well: Think differently, believe in yourself, and when you can, invest in yourself. But *pay your debts.*

Lucas showed similar business acumen when it came to managing his allowance. Under George Sr.'s roof, money was to be *earned*, and George Jr. and his sisters were expected to do chores in exchange for their allowances. George Jr.'s big weekly chore was to mow the lawn with a gigantic rotary push mower, a task he struggled with and quickly came to dread. "The frustrating thing was that it was tough grass to mow, and I was a little kid," Lucas said.[87] He eventually saved enough money from mowing so that, with a small loan from his mother, he was able to buy a gas mower, which made the task much easier. Lucas had figured out what he needed to solve a problem, and then put up his own money to do it. *Invest in yourself.* His father was grudgingly impressed.

But as well intentioned as George Sr. might be, doling out allowances with lectures on frugality and hard work, he and his son would never quite appreciate each other. "He never listened to me. He was his mother's pet," said George Sr. of his only son. "If he wanted a camera, or this or that, he got it. He was hard to understand."[88] The more George Sr. tried to impart his old-school Methodist values to his son, the more his son rebelled or frustrated him. "He is a conservative, self-made kind of man," Lucas later said of his father, "with a lot of prejudices which were extremely annoying."[89]

For George Sr., tensions between father and son must have been particularly frustrating—especially as the company that he was hoping to pass down to his son was thriving. In 1956, in fact, business was positively booming. That year, George Sr. moved L. M. Morris to a new space at 1107 I Street—the company's first address change in five decades—and opened the Lucas Company, the area's only supplier of the new copying machines. With the company growing, George Sr. also went looking for a more suitably upscale home address. The house on Ramona Avenue was sold, and the Lucases moved into a ranch house with a swimming pool on thirteen sprawling acres of walnut trees at 821 Sylvan Road. The new Lucas home was only about five miles away from Ramona Avenue—but in Modesto miles, and to George, it might as well have been on another planet.

Lucas was "very upset" about the move, he said later. "I was very attached to that [Ramona Avenue] house."[90] His mood blackened. "He started changing," recalled John Plummer. "He started paying more attention to records. He was becoming more introspective. He started to almost become a little bit of a ruffian...to follow some of the bad kids." Lucas bristled at that particular suggestion. "I was with *all* the crowds," he said. "I was little and I was funny. I was easy to get along with. I made friends pretty easily."[91] Or so he thought. What *was* true, however, was that Lucas—like millions of teenagers—had discovered rock and roll.

Lucas had taken music lessons on a wide variety of instruments, and while nothing ever stuck, he loved music. As a child, he adored the marches of John Philip Sousa, intuitively realizing the importance of themes and loving the way a good, loud march could thrum excitingly in the chest cavity. But his life changed in September 1956, when Elvis Presley swaggered and snarled his way through four songs on *The Ed Sullivan Show*. When Elvis performed in San Francisco in October 1957, Lucas was there.[92] For Lucas, rock and roll—and Elvis—was here to stay. Every day after school, Lucas would shut himself in his new room on Sylvan, read his beloved comics, and eat Hershey bars and drink Cokes while rock and roll throbbed from his little record player. Over the next decade, he would amass a "gigantic" collection of rock and roll records.[93]

Once Lucas began classes at Thomas Downey High School in 1958, his best grades, perhaps predictably, were in art and music. Otherwise, he quietly sank toward the bottom half of his class. "I was not a bad student; I was an *average* student," Lucas explained. "I was a C, sometimes a C-minus student. I was definitely not an achiever."[94] That was putting it mildly; by the end of his freshman year, he was getting Ds in science and English. "I daydreamed a lot," Lucas said later. "I was never described as not a bright student. I was always described as somebody who could be doing a lot better than I was doing, not working up to potential. I was so bored."[95]

His real classroom was probably back at home, where Lucas took up photography, and converted a spare bathroom in the new house into a darkroom. He taught himself the basics, shooting airplanes as they soared overhead and eventually becoming savvy enough that he could catch his cat frozen in mid-leap. But just as his classes had taken a backseat to art and music, his photography would vie for time with a new passion that would take up nearly all of his next six years—and would very nearly take his life. "My teenage years, they were completely devoted to cars," recalled Lucas. "That was the most important thing in my life from about the ages of 14 to 20."[96]

It was motorcycles first, which the thirteen-year-old Lucas would ride at a breakneck speed—engine roaring, tires squealing—through the rows of walnut trees on the Sylvan ranch. ("I've always liked speed," he admitted later.)[97] At fifteen, "cars kicked in," said Lucas. "I started hanging out at a garage, doodling with cars and working on engines."[98] He was good at it, too—the kid who had tinkered with toy trains and made a roller-coaster run with a reel of phone cable found himself right at home under the hood of a car. It wasn't long before Lucas was yearning for a car of his own—and George Sr., who had already watched his son race dangerously around the ranch on a motorcycle, made a preemptive purchase that he thought was in his speed-demon son's best interest: a tiny yellow Fiat Bianchina with a two-cylinder engine. "He figured that would be safe because it couldn't go that fast," Lucas said.[99] But the engine, he groaned, was "a sewing machine motor....It was a dumb little car. What could I do with that? It was practically a motor scooter."[100]

What he could do was take it apart and, after making a few adjustments, put it back together again. "I made it extremely fast," Lucas said proudly.[101] "I'd race around the orchard and spin out and smash it up."[102] Then he'd start all over again, hauling his car down to Foreign Car Service, a local garage that specialized in European cars, where he'd rebuild the Fiat, cutting off the roof and lowering the front windshield to a mere sliver, punching up the engine, installing a racing belt and roll bar, and tinkering with the suspension. Like Han Solo's *Millennium Falcon*, Lucas's Bianchina wouldn't look like much, but it would have it where it counted—and he would make a lot of the special modifications himself.

In May 1960, George Lucas turned sixteen. There would be no more spinning out and smashing up the Bianchina in the walnut groves; now, said Lucas, "I could really drive around, out on the streets."[103] School, never a priority, was all but forgotten. "I wasn't paying much attention at high school," he admitted later. "I found it all pretty boring and spent all my free time working on my car."[104] From that point on, said Lucas, "cars were all-consuming to me."[105]

As his grades suffered, Lucas began to look more and more like the juvenile delinquent his teachers were already convinced he was. The crew cut was grown out, and Lucas combed and greased his hair back in the style everyone called a "duck's ass," or sculpted his already wavy hair upward into a shiny California variation on the pompadour called the "breaker." Lucas didn't develop a lot of the bad habits typical of actual thugs—he wasn't a drinker, and his biggest vice was gorging himself on Hershey bars—but he definitely looked the part, wearing unwashed Levi's and pointy-toed boots with metal tips. At only five-foot-six, however, Lucas seemed more surly than intimidating— and John Plummer thought his friend simply looked lost, hanging out with "the undesirables and low-riders of [the] town."[106]

By reputation alone, one of the biggest groups of "undesirables and low-riders" in Modesto were members of a car club known as the Faros. Their nightly objectives, as one member later described it, were simple: "girls, beer, and cars."[107] They were probably more swagger than threat—by their own admission there was little smoking or swearing—but they looked dangerous and could always find their share of trouble with rival gangs and car clubs. Lucas, who had already made a habit of befriending older and stronger protectors, hovered around the Faros, though more as a mascot than as a full-fledged member. "The only way to keep from getting the shit pounded out of you was to hang out with some really rough guys who happened to be your friends," he said. Mostly, the Faros saw Lucas as the perfect decoy for churning up rival gangs, then luring them right into the Faros' waiting fists. "They'd send me in and wait until somebody would try to pick a fight with me, then they would come in and pound 'em," said Lucas. "I was the bait. I was always afraid I was gonna get pounded myself."[108]

For Lucas, however, being out on the street was never about fighting. Having his own car meant two things: racing and cruising. And Modesto, with its streets laid out in long grids, was ideal for both. "[George] was addicted [to cruising], more than anyone, I think," recalled Plummer.[109] For Lucas, cruising was more than an addiction; it was "a very distinctive American mating ritual," he said later. "[It's] very unique because it's all done in cars."[110]

The ritual was elaborate but predictable: usually Lucas and his fellow cruisers would troll down Tenth Street—"dragging Tenth," they called it—then cut one block east over to Eleventh Street, where they would cruise back up before cutting over to Tenth again, round and round all night. At times they'd park at the drive-in, order food, and move from car to car, blasting Buddy Holly or Chuck Berry, chatting through open windows or, if one got lucky, sliding into the backseat for a quick make-out session. It was a ritual that began to consume nearly all of Lucas's waking hours. "[It] was the main entertainment, sort of just going around in circles chasing girls all night," said Lucas. "You'd come in at four in the morning, get a couple hours of sleep, and go off to school."[111]

Despite his regular efforts, however, Lucas didn't actually catch that many girls. "I never really had any high school kind of girlfriends or anything," he said. "I was always going around picking up girls and hoping for the best."[112] While he allegedly lost his virginity in the backseat of a car, he seemed to enjoy the chase—the *ritual*—more than the conquest.[113] "Cruising is like fishing," Lucas explained later. "Unless...you happen to catch a shark, there are no real great moments. Mostly it's just sitting around talking, having a good time....[O]ccasionally you get a fish, but it's never that exciting."[114]

What *was* exciting, though, was racing. With his souped-up Bianchina, Lucas was a force to be reckoned with on Modesto's long straightaways; the little car was now built for speed, low and light-weight, with a driver who still weighed barely a hundred pounds. "George could drive 'em," said Plummer admiringly. "He was really good at that." Lucas loved gunning the engine then "peel[ing] rubber through all four gears with three shifts....It was the thrill of doing something really well."[115] It was no wonder the Modesto police found him an easy target, issuing him so many speeding tickets that he even-tually had to appear in court—and in a dreaded *suit*, no less.

After his immersion in the car scene, Lucas now knew what he wanted to do with his life. He didn't just want to race on Modesto's back roads; he wanted to drive a race car for a living. Unfortunately, California law prohibited him from officially racing until he reached the age of twenty-one. So Lucas made the rounds at northern California autocross events instead, putting his little Fiat through its paces on tightly controlled parking lot or airfield courses marked out with red cones. He even managed to win a few trophies, giving him bragging rights among the other car enthusiasts at the Foreign Car Service garage.

But there was an autocross driver at Foreign Car Service who was even better than Lucas, a fellow Modestan named Allen Grant, four years older than George, who seemed never to lose a race. Lucas, who loved speed, was impressed. "Since I was the fastest driver, George took a liking to me, and we became friends," said Grant.[116] In Grant, Lucas had found yet another big brother figure to whom he could attach himself. He joined Grant as his mechanic and, when needed, co-driver. As they leaned over the engine of Grant's car, Lucas could quickly make Grant, and the rest of the Foreign Car Service crew, a bit crazy. "He was always jabbering...'What about this? And doing this?'" said Grant. "And you know, we didn't take him very seriously. But we liked him."[117]

The racing community gave Lucas some much-needed structure. It wasn't school, but it was social, organized, and respectable in an underground way. Lucas joined the newly formed Ecurie AWOL Sports Car Competition Club—created almost solely so its members could compete at autocross—and edited its newsletter, writing its lead commentaries and filling its pages with drawings of cars. And he got his first real job, working as a mechanic at Foreign Car Service. He still looked like a greaser, but he was acting more like a professional grease monkey now, fixing cars, rebuilding engines, and acting as Grant's pit crew at the races Grant seemed to win almost effortlessly.[118]

It wasn't all cruising and racing, however. A car also gave Lucas "my own life," he said—freedom to explore the world beyond Modesto.[119] What he saw intrigued him. For one thing, there were art house cinemas showing films he'd never heard of, their marquees glowing with strange and glamorous titles like *Les quatre cents coups* or *À bout de souffle,* and directors with names that were exotic to him, like

Truffaut and Godard. With their existential themes, social relevance, frequently jittery camera movement, and a self-awareness in which characters often directly addressed the audience, these and other films of the so-called French New Wave just *felt* different from any of the films Lucas had seen at Modesto's Strand Theatre. "I *loved* the style of Godard's films," Lucas would say later. "The graphics, this sense of humor, the way he portrayed the world—he was very cinematic."[120] In 1962, Lucas couldn't quite articulate what he thought of the cresting French New Wave films; he just knew that they were something very different from *The Blob* or *Cinderfella*.

Lucas and John Plummer were also making regular trips north to the Berkeley area to attend the recently founded Canyon Cinema, a "floating *cinematheque*" established by avant-garde filmmaker Brice Baillie and several other like-minded colleagues to showcase underground, experimental, and avant-garde films. Lucas had never seen anything like it. Baillie had set up the original Canyon Cinema in his Canyon, California, backyard, serving free popcorn and wine as he projected movies from his kitchen window onto an army surplus screen; at other times and locations, films might simply be projected onto sheets.[121] While Baillie was promoting largely local filmmakers whose films had little chance of making it into theaters, films by foreign directors like Federico Fellini, Ingmar Bergman, and Jonas Mekas often crept into the rotation as well. Lucas found them all interesting, but he liked the more avant-garde films best—"the ones that were more abstract in nature."[122] Lucas would drive back to Modesto in his Bianchina after a screening, head swimming with images and sounds.

His parents knew nothing of it—not of dragging Tenth all night, nor the autocross races with Allen Grant, nor the art films in San Francisco. "He just disappeared in the evenings," said his sister Wendy.[123] Lucas thought his father's lack of interest in him was typical—and, looking back, probably understandable. "I was a hell raiser," Lucas said. "I didn't do very well in school. My father thought I was going to be an automobile mechanic, and that I wasn't going to amount to anything....My parents—not my mother, mothers never write off their sons—but my father wrote me off."[124]

The powder keg of tension between father and son finally exploded when Lucas was eighteen. Both knew that the fuse had been lit and sputtering for a long time. Lucas, however, in addition to the long hair, bad grades, and nighttime disappearing act that already so irritated his father, hadn't done himself any favors when he truculently, and briefly, went to work for George Sr. at L. M. Morris. Lucas hated dragging around gigantic boxes, sweeping the floors, cleaning the toilets. He even hated getting into his Bianchina to deliver packages. And so Lucas had quit—and his father was furious.

Lucas was furious too. "I got really mad at [my father] and told him, 'I'll never work in a job where I have to do the same thing over and over again every day,' and he just didn't want to hear that," said Lucas. The argument was on. "He had worked very hard to be able to give this [family business] to me, and so for me to refuse it was a big deal," Lucas said. "He thought that I would go off and starve to death as some kind of artist, living in a garret."[125]

"You'll be back in a few years," George Sr. told his son knowingly.

"I'll never be back," Lucas shot back. "And as a matter of fact, I'm going to be a millionaire before I'm thirty!"[126]

Recalling their spat forty years later—well after he'd become one of the most successful and wealthy businessmen in the world—Lucas could only smile at the irony of telling off his own prosperous entrepreneur father, as well as his own surprising resolve. "We had this big break, when he wanted me to go into the business and I refused," Lucas said in 1997. "And I told him, 'There are two things I know for sure. One is that I will end up doing something with cars, and two, that I will never be president of a company.' I guess I got outwitted."[127]

For now, Lucas would only concede that he was willing to finish high school before leaving L. M. Morris, and maybe Modesto, behind for good. He and Plummer were already planning to spend the summer in Europe, perhaps heading for France to watch Le Mans, or to Germany, where they could roar down the autobahn without any regard for speed limits. After that, Lucas would go to art school—which earned another scowl of disapproval from his father and another round of arguments—or become a full-time mechanic or race car driver. But first he had to graduate from Thomas Downey High School—and as his June graduation date approached, even that was looking less and less likely. With only a few weeks left of school, Lucas was failing several classes—and with final exams looming, he still had three term papers to turn in. Flunking out was a very real possibility.

Then on June 12, 1962—a sweltering hot Tuesday—with his graduation only three days away, Lucas piled into his Bianchina with an armload of schoolbooks and headed for the library, about twenty minutes away, where he planned to spend the afternoon studying for finals and writing the papers that were still due. Predictably, it didn't take him long to get bored, and at about 4:30 p.m. or so, Lucas climbed back into his little car and pointed it toward home. By 4:50 he was hurtling down Sylvan Road, with the dirt road entrance to the Lucas ranch coming up on his left. Lucas slowed the Bianchina to a crawl, then began to ease the little Fiat into a left turn.

Lucas neither saw nor heard the Chevy Impala, driven by seventeen-year-old Frank Ferreira, roaring up the road from the opposite direction. As Lucas turned across Sylvan, Ferreira's Impala T-boned the little Fiat, hitting it fast and hard. The Bianchina rolled several times, then smashed into an enormous walnut tree, wrapping itself around the trunk in a mangled metal death grip. Lucas's carefully juiced-up engine tumbled from the car's shattered husk, dripping oil and radiator fluid onto the hard-baked Modesto soil.[128]

2

Geeks and Nerds

1962-1966

Inside the Lucas house, Dorothy Lucas heard the squeal of tires and the sickening sound of the Bianchina rolling and then crashing into the walnut tree. "For my parents, it was devastating, because it was right at the end of their road, and my mother heard it," recalled Kate Lucas. "And she...went down to see what had happened....It was her son."[1]

The wreckage was terrible—a photograph of it would run on the front page of the *Modesto Bee* the next morning—but miraculously, Lucas wasn't inside the car when it hurtled into the tree. As the Bianchina rolled for the third time, Lucas's racing belt—the one he had so carefully installed himself, bolting it to the floor of the car with a thick metal plate—failed and snapped. He was flung clear of the car just before impact, landing on his chest and stomach with such force that he was immediately knocked unconscious. As he hit the ground, Lucas's left scapula fractured and his lungs were bruised; his heart rate plummeted, and he went into shock. He had been hurt badly—but had his racing belt held, he would have been mangled and likely killed inside the Bianchina, which hit the walnut tree hard enough to leave it leaning at a forty-five-degree angle, roots torn and exposed.

An ambulance arrived, sirens blaring, and Lucas was rushed to Modesto City Hospital a short distance away. En route, Lucas's color went from pale to blue, and he started to vomit blood. An open gash in his forehead continued to bleed, smearing blood across his face and staining his shirt collar crimson. It didn't look good—and on Lucas's arrival at the hospital, the facility's ace diagnostician, Dr. Paul Carlsen, was hastily called in to determine the extent of his injuries. To Carlsen's surprise, Lucas was actually in better shape than he looked; while there was some hemorrhaging from his bruised lungs, further testing showed no other internal bleeding. And apart from a few minor fractures, everything else was intact.

When Lucas awoke several hours later, he found himself in a hospital bed with an oxygen tube in his nose and several more tubes attached to a needle in his arm where he was receiving a blood transfusion. His mother, who had nearly fainted at the sight of his injuries, stood nearby with his sister Wendy. Groggily, Lucas could only ask, "Mom, did I do something wrong?" Dorothy Lucas burst into tears.[2]

Lucas's smashed Fiat was dragged onto a flatbed truck and hauled off for junk. "Most of the kids at school thought I had died," said Lucas later. "My car was this little mangled hulk that was driven down the main street where I cruised....Everybody thought I'd been killed."[3] His teachers at Thomas Downey High School took pity on what they thought for certain was a doomed young man. "All the teachers that were going to flunk me gave me a D," said Lucas, "so I managed to get my diploma by virtue of the fact that everybody thought I was going to be dead in three weeks anyway."[4]

Lucas would spend most of the next four months in bed, recuperating from his injuries. He did a lot of thinking—about the accident, about life, and about the universe and his place in it. It wasn't lost on him that he'd been saved by the failure of the very racing belt he had installed to protect himself. "I realized more than anything else what a thin thread we hang on in life," Lucas said, "and I really wanted to make something out of my life." It was similar to the existential crisis he'd experienced at age six—*What am I? How do I function in this, and what's going on here?*—only now it seemed he might finally be on his way to finding some answers. "I was in an accident that, in theory, no one could survive," he said. "So it was like, 'Well, I'm here, and every day now is an extra day. I've been given an extra day so I've got to make the most of it. And then the next day I began with *two* extra days.'... You can't help in that situation but get into a mindset like that.... You've been given this gift and every single day is a gift. And I wanted to make the most of it."[5] It was, he said later, "like almost starting a new life."[6]

The question of what to do with that new life, then, was not to be taken lightly. Driving a race car, however, was probably out of the question. "Before that first accident, you are very oblivious to the danger because you don't realize how close to the edge you are," said Lucas. "But once you've gone over the edge and you realize what's on the other side, it changes your perspective.... You see what the future is there [in racing], and you realize that you'll probably end up being dead. And I just decided that maybe that wasn't for me."[7] Lucas would always love cars, but his racing days were over—and "I was going to have to figure out something else to do," he said, "if I didn't want to be a car mechanic."[8]

And so, in the fall of 1962, the young man who had never given his studies much thought decided to go back to school, enrolling in Modesto Junior College—"which was fairly easy to get into," Lucas noted.[9] With his new outlook, he vowed to "apply myself at school"— a choice of words his father likely approved of, even if he thought his son was wasting his time taking arts and humanities courses.[10] Now that Lucas was in charge of his own educational destiny and no longer subject to the requirements of the California public school system, he could choose courses that truly interested him: Sociology. Anthropology. Psychology. "Stuff you didn't get in high school," Lucas said.[11] "These were things I was really interested in, and that sparked me," though he admitted, "It was very hard, and I didn't have [the] background I needed—I couldn't even spell."[12]

For the first time, Lucas was taking a genuine interest in school. John Plummer noticed the change in his friend immediately: "You could see he was now a serious student and those things [sociology and anthropology] really meant something to him."[13] Lucas worked hard and was proud of his efforts. "I was into something I really cared about and my whole grade situation just turned around," he said. "I had thought I was a terrible student, and then suddenly I was a great student."[14] "Great" was perhaps relative; while he received an A in astronomy and Bs in speech, sociology, and art history, his grades were mostly Cs. Still, all things considered, it was a remarkable turnaround.

Lucas received his associate in arts degree from Modesto Junior College on June 9, 1964. While anthropology had been his primary academic focus over the previous two years, Lucas had also become more serious about illustration and photography, and he was determined to go to art school, preferably the Art Center College of Design in Pasadena. There was one person, however, who had a problem with that particular plan: George Lucas Sr., who made it abundantly clear that there would be no artists in the Lucas family—especially if *he* was bankrolling it. "No way," George Sr. told his son flatly. "I'm not going to pay for that. Do it on your own if you want. You'll never make a living as an artist."[15]

Lucas knew that his father, with the power of the checkbook behind him, had him outgunned. "Aware, I think, that I'm basically a lazy person," Lucas said, "[my father] knew I wouldn't go to art school if I had to work my way through."[16] Boxed in, Lucas decided to apply instead to San Francisco State University—which was tuition-free, like most of California's state-funded institutions at the time—to pursue a major in anthropology, the one academic subject for which he had a genuine passion. That plan, at least, met with his father's approval, and Lucas's grades at junior college were good enough for San Francisco State to accept him. His path seemed set—and then, almost immediately, it suddenly wasn't.

It was partly John Plummer's fault. That summer, Plummer had decided to apply to business school at the University of Southern California in Los Angeles, and invited Lucas to accompany him to Stockton to take USC's entrance examination. Lucas scowled. "What am I going to do down there?" Plummer explained that USC had a cinematography school—which, Plummer thought, sounded close enough to photography for Lucas to find it interesting.[17] Lucas *was* interested; *cinematography* sounded so much more serious than *art school* that it just might meet with his father's approval. "So we drove to Stockton and took the...entrance exams. And I applied," said Lucas. While Plummer had assured him that the entrance exam was easy—and that the cinematography program would be even easier—Lucas wasn't so sure. "I didn't think I'd get in—because even though my grades had come up considerably in [junior] college, I didn't think they were good enough."[18]

Lucas bought a silver Camaro that summer, ready for his fall relocation—though whether it would be to San Francisco or Los Angeles he didn't yet know. And while he had sworn off racing, that didn't mean he had forsworn cars altogether. From time to time he would still hang around with Allen Grant, loitering in the pits and helping him prepare his car for races.[19] At this point, however, Lucas was more likely to photograph the race—or, better yet, film the speeding cars and their drivers, using a small 8 mm camera his father had given him. And while shadowing Grant, Lucas was introduced to another racing fan who knew his way around a movie camera: cinematographer Haskell Wexler.

The forty-two-year-old Wexler had recently wrapped the Henry Fonda political drama *The Best Man,* and was prepping his civil rights documentary *The Bus* for a 1965 release. Between films, Wexler headed his own racing team, and he was in the pits when a crew member steered Lucas his way. Talking cars and photography together, Lucas and Wexler quickly struck up a friendship—another older brother figure Lucas could attach himself to and learn from—and Lucas mentioned that he had recently applied to USC and was nervous about his prospects. Wexler promised to call a friend of his at the university and ask him to keep an eye out for the kid from Modesto. "I sensed a guy who had a burning desire to explore unique visual graphics, filmic things," Wexler said later.[20]

Lucas learned of his admission to USC shortly thereafter. While the story would be retold later with Wexler pulling strings to get Lucas into USC, the timing was coincidental. Even Wexler himself would say that he had only "encouraged [Lucas] to go to film school."[21] Lucas, to his great surprise and credit, had passed the entrance exam and gotten into USC on his own merits. But he would later remember, and repay, Wexler's support.

The decision to attend USC met with the approval of George Sr. as well. It had a solid reputation—and while it might be a bit too liberal for his taste, it was still a *private* school. As a private school, in fact, USC wasn't free, but Lucas's father agreed to pay for his son's tuition, as well as books and fees—and even send along monthly spending money—on the condition that Lucas take school seriously and treat it like a job. Failure, he made clear to his son, meant Modesto and L. M. Morris. So intent was the senior Lucas on teaching his son a life lesson that he hardly seemed to notice his son's declared major, just as Lucas had predicted. "I couldn't be an art major—that would have upset my father—but cinema, that's obscure enough," said Lucas. "He didn't know what it was and he didn't care as long as I wasn't in the art department."[22] Or at least as long as he didn't read too far into the school's description: Lucas would be enrolled in USC's Division of Cinema at the School of Performing Arts.[23]

There weren't many film schools in the United States in the mid-1960s, but the three largest and best were located at USC, at New York University in Manhattan, and at USC's crosstown rival, UCLA. The program at USC was the country's oldest and largest, founded by the Academy of Motion Picture Arts and Sciences in 1929, with a founding faculty that included some of Hollywood's biggest names, including actor Douglas Fairbanks and producer Irving Thalberg. It took its curriculum seriously and embraced new media without bias—it began offering television courses as early as 1947—and, by the late 1950s, offered the nation's only Ph.D. in film studies. The school was highly regarded for turning out educational films and documentaries. In 1956, cinema instructor Wilbur T. Blume had even won an Academy Award for Best Live Action Short Film for *The Face of Lincoln*.[24] Without quite meaning to, Lucas had chosen well. But even more than the school's professors, it was the other students he met, and access to moviemaking equipment, that really set him off running.

In mid-summer, Lucas packed his Camaro and headed for Los Angeles to stay with John Plummer in an apartment Plummer was renting in Malibu. Before classes started in the fall, Lucas planned to spend some time working in restaurants near the beach, drawing girls—for money, if he was lucky, and picking some up, if he was even luckier—and looking for summer work in the film industry. He would be disappointed; every film company door he banged on along Ventura Boulevard was closed in his face. Film was strictly an old boys' network, an insiders' game, closed off to those with no industry connections, relations, or contacts. "Every one I went into, I said I was looking for a job and I'd do anything," said Lucas. "No luck."[25]

What was more frustrating was that Lucas actually *did* have a connection in the film industry: Haskell Wexler. The seasoned cinematographer, already a fan of Lucas's in only a brief amount of time, had allowed Lucas to hang out that summer at his own commercial film company, Dove Films, to watch movies being made. But not even Wexler could get Lucas a job working in his own company unless Lucas was in the union. Lucas, never a joiner—and with an antipathy to unions learned from his conservative father—bristled. It was another lesson he wouldn't soon forget: to get into the movie machine, one had to be part of the system. And Lucas had already decided he didn't like the system—or the machine, for that matter. "I was disposed against it, mainly because of my first experience trying to get a job with Haskell and not being able to," Lucas said in 1971, still smarting from the rejection. "Being shut out...I thought that was extremely unfair."[26]

When it came down to it, going to film school didn't seem like a way into the system either. At that time, "nobody from a film school in the United States had ever worked in the film industry," said Lucas. "If you went to film school, it was a silly thing to do because you would never get a job. The only people who ended up there were people who loved movies. So there was this underground movement of film nerds who weren't going to amount to anything. As far as we knew, the studios didn't know we existed."[27] That was likely true: at that time, a degree in film meant nothing to the studios. Getting a job was hard enough; getting one working on a feature film was nearly impossible. Most students assumed they would probably make documentaries, commercials, or industrial films after graduation—if, that is, they worked in film at all. Even USC's most famous alumnus at that time, forty-one-year-old director Irvin Kershner, had scratched and clawed his way from government documentaries to television before finally getting a break from schlockmeister Roger Corman to direct *Stakeout on Dope Street* in 1958, then sliding into respectability with *A Face in the Rain* in 1963. It was a long road to success. Lucas's classmate Walter Murch, later an Academy Award–winning editor and sound designer, remembered being given the frank lay of the land his first day at USC. "The very first thing our film teacher told us...was, 'Get out of this business now. There's no future in it. There are no jobs for any of you. Don't do this.'"[28]

Lucas, too, heard the same grumbling and naysaying. "But I wasn't moved by that," he said. "I set the goal of getting through film school, and just then focused on getting to that....I didn't know where I was going to go after that." But he knew that "everybody was thinking I was silly."[29] Lucas's father, while giving tight-lipped approval to his son's curriculum, worried he'd never find a real job—and still had the doors of the Lucas Company propped open to welcome the prodigal son back home to Modesto. Lucas had even taken a razzing from the guys in the pits at the racetrack. "I lost a lot of face," Lucas said, "because for hot rodders, the idea of going into film was a really goofy idea."[30]

Lucas came into USC's film school as a junior in the fall of 1964. If he was expecting the campus to possess even a touch of Hollywood glamour, he was surely disappointed. Despite its long tenure at USC, the film school appeared to have been glued onto the outer edges of the USC campus almost as an afterthought, accessible through an ornate Spanish gate, and squeezed between the main campus and a girls' dormitory. And the buildings containing the classrooms themselves were famously low-rent: a smattering of Quonset huts and a group of bungalows built with lumber salvaged from World War I army barracks. In a way, said one USC film school dean, it "looked like a lot of movie studios. It had the feel of them, with its little corridors and wings and adjacencies. The story department was here, the editing department there, the sound stage around the corner, and so on." That didn't necessarily make them any more appealing. Even Steven Spielberg, who attended Long Beach State, twenty-five miles away, was well acquainted with the school's lack of charm. "A cinema ghetto," Spielberg said with a shudder, "the film equivalent of housing in the South Bronx."[31]

And yet, something about the school's ragtag, run-down appearance also inspired a sense of camaraderie, a sense of community, among its students—most of whom, said Lucas, "were kind of the geeks and nerds of our era."[32] For many, it was the first time they'd had a clique of their own, or a gathering place where they could talk about their interests—film—without sniggering or eye-rolling from the cool kids. The buildings might have been run-down, but they were *their* buildings, crammed with the loud, clattering equipment—cameras, projectors, Moviolas—they needed to bring their own visions to life. Over the entrance to one of the classrooms, someone had scrawled *Reality Ends Here,* and in a creative sense, that was certainly true; but for many, reality finally *began* when they entered film school. Lucas, for one, knew he had found his way. "I was sort of floundering for something," he said. "And so when I finally discovered film, I really fell madly in love with it, ate it and slept it 24 hours a day. There was no going back after that."[33]

The same could be said for many of Lucas's classmates, who had found a similar calling. The mid-1960s to early 1970s, in fact, marked an extraordinary moment for the major American film schools—a narrow sliver of time that gave birth to some of film's most enduring and prolific directors, editors, writers, producers, and craftsmen. Schools in New York were turning out artists with a grittier, harder-edged approach to film, like Martin Scorsese and Oliver Stone at NYU, and Brian De Palma at Columbia. In California, the versatile Francis Ford Coppola was working his way slowly through UCLA—even as he was writing and directing low-rent horror films for Roger Corman—while Steven Spielberg was at Long Beach State, ad-libbing his own cinema program, from which he would drop out in 1968, just shy of his degree. But it was USC that would produce one remarkable class after another for nearly a decade.

"I always call it 'the class the stars fell on,'" said Lucas classmate John Milius, a reference to the West Point class of 1915 that famously produced an unusually large number of multi-star generals as well as one U.S. president.[34] At USC, Lucas would be one of a group of highly motivated and talented young filmmakers, all friends, who would have a lasting impact on film and culture—and if they could indeed be said to be akin to the famous West Pointers, it was Lucas who ultimately held the presidential spot, the wealthiest and most successful filmmaker of the group, surrounded by a cohort of capable, clever Academy Award–winning generals. It was an assemblage who would eventually dub themselves "The Dirty Dozen," after the 1967 film about an eclectic and slightly dangerous group of Nazi-smashing American soldiers. Lucas, however, generally referred to them all as "the USC Mafia."[35] That would end up being a more appropriate designation, as they would all regularly hire, fire, and conspire with one another on countless projects over the next five decades, putting together a kind of "system" of their own.

"George made a few friends at USC and decided that's about all he needed for the rest of his life," said classmate Willard Huyck, who would become one of those friends, as well as Lucas's go-to writer on films like *American Graffiti* and *Indiana Jones and the Temple of Doom*.[36] There was also Randal Kleiser, a good-looking kid from Pennsylvania Dutch country who partly paid his tuition by modeling for print ads and billboards all over southern California. After graduation, he'd start out directing TV shows like *Marcus Welby, M.D.* and *Starsky & Hutch* before breaking into film in 1978 as the director of the most successful movie musical of all time, *Grease*.

And then there was John Milius, another of Lucas's lifelong friends and one of USC's most colorful students. Even in his early twenties, Milius was already a larger-than-life character, loud and barrel-chested, and as committed to surfing as Lucas had been to cruising. A fan of gunfighters and samurais, Milius lived in a bomb shelter, dressed like a Cuban freedom fighter, and, after film school, planned to join the marines and die gloriously in Vietnam. Chronic asthma would keep Milius out of the draft and thus out of the marines, and out of Vietnam; instead, he would write, punch up, or direct one hard-hitting screenplay or movie after another, from *Apocalypse Now* and *Dirty Harry* to *Conan the Barbarian* and *Red Dawn*.

Slightly older than Lucas was Walter Murch, who had come to USC's graduate film program from Johns Hopkins, along with Hopkins classmates Caleb Deschanel and Matthew Robbins. As driven as he was droll, Murch was fascinated with sound even as a boy, and had dangled microphones out of windows, banged on metal sculpture, and cut and spliced tape to make his own unique sounds; later, he would practically reinvent the art of movie sound, winning the Oscar for his work on *Apocalypse Now* and *The English Patient*. Deschanel, meanwhile, would be nominated for the Academy Award for cinematography five times, while Robbins would write or direct more than a dozen films, including *Dragonslayer* and **batteries not included*.

Murch's first encounter with Lucas had been a brusque one. Murch was developing photos in a darkroom when Lucas entered, watched him a moment, then told him matter-of-factly, "You're doing it wrong." Murch harshly shooed him away, but he had to admire the younger man's gall. "[That] was very typical of George at that time," said an amused Murch. "He knew how to do it, and he was going to make sure everyone knew that he knew that."[37] It was the beginning of a lifelong friendship.

Despite that kind of particularly rocky introduction, Lucas and the film students were a tight group, all roughly the same age, and with the same passion for film. Early on they were committed to helping one another with their films—lending a hand with editing, shooting, acting as extras, or just carrying equipment—no matter what the genre or subject matter. And their specific interests could vary widely. Lucas liked the esoteric art films he'd seen at Canyon Cinema, Murch adored the films of the French New Wave, while another classmate, Don Glut, couldn't get enough of monsters and superheroes. "Even though I was going into completely abstract filmmaking, I got involved in all kinds of filmmaking," said Lucas. "And the great thing about being in that film school was there were filmmakers that were interested in comic books, there were filmmakers that were interested in Godard, there were filmmakers that were interested in John Ford, and there were filmmakers that were interested in commercials and surfing movies. And we all got along together."[38] As Caleb Deschanel put it, "We really felt like we were part of a certain select group going in to make movies."[39]

They also felt they were better filmmakers than their crosstown competition at UCLA—a good-natured rivalry that continues to this day. The perception, explained UCLA alum Francis Ford Coppola, was that USC produced documentarians, filmmakers proficient in the technical side of filmmaking, while UCLA's students were better suited for producing the mainstream "fiction film."[40] That, snorted Walter Murch in mock disdain, was nonsense. "We all knew each other," said Murch. "UCLA accused us of being soulless sellouts to technology, and we accused them of being drugged-crazed narcissists incapable of telling a story or wielding a camera."[41] Each took great pride in attending movie screenings and hooting at or shouting down films produced at the rival school.

Like all new students, Lucas was required to live on campus, and was placed in Touton Hall, a worn-out all-male high-rise dormitory in the middle of campus, with no cafeteria. To make things worse, Lucas—who had always had a bedroom to himself—had to share his cracker-box-sized dorm room with a roommate, in this case a genial kid from Los Angeles named Randy Epstein. Lucas got along with Epstein fine, but he vowed to escape from the dorms as soon as he could. In the meantime, he wasn't planning on spending much time there anyway, preferring to buy his lunches and dinners from the candy machines at the Delta Kappa Alpha cinematography fraternity, and socializing over at the film school's central patio, where a circle of picnic tables surrounded a tired-looking banana tree. Here, said Milius, he and Lucas "would sit on the grass and try to hustle the girls as they went by."[42] They had little luck. "The girls from the dorms all gave a wide berth to film students, because they were supposed to be weird," said Lucas.[43]

And yet Lucas *was* weird, even among the film students. He had stopped dressing like a greaser and abandoned the duck's ass hairstyle, but now he just looked small and somewhat nebbishy in a silver-threaded sports jacket that appeared to be two sizes too large. When he added his thick-rimmed glasses, some thought he looked like a diminutive Buddy Holly. To Don Glut, he was even "conservative looking…like a young businessman."[44] Others thought Lucas looked stuck halfway between hipster and dude, his mistaken version of Los Angeles cool. And he *sounded* different, too, with a high-pitched, somewhat reedy voice that could arc even higher when he was excited or annoyed. "Just like Kermit the Frog," snickered Epstein.[45]

It is understandable, then, that Lucas was hoping to keep a somewhat low profile at USC. He'd come to *work,* not to worry about his wardrobe. Like many transfer students, Lucas had to fill his schedule with courses that met USC's basic requirements for graduation, taking classes such as English, history, and astronomy. In his first semester, his only film classes were a history of film and a history of animation. But it was enough. "Within one semester, I was completely hooked,"[46] said Lucas—though he later admitted that he hadn't known *exactly* what cinematography was until he actually started taking classes. "I discovered the school of cinema was really about making movies. I thought this was insane. I didn't know that you could go to college to learn how to make movies."[47]

Unlike rival film school UCLA, where students were almost immediately given a camera and permitted to begin making films, USC immersed its students in all the details of filmmaking first. "They didn't teach you *a* craft, but taught you *all* the crafts," said Bob Dalva, a Lucas classmate and later an Oscar-nominated film editor. "You learned how to shoot, you learned how to expose [film], you certainly learned how to edit."[48] In other classes, students would watch movies and talk about them—or, in teacher Arthur Knight's class, the well-connected Knight would bring in noted directors like David Lean, who discussed his film *Doctor Zhivago*. Lucas would later compare much of his film school experience to watching a movie on DVD while listening to the various commentary tracks. It was no wonder students in other departments eyed the film students with such disdain. "At the time, studying film was kind of like studying basket weaving," said Randal Kleiser. "Everyone on campus thought we were just trying to get easy A's by watching movies."[49]

For Lucas, it actually *wasn't* all that easy. "I had to take my film writing classes, but I suffered through them," he said. "I had to go into the drama department and do drama and stage work, but I hated getting up and acting. I really wanted to be in a real situation with a camera on my shoulder following the action. That was exciting to me."[50] Lucas, like his classmates, was itching to make a film—but they would all have to run the gauntlet of prerequisites first, making it through writing, editing, sound, lighting, even film criticism, before they could begin making their own movies. Eventually they'd make it to Mecca: a 480-level class called Production Workshop, where they'd at last be permitted to make films, though with strict rules on budgets, schedules, locations, and type of film. "The 480," then as now, was what it was all about.

Lucas, however, would make his mark well before that—and

despite his best efforts to remain under the radar, he'd almost immediately become one of USC's rising stars before he ever found his way into a film production class. "All the other guys were going around saying, 'Oh, I wish I could make a movie. I wish I was in a production class,'" said Lucas.[51] But he wasn't inclined to wait; he had already decided that the moment someone dropped a roll of film in his hands, he was going to make a movie, no matter what the assignment might be.

The opportunity came in his first-year animation class—actually Animation 448—where instructor Herb Kosower gave each student one minute of film for the animation camera and asked that they make a short movie to demonstrate a basic grasp of the equipment. "It was a test," Lucas recalled. "You had certain requirements that you had to do. You had to make it [the camera] go up and had to make it go down, and then the teacher would look at it and say, 'Oh yes, you maneuvered this machine to do these things.'"[52] While most students diligently put together short stop-action clips or brief hand-drawn cartoons, Lucas had something very different in mind.

In his short time at USC, Lucas had already become a fan of the work of the Serbian director and montagist Slavko Vorkapich, a former dean of the USC film school who had also been a colleague of the groundbreaking Russian director Sergei Eisenstein. Like Eisenstein, Vorkapich preferred psychological impact over straight-ahead narrative, creating complex montages from seemingly random and unrelated images and sounds, some of which conveyed a story while others concentrated more on mood. Lucas, already engrossed by the esoteric films at Canyon Cinema, was captivated, and watched the Serbian's films again and again. "Vorkapich's influence was everywhere at the school," said Lucas. "We focused a lot on filmic expression, filmic grammar. I was not into storytelling."[53]

Vorkapich's work would have a strong influence on Lucas's student films. The Serbian excelled at "pictorial fantasies" like the 1941 *Moods of the Sea*, in which waves crash into rocks, gulls take flight, and seals dive and frolic over the music of Felix Mendelssohn. The same year also saw the release of Vorkapich's *Forest Murmurs,* eight minutes of bears, trees, mountains, lakes, and chipmunks, all seemingly leaping, waving, and gushing in odd synchronicity with the music of Richard Wagner. But even his more story-oriented pieces didn't look like anything else; his 1928 film *Life and Death of 9413: A Hollywood Extra* intercut footage of live actors with miniature sets—most of which were cut from cardboard—and a bit of shadow puppetry to tell the story of an aspiring actor consigned to roles as an extra, and referred to by the uncaring Hollywood machine only by an impersonal number stamped on his forehead.

Lucas responded strongly not only to Vorkapich's medium but also to his message: he could already relate to the filmmaker's disdain for the Hollywood system, and the hero with the number-as-name, straining against a passionless society, was a device Lucas connected with strongly enough to borrow later for *THX 1138.* But at USC, Lucas would look to Vorkapich for inspiration for his one-minute film, searching through issues of *Look* and *Life* magazines for images he might sweep the animation camera over and across, up and down, back and forth—complying with instructor Herb Kosower's assignment, certainly, but far beyond what Kosower, or anyone else, could have expected.

Following the opening title card reading LOOK AT LIFE, Lucas made his intentions immediately clear with his first on-screen credit. This was no student assignment; it was A SHORT FILM BY GEORGE LUCAS. Furthermore, Lucas had chosen to set his film to music—in open defiance of Kosower's instructions—selecting Antônio Carlos Jobim's furious percussion piece "A Felicidade-Batucada" from the sound track of the 1959 film *Black Orpheus.* Over the next fifty-five seconds, in perfect sync with an explosion of drums and other percussion instruments, Lucas barraged viewers with a machine-gun fire of images hurtling across the screen one after another. The images are mostly of unrest and disorder: Race riots. Police dogs attacking protesters. Gesturing politicians. Dead bodies.

For a moment, the *whoosh* of images of protesters and riots gives way to the word LOVE, followed by couples kissing and young women dancing. Images seem to throb and pulse with the rhythm of the drums—a page right out of Vorkapich's book—until Lucas finally pulls slowly back from a photo of a young man with his hands up, blood streaming from his nose, as a preacher loudly quotes from Proverbs: "Hate stirreth up strife / While love covereth all sins." Lucas ends on an equivocal downbeat, with a clipping reading ANYONE FOR SURVIVAL, which fades first into END and then trails off into a lone question mark, which slowly recedes into a blur. *Finis.*

Even fifty years later, *Look at LIFE* is an impressive debut: aggressive, political, and utterly confident. "As soon as I made my first film, I thought, 'Hey, I'm good at this. I know how to do this,'" said Lucas. "From then on, I've never questioned it."[54] Even in his first sixty seconds of film, Lucas's talent for astute and clever editing is on full display: he cuts from one figure's upward-pointing finger immediately to another's waving hand; moments later, he follows a photo of a kissing couple with a still of Dracula sinking his teeth into a woman's neck. At other times, Lucas gives the illusion of movement by panning his camera quickly across a photo of fleeing protesters or of a young woman dancing. "[With this film] I was introduced to film editing—the whole concept of editing," said Lucas, "and I think ultimately that film editing was where my real talent was."[55]

His animation class was stunned. "It completely energized the class just looking at this thing," said Murch. "Nobody expected anything like this.... Everyone turned around and said, 'Who did that?' And it was George."[56] Lucas was suddenly the Boy Wonder. "Nobody there, including all the teachers, had ever seen anything like it," he recalled. "It made my mark in the department. That was when I suddenly developed a lot more friendships, and the instructors said, 'Oh, we've got a live one here.'"[57] It was the first time, too, said Murch, when "we saw that spark that George had that nobody else had in quite the same way."[58]

Lucas finished his first year at USC in triumph, but the work had taken a toll on his health; he came down with mononucleosis. It probably hadn't helped that most of his meals still came from the DKA vending machines and snack bar, but it's unlikely he had contracted mono in the usual way college students do. "George was chasing girls," said Milius cheekily. "He didn't catch them, but he *was* chasing them."[59] While the USC Mafia may have tittered over Lucas's coming down with the so-called kissing disease, they all knew it was stress, and not smooching, that had worn their young friend out.

With his first year behind him, Lucas could finally abandon dorm life, and he literally headed for the hills, renting a three-story, two-bedroom wood-frame house at 9803 Portola Drive, in the hills of Benedict Canyon, about a half-hour drive from USC. The place was low-rent in every sense of the word, perched at the top of a steep set of concrete steps poured into the hillside, with cramped bedrooms, closet-sized bathrooms, and a top-floor bedroom accessible only by an outside ladder. Lucas's father grudgingly agreed to pay the $80 monthly rent—and Lucas, feeling slightly guilty, eventually decided to bring in Randal Kleiser as his roommate, thereby splitting the costs and reducing his father's out-of-pocket expenses.

Kleiser was a good influence on Lucas—clean-cut, self-effacing, outgoing, and inclined to bring Lucas into social situations, whether Lucas liked it or not. Kleiser, in fact, made Lucas a founding member of what he dubbed the Clean Cut Cinema Club, also bringing in Don Glut, former Lucas roommate Randy Epstein, and a young man named Chris Lewis—the son of Oscar- and Emmy-winning actress Loretta Young—as the club's first members. While it was set up mostly as a support group for talking about and working on one another's film projects—"George's relationship with his friends was more about making films," Lucas's first wife would later remark—it was still the most outgoing Lucas had been... well, pretty much *ever.*[60]

Still, Kleiser wasn't going to be able to change Lucas *too* much. Despite his best efforts, Kleiser found that Lucas preferred shutting himself in his top-floor bedroom, sitting at the drawing board, planning his films, and sketching out ideas. "I would always try to go out to parties and to clubs and stuff," said Kleiser, "and George would usually stay upstairs in his room," drawing "these little star troopers." But for Lucas, that was even better than partying. "I'd be working all day, all night, living on chocolate bars and coffee," said Lucas. "It was a great life."[61]

Even as drugs were becoming more prevalent on college campuses, chocolate bars and coffee—as well as chocolate chip cookies and Coca-Cola—would be the worst junk Lucas put into his body. "I had all that young enthusiasm, and I was too busy to get into drugs," he said. "After a while, I could see it was a bad idea anyway."[62] For Lucas, movies, not marijuana, were his addiction, and if he had a moment to spare, he—and most of his film school friends, actually—thought the films of Akira Kurosawa and George Cukor provided the best kind of high. "We were passionate about movies....It was like an addiction," he said. "We were always scrambling to get our next fix, to get a little film in the camera and shoot something."[63]

Lucas was even working on projects that went beyond those assigned in class; during his senior year, he, Kleiser, and Lewis would form their own production company, Sunrise Productions, "with offices on Sunset Boulevard," Kleiser stressed—and in the spirit of the *cinéastes* they imagined themselves to be, Kleiser made up "snappier stage names" for himself and Lucas. "I was 'Randal Jon,'" said Kleiser, "and he was 'Lucas Beaumont.'"[64] Sunrise Productions would produce exactly one short film, *Five, Four, Three*—the title was a self-aware nod to the countdown seen at the front end of a film—a "mockumentary" on the making of a satirical teen beach movie called *Orgy Beach Party*. Lucas shot in a documentary style, following Kleiser around as he rescued his bikini-clad girlfriend from Don Glut's monster, while on the sound track, studio executives hooted at the film. It was self-referential and self-deprecating, and never completed.

Lucas began his senior year in the autumn of 1965. With most of the preliminary requirements out of the way, he could at last immerse himself entirely in film-related classes. Finally, he could enroll in Cinema 310—a film production class with the arty name "The Language of Film"—where he would be able to make real films, using real film equipment, rather than hijacking an animation camera as he had with *Look at LIFE*. Students were permitted to assemble small teams to serve as their film crews, and Lucas—already determined to do as much of the work himself as he could—looked no further than the Clean Cut Cinema Club, tapping Kleiser and Lewis to perform mostly as actors and equipment managers.

Lucas's Cinema 310 film was a three-minute Cold War thriller *cum* political statement called *Freiheit*, the German word for "freedom." Filmed entirely in Malibu Canyon, *Freiheit* starred Kleiser—in shirtsleeves and loafers, necktie askew, glasses slightly crooked—as a terrified young man being chased by unseen pursuers as he makes his way toward the line of fence separating communist East Germany from democratic West Germany. With the border and freedom in sight, Kleiser's student sprints across an open space, only to be cut down agonizingly by machine-gun fire within feet of his destination. As a voice-over oozes platitudes—"Freedom's a thing you have to deserve," says one voice. "You have to work for it"—Kleiser makes one last lunge for the fence before being brought down by another hail of bullets. As the credits roll, Chris Lewis, decked out like a Soviet soldier, stands over the fallen Kleiser, weapon in hand. "Of course freedom's worth dying for," intones an off-screen voice. "Because without freedom, we're dead."

"I went to marches [in the sixties]," said Lucas, "but I wasn't an instigator of anything."[65] And yet, with *Freiheit*, Lucas is clearly and aggressively making a statement. It's very much a film by a young man who wants to be taken seriously as an artist and insurgent—and to his credit, it sort of works. "He was able to do something that was artistic but also commercial," noted Kleiser. "It had a lot of slick style to it."[66] In *Freiheit*, Lucas is working in a more straight-ahead narrative style than in *Look at LIFE*, using a blue-tinted monochrome to give the film an otherworldly, slightly sinister look. And once again, it's Lucas's feel for editing that makes the film pop: as Kleiser waits in the brush for his chance to run for the fence, Lucas holds on the panting Kleiser for almost too long, which makes his failed break for freedom even more excruciating. And as Kleiser sprints, Lucas briefly cuts in a joggling shot from Kleiser's perspective, making the viewer, for one brief moment, the runner and victim.

As a political piece, it's a young Lucas being intentionally provocative, if heavy-handed, from the slow-motion shots of the anguished Kleiser running for the fence, all the way down to a title sequence that solemnly identifies *Freiheit* as A FILM BY LUCAS. "In the fifties, I was not very aware of the events that were going on around me," said Lucas. "It wasn't until Kennedy was killed that I became involved in a lot of things that I hadn't paid much attention to before."[67] Kleiser recalled Lucas being annoyed by students who romanticized dying in Vietnam in the name of freedom. "George wanted to make a statement about how easy it is to say that, but how in reality people were getting killed."[68] Ultimately, *Freiheit*'s underlying question—"What price, freedom?"—was one Lucas would explore and struggle with in the decades to follow, both as an artist and as a businessman.

Inside and outside the classroom, Lucas continued to immerse himself in films by a wide variety of filmmakers. Film school "was a perfect place for me to be exposed to a lot of different kinds of films," said Lucas. In the days before DVDs or streaming video, a small art film or foreign film "had to come to some art house." Otherwise "you had to see it at two o'clock in the morning on television, or you could see it in film school."[69] When it came to American directors, Lucas was particularly interested in the films of John Ford and William Wyler, the latter an influential director and cinematographer remembered not only for winning three Academy Awards but also for his inability to relate to actors—a criticism that would later be leveled at Lucas. Godard and Fellini remained Lucas's foreign gods. He was a particularly big fan of Godard's latest, the sci-fi film noir dystopian thriller *Alphaville*, in which the director used modern-day Paris as a stand-in for the futuristic title city. But lately he'd discovered a new idol: Japanese director Akira Kurosawa.

At the encouragement of John Milius, Lucas went to see several

Kurosawa films at the La Brea Cinema in Los Angeles, and remembered being "really blown away" by the director's 1954 film *The Seven Samurai.* "It really had a huge influence on my life in terms of seeing something that brilliant and something that emotional, and at the same time so exotic," said Lucas.[70] He loved Kurosawa's style, "so strong and unique,"[71] with the horizontal "wipes" to transition between scenes, the rat-a-tat editing, and the dusty, slightly worn look of his sets and costumes. Everything in a Kurosawa movie looked as if it had been used, repaired, then used again—a design aesthetic that Lucas would bring to *Star Wars.* Lucas also liked that Kurosawa was confident enough in his storytelling to plunk audiences down in the middle of medieval or nineteenth-century Japan without the benefit of backstory. Give audiences a bit of time with the mythology, thought Kurosawa, and the foreign would feel familiar—another conceit Lucas would bring to *Star Wars.*

And yet, even with his filmic vocabulary expanding, Lucas would return to the more familiar language of Vorkapich for his third film, *Herbie,* completed for his Cinema 405 class. This time, instructor Sherwood Omens paired the senior Lucas with junior Paul Golding. Lucas likely grumbled; he was becoming increasingly cranky about the idea of working with others and preferred doing everything himself. He could be easily irritated if he was saddled with crew members who couldn't keep up with him. "I was really incensed at the democratic process of filmmaking, where we helped the student who couldn't quite make it," Lucas said later. "I was into making it a competition, who can get it done first and best. If they couldn't cut the mustard, they shouldn't have been there."[72]

Golding, however, would pass the Lucas litmus test; he was an enthusiastic collaborator who also happened to bring to the table the keys to the film school stockroom, thereby ensuring that only he and Lucas had access to the highly coveted Arriflex camera.[73] That was the sort of go-getting defiance Lucas could rally behind, and he and Golding—who also prided himself on his editing abilities—would collaborate on several more films at USC.

After the politics of both *Look at LIFE* and *Freiheit, Herbie* is positively mellow: gorgeous black-and-white shots of nighttime lights reflected in the curves of cars—finally, Lucas could feature a car!—as the smooth jazz of the Miles Davis Quintet, playing "Basin Street Blues," fills the sound track. The name *Herbie,* in fact, comes from pianist Herbie Hancock, who Lucas and Golding mistakenly thought was playing piano on the piece. (It was actually Hancock's predecessor in the quintet, Victor Feldman.) Like Vorkapich's "pictorial fantasies," *Herbie* enjambs unrelated images and music to create an entirely new yet somehow cohesive piece. It's film jazz, in every sense—and as the final note of music fades, the lone on-screen credit quietly states that THESE MOMENTS OF REFLECTION HAVE BEEN BROUGHT TO YOU BY PAUL GOLDING AND GEORGE LUCAS.

After his first three films, it was becoming impossible for Lucas to keep a low profile, despite his best efforts. "George was always quiet," said Walter Murch. "He wasn't one of the people who would always be speaking out in class. He tended to keep his own counsel and to express himself through his films."[74] But now, after his first short productions, "he was recognized as being the star."[75] As Matthew Robbins remembered, Lucas was "highly regarded by all the students and a source of puzzlement to much of the faculty."[76]

Regardless of what the faculty may have thought of the tight-lipped young man, his films got their attention—and it was clear he was also becoming one of USC's most dexterous editors. While other students griped and complained about bad acting, absent crew members, unreliable equipment, or lack of adequate time to get the shots they wanted, Lucas worked quickly and without complaint; he'd cover up any defects, shortages, or missing shots in the editing room.

It's little wonder that Lucas would be at home both in the editing room and on editing equipment. The USC editing room looked like an auto shop class, with high ceilings, buzzing overhead lights, graffiti-covered walls, and equipment taking up most of the floor space. And the Moviola editing machines were Lucas's kind of contraption, as comfortable for him as sliding behind the wheel of a car, with foot pedals to control the speed of the film, a hand brake, a variable motor switch, and a viewing screen the size of a rearview mirror. Small motors whirred as students spooled film back and forth; discarded snippets of film were simply dropped to the floor to be swept up later. It became as familiar as working on his own car at the Foreign Auto Service. Plus, knowing his way around engines as he did, Lucas didn't need long to figure out how to fix the notoriously unreliable Moviolas, which broke down with frustrating regularity.

Some envious members of the DKA fraternity regarded Lucas as little more than a showboat and a dilettante, but DKA president Howard Kazanjian stuck by Lucas and even threatened to resign if Lucas wasn't voted in. It was an act of friendship and loyalty that Lucas would reward years later, when Kazanjian became a vice president of Lucas's own company, as well as his go-to producer for films like *Raiders of the Lost Ark* and *Return of the Jedi*. Despite his official status with DKA, though, Lucas's only real involvement with the fraternity was using it as a source of fuel for his marathon work sessions, as he continued to ransack the vending machines and snack bar for cookies and Cokes.

Lucas reached the Cinema 480 class in the final semester of his senior year. Here, instructor Douglas Cox would break the class into small crews to complete a ten-minute film, with three-track synchronized sound, in a period of ten weeks. The problem with working in an assigned crew meant, as classmate Don Glut noted testily, "not all of us were granted the esteemed privilege of actually directing a project."[77] Lucas, however, would both write and direct his senior project, heading up a crew that would eventually swell to fourteen, some of whom would receive on-screen credit, some of whom wouldn't. They'd all be working together closely, sure, but ultimately they'd be doing it Lucas's way.

Cox also imposed some terms and conditions on the project, most of which Lucas shrugged off or disregarded entirely. Teams could film in either color or black and white, for instance, but if they chose color, they'd receive only half the amount of film. "They discouraged us from shooting color," said Lucas, "because it takes so long to get it developed."[78] Challenge accepted: Lucas would shoot in color. Cox also required teams to shoot their films close to campus; Lucas would ignore that one altogether and take his team out to a location eighty miles away. The rules were of no concern to him. "I broke them all—all of us did," said Lucas. "Whenever I broke the rules, I made a good film, so there wasn't much the faculty could do about it."[79]

The rule breaking even extended to a bit of pilfering, as well as some breaking and entering. With only a limited amount of time and equipment, competition was fierce for the best cameras and editing machines. Lucas, said Matthew Robbins, "was very resourceful. He always would find a way to get what he needed in terms of equipment and bodies to put together a crew."[80] Paul Golding had hoarded the Arriflex for Lucas to use on *Herbie;* this time it was John Milius, always game for a bit of delinquency, who broke into the equipment room and "borrowed" for Lucas the Éclair NPR camera that Lucas loved. "He really wanted to use that camera," said Milius, "and I stole it, and hid it in my car, and slept in my car with the camera for a week while we used it."[81] And once it came time to edit, Lucas didn't want to limit his use of the equipment to the building's regular hours either. "We'd shimmy up the drain spout, cross over the roof, jump down into the patio, and then break into the editing rooms so we could work all weekend," said Lucas.[82]

For his film, Lucas would combine two of his passions, one old—racing—and one new. "*Cinéma vérité* was just coming in at that point," said Lucas. "We studied that a lot."[83] *Cinéma vérité* (French for "truth cinema") was a new kind of documentary filmmaking in which the camera observed real people, in uncontrolled situations, with no preconceived notions or scripted outcomes. At its purest, it involved little more than using a camera and sound-recording equipment to shoot and then present raw, nearly unedited footage. Most of it, however, had a little more flash than that—and Lucas was strongly influenced by the films coming out of the French unit of the National Film Board of Canada, which produced *cinéma vérité* with verve and attitude.

Lucas was particularly fond of director Jean-Claude Labrecque's 1965 film *60 Cycles,* following bicyclists in the Tour de St. Laurent as they wound their way through 1,500 miles of Canadian countryside to the music of Booker T. & the M.G.'s. Lucas "flipped out over it," said classmate Charley Lippincott, who had procured the film from the Canadian consulate.[84] Part documentary, part slice of life, part experimental film, at sixteen minutes it did all the things that Lucas wanted to do with his 480 film: long shots, aerial shots, crowds, and—best of all, in the spirit of genuine *cinéma vérité*—no actors. Lucas couldn't get enough of it, borrowing it from Lippincott and watching it over and over again until Lippincott finally had to return it, long overdue, to the impatient Canadians.

For his own bit of flashy *cinéma vérité,* then, Lucas took his crew to Willow Springs Race Track in Rosamond to film driver Peter Brock as he put his yellow Lotus 23 through its paces. Lucas captured it all from carefully chosen angles; sometimes the car seems incidental, glimpsed only as it speeds behind a series of signs, in an aerial shot, or seen off in the distance, where the chirp of birds is almost louder than the roar of the engine. Other times, Lucas puts the camera in the car for Brock's perspective from behind the wheel, one eye on the speedometer, or turns the camera on Brock as he works the stick shift, or—in one glorious, unscripted moment—grimaces as he cranks the engine after the Lotus spins out and stalls. Finally, Lucas closes in on the face of a stopwatch as a member of the pit crew snaps it to a stop with an audible mechanical *click,* its hands frozen on Brock's best lap time: 1:42.08. Lucas would use it as the title of his film.

Lucas called *1:42.08* a "visual tone poem,"[85] reflecting his interest in cars as well as "the visual impact of a person going against the clock"—a theme he would take up later in *THX 1138.*[86] At its heart, it's also about man and technology—another theme Lucas would explore—and our efforts to master technology without letting it master us first...even if we *do* spin out once or twice. To Lucas's surprise, too, he found he had enjoyed working with a crew, and was proud they had brought their project in right on time. "We had only ten weeks to make the film, from the point that you start the script to the point where you actually have to have print," he said. "For students, that's quite an achievement."[87] And that wasn't all that happened out at Willow Springs. While there, Lucas had run into another film crew, an advance team for the racing film *Grand Prix*, trailing along after star James Garner as he trained with a stunt driver. With only a minimal amount of sweet-talking, Lucas landed a job as a camera operator on the film's second unit, picking up a few bucks, and his first professional Hollywood credits, for a few additional days' work at the track.

In the end, *1:42.08* might have been a group effort, but Lucas had made his mark by breaking the rules and doing it his way. Again. The film didn't wow Lucas's professors quite as much as his previous work, but he was in good shape; instructor Douglas Cox was a fan of art films—he would clash with Glut over making pulpy monster movies like *Wrath of the Sun Demon*—and appreciated what Lucas was trying to do.[88] *Cinéma vérité* aside, *1:42.08* shows Lucas finding his own style as a director, content to let a well-placed camera almost casually catch the action. And Lucas is almost too creative an editor to ever really do pure *cinéma vérité*; he can't resist using a rapid series of flickering cuts to make Brock's Lotus seem to move even faster, or inserting a brief shot of a sign advertising a restaurant named George & Aggie's—a cameo so coy that if you blink, you'll miss it. And in his first true sound film, Lucas already takes great pleasure in seat-rumbling audio as Brock's Lotus screams by again and again like one of *Star Wars'* TIE fighters.

Lucas graduated from the University of Southern California with a bachelor's degree in cinema on August 6, 1966, and he would always have warm feelings toward USC. "I discovered my talent here," he said during a ceremony at the university in 2006.[89] His future, however, was uncertain. "I assumed I would make the kind of avant-garde films that were being made in San Francisco at that time," he recalled. "You can't make a living making those films, so I figured I'd also work as a documentary cameraman. That's really what I wanted to do anyway. I would be a documentary cameraman for my livelihood, and make movies on the side. That was going to be my life."[90] Or so he thought.

Like most film school graduates, Lucas found the doors of mainstream movie studios closed to him. "It was impossible to break into the industry in any of the guilds or unions," said Gary Kurtz, who had graduated from USC in 1962 and by 1966 was still working on low-budget films like *Beach Ball*. "A lot of film school graduates just got tired of that process and did other things.... [T]hey went into educational or documentary films, which weren't so rigidly unionized."[91]

The military loomed as well. As an unemployed college graduate, Lucas was eligible for the draft, with a very real possibility of being sent to Vietnam. Lucas considered himself an activist — "I was angry at the time, getting involved in all the causes," he said — and was opposed to the war, but his friends told him that with his degree and skill set, he could likely be an officer in the air force photography unit. Lucas found the idea creatively intriguing. Unlike his classmate John Milius, Lucas saw nothing romantic in the military or war, but he *did* have to admit that Vietnam had filmic possibilities; if he went to war and survived, the stories of what he saw and did there would make a hell of a film. "I was going to spend two years somewhere slogging around in the mud," he figured, "hoping to get assigned to something reasonable, and using the experience to write about in later years." Still, he admitted: "I wasn't really that enthusiastic about going in the first place. I was just doing it out of desperation."[92]

Enthusiastic or desperate, it never happened. Lucas reported for his induction physical, where, to his utter astonishment, he was rated 4-F; he had failed his physical. Doctors had found diabetes, the same disease that had killed his grandfather Walton. Lucas was put on Orinase and would have to manage his disease with medication for the rest of his life. That also meant no drugs or alcohol, a condition he could easily handle; his clean-cut image would now be true out of necessity. But diabetes also meant giving up the chocolate chip cookies, Hershey bars, and Cokes that he had lived on for pretty much the last ten years. That would be tougher.

With any chance of a military career now off the table, Lucas let his hair grow out—which for him meant it tended to pile up higher on his head rather than trail down his back. He also grew a beard, a dark and neatly trimmed Vandyke that surrounded his mouth. While he looked more beatnik than hippie, he also looked *cool*—even with his ears still sticking straight out from his head. Lucas was finding his look.

Being rejected for military service also meant that Lucas could return to USC for graduate school, but that too would have to wait; he had missed the chance to enroll for the fall 1966 semester. For a moment, Lucas was aimless, with no job and no real prospects. Finally, he capitalized on one of the only real contacts he had in the film industry, calling on graphic designer Saul Bass, whom Lucas had gotten to know while shooting second unit footage for *Grand Prix*. Bass, who had designed the visually stunning opening sequences for Hitchcock's *North by Northwest* and Otto Preminger's *The Man with the Golden Arm*, had been tapped by director John Frankenheimer to put together a similarly vibrant title sequence for *Grand Prix*, slotted for release in December. Lucas, a lover of montages, helped Bass cut together the footage for the film's exciting, roaring opening moments. That same summer, Bass was working on a documentary of his own called *Why Man Creates*—which would win an Academy Award in 1968—and would rely on Lucas to serve as a cameraman and jack-of-all-trades.

By early fall, Lucas's work with Bass was finished and he was looking for a job again. He was still living in the house on Portola, still shutting himself in his top-floor room, though from time to time, he *could* be persuaded to join a party of film school students and graduates. At one party that autumn, Lucas and Matthew Robbins were standing in the kitchen talking films when Lucas mentioned that he wanted to "make a movie about someone escaping from the police," as Robbins recalled, "from an all-pervasive Big Brother, eye-in-the-sky" point of view.[93] Robbins thought the idea sounded exciting and offered to take a crack at writing the story for it, eventually looping in Walter Murch to collaborate on a two-page treatment called *Breakout,* which they completed in early October. Mostly an extended chase sequence, the final scene describes the hero emerging from a trapdoor in the desert, yelping for joy and running for freedom into the sunset—the happy ending that had been denied Lucas's young hero in *Freiheit*. "As the man recedes," continues Robbins's treatment, "[a] hand reaches out of the underground room, finds the handle on the trap door and slowly closes it."[94] The visual stuck with Lucas. He wanted to see that film. As soon as he could, he was going to *make* that film.

But first, a job. After applying unsuccessfully for employment at the Hanna-Barbera animation studios, Lucas finally landed a position with the U.S. Information Agency as a grip—the person responsible for maintaining and carrying the camera equipment—for its teams working on education and propaganda films. It wasn't much, but it was still the kind of opportunity most film school graduates would have killed for.

George Lucas, heir to a stationery store, car crash survivor, lover of photography and film, was officially working in the film industry, albeit just barely.

3

The Right Horse

1967

L ucas returned to USC in January 1967, taking a few graduate film courses, including a class on film direction taught by comedian Jerry Lewis—a class he quickly came to loathe. "Lewis had such an outrageous ego," said one classmate.[1] Lucas would sink down into a seat in the back row of the classroom, glowering. Rather than seeking Lewis's instruction, most of the students had taken the class merely hoping the comedian could help them get into the vaunted Directors Guild of America. They would all be disappointed.

At almost the same moment that Lucas started back at USC, he caught a lucky break: his friend Bob Dalva, who was editing and logging documentary footage at the U.S. Information Agency, was leaving his position and recommended Lucas as his replacement. Lucas, eager to start using USIA's equipment rather than lugging it, accepted and reported to the studios of veteran editor Verna Fields, who was working out of a facility she had set up in the garage of her San Fernando Valley home.

Short and slightly stocky, with owlish glasses and a messy mop of dark hair, Fields—despite her unassuming looks and diminutive stature—was a larger-than-life personality, loud and brassy. As an editor, she was fast and very, very good—largely because, as one of the few women in a male-dominated profession, she had to be. "I got into movies by accident," she said later, and that was partly true; in the 1930s, while loitering around a movie studio with her boyfriend, she had been spotted by director Fritz Lang, who asked in his heavy German accent, "Who is dat yung gurl always hanging around?" and hired her as a sound-editing apprentice. Four years of work got her into the unions—the golden ticket to the inside that so many others coveted.

Fields stopped editing when she married and had children, until her husband died of a heart attack at age thirty-eight in 1954, leaving her a single mother with two kids to support. Fields constructed editing rooms in her house, and took jobs editing TV programs like *Sky King* and *Fury*. ("I'd tell the kids I was the Queen of Saturday morning," she laughed.) Soon she moved into motion pictures, working on films like the experimental documentary *Savage Eye* and the Charlton Heston blockbuster *El Cid*. But the politically liberal, outspoken Fields was a crusader—"I was interested in using film for social reform," she said—and got enthusiastically caught up in President Johnson's Great Society, editing films for the U.S. government's Office of Economic Opportunity and the USIA.[2] At the moment, she was editing a USIA film called *Journey to the Pacific*, about Johnson's visit to the region for the 1966 Manila summit conference, and she needed all the good editing hands she could get.

Lucas—like nearly everyone else who worked for Fields—quickly came to adore her, but he just as rapidly learned to hate editing government films. "If you make a picture for the government, it wants to look good," said Lucas. "It's Hollywood invading everything." He was told that Lady Bird Johnson couldn't be shown at unflattering angles, while no shot could be used in which President Johnson's bald spot was visible. Even shots Lucas thought were artistic were scrutinized for potential offense. "I had put in a shot of a bunch of horses in Korea running down the street to help control the huge crowds," he said. "Someone thought it looked a little too fascist—which it wasn't—and made us take it out. I just liked the shot."[3]

While Lucas didn't like cutting together footage of someone "saying things I didn't really believe in just because I had to make a living," more than anything else, he just didn't like being bossed around.[4] Being told which shots he could and couldn't use annoyed him. "The director would come over and say, 'You can't cut this this way; you've got to cut *this* way,'" said Lucas. "And I said, 'I don't like this.' At that point, I was really wanting to be an editor and a cameraman...[and] in the course of...doing this, I sort of said, 'You know, maybe I want to be a director. I don't want people to tell me what to do."[5]

Lucas wasn't the only one working in Fields's editing rooms. While Fields had plumbed the classrooms at USC for students willing to edit and log footage, she had also hired more experienced professional editors from small production companies and paired them with the less experienced students. Lucas was placed alongside a young assistant editor from Sandler Films named Marcia Griffin, a year younger than Lucas, but who had already been supporting herself as a professional editor for more than a year. Griffin was a talented, intuitive editor—and, said John Plummer, "she was cute as hell," with straight brown hair and a wispy voice—but Lucas was more threatened than impressed by her presence in the editing room. "Marcia had a lot of disdain for the rest of us, because we were all film students," Lucas recalled. "She was the only real pro there."[6]

She had worked hard to get where she was. Born in Modesto to an air force officer who abandoned his family when Marcia was two, she and her sister had been raised by their single mother in a small apartment in North Hollywood. With no child support coming in, Marcia's mother managed as best she could on her meager income as a clerk in an insurance agency, but money would always be tight. "We had a lot of love and a supportive family," Marcia remembered. "But economically, it was real hard on my mother."[7] When she was a teenager, her father reentered her life, and Marcia moved to Florida to live with him and his new family, a well-intentioned experiment that turned out to be a failure. After two years she moved back to Hollywood, finished high school, then enrolled in evening chemistry classes at Los Angeles City College while working full-time in a mortgage banking firm to help support her mother and sister.

Like Verna Fields, Marcia got into editing almost by accident: "I just walked in off the street," she said.[8] She had gone down to the California state employment office to apply for work as a librarian, and was sent to the Sandler Film Library, which was looking for an apprentice film librarian. The job didn't pay as much as she was making at the bank, but she found she liked the work and was good at it. "I would have cut film for free because I enjoyed it so much," she said. So far, her work was paying off; she had gotten into the union. Furthermore, she was willing to put in the effort to work her way through the apprentice editor system, an often frustrating eight-year process in which she was likely to see most of the higher-profile editing jobs go to men — mainly because female editors were considered either too fragile to carry heavy film cans or too delicate to put up with the web of foul language that film editors typically wove while on the job.

Working alongside Lucas, however, she was unlikely to hear much profanity — or much conversation at all, for that matter. When he was editing, Lucas preferred listening to music and rarely engaged in chatter — and when he did, he preferred to talk about film instead of anything personal. While Lucas remained wary and a bit daunted by this unwanted presence in the editing room, in truth Marcia was slightly intimidated by him as well. She could see right away how good he was. "He was so quiet and he said very little, but he seemed to be really talented and really centered, a very together person," said Marcia. "I had come out of this hectic commercial production world and here was this relaxed guy who threaded the Moviola very slowly and cautiously. He handled the film with such *reverence.*"[9] For now, Lucas would remain aloof. But despite his wariness, Marcia intrigued him; in time, he thought, he might even talk to her.

* * *

After spending his days in class, then sitting for hours at a Moviola for Verna Fields, Lucas spent his evenings standing in front of a classroom at USC, serving as a teaching assistant for cinematography instructor Gene Peterson, a job he had taken to help defray some of his tuition costs. The evening class that Lucas taught had a unique enrollment; Peterson had a contract with the military to teach its cameramen, mostly navy men and air force representatives, how to "loosen up a bit," as Lucas put it. "These veteran Navy cameramen had been taught to shoot film by the book." Lucas's job, then, was to make them think more like artists. "I had to train the Navy guys to shoot using available light, to think about composition, and to try to get them to make a movie in a different way."[10]

Lucas likely caught a bit of razzing from the USC Mafia; with the war in Vietnam taking up more and more of the front page each day, and student protesters taking out their frustrations on both politicians and returning soldiers alike, teaching a class full of crew-cut servicemen seemed to some like fraternizing with the enemy. "They sent these military guys to join all of us who had shaggy hair and who were protesting and marching," said Willard Huyck. "And we would have nothing to do with the military guys."[11] Lucas, however, saw things a bit differently. Because the class he was teaching was sponsored and subsidized by the federal government, the navy crews had better equipment than the average USC film class—and, more important, they had nearly unlimited access to color film with sound. What Lucas saw, then, was a classroom filled with great equipment, limitless supplies of film, and a crew that could take orders well. He could do things entirely his way, with all the equipment and film he needed.

Lucas's gut instinct was correct: the military crews did take orders well; they just didn't want to take them from *him*. Astutely reading the mood of the room, Lucas decided to play to their competitive spirit. He broke the class into two teams, one of which he would lead to make *his* film, while the other group would follow the lead of their ranking officer. It was a contest the opposing team was destined to lose right from the beginning—for Lucas already knew what film he was going to make. He was going to make that movie he'd discussed with Matthew Robbins and Walter Murch in a Hollywood kitchen—the one about the man emerging from underground and running for freedom.

There was going to be very little plot; with only twelve weeks to complete the project, Lucas wanted to concentrate more on the look and feel of the film rather than plot or characters—a criticism that would be lobbed at some of his later films as well. "I liked the idea of doing something futuristic," Lucas said. "I wanted to do something extremely visual that had no dialogue and no characters—a cross between a theatrical and a nontheatrical experience. Something a little experimental."[12] Actually, it was going to be a *lot* experimental, as Lucas had some unconventional ideas that had, he said, been "boiling around in my mind for a long time."[13]

First, as in Godard's *Alphaville,* Lucas was going to use the present to represent the future. There would be no need to build space-age sets or props; with some clever camerawork and a bit of tape and fabric, Lucas could make 1960s-era clothing and machinery look futuristic yet still somehow shopworn and vaguely familiar—the "used universe" mentality he would later bring to *Star Wars.* Plus, with the power of military clearances behind him, Lucas could access computer rooms and other facilities at locations that would normally be closed to him, including LAX, Van Nuys Airport, and an underground parking area at UCLA. To the greatest extent possible, too, he was going to use only natural lighting, which would give the film a documentary sensibility, almost a feeling of "found footage" that had somehow made its way back to 1967 from the future.

He had a new cinematic muse as well, yet another product of the National Film Board of Canada: an eclectic black-and-white film called *21-87,* by a brilliant thirty-year-old montagist named Arthur Lipsett. Lucas admitted to watching the film "twenty or thirty" times.[14] It "had a very powerful effect on me," Lucas said later. "It was very much the kind of thing that I wanted to do. I was extremely influenced by that particular movie."[15] Not only would it have a profound impact on the way he thought about and used sound in his films but also it would even subtly inspire a key part of Lucas's *Star Wars* mythos.

For *21-87*, Lipsett created a nearly ten-minute film montage, using short movies he had taken in New York City along with random bits of film picked up off the editing room floor at the National Film Board. The result is jarring and fascinating: regular people going about their everyday lives—walking in the park, talking on phones, commuting to work—intercut with bizarre, often unsettling footage, like a horse jumping from a diving board, an autopsy, or a smiling, disembodied prop head advertising cigarettes in a store window. But it's Lipsett's unique sense of sound that gives the images their vivid, almost subversive feel, infecting everything on-screen with mood and personality: Lipsett's sound track buzzes and whirs with fragments of conversations about morality, the Bible, and ruminations on God. Blues and gospel play over couples dancing and young men shooting one another with toy pistols. A choir exults as people laugh at their distorted images in funhouse mirrors and as commuters exit an escalator. "When George saw *21-87*, a lightbulb went off," said Walter Murch. "One of the things we clearly wanted to do...was to make a film where the sound and the pictures were free-floating."[16]

In one memorable moment—especially as it affected Lucas—Lipsett inserts over images of fluttering pigeons a snippet of an existential discussion between Warren S. McCulloch, a pioneer in artificial intelligence, and cinematographer Roman Kroitor. As McCulloch contends that human beings are merely complicated machines, Kroitor counters that it can't be that simple or soulless, arguing that as humans contemplate the world around them, "they become aware of some kind of force...behind this apparent mask which we see in front of us, and they call it God." A decade later, Lucas would acknowledge that his own version of the Force, while based on the universal idea of life forces, was a tip of the hat to Lipsett, "an echo of that phrase in *21-87*."[17]

Lucas would borrow one more conceit from *21-87*: "I think that's one reason I started calling most of my [college] movies by numbers," he said.[18] This film, then, would be named for its main character, designated in Lucas's dystopia as *THX 1138 4EB*. As Vorkapich had done with his main character in *Life and Death of 9413: A Hollywood Extra*, Lucas would emblazon his hero's identifying number across his forehead. Although Lucas always insisted that the letters THX "[don't] mean anything,"[19] Matthew Robbins—who had left the protagonist unnamed in his first treatment—thought Lucas might simply have liked the look of the three letters, pointing out that "the letters T, H and X are all symmetrical."[20] Others speculated that Lucas had coyly lifted the title from his phone number, 849-1138, with the letters THX corresponding to the numbers 8, 4, and 9 on the phone's dial.[21]

Lucas filmed *THX 1138 4EB* over three long, grueling days in January 1967. He would work his navy film crew hard all night, lugging equipment into computer labs and parking lots to catch his main character sprinting down one hallway after another as his pursuers monitor him from a control room. At times it was practically guerrilla filmmaking, as Lucas and his crew would shoot as much as they could in a parking garage before the light changed or they ran out of time. And even with the military's equipment at their disposal, there were still shortages and equipment failures. Through it all, Lucas simply coped and improvised, with a resilience that impressed the hardened navy officers. Lacking a proper dolly for moving shots, for instance, Lucas and cameraman Zip Zimmerman simply mounted the camera sturdily onto their shoulders and sat stone still on a rolling platform as it was towed slowly backward.

Making things even tougher, Lucas was still working full-time for Verna Fields, sorting and editing footage of President Johnson for *Journey to the Pacific* during the day before returning to his own film at night. The pace was exhausting; Fields would often catch Lucas asleep at his Moviola, head down, as film slowly unspooled onto the floor. At night, he often barely had the strength to carry the movie camera, opting instead to cradle it in his arms rather than perching it on his shoulder. Much of the time he would leave the camerawork to Zimmerman, preferring to direct from one side. The three-day shoot was going to be the easy part anyway; Lucas would be doing the *real* work on his film all by himself, in the editing room, where he would add optical effects, on-screen chroma key, and an interesting, aggressive sound track. With filming complete, an exhausted Lucas took his film cans over to Fields's place, where he planned to spend the next ten weeks editing the film on her Moviolas at night.

With filming on *THX* complete—though there were still weeks of editing to be done—Lucas turned to his next project, *anyone lived in a pretty [how] town,* an arty six-minute film inspired by the e. e. cummings poem of the same name. For the first time, Lucas had full-color 35 millimeter Cinemascope at his disposal, though it hadn't been easy. "On this one, we weren't even allowed to shoot in color," Lucas said. "It was a five-week project and they said we couldn't possibly do color in five weeks because it took almost a week just to get the dailies back." But Lucas decided to do it anyway, working again with Paul Golding, his collaborator on *Herbie,* and a good-sized crew, including several actors, with costumes and props. Lucas shot the film over twelve days—nine more than it had taken to shoot *THX*—on a budget of only $40, and finished the film in the five-week deadline. "We were one of the only crews to finish," Lucas said, though he admitted he and his team *had* received a dressing-down at the hands of instructor Douglas Cox for shooting in color after he had advised against it.[22]

Lucas continued to edit *THX* late into the evenings, paying particular attention to the way the film sounded. He and Walter Murch—who found editing sound "intoxicating"—had talked about the importance of sound often, and both knew that the right sound track could transform a film into an *experience*.[23] They had seen it firsthand at USC, where the screening room was situated in such a way that sound would funnel down the hallway and out onto the open patio—and "when there was a really interesting-sounding film," Lucas explained, "the whole department would come rushing in to see what it was."[24] Lucas, then, would always want the sound and music in his movies to be as clear and immersive as possible—a campaign he would deftly wage through his entire career, not only choosing the dynamic conductor John Williams to score his films but also successfully advocating for theater sound systems with better speakers and acoustics.

As Lucas hunched over the Moviola in Fields's editing room—culling through footage of Lyndon Johnson during the day, then spooling *THX 1138 4EB* back and forth all night—he found himself talking more and more easily with Marcia. Their casual chatter was still mostly about films, but Lucas *liked* that she could talk about film-making with the same excitement, the same appreciation for the technical side of things, that he could. Until Marcia, the few women Lucas had dated in college were mostly into what he thought were "a lot of dumb things."[25] Here was someone who wanted to talk story lines and film mechanics, and who also shared his disdain for the Hollywood system even as she was trying to work her way up through it. She was smart and easy to talk to—so Lucas finally summoned the nerve to ask her out. Sort of.

"It wasn't really a date," Lucas said of their outing to the AFI headquarters in Beverly Hills to watch a film by a mutual friend. "But that was the first time we were ever alone together." There were more conversations in their apartments, followed by more movies, and suddenly, before either quite realized it, they were dating. "Marcia and I got along real well," said Lucas plainly. For her part, Marcia was attracted to his drive and intensity, but she also found him surprisingly "cute and funny and silly."[26]

They seemed an unlikely couple. Whereas Lucas was serious and brooding, Marcia, said classmate Richard Walter, "was very bright and upbeat. Just the loveliest woman you ever saw in your life."[27] Milius, never one to mince words, thought Lucas was clearly outclassed. "We all wondered how little George got this great looking girl," Milius snorted, though he thought he knew the answer: Marcia was "smart, too, obsessed with films." And, he added impishly, "she was a better editor than he was."[28] Golding, however, thought they looked great together. "They're both so little," he said matter-of-factly.[29]

Lucas's next student film was an ambitious black-and-white documentary spotlighting Los Angeles radio personality Bob Hudson, a blowhard of a deejay who called himself "the Emperor." Lucas, who had spent most of his teens listening to deejays chatter as he cruised Modesto, had wanted to make a documentary about a radio personality for some time. "People develop this relationship with people on the radio," said Lucas. "They think of them as [being] one way and they create a sort of ambiance about themselves. People get very close to the people on the radio except, of course, they're not close at all."[30] He had initially wanted to make a film about the enigmatic Wolfman Jack—who in 1967 was burning up American airwaves with 250,000 watts from Tijuana radio station XERB behind him—"but I didn't know where he was," said Lucas.[31] Hudson, then, had been a happy accident. "[George and I] were both listening to the Emperor Hudson radio show at the time," said Paul Golding, "and we both tried to call each other at the exact same time that we were listening to his show because we both knew that we had to make a film about this guy."[32]

Lucas and Golding regrouped with their small team from *pretty [how] town* for their documentary, which was originally to have been ten minutes long, except that Lucas and Golding were "rather ambitious," and envisioned the film as a kind of half-hour television show, complete with commercials.[33] Lucas badgered their instructors for more film, getting into several loud arguments before he succeeded in prying loose enough film to shoot additional footage, on the condition that the final project be edited down to no more than ten minutes. "I got used to shooting a ton of material and making a movie out of it in the editing room," said Lucas.[34] He had no intention of complying with the demand that he limit the film to ten minutes.

Lucas would shoot *The Emperor* throughout most of March and April 1967, filming Hudson as he ranted on the air and over the phone, and even getting him to sit for interviews. "He had no idea what was going to happen with us being in his studio," said Golding, "and he didn't want anyone in there screwing up his radio show."[35] Hudson eventually came to trust and enjoy Lucas and his film crew, even taking part in an on-screen gag in which Hudson emerges from his car flanked by jackbooted bodyguards played by Lucas and Golding in Hitchcock-style cameos. When they weren't trailing along after Hudson, Lucas shot fake ads that gave off a whiff of *Mad* magazine and an even more distinctive scent of pot, including an ad for a Camaro that turns out to be a rhinoceros instead of a car, and bananas that could be smoked—the latter featuring Milius playing a Mexican *bandito* with smirking relish.

It was a good experience for everyone involved. "It was filmmaking at its purest," recalled Golding. "We all worked together wonderfully and we were all very open to each other's ideas."[36] Milius, too, would always regard *The Emperor* as one of Lucas's defining films. "He was a great graphic kind of artist in a way," said Milius. "He had a definite kind of visual orientation towards things...a great sense of what he wanted to do, you know, and he did unusual things."[37] Indeed, one of *The Emperor's* most unusual and jarring moments comes halfway through the film, when the credits begin to roll, seeming to mark the end of the movie. It was actually a fake-out aimed at naysaying USC instructors, making it appear as if Lucas had complied with their demands to end the movie after ten minutes. At the film's first screening, recalled Golding, "you could hear this wave of sadness and disappointment in the crowd, because everyone knew...about the battles that we had been fighting with the school to shoot this, and they had thought that we had caved in on the school's demands." When the audience realized that the film continued for another twelve minutes after the credits, the theater erupted with excitement. "Every minute of it past those titles," said Golding puckishly, "was our deliberate attack on the facility."[38] Lucas soaked in the applause with satisfaction. He'd been right. *Again.*

That spring, Marcia moved in with Lucas in his hilltop apartment on Portola. Friends scratched their heads; the two of them seemed so unalike. But both Lucas and Marcia thought that was exactly what made them perfect for each other. "I always felt I was an optimist because I'm extroverted, and I always thought that George was more introverted, quiet, and pessimistic," said Marcia. Lucas was typically inscrutable. "Marcia and I are very different and also very much alike," he said. If pressed, he also had to admit he liked that she made him dinner every night. When Lucas's parents saw the two of them together, they could tell by the relative ease with which he acted around her that she was the one. Cementing the deal in the minds of many Lucas family members, Lucas confessed to his brother-in-law, "Marcia is the only person I've ever known who can make me raise my voice."[39] Coming from the low-key Lucas, that was high praise indeed.

In the weeks after the release of *The Emperor*, Lucas finally completed work on *THX 1138 EB*. He was pleased with it — "I didn't expect it to turn out so well," he admitted — and had worked hard to make the film a senses-swamping experience.[40] Visually, Lucas had filled the screen with plenty of high-tech tricks: images are distorted or streaked with static, like the flicker of a barely tuned-in television channel; numbers run down the sides and across the bottom of the screen, giving the viewer a disorienting feeling of watching everything on a video monitor, just as THX's pursuers do. Some sequences appear to be filmed by a surveillance camera, while others are tinted orange, as seen through the visor of a policeman's helmet, with an on-screen display indicating we're seeing the view from PERFECTBOD2180. At one point the date flashes past: 5-14-2187 — Lucas's on-screen nod to Lipsett's influential film.

Lucas's weeks of attention to the sound track had paid off, too, for even today, few other films sound like it. "There was this wild mixture of Bach," said Walter Murch, "and skittering around in that were the chatterings of almost undistinguishable voices in air traffic control, or something like that."[41] Lucas borrowed interesting music from any place he could find it, using the Yardbirds' haunting "Still I'm Sad" over the opening credits, and loud organ chords reverberating over THX's triumphant sprint into the sunset in the movie's closing moments. Plotwise, Lucas added an additional undercurrent of paranoia, with THX's mate YYO 7117 being interrogated by the state —

represented by a Christ-like figure with 0000 across his forehead—for the crime of "SEXACTE." There are lots of extended sequences of people pushing buttons and operating machinery, as well as shots of THX running down endless hallways, arms flailing—and yet, with Lucas's rapid-fire editing, on-screen effects, and surreal sounds, it's all somehow exciting. Quite simply, *THX 1138 4EB* works.

"I was into trying to create emotions through pure cinematic techniques," Lucas said later. "All the films I made during that time center on conveying emotions through a cinematic experience, not necessarily through the narrative. Throughout my career, I've remained a cinema enthusiast; even though I went on to make films with a more conventional narrative, I've always tried to convey emotions through essentially cinematic experiences."[42] It was indeed a cinematic experience; its debut was nothing short of a happening. Students cheered from the moment the USC logo appeared on-screen, and elevated to a roar as its color slowly transitioned from yellow to blood red.

The success of *THX* also went a long way toward mitigating some of the continuing tension between father and son. While George Lucas Sr. had long accepted that his son was determined to be a filmmaker, that didn't mean he had to be happy about it. But watching his son's films at a USC student film festival, with the audience buzzing enthusiastically around him, he could appreciate that his son had not only found his calling but also earned the respect of his peers. "Now, I had been against this thing of his going to the cinema school from day one, but we guessed he had finally found his niche," said George Sr. "As we drove home, I said to Dorothy, 'I think we put our money on the right horse.'"[43]

Feeling both confident and vindicated by *THX 1138 4EB*, Lucas applied for a student scholarship offered by Columbia Pictures and writer-producer Carl Foreman, who was overseeing production on the Gregory Peck film *Mackenna's Gold* in Utah and Arizona. Foreman was offering an opportunity for four students—two from UCLA, two from USC—to watch his film crew at work and, more important, to spend their time producing short films on the making of *Mackenna's Gold* that Foreman could later use to promote the movie. To Lucas's likely disappointment, he wasn't one of the two USC students selected; instead, scholarships went to classmates Charley Lippincott and Chuck Braverman. At the last moment, however, Lippincott backed out after landing a job with an assistant director at Columbia Pictures and recommended Lucas as his replacement—and off Lucas went to the Arizona desert to hook up with Foreman and the crew of *Mackenna's Gold*. It was the first time he had the chance to see a major motion picture being made—and Lucas, never a patient bystander to begin with, wasn't impressed.

"We had never been around such opulence, zillions of dollars being spent every five minutes on this huge, unwieldy thing," Lucas said later. "It was mind-boggling to us because we had been making films for three hundred dollars, and seeing this incredible waste—that was the worst of Hollywood."[44] Lost on Lucas, however, was the fact that he was benefiting from such largesse, for Foreman had provided his four young filmmakers—besides Lucas and Braverman from USC, there were J. David Wyles and David MacDougall from UCLA—with the equipment and transportation they would need to make their own short films, and was even paying each of them a weekly stipend, most of which Lucas would pocket. Lucas could still work in the guerrilla style he preferred, but Foreman was providing him with some of the best equipment of his fledgling career to do it.

Despite his distaste for the "opulence" on set, Lucas was privately hoping that his experience on *Mackenna's Gold* might finally pry open the doors to a job in Hollywood, and he wanted to make a good impression on Foreman. It would be an uphill battle, for Foreman—who had written *High Noon* and overseen the highly profitable films *The Guns of Navarone* and *Born Free*—had a reputation for being prickly. And perhaps for good reason: he had been blacklisted during the Red scare in the 1950s, and had exiled himself to London for more than a decade. *Mackenna's Gold* marked his first major project since his return to the United States.

If Lucas was hoping to ingratiate himself with Foreman, however, he got off to a shaky start. Although Foreman had essentially given his four young filmmakers carte blanche for making their films—they would have no supervision, no one spot-checking their work—he *did* ask for approval of their subjects. Wyles offered to make a film about the horse wranglers, while MacDougall would shadow director J. Lee Thompson, and Braverman would follow around Foreman himself. Lucas, who admitted to being "a very hostile kid in those days," wanted nothing that conventional, and offered to make a "tone poem," in the vein of *1:42.08,* instead. Foreman tried to talk him out of it, but the more he objected, the deeper Lucas dug in. "If they were going to give a scholarship to make a movie, then I wanted to make a movie," Lucas protested. "I wasn't going to do some promo film to advertise the picture."[45]

Lucas would go off on his own—Foreman would later accuse him of "snubbing" his fellow filmmakers, a charge Lucas denied—filming the desert scenery, the enormous skies, the windmills and prairie dogs, with mere glimpses of the film crew for *Mackenna's Gold* in the background, trespassers visible only from afar. Lucas named his movie for the date he completed filming, calling it *6-18-67*—another numerically named film. Part John Ford western, part tone poem, it was also, Lucas told Marcia, "a film about you, because no matter what I'm photographing, I pretend and wish that it is you." But Foreman wasn't impressed, complaining that Lucas's arty four-minute film was in direct defiance of the original assignment and had little to do with *Mackenna's Gold.* A year later, however, when *6-18-67* was shown on a Los Angeles PBS station, Foreman grudgingly admitted that Lucas had made a statement. "Life [in the desert] went on before us, and life went on after us," said Foreman, "and that's what George's film was all about."[46]

Lucas returned to Los Angeles in June, where, to his surprise, he found that he and Walter Murch had been nominated for the highly coveted Samuel Warner Memorial Scholarship. The scholarship was another of those opportunities to observe—"watching doesn't teach you anything," Lucas grumbled—but it *did* send the winner to the Warner Bros. studios to work for six months in any department of his choosing, and even paid a weekly stipend of $80. "It was a big deal," Lucas admitted, and, given his lost opportunity with Foreman, it might even offer another chance to break into the tightly closed Hollywood system. As he and Murch waited on the USC patio for the scholarship's selection committee to inform them of the winner, the two of them vowed that whoever won the scholarship would somehow use the opportunity to help the other. Lucas won—and, years later, would make good on their pact, hiring Murch to edit sound for *American Graffiti*. "We were good friends throughout my time at the department, and I was able to help him out later," said Lucas warmly. "In those days, everybody was helping each other."[47]

As Lucas quickly discovered, it wasn't a good time to be at Warner Bros. Warner, like most of the major studios, was a dinosaur that appeared to be slowly lumbering toward extinction. Attendance at movies had plummeted over the previous two decades—in the early 1950s, movie theaters in the United States were already selling 34 million fewer tickets *each week* than they had only three years earlier—largely because of an upstart invention called television that provided viewers with more entertainment options, and made them available in the comfort of their homes. Looking for audiences, studios began making sprawling big-budget films, many of which dragged the studios down when they failed to take hold at the box office—including, most famously, director Joseph Mankiewicz's 1963 film *Cleopatra*, which nearly bankrupted 20th Century Fox. In 1967, the musical bomb *Camelot* would cripple Warner in a similar manner.

Furthermore, the moguls were dead or retiring. At Warner, in fact, seventy-five-year-old studio head Jack Warner had recently sold his stock to Seven Arts and was preparing to head across town to set up his own production company. As the studios hemorrhaged money, in-house actors and writers were let go. Making things worse, as the vise grip of unions squeezed studio bottom lines, many studio heads found it cheaper and easier to abandon making films in the studios in favor of filming on location or with foreign film crews. Soundstages were shuttered. For a moment, Lucas held out hope that he might be able to pursue animation at Warner's famous animation unit, which had produced a seemingly endless stream of quality Looney Tunes cartoons for decades—but that, too, had been closed since 1963 and would not reopen. "Everything was shut down," said Lucas. "It was like a ghost town."[48]

As it turned out, not *everything* was shut down; there was one movie in production on the lot, just starting a twelve-week shoot under a rookie director: a film adaptation of the shopworn musical *Finian's Rainbow,* starring an equally shopworn sixty-eight-year-old Fred Astaire. Lucas groaned as he reported to the set. "I wasn't really interested," he said. "I had just finished one scholarship watching *Mackenna's Gold,* and by this time I had pretty much decided I didn't want to go into the theatrical film business anyway. I wanted to be a documentary cameraman."[49] And now here he was, stuck at a nearly deserted Warner Bros. lot, playing the dreaded role of *observer* again—and to a greenhorn director, no less.

Lucas loitered around the set of *Finian's Rainbow* for several days, quietly watching—*observing*—with his arms folded, mouth set tight. Eventually, the director noticed the "skinny young man" watching him, and asked someone who it was. Learning that his guest was a "student observer from USC," he coyly sidled over to the stone-faced Lucas between takes.

"See anything interesting?" he asked Lucas.

Lucas shook his head slowly. "Nope," he said flatly, making a quick sideways cut with his hand, palm down. "Not yet."

And "this," said the director—a burly, bearded twenty-eight-year-old named Francis Ford Coppola—"is how I met George Lucas."[50]

4

Radicals and Hippies

1967–1971

rancis [Ford Coppola] and I were very good friends right from the
moment we met," said Lucas.[1] In spite of Lucas's typically brusque
opening salvo—it wasn't quite the gruff "you're doing it wrong" with
which Lucas had once greeted Murch, though it was close—Coppola,
too, felt an immediate kinship with Lucas. Partly, it had something to
do with their closeness in age: Lucas was twenty-three, Coppola
twenty-eight. "In those days, film directors were not young people.
They were pretty much older men in suits, smoking pipes," said Coppola. "When I saw George, it was sort of like seeing one of my own,
someone more my age...with my background and with my attitudes
toward filmmaking."[2]

At first glance, the two of them didn't seem to have much in common. Unlike Lucas, Coppola had been raised in a household that tol-
erated, even encouraged, artistic expression. Coppola's father, Carmine,
was a musician with the Detroit Symphony Orchestra who happened
to be playing the flute on the radio show *The Ford Sunday Evening*

Hour on the evening Francis was born on April 7, 1939—and hence adopted the name of the show's sponsor for his new son's middle name. Unlike in the Lucas household, there would be little strife between Francis and his own father—and when Francis contracted polio at age ten, his father was nearly "wiped out" with anguish, a show of emotion that would have been out of character for George Lucas Sr.[3] Francis would recover from the disease after nearly a year of being quarantined on bed rest in his own room—a confinement he never forgot. "A lot of my getting into the movie business stems from me feeling this isolation," Coppola said later.[4]

After graduating from Jamaica High School in New York, Coppola enrolled at Hofstra University in 1956, where he quickly took over the theater arts program on the strength of his ability to do it all: write, direct, act, and produce. He also honed a defiantly independent streak. "The whole tone of my regime—and it was a regime," said Coppola, "was to turn control of the Theater Arts Department into the hands of students," which he successfully did. After graduation—"I left Hofstra as really the top guy," Coppola recalled proudly—he discovered the films of Soviet director Sergei Eisenstein and immediately transferred his love from theater to cinema. "On Monday I was in the theater," he said, "and on Tuesday I wanted to be a filmmaker."[5]

Inspired, Coppola enrolled as a graduate student at UCLA film school in the fall of 1960. With his talent for screenwriting, he won the prestigious Samuel Goldwyn Award and soon found himself—like so many aspiring filmmakers at the time—working for Roger Corman, for whom he wrote and directed the low-budget horror film *Dementia 13* in 1963. That same year, his screenwriting also brought him to the attention of Warner Bros.–Seven Arts, which put him under contract to write or punch up scripts, one of which, *Patton*, would later win him an Academy Award. Coppola, however, quickly grew frustrated with writing movies for others. He wrote a screenplay based on the novel *You're a Big Boy Now*, which he shot on location in New York City in a speedy twenty-nine days in 1966. At twenty-seven, Coppola had officially made a major motion picture. It was a big deal, and Coppola knew it. "In those years, it was unheard of for a young fellow to make a feature film," he said later. "I was the first one!"[6]

To frustrated film students and graduates, who regularly found the doors of mainstream Hollywood closed and barred, Coppola was already "a legend," said Walter Murch.[7] "Because of his personality, he actually succeeded in getting his hand on the doorknob and flinging open the door, and suddenly there was a crack of light, and you could see that one of us, a film student without any connections to the film business, had put one foot in front of another and actually made the transition from being a film student to being somebody who made a feature film sponsored by one of the studios."[8] To Steven Spielberg, Coppola was "my shining star.... Francis was the first inspiration to a lot of young filmmakers because he broke through before many others."[9]

Convinced by his work on *Big Boy* that Coppola was the real deal, Warner had now placed him at the helm of *Finian's Rainbow,* their lone project at the near-empty studio. As two of the youngest people on the set, Lucas and Coppola soon found themselves spending plenty of time together—another big brother figure to whom Lucas could attach himself. In this case, however, it was a role Coppola was happy, even eager, to play. "I was anxious to have a friend," said Coppola, "and, as things turned out, something I had never had, which was a younger brother."[10] And as brothers tend to do, the two of them would bicker, sometimes furiously, then reconcile over and over again as the years went by.

At the moment, however, Lucas was bored. Coppola was good company, but Lucas wanted to do anything other than "observe." He'd had enough of standing around during the production of *Mackenna's Gold* earlier that spring. So Lucas began leaving the back lot—and Coppola—to poke around in the vacant animation building, looking for any abandoned scraps of film that he might use to make a short movie. "The cameras were still there," said Lucas, "so I figured I'd find some short pieces of film and spend the six months of my work time there making an animated film."[11]

Coppola noticed the young man's absence and was not amused. "What are you doing?" he demanded of Lucas. "Aren't I entertaining enough for you?"[12] When Lucas explained that he preferred *doing* to watching, Coppola nodded sympathetically and gave Lucas a job as his administrative assistant, promising $3,000 for six months' work. While Lucas took care of many of the day-to-day details on the set, dutifully shooting photographs to ensure continuity of props and furniture over a variety of takes, Coppola expected more out of the young man he was quickly coming to see as a protégé. "I used to tell him things like 'George, every day you need to come up with a brilliant idea. That's your assignment,'" recalled Coppola. "And every day he would come up with a brilliant idea, so I very quickly understood this was an exceptional person."[13]

They made an odd-looking pair. Lucas was short and unassuming, while the nearly six-foot Coppola was jovial and outgoing. But the more they got to know each other, the better they liked each other—and the more they came to appreciate their differences. "[George's] strengths were in areas different than mine," said Coppola. "I had come out of theater, and I had been trying to be a writer for so long, and he had come more out of design, and was very strong in editing. So there was a kind of mutual joining of these specialties."[14] Whereas Lucas, for example, had little interest in dealing with the daily dramas of actors, Coppola, with his background in acting in the theater, jumped willingly into the fray, unconcerned about feelings or egos. At one point during the production of *Finian*, Coppola made a point of loudly firing Hermes Pan, Fred Astaire's choreographer of choice, even over the objections of Astaire, who quietly grumbled that he "hated the things he saw Coppola doing."[15]

For Lucas's part, it was easy to get swept up in the charismatic Coppola's loud enthusiasm. "Francis is very flamboyant, very Italian, very 'go-out-there-and-do-things.' I'm very 'let's-think-about-this-first,'" Lucas said later. "But together we were great, because I would be the weight around his neck that slowed him down a little bit to keep him from getting his head chopped off. Aesthetically, we had very compatible sensibilities…but we were very much the opposite in the way we operated and the way we did things. And that, I think, allowed us to have a very active relationship."[16] At times Coppola could even run his crew with a gleeful disregard for the rules that Lucas admired. For one scene in *Finian*, Coppola had hauled a film crew up to San Francisco to film Fred Astaire on the city's famous Golden Gate Bridge. Lacking the proper permits, Coppola simply shot until a state police car chased them off—a bit of insurrectionary moviemaking Lucas could appreciate.[17]

They may have been complementary personalities even in their twenties, but there was one thing about Lucas that Coppola was determined to change. "You're going to have to learn to write if you're ever going to learn to direct," Coppola told him.[18] "Nobody will take you seriously unless you can write."[19] Lucas groaned, shuddering at the memory of the long evenings he had spent laboring over high school and college papers, struggling with spelling and basic grammar. "I'm not a writer," he protested. "I *hate* writing."[20] Besides, he told Coppola, "I like *cinéma vérité*, documentaries…non-story, non-character tone poems."[21]

But Coppola stood firm; any director worth his salt had to know how to put together a screenplay. Coppola promised to help in any way he could, and even had a project in mind for Lucas's first script: Lucas's own *THX 1138 4EB*, the short student film ending with the escape into the desert, which Coppola was convinced could be expanded into a full-length feature. To sweeten the deal, Coppola thought of a way Lucas could write his script *and* get paid for it. All it would take was a bit of subterfuge, Coppola-style.

As Coppola wrapped filming on *Finian's Rainbow* that autumn, he was already eager to get started on his next film, this time from one of his own scripts called *The Rain People*, inspired by a childhood experience when his mother had run out on his father after a fight and checked in to a local motel, effectively disappearing for several days. Coppola envisioned it as a much more intimate and personal film than any he had made previously and wanted to bring a grittier style of filmmaking to it. "I've got this plan to do a tiny movie with just a small group of people, a bit like making a student film," he told Lucas, "get in a truck and drive across the United States, making a movie as I go. No planning, no nothing—just do it."[22] Coppola wanted Lucas to serve as his right-hand man for the project. Lucas *was* intrigued, but slightly skeptical. He thought that Coppola needed to think things through first; Coppola thought that Lucas lacked a sense of adventure. "He used to call me the eighty-five-year-old man," sighed Lucas.[23]

With his typical swagger, Coppola dangled *The Rain People* in front of Warner Bros.–Seven Arts for several weeks, then coyly went missing, a strategic feint meant to convince the studio that he was taking his project somewhere else. It worked: in a flurry, Warner Bros.–Seven Arts agreed to give Coppola $750,000 to shoot *The Rain People* exactly as he wanted—on the road, away from the studio, and without script approval. Additionally, as part of the deal, Coppola had persuaded the studio to include $3,000 for Lucas to write the script for *THX 1138*. Coppola told Lucas to think of it as his salary; he could work with Coppola on *The Rain People* by day and write *THX 1138* at night.

An impressed Lucas could only shake his head in awe at Coppola's colossal nerve. "Francis could sell ice to the Eskimos," Lucas said later. "He has charisma beyond logic. I can see now what kind of men the great Caesars of history were, their magnetism."[24]

Coppola had good reason to believe in the potential of *THX* as a feature-length film. Throughout 1967 and early 1968, Lucas's *THX 1138 4EB* was still making the rounds of the student film circuit, where it was winning praise—and prizes—from students, critics, and even Hollywood insiders. Ned Tanen, a young producer at Universal, remembered leaving the theater in a near daze. "You looked at the movie, and said, 'Jesus, who the hell did *this?* I don't know where he stole the footage, but he is someone very special.'"[25]

The pinnacle for *THX*—and for Lucas as a student filmmaker—came in January 1968, when *THX* was selected as the best dramatic film at the third National Student Film Festival, held at UCLA's Royce Hall. Lucas actually had films entered in three of the four major

categories; besides *THX, The Emperor* had been competing in the documentary category, while *6-18-67* was entered as an experimental
film—and rumor had it that Lucas had actually *won* in those categories as well before being downgraded to honorable mention status to
prevent a sweep by a single student filmmaker. As it was, Lucas even
had a hand in the winning entry in the animation category, USC classmate John Milius's *Marcello, I'm So Bored*, for which Lucas had edited
the sound. It was enough to get him a mention in *Time* magazine and
applause from the *Los Angeles Times* as "the most impressive young talent to emerge from a university cinema department in the past five
years."[26] Film critic Charles Champlin went even farther, declaring
that "for ingenuity, power, and professionalism, Lucas's *THX 1138
4EB* is a knock-out and must be seen."[27]

Beyond the accolades and attention, the competition proved pivotal to Lucas—and filmmaking—for a very different reason. When
the curtain at Royce Hall went up on Friday, January 19, 1968, for the
first night of the festival, sitting in the audience was a twenty-one-year-
old junior from California State Long Beach named Steven Spielberg.
"I didn't know ahead of time about any of the films...so I anticipated
nothing," Spielberg remembered. "I saw a number of shorts first—but
when *THX* came on, there was so much virtuosity in the craft and the
vision and the emotion of that story that...I couldn't believe it was a
student film....It absolutely stopped the festival. You could have heard
a pin drop in that theater."[28] Spielberg was awestruck—and practically
jade green with envy for its young director. "My first impression was 'I
hate you!'" said Spielberg later, laughing. "'I hate that guy, man! He's
so much better than I am!'"[29]

Afterward, Spielberg headed backstage, where he found Lucas
with Coppola—and their individual recollections years later of their
first encounter is reflective of both of their personalities and narrative
styles. Spielberg remembered the moment warmly and vividly. "George
was a really friendly guy," according to Spielberg. "[He said], 'Hey,
how are you?' and we shook hands and became friends from that
moment on. The friendship actually began with a handshake."[30] In his

telling of events, however, Lucas wasn't willing to confirm either the emotion or the details. "I think I may have met him. There were a lot of people afterward," Lucas said. "But," he conceded, "if we met, it was definitely [just] a handshake, 'Hi, how are you?'"[31]

However memorable—or unmemorable—its start, a friendship between Lucas and the man he would later refer to affectionately as "my partner, my pal, my inspiration, my challenger"[32] was perhaps inevitable, for the two of them were much alike. As teenagers, both had been outsiders, though in Spielberg's case, he was more nerd than greaser. "I was a loner and very lonely," Spielberg recalled of his years growing up in Arizona. "I was the only Jewish kid in school, and I was very shy and uncertain."[33] Spielberg, too, was an apathetic student, a devotee of comic books, and a self-proclaimed "TV junkie." Unlike Lucas, however, Spielberg had known since elementary school that he wanted to be a filmmaker, shooting his own westerns, mysteries, even a World War II fighter pilot film called *Fighter Squad.* "I've been really serious about filmmaking since I was twelve years old," Spielberg said later. "I don't excuse those early years as a hobby....I really did start then."[34]

Poor grades kept Spielberg out of film school at USC, so he enrolled at Cal State Long Beach instead, where he had to ad lib a cinema curriculum since Long Beach had no formal film school. It probably didn't matter anyway; Spielberg spent most of his college years sneaking into Universal Studios to watch films being made, sitting with editors in cutting rooms, and, from time to time, getting thrown off soundstages. While he had completed several amateur films— including a feature-length film called *Firelight* that had premiered at a real movie theater in Phoenix when he was seventeen—at the time of his first encounter with Lucas in early 1968, Spielberg's filmmaking was still more aspiring than actual. But Lucas and his work had inspired him anew. "No longer were John Ford, Walt Disney, David Lean...my role models," said Spielberg. "Rather, it was someone nearer my own age, someone I could actually get to know, compete with, draw inspiration from."[35] Motivated in part by what he had seen on-screen at Royce Hall, Spielberg would raise the money to write and direct an impressive twenty-five-minute film called *Amblin'*—and by the end of the year would be under contract with Universal, an observer no more.

In February 1968, Lucas left California for Long Island, New York, to begin scouting locations for *The Rain People*. Coppola was planning to begin filming in March and had headed to New York ahead of Lucas, shooting B-roll at Hofstra and preparing his seven-vehicle caravan for its slow trek across the county. Coppola had already announced that wives and girlfriends would not be permitted on the trip, so Lucas had brought Marcia to New York for a bit of time together before he left on his extended adventure with Coppola. As he prowled nearby Garden City, scouting sites where Coppola would later film a wedding sequence, Lucas proposed to Marcia.

For Lucas, the decision to marry Marcia was as inexplicable as it was obvious. "It wasn't that I saw her in the editing room and said, 'I'm going to get that girl,'" said Lucas. "It was more like, 'This is another girl and we'll have fun and what the heck.' I certainly never expected I would marry Marcia." But, he said, "Marcia and I got along real well. We were both feisty and neither one of us would take any shit from the other. I sort of liked that. I didn't like someone who could be run over."[36] John Plummer, who had been there from the beginning, wasn't at all surprised. "She had a lot of the same beliefs that George did," said Plummer. "As a couple, [they were] very supportive. They had a mission together, what they wanted to do. It seemed like it was a very good relationship."[37]

That mission, at least as envisioned by George, involved their eventually moving back to northern California, where Marcia could continue to edit commercials and the odd film project while he pursued a career as an independent avant-garde filmmaker. "We'll make [films] together and sell them there," he told her. "It's probably going to be very hard." But Marcia admired that kind of forward thinking. "George has always planned things very far in advance," she said. "He always works out in his head what may happen in a year or two and figures out what all the possibilities are so that he can handle whatever situation pops up. He's very good at capitalizing on all the options."[38]

As in his friendship with Coppola, Lucas viewed his and Marcia's differences as the underlying strength in their relationship; typically, however, he had a tough time articulating it. "I say black, she says white," explained Lucas. "But we have similar tastes, backgrounds, feelings about things, and philosophies." Marcia put it a bit more elegantly, noting that "we want to complete ourselves, so we look for someone who is strong where we're weak." If there was one thing that truly made them compatible, however, it was their mutual love of editing. "That's one of the reasons our relationship works—we both love the same thing."[39] In hindsight, it was probably not the best foundation on which to build a marriage.

Officially engaged, Marcia headed back to California while Lucas piled into one of the several station wagons Coppola had wrangled to transport his entire twenty-person film crew—director, actors, stuntmen, grips, soundmen, everyone—on a nearly five-month crawl through eighteen states. Coppola also planned on carrying all the equipment he needed, including a full-size, state-of-the-art Steenbeck editing table he had purchased at his own expense, deducting the cost from his director's fee. The process of shooting *The Rain People* was "a labor of love," Coppola said later. "We had a very small crew in a remodeled Dodge bus that we rebuilt ourselves and filled with the most advanced motion picture equipment available."[40] Ultimately, the plan was *there was no plan:* while Coppola had a shooting script, he had no established shooting schedule and no specific locations in mind; if he saw a place that looked promising for a certain scene, he'd stop and roll film. Inspiration would define their direction each day. It was shooting without a net—the sort of guerrilla filmmaking Lucas loved.

But there was nothing easy about it. The schedule was particularly grueling for Lucas, who would get up every day at 4 a.m. to agonize over his script for *THX 1138* for two hours, then head out at 6 a.m. to spend the rest of the day as Coppola's third assistant director, right-hand man, and all-around gofer. The writing process was particularly slow and miserable. "Francis...practically handcuffed George to the desk," Marcia remembered.[41] But Lucas persevered. "[Francis] sort of took me under his wing," as Lucas later put it. "He said, 'I'll help you.'"[42] Coppola's first bit of advice: "Don't ever read what you've written. Try to get it done in a week or two, then go back and fix it...you just keep fixing it."[43]

At the same time, Lucas—never one to pass up the opportunity to grab any bit of film and start shooting—had begun working on a behind-the-scenes documentary about the making of the film, tailing along after Coppola with a 16 mm camera and a Nagra tape recorder. "George was around in a very quiet way," said producer Ron Colby. "You'd look around and suddenly there'd be George in a corner with his camera. He'd just kind of drift around. But he shot the camera, did his own sound. He was very much a one-man band."[44] He also found in the boisterous Coppola an ideal subject; it was easy to catch the director arguing with his actors—among them James Caan and Robert Duvall—squabbling with local authorities, or grousing loudly into the telephone about union interference and daring Warner executives to call the police on him. But Coppola loved what Lucas was putting together, and even managed to re-appropriate $12,000 from the film's publicity budget to pay for the documentary, which Lucas would eventually title *filmmaker*.

As the Coppola convoy rolled out of New York, through New Jersey, and into Pennsylvania, Coppola ordered the entire crew to shave off their beards—himself included, which Lucas thought made Coppola "unrecognizable"—to give themselves a more conservative look that might come in handy when dealing with local authorities.[45] Sometimes the ploy paid off, as Coppola was able to sweet-talk his way into shooting in the middle of an Armed Forces Day parade in Tennessee. In Kentucky, however, a prickly ferry operator refused to permit Coppola to film onboard, while in Nebraska, he clashed with local cops over his use of police insignia. Through it all, Lucas stood quietly by, camera rolling—and when he wasn't filming, he *still* stood near Coppola, hands jammed in his pockets, Coppola's silent shadow. "There was definitely a joining of the hip there between those two guys," remembered Colby. "George was very withdrawn, very quiet, very shy. And Francis was quite ebullient and outgoing."[46]

Still, Lucas and Coppola weren't so joined at the hip that they couldn't squabble from time to time; Lucas found it particularly galling when Coppola exempted himself from all the terms and conditions he'd imposed on the rest of the crew in the spirit of their adventure. Though Coppola had decreed, for instance, that there would be no wives or girlfriends permitted on the trip, he brought along his wife, Eleanor, and their kids anyway, putting them at the rear of the convoy in a Volkswagen minibus. That particular offense Lucas was able to brush off, though he did make a point of showing Coppola's family in *filmmaker*, under a bit of fawning narration. But when Coppola abandoned their convoy at a run-down motel in Pennsylvania in favor of spending a relatively comfortable weekend in New York—there were whispers that Coppola was visiting a mistress—Lucas was furious. "Francis was saying all this 'all for one' stuff, and then he goes off and screws around in New York," said Lucas. "He felt he had a right to do that, and I told him it wasn't fair. We got into a big fight over it."[47] *Fair* would always be a big deal to Lucas.

Such disagreements aside, both Lucas and Coppola found the whole seat-of-the-pants process of making *The Rain People* invigorating. No sets were needed, no studio facilities were needed—and anything Coppola *didn't* have on hand he could get on his own terms. While he didn't have equipment with him to print each day's footage, for instance, Coppola would simply have the film flown to New York each evening for printing so he could view the footage several days later. And better yet, he could do it all without having the Hollywood suits looking over his shoulder or visiting the set and offering useless advice. "We began to feel like Robin Hood and his band," said Coppola. "We really had a filmmaking machine in our hands, and it didn't need to be in Hollywood. It could be anywhere."[48]

Anywhere could even be the middle of nowhere. By late June, Coppola had so much footage in his hands that he decided to hole up for a few weeks in Ogallala, Nebraska, to sort through it all. Coppola converted an old shoe store into an editing room, where he huddled over the Steenbeck with editor Barry "Blackie" Malkin to assemble a working cut. Lucas suggested that things might move along faster if Malkin had an assistant, and recommended Marcia for the job, coyly subverting Coppola's rule against girlfriends in the name of practicality. But when Lucas called her with the offer, Marcia was torn; she had an offer from Haskell Wexler to work on his film *Medium Cool,* which Wexler was planning to shoot at the 1968 Democratic National Convention in what would turn out to be a most tumultuous summer. Lucas had his projects, she had hers—but newly engaged, Marcia felt she was obligated to choose Lucas's project over hers, and dutifully showed up at the shoe shop in Nebraska. As things turned out, a delay in Wexler's shooting schedule would ultimately permit her to work on both films, but a pattern was already forming: Lucas's work came before her work. And sometimes before *her.*

Still, Lucas was glad to have Marcia around—and so was Coppola, who admired more than just her editing skills. "Everybody wanted Marcia," said John Milius flatly, and Coppola—married, but with a reputation, as Marcia put it, as "a major pussy hound"[49]—"attempted to hit on Marcia," according to Milius, "because he attempted to hit on the wives of everybody." Lucas could only watch in tight-lipped annoyance, filing this new offense away for future reference, even as Marcia politely rebuffed Coppola's overtures. "That was Francis," said Milius. "Francis was for Francis—but Francis was great; a truly great man."[50] Sometimes that was enough, sometimes not. Lucas might forgive, but he wouldn't forget.

Coppola returned to the rough cut of *Rain People,* and was so intent on the process, in fact, that in late June he decided to blow off a prior commitment he'd made to participate in a teachers' conference in San Francisco. He'd agreed to sit on a panel called "Film in Relation to the Printed Word," along with several other filmmakers who had adapted books into movies, as Coppola had with *You're a Big Boy Now.* At the last moment, Coppola decided he *wasn't* going—but rather than drop out altogether, he decided to send Lucas in his place.

Lucas arrived at the San Francisco Hilton just in time for the panel, sliding into a seat on the dais behind a placard that still had Coppola's name on it. Sitting next to him was a thirty-one-year-old independent filmmaker from northern California named John Korty, who had adapted his film *The Crazy-Quilt* from psychoanalyst Allen Wheelis's short story "The Illusionless Man and the Visionary Maid." While Korty spoke eloquently on the topic at hand, it was when he digressed into the details of his filmmaking that Lucas really took an interest.

For the past three years, Korty had been running his own film-making facility out of his barn at Stinson Beach, a small ocean resort town just north of San Francisco. He had privately raised the $100,000 for *Crazy-Quilt* by hitting up friends, colleagues, and even his actors for money, shot the movie locally, then edited it on his own equipment. At the film's premiere at the Museum of Modern Art in San Francisco, it received a lengthy standing ovation, and Hollywood executives fell over themselves scrambling to distribute it and recruit Korty, with producer David Wolper wooing him particularly hard. But Korty was having none of it. "From what I saw of Hollywood, they can keep it right now," Korty said. "I would rather work for myself.... [In Hollywood] you have a producer breathing down your neck. Hollywood is dying slowly. Here [in northern California] I am happier working with less money. The risk of failure is far less. We can complete a film in maybe a year... getting the results we want."[51]

It was a speech Coppola or Lucas could have made—and probably had. As soon as their session ended, Lucas excitedly pulled Korty aside. "You've gotta talk to Francis," he said, and the two of them found a pay phone in the lobby so they could call Coppola in Nebraska.[52] Coppola was ecstatic; he wanted to meet Korty as quickly as possible—and on July 4, Coppola, Lucas, and Ron Colby drove up to meet Korty at his Stinson Beach headquarters.

Korty and his wife lived in a two-story house overlooking the beach, only steps away from a slate-gray barn with broken windows that Korty used as his all-purpose film studio. The view was gorgeous. "Where else can you walk out the door and be in the ideal place to start shooting?" said Korty.[53] The barn was packed with "all of the toys of a young filmmaker," recalled an impressed Colby.[54] A large movie screen hung over a stage at one high end of the barn, faced by a sound-proofed projection room housing a 35 mm projector. Korty was finishing work on his newest film, *Funnyman,* and showed Coppola the recording, editing, and dubbing equipment tucked away under the eaves. It wasn't necessarily all state of the art, but it was all *his,* and Coppola and Lucas were dazzled. This was exactly what they had in mind for themselves. "[Korty] inspired us both," said Coppola. "He was a real innovator."[55]

Coppola, Lucas, and Colby piled into their station wagon to begin their drive back to Nebraska, where *The Rain People* was still spooled on the Steenbeck. But Coppola and Lucas had seen the future in Korty's barn on the beach—and when they finished living out of their *Rain People* caravan, Coppola was going to build his own cinematic community…somewhere. "If you can do it," he had told Korty enthusiastically, "we can."[56]

Coppola finally completed the first rough cut of *The Rain People* in San Francisco in mid-October. While Francis was finishing his film, George and Marcia were cutting together Lucas's documentary, now officially called *filmmaker: a diary by george lucas,* in their little house on Portola. As always, film editing, no matter how long the hours, was the fun part—and it was great that he and Marcia could do it together. The rest of the time, however, Lucas was toiling over the script for *THX 1138.* Coppola had continued to lecture Lucas that it was the ability to write original material that separated *filmmakers* from mere *directors.* "Write the screenplay, and then execute it as a producer and director," admonished Coppola.[57] The irony would be that over the course of their careers, it would be Lucas, the self-proclaimed "terrible writer," who would write and direct his own original material—and create two iconic film franchises along the way—while Coppola would largely make his name adapting other people's work for the big screen. At the moment, however, Lucas was taking his mentor's advice seriously, writing and rewriting, getting it all down, just as Coppola had directed.

By November 1, the first draft was complete. "This is terrible," Lucas told Coppola as he handed him the script, and Coppola didn't disagree.[58] After several weeks of working with Lucas on a second draft, Coppola finally admitted he was stumped. "I just don't understand your vision," he told Lucas. "Maybe what we'll do is hire a writer and let him try to do it." Coppola then handed off the first two drafts to television writer Oliver Hailey, but after reviewing Hailey's work, Lucas was even more frustrated, grousing, "His script wasn't at all what I wanted."[59] Lucas would keep revising. And he'd stay unhappy.

For Lucas, writing would always be hard—unless someone else was doing it, at which point Lucas was brimming with ideas and suggestions. Lately, Lucas had become more and more intrigued by a script John Milius was tinkering with for a war movie set in Vietnam— a dangerous topic in 1968, to be sure. It was a mashup of *Dr. Strangelove*—a film both Milius and Lucas loved—and Joseph Conrad's *Heart of Darkness,* a novel Milius was eager to adapt because it seemed so impossible. (A successful film adaptation, said Milius proudly, "had stumped all these great writers.") At first, Milius called his script *The Psychedelic Soldier* but then settled on *Apocalypse Now,* an inspired swipe at the NIRVANA Now buttons being worn by the hippies Milius despised. Lucas loved the script, and as Milius continued writing, Lucas would throw out one idea after another about how the film should be made. Naturally, he would direct it, and would do it in a documentary style on 16 mm film, to give it almost a newsreel effect. "George said, 'Put all the neat stuff in there, all the helicopters,'" laughed Milius. To Lucas's mind, "the big hero thing to be was the director,"[60] said Milius, not the writer.

That winter, even as *THX* was still simmering, Lucas began scouting around Marin County for possible places to establish Coppola's grand cinematic community. Coppola was looking, too. While Francis was leaning toward San Francisco for his new headquarters—he had come to appreciate the area's "political and cultural ferment"—he was casting a wide net when it came to inspiration.[61] Late in 1968, Coppola and Ron Colby left for Denmark to visit another independent film company, Lanterna Film, from which Danish filmmaker Mogens Skot-Hansen had been overseeing film production—mostly commercials and soft porn—since 1955. Coppola and Colby arrived to find Skot-Hansen working out of an old mansion tucked up on a hillside overlooking a lake, filled with state-of-the-art equipment, staffed by beautiful blond women, and housing a bohemian community of filmmakers. Coppola wanted it all, from the house to the equipment to the camaraderie. He and Skot-Hansen struck up a friendship—he would stay with Skot-Hansen and his family for nearly three weeks—and when Coppola left, the Dane presented him with a nineteenth-century optical toy, a cylinder that, when spun and squinted at through a series of slits, produced an illusion of movement.[62] While Coppola liked the toy, he loved its name even more: *zoetrope,* from the Greek words meaning "life movement."

On his way home, Coppola stopped at a Photokina trade fair in Cologne, where he eagerly spent $80,000 on a new editing console and sound mixers, despite the fact that he couldn't afford any of it—and once the equipment was shipped back to the States, he had nowhere to put it. It didn't matter; Coppola was too fired up in pursuit of his dream of his own cinematic commune, his own creative freedom, to bother with such details. "It's mine," Coppola said proudly of his new equipment.[63] "If you're not willing to risk some money when you're young, you're certainly not ever going to risk anything in the years that follow."[64] Arriving back in San Francisco, he excitedly called Lucas to tell him about Skot-Hansen, the mansion, and his new toys. "This is what we need to do," he told Lucas. "We need to get a big old house, like a fraternity, and make movies. And do it here, somewhere outside of Hollywood."[65] That sounded just fine to Lucas, who wanted to stay as far away from Hollywood as possible.

As Lucas drove around Marin County, in fact, he was looking for more than just a location for Coppola's studio; he and Marcia were planning to move to northern California together—just as Lucas had sworn they would when they got engaged—and he had spotted a little house perched at the top of a sloping hill in Mill Valley. The place was small but picturesque—with its white picket fence, it looked like something out of a Norman Rockwell painting—and at $120 a month, it was definitely affordable. It was just the kind of place where a young couple could settle down together. "We were really happy and optimistic," Lucas said later of their time together in Mill Valley. "In our lifestyle there were only two rooms we used, the kitchen and the bedroom. We were in either one or the other."[66]

George and Marcia were married on Saturday, February 22, 1969—almost exactly a year after they had announced their engagement—at the First United Methodist Church in Pacific Grove, California. Lucas, in his darkest suit and tie, was rail thin but beaming from ear to ear as he and Marcia said their vows. Coppola was there in a plum-colored jacket and matching shirt, along with USC classmates Walter Murch and Matthew Robbins, and Verna Fields, who had been present at the beginning of their unexpected courtship. "It was a small wedding, it was informal," said John Plummer. "It was friends, it was a terrific time."[67] The newlywed Lucases sprinted off for a brief honeymoon at Big Sur, then returned to Mill Valley, where Marcia hoped to settle in and start a family, while Lucas headed for San Francisco to play businessman with Coppola.

Over the past several months, Coppola had come close to landing a home for his company. At one point Lucas had spotted in the tiny town of Ross what seemed to be an ideal property, an old mansion known locally as the Dibble Estate. Coppola excitedly sold his house and nearly everything else he had on hand to raise the money for the down payment, then was beaten to the punch by another buyer ("which was very disappointing," sighed Coppola).[68] Negotiations then began on another property, which *also* fell through, leaving Coppola in the lurch as the editing console and sound mixers he had purchased in Cologne were finally on their way to San Francisco with no place to house them. With time running out, John Korty helpfully located a three-story loft in a warehouse at 827 Folsom Street in San Francisco—"a big kooky brick building," Coppola called it—just in time for Coppola to load in his bulky new equipment.[69] Lucas enthusiastically suggested calling their upstart company Transamerican Sprocket Works, but Coppola overrode that particular proposition, arguing that it sounded too much like a rock group. Coppola had another name in mind anyway, a tip of the hat to Skot-Hansen and his wonderful optical toy: American Zoetrope.

Coppola named himself president of Zoetrope, of course, and appointed Lucas his executive vice president. And why not? "George was like a younger brother to me," said Coppola. "I loved him. Where I went, he went."[70] But this was more than just another moviemaking venture together; Zoetrope was *freedom*, a deliberate thumb in the eye of Hollywood and its stranglehold on filmmaking—and Lucas loved playing the role of revolutionary. "Francis said, 'This is what we want to do,' and I said, 'Yeah, this is what we want to do,' so we immediately moved here [to San Francisco] and set up American Zoetrope," Lucas recounted later. "When we got up here, they [the Hollywood studios] said, 'You can't possibly make movies up here.' And we said, 'Well, we don't care.' I said, 'I love San Francisco and that's where I want to live and I don't care.' I kept being stubborn and persistent."[71]

One of Lucas's first acts as Coppola's vice president was to bring compatible talent into their ranks. Right away Lucas placed a call to Walter Murch, who was working on commercials with Haskell Wexler down in Los Angeles, and asked him to drop everything, move to San Francisco, and begin editing sound for *The Rain People* on Zoetrope's newly installed equipment. "I remember George saying, 'Well, we may all be back in a year with our tails between our legs, but at least it'll be fun while we're doing it. Who knows what will happen?'"

recalled Murch. "Most people in Hollywood thought what we were doing was crazy. But it was the late sixties, it was San Francisco, it was all part of what we saw then as the beginnings of the technical democratization of the filmmaking process—with comparatively little money, you could actually go on the road and shoot a feature film."[72] Off Murch went to San Francisco.

John Korty, too, had come along on the adventure, though he was more interested in leasing offices and using Coppola's state-of-the-art equipment than in becoming one of Coppola's Merry Men. Haskell Wexler also expressed an interest in working out of Zoetrope, attracted by the idea of using small crews with portable equipment. Coppola, in fact, was willing to do business with any like-minded filmmaker, screenwriter, editor, or technician, and he and Lucas eventually recruited other eager friends and colleagues, including Matthew Robbins, Willard Huyck, John Milius, and Carroll Ballard. Coppola, delighted to have apostles, sealed most of their deals with a handshake instead of a formal contract—because contracts, said Coppola, in a typical bit of antiestablishment bluster, were "sort of immoral."[73]

There was one friend, however, who wouldn't be invited into the Zoetrope circle. At one point Lucas brought in Steven Spielberg to show Coppola *Amblin'*, Spielberg's recently completed twenty-six-minute student film. Coppola may have been impressed, but he wasn't convinced Spielberg was worthy of Zoetrope; there was too much Hollywood stink on him for Spielberg to be a true revolutionary. "I wasn't really in Francis's circle. I was an outsider, I was the establishment," said Spielberg. "I was being raised and nurtured at Universal Studios, a very conservative company, and in his eyes, and also George's eyes, I was working inside the system."[74] Spielberg would remain on the outside looking in—for now.

Despite his swagger, Coppola admitted that he worried about financing Zoetrope, especially since *Finian's Rainbow* had quickly faded from sight on its release in late 1968. Coppola couldn't make money without a project on hand. "I don't want to have to make success," he groused to the press. "You know, if it means I've got to work on $6,000 films in San Francisco, then I guess that's what I have to do. I don't know. I'll probably do another big picture now. I really need the money."[75]

Money, Coppola decided, could probably be squeezed from Warner Bros.–Seven Arts, where he still had some influence. Despite the failure of *Finian*, the studio was high on *The Rain People*, scheduled for release in September 1969, and Coppola enthusiastically submitted Lucas's latest draft of *THX 1138* to executives in the office of studio head Eliot Hyman. To Coppola's dismay, Hyman and his team weren't impressed; they rejected the script outright, plunging Lucas into a funk. But the savvy Coppola knew something Lucas didn't: Warner Bros.–Seven Arts was about to be bought out by Kinney National Services, which until 1969 was known largely for its parking lots and cleaning services. "What we'll do is we'll wait until these new guys come on board," Coppola told Lucas. "We won't tell them [*THX*] has already been turned down. We'll just pretend that we've already started it."[76]

The imminent change in leadership at Warner was one lucky break. In July 1969, Coppola caught another.

July 14, 1969, saw the release of the film *Easy Rider*, a counterculture road movie directed and co-written by thirty-three-year-old Dennis Hopper, and produced completely outside of Hollywood. Filmed on the road—like *The Rain People*—on a shoestring budget that hovered around $350,000, *Easy Rider* would go on to become one of the most profitable films ever made. Its only contact with the Hollywood system had been for distribution—"the last great mystery with which studios held everyone at bay," lamented one director—the rights to which had eagerly been snatched up by Columbia.[77] "There was a breakthrough with *Easy Rider*," said Walter Murch, "which finally suggested to the studios that there might be something to the way we were thinking."[78] Hopper may have beaten Coppola to the punch, but he had proved Coppola's revolutionary instincts right.

The studios didn't care who had gotten there first; they merely smelled money. Why invest millions bankrolling production of an enormous film on a studio back lot when you could simply distribute independently produced films? Suddenly, independent films—made by young directors, writers, actors, and producers—were in demand. The studios wanted young talent, at times even recruiting directly from film schools. It was a movement Lucas applauded. "I think the student films are the only real hope," Lucas told one reporter. "I think [the studios are] slowly beginning to realize that students know what they're doing, you know? That they're not just a bunch of silly kids out there playing around."[79]

Hollywood was shifting—at least for the moment—toward a new wave of dynamic American filmmaking, largely defined by the personal visions of the *auteur* directors—as integral to a film, went the argument, as a poet was to a poem. "'Personal filmmaking,' that was a phrase we used a lot," explained Coppola. "A personal film was something that you wrote and directed about things that maybe you didn't fully understand, that the filmmaking would answer, that would be not just the repeating of a genre film over and over again... to try to make films that would shed light on life."[80]

It wouldn't take long for the movement to sputter out—and Lucas, to his dismay, would be largely responsible for the gradual shift away from grittier, more personal films, toward more easily accessible pop blockbusters.

For the time being, however, *Easy Rider* had created a tsunami of independent enthusiasm, and in August, Coppola decided to ride the wave right into the offices of Warner Bros.–Seven Arts—he allegedly came roaring into the studio on a motorcycle—to make the new regime an offer it couldn't refuse. Following Warner's takeover by Kinney, the studio had installed former talent agent Ted Ashley as its new chairman, and Ashley had cleaned house, bringing in film producer John Calley as his head of production. Coppola was all but certain that he could pry Calley's wallet open with a bit of the famous Coppola charm—and he pitched Calley and the Warner executives hard, offering them a "multipicpac" of seven screenplays, few of which had actually been written. But Coppola confidently promised Calley that not only was every one a sure-fire hit, but also, in the spirit of low-budget independent films like *Easy Rider*, they could be produced for under $1 million each. Included in the mix was a script of his own called *The Conversation*—Coppola assured Calley that Marlon Brando was interested in it (he wasn't)—and, of course, Lucas's *THX 1138*, which Coppola, just as he had promised, claimed was already in production.

As it turned out, that was actually nearly true. After several false starts, Lucas had finished up the final draft of *THX* with Walter Murch—a good choice, since Murch had worked with Lucas on the outline for the original student film—but Coppola wasn't about to let anyone at Warner have a peek at Lucas's esoteric script. "You've got to understand something," Coppola told Warner. "I can't get Lucas involved in working with a studio about developing a script. He trusts me, we can do it together, he and I, it'll be great, but stay out of it. We'll bring you the finished film."[81] And not to worry, Coppola told Calley: Lucas was a genius and "a gigantic talent"—a designation Calley didn't argue with. "All that knew him felt that [Lucas] was a sort of potential cinema genius," said Calley, "certainly revolutionary."[82] Coppola's word, and Lucas's reputation, were good enough for Calley.

Lucas was also casting and scouting locations. Initially he had envisioned shooting *THX* in Japan, using the country's distinctive modern architecture to convey a surreal sense of the future. After sending art director Michael Haller to Japan to take pictures, Lucas had finally gone there himself—on Zoetrope's dime—to choose locations. Local officials were excited about the idea of Lucas filming inside several industrial complexes—including a nuclear power plant—but it quickly became clear that securing the official permissions was going to be a nightmare. Back Lucas went to San Francisco, where he'd keep looking for locations locally even as he was overseeing casting.

Lucas was in an open casting call, in fact, when Coppola burst into the theater and pulled him aside to tell him he'd reached a deal with Calley to finance seven films. (Since his birthday was April 7, Coppola always considered seven his lucky number.) Warner had agreed to give Coppola $300,000 for the development of *THX* and six other scripts — one of which, he told Lucas, was his and Milius's *Apocalypse Now.* It was a film Coppola really had no right to barter with; he hadn't seen the script, and had nothing to do with it, apart from knowing of Lucas's involvement, but his own excitement had carried the day.[83] "I was shocked," Lucas said later. "It was great about *THX,* but Francis hadn't even asked me or talked to me about *Apocalypse.*"[84] There was no talking Coppola down, though, and there was no going back. "Nobody can pick holes in this [deal]," Coppola said. "It's right. I can feel it....I know this is good."[85]

"That was the moment that American Zoetrope was really born," Lucas said later.[86] "Once *THX* was a go, we were able to pay people, and everybody suddenly had a job."[87] Publicly, Calley had been supportive, even excited about Warner's relationship with Zoetrope. "We're inclined to take enlightened gambles on young people," Calley told one writer.[88] But being enlightened didn't mean he was naïve or stupid. Calley had given Coppola the money on one very shrewd condition: these scripts weren't being optioned; this was a *loan.* The moment Warner Bros.–Seven Arts lost faith in Coppola or any of his films, they could call in their loan and Coppola would have to pay back everything.

Coppola was confident that was never going to happen, publicly vowing that his company would be worth $10 million by 1975.[89] Flush with Calley's money, Coppola spent the late summer of 1969 making Zoetrope resemble a proper company, charging his wife, Ellie, with the task of turning Zoetrope's eight editing rooms and three floors of offices into "a homey place, not lush or anything."[90] Ellie filled it with inflatable couches and furniture, painted the brick walls red, white, and blue — or covered them with orange and blue fabric — and mounted gigantic black-and-white photos of old-time directors in every room. Coppola took particular pride in the reception area, where he set up an antique pool table and a polished silver espresso maker, lined the walls with display cabinets filled with old movie equipment, and hired only the most beautiful and most miniskirted of receptionists.[91]

Most of the money, however, went into equipment. In addition to his expensive German editing machines, Coppola owned the only three-screen Keller mixer in California, a beast of a machine—it looked like it belonged on the bridge of *Star Trek's Enterprise*—that could edit three sizes of film at three different speeds. There were portable lights and sound equipment, and cameras with personalities as distinct as filmmakers', from Super 8 to Arriflex to a $40,000 Mitchell BNCR.[92] All were available for any filmmaker to rent—and over the next year, most of it would be misplaced, lost, or flat-out stolen.[93] "The studio wasn't always run prudently," Coppola admitted later. "The company was created out of idealism more than anything."[94]

That was certainly true—and he and Lucas often clashed over exactly whose idealism should prevail. "I think Francis always looked at George as sort of his upstart assistant who had an opinion," laughed Steven Spielberg. "An assistant with an opinion, nothing more dangerous than that, right?"[95] While Coppola envisioned Zoetrope as a corporate compound, with its own airport and fleet of helicopters, Lucas wanted something smaller, even cozy, and less oppressive. "What we're striving for is total freedom, where we can finance our pictures, make them our way, release them where we want them released, and be completely free to express ourselves," explained Lucas. "That's very hard to do in the world of business. In this country, the only thing that speaks is money and you have to have the money in order to have the power to be free. So the danger is—in being as oppressive as the next guy to the people below you. We're going to do everything possible to avoid that pitfall."[96]

Still, both Coppola and Lucas proclaimed to anyone who would listen that independent filmmaking was the wave of the future, with Zoetrope as the standard-bearer. The Hollywood studio system was dead, Coppola thundered to the *Christian Science Monitor*. "It's like

Czarist Russia had toppled itself....[I]n ten years there won't be a major studio left."[97] Lucas put it in slightly less heated terms, telling one reporter: "The only thing they've got that we need is money. And they're getting less and less. The most exciting thing about film is that it's just starting. Everyone in Hollywood is over 50 and creaking. They see movies as the past. We see it as the future."[98]

Ultimately, Coppola saw Zoetrope as occupying the same space in film that the Beatles' Apple Corps did in music—a company in which creativity trumped commerce, and every voice deserved to be heard. "We value the fact that young people come to us," Coppola said. "We will look at anyone's film and read anyone's manuscript."[99] Lucas agreed with that approach to a certain extent—"We say, 'We think you are a talented, functioning person and we are hiring you because of your abilities, and whatever you come up with, we're going to take,'" he said—but he didn't see Zoetrope as quite the artistic Eden that Coppola did. To Lucas, it was more of "a loose confederation of radicals and hippies."[100] As he put it: "It was very rebellious. We had very off-the-wall ideas that never would have been allowed to infiltrate the studios."[101]

Some of those off-the-wall ideas extended beyond what was on the screen to how movies should be made, distributed, and sold. Both Coppola and Lucas predicted a bold, high-tech future, with movies "sold like soup," said Coppola. "You'll be able to buy it in cartridges for $3 and play it as you would a record, at home."[102] Sitting in conversation with Mel Gussow of the *New York Times* in his Zoetrope office one afternoon beneath a wall-sized photo of Eisenstein, Lucas seconded Coppola's enthusiasm for videocassettes—a technology that would arrive in nearly every home more than a decade later—and confidently predicted that movies would eventually be produced in a 3-D format, perhaps even as holograms. He was, however, even more excited by the idea that cameras and other filmmaking equipment might eventually become so compact and inexpensive that anyone could make a movie, thereby cutting out the need for the Hollywood machine altogether. "The joke here is that Mattel will come out with a complete filmmaking kit. It will be all plastic, and any ten year old can make a film," said Lucas. "I look forward to the dispersal—when you don't need a place like this."[103] Lucas loved the idea of democratizing the filmmaking process: to him, that was what Zoetrope was really all about.

Lucas began filming *THX 1138* on Monday, September 22, 1969, shooting from 8 a.m. to 7 p.m. in the still unfinished Bay Area Rapid Transit system. Fleshing out his fifteen-minute student piece into a more fully realized ninety-minute film had required Lucas to plumb a few of his own experiences to frame the look and feel of his protagonist THX's environment. "[George] said he got part of the idea for the world of sterile living when he was commuting on Southern California's concrete freeways," his mother, Dorothy, recalled, "and as he glanced over all its concrete buildings, 'What a world,' he would say."[104] For *THX*'s distinctively stark look, Lucas would make the most of his well-scouted locations—he would build only one interior set—filming not only in the empty BART system but also at the Oakland Arena, the Marin Civic Center, and the campus of Berkeley. With a strategically placed camera, Lucas could make even a normal escalator look vaguely exotic. And as with his experience shooting the first version of *THX*, there were days when he and his crew had to film quickly and without permits. "Sometimes we'd only have about two hours to shoot in a particular place," said Lucas. "There were lots of things that made it feel like a street film—we would get in there, get our shots before the police came, and then run away as fast as we could."[105]

THX's impersonal, imperfect, mechanized society was inspired by an experience at USC in which the university's new computer system had garbled every student's course schedule. "That really made an impression on his mind," said Dorothy Lucas.[106] The final script, then, established the world that had only been hinted at in Lucas's student film, setting THX in a cold, oppressive society in which the government monitored its residents, set priorities based on budgets, and required its citizens to live and work in a drug-induced, emotionless stupor.

Lucas and Murch had also fleshed out the role of THX's mate, LUH 3417, who decreases THX's state-sanctioned drug intake. As THX gradually shakes himself loose from the influence of drugs, he becomes more aware of and conflicted by emotions, until he and LUH finally make love—a criminal offense that puts him on trial for sexual perversion and drug evasion. THX is sentenced to be conditioned and held in detention: an endless white expanse populated by other nonconformists—some dangerous, some merely different—including the speechmaking SEN 5241, who may or may not have a prurient interest in THX. Tired of imprisonment, THX simply walks out of confinement and into the white void. It was a major turning point in the plot, and Lucas wanted everyone to appreciate the message he was trying to convey. It was "the importance of self and being able to step out of whatever you're in and move forward rather than being stuck in your little rut," Lucas explained in 1971. "People would give anything to quit their jobs. All they have to do is do it.... They're people in cages with open doors."[107]

When authorities become aware of THX's disappearance, they announce a projected time and budget for his capture—and Lucas devotes the final third of the film to the pursuit of THX, finally placing the extended chase sequence of his student film into a larger context. With chrome-faced robot policemen in pursuit, THX eventually steals a car—Lucas would always love the opportunity to film racing cars—and speeds down an endless series of tunnels, finally crashing into scaffolding. He continues on foot, harassed for a moment by the squat shell people, until he reaches a ladder and begins climbing, with a robot policeman nearly on his heels, only a few rungs below him. As THX nears the top, the policeman is ordered to abort the chase, as the budget for his capture has been exceeded. Finally free from pursuit, THX climbs to the surface, where he stands against a backdrop of a blazing sunset—the shot Lucas had envisioned since at least 1966, now in full color *and* wide-screen.

At its core, *THX 1138* was about refusing to accept the status quo. "[It's] about a hero who lives in an anthill and dares to go outside,"

Lucas would say later. In a way, that was what he and Coppola were doing with Zoetrope. Like THX, they too had broken away from the system in pursuit of a freedom that could be had if one was simply willing to walk away from the status quo. As Lucas noted, "this issue of leaving a safe environment and going into the unknown" would be an underlying premise of his first three films, running in a thematic straight line from *THX* through *American Graffiti* and on into *Star Wars*. "I was very consistent in my cinematic obsessions," he admitted.[108] While critics would later pick apart *THX*, it and his other movies would come from the same emotional and psychological core.

Lucas's real strength, as always, was his visual and artistic sense. At times Lucas could be deliberately arty, showing a lizard crawling through the internal wires of a piece of machinery—an image Lucas insisted was a metaphor, but one that Walter Murch felt worked better if it went unexplained. Lucas would often be accused of favoring machinery over people in his films, and of being cold and emotionless—or, at the very least, uninterested—but he really wanted his images to convey feeling. He was convinced, in fact, that *THX* was all *about* emotions—about squashing and suppressing them, struggling to control them, then releasing and embracing them, regardless of the consequences. It was "pure filmmaking," he insisted; it didn't always have to make sense, but it definitely had to provoke a feeling or response.

It was also important to Lucas that *THX* look like nothing else. "My primary concept in approaching the production of *THX 1138* was to make a kind of *cinema verité* film of the future," he explained to *American Cinematographer*, "something that would look like a documentary crew had made a film about some character in a time yet to come."[109] For that reason, he had tapped for his directors of photography two documentary filmmakers—newsreel cameraman Albert Kihn and Dave Meyers, who had shot footage for the documentary *Woodstock*—and insisted they work almost exclusively with available light, just as he had done for his student film. Things could be especially challenging in the detention sequence, which featured actors in white costumes on white furniture against a white background. Lucas was pleased with its distinctive look—fearful of leaving tracks on the white floor, he walked the set in his socks—and asked Kihn to keep the camera still, letting actors move almost casually in and out of the shot, much as in a documentary. At other times, Lucas would place his cameramen in almost total darkness, then order them to "put on your fastest lens, open it up all the way and shoot."[110] To Lucas's surprise, most of the dailies "looked good." But there was no way he was going to show them to the studio—not even if asked. "They'd have fired me on the spot," he said later.[111]

That might have been true. Fortunately, Warner executives had promised to hassle Lucas as little as possible, though they did insist on Coppola's assigning a line producer to keep an eye on Lucas and this arty science fiction film they were becoming increasingly nervous about. Coppola appointed Larry Sturhahn, his assistant director from *You're a Big Boy Now,* to the job, largely because he felt Sturhahn was just abrasive enough to keep Lucas on schedule. The ploy would work—Lucas would bring the picture in on time and on budget—but he seethed constantly about Sturhahn, who seemed always to be on the phone instead of on the set helping him out. In the words of Matthew Robbins, "Sturhahn was assigned to *THX* so George would have someone to hate."[112]

Even if he hated his line producer, Lucas loved his "very professional cast of excellent actors."[113] He knew he was asking a lot of them; everyone would be required to shave their heads, makeup and wardrobe would be minimal, and, at Lucas's direction, the affect expressed by the characters would be "confused emotion." Even the dialogue, Lucas said, was "intentionally abstract," often unrelated to the on-screen visuals, much like Lipsett's use of dialogue in *21-87.*[114] "For the actor," said Lucas, "the less you have to do, the harder it is."[115]

Fortunately, Lucas had chosen his actors well; for the title role he had hired Robert Duvall, with whom he'd become friendly during *The Rain People.* "I'd decided on Bobby before I'd even finished the script," he said later.[116] The role of LUH went to Maggie McOmie, a former Kelly girl who had little acting experience but was eager to shave off her long strawberry blond hair for the role—a decision that upset Lucas more than it did her. The role of SEN, meanwhile, went to the edgy Donald Pleasence, who excelled at playing a combination of smart and sinister.[117] Lucas would always admit that working with actors was never his strong suit—"I'm not very good with people, never have been," he said—and during the shooting of *THX* he opted not to do much rehearsing, preferring to set up the scene, rehearse it once, then shoot, with no marks and little measuring.[118] But Duvall found such a hands-off approach refreshing. "[Lucas] leaves you alone," said Duvall. "That's always a welcome thing.... [Y]ou felt you were in safe hands."[119]

It didn't matter much to Lucas anyhow; he'd take care of everything during the editing process.[120] Lucas finished shooting *THX* on the night of November 21, 1969, filming cars crashing in chilly Caldecott Tunnel in Oakland. With shooting complete, he took his film—all 250,000 feet of it—home to Mill Valley, where he planned to edit the movie in his attic rather than at the new facilities at Zoetrope. The Folsom Street offices were too busy and noisy, Lucas explained, with too many distractions—"like trying to write a novel in a newspaper office."[121]

It was a decision that didn't surprise Coppola one bit. "You know what George is like," he sighed.[122]

After spending the last part of 1969 renovating and decorating the Zoetrope offices, Coppola was ready to officially open the doors—and on Friday, December 12, he did so with his usual panache, throwing an enormous party to which pretty much the entire city of San Francisco was invited. "All of the rock groups" were there, recalled Milius. "There was a lot of dope being smoked, a lot of sex. It was great."[123] John Calley was there too, hands in his pockets, mouth slightly agape, and probably wondering what in the world he had gotten himself and Warners into.

Coppola didn't care. With Lucas at work editing *THX 1138* and the rest of his apostles developing scripts and planning projects, Coppola at last had his cinematic Eden—part hippie commune, part art-ists' colony, and all his. "It was like a dream," he said. "It was like a film school that never existed." Lucas, too, thought it was about as near to nirvana as a filmmaker could get. "The closest we came to the dream was when we were doing *THX* and everybody was writing their scripts," said Lucas, "and everybody was hanging out at the pool table drinking cappuccinos and waxing philosophic about the new world order and everything." John Milius agreed. "It was," he said enthusias-tically, "the best thing we ever did."[124]

It wouldn't last long—and it would be largely Lucas's and *THX*'s fault.

After completing filming on *THX* in November 1969, Lucas, Marcia, and Walter Murch spent nearly six months editing the film, working almost nonstop seven days a week. "The clatter of film was heard twenty-four hours a day," noted Murch.[125] George and Marcia would edit all day, then stop each evening when Murch arrived on his motorcycle, roaring in from Sausalito, five miles away, where he was living on a houseboat. They would discuss the film over dinner, then Murch would spend all night editing the film's sound. Each day, Lucas hoped he had left Murch with something in the film's visuals that would inspire him in the way he cut together the sound; similarly, when Murch handed off the film each morning, he hoped Lucas would hear something in the sound track that would influence the way he assembled the film. It was a marriage of sound and image, and Lucas loved the way they played off each other—and they would all talk over the film's continuing evolution at breakfast, before Murch headed back to Sausalito and the Lucases climbed up the stairs to the editing room.

And so it went, on into the spring of 1970. The pace was exhaust-ing, but Lucas loved the editing process, and he was pleased with the way the movie was coming together. Marcia wasn't so sure. While Lucas continued to insist that *THX* was all about emotion, Marcia didn't think it was working. "I like to become emotionally involved in a movie," she said. "I never cared for *THX* because it left me cold." But that sort of criticism only made Lucas angry; he told Marcia she didn't understand. Marcia nodded and continued to edit the film in line with Lucas's vision, but she wasn't happy about it. "All he wanted to do was abstract filmmaking, tone poems, collections of images," she sighed.[126]

In May 1970, nervous executives at Warner Bros. finally asked to see *THX 1138* for themselves. It had been seven months since Lucas had completed filming, and Coppola had continually promised the studio that Lucas was taking the time he needed to give them something truly great. Now it was time for Coppola to put up or shut up. The night before his meeting with Warners, Coppola came by Lucas's house for his first look at *THX*.

When it was over, Coppola sat in silence for a moment. "Well," he said slowly, "this is either going to be a masterpiece or masturbation."[127] But he told Lucas not to worry—he would assure Warners that the film was still a work in progress, and that Lucas could fix anything they didn't like in the next edit. "This is your first film, we're all learning, we're trying something new here," he told Lucas. "It would be crazy to think we're going to hit the bull's-eye the first time."[128] Coppola took the film and headed for Hollywood. All Lucas could do was stay in Mill Valley with Marcia and wait.

The next day, Coppola screened *THX* at the Warner Bros. lot. Besides Ashley and Calley, the studio had brought in several heavy hitters for the session, including Frank Wells, the head of business affairs, Dick Lederer, vice president of production, and story editor Barry Beckerman. Their response, to say the least, wasn't encouraging. Mostly, the executives were baffled. "Wait a minute, Francis," asked one, "what's going on? This is not the screenplay we said we were going to do. This isn't a commercial movie." Coppola could only sink down into his seat and mutter, "I don't know what the fuck this is."[129]

Lucas had expected, and prepared for, such a response. "[Francis] doesn't look at the downside," Lucas explained later. "I'm *always* looking at the downside. And he's going, 'Oh...you're an eighty-year-old kid....Why are you always worried about everything going wrong? Why don't you just think about all the success we're going to have?'"[130] In this case, however, Lucas was right to worry, for there was a very real chance the Warner executives were going to take the film and re-edit it themselves. Lucas vowed that wasn't going to happen—and he even co-opted several Zoetropers into a contingency plan. As the film rolled, Murch, Caleb Deschanel, and Matthew Robbins waited at the base of the famous Warner Bros. water tower, just outside the screening room. The moment the movie ended, they ran up to the projection booth, took the film cans, and sped away in Robbins's Volkswagen minibus.

While Ashley wasn't actually planning to take the film from Lucas—at least not yet—he did tell Coppola that the film somehow needed to be made more "accessible" to audiences. Lucas was stunned; in his view, he'd made a movie that was *much* more accessible than the original student film. It was "accessible, but also stylized and two-dimensional," Lucas said later, and it frustrated him that the studio executives just didn't get it.[131] "They didn't understand it at all," he complained. "They were completely confused by it."[132] Marcia tried not to remind him she had told him so. "When the studio didn't like the film, I wasn't surprised," she said later. "But George just said to me, I was stupid and knew nothing. Because I was just a Valley Girl. He was the intellectual."[133]

Intellectual or not, Lucas had a very real problem. Ashley was willing to give Lucas the opportunity to recut the film himself, and asked that he work with Fred Weintraub, the studio's vice president of creative services, to find a middle ground. Weintraub was a big, bearded man with a bohemian streak, but at age forty-two, he had little patience with the avant-garde; he wanted mainstream appeal. In 1975, he would produce Bruce Lee's *Enter the Dragon*, a film that was much more his speed. One of Weintraub's first recommendations, then, was for Lucas to take the diminutive shell people, who appeared in the last half of the film, and move them to the beginning of the movie instead, and then tell the rest of the film as flashback. "Put the freaks up front," he told Lucas matter-of-factly—and to this day, Lucas can only repeat the phrase with contempt: *Put the freaks up front.* "Forget it," Lucas told Coppola, "I'm not doing any of this stuff," and he and Weintraub would go around and around again. "[George] had to sit in the same room as one of the monsters, one of the freaks, who had the power to tell him what to do," said Murch.[134]

Weintraub eventually stopped talking about freaks and flashbacks and agreed to let Lucas pare down some of the scenes in the white limbo detention sequence. But Coppola knew that the film was likely in trouble, and that his own capital with Warner Bros. was in rapid decline. It got even worse with the release of *The Rain People* in late August; while well reviewed, the film landed with a thud. With Warner running out of patience, and Zoetrope hemorrhaging cash, Coppola was in desperate need of money.

Then, in the late summer of 1970, came an offer he couldn't refuse.

For much of 1970, executives at Paramount had been wooing Coppola to take the helm of a low-budget action film based on one of the biggest books of 1969, a sprawling gangster novel by Mario Puzo called *The Godfather*. Coppola was with Lucas, recutting *THX* in the Mill Valley editing room, when Paramount executive Peter Bart called once more to offer him *The Godfather*. "They've just offered me this Italian gangster movie," Coppola told Lucas. "It's like a $3 million potboiler based on a best-seller. Should I do it?"[135] To Lucas, whose father had always reinforced the concept of staying in the black, the answer was obvious. "I don't think you have any choice," he told Coppola. "We're in debt. You've gotta get a job."[136] On September 28, Coppola signed the deal with Paramount to direct *The Godfather*, with production to begin in the spring of 1971. He was offered $75,000 to direct it, plus 6 percent of the profits—not much, especially if the film didn't work, and given that Coppola was a lavish spender.[137] "It takes no imagination to live within your means," Coppola liked to say.[138] But it was a job.

On Thursday, November 19, 1970—a date that came to be known among Zoetropers as "Black Thursday"—Coppola reported to Warner Bros. to present the final edit of *THX*, as well as all of the scripts that had been written over the past year, to the Warner top brass. Coppola, knowing he was already on thin ice, wanted to make a good impression, and had twelve copies of each script, bound in leather—one for each executive at the table—which he then put into a long silver box embossed with the American Zoetrope logo. Decades later, Korty still rolled his eyes at the showmanship. "Anyone who came and looked at it would say, 'gee, that looks like a coffin.'"[139]

He had no idea.

The screening of *THX* was up first. The executives' response was the same as at the May viewing. "[They] went ballistic.... That's when the shit hit the fan," said Lucas. "Suddenly it was the crash of '29."[140] Calley had hated the first cut of *THX,* and in his opinion, this one was no better. "There was nobody in the room...that thought they knew what to do with *THX 1138,*" Calley recounted later. "Everybody thought it was a loser."[141] "It was insane," Lucas said of the screening. "I wish I had filmed it. It was like bringing an audience to the Mona Lisa and asking, 'Do you know why she's smiling?' 'Sorry, Leonardo, you'll have to go back and make some changes.'"[142]

It was over. Ashley and Calley had lost all confidence in Coppola and his band of hippies. They'd still distribute *THX* under the Zoetrope imprint, but after that, the deal was off. Ashley wanted none of Coppola's scripts—essentially tossing away *The Conversation* and *Apocalypse Now*—and to make things worse, they wanted their $300,000 back. Finally, this time they had no intention of letting the film disappear into the back of a VW bus. They took *THX 1138* away.

Coppola left the meeting completely stunned. "Warners didn't like it and totally dumped on it. They said it didn't have any appeal," said Coppola later. "They could've helped it a lot if they'd wanted to, but by then they were too mad at us." He admitted that *THX* "was unpredictable—it wasn't a stock science fiction film, but Warners was so angry they broke off all relations."[143] It would turn out to be a staggeringly shortsighted move on the part of the studio. "They had turned down what became the whole 70s cinema movement," said Coppola.[144] "They didn't get it. And they didn't get this wonderful group of young people who were going to clearly make the films for the next couple of decades.... They rejected every project we had and then they basically just abandoned us."[145]

Lucas was furious. "They don't respect talent," he groused to one journalist. "They don't know what an idea is, and they just walk all over it, and it's that kind of a thing that really makes you angry."[146] He wouldn't speak to Ashley again; more than a decade later, when Lucas was shopping around distribution rights for *Raiders of the Lost Ark,* he demanded an apology from Ashley before he'd even consider giving the rights to Warner Bros. Ashley apologized; Lucas gave the rights to rival Paramount anyway.

In fairness, it wasn't entirely *THX* or Lucas that had scuttled the deal. By mid-1970, the film industry had shifted again, pivoting largely on the phenomenal success of overproduced star-studded blockbusters like *Airport* (dismissed only a year later by star Burt Lancaster as "the biggest piece of junk ever made") or sentimental treacle like *Love Story,* which would be the highest-grossing movie of 1970.[147] As quickly as they'd tidal-waved in, independent youth-oriented movies like *Easy Rider* were now decidedly out. "There was a change in the whole industry," said John Korty. "It was a gamble Francis made when he opened Zoetrope at a time... [when] *Easy Rider* was the freshest thing on everyone's mind. Then *Airport* came along, management policies shifted and the ground beneath Zoetrope started shaking."[148]

"When I started the feature *THX,* we were in a real, real eight-month Renaissance there [at Zoetrope]," Lucas explained in early 1971. "All of a sudden there was freedom, mainly because of *Easy Rider.... Easy Rider* did a great thing, but it didn't last very long.... The studio saw [*THX*] and went crazy because that was when *Airport* had come out... and then *Love Story.*"[149] Warner "decided not to finance any more youth-oriented, adventurous, crazy movies. They went back to hardcore entertainment films. For them it was a good decision because they made a lot of money on that decision. But they sold us completely down the river."[150]

THX 1138 was handed off to veteran editor Rudi Fehr, who

excised a little more than four minutes from Lucas's final cut. It was another move Lucas never forgot or forgave. "This was George's first experience with 'studio interference,'" said Murch. "And so George spent a season in Hell because this was his baby, this was his very first film, and he felt the studio was mangling it."[151] Those four minutes turned Lucas's cynicism toward Hollywood into outright rage. "There was no point for them to do it, other than [to] exercise some power," he said. "[Their attitude was] 'We can screw around with your movie, so we're going to.'...We fought it, and they did it, and I was angry about it."[152] And he had no patience with executives who argued that they had cut only four minutes from a ninety-minute film. "They were cutting the fingers off my baby," he fumed.[153]

"It was unbelievable," said Matthew Robbins. "How is it possible they would have the right to go and tell the filmmaker what to do? It was an injustice."[154] For Lucas, it was more than unjust; it was immoral. "The terrible thing about this country is that the dollar is valued above the individual," said Lucas. "You can buy another person no matter how talented he is and then tell him he's wrong. They do not like to trust people."[155] Lucas wouldn't trust studios again. Ever.

Black Thursday left Zoetrope in a financial and creative free fall from which it wouldn't recover—"the death of a dream," lamented Ron Colby.[156] "Zoetrope was picked clean," Coppola said sadly. "Everyone had used it, no one had contributed, and there was a time when I literally was staving off the sheriff from putting the chain across the door."[157]

"Everybody scattered to the wind at that point," said Lucas—including him.[158] Coppola was disappointed and somewhat hurt by his followers' loss of faith. "I had always regarded George as my heir apparent," Coppola said. "He'd take over Zoetrope for me while I went out and did my personal films. Everybody utilized Zoetrope to get going, but nobody wanted to stick with it."[159]

The collapse of Zoetrope—and especially the experience with *THX* and Warners—would cause some hard feelings between Lucas and Coppola. "I've had a very volatile relationship with Francis," Lucas said later. "It's on both sides, like we were married and we got divorced. It's as close a relationship as I've had with anybody."[160]

Mostly their disagreement was sparked by their differing management styles and attitudes toward money. "I'm very cautious," said Lucas. "I don't borrow money. I'm very protective of the things that I build."[161] Lucas, always tight with a dollar, had watched in dismay as Coppola continued to spend money recklessly, sometimes gleefully, on exotic equipment and expensive invitations. "George became very discouraged by my 'bohemian' administration," said Coppola.[162]

Even more galling, at least in Lucas's eyes, was that Coppola often had the nerve to act like one of *those people,* the dreaded Hollywood suits that Lucas loathed. He resented it when Coppola billed some of Zoetrope's expenses against *THX's* budget. To Lucas, that was *his* money, purely for *THX,* and not for Coppola's use. And when Zoetrope administrator Mona Skager discovered that Lucas had been making long-distance phone calls from the Zoetrope offices in an effort to wrangle editing jobs for Marcia, she presented Lucas with a bill for $1,800, since the calls couldn't be considered Zoetrope business. Even Coppola knew that was going too far. "I would never have done that to a friend," Coppola said later. "Mona was way out of line. I always believe that that incident was one of the things that pissed George off and caused a breach."[163]

For his part, Lucas would never let the demise of Zoetrope be draped around his shoulders. He would never apologize for *THX*— not then, not ever. "[It was] my one chance to make an avant-garde movie," Lucas said later. "It almost brought American Zoetrope down...[and] almost destroyed my career. But it was definitely worth it at the time."[164] He made up his mind now to break away from Coppola—who was already on his way to Italy to scout locations for *The Godfather*—and make it on his own. "I needed to go and develop another project," Lucas said. "I couldn't rely on Zoetrope to do that for me. It fell apart."[165]

Determined to control his own projects—no studio, he vowed, would ever force him to compromise his vision again—Lucas enlisted

the help of entertainment lawyer Tom Pollock to draft the incorporation papers for his own company. In 1971 Lucas officially opened
Lucasfilm Ltd., his own independent production company run out of
his little house in Mill Valley. Its lone employees were him and
Marcia.

Warner Bros. finally released *THX 1138* in March 1971. The studio
had stuck by its promise to distribute the film, but they didn't have
much hope for it.

Still, the film had its fans, most of whom admired Lucas's visual
sense. "The strength of *THX 1138* is its complete faithfulness to a very
personal vision," wrote Kenneth Turan in the *Washington Post*, "a vision
strong enough to transform what may sound like a collection of cheap
effects into a visually gratifying science fiction film."[166] Roger Ebert,
writing in the *Chicago Sun-Times*, noted that "Lucas doesn't seem to
have been very concerned with his plot...but as a work of visual imagination it's special," and awarded the film three out of four stars.[167]
Critics for the *New York Times* were particularly effusive, with one
reviewer applauding Lucas's "technical virtuosity that...achieves exceptional emotional intensity" (finally, someone who got it!),[168] while
Vincent Canby called the film "a Wow." *THX 1138*, wrote Canby, "is
practically an iconography of contemporary graphics, in which actors
are, intentionally, almost but not quite indistinguishable from the
décor."[169] It was a sentiment that would be lobbed at Lucas, sometimes
derisively, for most of his career.

Other reviews were tougher. *Variety* immediately sniped that the
film was "likely not to be an artistic or commercial success."[170] A commercial success it definitely wasn't; positive nuggets aside, reviewers
and audiences alike were generally baffled by *THX*'s theme and its
sparse, avant-garde look, and the film landed with a thud. Lucas didn't
even tell his parents about it; they wouldn't see it until it opened at the
Covell Theatre in Modesto in June.

Lucas took it all personally. "Critics are the vandals of our time,
like spray painters who mess up walls," he complained. He vowed to

stop caring what critics thought; he lumped them in with those passionless film executives who knew nothing about filmmaking and told him to *Put the freaks up front!* Who were they to criticize anyway? "I basically said, 'To hell with reviews.'"[171]

Friends tried to be supportive and sympathetic. "George thought not only had he managed to make a movie which was visually exciting, but it was really about something," said Matthew Robbins. "He was disappointed that there was no audience for American art films."[172] Ron Colby thought he understood why audiences had stayed away. *THX,* said Colby, "was beautifully realized. But it's a bummer."[173]

Marcia thought so too. "After *THX* went down the toilet, I never said, 'I told you so,'" she recalled, "but I reminded George that I warned him it hadn't involved the audience emotionally." Lucas hated that sort of criticism. "Emotionally involving the audience is easy," he told her. "Anybody can do it blindfolded. Get a little kitten and have some guy wring its neck."[174]

But Marcia persisted, until George finally threw up his hands in mock surrender.

"I'm gonna show you how easy it is," he told her. "I'll make a film that emotionally involves the audience."[175]

5

American Graffiti

1971–1973

The weeks following the implosion of Zoetrope had been tough on Lucas. He was feeling abandoned by Coppola, who by early 1971 was already deep in pre-production work on *The Godfather*, part of his ongoing effort to earn enough to pay Warner back its $300,000. But while Coppola had a job, Lucas didn't. For now, he and Marcia were getting by, albeit just barely, on what Marcia was making editing Michael Ritchie's film *The Candidate*. In the meantime, Lucas was considering taking side jobs as a documentary cameraman, or raising the money needed to make more of the small, arty "tone poems" he loved.

There was also *Apocalypse Now*, still in free fall since its abandonment by Warner on Black Thursday. It was the only project Lucas had that was actually in script phase, and he still had big plans for it even as he and Milius continued passing the pages back and forth. Lucas had recently brought in another collaborator for the project as well: a serious, soft-spoken thirty-year-old producer named Gary Kurtz.

Like Lucas and Milius, the Los Angeles–born Kurtz was a graduate of USC film school, though he liked to point out that when he graduated in 1963, the film school "was a poor cousin" to the one Lucas and Milius attended a year later.[1] Like most film school graduates, Kurtz couldn't find a job in Hollywood, so he simply stayed at USC as an employee, working on medical information films for the U.S. Public Health Service and running the school's film library. Eventually he also found a job working for Roger Corman, where he became a jack-of-all-trades, managing sound, cinematography, even special effects.

Unlike Lucas and Milius, however, Kurtz didn't escape the war; in 1966, Kurtz was drafted by the marines and sent to Vietnam. He was halfway through his basic training, he remembered, when "basically I realized that I was a conscientious objector."[2] A sympathetic and savvy superior advised Kurtz to keep his objections to himself, and put a film camera in his hand instead of a rifle. Kurtz spent two years in Vietnam in a film unit, squinting through the eyepiece of a camera at blood and burning villages, an empty holster on his hip. He returned home in 1968 with a newfound spirituality, carrying himself with the quiet dignity of a Quaker, even growing a chin-curtain beard that gave him a slight resemblance to Abe Lincoln or Captain Ahab.

Kurtz made his way back into film, and by 1970 he was working with director Monte Hellman—another Corman disciple—on the road movie *Two-Lane Blacktop*. The film was decidedly low-rent, hurriedly financed by Ned Tanen at Universal to surf the *Easy Rider* wave—and Kurtz, trying to stretch his budget as far as he could, wanted Hellman to shoot *Two-Lane Blacktop* in the inexpensive 35 mm Techniscope format. The only problem was that neither Kurtz nor Hellman had ever worked in Techniscope before. So Kurtz called on Coppola—yet *another* member of the Corman fraternity—for a bit of help. Coppola, with his typical bombast, told Kurtz that he needed to visit one of his protégés who had just finished shooting his first film, *THX 1138,* in Techniscope, and was editing the movie in his attic in Mill Valley.

As instructed by Coppola, Kurtz drove out to Mill Valley and knocked on the door. When Lucas answered, Kurtz thought he looked like a film student. "He was just this little guy," said Kurtz, in jeans and tennis shoes and an untucked dress shirt that seemed two sizes too big for him. But the more he and Lucas talked—and the more he watched Lucas deftly work the controls of the Steenbeck editing table—the more Kurtz liked him. "We both came up in the school of doing everything ourselves," said Kurtz. "He was my kind of film-maker."[3] Kurtz left impressed, and went off to make *Two-Lane Blacktop* in Techniscope, while Lucas continued to wrestle with Warner over *THX* for the rest of 1970. But it was the beginning of one of Lucas's most important creative partnerships—Lucas and Kurtz would oversee three gigantically successful films together in the span of ten years—and it was perhaps only fitting that Coppola had been the one to connect Lucas with his next big brother figure. "I knew George Lucas by reputation—I'd seen some of his student films," remembered Kurtz, "but it was Francis who brought us together."[4]

It was Coppola, in fact, who now brought them together again as Lucas was mulling over *Apocalypse Now.* Coppola had seen some of the footage Kurtz had shot in Vietnam, and suggested to Lucas that Kurtz might be the ideal collaborator on a war movie. Kurtz, however, wasn't so sure. Unlike the polar opposites Lucas and Coppola, Lucas and Kurtz were cut from the same temperamental cloth; both were quiet and low-key, and Kurtz worried that neither of them had a forceful enough personality to run a movie set. But he and Lucas got on well enough that they decided to move ahead anyway.

Kurtz was genuinely intrigued by *Apocalypse;* he saw it as their opportunity to make a dark comedy in the same vein as Robert Altman's 1970 film *M*A*S*H.* But the more they talked, the more Lucas waffled. There was some question as to whether it was really their film to shop around anyway; technically, it was the property of Zoetrope, though the typically defiant Lucas continued to argue that the film actually belonged to him and Milius and that Coppola had had no right to use it as a bargaining chip in the first place. More than anything else, however, Lucas was having second thoughts about making a war movie at all. With a highly unpopular war still splattered across the front pages of the newspapers each day, Lucas shuddered at the idea of taking part in some insidious cynical trend. "I was working on basically negative movies—*Apocalypse Now* and *THX*, both very angry," Lucas said later.[5] "I realized after *THX* that people don't care how the country's being ruined. All that movie did was to make people more pessimistic, more depressed, and less willing to get involved in trying to make the world better." He decided, "We've got to regenerate optimism."[6]

After *THX*, Lucas was driven to make a movie that was not only optimistic but also mainstream, marketable, and exciting. *Apocalypse Now* was shelved, but Lucas definitely wanted to keep working with Kurtz. So while vowing they would come back to *Apocalypse Now* at some point in the future, he and Kurtz continued to kick around ideas for a new film. What kinds of movies did *they* like? What did *they* think was exciting? For a moment, they considered a remake of the Kurosawa classic *The Hidden Fortress*, reimagining it in a more modern setting in the same way director John Sturges had transferred another Kurosawa film, *The Seven Samurai*, from ancient Japan to the Old West in his 1960 picture *The Magnificent Seven*.

What *really* got them both fired up, however, was Flash Gordon. Lucas animatedly described the Flash Gordon serials he had loved watching on KRON as a kid, but he didn't need to bother: Kurtz was a fan too, and excitedly discussed with Lucas the possibilities of acquiring the rights from King Features. Lucas reached out to the syndicate, even making a quick trip to New York to plead his case, but "they were way too expensive for us," recalled Kurtz. King Features had perhaps intentionally priced Lucas out of the market, holding out hopes for a big-name director to take on their franchise, since they were also coyly dangling the rights in front of Federico Fellini. Lucas kept the pressure on, and "they weren't averse to discussing it," said Kurtz, "but their restrictions were so draconian that we realized right away that it wasn't really a great prospect at the time."[7] The syndicate ended up overplaying its hand, as Fellini, too, would pass.

Both Lucas and Kurtz knew that what they really wanted to do was "some kind of Flash Gordon–like science fiction story," said Kurtz.[8] It was "something that we wanted to see, that we would pay to go see! And no one was making it!"[9] If Lucas couldn't get the rights to Flash, then he'd simply create a world of his own that didn't have to adhere to someone else's rules or work with someone else's characters. By denying Lucas Flash, King Features had inadvertently sent him down the path toward creating *Star Wars*. Flash Gordon, in fact, wouldn't appear on the big screen until 1980, in a Dino De Laurentiis–produced stinker trying hard to cash in on the science fiction craze Lucas had spawned with *Star Wars*—an irony that was never lost on Lucas.

But Lucas wasn't ready to start on another science fiction movie just yet. "After *THX*, I was considered a cold, weird director, a science fiction sort of guy who carried a calculator. And I'm not like that at all," Lucas said later.[10] In addition to Marcia, Coppola, too, had challenged Lucas to try something different. "Don't be so weird," Coppola told him. "Try to do something that's human. Don't do these abstract things."[11] He advised Lucas, "Why don't you try to write something out of your own life that has warmth and humor?"[12]

Challenge accepted. "If they want warm human comedy," said Lucas, "I'll give them one, just to show that I can do it."[13] He thought he knew exactly how to go about it. Lucas would later claim it was his growing interest in anthropology that was the impetus behind *American Graffiti*. "I became fascinated with the modern mating rituals of American youth who did their dance in cars, rather than in the town square or in other ways that societies have done these things," he would tell reporters forty years later. And yet, that was probably only partly true. Mostly, the writer who hated to write was following the path of least resistance—by writing, as Coppola had suggested, something out of his own life. "If you're a writer and a director," said Lucas, "you make movies about the things you know about." For Lucas, then, that meant there was never any doubt what he would write about: "Growing up in Modesto, I spent many years cruising Tenth Street, and I was enamored with the experience."[14]

That still didn't mean the actual writing process was going to be any easier. "As I started out with *American Graffiti*, I said to myself, 'I don't want to write this. I can't stand writing,'" Lucas confessed later, "and I frantically went around trying to get a deal to develop the script."[15] Getting a deal, however, would require at least an outline, so Lucas wrote a five-page treatment about four young men, most of them cruisers or cruiser wannabes, getting ready to leave high school, with their lives veering off in very different directions. Lucas envisioned a coming-of-age film in the same vein as Fellini's *I Vitelloni*, which follows five young men as they go through pivotal points in their lives. "[It was] kind of the same issue about growing up," said Lucas. "It was one of the themes in my first film, *THX*, and I wanted to expand on it."[16] With some help from film school pals Willard Huyck and his wife, Gloria Katz, Lucas's five-page proposal was eventually fleshed out to eighteen pages. Lucas promised the Huycks that if the proposal sold, they'd get the screenwriting job, then handed the proposal off to another new partner in his creative life, a twenty-two-year-old agent named Jeff Berg, for Berg to shop to the studios. For Lucas, looking to studios to back a project was like tucking his tail between his legs; he'd vowed never to be a part of the Hollywood machine again. But with no money and no prospects, Lucas was going to take whatever he could get.

Unfortunately, his timing couldn't have been worse. In March 1971, just as Berg was taking *American Graffiti* around for review, *THX 1138* had landed in theaters, and despite an appealing proposal for his second film, Lucas was damaged goods. "The easiest job you'll ever get is to try to make your first film," Lucas ruefully noted later. "That's the easy one to get...because nobody knows whether you can make a film or not....After you've done that feature, then you have a heck of a difficult time getting your second film off the ground. They look at your first film and they say, 'Oh well, we don't want you any more.'"[17] And they didn't. Nearly every door was closed in Berg's face; only David Chasman, a producer at United Artists who'd overseen the James Bond films and *A Hard Day's Night*, took a passing interest.

THX 1138 did have its fans, and most of them were in France, where *THX* had been selected as one of fifty-two films to be shown as part of the Directors' Fortnight at the Cannes Film Festival. So it was in this roundabout way that Lucas's first film helped him get his second one made. "Of course Warners wouldn't pay for us to get there," grumbled Lucas.[18] But Lucas decided to go to Europe anyway. "What the hell," he told Marcia, "let's go."[19] He and Marcia took their last $2,000 out of the bank to pay for an extended trip. They planned to live as cheaply as they could, staying in hostels or with friends, and backpacking most of the way; their largest expense would be a set of Eurorail passes. Walter Murch and his wife, Aggie, gamely agreed to join them.

The Lucases left California in early May, headed for London, where they planned to stay a few days in a cheap pension before heading to Cannes. Their first stop: an extended layover in New York City, where George and Marcia would spend the night with the Coppolas. Lucas was determined to make the most of his brief time in New York by paying a visit to the offices of David Picker, president of United Artists, the one film studio that had expressed even remote interest in *American Graffiti*. "If I could just get to him," Lucas figured, "maybe I could pitch this and they can make it happen."[20] Lucas did get to him — and he pitched *American Graffiti* hard, reminding the mogul of David Chasman's interest in the project as well. Picker nodded, took a copy of Lucas's *American Graffiti* proposal, and said he wanted to think about it. Picker, too, was heading for Cannes later in the week, and asked Lucas to check back in with him once he arrived in London.

Lucas spent a restless night with the Coppolas. "Francis was in severe trauma," he said, deeply embedded in work on *The Godfather* and hating nearly every moment of it. ("It was just non-stop anxiety," said Coppola, "and wondering when I was going to get fired.")[21] Adding to the tension, Ellie Coppola was nine months pregnant with their daughter, Sofia. "We had to leave at around 7 a.m. to catch the plane to London," recalled Lucas, "but Francis and Ellie got up at four in the morning, running through the room on the way to the hospital, because she was in labor. She had Sofia that day. When we got to London...I found a pay phone and called David Picker, who said, 'I've thought about this and you can have some money and you can write [*American Graffiti*]. I'm going to be at the Carlton [Hotel in Cannes]. Come visit me there and we'll talk about it.'" It was May 14—Lucas's twenty-seventh birthday. "So it was my birthday, it was Sofia's birthday, and I got *American Graffiti*, all on the same day."[22]

Picker didn't have a lot of money to offer—only $10,000 to develop the full screenplay—but it was enough for Lucas to call the Huycks in California to let them know he had a deal. "I got the money," he told them. "We can start working on the screenplay." To his disappointment, the Huycks declined; they were preparing to make their own low-budget horror film in London, and couldn't commit to writing a full screenplay. Lucas hung up and called Gary Kurtz. "I want to get this thing off the ground," he told Kurtz, and the two of them agreed to give the assignment to Richard Walter, another USC classmate. But Lucas wanted Walter to work fast; ideally the screenplay should be complete when Lucas returned home from Cannes. Kurtz told Lucas he would take care of it.

Satisfied, the Lucases headed for Cannes, already several days into its twenty-fifth anniversary celebration. Charlie Chaplin was there. John Lennon and Yoko Ono strolled the boardwalk, as did most of the Rolling Stones, who were there to catch the premiere of the rock documentary *Gimme Shelter*.[23] Lucas was in awe, but with no money, he couldn't even get tickets to the showing of his own movie; he and Marcia had to sneak in a back door. To his delight, French audiences loved *THX*, and Cannes officials put together a press conference where Lucas could talk about the movie—an event Lucas didn't even know about, and thus failed to attend, much to the annoyance of his hosts. "I was barely able to get into my own picture, let alone get to a press conference," Lucas explained. "But for a number of years, the French thought I was a real snob."[24]

Lucas did keep his appointment with Picker, however, showing up at the Carlton Hotel as directed, and meeting the studio president "in one of those big suites," he remembered. "That was my first big-time movie experience." Here they sealed the deal on *American Graffiti*— and did Lucas have anything else? In a moment reminiscent of Coppola enthusiastically giving away the unfinished *Apocalypse Now* in his pitch to Warners, Lucas told Picker all about his ideas for his unnamed "space opera fantasy film in the vein of Flash Gordon."

"Great," said Picker, "we'll make a deal for that, too."

"And that," said Lucas later, "was really the birth of *Star Wars*. It was only a notion up to then—at that point, it became an obligation!"[25]

As Lucas left the meeting, Picker handed him his own tickets for Cannes events so the young couple could enjoy the rest of the festival in style. When it ended on May 27, the Lucases spent the next several weeks riding trains across Europe, and in a reminder that you could take Lucas off the drag strip but you could never quite take the drag strip out of Lucas, they caught as many car races as they could, including the Le Mans endurance race and the Monaco Grand Prix, before getting back to the States and their movies.

When Lucas returned to California in late summer, he called on Richard Walter to check on his progress with the script for *American Graffiti*. Right away he knew he had several problems. First, Kurtz had promised Walter the entire $10,000 Picker had provided for script development—meaning Lucas was already out of money before he'd even read a page of the script. The other problem was the script itself. As Lucas sat reading it, "he really looked grim," recalled Walter. "George always looked as if he was ready to be executed—and I can tell he doesn't like this draft."[26]

According to Walter, Kurtz had given him the eighteen-page proposal, described the basic plot, and then told Walter to "pay no attention to these pages." Walter, thinking he had been given free rein, offered to base the screenplay on a rock and roll novel of his own set in New York called *Barry and the Persuasions*—hardly the California cruising scene Lucas had outlined. ("I'm a Jew from New York,"

Walter said later. "What do I know from Modesto? We didn't have cars.")[27] Kurtz had wisely nixed that idea, but Lucas still hated the final script that Walter turned in. "I ended up back home with a completely worthless screenplay about drag racing that was basically *Hot Rods to Hell*," said Lucas. "It was completely different than the original treatment....My intense desire to get a writer had backfired on me, and I ended up with an unusable script and no money."[28] Excruciating as the experience might be, then, Lucas would write it himself. So over the next three weeks, Lucas wrote from eight in the morning until eight in the evening, seven days a week, *bleeding* on the page, as he would always put it.

In late summer, agent Jeff Berg took the completed script back to David Picker at United Artists, and Picker rejected it outright. While he was still intrigued by the idea, he was disappointed with Lucas's execution: four different yet interwoven story lines, carried along by a rock and roll sound track. While common and nearly a cliché today, back in 1971 no one had ever seen or heard of such an approach to filmmaking. "The kind of structure I had presented just wasn't done in those days," said Lucas.[29]

With a failed science fiction film to his name and a new script no one wanted, Lucas had no real prospects and no money. Desperate, he borrowed money from Coppola and—the ultimate humiliation— from his father. "Financially, he was struggling," recalled his sister Kate. "It was a difficult time for him. I think being my father's son, he didn't believe in debt."[30] But Lucas was also determined not to take no for an answer. Berg was to keep shopping the script until he found someone, anyone, who could appreciate what Lucas was trying to do. In the meantime, he picked up a bit of work from Coppola shooting a montage for *The Godfather* in early 1972—the sequence of spinning newspaper headlines and crime scene photos as the Five Families go to war—but not much else.

Still, Lucas was determined to keep pressing ahead, working with his attorney to file the necessary paperwork to officially incorporate Lucasfilm Ltd., at the moment little more than a shell corporation with a placeholder name. As he and Kurtz filled out the forms, Lucas nearly balked at the continued use of the very British extension "Ltd." instead of its Americanized counterpart, "Inc." "He was a bit leery of it," said Kurtz. "He thought it was kind of an ego thing. But we thought we'd just call it that for the incorporation and worry about it later."[31] They would never worry about it again. It would remain Lucasfilm Ltd. in perpetuity.

As Berg shopped around the *American Graffiti* script, he found that while there were few takers for the film, there *were* studios interested in Lucas as a director. Tomorrow Entertainment in particular wanted Lucas to direct a feature the studio had in the pipeline, a heist film starring Donald Sutherland called *Lady Ice*. The studio made Lucas an attractive offer, upping his directing fee to $100,000 as well as a piece of the net profits. There were other offers, too, to direct movies based on the Who's concept album *Tommy* or the rock musical *Hair*. "I had all these producers calling me saying, 'I hear you're really good at material that doesn't have a story. I've got a record album I want you to make into a movie,'" Lucas recalled. "And they were offering me a lot of money...but they were terrible projects."[32]

Still, he *did* need the money. Lucas talked it over with Marcia, who encouraged him to remain steadfast in his pursuit of *American Graffiti*. After all, if *Graffiti* sold, he couldn't be in the middle of a project for someone else. Lucas, then, turned every offer down—but it wasn't easy. "That was a very dark period for me," he said later.[33] "We were in dire financial straits....I turned that down [*Lady Ice*] at my bleakest point, when I was in debt to my parents, in debt to Francis Coppola, in debt to my agent; I was so far in debt I thought I'd never get out."[34] It took years "to get from my first film to my second film, banging on doors, trying to get people to give me a chance," remembered Lucas. "Writing, struggling, with no money in the bank...getting little jobs, eking out a living. Trying to stay alive, and pushing a script that nobody wanted."[35]

Two hurdles were making *Graffiti* a tough sell for Berg. One was the title, which studios found baffling; it sounded, they thought, like an Italian movie about American feet. The larger problem, however, was that Lucas was pushing *American Graffiti* not just as a movie but as some sort of musical, actually writing across the first page of the script: "*American Graffiti* is a MUSICAL. It has singing and dancing, but it is not a musical in the traditional sense because the characters in the film neither sing nor dance." It was no wonder studio executives were confused. Making things worse, *Graffiti* was seen as yet another movie trying to cater to the youth market—a movement Dennis Hopper had crashed just as spectacularly as he had created it when his *Easy Rider* follow-up, *The Last Movie*, tanked at the box office.

And then, in early 1972, the script landed on the desk of Ned Tanen at Universal. Tanen, an early fan of Lucas's *THX* student film, was also a car lover—though he was a southern rather than a northern California cruiser—and so he thought he knew what Lucas was trying to do in his script. Tanen and Kurtz had a relationship as well, having worked together on *Two-Lane Blacktop* several years earlier. Tanen thought this was a team he could probably work with. He called Berg and told him he wanted to meet with Lucas to discuss *American Graffiti*.

Lucas showed up in Tanen's office with a cassette filled with music recorded from his own exhaustive collection of 45s: Buddy Holly. The Beach Boys. Elvis. The Platters—everything he had listened to cruising Modesto as a teenager. Just as the front page of his script promised, Lucas pitched *American Graffiti* as a musical—and as he described to Tanen the stories of each of his four main characters, Lucas played a corresponding song from his cassette. Each song, he knew, would evoke a particular moment in time—"what a certain generation of Americans thought being a teenager was really about—from about 1945 to 1962," he said later.[36] And it worked; Tanen immediately got it. "It's about every kid you ever went to school with," enthused Tanen. "It's about everything that ever happened or didn't happen to you, or that you fantasize or remember as having happened to you."[37] Yes, he and Lucas could do business—but there were some conditions.

First, Tanen generally produced only films budgeted at $1 million or less. *Graffiti* would be budgeted at $750,000. And Lucas would have no studio space at his disposal; the film would have to be made on location. More critically, there would be no additional budget set aside to cover the costs of clearing the music rights. If Lucas wanted to use Elvis songs in *American Graffiti,* that was fine—but he'd have to pay for it out of his $750,000. That was less money than Lucas had received for *THX 1138,* and he knew it might take as much as $100,000 to cover the music. Before he could shoot a single frame of film, Lucas knew at least 10 percent of his budget would be gone.

Making things even more challenging, there was one final, and perhaps more difficult, demand: the studio wanted a well-known actor involved, someone whose name on a movie poster would capture the attention of an audience. Lucas argued that since the movie was about teenagers, the cast would likely be made up mostly of young, unknown actors, and he had no intention of compromising the story to arbitrarily insert a marquee-grade star. Tanen conceded Lucas's point and suggested finding a big-name producer instead. And in the spring of 1972, following the release of *The Godfather* to outstanding reviews and box office numbers that stunned even its director, there was no bigger name than Francis Ford Coppola.

Tanen and Coppola had tangled in the past—Tanen would always call Coppola "Francis the Mad"—but the idea of promoting *American Graffiti* with Coppola's name attached to it dazzled Universal executives.[38] Lucas was still nursing a grudge against Coppola over the demise of Zoetrope—and, if put on the spot, would likely have admitted he was hoping to be regarded as an independent filmmaker and the head of Lucasfilm Ltd. rather than as Coppola's young apprentice yet again. But knowing Coppola as well as he did, he knew Francis would stay out of his way, leaving the day-to-day, on-location producing to Kurtz. Lucas told Tanen he'd be more than happy to have Coppola as his producer—and then went to discuss it with him.

"Yeah, sure, great," Coppola told Lucas—then threw out what he thought was an even better idea. "You know, *we* should be doing this picture," said Coppola. "Let's get it out of Universal. I'll finance it myself."[39] Lucas, on the verge of a deal with Universal, thought that was a bad idea; if Tanen found out Coppola was trying to take the movie away from him, it might scuttle the deal altogether. But it was Francis being Francis again. Lucas decided to give Coppola a bit of time to see what he could do, and with his profits from *The Godfather* as collateral, Coppola went to the City Bank in Beverly Hills to secure a loan for $700,000 that he could put toward *American Graffiti*. But both his accountant and his wife put an immediate stop to Coppola's plan before it could even get under way. Ellie Coppola didn't like the script, and informed her husband in no uncertain terms that if he was going to gamble his profits on a film, it would be one of his own and not one by a protégé. Chastened, Coppola decided not to pursue the loan. He'd take Universal's money instead.

"We didn't get the [okay from Tanen] with the [script]," Kurtz recalled later. "We got it with Francis's name....They [Universal] thought the concept might work, but they wanted to be a little more certain, and his reputation provided the certainty."[40] With Coppola officially aboard, Tanen could ink the deal. As producer, Coppola would earn $25,000 plus 10 percent of the net; Lucas, meanwhile, would be paid $50,000 to write and direct, as well as 40 percent of the net profits.[41] While the figures were small, the deal was generous, and one that promised to make both Lucas and Coppola quite a bit of money if—and this was a big if—*American Graffiti* could turn a profit. Finally, as he had in his initial agreement with United Artists, Lucas also rolled his untitled space opera—"the Flash Gordon thing"—into the deal with Universal. If all went well, it would be his next project.

Lucas was generally happy with the arrangement, and it was Tanen, in fact, who'd gone to bat for Lucas with studio head Lew Wasserman, who was skeptical of *American Graffiti* and even more suspicious of the Flash Gordon thing. Tanen later said he simply had had a hunch about Lucas. "You could just feel something big was going to happen to him," said Tanen.[42] Lucas liked Tanen, too, and particularly appreciated the way he worked. "[Universal] in effect wrote you a check and told you to go away and come back with a finished movie,"

Lucas said later. "They never bothered you at all. It was a very, very good atmosphere."[43]

Well, mostly. There was really only one thing Lucas didn't get in the deal: control over the final edited version of the film. After the relative failure of *THX*, there wasn't much room for Berg to negotiate the point on his behalf. Lucas grudgingly agreed to give Universal editorial control. And once again, he would end up regretting it.

With Universal behind him, and Kurtz watching his back, Lucas put *American Graffiti* into pre-production immediately. He set up a production office in San Rafael, about fifteen minutes away from Mill Valley. Lucas liked the look of San Rafael's main streets — unlike in Modesto, storefronts still looked much as they had a decade earlier — and he planned to shoot most of the movie's exteriors there. Searching for cars from the appropriate era to cruise the streets during filming, Lucas put ads in Bay Area newspapers promising owners $20 a day to drive 1962-era cars in the background.[44] Kurtz's assistant Bunny Alsup — who was also his sister-in-law — photographed every car and driver who responded to the ads so Lucas would have a variety of cars to choose from. It was Kurtz, however, who found the 1932 deuce coupe with the chopped top that would be cleaned up and painted yellow — yet another yellow sports car! — to create *American Graffiti*'s most iconic automobile.

Perhaps the most pressing business at the moment was getting the rights to the music. Without the music, insisted Lucas, there *was* no film; it was, he reminded everyone, a *musical*. Lucas had made up an extensive song list, selecting at least three songs for each scene in the event he couldn't clear one or two of them. When Kurtz ran the list by executives at Universal, they "practically had a heart attack," said Kurtz, and urged Lucas to record the songs with an orchestra or a cover band instead. Kurtz blanched. "We can't do that," he said. "We have to use the original records."[45] Executives eventually agreed, but warned Kurtz that if clearances exceeded 10 percent of the budget, the difference was coming out of Coppola's pocket.

Lucas wasn't going to be able to afford about half of the songs he wanted anyway. Right away, Elvis's music was out; the rights were too expensive, and the King's label refused to negotiate. Kurtz had better luck with the Beach Boys, mainly because he knew drummer Dennis Wilson personally, after working with him on *Two-Lane Blacktop*. Kurtz eventually secured a number of Beach Boys songs, including "Surfin' Safari" and "All Summer Long," for a reasonable fee—and once Kurtz and Lucas could point to the involvement of the Beach Boys, clearing song rights became much easier. Eventually Lucas would clear forty-three songs for the movie, including hits by Buddy Holly, Chuck Berry, Fats Domino, the Del-Vikings, and Booker T. & the M.G.'s. Lucas had just secured the sound track that would make the film—and he and Kurtz had brought the clearances in for around $90,000. Right on target.

Casting, too, was critical. Lucas still intended to use young actors, close in age to the characters they were playing, even scouring local high school drama productions looking for promising talent. On the recommendation of both Coppola and Kurtz, Lucas turned to veteran casting director Fred Roos to help him through the process. For Lucas, the casting wasn't just important; it was personal: each of the four main characters was rooted in his own personality and life experiences. "I'm sort of everybody," Lucas said later.[46] "They were all composite characters, based on my life, and on the lives of friends of mine," he told a reporter.[47] "I was Terry the Toad, fumbling with girls, then I became a drag racer like John.... And finally I became Curt. I got serious and went to college."[48] Really, the only character he had struggled with in his script was the overachieving Steve. "[That was] the only character I really wasn't," he said. Nevertheless, "I have a lot of friends who were the Steves, who stayed and just sort of followed the path that was laid out for them."[49]

For weeks, Lucas held open auditions so he could sift through as many actors as possible. With Roos next to him, Lucas saw thousands of young performers in ten-minute increments, six days a week, twelve to fourteen hours a day. Lucas took notes on everybody, scratching his thoughts down in notebooks in his crabbed handwriting and rarely saying much of anything. His silence distressed some of the young actors. "He hardly said two words to me," said Candy Clark, who would end up with the role of the ditzy but well-intentioned Debbie. "He was mostly looking at me, which makes for a very uncomfortable audition when someone is just sizing you up, not interacting."[50]

Once the first round of auditions was complete, Lucas picked four or five actors for each of the major roles, paired them up into boy-girl couples, then videotaped them so he could watch their performances closely, over and over again—a practice that would become an industry standard. After poring over the videos, Lucas would then take the best two or three from each couple and record their performances again, this time on 16 mm film. It was a long, excruciating process, but Lucas was determined to make exactly the right choice for each role.

The weeks of hard work paid off, as Lucas was able to assemble a note-perfect cast, the majority of whom would go on to long careers. Lucas had been impressed enough with Richard Dreyfuss to offer him his choice of playing either the intellectual but adventurous Curt or the popular but conflicted Steve. (Dreyfuss chose Curt, believing he was much more like that character.) Suzanne Somers, in her first real film role, was given the part of the enigmatic Thunderbird-driving blond bombshell who nearly persuades Curt not to leave his small town—to *escape*, as Lucas explained it, the same theme that had driven *THX 1138*. Curt's all-night quest for the blonde in the hot car has more than a whiff of Lucas's own truth to it; according to his mother, "George always wanted to have a blonde girlfriend. But he never did quite find her."[51] Curt wouldn't either.

The character who *did* land the blonde, however, was probably the one the most like Lucas: Terry the Toad, played with geeky enthusiasm by Charles Martin Smith. "There's so much of George in Terry the Toad, it's unbelievable," said John Plummer. "The botching of events in terms of his life, his social ineptness in dealing with women."[52] Smith had missed the first rounds of *Graffiti* auditions, but Lucas ran into him in a studio office building and asked him to try out. And it probably didn't hurt that with his thick-rimmed glasses, Smith even *looked* a little like Lucas.

Cindy Williams, who landed the role of Laurie—the ingenue role, Lucas called it—was jet-lagged and bleary-eyed throughout the audition process and thought she'd be so bad in the role that she very nearly didn't accept it until pressed by Coppola. "I was just awestruck that Francis Coppola would call me," Williams said. "I was, like, hypnotized: *Yes, evil master, I will do the film*, I said. *Of course I will.*"⁵³

The role of Steve, the character Lucas had struggled with the most on the page, went to one of the more experienced, and youngest, actors in the film, eighteen-year-old Ron Howard. While Howard had more than a decade of acting experience—including an eight-year run on the highly successful *Andy Griffith Show* and a memorable role in the film *The Music Man*—it was still uncertain whether he could carry a film as an adult, mainly because it wasn't clear whether audiences would accept that *Andy Griffith*'s precocious Opie had grown up.

In 1972, in fact, Howard was preparing to enter film school at USC, determined to become more than just an actor—but when he heard that Lucas was holding open auditions, Howard decided to read for the part. He did so "with some trepidation," he said later, mainly because he too had been confused by Lucas's insistence on calling *Graffiti* a musical. "George, I have to admit one thing," Howard told Lucas during his audition. "I know I was in *The Music Man*, but I think they cast me because I couldn't sing—because I really can't. And I certainly can't dance. In fact, I can just barely carry a tune." Lucas shrugged. "Oh, don't worry about it," he told Howard. "You wouldn't have to sing. No one really sings, but it *is* a musical."

"And that was it," said Howard, who landed the part and never asked about singing again. But he would remain baffled, at least for a while, by Lucas's "musical."⁵⁴

It was casting director Roos who would bring in one of the more unconventional cast members, a self-taught carpenter named Harrison Ford. Struggling as an actor, Ford had taken up carpentry to pay the bills—and was so good that he had earned a reputation as the

"Carpenter to the Stars," building a recording studio for Sergio Mendes and a deck for Sally Kellerman, and doing odd jobs for the art rock group the Doors. Ford was doing so well, in fact, that he very nearly didn't take the role playing hot-rodder Bob Falfa, since it paid less than half of what he was making doing carpentry jobs. While Ford eventually settled for a little more than scale, he drew the line at having his hair buzzed into a flattop. Lucas agreed to permit Ford to tuck his hair up into a white cowboy hat instead. It would not be the last iconic hat Ford would wear for Lucas.

It had taken five exhausting months to cast the film. Working with actors was never Lucas's strong suit anyway, but he had set himself a particularly grueling schedule, flying from San Francisco to Los Angeles each week to sit through auditions all day, then crashing on the couch at Matthew Robbins's house in Benedict Canyon at night. Fortuitously, Lucas wasn't the only one in Robbins's house; that spring, Robbins was at work on a script for Steven Spielberg called *The Sugarland Express,* and Spielberg would drop by every evening to talk about the script over dinner. "So they'd still be around the kitchen table discussing their script," said Lucas, "and we'd have dinner, talk, and hang out. That's where we really got to know each other."[55]

From the moment of their first meeting at the student film exhibition at UCLA in 1969—when Spielberg joked he'd been "insanely jealous" of Lucas as a filmmaker—Lucas and Spielberg's relationship would always be a mixture of good-natured competition and warm admiration. In January 1971, for instance, after Spielberg had flashily directed an episode of the NBC series *The Name of the Game* titled "L.A. 2017," Lucas had taken wry delight in pointing out that its setup—a vaguely dystopian future in which residents of Los Angeles live underground—bore more than a passing resemblance to *THX 1138.*[56] But Lucas had nothing but praise for Spielberg's most recent effort, an edge-of-the-seat made-for-TV thriller called *Duel,* about a mild-mannered motorist being stalked by the unseen driver of a tanker truck. Lucas had watched it at Coppola's house during a party, shutting himself into an upstairs room while the festivities raged below him. "I ran downstairs and said, 'Francis, you've got to come see this movie. This guy's *really* good.'...I was very, very impressed with his work."[57]

Spielberg, too, would always look back fondly on those long evenings in Benedict Canyon, swapping stories with Lucas and grousing about the challenges of getting a film made. "We were the movie brats who got together a long time ago and decided to talk about how hard it is to make movies," said Spielberg. "I mean, we're constant complainers. We love complaining to each other."[58] The dinner table conversation at Robbins's place—complaints and all—would cement their blossoming friendship for good.

The last big task on *American Graffiti* was to get into shape the troublesome Lucas-penned script that had so annoyed Ellie Coppola. Lucas checked in with the Huycks again, and was relieved to find out they were available to work on the screenplay. Lucas and the Huycks began passing pages back and forth, writing and rewriting, at times even typing right over pages of an earlier draft. The Huycks wrote quickly, and Lucas was grateful for their help and generous in praise of their talent. "What they did was improve the dialogue, make it funnier, more human, truer," Lucas explained. Still, he said, "it was basically my story. The scenes are mine, the dialogue is theirs."[59] The final script was finished on May 10, 1972, and just in time—for Lucas had his cameras ready to roll in San Rafael on Monday, June 26, the first day of a breakneck twenty-eight-day shooting schedule.

He had trouble almost from the start. "The hardest thing is that it was all at night," said Lucas later. "It was a very short schedule...in that the sun went down at nine at night and came up at five in the morning. That left a very short day, and...I only had twenty-eight of them, so it was a very, very, very fast and short schedule, especially considering it was all on location with cars that broke down and all the other drama that would go on....It was just physically a very difficult thing to get through."[60] On the first night of shooting, Lucas gathered his crew on Fourth Street in San Rafael at 4 p.m. to begin the task of installing camera mounts onto the hoods and sides of several vehicles—a time-consuming process that ate up so much of the evening that Lucas didn't begin filming until nearly midnight. After breaking for dinner—or maybe it was breakfast—at 1 a.m., Lucas shot nonstop until the sun came up at 5 a.m., but only barely managed to complete about half the scenes on his schedule. Already "we were half a day behind," lamented Lucas, "and to fall half a day behind on a 28 day schedule is like the end of the world."[61]

The second night was no better. Despite the agreement he had negotiated with the town of San Rafael under which he would pay $300 per night to film on Fourth Street, local businesses were already complaining about closing the street. When Lucas and his crew arrived in San Rafael on Tuesday evening, they learned the local council had withdrawn permission for him to film and would not permit the police to clear or control traffic on Fourth Street. Lucas made the most of the evening anyway, rapidly shooting his way through nineteen setups while Kurtz scrambled to find them a new location. "Then we had focus problems on the camera, and the assistant cameraman was run over by a car," Lucas recalled with a sigh. "Then we had a five alarm fire. That was a typical night."[62]

Kurtz managed to find a more receptive shooting location in the town of Petaluma, about twenty miles north of San Rafael, but that didn't mean things were going to get any easier. San Rafael, to its credit, would permit Lucas to return for two more nights of shooting to film most of *Graffiti's* cruising scenes, but Lucas was having problems beyond mere location. For one thing, he was exhausted. After shooting all night, Lucas would try to sleep during the day; but instead he generally spent the daylight hours watching footage shot the previous night, writing notes that he would pass along to Marcia, who was editing a rough cut of the film with Verna Fields as quickly as Lucas could bring it to them. By the time he arrived in Petaluma each evening to start filming, he'd hardly slept at all. Some nights Lucas would be found sound asleep in a chair, wrapped up cozily in Kurtz's jacket;

other times he'd fall asleep as he dangled in a harness off the side of a moving car, head lolling. "Night after night took its toll on George," recalled Harrison Ford. "George was often asleep when it came time to say 'Cut.' I often woke him up to tell him it was time to try it again."[63] Even in June, northern California evenings could get chilly, and despite wearing his USC varsity jacket, Lucas shivered from the cold all night long. He eventually came down with the flu, and his diabetes, which he normally kept under control, was troubling him. "I don't think I can last at this," he told Milius shakily.[64]

Worse, he wasn't happy with what he was seeing. Lucas was shooting *American Graffiti* in a documentary, almost disengaged style— setting up the camera, then letting it roll as the actors moved in and out of the shot. He was also filming in inexpensive Techniscope again, mostly because he loved the grainy look it gave everything. But his documentary approach still also extended to using mostly natural light, relying mainly on streetlights, headlights, and neon signs. With such poor lighting, however, nothing would stay in focus. "It just looked mushy," said Kurtz.[65] After watching a week's worth of footage, Lucas knew he had a serious problem.

When it came to solving lighting problems, Lucas knew exactly who to call for help: Haskell Wexler. He had actually wanted Wexler at his side as a cameraman right from the start, but Wexler had refused; he didn't like shooting in Techniscope, and he already had his hands full shooting commercials in Los Angeles. "But when we got in trouble and I asked him to do it, he did it—as a friend, to help me out," said Lucas fondly.[66] Wexler's schedule would be nearly as rough as Lucas's; every day he would shuttle back and forth between Los Angeles and San Francisco, shooting commercials all day and *American Graffiti* all night. While Kurtz worried that the pace might take a toll on Wexler's health, Wexler claimed it didn't bother him a bit. "It didn't affect me," he said with a shrug. "I loved it. I loved working around those kids, around George, and the story....It was a great experience."[67]

Wexler's expertise would make a difference immediately. Lucas had instructed Wexler that he wanted *American Graffiti* to look like a jukebox, "very garish, bright blue and yellow and red"[68] — "ugly," muttered Marcia[69] — and Wexler had delivered, installing brighter bulbs in signs and streetlights, and strategically placing low-wattage lights in cars to directly illuminate the faces of actors. Wexler, said Lucas, was "a lifesaver."[70] Lucas couldn't praise him enough. "He's really terrific so I just let him do it and I didn't worry about it anymore…and he did a fantastic job. The movie looked exactly the way I wanted it to look."[71]

With the technical problems in Wexler's capable hands, Lucas could concentrate on setting up his shots, guiding his actors, and bringing the film in on time. Lucas was well aware that working with actors was his biggest weakness, so he was fortunate to have chosen a cast that needed very little real direction. "George was given this cast, and he had to shoot so fast that there wasn't any time for directing," said Coppola. "He stood 'em up and shot 'em, and they were so talented.…It was just lucky."[72] Richard Dreyfuss thought there was more than just luck involved. "He trusted us," said Dreyfuss. And why not? In Lucas's view, he had hired the best actors, carefully chosen for each part, so why *shouldn't* he trust them to deliver?

Lucas's style as a director, however, could be wildly unpredictable. Sometimes he would talk briefly with the actors before a scene, run through a number of options or variations, then finally nod and ask, "Is that the way you wanna do it?" before disappearing to set up the shot. After a scene, Lucas wouldn't offer any feedback beyond "Great! Terrific!" and maybe "Let's try again!" It was "a little unnerving," said Ron Howard, "because George didn't really particularly talk to us much."[73] Other times, Lucas wouldn't talk at *all*, and would simply set up several cameras without telling his actors which one would be filming the master shot. Partly this was a matter of speed and economy; with two cameras rolling, Lucas was essentially getting two different versions of every scene to choose from in the editing room. But it also gave the film a documentary style, almost a "found footage" look, that Lucas loved. With multiple cameras rolling, actors were often uncertain which one to play to. "Just keep doing the scene!" Lucas would shout—an approach Ron Howard found as thrilling as it was confusing. "Often we couldn't tell where the cameras were. You didn't know if it was a long lens getting you in close-up at any given moment," said Howard. "So at first it was disorienting—but ultimately it was incredibly liberating."[74]

"[George] was sort of a control freak," said Willard Huyck sympathetically, "and directing was out of his control."[75] And it was those out-of-control moments that could result in cinematic perfection. In *Graffiti*'s opening scene, Terry the Toad cruises into Mel's Drive-In on a Vespa moped, then lurches up over a curb, engine sputtering, and crashes into a row of vending machines. It had all been accidental on the part of actor Charles Martin Smith, who had merely tried to let the clutch out quickly on the Vespa so the moped would stop with a jerk. "Instead it took off with me still hanging onto it," said Smith, who limped away from the bike, still in character, with his pride intact—an unintentionally note-perfect entrance for *Graffiti*'s resident nerd.[76]

As the weeks wore on, even with Wexler's steady presence behind the camera and Kurtz's stoic calm behind the scenes, there were problems Lucas couldn't avoid. Axles broke on several of the cars, the yellow '32 coupe blew its reverse gear, and Lucas's beloved Éclair camera—the one he cradled in his arms and carried like a prize pig— was badly damaged when it fell off a tripod.[77] And away from the set, some of his cast members were misbehaving. "If you put a group of young people together in a Holiday Inn, what's going to happen?" said Candy Clark. "There is going to be some drinking! When they weren't working, they would just hang out and drink beer or whiskey. It wasn't abnormal behavior or anything scandalous."[78] Harrison Ford in particular could be a mischievous drunk, throwing beer bottles into the hotel parking lot just to watch them explode, and scaling the Holiday Inn sign to place a bottle on top. Eventually Kurtz pulled the actor aside to read him the riot act—a scolding a contrite Ford never forgot. "[Kurtz] was the guy who told me no more drinking beer on the streets," said Ford, "and then no more drinking beer in the trailer, and then no more drinking beer."[79] Fortunately, neither Ned Tanen nor any of the suits at Universal showed up in Petaluma very often to check on things—and when Tanen did visit the set, Lucas made a point of ignoring him. "George has no social graces," said Gloria Katz. "And in his psychology, the suits had no business other than writing the checks. He didn't want to hear what they said, he didn't respect them, nothing."[80]

If there was anyone on the set who *did* have Lucas's utmost respect, it was probably the larger-than-life personality Lucas had chosen to serve as the film's Greek chorus and conscience: a thirty-four-year-old deejay named Robert Smith, better known as Wolfman Jack.

While Lucas always claimed to remember listening to Wolfman Jack while cruising in high school, that wasn't quite true; Smith didn't create his Wolfman persona until at least 1962, when he was still spinning discs as "Big Smith with the Records" on KCIJ-AM in Shreveport, Louisiana—and even then, his voice couldn't be heard much beyond the borders of the state. In 1964, however, Smith moved to Mexican radio station XERF-AM—which blasted its signal across most of North America with 250,000 watts behind it—and then, in 1965, over to XERB in Tijuana, another "border blaster" that nearly anyone in the United States could tune in to at 1090 on the AM dial. This is where Lucas, in his early days at USC, would have first heard the Wolfman as he yelped and howled his way into stardom, fascinating listeners with his raspy voice and hipster delivery: "Are you wit' me out deh?" he would ask every night. Listeners didn't know if he was white or black, or whether he was broadcasting from Mexico, California, a boat in the Pacific, or the moon, for that matter.[81]

Lucas loved every minute of it. "He was a really mystical character, I'll tell you," said Lucas. "He was wild, he had these crazy phone calls, and he drifted out of nowhere. And it was an outlaw station. He was an outlaw, which of course made him extremely attractive to kids." Lucas, too, understood better than most the power of a deejay; it was with good reason that he had chosen deejay Emperor Hudson as the subject of his first USC documentary: "A lot of teenagers have a make-believe friend in a disc jockey, but he's much more real because he talks to them, he jokes around.... He's part of the family. You listen to him every day, you're very close to him, you share your most intimate moments with him."[82]

Wolfman Jack's involvement was critical to the film; it would be the music from his radio show, intercut with the Wolfman's on-air patter, that would carry the movie from scene to scene. In fact, Lucas sat down with Jack to record an entire radio show, which Lucas planned to edit into the film's sound track, including real radio footage of the Wolfman taking phone calls and bantering on the air with actual listeners. Lucas was grateful to the enigmatic Jack for agreeing to take the role. It would be the first time most of his listeners would see him, which Jack worried might remove some of the luster from his on-air personality. While Lucas's limited budget meant he could pay the deejay only $3,000, Lucas gave Wolfman one of his points in the film. If the film turned a profit, so would the Wolfman. It would turn out to be one of the best-paying gigs Jack ever had.

Lucas also put the deejay at the center of one of *Graffiti*'s most important moments, as it would be the Wolfman who would deliver the film's central message: "Get your ass in gear," he tells Curt serenely, dispensing wisdom in thoughtful sound bites much as Yoda would advise Luke Skywalker a decade later. For Lucas, it was a similar though more mature message than that of *THX 1138*. That film had been about escaping; *Graffiti* was about growing up. For Lucas, and so many others of his generation, 1962—the year before the Kennedy assassination—was the year before the world changed forever, for better or for worse. Those who lived through it had a simple choice: evolve or face extinction.

For that reason, Lucas was never going to change the title, no matter how much studio executives fussed over it; even Coppola would encourage the cast and crew to try to come up with an alternative, with Coppola himself floating *Rock Around the Block*. But Lucas knew *exactly* what the title meant. The film itself truly *was* American graffiti—a unique moment in time, preserved on celluloid, scratching its essence on the movie screen like the etchings on Egyptian monuments, to ensure its memory wouldn't be lost forever. "It's about a period of transition in history in America where in one year you had a President that a lot of kids admired....[Y]ou had a certain kind of rock'n'roll music, a certain kind of country where you could believe in things....You had a certain kind of life," Lucas explained in 1974. "But in the next two years everything changed: no longer were you a teenager; you were an adult going to college or doing whatever you were going to do. The government changed radically, and everybody's attitude toward it changed radically. Drugs came in. Although it had always been there, a war surfaced as an issue. The music changed completely. *Graffiti* is about the fact that you have to accept these changes — they were on the horizon — and if you didn't, you had problems.... You try to fight it...and you lose."[83] *Get your ass in gear.*

Lucas completed filming on *American Graffiti* on Friday, August 4, 1972. Perhaps predictably, the final two weeks had been bogged down by one mechanical failure after another, with a broken tie rod hampering the shooting of a stunt car, underexposed film requiring a long round of retakes, and a flat tire that kept the airplane in the final scene firmly on the ground. While Lucas had lightened things up in the last week of shooting with a real sock hop in the gym of Tamalpais High School — Coppola had shown up for that one, as had Marcia — Lucas was glad that it was over. "You couldn't pay me enough money to go through what you have to go through to make a movie," he complained to the *New York Times*. "It's excruciating. It's horrible. You get physically sick. I get a very bad cough and a cold whenever I direct. I don't know whether it's psychosomatic or not. You feel terrible. There is an immense amount of pressure, and emotional pain....But I do it anyway, and I really love to do it. It's like climbing mountains."[84]

True to form, Lucas was looking forward to the editing process. "I'm really gonna direct it in the editing room," he told Ron Howard. "That's when I'm going to make my choices."[85] Most of the actual editing responsibility was in the hands of Tanen's editor of choice, Verna Fields, who was assembling the movie in the garage of Coppola's house. But because Fields had another, higher-profile job—she was editing Peter Bogdanovich's *Paper Moon*—she'd been assigned an equally capable assistant editor in Marcia Lucas. That, at least, ensured that Lucas would have *some* say in the edit. And just to make certain, he'd taken over another critical component of the editing process as well: the music. Lucas knew exactly which songs he wanted playing over particular scenes, but actually cutting the songs into the film so that they blended seamlessly into the scene was going to require a certain kind of flair. Lucas, who had called on Haskell Wexler when stuck with a lighting problem, knew exactly who to call when it came to finessing difficulties with sound: Walter Murch.

Lucas knew he couldn't just dub the songs in behind the action in the film. "You would drive your audience mad if you did that," agreed Murch. Instead, he wanted the music in the film to sound like it was being broadcast over car radios, on public address systems in gyms, or out of tinny transistor radio speakers. They would have to figure out how to "worldize" their music, Lucas said—and Murch couldn't wait to get his hands on it. Together he and Lucas recorded the entire sound track for the film—all the way down to Wolfman Jack's patter—on speakers reverberating across gymnasiums, warbling out of old PA systems, or even in Lucas's own backyard, where Lucas would slowly and randomly walk a speaker around the yard, blasting the sound track as Murch's tape recorder rolled.[86] "We took all of the music and made it so it would bounce around the environment…as a sound effect," explained Lucas. "Then we took sound effects and used them in the places where we really needed tension and drama."[87]

It was the first time a pop sound track had been given its own dramatic presence in a film—an innovation that filmmakers like Quentin Tarantino and Joel and Ethan Coen would embrace as they practically built films like *Pulp Fiction* and *O Brother, Where Art Thou?* around carefully selected songs from established pop and folk songbooks. In his desire to turn his sound track into a sound effect, Lucas had made the sound track—and the sound track album—a vital part of the movie experience. Editing the sound track into the film was hard work—it would take nearly five weeks just to cut in the sound—but Lucas loved every moment of it. "I love rock 'n' roll," he said. "Making *Graffiti*, I could sit down at my Steenbeck and play all this rock 'n' roll all day; that was my job in editing. The editors were cutting the scenes and I was putting in the rock 'n' roll saying, 'Wow, that's really great.' It's like carving something; it takes shape, and it's a lot of fun."[88]

So much fun, in fact, that the first edit of the film came in at nearly three hours long. Lucas agonized over the next round of editing—keeping the music aligned even as scenes were pared down was a major challenge—but managed to excise only another hour. "With all the cars and the music in it, [it originally] came out to 160 minutes," Lucas said. "We knew it couldn't be that long because the contract said 110 minutes."[89] Back again he went, with Marcia cutting the film as Lucas and Murch worked on the sound, until they finally pared the film down to 110 contractual minutes. The cuts had been difficult to make, but at least *he* had overseen them, not some studio bureaucrat who didn't understand the film.

He sent the completed print to Universal in December 1972. Lucas was happy with it. Executives at Universal, however, weren't so sure.

In late January 1973, Ned Tanen boarded an airplane in Los Angeles, bound for San Francisco—and he wasn't happy. Universal was still uncertain about *American Graffiti* and had scheduled a public screening of the film in San Francisco at 10 a.m. on Sunday, January 28, to gauge audience reaction. But Tanen was already in a dark mood; the studio was losing faith in *Graffiti* fast, preferring to pour their time and money into promoting *Jesus Christ Superstar* instead. ("They'd forgotten about us," sighed Lucas.)[90] And while Tanen himself had yet to see more than a few minutes of the film, he was less and less inclined to be enthusiastic about it. It might be salvageable, he thought, as a television movie, but that was about it.

As Tanen made his way to his seat, he pushed past Matthew Robbins, screenwriter Hal Barwood—yet another of the USC "Dirty Dozen"—and Lucas's agent Jeff Berg, all of whom were also headed north for *Graffiti's* debut. "We greeted him and he greeted us, but I remember vividly how unfriendly he was," said Robbins.[91] "Ned wouldn't sit with us on the airplane and he wouldn't share a cab to the theater. He was furious before he even saw the movie."[92] In San Francisco, Tanen's mood didn't improve, even as his cab dropped him off outside the Northpoint Theater on the corner of Bay Street and Powell in the city's North Beach section.

Inside, the eight-hundred-seat theater was filled to capacity. But Tanen was still skeptical. The theater was practically in Lucas's backyard, and the executive was convinced that Lucas had packed the house with friends and family willing to applaud anything. While Lucas *had* invited friends, cast members, and family—his parents were there, ready to see the film their son had pursued so devotedly with borrowed money—the crowd was mostly a young one, Lucas's age or younger, a new kind of filmgoer, raised on rock and roll and weaned on *Easy Rider.* Tanen took it all in with a scowl, then sank into a seat near the front of the theater; George and Marcia, Coppola, and Kurtz retreated to their seats in the back.

"The movie started," said Marcia, "and the minute 'Rock Around the Clock' came on, people just started whooping and hollering. And when Charlie Martin Smith drives in on the Vespa and bangs into the wall, the audience laughed. They were with the film all the way."[93] Ron Howard agreed. "The audience just went nuts," he said, and by the time the final credits rolled under the music of the Beach Boys, "there was applause and there was cheering and chatter," recalled Robbins, a "feeling of such generous goodwill and astonishment. It was a fabulous screening."[94]

Lucas exhaled in relief. "Francis and George and I were all euphoric," remembered Marcia.[95] And then here came Tanen, striding purposefully up the aisle toward them. As he passed, he angrily collared Kurtz and Coppola and dragged them into the dark walkway between the last rows of seats. "[Tanen] was livid; he thought [the film] failed," said Murch. "He was saying as much to Francis...and George was sitting there thinking, 'Oh my God, it's *THX* all over again, they're gonna take the film away from me.'"[96] Marcia, too, was stunned by the executive's dismissive response. "I was in a state of shock," she said.[97]

Coppola had worked himself into a lather. "What are you talking about?" he shouted at Tanen. "You were just in the theater for the last two hours! Didn't you just see and hear what we all just saw and heard?"

"I'm not talking about that," said Tanen flatly. "We'll see if we can release it."

"You'll see if you can *release* it?" fumed Coppola. "You should go down on your knees and thank George for saving your job! This kid has killed himself to make this movie for you. He brought it in on time and on schedule. The least you can do is thank him for that!" Coppola reached dramatically for a nonexistent checkbook and offered to buy the film from Universal outright. "If you hate it that much, let it go," he told Tanen. "We'll set it up someplace else, and you get all your money back."[98]

Tanen refused to rise to Coppola's bait and stormed out of the theater. Coppola was furious and would bear the grudge a long time; he and Tanen wouldn't speak to each other for nearly twenty years. (Years later, Coppola looked at the numbers and determined that had Tanen permitted him to finance *American Graffiti*, he'd have made $20 million.)[99] For his part, Lucas was touched by Coppola's chest-thumping defense. "Francis really stood up to Ned," said Lucas later. "I had given [Francis] a bad time when the Warners thing came down over *THX*, I really held that against him — 'You're gonna let them cut it, you're not gonna go down there and stop 'em?' — and when *Graffiti* came along, I said, 'Here we go again.' But Francis did what he was supposed to do. I was pretty proud of him."[100]

Robbins tried as best he could to console Lucas as he staggered out of the theater in shock. "That the studio, with a capital 'S,' could still represent itself in such a blind, insensitive, and obtuse way only reaffirmed so many of George's feelings about what Hollywood was made of," said Robbins.[101] Tanen, however, wasn't concerned about Lucas's feelings; he was worried that he had another one of Lucas's art movie bombs on his hands, this time with an expensive rock and roll sound track. *American Graffiti* was taken away from Lucas to be reexamined and recut.

Lucas slunk home to fume to Marcia, to friends, to anyone who would listen. "I don't know what to do," he moaned to Willard Huyck. "This picture — people are responding off the wall, and they keep telling me they're going to put it on television."[102] Marcia was sympathetic, but only to a point. "George was just a nobody who had directed one little arty-farty movie that hadn't done any business," she said later. "He didn't have the power to make people listen to him."[103] Still, she encouraged him to fight, to talk with Tanen and make the case for his own film. But Lucas sulkily refused to have anything to do with Tanen, and left the negotiations with Universal up to Kurtz. Producers, not artists, were the ones who should fight with the studio suits.

Kurtz eventually persuaded Tanen to allow Lucas to reedit the film himself as long as it reflected Tanen's recommended changes. Lucas spent the next three months recutting the film, gleefully ignoring Tanen's suggestions altogether, with a predictable result: an unamused Tanen handed the film off to Universal's in-house editors. With a bit of persuasion from Coppola, however, even Universal's editors could see that Lucas had been right: the film flat-out worked. In the end, Universal pulled only three scenes, totaling a little more than four minutes, out of *American Graffiti*. But Lucas was apoplectic. "There was no reason for the cutting," he complained. "It was just arbitrary."[104]

It was a "formative experience" for Lucas, said Walter Murch.[105] Lucas had seen Hollywood tamper with — no, *mutilate* — his art, not once, but twice now. He wasn't going to let it happen again. "It's more a moral issue than anything else," Lucas said plainly.[106] "That was the beginning of his passion to become an independent filmmaker," said his sister Wendy, "so that he would have total control over his films and not be under some MBA studio executive who himself had never written or directed or edited a film from the ground up."[107]

"They're people who have never made a movie in their lives — agents and lawyers with no idea of dramatic flow," said Lucas derisively. "But they can come in, see a movie twice, and in those few hours they can tell you to take this out or shorten that. The movie industry was built by independent entrepreneurs, dictators who had a very strong feeling about movies. They knew what they wanted and they made it happen."[108] Those four excised minutes would spawn an empire that would answer to the one independent entrepreneur and dictator who mattered: George Lucas.

Kurtz spent much of the spring of 1973 ensuring that the newly recut *American Graffiti* was seen by Universal executives in the best possible light, showing the film in theaters packed with young viewers rather than in Universal's cramped viewing rooms. "Normally, fourteen stodgy old men sit in a room and that's it," said Lucas. Steven Spielberg, who attended a May 15 screening in Beverly Hills, was certain his friend had a smash on his hands. And yet Tanen *still* wasn't sure. But the film was building a following, and several other studios, including 20th Century Fox and Paramount, expressed an interest in distributing the film if Universal lost its nerve. Suddenly, said Lucas, Universal "knew they had a movie."[109]

American Graffiti opened on Wednesday, August 1, 1973, in limited release, seen only in theaters in New York and Los Angeles. At the Avco Theater on Wilshire Boulevard, there were lines around the block that first night. *Graffiti* would perform strongly from the moment of its premiere, earning good reviews and strong word of mouth. When it finally opened in theaters across the nation two weeks later, it would already have a slow momentum behind it that would build it into a certified smash. "It didn't actually explode, it was never that huge of a hit," said Tanen. "It just stayed in theaters for, like, two years."[110]

Critics fell all over themselves reviewing *American Graffiti* in the most glowing of terms. *Time* magazine hailed it as "superb and singular,"[111] while the *Washington Post* called it "a lovely nostalgic conception... [which] promises to become that increasingly rare but heartening commodity, a new American movie that almost everyone is going to like."[112] Charles Champlin, the influential critic of the *Los Angeles Times*, called it "one of the most important films of the year" and declared that "to miss it is to miss something quite special."[113]

One of its biggest fans was the *New York Times*, which featured both the film and Lucas in several stories over two months and hailed *American Graffiti* as "a work of art."[114] Lucas wasn't sure whether to bristle at that label or not. "My thing about art is that I don't like the word *art* because it means pretension and bullshit, and I equate those two directly," he told *Filmmakers Newsletter.* "I don't think of myself as an artist, and I don't think I ever will....I'm a craftsman. I don't make a work of art; I make a movie. If it does what I want it to do then somebody else can come along and figure it out."[115]

The only critics, really, who couldn't figure it out were those in his own backyard. The reviewer for the *San Francisco Chronicle* hated the film, calling it "without a doubt the most tedious film I have ever seen."[116] It was given an "empty chair" rating—the equivalent of zero stars. Even with all the other positive reviews behind it, for Lucas, the *Chronicle* review was the only one that mattered—because it was the one his parents read, and the only one his family and friends in northern California saw. "Because of those lousy reviews in San Francisco," said Coppola sympathetically, "all his friends and neighbors think he's a flop."[117]

The *Chronicle*'s opinion, however, was decidedly in the minority. Apart from some grumping from critics like the *Chicago Tribune*'s Gene Siskel, who accused Lucas of laying on the nostalgia a bit too thick, Lucas's little film was the darling of the critics—and so was Lucas.[118] "One of the world's master directors," declared the *New York Times*, "the current wunderkind of the film world."[119] *Time* magazine noted that after the relatively antiseptic *THX*, *American Graffiti* showed Lucas with "a new and welcome depth of feeling,"[120] while the *Washington Post* thought Lucas had become "a whole movie director,"[121] a description Lucas thought was fitting. "Oh, he *loved* it," teased Marcia.[122] But Lucas insisted that he "[didn't] listen to any of that stuff. If you believe that, then you have to believe the bad stuff."[123]

Still, he wasn't about to be too modest. "I know how good I am," he told the *New York Times* matter-of-factly. "*Graffiti* is successful because it came entirely from my head. It was *my* concept. And that's the only way I can work."[124]

American Graffiti would end up on countless "Best of" lists for 1973 and would win a number of awards, including the Golden Globe for Best Musical or Comedy, and a New York Film Critics Circle Award for Lucas and the Huycks for Best Original Screenplay. When Oscar season rolled around, it would be nominated for five Academy Awards, including Best Picture, Director, and Editing. It would win none, losing to *The Sting* in nearly every category. Marcia cried; George shrugged it off. He never expected his little film to win *anything*.

It did, however, make a lot of money. With direct costs of a little over $1 million, *American Graffiti* earned more than $55 million in rentals, making it one of cinema's most profitable returns on investment, then or ever. With his points in the film, Lucas earned nearly $4 million, after taxes. As he had vowed to his father more than a decade before, Lucas was a millionaire before the age of thirty. In fact, he had done it with two years to spare.

Lucas wasn't the only one who got rich off *American Graffiti*. Lucas split one of his profit points equally among the film's actors—only fair, he thought, since most of them had worked for little more than scale. "When you have a big hit film, it adds up," said Candy Clark. "We didn't ask him for it; he just did that."[125] Wolfman Jack kept his point, as well as a piece of *Graffiti*'s enormously successful sound track.[126] Haskell Wexler, who had provided Lucas with his services for free, was also given a point, as were Kurtz, the Huycks, and lawyer Tom Pollock—a percentage that would earn each of them more than $1 million in the coming decades.

As the film's distributor, Universal, too, earned its piece of the movie—and Lucas gagged on every cent. "The idea that the suits actually made a profit on his movie was just appalling to him," said Gloria Katz.[127] But it wasn't just Universal that galled Lucas; he was annoyed with Coppola as well. As the film's producer, Coppola received ten points—that was all well and good. But he and Lucas had also agreed to split forty other points equally between them, and the details of that arrangement were causing friction between master and upstart apprentice. "George is just like an accountant when it comes to money," said Willard Huyck. "The amount of money that George had to send to Francis upset him."[128]

Out of his twenty points, Lucas had agreed to pay the actors, Pollock, and the Huycks. Lucas expected Coppola to pay Kurtz from his share—producer looking out for producer, after all—and to split a payment to Wexler. But Coppola hadn't liked that, arguing that it was Lucas who had hired Kurtz, not him, and therefore Kurtz was Lucas's responsibility. As for Wexler, Lucas had brought him on in the middle of the film, and Coppola thought the cameraman should be Lucas's responsibility as well. Coppola, however, was planning to work with Wexler on *The Conversation,* so he suggested that Wexler be paid three points, with one coming from Lucas's share and two from his own. Lucas paid his share promptly; Coppola didn't.

Lucas angrily accused Coppola of reneging on their deal. After much negotiation, Coppola finally paid both Kurtz and Wexler from his share, but the damage was done. The relationship between Lucas and Coppola would sour again, and stay that way for the better part of a decade. For Lucas, it had never been about profits; it was about *principle.* "Francis was questioning my honesty," Lucas said in 1983. "He thought that I was operating the same way he was operating. He was accusing me of being like him, and that upset me. We really didn't have any kind of giant falling out," he added carefully. "But it was one of the reasons we drifted apart more than anything else."[129]

With the profits from *Graffiti,* Lucas quickly paid back all the money he had borrowed from friends, colleagues, and parents during the dark days of trying to sell his own movie less than two years earlier. George Sr. took the payment from his son proudly; he had backed the right horse again. But even with $4 million in the bank, Lucas was still convinced he could lose everything if he wasn't careful—and the money was already going fast. "He had this idea of being a flash in the pan," said Marcia. "You hit it once and that's all you're ever going to have. There are no guarantees."[130] Wealth, then, wasn't going to change him *too* much. "Money is not the most important thing to him," said John Plummer. "He's not a conspicuous spender....For a long time after *American Graffiti*, he still drove a sixty-nine Camaro."[131] Instead, Lucas quietly invested in property and bonds, and socked money away in savings accounts—nothing too flashy. Unlike Coppola, he wouldn't be buying showy cars or sprawling mansions in the hills.

Or at least, nothing *too* showy or sprawling. In the autumn of 1973, Lucas purchased a one-story Victorian mansion at 52 Park Way in the tiny town of San Anselmo, not far from a little colonial house he and Marcia had moved into earlier that summer at 30 Medway Road. The place was run down—it had been built in 1869 and was already a Marin County landmark—and it looked a bit like a haunted house, with its dark shingles and drooping gables. But he and Marcia loved it; Marcia would name it Parkhouse, and George would quickly have it fitted out with a screening room, offices, and an editing room in the attic. Filmmaking friends and USC Mafia members such as Carroll Ballard, Matthew Robbins, and Walter Murch were offered offices and workspace for no charge. "It was a little filmmaking complex," said Lucas proudly—his own miniature Zoetrope.[132]

The most important workspace, however, was probably at their house on Medway, where Lucas—always an aspiring architect—was reconstructing a second-floor tower using old photographs for reference. In here he would build a cozy office with a fireplace and with windows on three sides, offering a heavily wooded view that gave the room the appearance of being in a treehouse.[133] Most of the floor space would be taken up by a gigantic desk Lucas had built himself, using three large doors for the desktop. This was his room for writing, and Lucas was currently laboring over the first drafts of the script for his "Flash Gordon thing." It was a mishmash, he told *Filmmakers Newsletter*, "[a] science fiction–Flash Gordon genre, *2001* meets James Bond, outer space and space ships flying in it." It was "a much more plotted, structured film than [*THX*] or *American Graffiti*," he said. "Since I've never done that before, it's hard to say exactly what it is."[134]

He did, however, have a two-page treatment, handwritten on notebook paper, and a title, scrawled in cursive on the center of the treatment's cover page: *The Star Wars*.

PART II

EMPIRE

6

Bleeding on the Page

1973–1976

I don't have a natural talent for writing," George Lucas confessed to *Filmmakers Newsletter* in 1974. "When I sit down, I bleed on the page, and it's just awful. Writing just doesn't flow in a creative surge the way other things do."[1]

No other project would make Lucas bleed more than *Star Wars*. For nearly three years he would agonize over plots and characters, plumbing science fiction novels, folklore, comic books, and movies for inspiration. He would struggle through draft after draft, writing and rewriting, lifting scenes and subplots he liked from earlier drafts, fussing with the spellings of planets and characters, and trying to make sense of an ever-expanding script that was starting to spin out of his control. And time and time again, he would find both friends and studio executives baffled by his story, skeptical he could ever get any of it on film.

Lucas would treat the writing of *Star Wars* as a full-time job, trudging up the stairs to his writing room each morning at 9 a.m., where he would then lower himself slowly into his wooden desk chair and stare at a blank page for hours, waiting for the words to come. "I sit at my desk for eight hours a day no matter what happens, even if I don't write anything," he explained. "It's a terrible way to live. But I do it; I sit down and I do it. I can't get out of my chair until five o clock or five thirty.... It's like being in school. It's the only way I can force myself to write."[2]

Over his desk, he hung a wall calendar to track his progress, vowing to write five pages daily and marking off each day with a big dramatic X. On a good day, he might have one page completed by 4 p.m.—then, with an eye on the clock, he would scramble to write the four remaining pages over the next hour. If he could finish his pages early, he would permit himself to knock off for the rest of the day, and maybe reward himself with a bit of music from one of his most prized possessions: a glowing, garish, fully functional 1941 Wurlitzer jukebox, which Lucas had loaded with his own collection of rock and roll 45s. As The Diamonds' "Little Darlin'" wailed from the Wurlitzer's throbbing speakers, Lucas would kick back in his chair, tennis shoes off and shirttail untucked, lost in the music and grateful to be done for the day.

Most days, however, the jukebox would remain quiet, its neon lights dark—and no words would be written at all. At 5:30 he would tromp downstairs to watch the evening news with Walter Cronkite, glaring with anger over a TV dinner as he stewed about the blank pages he'd left upstairs. "You go crazy writing," Lucas said later. "You get psychotic. You get yourself so psyched up and go in such strange directions in your mind that it's a wonder that all writers aren't put away someplace."[3]

It could be said that *Star Wars* was partly Coppola's fault.

In late 1972, with *American Graffiti* in post-production, Lucas was ready to begin work on his next project, which he was convinced would be *Apocalypse Now*. For Lucas, the fact that Coppola still owned the film was just a technicality. "All Francis did is take a project I was working on, put it in a package deal, and suddenly he owned it," groused Lucas.[4] As far as he was concerned, intention was nine-tenths of the law—and he fully intended to make *Apocalypse* his next film, sending the script around to several studios, and, to his surprise, "pretty much got a deal" at Columbia.[5] In November, then, Gary Kurtz was dispatched to the Philippines and Hong Kong to scout suitable locations, "and we were all ready to go," said Lucas. Ready, that is, until Columbia, still trying to ink an agreement, began to haggle over percentages.

Coppola refused to hand over any of his own interest in the film; if Columbia wanted a larger piece of the movie, they were going to have to take it out of Lucas's share. "My points were going to shrink way down," complained Lucas, "and I wasn't going to do the film for free." Lucas would cede *Apocalypse Now* back to Coppola, at least for the moment—but he wasn't happy about it. "[Francis] had a right to do it, it's in his nature," Lucas said later, "but at the same time, I was annoyed about it."[6]

Had Coppola chosen to negotiate instead of digging in his heels, Lucas's next project might very well have been *Apocalypse Now*, and *Star Wars* would have continued to be a contractual add-on, to be developed at a later time, perhaps—or perhaps not at all. Instead, Lucas grudgingly abandoned the project, grumbling about Coppola's stinginess. *Star Wars*, then, would be spawned by Lucas's need to fill both a creative and a financial void. "I was in debt," Lucas recalled later. "I needed a job very badly. I didn't know what was going to happen with [*American*] *Graffiti*."[7] With *Apocalypse Now* shelved, Lucas turned to his only other viable project, the one still embedded in his two-picture deal with Universal. "I figured what the heck, I've got to do something," said Lucas. "I'll start developing *Star Wars*."[8]

Only at this point, it wasn't *Star Wars*. Not even close.

As Lucas sat down to write in his little office in Mill Valley in February 1973, all he had was the merest spark of an idea. After a skeptical King Features had declined to sell him Flash Gordon, Lucas decided he could just as easily make up his own characters in a similar vein. "It's your basic superhero in outer space," he explained. "I realized that what I really wanted to do was a contemporary action fantasy."[9] As would become his habit, Lucas began the writing process by making lists of names and locations for his fantasy, scrawling *Emperor Ford Xerxes XII*—a suitably heroic-sounding name—at the top of one of his notebook pages, followed by single names like *Owen, Mace, Biggs*, and *Valorum*. After trying various combinations, Lucas then divided his list into names of characters and planets, giving each a brief title or description. Luke Skywalker was on the list from the very start, but he was "Prince of Bebers," while Han Solo was "leader of the Hubble people." The planets Alderaan and Yavin were there too, as were locations named after Herald Square and the Japanese actor Toshiro Mifune.[10]

Next, Lucas began inserting his names and places into a short narrative, not much more than a story fragment, called "The Journal of the Whills." He envisioned borrowing a storytelling device from the old Disney cartoons, showing a storybook—in this case the *Journal of the Whills*—"falling open in the opening moments of the movie to emphasize that whatever story followed came from a book,"[11] he told an interviewer. "This is the story of Mace Windy," wrote Lucas, underlining the name for emphasis, "a revered Jedi-bendu of Opuchi, as related to us by C. J. Thorpe, padawan learner to the famed Jedi." Over two densely written pages, Lucas crammed in plenty of names and backstory, and was only just starting to wind himself into the barest hint of a plot—his heroes were "summoned to the desolate second planet of Yoshiro by a mysterious courier from the Chairman of the alliance"—when he trailed off practically in mid-sentence, already out of gas. It was a nonstarter, and Lucas knew it.

So he began again, making another list of names, scribbling out bits of plots and scenes he knew he wanted to include. "One of the key visions I had of the film when I started was of a dogfight in space with spaceships—two ships flying through space shooting each other. That was my original idea. I said I want to make that movie. I want to see that." Trying to get the dogfight in his head down on paper was difficult, however, so Lucas began taping old war movies on television, compiling footage of airplane battles from films like *The Bridges at Toko-Ri* and *Tora! Tora! Tora!* "I'd just edit it according to my story," he said later. "It was really a way of getting a sense of movement of the spaceships."[12] Eventually he would have more than twenty hours of tape, which he would transfer to 16 mm film, then tightly edit down to a reel about eight minutes long. "I would have the plane going from right to left," explained Lucas, "and a plane coming toward us and flying away from us, to see if the movement would generate excitement."[13] While he didn't know it yet, the reel of dogfighting, swooping, tail-spinning aircraft would be one of the most important bits of film he would ever put together—the wet concrete he would pour into the mold for the cornerstone of his own film empire.

On April 17, Lucas began writing another treatment, this one titled *The Star Wars*. This draft contained the dogfight in space that Lucas wanted to see, as well as a more fully realized plot that channeled bits of *Flash Gordon* and Kurosawa's *The Hidden Fortress*. Lucas poured everything he had ever loved about the Saturday morning serials into his treatment, with plenty of chases, close scrapes, exotic creatures, and general derring-do. From *The Hidden Fortress* he borrowed a few key plot points—namely, a princess being escorted through enemy territory by a wise and battle-scarred general and, more important, two bumbling, bickering bureaucrats to serve as comic relief.

Luke Skywalker makes his first appearance, though in this early draft he's an aged general guarding a young princess on the planet Aquilae. He and the princess meet two squabbling bureaucrats who have escaped from an orbiting space fortress, and the four of them travel to a spaceport to find a pilot to take them to the planet Ophuchi. Skywalker—handy with a "lazer sword"—recruits and trains a band of ten boys to be warriors before escaping the planet in a stolen ship. There's a dogfight—there would *always* be a dogfight—a chase through an asteroid field, and a crash on Yavin, a planet of giant furry aliens. The princess is captured, and Skywalker leads an assault on the Imperial prison, escaping amid yet another spectacular dogfight.

There's an awards ceremony—and there would *always* be an awards ceremony as well—where the princess is revealed "as her true goddess self."[14]

Even at fourteen handwritten pages, this rather busy proposal still seemed too "vague" to Lucas.[15] But he nonetheless had it bound in a black leather binder with *The Star Wars* embossed in gold on the cover and gave it to agent Jeff Berg to take to United Artists for a look. Berg confessed that he didn't understand a word of it, and didn't really know how to pitch it. Lucas did, even if his description was all over the place. "[It's] a space opera in the tradition of Flash Gordon and Buck Rogers," he explained. "It's James Bond and *2001* combined—super fantasy, capes and swords and laser guns and spaceships shooting each other, and all that sort of stuff. But it's not camp," he insisted. "It's meant to be an exciting action adventure film."[16] For Lucas, enthusiasm always trumped clarity.

On May 7 Berg brought Lucas's treatment to United Artists, putting it in the hands of David Chasman, the same executive who had believed in *American Graffiti*. Lucas knew the treatment he was giving Chasman was a lot to comprehend—getting the images in his head to come through on the page would always be difficult—so he had included ten pages of illustrations to try to convey the look and feel of what he had in mind: photos of NASA astronauts, amphibious tanks, and drawings of space heroes clipped from comic books. Chasman was intrigued, but he was also on his way to Cannes, and promised Berg he'd review the materials and be in touch shortly. It took three excruciating weeks for Chasman to wire his answer: No.

Glumly Lucas asked that Berg submit the proposal to Ned Tanen at Universal. "I hated Universal," said Lucas, "but I had to go to them. Part of my deal to make *American Graffiti* was that I had to sign my life over to them for seven years....They owned me."[17] Making things worse, Lucas and Tanen were still bickering over *Graffiti*, which Tanen was demanding be recut even as Lucas was approaching the studio, hat in hand, with a proposal for his next film. "It was right in the middle of Ned's most angry period," said Lucas's attorney Tom Pollock. "It was not submitted with enthusiasm."[18] Nevertheless, Berg dutifully sent the treatment over to Tanen in early June, promising the film could be made on the cheap. Lucas grudgingly described it as "a $6 million idea, which I'll make for $3 million."[19] Like Chasman before him, Tanen took the binder from Berg and promised he'd be in touch shortly.

Even as Tanen was ruminating, Berg had begun an informal discussion with 20th Century Fox and the studio's new vice president for creative affairs, Alan Ladd Jr. "Laddie," as he was called by nearly everyone, was the son of actor Alan Ladd. Show business was in his blood and he had an intuitive feel for commercial hits, as well as an appreciation for talent, no matter how quirky. He had recently rescued writer-director Mel Brooks from a panicky Warner Bros. after the studio had lost faith in the unreleased *Blazing Saddles,* and Berg thought Ladd might appreciate both the talent and travails of his own client, who was fighting a similar creative battle with Universal over the still unreleased *American Graffiti.* Over drinks one afternoon, Berg offered to show *Graffiti* to Ladd and sent a smuggled print to his office. "I saw it on the Fox lot at nine one morning, and it absolutely bowled me over," recalled Ladd. "That's when I just said to Jeff [Berg] that I'd like to meet George and hear about what ideas he's working on."[20]

Lucas flew to Los Angeles, eager for the conversation. More than any other studio at the time, Fox seemed to know what to do with science fiction. In 1968 it had released the widely popular *Planet of the Apes,* which it grew into a five-picture franchise. Beyond *Apes,* however, Fox was in need of a hit. Following the 1971 departure of mogul Darryl F. Zanuck, who had steered the company on and off since 1935, the studio was now being run by Dennis Stanfill, a former Lehman Brothers executive. More accountant than innovator, Stanfill was nevertheless savvy enough to follow a trend when he saw one; in addition to steering *Planet of the Apes* through its several sequels, he had successfully banked on the disaster movie fad, distributing films like *The Towering Inferno* and *The Poseidon Adventure.* But the studio was still losing money rapidly, and morale was low. "It was grim," said one Fox executive. "A very demoralizing place to go to every day."[21]

For Lucas, it must have been reminiscent of the day six years earlier when he had walked onto the virtually abandoned Warner lot. There he had found Coppola, the supportive but stormy big brother who would encourage, inspire, and infuriate Lucas as he made his way as a young filmmaker. Now at Fox, he would find Ladd, his next big brother, advocate, and defender, who would lead him through the next stage of his career. Unlike with Coppola, however, there was little bombast in the low-key Ladd, which made him a good temperamental fit with the equally restrained Lucas. "He and I together don't make one-half an extrovert," remarked Ladd.[22] Like Lucas, Ladd didn't talk very much—and when he finally did speak, he did it so quietly and calmly that some thought he sounded eerily like the rogue computer HAL from *2001: A Space Odyssey*.[23] Though Lucas derisively referred to most Hollywood executives as "used-car dealers," there was something about Ladd that he liked right away.[24]

For one thing, he and Ladd both spoke the same language: film. Rather than laying out his photos of astronauts or attempting to describe the plot or mood, Lucas spoke to Ladd about the films they both loved. "This sequence is going to be like *The Seahawk*," he told Ladd excitedly, while other scenes would be reminiscent of *Captain Blood* or Flash Gordon. "I knew exactly what he was saying," said Ladd. And he liked Lucas, too. "I knew... from spending time with him that he was a dead honest person who knew what he was doing."[25] Ladd was interested—but at the moment, Lucas was still contractually bound to wait for the word to come back from Universal. If Tanen and Universal said no to *The Star Wars*, Ladd and Fox could have it.

Ladd wouldn't have to wait long. At the end of June, Universal passed. While Tanen had issues with the proposed budget, mostly he was just baffled by the proposal itself, admitting he had "a very tough time understanding [it]."[26] Berg thought that perhaps "psychologically, they [executives at Universal] weren't prepared" to invest in a big-budget, special effects–heavy movie. More likely, they probably weren't prepared to invest in Lucas, whose still unreleased *American Graffiti* was being recut—and, in the minds of many at the studio, seemed destined for failure. Why in the world would they back a $3 million film by an artsy director who had likely bungled a film with a budget of $750,000? Universal's answer was no.

With Universal out of the way, Lucas's agents began negotiating with Fox in earnest in mid-July, passing back and forth an eight-page memo of agreement. Lucas would receive $50,000 to write the script, $100,000 for his duties as director, and $15,000 for "development" of the project, with a filming budget of $3 million. The most important figure in the deal, however, was the $10,000 Lucas would receive upon signing the agreement memo. That was money that would go in his pocket immediately—and he needed it. "I was so far in debt," recalled Lucas. "That was why I made the deal."[27] Without it, he said later, "I don't know what I would have done. Maybe take a job. But the last desperate thing is to 'take a job.' I really wanted to hold on to my own integrity."[28]

To Lucas, integrity would always be more important than the money, and he defiantly insisted his contract give him as much control as possible over his own film. He explicitly assigned producer duties to Gary Kurtz, gave editing to Verna Fields and Marcia Lucas, and named Walter Murch his post-production supervisor—and further stipulated that Fox couldn't assign him an executive producer or control production. "I was not that willing to listen to other people's ideas—I wanted everything to be my way," Lucas said. "I didn't mind getting input from the creative people around me, but not the executives....I fought for many years to make sure no one could tell me what to do."[29]

Despite his swagger, Lucas knew he had been lucky to get the deal. "We had no negotiating power," recalled attorney Tom Pollock. "They [Fox] were the only ones that wanted it."[30] Part of the problem was the genre itself. While science fiction films were in the middle of a slow climb to respectability in the early 1970s, they were still seen as a risky venture. On its release in 1968, *2001: A Space Odyssey*—which Lucas loved, calling it "the ultimate science fiction movie"—had been a critical hit but a financial failure, and would take years to turn a profit.[31] Ladd, then, was taking a real chance on Lucas and his some-what incoherent proposal—but unlike the skeptics at Universal, Ladd was convinced enough of Lucas's talent to make the creative leap of faith. "It was a gamble," said Ladd, "and I was betting on Lucas."[32] Agreed Lucas, "[Ladd] invested in me, he did not invest in the movie."[33]

It didn't take long before Ladd would look positively brilliant. On August 1, 1973—as Lucas was still in the middle of negotiating his deal memo with Fox—came the release and near-overnight success of the underdog *American Graffiti*. Suddenly, Lucas was the hottest direc-tor in the industry. Fox executives might have worried that Lucas would attempt to leverage his newfound reputation into a higher direc-tor's fee for *The Star Wars*—agent Jeff Berg was convinced they could easily negotiate a fee of half a million dollars—but typically, Lucas didn't want money; he wanted *control*. "He had been burned on control by studios," said Pollock later. "He really saw it first as a control issue rather than a money issue."[34]

"Fox thought I was going to come back and demand millions of dollars and all these gross points," recalled Lucas. "I said, 'I'll do it for the deal memo, but we haven't talked about things like merchandising rights, [and] sequel rights."[35] He would insist that those particular clauses—normally considered underbrush in a contract—remain nego-tiable as he and Fox moved forward with the formal contract. He would also insist that *The Star Wars* be produced by Lucasfilm, thereby ensuring that he could keep an eye on the bottom line and that any expenses billed against the film were really his—for, even three years after completing *THX 1138*, he was still irked with Coppola for bill-ing Zoetrope's costs against his movie.

Lucas signed the agreement memo with Fox in late August. While Fox claimed public bragging rights for landing a hot commodity—it was excitedly announced in the *Los Angeles Times* that Lucas had been signed to "quickly" complete *The Star Wars*, followed by the Huyck-penned period piece *Radioland Murders*—behind the scenes, the studio had been cautious in wording its agreement.[36] This was only a memo, not a contract. There was no agreed-upon budget, and no guarantee the film would even be made—and Fox had left itself an escape clause allowing it to back out at any time after reading the screenplay. But Lucas nonetheless set up a new company, called The Star Wars Corporation, to manage the financials and then had Lucasfilm formally "loan" the corporation his services as director. Pocketing the $10,000 he had been given on signing the agreement, Lucas set to work writing the first draft of the script—which, according to the agreement, he had promised to deliver by October 31, 1973. Lucas fretted that he'd never be able to finish on time—and, in fact, he wouldn't even come close to making it, citing "an infinite number of distractions."[37]

Partly, he had the success of *American Graffiti* to blame. With a genuine hit on his hands, Lucas, for the first time in his life, had a regular flow of income, coming in almost faster than he could figure out what to do with it. Mostly he saved it. But he did make three large purchases, one of them personal, two of them practical. First, Lucas bought a partnership in a comic book store in New York City called Supersnipe, owned and managed by a New York University film school graduate named Edward Summer.

Even though Lucas would never share his father's enthusiasm for retail, he loved browsing the rows of comics in the little shop anytime he was in New York, and he enjoyed the company of Summer, who could talk films and comics with the same ease and enthusiasm as Lucas. For the kid who had once spent summer evenings reading torn copies of *Tommy Tomorrow* on John Plummer's dimly lit front porch, owning a comic shop was a dream come true.

On the practical side were the houses on Medway and Park Way that he purchased in San Anselmo and where he planned to draft the script for *The Star Wars* in earnest—if, that is, he found the time. He was enjoying overseeing the work of the carpenters and electricians as they installed the screening room and offices in the old Victorian house at Park Way. It was slowly becoming his very own clubhouse, the new headquarters for Lucasfilm Ltd.—and it was *much* more fun to work on than the script for *The Star Wars*. "I was restoring my office," Lucas recalled with a shrug. "Building a screening room kept me going for nine, ten months."[38]

Lucas wasn't buying and renovating houses just so he could build his own filmmaking complex; he and Marcia were hoping to start a family. But it was difficult. Lucas had worked himself to exhaustion during the nearly two years it had taken to write, film, edit, and fight for *American Graffiti*. Writing *The Star Wars* was sapping his motivation and energy too, but mostly he and Marcia were simply apart too much. For much of the winter of 1973 and spring of 1974, Marcia was working on location in Los Angeles and Arizona, editing *Alice Doesn't Live Here Anymore* for director Martin Scorsese. It was a big job, the first on which she would be the lead editor, not an assistant—and at the time she had taken it, she and George had desperately needed the money. That was no longer a concern, but now Marcia found she wanted more than just the money; she wanted to be taken seriously as a film editor, and not just as an editor of films by George Lucas. "I thought, If I'm ever going to get any real credit, I'm going to have to cut a movie for somebody besides George," said Marcia. "'Cause if I'm cutting for my husband, they're going to think George lets his wife play around in the cutting room. George agreed with that."[39]

George may well have agreed that Marcia needed to take on projects other than his movies—"it is hard for a film editor to come home and call the director a son-of-a-bitch when she happens to be married to him," he told the *New York Times*—but that didn't mean he had to like it.[40] While Lucas could often be cool or even brusque to Marcia when they were in the same room, he would always miss her terribly when she was gone. During the months when Marcia was in Arizona, Lucas would shuttle back and forth between San Francisco and Tucson, where he would spend his days sitting on a patio, reading science fiction and fantasy novels, writing his script, and—if pressed to admit it—keeping his eye on Scorsese. While never exactly the jealous type, Lucas was hopeful his presence might at least put a damper on Scorsese's fast hands. The approach would mostly work, though it didn't necessarily keep the wily Scorsese from trying. Ultimately, however,

Scorsese would respond most strongly to Marcia's talent, and would make her his editor of choice for his next two films, *Taxi Driver* and *New York, New York*. Those jobs, too, would keep Marcia away for weeks or months on end.

Even as he sat in the Tucson sun, Lucas was reading all he could now, soaking up themes, tropes, and plot devices. There was Edgar Rice Burroughs's novel *A Princess of Mars*, whose hero, John Carter, rescues the spunky princess of the title, and E. E. "Doc" Smith's series of Lensman novels, about superpowered space cops, a variation on Lucas's beloved *Tommy Tomorrow* comic books. Lucas also devoured anything written by Harry Harrison—his 1966 novel *Make Room! Make Room!* had recently been adapted to film as *Soylent Green*—and Lucas particularly loved his rambunctious sci-fi comic novels like *The Stainless Steel Rat* and *Bill, the Galactic Hero*, whose title character was a frustrated farm boy. There were books on mythology and religions—Scorsese remembered Lucas reading Isaac Asimov's *Guide to the Bible*, as well as Sir James George Frazer's tome *The Golden Bough: A Study in Comparative Religion*—and comic books like Jack Kirby's energetic, vibrant, and somewhat psychedelic *New Gods*, in which Orion, the hero, was the son of the villainous Darkseid.

Lucas took it all in, reading books and comics, watching movies, filing away the bits and pieces he liked, discarding what he didn't. "I researched kids' movies and how they work and how myths work," Lucas said, "and I looked very carefully at the elements of films within that fairy tale genre which made them successful. I found that myth always took place over the hill, in some exotic, far-off land. For the Greeks, it was Ulysses going off into the unknown. For America it was out West. . . . The last place left 'over the hill' is space."[41]

Even Vietnam would work its way into his thinking, a by-product of the abandoned *Apocalypse Now*. "I figured that I couldn't make that film because it was about the Vietnam War," said Lucas, "so I would essentially deal with some of the same interesting concepts that I was going to use and convert them into space fantasy so you'd have a large technological empire going after a small group of freedom fighters."

As Lucas made notes for his next draft, then, the planet Aquilae was now "a small independent country like North Vietnam threatened by a neighbor or provincial rebellion," while the Empire "is like America ten years from now...allowing the crime rate to rise to the point where a 'total control' police state was welcomed by the people."[42] This was Lucas coyly hiding his liberal politics in plain sight. "Most people," said one associate later, "have no realization that part of it [*Star Wars*] is about a Vietnam situation."[43]

In May 1974—nearly eight months past his deadline—Lucas completed the rough draft of *The Star Wars*. At 191 scenes and 33,000 words, it was crammed full of politics and backstory, but even in this early draft, parts of it sound familiar. The main character in this draft is a young man named Annikin Starkiller, who trains to become a Jedi Bendu under seventy-year-old general Luke Skywalker. There are two droids providing comic relief, one short and squat, the other a gleaming "*Metropolis* style" robot, a reference to director Fritz Lang's mechanical woman in his 1926 art deco film. There's a "huge green-skinned monster with no nose and large gills" named Han Solo, a feisty fourteen-year-old Princess Leia, references to "lazerswords" and Wookiees, as well as to a "tall, grim-looking general"—and relatively minor character—named Darth Vader. And for the first time, one character bids good-bye with "May the Force of Others be with you." Lucas was still holding on to elements from his first treatment that he liked, including a fight in a cantina, a chase through an asteroid belt, a rescue from a prison, and the concluding awards ceremony. But he was also struggling with parts of it: he wasn't quite sure yet what the Empire was searching for, and there were still too many characters, too many locations, too many backstories to sort through.[44] But at least it was finished.

The script—with EYES ONLY! stamped playfully across the title page—went over to Alan Ladd at Fox. "It was a long time coming," said Ladd.[45] But he liked what he read—at least what he could understand of it—and, to the likely bafflement of some Fox executives, asked Lucas to begin working on a second draft. Back Lucas went to his writing room, to sit at his desk for eight hours each day, turning a pencil over and over in his hand, staring out the window, waiting for the muse. As the son of a stationer, Lucas was picky about his writing supplies; he would use only number-two pencils and regular blue-and-green-lined notebook paper. Drafts would be written out in his hunched cursive, the words growing fatter as his pencil dulled against the page. He was also carrying a little notebook with him at all times so he could write down names and ideas just as quickly as they came to him.

And inspiration, it seemed, could come from anywhere. One afternoon, Marcia drove away from the house with their dog — an enormous Alaskan malamute named Indiana — sitting happily in the passenger seat next to her, his head brushing the ceiling of the car. Lucas thought the dog, nearly as big as a person, looked like Marcia's copilot — an image that would eventually evolve into Chewbacca, the copilot of the *Millennium Falcon*. Another important character had found his name in a throwaway comment from Walter Murch while he and Lucas were editing *American Graffiti*. The two of them had devised their own system for making sense of the racks of film reels and miles of film, assigning each of the reels, dialogue tracks, and sound tracks its own identifying number. During one late-night session, Murch asked Lucas for Reel 2, Dialogue 2 — but shortcut the request by asking for R2 D2 instead. Lucas loved the sound of it — the way a name sounded would always be important to him — and after handing Murch the film cans, quickly scribbled *R2D2* down in his notebook. "As I was writing, I would say the names to myself, and if I had a hard time dealing with a name phonetically, I would change it," he said later. "It had to do with hearing the name a lot and whether I got used to it or not."[46] At the moment, however, it seemed he hadn't gotten used to *any* of them — for in July 1974, as Lucas went through his rough draft again, he suddenly decided to change nearly every name in the script. R2-D2 became simply A-2. The Jedi Bendu became the Dai Nogas. Annikin Starkiller was redubbed Justin Valor, Leia became Zara, Wookiees became Jawas.

Still, changing character names was the easy part. Revising the story was harder—and for weeks, Lucas would stare at his notebook, then at the typewriter page, waiting for something, anything, to fire his imagination. "I sit there and wait for the mail to come," he sighed, "then I sit and wait for 5 o'clock to come."[47] Gray hairs began to fleck his beard. At times, he would snip absently at his hair with a pair of scissors, filling his trash can with the clippings. His mind wandered. "I can't help but think about things other than what I'm supposed to be thinking about," he admitted—and one morning, as he thought about the old Flash Gordon movie serials that had initially inspired *Star Wars,* he realized that he liked plenty of other old serials too. He was especially fond of *Don Winslow of the Navy,* about a naval intelligence officer who fights spies as he locates and explores a secret submarine base. Lucas liked that Winslow relied as much on his brains as his fists. "I began thinking it'd be a good idea to have an archaeologist in a 1930s-style serial," Lucas said. "So I'd make little notes about what it would be, who his character was, and how all that would work out. That's how I came up with the idea of Indiana Smith."[48] That name—taken from his beloved malamute—he would also slightly change.

Progress was slow; his mood blackened, but Marcia remained upbeat and supportive, patiently bringing him his dinner in front of the television set each night, either a TV dinner or tuna sandwiches with the crusts removed, just like his mother had made them. Marcia didn't always understand exactly what was going on as the drafts progressed, but she encouraged George to keep working, and to stay true to his own vision for the film. "George knows who his audience is," she explained. Still, she wasn't afraid to speak her mind when she thought the script dragged or got overly confusing. "I'm real hard," she admitted, "but I only tell him what he already knows."[49] George might set his mouth tightly, but he would take her suggestions seriously. As she would prove time and again, when it came to story, Marcia's instincts were almost always right.

Lucas also sought the opinions of friends whom he trusted, including Milius, the Huycks, and Coppola. Lucas was genuinely interested in their comments, flying down to Los Angeles with nothing more than deodorant and a change of underwear so he could spend the night talking over his pages with the Huycks. "He'd take his notes, and he'd go and visit all his friends," said Huyck. "Then he'd fly back home and rewrite [*Star Wars*] some more." Most of them still found the script incomprehensible; Coppola, however, offered few changes. "I thought it was terrific," he reassured Lucas.[50]

In fact, Lucas and Coppola's relationship was warming again; in an interview published in *Film Quarterly* that spring, Lucas described their relationship in genuinely affectionate, almost brotherly terms. "We more or less work together as collaborators.... We can bounce ideas off each other because we're totally different. I'm more graphics-filmmaking-editing oriented, and he's more writing and acting oriented. So we complement each other, and we trust each other," explained Lucas. "Half the time he says I'm full of shit, and half the time I say he's full of shit. It's not like a producer telling you that you have to do something. Francis will say, 'Cut that scene out, it doesn't work at all.' And I may say, 'No, you're crazy. That's my favorite scene. I love it.' And he'll say, 'Okay, what do I care? You're an idiot anyway.' Actually, he calls me the stinky kid. He says, 'You're a stinky kid, do what you want.' And I say the same thing to him. It works very well, because you really need somebody to test ideas on. And you get a piece of expert advice that you value."[51]

Another friend whose opinion he valued was Steven Spielberg, whose company Lucas was enjoying more and more. In the summer of 1974, Spielberg was at work on *Jaws* for Universal, a project that would feature a gigantic mechanical shark that was still being constructed in a North Hollywood hangar. One afternoon, Spielberg took Lucas, Milius, and Scorsese out to the warehouse to have a look at the half-completed monster shark, still on struts and suspended in slings. The thing was enormous—so big, in fact, that Milius thought the craftsmen were "overdoing it." As Lucas looked over the storyboards the artists were using for reference, he felt himself becoming slightly envious. "If you can get half of this on film," he told Spielberg, "you're gonna have the biggest hit of all time." (He would be right: soon after its 1975 release, *Jaws* would indeed become the highest-grossing film of all time — at least until Lucas surpassed it with *Star Wars* two years later.) Ever the gadget freak, Lucas climbed a ladder and leaned into the gigantic open mouth of the shark to see how it worked — at which point Spielberg mischievously seized the controls and slowly closed the mouth on Lucas . . . and then couldn't get it to open again. Lucas eventually shook himself loose and the four filmmakers fled, convinced they'd broken Universal's prized prop.[52]

By August of 1974, it had been nearly a year since Lucas had signed the deal memo with Fox for *The Star Wars* — and he *still* didn't have a formal contract. Although he had delivered the first draft of the script late — and was in danger of missing the September deadline for the second draft — that wasn't the cause of Fox's hesitation. Mostly, Fox executives were still uncertain about the budget — how much were these special effects going to cost, and how many sets would need to be built? — and were foot-dragging rather than making a decision. "Fucking slow," said attorney Tom Pollock bluntly. "I got mad," said Lucas.[53]

Still, sensing an opportunity in the unfinished agreement, Lucas had Pollock fire off a letter to Fox on August 23 asking for what would turn out to be two crucial concessions. "I was very careful to say, 'I don't want more money,'" Lucas explained later. "[I said], 'I don't want anything financial, but I do want the rights to make these sequels.'"[54] Friends like the Huycks were aghast at Lucas's stubbornness — but then, they didn't share, or even understand, his vision for the film. "He would say, 'They're not giving me control, they're not giving me the rights to the sequels,'" recalled Willard Huyck. "And I'd pause and I'd say, 'George you're lucky to get ten million dollars to make this movie. Let's just make the first one.'"[55]

As negotiations with Fox dragged on, Coppola stepped in with an offer Lucas found almost too attractive to ignore. After trying for the past year to land studio backing for *Apocalypse Now*, Coppola had finally decided to finance the movie himself — and he wanted Lucas to direct it. Coppola may have envisioned it as a collaboration of Hollywood's two hottest filmmakers—"I was anxious for George Lucas to do the picture on any basis at all," Coppola told an interviewer—but Lucas wasn't ready to hitch himself to Coppola again, at least not yet.[56] While Lucas had been working on *Apocalypse Now* off and on for more than four years—pushing it through screenplay revisions with John Milius, pitching it to glassy-eyed studio executives, and sending Kurtz to scout locations—he found he was suddenly much more interested in *The Star Wars*. "I had this huge draft of a screenplay," said Lucas, "and I had sort of fallen in love with it."[57] Lucas turned the offer down—and while he may have hoped Coppola would still give him the opportunity to direct it later, his time for *Apocalypse* had passed. Coppola would take the director's chair himself, eventually spending two nightmarish years in the Philippines on the problem-plagued production.

Lucas had other reasons to pass; for one thing, he just didn't think moviegoers needed one more "angry, socially relevant film." With Watergate and Vietnam still leading the nightly newscasts and splattered across front pages everywhere, the real world already seemed angry enough. "I thought, 'we all know what a terrible mess we have made of the world,'" said Lucas. "We also know, as every movie made in the last ten years points out, how terrible we are, how we have ruined the world and what schmucks we are and how rotten everything is. And I said, what we really need is something more positive."[58]

For Lucas, the idea of *The Star Wars* offered a different, even higher calling. "I realized there was another relevance that is even more important—dreams and fantasies, getting children to believe there is more to life than garbage and killing and all that real stuff like stealing hubcaps—that you could still sit and dream about exotic lands and strange creatures," Lucas explained to *Film Quarterly* in 1977. "Once I got into *Star Wars*, it struck me that we had lost all that—a whole generation has grown up without fairy tales. You just don't get them any more, and that's the best stuff in the world—adventures in far-off lands. It's *fun*."[59]

At this point, then, *Star Wars* had become more than just a passion; it was a moral obligation—and Lucas, in his negotiations with Fox, was determined to keep hold of as much of it as he could, going after merchandising rights and commercial tie-ins, making it clear that his company would have the "sole and exclusive right" to use the name *Star Wars* for merchandising. "When I was writing, I had visions of R2-D2 mugs and little windup robots, but I thought that would be the end of it," Lucas recalled. "I went for the merchandising because it was one of the few things left that we hadn't discussed."[60] But Lucas also shrewdly recognized that Fox and other studios had underestimated—and, in many cases, wasted—merchandising opportunities to market their films. "We found Fox was giving away merchandising rights, just for the publicity," said Lucas. "They gave away tie-in promotions with a big fast food chain. They were actually paying these people to do this big campaign for them. We told them that was insane."[61] Lucas seized his opportunity: "I simply said, 'I'm gonna be able to make T-shirts, I'm gonna be able to make posters, and I'm gonna be able to sell this movie even though the studio won't.' So I was able to get everything that was left over."[62] John Milius remembered Lucas talking about the money he was certain he'd make from merchandising, bragging: "I'm going to make five times as much money as Francis on these science fiction toys. And I won't have to make *The Godfather*."[63]

Fox took its time responding to Lucas's two demands; while sequel and merchandising rights were generally bottom-tier clauses, Fox was still careful enough to ensure they didn't just give them away. Ultimately, however, the studio agreed with Ladd. They were willing to sign over the sequel and merchandising rights mainly because they'd gotten the director of *American Graffiti* so cheaply. "George never once came in and said, 'Now I'm worth ten times more than I was when you made a deal with me,'" said Ladd. "His attitude was, 'I made a deal. I'll stick with it.'"[64] As Lucas put it, "I didn't ask for another $1 million, just the merchandising rights. And Fox thought that was a fair trade."[65] Fox wasn't prepared to draw up the contracts just yet—there was still the question of the film's final budget to nail down—but things were at least moving again. And no one, not even Lucas, appreciated that by securing sequel and merchandising rights, he had just negotiated for himself a billion-dollar clause. Decades later, Fox executive Gareth Wigan would shake his head in wonder at Lucas's instincts and audacity. "George was enormously far-sighted, and the studio wasn't, because they didn't know the world was changing," said Wigan. "George *did* know the world was changing. I mean, *he changed it.*"[66]

When it came down to it, *American Graffiti* saved *Star Wars* more than once.

"The financial return [from *American Graffiti*] is nice," Kurtz remarked in 1973, "but money isn't the important thing. The success of *Graffiti* allows us to do what we want and have some influence in the business."[67] That was true to some extent; the enormous success of *American Graffiti* had given Lucas the leverage he needed to muscle some key concessions out of Fox during contract negotiations. But Fox's concessions still hadn't produced a formal contract—and without a contract, there was no money for further development of *Star Wars*. At this point, then—Kurtz's statement of principle notwithstanding— money really *was* the important thing. If Fox wasn't going to invest in *Star Wars,* then Lucas would. The profits from *American Graffiti* would help Lucas throw *Star Wars* a number of lifelines critical to its further development.

In late 1974, one of his first investments was in a talented model maker named Colin J. Cantwell, who had built the miniatures for *2001: A Space Odyssey* and *The Andromeda Strain*. It would be Cantwell's job to design and build the prototypes for the many spaceships and vehicles mentioned, but only vaguely described, in Lucas's script. Lucas usually had a general idea of how a ship or vehicle should look— he wanted his spaceships to look realistic, he told Cantwell, but with "a comic book nobility"—and he and Cantwell would pass drawings back and forth, tinkering with details, until eventually Cantwell had a final sketch to work from.[68] Cantwell was a real kitbasher, combining parts from various plastic model kits—cars, boats, airplanes, tanks, anything—to create spaceships with an incredible amount of technical detail which looked as if they might really work. But the model maker had a keen sense of the dramatic as well; it was Cantwell who would come up with the designs for the X-wing and TIE fighters, treating their distinctive look as a storytelling device. "My premise," Cantwell explained, "was you had to instantly know the bad guys from the good guys...by how [a ship] looks and feels."[69]

Once Cantwell's models were complete, Lucas would take them to his second, and perhaps even more important, new employee: artist Ralph McQuarrie, a former illustrator for Boeing whom Lucas had met through Hal Barwood and Matthew Robbins several years earlier. "I'd seen some of his paintings," said Lucas, "and I thought he was really brilliant."[70] Everything in a McQuarrie painting, from characters and their clothing to buildings and battleships—looked elegant yet slightly worn, giving his work the same "used universe" aesthetic that Lucas had brought to *THX* and was hoping to repeat again in *Star Wars*. McQuarrie, then, was just the artist to help visualize the countless worlds and characters contained in Lucas's ambitious script. Typically, however, Lucas wasn't going to give McQuarrie entirely free rein. "I just describe what I want and then he does it," was how Lucas explained their collaboration. Just as Lucas had insisted on hovering over Cantwell's work, so too would he fuss with and modify McQuarrie's rough sketches until he was at last happy with them. Only at that point would McQuarrie be permitted to paint the final image.

Still, it was McQuarrie who would establish the artistic coherence of the *Star Wars* universe, painting fully realized exotic locations like Tatooine and Cloud City on the planet Bespin, and creating iconic character designs like the Tusken Raiders, C-3PO, R2-D2, and Darth Vader. Vader's design, in fact, had been a happy accident. The artist had given the "grim-looking general" a spacesuit he thought the character would need to board a spacecraft—but Lucas loved the look so much it became the villain's regular uniform. More than anything else, however, McQuarrie's paintings would make Lucas's imagined and sometimes confusing universe that much easier for executives and others to comprehend. For Lucas, there was never any doubt about the value of McQuarrie's contribution. "When words could not convey my ideas," said Lucas, "I could always point to one of Ralph's fabulous illustrations and say, 'Do it like this.'"[71]

McQuarrie's first painting—of primitive versions of R2-D2 and C-3PO on a desert planet—was completed on January 2, 1975, just in time for Lucas to include it in the gold-embossed binder containing the latest revision of his script, which now had the lengthy title *Adventures of the Starkiller, Ep. I: The Star Wars.* "I think they [the paintings] were done as a substitute for arm waving and verbal descriptions and to start budget talks," said McQuarrie.[72] That was probably true, as Lucas and Fox were still squabbling over the projected costs of the film. Part of the problem was that the script kept growing, with new locations, new characters, and new battles added in every draft. "It got to be a very fat script," agreed Lucas, "and the story had gotten away from me."[73]

In this latest draft, Lucas had more carefully fleshed out the concept of the Force—still called the *Force of Others* in this version—dividing it neatly into a good side called Ashla and a bad side called Bogan. He had also decided that the Force could be intensified through the possession of a mystical Kiber Crystal—Lucas's first, but by no means last, great MacGuffin. "The concept of the Force was an important one in the story," said Kurtz, "and the difficulty is trying to create a religious spiritual concept that works in a very simple way without heavy exposition."[74] Unfortunately, Lucas's reliance on heavy exposition was still a problem, though things were getting better. Lucas had decided to make Threepio and Artoo more central to the story—his ongoing nod to the two peasant farmers who had held together *The Hidden Fortress*—but it was a decision that annoyed Coppola, who thought Lucas was turning the story into comedy. "He had a whole... script that I thought was fine, and then he chucked it," said Coppola. "He was interested in the two servants."[75] Coppola remained more intrigued by the idea of a teenage princess at the center of the story—but Lucas had thrown that out, too, downgrading Leia to Luke's cousin in the new draft, and then all but writing her out of the plot. Instead, he chose to concentrate on a mighty Jedi warrior known as "the Starkiller" and his family of sons.

This time Luke is prompted into action when he receives a hologram message from his brother Deak, who asks Luke to bring the Kiber Crystal to their wounded father, the Starkiller. Luke hires Han Solo, now a "burly-bearded but ruggedly handsome boy"—pretty much Coppola as a starpilot—and his copilot Chewbacca ("resembling a huge gray bushbaby monkey") to take him to Cloud City, where Deak is now being held prisoner. Luke and Han rescue Deak, escape with the Death Star in pursuit, then head for Yavin, where they use the Kiber Crystal to revive the Starkiller. Luke leads an assault on the Death Star—and though he isn't the one to fire the fatal shot that destroys the space station, Luke returns to Yavin a hero, to lead a revolution at the side of his father. And now that Lucas had bought up the sequel rights, he wanted to make it clear that he intended to use them, as a final roll-up title promises that the Starkiller and his family will be back soon in "the perilous search for THE PRINCESS OF ONDOS."[76] He'd get to the princess in the *next* film.

Still, the bones of *Star Wars* were falling into place: the droids are looking for their old master; Luke hires Han and Chewie; there's a rescue mission, a fall into a garbage chute, and an assault on the Death Star. But there are still too many locations, too many names, too many planets, and—one of Lucas's biggest problems—too much backstory and too many long speeches. Ladd was confused by it—it wasn't much like the rough draft he'd seen in May 1974—and Coppola, too, made it clear that he thought it was a mess, wondering aloud why Lucas was "dumping" all the elements that he had liked in the first draft.

Worse, even with McQuarrie's paintings providing a better feel for the look of things, the new script did little to help Fox executives decide on a final budget. With Fox stalling, Lucas asked Kurtz to put together a budget that they could bring to Ladd, essentially telling the studio what the budget should be. That was fine with Kurtz, who had wanted for months to get started on production. Privately, Lucas and

Kurtz thought they could probably make the movie for less than $4 million, with Kurtz spitballing costs at $2.5 million and Lucas—who was convinced he could make a science fiction film in the handheld documentary style he loved—estimating a budget of $3.5 million. At Fox, however, the response was one of continued bewilderment. One Fox budget analyst estimated that special effects alone would drive costs over $6 million. Kurtz threw up his hands. "I came up with a $15 million and a $6 million and a $10 million budget," said Kurtz. "And it was totally arbitrary. You have to design the sets before you know how much things are going to cost."[77]

Shrugging off the indecisive Fox, Lucas and Kurtz were determined to move forward as if they had a deal in place, continuing to pour their own *American Graffiti* profits into developing Lucas's "Flash Gordon thing." In April, Kurtz began looking for studio space. Even without formal set designs, Kurtz estimated they would need eleven soundstages, including a gigantic one for the final awards ceremony Lucas was still determined to keep in his story.

Soundstages at Columbia and Warner Bros. were too small, so Kurtz headed for London, where one of the largest facilities was at Pinewood, home to several James Bond films. But officials at Pinewood required filmmakers to use Pinewood staff—a concession Lucas, ever the control freak, wasn't willing to make. Finally, Kurtz took a look at Elstree Studios, a run-down facility just north of London all but abandoned since completion of *Murder on the Orient Express* in 1974. Elstree had plenty of space and—even better—Lucas could bring his own crew to handle everything from cinematography to catering. Kurtz booked Elstree for a seventeen-week period, to begin in March 1976, a little less than a year away. But even Kurtz, who prided himself on lowballing his budgets, could see that this wasn't going to be a film that could be made on the cheap. He guessed it would cost around $13 million. Lucas grimaced; that was *way* beyond what he initially thought it might cost—and at that point $13 million sounded too high. An even $10 million sounded more reasonable. That would be the number he submitted to Fox as the proposed budget. Fox promised to get back to him. Lucas would have to keep waiting—but he was growing more angry and impatient by the day.

Necessity would force Lucas to make perhaps *the* investment that would become the cornerstone of his self-made empire. From day one, Lucas had wanted his film to feature a dramatic dogfight in outer space, with spaceships tumbling and spiraling in a manner similar to real warplanes. But visuals like that were going to require some exceptional special effects—and Fox, like every other major studio, no longer produced special effects in-house. In the past, studios had used visual effects primarily to keep costs down, producing miniatures, models, and matte paintings to make back lots look larger, or to re-create exotic locations. But films like *Easy Rider* and *The Rain People* had changed the Hollywood production mentality. Why create an alternate reality on a back lot when you could simply film on location? Effects shops were shuttered, effects men—and they were almost entirely men—retired. With no real special effects shops to utilize, then, Lucas decided he had no choice but to create his own. He just needed the right person to run it: someone creative and aggressive, who shared his vision for the film but wasn't *too* visionary, since Lucas still intended to control things as much as he could. Speed mattered, too; Lucas would need his manager not only to set up shop as quickly as possible but also to begin producing effects almost immediately.

First, Lucas approached Jim Danforth, a stop-motion animator best known for his work on the 1970 film *When Dinosaurs Ruled the Earth*. But Lucas rubbed the animator the wrong way, and Danforth was unsettled by the seat-of-the-pants nature of the project. "I liked the idea of the film, sci-fi with a sense of fun, but just didn't want the problems of working with Lucas," said Danforth. "He was right out front with me, told me, 'I don't know how we're going to do all this stuff, maybe we'll darken a studio and throw models at a camera, but whatever we do, I'll be right there with you.' I can't work like that, so I turned it down."[78]

Next Lucas turned to veteran Douglas Trumbull, who'd overseen special effects for *2001: A Space Odyssey*, *Silent Running*, and *The Andromeda Strain*. Trumbull, too, said no, most likely to accept a better offer from Steven Spielberg to produce visual effects for *Close Encounters of the Third Kind*—which, unlike Lucas's movie, actually had a budget and a shooting schedule. Privately, Lucas was likely relieved, as he had quickly come to realize that handing the project to Trumbull would mean losing control altogether. "If you hire Trumbull to do your special effects, he does your special effects. I was very nervous about that," Lucas said later. "I wanted to be able to say, 'It must look like this, not that.' I don't want to be handed an effect at the end of five months and be told, 'Here's your special effect, sir.' I want to be able to have more say about what's going on. It's really become binary—either you do it yourself, or you don't get a say."[79] So Lucas didn't get Trumbull either. But Trumbull did recommend one of his assistants from *Silent Running*, an opinionated and fiercely independent young man named John Dykstra.

What the twenty-seven-year-old Dykstra didn't have in years of on-the-job experience he more than made up for with brilliance, enthusiasm, and a belief that no project was impossible. Lucas and Kurtz went to interview Dykstra together in a bungalow on the Universal lot and were immediately impressed. Lucas explained the plot of the newest draft of *The Star Wars* to Dykstra as best he could (which involved "a lot of hand flying," Dykstra recalled later) and showed the reel of dogfights he had edited together from old war movies.[80] Dykstra was immediately intrigued. "[George's] initial concept was that he wanted something very quick and dirty," said Dykstra. "He wanted something we could grind out quickly and cheaply."[81]

Still, as the two of them watched the dogfight reel and talked through some of the visual effects, Lucas was adamant that he didn't want "men in black suits with models on sticks." He was already spending money on Colin Cantwell and Ralph McQuarrie to design and build realistic-looking spaceships; he didn't want that illusion broken the moment the ships took flight. "We're going to have to make something more sophisticated," Lucas told Dykstra.[82] That was fine with Dykstra, who thought he knew just what Lucas needed. Several years earlier, Dykstra had worked with motion control technology at the Institute of Urban and Regional Development at Berkeley, where, as part of a planning project, he had programmed a PDP-11 computer to guide a small 16 mm camera through a model city. Unlike stop-action effects, which require the shutter of the camera to be opened and closed every time a model is moved a fraction of an inch, motion control is all about moving the camera, not the model. Motion control, then, would give Lucas exactly what he needed, allowing the camera, with computer-programmed precision, to do the diving and swooping needed for his space battle. What Lucas really wanted, recalled Dykstra, was "fluidity of motion, the ability to move the camera around so that you could create the illusion of actually photographing spaceships from a camera platform in space."[83] It was almost like documentary-style special effects, with the camera as an observer. No wonder Lucas loved it.

There was only one real problem: the camera needed to film a project on the scale of *The Star Wars*—with multiple models requiring multiple passes by the camera—didn't yet exist. "[Dykstra] was anxious to actually build one," said Lucas, "because it was an idea that John had had for quite a while and this seemed like the perfect opportunity to exploit that."[84] But the clock was ticking; Lucas wanted work on effects to start as quickly as possible, and ideally be finished by late 1976 or early 1977 so he could edit them into the live action sequences. In that time, Dykstra would not merely have to produce the visual effects; he would have to develop the technology needed to shoot them in the first place. "At that point," recalled Dykstra, "I said, 'This is going to be hard to do in a year, George,' and he said, 'I don't care, kid, just do it.' So, we did it."[85]

It wasn't quite as simple as *that*, however. First, Lucas had to find a building to house his special effects shop. Lucas wanted his facility close to home, preferably near Parkhouse in Marin County, but Dykstra persuaded him to stay close to Hollywood, where they would have ready access to film development and processing. Kurtz, who always seemed to know how to scout for locations, found an unassuming and newly constructed warehouse at 6842 Valjean Avenue in Los Angeles, across from the Van Nuys Airport. The building was essentially a sweltering cavern—"probably 1,300 square feet, and smelled like a gym locker," as Dykstra put it—with no interior walls, no offices, no equipment, not even air-conditioning.[86] Lucas thought it was perfect.

Jim Nelson, a post-production ace and old friend of Kurtz's from *Two-Lane Blacktop*, was put in charge of banging the warehouse into shape, and spent six hot weeks outfitting three major departments: model building, camerawork, and optical compositing, where all the shots would eventually be combined. As far as hiring staff, "we approached the visual effects as a grand experiment," said Kurtz, "[asking ourselves,] 'Can we do this with a lot of people who work on architectural models and commercials and had never made feature films before?'"[87] Finding employees would never be a problem; every model maker, artist, and film geek who loved science fiction—especially those who had seen *THX 1138*—wanted to work for Lucas. Cinematographer Richard Edlund and effects artist Dennis Muren had made only short films and a few commercials, and done some TV work. Storyboard artist Joe Johnston and animator Peter Kuran were both still in college, and Kuran wanted the job so badly he offered to work for free. It was "a lot of young kids, basically," said Lucas. "Very few of them had worked on a feature film."[88]

Nelson, while technically in charge, was really just one of the inmates running the asylum, and he and Dykstra openly encouraged an atmosphere of goofball collegiality that sparked both inspiration and collaboration. "I hired people who were young, people who had not really had a lot of industry experience, but were talented people, people that I'd worked with before," said Dykstra. "And we formed a group that was cooperative....I can't stress that enough: cooperative."[89] It helped, too, that Lucas had actively discouraged hiring from the unions; they had always left a bad taste in his mouth anyway, and he had no patience with the rules they would have imposed on a production that had no time to get bogged down in process. "Everybody sort of could cross-train and work in different techniques," as Dennis Muren put it. "That was different than a Hollywood system that had very strict union rules. There was no way this work could be done that way or no way that the Hollywood unions could understand what we were doing."[90]

Not that the unions didn't try. Later that fall, as Dykstra and his team were beginning to build their computerized motion control camera—which everyone was already referring to as the Dykstraflex, a name the wily Dykstra made no effort to change—union representatives stopped by to argue that Lucas should be hiring effects experts from inside the industry. Dykstra insisted that he had tried, but, "quite frankly, [I] didn't find anybody that I wanted." Lucas chose to simply ignore the unions. "George was absolutely adamant that we wanted to set up our own shop with our own people," explained lawyer Tom Pollock. "That was one of the control things that we'd been fighting about from the beginning."[91]

At the moment, however, special effects were yet another expense in which a nervous Fox was unwilling to invest. Lucas had assured Ladd that he could do the effects work for a little more than $2 million—a number that, in reality, wouldn't even come close to his costs—but Fox had continued to waffle, insisting Lucas cut his effects budget down to $1.5 million. "They just assumed that it would all get done somehow," sighed Lucas. "They just figured that we could do it for a million and a half, and that it was our problem, not theirs."[92] As Dykstra and his effects wizards went to work, Lucas continued to pour his *American Graffiti* money into the unassuming warehouse across from the Van Nuys Airport, spending nearly $88,000 in its first three weeks of operation.[93]

Lucas claimed later that the name for his new special effects company had simply "popped into his head" as he was drafting the organization's articles of incorporation.[94] "We said, 'What are we going to call this thing?'" They were in an industrial park, Lucas explained. "They were building these giant Dykstraflex machines to photograph stuff, so that's where the 'Light' came from. In the end I said, 'Forget the Industrial and the Light—this is going to have to be Magic. Otherwise we're doomed, making a movie nobody wants.'"⁹⁵ "Industrial Light and Magic" it would be, then, an official subsidiary of Lucasfilm Ltd. Born of necessity, seeded with his own money, and feeding off Lucas's need to control every aspect of production, ILM would stand as one of the cornerstones of Lucas's film empire—an investment that would set him well on the way to becoming a multi*billion*aire. "How many people think the solution to gaining quality control, improving fiscal responsibility, and stimulating technological innovation is to start their own special-effects company?" Ron Howard said admiringly. "But that's what he did."⁹⁶

On Friday, June 20, 1975, Steven Spielberg's *Jaws* opened in 409 theaters and changed movies forever. As Lucas had predicted, Spielberg had a colossal hit on his hands—one that surprised even Spielberg, who had brought the film in over budget and a hundred days late, and nearly had a nervous breakdown, all but convinced he'd just made a spectacular dud. But *Jaws* was more than just a great film; for the first time, a Hollywood studio—in this case Universal—had recognized that distribution and advertising mattered, especially advertising on television. Instead of opening in only a few theaters in select cities, *Jaws* opened in hundreds of theaters nationwide. And with nearly $2.5 million in marketing and promotion behind it—double the amount spent for most films—*Jaws* was an unavoidable presence in the summer of 1975, with terrifying prime-time television spots, a memorable poster, and marketing that included board games and beach towels.

Like the film's titular character, *Jaws* just kept slowly trolling along all summer, drawing crowds week after week. Spielberg remembered reading the returns each weekend and "waiting for the next weekend to drop off and it didn't, it went up and it went up."⁹⁷ In its first release, *Jaws* would set a record of $129 million in rentals. Studios watched with envy as Universal counted its profits. But those profits had come at a cost. Advertising was expensive, as were the prints needed for a nationwide release, and studios wanted those costs recovered as quickly as possible. The way to recover those costs? More advertising and release to even more theaters. It was a snake — or in this case a shark — devouring its own tail. The modern blockbuster was born.

While Spielberg savored his success, Lucas was hunkered down again, working his way through revisions to his script. As he read through the most recent draft, Lucas realized he had no leading female characters — he had shuffled Leia off to secondary status too quickly — and therefore decided that Luke was now a girl, a decision that lasted only long enough for McQuarrie to complete one painting with a female hero. By May, Luke was male again, and Lucas submitted to Ladd a new, hastily written six-page synopsis in which he'd added a new character, a mystical old man he had lifted straight out of the pages of Carlos Castaneda's 1968 *The Teachings of Don Juan: A Yaqui Way of Knowledge*. Castaneda, an anthropologist educated at UCLA, was in the midst of writing a series of books describing his own apprenticeship to the Yaqui shaman Don Juan Matus, and Lucas soaked up all the Castaneda he could as he struggled with themes of father-son and master-apprentice relationships in his script. "Old man can do magic, read minds, talk to things like *Don Juan*," Lucas wrote in his May 1975 treatment.[98] By the time Lucas completed the next draft in August, the old man even had a name: General Ben Kenobi.

In fact, by the third draft, completed in August 1975, Lucas had tightened and improved the script even further, moving Luke more firmly to the center of the script as the hero, and making Leia — instead of Deak — the character who gets captured and needs rescuing. Lucas still had the Kiber Crystal in the script but was beginning to realize that pursuing the stolen plans for the Death Star made for a much more interesting story. "I find plots boring," Lucas insisted, "because they're so mechanical."[99] Mechanical or not, the plot we generally recognize as *Star Wars* is falling into place here. After more than two years of writing, of bleeding on the page, Lucas knew he was finally close to getting it right. "Each story was a totally different story about totally different characters before I finally landed on *the* story," he said later with near-palpable relief.[100]

And yet even his own progress depressed him. While Lucas saw *Star Wars* as his response to a weary world in need of new heroes and mythologies, his friends saw it as a juvenile exercise unworthy of his talent. Wasn't this the boy wonder whose experimental films and "tone poems" had dazzled intellectuals and amazed audiences? "They said, 'George, you should be making more of an artistic statement,'" Lucas grumbled. "People said I should have made *Apocalypse Now* after *Graffiti.*... They said I should be doing movies like *Taxi Driver.*"[101] Marcia finally pulled aside one of Lucas's newer friends, the director Brian De Palma—who, like Lucas, had started in arty documentary-type films and was now trying for a more mainstream hit with an adaptation of Stephen King's 1974 novel *Carrie*—and begged De Palma to cheer George up. "George thinks he has no talent," she told him flatly. "He respects you. Tell him he does."[102]

Lucas began casting in August. De Palma was at his side, for both personal and practical reasons: De Palma wanted to begin casting *Carrie*, and he and Lucas—who was casting the parts of Luke, Leia, and Han—needed actors in roughly the same age bracket. Working out of the Zoetrope offices Coppola kept at the Goldwyn Studios in Los Angeles, Lucas and De Palma—along with Fred Roos, Lucas's shrewd casting director from *American Graffiti*—saw "thousands of kids," with auditions starting at 8 or 9 in the morning and running until well after 8 in the evening.[103] At that pace, most actors spent little more than a few minutes in front of the directors. "Brian did all the talking," remembered Carrie Fisher, "because George didn't talk then."[104] Most of those who auditioned assumed Lucas was De Palma's assistant.

Lucas may have been quiet, but he was taking casting seriously. He intended for there to be a love triangle involving the three main characters—an intergalactic *Casablanca*—so the chemistry among the three leads was critical. It mattered even more, in fact, in a film in which most of the cast were robots and aliens, or covered in full body armor. As in any of the countless *Road* movies of the 1940s, in which the interplay among Bob Hope, Bing Crosby, and Dorothy Lamour could carry a film when the plot sagged, Lucas needed his leads to help ensure the audience suspended its disbelief and didn't get bogged down in details. There would be no ham acting or knowing winks at the camera; *Star Wars* might have been an affectionate nod to the old science fiction serials of the 1930s and 1940s, but it wasn't camp. His actors, then, had to play it straight. Looks mattered, too. For a director, "your first impression of them is the same impression more or less as the audience's when they meet them," said Lucas.[105] As Mark Hamill put it, "They weren't going to [just] let us read. You had to look right first."[106]

Nearly every young actor in Hollywood and New York, it seemed, wanted to audition. John Travolta, Nick Nolte, and Tommy Lee Jones all came in during the first week. Lucas would immediately pass on all three, though De Palma would pick Travolta for a role in *Carrie*. Twenty-three-year-old Mark Hamill, who had a long résumé of small television parts, showed up to audition only after some prodding from his friend Robert Englund, who had unsuccessfully tried out for the part of Han Solo. (Despite missing out on the part of Han, Englund would take on another iconic role years later, playing Freddie Krueger in countless *Nightmare on Elm Street* films.) As a lifelong science fiction and comic book nerd, Hamill loved the idea of being the hero in a sci-fi film but had only barely sat down to introduce himself before Lucas waved him out of the room. Hamill—who had also unsuccessfully auditioned for *American Graffiti*—thought he had blown it again. Lucas seemed much more interested in Robbie Benson and Will Seltzer, both of whom he asked to come back.

Casting for Leia was harder, at least to the mind of Marcia, who only half-jokingly teased her husband about auditioning every young actress on the West Coast. "I knew he was going to be looking at the most beautiful eighteen- and nineteen-year-old girls in Hollywood for Princess Leia, and I felt so insecure," she recalled. "I said, 'George, are you going to be a good boy when you're down there?'" Lucas grimaced. "My first vow when I came to a film studio was never to date an

actress," he said. Lucas saw himself as "just a funny kid. [A]nd someone like a Playmate of the Month is coming after [me]? Life is too
short for that."[107] Marcia didn't have a thing to worry about; Lucas was
essentially a brain in a jar, sitting stoically through casting sessions,
and eventually passing on Amy Irving—another actress De Palma
would nab—Jodie Foster, and Linda Purl. While he was skeptical
about casting any of his *American Graffiti* stars in his current project,
he loyally sat through an audition with Cindy Williams before scratching her off the list of possibilities as well. Williams later heard that
Lucas told others he was looking for "a young Cindy Williams." "I just
about died," she sighed. "Every actress waits in anticipated horror to
hear those words."[108] After several weeks of auditions, Lucas thought
he'd found the perfect princess in a young actress named Terri Nunn,
who'd only just turned fourteen in June, though she looked much
older, and in fact often added several years to her age when out on
auditions.[109]

Finding the right Han Solo proved to be the trickiest task of all.
Solo had evolved on the page more than most of the other characters,
starting as a gilled, green-skinned alien, progressing through a burly,
Coppola-like phase, and finally becoming a world-weary, somewhat
cynical pirate, part James Dean, part Humphrey Bogart. It was a role
that was going to take just the right amount of swagger and sincerity.
Lucas had briefly considered casting an African American, looking
closely at twenty-eight-year-old actor Glynn Turman. But given that
he was contemplating a romance between Han and Leia, Lucas was
concerned that an interracial relationship might be too distracting for
1970s audiences. "He didn't want *Guess Who's Coming to Dinner*," said
Kurtz.[110] Turman remained on Lucas's short list for Han—but after
considering several other promising prospects, including Al Pacino
and Kurt Russell, Lucas had all but settled on a quirky, slightly dangerous New Yorker: thirty-two-year-old Christopher Walken.

Lucas's core cast wouldn't finally come together until December,
when he called back several groups of actors—mostly Lukes and
Leias—to sit for another three days of auditions. This time there

would be a camera rolling so Lucas, as he had done with tryouts for *American Graffiti,* could see how his actors looked on camera. While Lucas thought he was close to finding his cast, casting director Fred Roos had coyly salted Lucas's short list for Luke and Leia with some suggestions of his own. He had also cleverly planted another possibility for Han Solo right under Lucas's nose by hiring a carpenter to frame and hang a door in the Zoetrope offices: Harrison Ford. Ford had found acting jobs scarce since *American Graffiti,* and had returned to carpentry to feed his young family. But Roos liked Ford and thought he was worth a look. "Getting George to consider Harrison took some working around," said Roos.[111] For one thing, Ford didn't even want to be in the room working on his knees as a carpenter when there was a casting call; it was too humiliating. "I'm not working a fucking door while Lucas is there," he had groused to Roos.[112] But Roos had a plan: as actors came in to audition for other roles, Roos suggested to Lucas that Ford read Han's lines with them. Though still wary of hiring any of his cast from *Graffiti,* Lucas was willing to let Ford play off the other actors—and after watching Ford for several days, Lucas was intrigued. "I thought, *Here's a possibility,*" said Lucas. "But I had to go through the whole process. I wasn't going to take anyone just because I knew them, or I knew they could act well—I really wanted to see all the diverse possibilities and come at it fresh."[113]

On December 30, Ford would officially become one of those diverse possibilities when he read with two actors suggested by Roos, one of whom Lucas had already auditioned and dismissed and another he hadn't seen at all. Mark Hamill had left his August session with a confused shrug and had all but forgotten about *Star Wars* when his agent informed him he was going back to audition again, this time working off four pages from the latest draft of the script, heavy with Lucas's unique brand of technospeak. "There's a line I remember from the original test," said Hamill, "where...I say, 'We can't turn around. Fear is their greatest weapon. I doubt if the actual security there is any greater than it was on Aquilae or Sullust, and what there is, is most likely directed toward a large-scale assault.' [And] I thought, *Who talks like this?*"[114] But Hamill delivered the lines with just the right amount of excitement and naïveté that Lucas was impressed. "Okay, good," he said—about the closest Lucas would ever come to support and enthusiasm—but Hamill was still convinced he'd lost the part.[115] "I didn't feel bad or disappointed," said Hamill. "It was just a clean no-go."[116]

The other actor Lucas saw that day was Carrie Fisher, the nineteen-year-old daughter of Hollywood actors Debbie Reynolds and Eddie Fisher, who had made her acting debut only a year earlier in a small but memorable role in *Shampoo*. Fisher had missed the auditions in August, but Roos encouraged Lucas and Fisher to meet. Fisher received her pages of the script, and she too rolled her eyes, though for a different reason. "Leia was unconscious a lot," recalled Fisher. "I have an affinity for unconscious. But I also wanted to be involved in all of it."[117] Fisher read with Ford, her Leia responding aggressively, and at times with exasperation, to Solo's badgering. Though Lucas found Fisher a bit pushy for a princess, if he was looking for chemistry, he'd found it between Fisher and Ford.

Ford, too, was feeling better and better about his chances for the role he hadn't actively sought. In the course of a month, he'd rehearsed the same lines with enough actors that he knew the dialogue backward and forward, and could deliver it in a relaxed, almost cocksure manner. It was undeniable that over three weeks, Ford had molded Han Solo into his own character—and while Lucas was still interested in Christopher Walken for the part, Ford was quickly becoming a contender. Even the Huycks were pushing for Ford, telling Lucas that Ford "was more fun."[118] But Ford—like Hamill and Fisher—left the auditions in a cloud of uncertainty.

Lucas had narrowed his lead threesome down to two competing groups: in one was Walken, Will Seltzer, and Terri Nunn, a trio Lucas described as "a little more serious, a little more realistic"; in the other, Ford, Hamill, and Fisher, a group Lucas called "a little more fun, more goofy." It would take until January for him to make up his mind. Lucas liked both threesomes, but one trio seemed to entail more problems than the other. Nunn was a minor, first of all, which would severely limit the number of hours she could work each day. And Seltzer...well, Lucas just felt he was a little too "intellectual," whereas Hamill was "idealistic, naïve, and hopeful."[119] Lucas would go with the trio of Hamill, Ford, and Fisher, then, with only one condition: "I got [the part] with the proviso that I went to a fat farm," said Carrie Fisher drily, "and that I lose ten pounds."[120]

Lucas was happy with his cast—"I look for magic," he said later. "What can I say?"—but not everyone was so sure he had made the right decision.[121] "I disagreed with George's casting," said Coppola, "but it was not for me to say."[122] Said Ladd, "I'd be lying if I said, 'My god Harrison's perfect...' No, I was very nervous about the cast."[123] Ladd was also nervous that Lucas hadn't yet hired a big-name actor for the film. For Lucas, using unknown actors was important; he wanted audiences relating to the characters, not the actors. But he did have a name actor in mind for the role of Ben Kenobi, and asked casting director Dianne Crittenden to arrange a meeting with the English actor Alec Guinness, who was in Los Angeles wrapping work on the film *Murder by Death*. Crittenden managed to have a copy of the latest version of the script delivered to Guinness's dressing room, along with a bundle of McQuarrie's paintings. Guinness was annoyed from the start; he didn't like people pushing scripts on him, and he was particularly dubious about science fiction. But Guinness was preparing to produce a play in London and he needed the money. Looking at *Star Wars* as nothing more than a paycheck, he agreed to have lunch with Lucas.

Lunch went well enough. In his diary, Guinness described Lucas as "a small, neat-faced young man with a black beard...with tiny well-shaped hands, poorish teeth, glasses, and not much sense of humour. But I liked him."[124] One colleague had told Guinness that Lucas was "a real director," and after meeting him, Guinness was inclined to agree,[125] though he admitted he found him "[a] touch boring."[126] But he wasn't ready to commit; there was going to have to be enough money involved for Guinness to overcome his doubts about the script. "I *may* accept, if they come up with proper money," Guinness wrote in his diary. "Science fiction—which gives me pause—but it is to be directed by Paul [*sic*] Lucas who did *American Graffiti*, which makes me feel I should. Big part. Fairy-tale rubbish but *could* be interesting perhaps."[127] He and Lucas would keep talking, and Ladd was pleased that Lucas was at last adding a recognizable name to his cast. "Guinness didn't sell tickets on his own," said Ladd, "but it was nice that he was in the picture."[128]

In addition to his cast, Lucas spent much of the summer of 1975 assembling other key creative personnel, all brilliant in their own ways, and each handpicked by the control-craving Lucas. John Barry, a gifted set designer who had worked on *A Clockwork Orange*, had been a happy accident, discovered while Lucas was visiting the Huycks in Mexico, where director Stanley Donen was filming their 1930s-era script *Lucky Lady*. Lucas was stunned by how realistic the sets looked; as he stood in a set built to resemble an old salt factory, he even rolled up the sleeves of his plaid shirt to see if he could shovel the salt. To his delight, he could—and he called over Barry and set decorator Roger Christian to discuss having them design and decorate sets for *Star Wars*, telling them that he "wanted it all [looking] real and used." Christian was ecstatic. "My first conversation with [Lucas] was that spaceships should be things you see in garages with oil dripping," said Christian, "and they keep repairing them to keep them going, because that's how the world is."[129] Lucas nodded approvingly, but enthusiasm was only part of it. *Star Wars*, he explained, was a big project that was going to have to be made quickly—Lucas wanted to start filming in February 1976, only about seven months away—and cheaply. "I think anybody with more experience would have just said, 'I don't think I can do it in that amount of time,'" said Barry. But he decided, "I have just enough experience to be able to cope with the problems, and just enough inexperience so I should take it on."[130] Lucas hired them both, paying each with still more of his *American Graffiti* money.

Barry and Christian would help Lucas ensure his movie looked great; but Lucas also wanted to make certain his movie *sounded* like nothing else before it. Sound had always been important to Lucas, whether it was orchestrating the eerie undercurrent of whirrs and chatter he had embedded in *THX 1138* or making sure *American Graffiti* had a rock score that complemented, but didn't overwhelm, the action on-screen. When it came to sound, then, Lucas's go-to had always been Walter Murch—and Lucas had even ensured that his agreement memo with Fox specified that Murch would be in charge of sound. But that had been in 1973; by the summer of 1975, Murch was committed to several other projects and was unavailable for *Star Wars*. So Lucas went to USC and asked for "the next Walter Murch," and was referred to a twenty-seven-year-old graduate student named Ben Burtt—who, like Murch, had been sticking a microphone under pretty much everything since he was a kid. Burtt's first assignment, courtesy of Gary Kurtz: find the voice for a Wookiee.

Armed with a Nagra recorder and microphones borrowed from Zoetrope, Burtt recorded zoo animals, pored over sound collections at movie studios, and even rented animals, eventually crafting Chewbacca's distinctive roars, moans, and whimpers from a carefully mixed blend of sounds made by four bears, a lion, a seal, and a walrus trapped at the bottom of a dry pool at Marineland, near Long Beach.[131] Impressed, Lucas asked Burtt to put together an entire library of sounds for the film. "Collect weird, strange sounds," Lucas told him, and Burtt would loiter at airports, bang on guy wires, and record vibrating film projectors in the search for the best sounds for spacecraft, laser guns, and lightsabers.[132] Burtt thought assembling the sound library might involve "a few weeks' work…but twenty-nine years and ten months later, I finally came to the end of building that library."[133] What Burtt would eventually give Lucas would define not just six *Star Wars* films but science fiction sound effects for a generation of filmgoers.

But if Lucas truly wanted to give *Star Wars* a unique personality in sound, he would find it in the savvy choice he made for the composer of his film music. Lucas knew he wanted a classical-sounding score, something swashbuckling and with a personality of its own, to enhance the images on the screen. While visiting Spielberg on Martha's Vineyard in early spring, where Spielberg was in post-production on *Jaws,* Lucas mentioned he was on the lookout for a composer who could give him "a very sort of Max Steiner–type, old-fashioned, romantic movie score."[134] Spielberg immediately recommended John Williams, a forty-three-year-old Oscar nominee who had scored both *Jaws* and *The Sugarland Express.* "I've worked with this guy and he's great!" Spielberg told him.[135] The introduction was made, and after reading Lucas's script, Williams agreed to compose the score for *Star Wars*...but not until the following year, as he was already at work on music for two thrillers, Alfred Hitchcock's *Family Plot* and John Frankenheimer's *Black Sunday.* It would be Williams, perhaps more than any other collaborator, who would give *Star Wars* the air of excitement and dignity that Lucas envisioned—and his score would become iconic, its opening brass blare cheered by audiences through seven movies and counting. Lucas would always be open in his admiration for Williams. "He's right up there with Buddy Holly and the Drifters," Lucas would say later, the highest praise he could give any musician.[136]

As the summer wore on, Lucas was still slogging through rewrites on his script, still sitting down in front of the evening news with a scowl on his face. Marcia, however, was no longer there to make reassuring noises or beg friends to tell George he was brilliant. She had taken yet another job working for Martin Scorsese, this time as supervising editor for *Taxi Driver;* their plans to start a family would remain once again on hold. Not that Lucas was going to be home much, either; in late August 1975, he and Kurtz left for England to start pre-production at Elstree, looking over a landspeeder John Barry was tinkering with as well as a prototype of R2-D2, made of unpainted wood with a primer-gray swivel head. Lucas picked up several more members of his cast in London as well. Six-foot-seven Welshman and bodybuilder David Prowse was given his choice of either Darth Vader or Chewbacca, and chose the villain, leaving the role of the Wookiee to seven-foot-two Peter Mayhew, a genial hospital porter who was said to have a pair of the largest feet in London.

For the role of C-3PO, Lucas had to cast a much wider and more specialized net. He wasn't necessarily interested in the way the actor sounded—he planned on dubbing in Threepio's voice later, ideally with the cadences of a Bronx used-car dealer—but he needed an actor who could play a convincing robot, preferably someone with good mime skills. Twenty-nine-year-old Anthony Daniels, who hated science fiction and had walked out of a viewing of *2001: A Space Odyssey,* very nearly didn't try out for the part. He eventually met with Lucas and liked him, but remained skeptical of accepting the role until he spotted McQuarrie's painting of Threepio and Artoo and locked eyes with the golden droid. "He seemed to be saying, 'Come! Come be with me!' and the vulnerability in his face made me want to help him," said Daniels. "Isn't that weird?" Three decades later, after playing the droid in six films, Daniels yelled at McQuarrie in mock agitation, "You realize this is all your fault!"[137]

Pre-production in London was moving along, Dykstra and the wizards at ILM were starting work on the special effects—though mostly they were still building the cameras and other equipment needed to film them first—and Lucas had very nearly decided on his final cast. But there was one thing missing, something critical: he still didn't have the official green light for the project from Fox. That meant there was no budget yet, so he couldn't complete his sets, build the robots, or even design and assemble costumes and wardrobe. It had been more than two years since the agreement memo with Fox, and Lucas hadn't seen another dime beyond the $10,000 he'd been paid for the first draft of the script. "I had written four scripts [and] they had only paid me for one," groused Lucas. "The least they could have done in that time was crank out one contract."[138] Until that happened, he and Kurtz were continuing to lay out their own money to cover expenses, funneling most of it through The Star Wars Corporation; they would eventually spend nearly $1 million between them. Friends were worried Lucas might lose everything on his "Flash Gordon thing," but Marcia remained supportive. "George takes enormous risks. He's very determined," she said. "He invested that money because he knew he was going to make that movie. He knows what he wants and he knows how to get it. He's gambling, but he's gambling on himself and his own ability to come through."[139]

Still, costs were beginning to reach a level where even *American Graffiti* money couldn't keep paying for everything much longer; Lucas needed an official "go" from the studio, with the contract and budget that went with it—and he needed it now. Work at ILM alone was running about $25,000 per week. In the first three months alone, the company had soaked up more than $241,000 in costs. "I had to build my own studio, render the storyboards, devise the opticals, and I poured a lot of my own money into it," Lucas noted, adding: "I hate to waste money. I don't spend it lightly."[140] Neither did Fox—and in October, the studio was suddenly spooked into a paralysis that very nearly cost them *Star Wars* altogether.

It was actually *Lucky Lady*, the Huyck-penned project filming in Mexico, that had given Fox cold feet. The film's director, Stanley Donen, was much like Lucas: independent and visionary, with a penchant for doing everything himself. But halfway through the film's production, "he got into serious trouble," recalled Kurtz. "The studio had to keep flying down there and they eventually took over the entire production."[141] That experience had so startled Fox executives that they were determined not to be caught flat-footed again by another free-spending independent director. To keep Lucas in check, Fox halted production on *Star Wars*, pending further review by the board of directors at its meeting scheduled for December. Until then, Lucas was effectively shut down for two months.

Angry with Fox for waffling in its support, Lucas was determined to take the project elsewhere, even bringing the script back to United Artists and to Ned Tanen at Universal to see if either might reconsider picking up *Star Wars*. Both decided to give it a look—Lucas was too hot a commodity to ignore—but neither was convinced that Lucas could pull off his ambitious script, especially one that relied so heavily on special effects. Universal was particularly brusque in its brush-off, passing around a memo that dismissed both the story and Lucas's vision. "The question, in the end," wrote one executive in an internal document, "is how much faith we have in Mr. Lucas's ability to pull it all off."[142] The answer, apparently, was *none*. For the rest of his life, Lucas would remember Universal's slight—and he'd never let Ned Tanen forget it. He would later take considerable glee in knowing that Universal's lack of faith in him had cost the studio a billion-dollar franchise. "I hold grudges," he told *Rolling Stone* in 1980. "Universal tried to be nice to me, but I was really angry and I remain angry to this day."[143]

In the end, then, he was going to have to keep dealing with Fox, so he and Kurtz finally began putting together their own highly detailed budget, cutting costs and corners wherever they could to get the final number as low as possible. Working with set designer Roger Christian, they scrubbed the script for places where costs could be minimized by eliminating characters, changing the location of certain scenes to reduce the number of required sets, consolidating scenes, or eliminating some sequences altogether. In several instances, such decisions actually improved the script, as Lucas chose to remove Cloud City from the script and imprison Leia instead on the Death Star, making her rescue that much more dangerous and exciting. Lucas and artist Joe Johnston also carefully storyboarded out nearly every shot, trying to determine exactly how many scenes, sets, and special effects would be needed. Lucas was confident he had cut the fat out of the script, but feared that they were now cutting bone and sinew—a concern shared by Dykstra, who called the studio's notorious cheapness "bullshit."[144]

Even with production at a standstill, Lucas was a man in constant motion, jetting between London—where he was still consulting with Barry on sets and robots—and Los Angeles, where he would hunker down with the crew at ILM. Here he would scribble on drawings, move storyboards around, and tweak models even as they were being built. And to his dismay, he'd run into a major problem with one very important spaceship. In September 1975, the Lew Grade–produced science fiction series *Space: 1999* had debuted on American television.

Lucas watched it, and hadn't gotten much further than the opening credits when he realized that the show's central ships, the Eagle Transporters, looked a little too much like Han Solo's still unnamed pirate ship, which the ILM crew had only just constructed and rigged out with lighting. Lucas didn't want there to be even a whiff of an accusation that he had lifted his ship design from *Space: 1999,* so he insisted the ILM team start over. Lucas told the crew he wanted something like a flying saucer, but also "something with a lot more personality," essentially a flying hot rod, that looked like it was built for speed from junked parts of other ships.[145] So Lucas, Dykstra, and Johnston came up with a design for a ship they called the "Porkburger": essentially two inverted saucers with mandibles in the front and the cockpit off to one side. It wasn't until March 1976, only weeks before filming was to begin, that Lucas would hit on the ship's name. The Porkburger would become known as the *Millennium Falcon.*

The Fox board of directors held its winter meeting on Saturday, December 13, 1975. Fortunately for Lucas, Ladd did most of the talking. "I'm a believer in this," he told a skeptical and mostly quiet board listening to their *Star Wars* pitch—including Princess Grace of Monaco, who'd been appointed to the board over the summer. With Ladd pushing hard, giving each board member not just the script but reams of concept art by McQuarrie and Joe Johnston, the board gave its consent to green-light the project with a budget of $8.3 million— and hinted *very* strongly that it expected the final budget Lucas proposed to come in under that. After a great deal of negotiating on the part of Kurtz, the final projected budget was set at a very precise $8,228,228. Lucas groused that Fox was asking him to make a $15 million movie on half the budget.

Nevertheless, with the project officially a go, Lucas—through The Star Wars Corporation—could finally get down to negotiating an official contract with Fox. Lucas had rightly grumbled about Fox's foot-dragging for two years, but the delay had actually worked in his favor. With both his reputation and finances enhanced by *American*

Graffiti, "George didn't need the money anymore," said attorney Tom Pollock, "so we went after all the things we wanted in the beginning...[w]hich is control—control over the making of the picture and control over the exploitation of all the ancillary rights."[146] Additionally, Lucas would own—*control*—about 40 percent of the gross profits from the film; but what he really was after was buried in the details. As a result, the nine-page deal memo ballooned to a forty-page production and distribution contract, according to which Lucas would own the rights to sequels, television, publishing, and merchandising—"areas that were important to George," said agent Jeff Berg, "because he knew the life of *Star Wars* would exist beyond making the first theatrical motion picture."[147] It took until nearly February 1976—about two weeks before cameras were to begin rolling—for the contract to be signed, and Pollock, who had seen his share of hardball tactics, thought the final document was "one of the most brilliantly written movie contracts I have ever read. Not from the standpoint of the studio, but of a filmmaker getting what they want."[148]

What Lucas really wanted now was to get started. By the end of 1975, he had been struggling with *Star Wars* for nearly three years, suffering through rejection at the hands of two studios, dealing with skepticism from his friends, a depletion of his savings, and an almost lethal lack of faith from 20th Century Fox. Now he was close to finalizing his contract and his budget, his cast was falling into place, locations were being scouted, and his soundstages in London were reserved for March. Meanwhile, the crew at ILM were building cameras and storyboarding effects shots in California, John Barry and Roger Christian were working on sets in London, and Ben Burtt was collecting sound effects just about anywhere. Things looked to be on track to begin filming in March 1976, except for one thing: the always troublesome script. "This film has been murder," Lucas complained in December 1975. Compared with this, writing *American Graffiti* had been a cakewalk. "It's very hard to write about something you make up from scratch. And the problem was that there was so much I could include—it was like being in a candy store, and it was hard to not get a stomach ache from the whole experience."[149]

As 1976 approached, Lucas was finishing up his fourth draft, now officially titled *The Adventures of Luke Starkiller, as Taken from the Journal of the Whills, Saga I: Star Wars.* Lucas was still paring down subplots and characters, removing elements that either slowed things down or required too much backstory. He had a much better handle on the Force at this point, and had wisely decided to remove the Kiber Crystal from the story altogether, making the Force "more ethereal," he explained, rather "than to have it solidified in a thing like a crystal."[150] The Force was "a big idea," he told science fiction writer Alan Dean Foster, whom he had personally tapped to write a novelization of the film. "[Luke] has to trust his feelings rather than his senses and his logic—that's essentially what the Force of Others comes down to."[151]

There is no indication that Lucas ever intended for Darth Vader to be Anakin Skywalker, or that he would be the father of Luke and Leia, twins separated at birth. While Lucas would, over the course of three decades, perpetuate a kind of retroactive continuity by asserting that this had been his plan all along, in 1975 he still clearly intended for Vader and Luke's father to be separate characters. Vader's backstory, he explained, was "about Ben and Luke's father and Vader, when they are young Jedi knights. Vader kills Luke's father, then Ben and Vader have a confrontation, just like they have in *Star Wars,* and Ben almost kills Vader."[152] As for the name "Vader," Lucas has made much of the linguistic coincidence that *vader* is the Dutch word for "father"—but it was also a name he'd likely heard nearly daily at Downey High School, where he had a schoolmate one grade ahead, an all-conference athlete named Gary Vader. For Lucas, who loved the way words sounded, it was too good a last name *not* to use.

By the time Lucas completed his fourth draft on January 1, 1976, he had come a long way since the nonstarter *Journal of the Whills,* but he was still unhappy with it. "I had a lot of vague concepts," he remembered years later, "but I didn't really know where to go with it, and I've never fully resolved it. It's very hard stumbling across the desert, picking up rocks, not knowing what I'm looking for, and knowing the rock I've got is not the rock I'm looking for. I kept simplifying it, and I kept having people read it, and I kept trying to get a more cohesive story—but I'm still not very happy with the script. I never have been."[153]

"In the end," Lucas said later, "I really didn't think we were going to make any money at all on *Star Wars*."[154]

7

"I Have a Bad Feeling About This"

1976-1977

Barely two weeks into filming *Star Wars*, and George Lucas was ready to kill Sir Alec Guinness.

"It is quite a shock to an actor when you say, 'I know you have a big part...and all of a sudden I have decided to kill you,'" Lucas told a writer for *Rolling Stone* in 1977. But to Lucas's mind, killing off Guinness's character Obi-Wan Kenobi was vital to the film, correcting what Lucas saw as a major shortcoming in the latest draft of his always evolving script: "There was no real threat in the Death Star," Lucas explained. In his latest draft, Kenobi survived his lightsaber duel with Darth Vader by retreating through a blast door that slammed shut behind him. That not only left Vader "with egg on his face," as Lucas put it, but also made the assault on the Death Star little more than a bit of galactic breaking and entering, with Vader as a flummoxed shopkeeper shaking his fist in rage as the heroes escaped unharmed. "This was dumb," said Lucas flatly. "They run into the Death Star and they sort of take over everything and they run back. It totally diminished any impact the Death Star had."[1]

It was Marcia who had put Ben Kenobi's head on the block, pointing out to George that after escaping the Death Star, the old general didn't have much to do for the rest of the film. Lucas had to agree — "the character stood around with his thumb in his ear" — and Marcia suggested that Kenobi be killed in his lightsaber duel and then offer Luke advice as a spirit guide in the final act.[2] Lucas may have cringed at the idea of killing off his film's only Oscar-winning actor, but he knew Marcia was right. "Marcia was very opinionated and had very good opinions about things, and would not put up [with it] if she thought George was going off in the wrong direction," said Walter Murch. "There were heated creative arguments between them, for the good."[3] Debating the case with Marcia, however, was nothing compared with breaking the news to Guinness himself.

In early April 1976, Lucas was with Guinness in Tunisia, where they'd spent the better part of a week filming the scenes set on the desert planet of Tatooine. Lucas, his nerve finally steeled, pulled the actor aside to break the news about the fate of Ben Kenobi — but then waffled, telling Guinness he hadn't really made a final decision yet. According to Lucas, Guinness "kept it under control," but privately, the actor was fuming, "irritated by Lucas saying he hadn't made up his mind whether to kill off my part or not. A bit late for such decisions."[4] Lucas would make up his mind for good only a few days later. As filming began at Elstree Studios in London, Lucas informed Guinness that Ben Kenobi would die at the hands of Darth Vader. This time Guinness wouldn't keep it under control. "I'm not doing this," he told Lucas tersely, and threatened to leave the film altogether.[5]

Trying to smooth things over — and keep his biggest-name actor from walking out — Lucas took Guinness to lunch to make his case. "I explained that in the last half of the movie he didn't have anything to do, it wasn't dramatic to have him standing around, and I wanted his character to have an impact," said Lucas. Guinness considered carefully, listening as Lucas argued that having Kenobi as a spirit guide "was really a Castaneda *Tales of Power* thing."[6] Guinness agreed to stay—"I simply trust the director," he would explain later—but in truth, Guinness would never be entirely comfortable in Obi-Wan's cloak. Still, Lucas was paying him well—"lovely bread," Guinness admitted privately—and had thrown in two profit points to boot, which made the "rubbish dialogue" easier to say and swallow.[7] "I must confess I'm pretty much lost as to what is required of me," Guinness admitted to the *Sunday Times* a month later. "What I'm supposed to be doing, I can't really say."[8]

Publicly, however, Lucas reported that Guinness "took it all very well...and developed the character accordingly."[9] The crisis had been averted—but it would be far from the last. From day one, *Star Wars* would be a problem-plagued production that would blow through its budget, mentally and physically exhaust Lucas, and so try the patience of executives at Fox that the studio very nearly pulled the plug on the film altogether. "I forgot how impossible making movies really is," a weary Lucas wrote in a letter to Marcia during filming. "I get so depressed, but I guess I'll get through it somehow."[10]

Three months before filming began—and well before he was even considering killing off Guinness's Obi-Wan—Lucas left California in January 1976, headed for England, where he took over the production offices at sprawling Elstree Studios in northern London. Meanwhile, in Los Angeles, John Dykstra and ILM were supposed to be putting together the first of the 360 special effects shots Lucas had asked for. Unfortunately, most of their time was still devoted to building the cameras, optical printers, and other equipment that would be needed to film and assemble the visual effects. "We designed and built our own electronics from scratch," Dykstra said proudly.[11] But every day spent manufacturing the technology meant another lost day of filming the effects themselves. And with Lucas now in London, where he could no longer drop in unannounced or hover over the work, ILM would only fall farther and farther behind.

Lucas took with him the fourth draft of the script, which he had completed on January 1. Typically, he still wasn't happy with it, though he was pleased with the script's new opening line: *A long, long time ago, in a galaxy far, far away an incredible adventure took place...* The rest of the writing, however, he found "painful, atrocious" and decided that with filming scheduled to begin in twelve weeks, it was probably time to bring in a writer—or in this case *writers*—to give the script a once-over. "I never arrived at a degree of satisfaction where I thought the screenplay was perfect," he said later. "If I hadn't been forced to shoot the film, I would doubtless still be rewriting it now."[12] Lucas called on Willard Huyck and Gloria Katz, his reliable collaborators on *American Graffiti,* and brought them to London to work on a rewrite. The Huycks worked with their typical speed, sanding some of the jargon-heavy edges off Lucas's script, tightening the dialogue in a few key places, and paying particular attention to the banter between characters, especially the interaction between Han and Leia. (They would also add an in-joke in which Leia is held captive on the Death Star in cell number 2187, a nod to the Arthur Lipsett film Lucas loved.) In lieu of payment, Lucas gave them something that would eventually be much more lucrative: two percentage points.

Meanwhile, over at Elstree, Lucas had makeup artist Stuart Freeborn—who had created the convincing apes featured in the opening moments of *2001*—hard at work creating the makeup and prosthetics for Chewbacca and other aliens. In another workshop was costume designer John Mollo, a historian with a love of military uniforms, who had been put in charge of designing and making armor and costumes, a task he jumped into with such relish that he was producing them almost faster than Lucas could look at them. John Barry's sets were also under construction at all hours of the day, sprawled across eight of Elstree's soundstages, including one set taken up entirely by a full-sized *Millennium Falcon.* Most sets would still be under construction when filming began at Elstree in April.

The pace was exhausting, and Lucas hadn't shot an inch of film yet. Making things even more unbearable, Lucas hated London.

"George wasn't happy there—he doesn't like to be away from home," said Kurtz. "Everything is different enough to throw you off balance."[13] It wasn't just driving on the opposite side of the road that made him nervous; he didn't enjoy the food—he found it impossible to get a decent hamburger—and was irritated that the light switches were "upside down." Worse, the house he was renting in the Hampstead area of London was broken into, and his television set was stolen. Not that it mattered; he frequently complained that there was nothing decent to watch on TV anyway.

With only days to go before cameras rolled, Alan Ladd dropped in on Lucas and Kurtz to review the fine print in the budget. Fox executives had directed Ladd to warn Lucas that once costumes, makeup, armor, sets, and the costs of travel were folded in, the final budget needed to come in under $10 million. "This will only work if everything goes perfectly," Kurtz cautioned Ladd, "and it rarely does."[14] Duly chastened by Ladd and Fox, Lucas insolently pegged his budget at $9,999,999. It didn't matter; it would never be enough, and Ladd left London feeling less and less certain that Lucas had his production costs under control.

On the morning of Thursday, March 18, Lucas and much of the *Star Wars* crew departed London for Djerba, an island just off the coast of Tunisia in north Africa. From there, a six-hour drive into the interior of Tunisia brought them to the sun-bleached salt flats of Nefta, where John Barry's craftsmen, after slogging through the desert dragging their materials in the beds of trucks and on the backs of donkeys, had built Luke's homestead, as well as the bottom half of an enormous Jawa sandcrawler. In keeping with Lucas's "used universe" aesthetic, everything looked as if it had already been there for a century or more—and the sandcrawler, in fact, with its gigantic tank-like treads, had piqued the interest of the government in adjacent Libya, which had rushed inspectors across the border to ensure Lucas's crew wasn't constructing some newfangled military vehicle.

Filming on *Star Wars* began at 6:30 a.m. on Monday, March 22, 1976. It was a catastrophe almost from the start. "Things started going wrong," said Kurtz with typical understatement.[15] Wind and heavy rains—the first rainfall in the Tunisian desert in nearly a decade—damaged sets and props, and rapidly fading light made it nearly impossible for Lucas to film Hamill, as Luke Skywalker, quietly contemplating his dreams against a blazing desert sunset. (It would take three days before Lucas could get the now-iconic shot on film.) Remote-control robots malfunctioned, and Anthony Daniels, in his ill-fitting C-3PO costume, could barely see and hear, and couldn't take more than a few steps without falling over. "I was very, very tired and very cross," said Daniels.[16]

And then there was Lucas's own self-imposed misery involving the script and his hand-wringing over the decision to kill off Ben Kenobi. Guinness may have been annoyed with Lucas's indecision, but for the most part, Sir Alec eagerly, even enthusiastically, supported Lucas's vision for the film. On his first day of filming, he took great relish in rolling in the dirt to give his own wardrobe the same "used universe" look as the rest of the film. Lucas admitted he was in awe of the Englishman. "He's huge and I'm so small," said Lucas. "I didn't know where to put myself."[17]

By the end of the two-week Tunisian shoot, Lucas was "desperately unhappy." But with work wrapped on location, production would now move to Elstree, and what Lucas expected would be a much more stable and controllable studio environment.

"I was hoping things would go better," Lucas said later. "But they didn't."[18]

Things were very much under control at Elstree—but unfortunately, Lucas wasn't the one controlling them. British unions kept all activity to a heavily regulated and routinized schedule: an 8:30 a.m. start, tea at 10, lunch for an hour starting at 1:15 p.m., with another tea break at 4. And the crew would stop promptly at 5:30 p.m., whether the work was finished or not. The 5:30 quitting time was particularly galling to Lucas, who had never had much patience with unions anyway, and was used to working late into the evening to get just the right shot or finish a particularly long scene. Lucas would corral Kurtz to help him plead with the union representatives for additional time, almost always without success. "The crew got upset with both of us," said Lucas. "I ended up having to be nice to everybody, which is hard when you don't like a lot of people."[19]

The British crew members were also baffled by what kind of movie, exactly, these Americans were making, derisively referring to Chewbacca as "the dog," snickering as grown men and women fired weapons that made no noise, and watching in amusement as Lucas fumed over yet another stalled R2 unit. "The British crew thought we were all out of our minds," recalled Harrison Ford. "They just thought that it was ludicrous and stupid."[20] As Lucas put it, "I was just this crazy American who was doing this really dopey movie."[21]

Lucas had only himself to blame for some of the friction; his quiet, somewhat terse style grated on the British. "All film crews are a matter of chemistry," said Kurtz diplomatically. "George is not a particularly social person. He doesn't go out of his way to socialize. It takes him a while to know somebody, to get intimate enough to share his problems with them. It's easier for him to work with people he knows."[22] For Lucas, though, *people* were precisely the problem. "Directing is very difficult because you're making a thousand decisions—there are no hard and fast answers—and you're dealing with *people*, sometimes very difficult people, emotional people," he sighed. "I just didn't enjoy it."[23]

When filming began at Elstree on April 7, not only were the script and the sets still under construction, but also, apart from his decision to kill Ben Kenobi, Lucas had only recently settled on the last name "Skywalker" for his hero. It was a decision he fussed over—the "Starkiller" surname had been in his script for more than three years— but with the 1969 Charles Manson murders not yet a distant memory, Lucas worried that the name made Luke sound too much like a serial killer. The name of the film, too, was up in the air. While the crew would use clapper boards and notebooks emblazoned with a logo reading *The Star Wars*, Lucas had all but settled on dropping the definite article, preferring simply *Star Wars*.

Even as cameras rolled, Barry and his crew were still putting the finishing touches on nearly a hundred sets spread across the eight soundstages. One of the most impressive was over on Stage 3, where the full-sized *Millennium Falcon* sat, based on a detailed model sent over from ILM. Barry's construction crew quickly discovered, however, that scaled up, the entire ship wouldn't fit onto the soundstage, so only half was built against one wall; the rest would be added as a matte painting later, as needed. The ship was so enormous, in fact, that Lucas decided it was better just to leave it in place and build the needed sets around it, including the Docking Bay 94 hangar where Han Solo would confront Jabba the Hutt — a sequence Lucas would tinker with, shelve, then revive nearly twenty years later with the help of new filmmaking technology.

Everywhere he looked, all Lucas could see were the problems. Robots continued to malfunction and run into walls. Even after adjustment, Anthony Daniels's C-3PO costume still fit him poorly, leaving most of his upper body's weight resting so heavily on his hands that his thumbs went completely numb for the entire shoot. There was so little money that nearly all of the scenes on the Death Star were filmed on the same set, dressed several different ways — and John Barry squabbled with Lucas's director of photography over the best way to light them.

For perhaps the first time, however, Lucas enjoyed working with his actors — even if his actors couldn't always tell. Typically, Lucas gave little or no feedback after takes, leaving the actors grasping for guidance. If he liked a take, he would simply mutter: "Cut. Print it. Perfect." If he didn't, he would offer one of only two bits of direction: "Faster, more intense," or "Same thing, only better." It got to be something of a joke with the actors, who would look expectantly at Lucas after every take, waiting for his response with mock excitement. "George has such a clear vision in his head of what it is that he wants, actually trying to get that out of an actor is a bit of an inconvenience," said Harrison Ford. "That's not George's favorite part of a job."[24] As Mark Hamill put it, "I have a sneaking suspicion that if there were a way to make movies without actors, George would do it."[25]

And yet Lucas *did* like his actors. He was particularly fond of Hamill, who was exactly his kind of nerd: short, with a geek's gung-ho fondness for comic books and toys. In fact, it didn't take Hamill long to realize that Lucas had infused more than a little of himself in the character of Luke. "I'm really playing *him* in the movie," said Hamill, who had watched Lucas closely as he acted out the scene in which Luke finds the runaway Artoo.[26] "I was thinking, *He's doing it so small, so I'll do it just like him,*" said Hamill, *"and he'll see how wrong he is."*[27] But Lucas loved it, and Hamill would come to integrate a few of Lucas's quirks — smaller gestures, quieter dialogue — into his character. Lucas would take to warmly calling Hamill "The Kid," a slight variation on the *stinky kid* nickname Coppola had bestowed on Lucas.

Fisher, by contrast, reminded him of his own younger sister, tough and silly at the same time. Fisher had a wicked sense of humor and a foul mouth — fueled at times by a drug habit she managed to keep mostly hidden — and she had no trouble at all playing a tough-talking princess. And yet Lucas didn't want her looking *too* aggressively feminine, using gaffer's tape to hold down her breasts. "No breasts bounce in space, no jiggling in the Empire," Fisher snickered, adding: "Gary Kurtz had to tell me that. George didn't have the nerve."[28] Still, despite her swagger, Fisher was insecure about playing Leia; she never felt she was pretty enough, disliked her earmuff hairstyle, couldn't decide what accent she should be using, and fretted about dropping her prop gun during her swing over a chasm with Hamill — but also worried that if she expressed any displeasure or discomfort, she would be fired and replaced by Jodie Foster or any of the countless other actresses Lucas had rejected for the role.

Ford, however, had no such inhibitions. Displaying a *the-hell-with-it* attitude — and looking like he was having more fun than anyone else — Ford gave Han Solo just the right balance of smarm and charm. More than the other actors, Ford wasn't shy about voicing his displeasure with Lucas's jargon-heavy script and clunky dialogue. "You can type this shit, but you can't say it," he would tell Lucas brazenly — and Ford would go through his lines each day, slightly tweaking his dialogue, and warning Lucas when he intended to ad-lib in a particular take. "Stop me if I'm really bad," he would tell Lucas—but he was rarely stopped.[29] None of them were, really. Lucas even kept in Hamill's ad-lib in which he winkingly gave Chewbacca's cell block number as 1138, a coy nod to Lucas's other science fiction film. "In terms of changing their lines," said Lucas, "well, that's a matter of letting them have their way."[30]

The chemistry—the "magic," as Lucas had called it—among his cast continued off-screen as well, and Lucas was relieved that, for the most part, his actors were hassle-free. "I only want people who are good, talented, and easy to work with," Lucas once remarked, "because life is too short for crazy actors."[31] According to Hamill, the cast regularly went out of their way to try to make Lucas laugh, "because he really looked like he was ready to burst into tears, and you'd try to cheer him up."[32] Ultimately, they all came to trust in Lucas and his instincts as a director, even if they didn't always understand what was going on. "At times during *Star Wars* I was perhaps a bit puzzled," said Guinness, "but I never lost faith in the project. There were people around who doubted the sanity of the venture and who were critical of George and Gary [Kurtz]. 'Lucas doesn't know what he's doing,' they'd say, or 'Call this filmmaking?' But I had confidence in them."[33]

Still, even Guinness had his moments of rolling his eyes at what he called Lucas's "ropey" dialogue, as did Anthony Daniels and Mark Hamill, who bonded over their mutual snickering at their lines. When Hamill teased Daniels that Threepio's dialogue was worse than Luke's, Daniels pointed out that he, at least, was "behind a mask. None of my friends know I am in this movie, so it's fine."[34] Three-foot-eight Kenny Baker, anonymously ensconced inside R2-D2's aluminum shell when the script called for the little droid to shuffle or rock, also "wondered what the movie was about. None of us knew."[35] And yet he, too, would do his best to please Lucas, smiling broadly inside his R2 unit to convey R2's emotions, even though no one could see him. "You have to do something to get the feel of the thing," explained Baker with a shrug.[36]

Even Lucas's villains were relatively easygoing. Dave Prowse would walk forcefully around the sets between takes in his full Vader costume, doing his best to stay in character, but took it all in good stride when he learned that his castmates had dubbed him "Darth Farmer," in playful reference to the West Country English accent in which he delivered his fearsome lines, to be dubbed later by James Earl Jones. Meanwhile, Peter Cushing, playing the cold Grand Moff Tarkin, was such a warmhearted gentleman that Carrie Fisher found it difficult to rail angrily at him about his "foul stench." "The man smelled like linen and lavender," she said.[37]

On April 13, over on Elstree's Stage 6, Lucas would finally film the cantina sequence he'd been envisioning since the treatment for *The Journal of the Whills*, including the moment when someone loses an arm to a lightsaber. Unfortunately, it didn't live up to his expectations—and probably never would. Prior to filming, makeup artist and mask maker Stuart Freeborn became seriously ill and had to be hospitalized, leaving most of the cantina monsters unfinished. "The ones we did have were background monsters, which weren't meant to be key monsters," said Lucas. While he would shoot additional footage with some new monsters almost a year later, he would always be disappointed with the relatively unexpressive cantina creatures, most of whom could barely move their hands. Even the normally enthusiastic Hamill was unimpressed. "It was really imaginatively described, and then you go in there, and it looks like *The Nutcracker Suite*," said Hamill. "You know, a frog guy, a mouse girl.... [I]t was really disappointing."[38]

But what disappointed Lucas more than anything else was the feeling that he was losing control of his own movie. Partly it was due to the size of the crew needed for a $10 million film. This wasn't *American Graffiti*, a $700,000 film shot over twenty-eight days on the streets of Petaluma with a crew of fewer than twenty; *Star Wars* required a crew of over nine hundred. "The larger the picture, the less time you have to deal with detail," said Kurtz. "On a small picture, you can do everything yourself."[39] That was the way Lucas would have preferred it; with such a large crew, he had no chance of controlling everything. Instead, he had to follow a chain of command, a process he found excruciating. Once a decision was made, "I would tell a department head, and he would tell another assistant department head, he'd tell some guy, and by the time it came down the line, it was not there," complained Lucas. "I spent all my time yelling and screaming at people, and I have never had to do that before."[40] Ultimately, "I tried to be in complete control, to do everything myself, but it almost killed me," he said. "It was too difficult, and I was miserable because I agonized over things not turning out my way."[41]

That was particularly true of the film's editing—always Lucas's favorite part of the process, and the hardest task for him to turn over to another. As he had done with *American Graffiti,* Lucas was shipping off footage to be edited nearly as quickly as he was shooting it, this time sending each day's work to British editor John Jympson. Although Jympson was a veteran of more than twenty films, Lucas had hired him only grudgingly; Lucas's first choice, Richard Chew—who had edited for Coppola and Miloš Forman—was scuttled by Fox executives, who strongly recommended Lucas hire an editor based locally in London. Still, Jympson seemed like a good choice; one of the many films he had edited was *A Hard Day's Night,* and Lucas hoped he would bring that same quick-cut *cinéma vérité* style to *Star Wars.* It didn't happen. "I wasn't happy with it," said Lucas. "I tried to get the editor to cut it my way and he didn't really want to."[42]

In Lucas's opinion, Jympson was making each scene too long and using too many wide shots. Lucas insisted that he wanted *Star Wars* to look like a *documentary*—an odd description to apply to a science fiction film, but an apt one, as *Star Wars* would not look like any other science fiction film. His "used universe" sensibility already gave the film a realism and an intimacy missing in most science fiction films, but Lucas wanted what John Barry described as "a newsreel sort of feeling." As was his habit, Lucas had set up multiple cameras for each take, strolling the sets at night to figure out the best camera angles, and then filming every scene with three or four cameras rolling. And rather than beginning a new scene with a wide shot to let viewers see one of Barry's gigantic detailed sets, Lucas kept the camera in tight, letting the actors wander into the frame—"like it was shot on location," explained Barry.[43] "The film has to make us believe it really existed," explained Lucas, "that we've really gone to another galaxy to shoot. The success of the imaginary, it's to make something totally fabricated seem real…that everything be credible and totally fantastic at the same time."[44]

But Jympson hadn't captured any of that feeling in his edit, forcing Lucas to send lackluster footage back to Los Angeles for Alan Ladd and Fox executives to review. Worse, ILM still had no completed special effects shots, even as the effects budget kept pushing higher and higher. "My head was in the shit," groaned Dykstra, who did his best to plead his case.[45] "We were designing and building optical printers, cameras, and miniatures; as a result, the process didn't produce a lot of film at first," Dykstra explained later. "I can understand [Lucas] being nervous about it; he was helming the show—and the studio was nervous."[46]

It was no wonder, then, that Ladd decided to fly to London in early May to see exactly what was going on. "I had been getting very negative feedback from London about the picture," Ladd remembered. "And the picture was escalating in cost, so I thought I'd go see for myself."[47] Ladd watched a few days of filming, walked the sets, then huddled with Kurtz and Lucas, hoping for reassurance. Lucas admitted Jympson's footage looked terrible. "I just wish you had never seen this stuff," he told Ladd.[48] "This is *not* what I want," Lucas assured him, "and this is *not* what it's going to look like." Ladd went back to the studio and promised the board that things were fine—but "my real reaction," said Ladd, "was *utter and complete panic.*"[49]

He wasn't alone. As filming continued through May, Lucas—who had managed to stay relatively stable for eight weeks—finally buckled and fell ill, developing a hacking cough and a foot infection so painful he didn't even want to get out of bed. Partly it was the pace. "We worked like stink, twenty hours every day," said production supervisor Robert Watts.[50] As Carrie Fisher remembered, "It was like combat shooting...because we had no time, because there was no budget."[51] Mostly, though, the problem was that no matter how hard Lucas tried, nothing seemed to go right. "I cared about *every* single detail," said Lucas.[52] "It's very hard for me to get into another system where everybody does things for me, and I say, 'Fine.' If I ever continue to do these kinds of movies, I've got to learn to do that."[53] Not surprisingly, when it came time to film the scene in the trash compactor—another sequence Lucas had included in his script since practically day one—his vision had been compromised by the chain of command. The fearsome tentacled monster he had envisioned in his script had been stripped down to resemble nothing so much as "a big wide brown turd."[54]

Still, even Lucas's hectic pace couldn't overcome the endless delays caused by faulty props, malfunctioning robots, and the union-mandated quitting time. By June, Lucas had fallen more than a week behind schedule—and Dykstra and ILM weren't making things any easier, sending over front projection special effects shots that were out of focus, improperly lit, and completely unusable. "ILM was a mess," said Marcia Lucas. "They spent a million dollars, and the FX shots they'd been able to composite were just completely unacceptable, like cardboard cutouts, the matte lines were showing."[55]

And then there was editor John Jympson, who was still cutting each day's footage together into what Lucas thought was a completely unwatchable film. "I don't think he fully understood the movie and what I was trying to do," Lucas said.[56] Finally deciding enough was enough, Lucas dismissed the problematic editor in mid-June, groaning that the firing was "a very frustrating and unhappy experience."[57] The hour's worth of footage Jympson had already assembled would have to be completely recut.

Dykstra and ILM were a different kind of problem. While Lucas had no intention of dismissing Dykstra, it was clearly time to have a heart-to-heart with him and his ILM team. Dykstra arrived in London on June 23 to meet with Kurtz and Lucas at Elstree, with Kurtz doing most of the talking since Lucas, now sicker than ever, had lost his voice. "We sat down with John and went over the optical effects," recalled Kurtz. Because the front projection effects had been unusable, it was decided that Lucas would shoot against a blue screen instead, with the effects shots to be added later. But scrapping even the few front projection shots they had meant starting over—and the clock was ticking, with roughly a year left to finish the effects. "We have 360 shots, that makes one shot a day," Kurtz told Dykstra. "Are we going to finish on time or not?'" Dykstra took only a moment to consider, then hedged his answer. "If things go right," he told Kurtz, "yeah, we can do that."[58]

Back in Hollywood, Ladd was under similar pressure from his fellow board members at Fox, who were steadily losing faith in Lucas and his late, expensive film. Concerns ran the gamut from the serious to the silly—there was hand-wringing over whether Chewbacca should wear pants—but Ladd was continuing to put his own reputation on the line, defending the movie and doing his best to keep executives away from Elstree and off Lucas's back. "There were a lot of problems, yes," said Ladd wearily. "Every board meeting I attended, the subject was always about *Star Wars*....It was rather unpleasant."[59] Still, Ladd did such a good job keeping Fox executives in the dark that when *Los Angeles Times* film critic Charles Champlin traveled to London to write a story on Lucas, he was collared on his return by Fox board members who asked for a full report on what Lucas was up to.

By mid-July, however, with Lucas still fifteen days behind schedule, Ladd could no longer keep his board at bay with noncommittal reassurances. The plans for releasing *Star Wars* in time for Christmas 1976 had already been scrapped, and the board was losing patience. "You've got to finish in the next week," Ladd told Lucas, "because I've got another board meeting and I can't go in there and say we're still shooting."[60] Scrambling to finish, then, Lucas split production between several units, bicycling frantically between soundstages to supervise as much of it as he could. Spielberg, itching to get his hands on *Star Wars*, even offered to oversee one of the second units. "George wouldn't let me," said Spielberg, a refusal he attributed to their increasing personal and professional rivalry. "I was admiring and jealous of his style, his proximity to audiences. But he did not want my fingerprints anywhere around *Star Wars*."[61]

On Friday, July 16, 1976, Lucas completed principal photography. Though he ended up twenty days behind schedule, he was very nearly on budget, thanks to a devaluing of the British pound, which reduced his overages to about $600,000. Fox still grumbled, but Lucas was generally pleased that he'd survived Tunisia and Elstree pretty much on target. "For what it was, *Star Wars* was made very inexpensively," Lucas said later, "a real low budget movie."[62]

Still, that didn't mean he was happy with it. On Saturday morning, Lucas returned to the United States, stopping briefly in New York to see De Palma and then in Alabama to visit Spielberg, who was finishing work on *Close Encounters of the Third Kind*. Spielberg pored over a booklet of black-and-white *Star Wars* stills Lucas had brought with him and "was just amazed," said Spielberg, "but George was so depressed. He didn't like the lighting; he didn't like what his cameraman...had done for him. He was really upset."[63]

After leaving Spielberg, Lucas headed for Los Angeles to check on Dykstra and ILM. His mood would not improve.

Despite the heart-to-heart with Dykstra in June, ILM was still woefully behind schedule. "They'd spent a year and a million dollars and had one shot," recalled Lucas. While that shot—the escape pod ejecting from Leia's ship and spiraling down toward Tatooine—was a good one, Dykstra and his crew were showing no signs of picking up the pace. "Those guys didn't quite understand the critical nature of making a movie," Lucas said later. "You can't be a day late; it just doesn't work. It all fits together into a giant mosaic. All the pieces have to fall together." As Lucas saw it, the pieces were in danger of being lost altogether. "I thought, 'This is it. I really got myself into a mess I'll never get myself out of.'"[64]

He left Los Angeles for northern California in a state of near despondency—and shortly after landing in San Francisco, Lucas suddenly felt sharp pains in his chest. Fearing a heart attack, Marcia checked George into the hospital, where he was diagnosed with hypertension and exhaustion, and was ordered to cut down the stress in his life. "That's when I really confirmed to myself I was going to change, that I wasn't going to make any more films," Lucas said. "I wasn't going to direct anymore. I was going to get my life a little more under control."[65]

But not yet. Lucas had no intention of relinquishing control over this film, even if it killed him. "If I left anything for a day," he feared, "it would fall apart, and it's purely because I set it up that way and there is nothing I can do about it," Lucas said. "It wasn't set up so I could walk away from it. Whenever there is a leak in the dam, I have to stick *my* finger in it."[66]

It was time, then, to stick his finger in the dam. The first order of business was to get ILM to shape up, which meant a change in leadership at the workshop. Dykstra, with his laid-back, collegial style, ran the place like a frat house—"a quasi-hippy mentality," Kurtz called it. The staff was fiercely loyal to Dykstra, but to Lucas, that was part of the problem: he wanted them loyal to *him*, not Dykstra. After all, it was his film, his vision, and his money they were burning through. The best way for Lucas to control production, then, was *literally* to control production. Lucas announced he would personally oversee work at ILM on Mondays and Tuesdays, and brought in George Mather, an experienced production supervisor, to watch over things for the remainder of the week. For the ILMers, it was like bringing the principal into an unruly classroom. "There was a certain amount of resentment at first," said Kurtz. Dykstra considered it "an unnecessary hindrance to my work," but tried to be pragmatic.[67] "George brought in people meant to crack the whip," Dykstra said later. "Whether they felt like they succeeded or not, I don't know. They wanted to go from zero to 60 in 1.2 seconds, and that wasn't in the cards."[68]

Even with Lucas and Mather overseeing things, there were still cost overruns—explosions came in at $65,000 instead of the budgeted

$35,000—but gradually ILM began to fall into a more productive rhythm. "We finally got up to sixteen people in the optical department, working on two shifts, eleven hours a day, six days a week," recalled one ILM artist.[69] Still, there was a reason why ILM had come to be called derisively "The Country Club": staff still kept irregular hours, working mostly at night to make conditions bearable in a building without air-conditioning. During the days, Dykstra would often be found beating the heat by soaking in a large tank filled with cold water, along with as many of ILM's employees as could possibly fit, or leaping onto a water slide made from an airplane escape chute salvaged from the airport across the street. "Our reputation wasn't stellar," admitted Dykstra, "because we were breaking a lot of rules."[70] That wasn't all they were breaking: one afternoon, Lucas and Kurtz pulled into the ILM parking lot just in time to see Dykstra, fumbling with the controls of a forklift, send a refrigerator plunging to the pavement. Lucas got out of the car, stepped around the wreckage, and walked into the warehouse. He never said a word.

ILM's first real task had been to assemble the shots needed for the assault on the Death Star—especially since Fox, citing potential costs of the effects, was pressuring Lucas to remove the sequence from the film altogether. Lucas had explicitly described the sequence through fifty pages of his script, but he was still concerned it wouldn't look the way he envisioned it. "I'm trying to make everything look very natural, a casual almost *I've-seen-this-before* look," he explained. "Like the X-wing and TIE fighter battle, you say, 'I've seen that, it's World War II—but wait a minute—that isn't any kind of jet I've ever seen before.' I want the whole film to have that quality. It's a very hard thing to come by, because it should look very familiar but at the same time not be familiar at all."[71] For guidance, the ILM crew looked to Lucas's reel of dogfight footage to get a better feel for how Lucas expected the ships to move, beyond what was described on the page. "It was hugely helpful," said ILM artist Ken Ralston. "To describe that abstract world of a battle is impossible.... [T]hat [footage] was a great thing."[72]

The footage would also be of enormous use to the editor Lucas had recently installed at Parkhouse to replace Jympson: Marcia Lucas. George hadn't wanted Marcia editing *Star Wars*—and, truth be told, Marcia didn't really want to edit it, either. Not only was she still trying to be seen as more than just an editor of her husband's films, but also, as far as she was concerned, *Star Wars* was beneath George's talents. She wanted him working on more serious, artistic films—the kind Coppola made, for example, and the kind she had edited for Martin Scorsese and Michael Ritchie. For his part, Lucas had wanted Marcia to take some downtime after completing *Taxi Driver,* with the hope they could conceive a child. But the pregnancy never happened, and Lucas, agonizing over a replacement for Jympson—and needing an editor who knew and understood his rhythms as a director—had finally asked for her help.

As Marcia waited for ILM to complete its shots, she would splice in footage of swooping Tomahawk airplanes and tailspinning Messerschmitts between shots of X-wing pilots chattering at one another in their cockpits and Leia monitoring the fight from the base on Yavin— and the moment the effects came in from ILM, she would replace the black-and-white shots with the new footage. More often than not, she had to use every last inch of film ILM had shot, some of which took up no more than a few seconds of screen time. Lucas may have intended to hover over Marcia as he had during *American Graffiti,* but there just wasn't enough time; he had to relinquish the tough work, and control, to her—and ultimately, Lucas had to admit he was impressed. "I think it took her eight weeks to cut that battle," he said later. "It was extremely complex and we had 40,000 feet of dialogue footage of pilots saying this and that. And she had to cull through all that, and put in all the fighting as well."[73]

Lucas would later compare the editing of *Star Wars* to sleight of hand, pointing out that there actually weren't very many ships in a given shot, and noting a lack of continuity between some cuts. But the effects footage was edited together so carefully and seamlessly with the live action shots that the technicalities hardly mattered; the quick cutting of the effects shots is part of what makes the sequences so exciting.

Unlike in *2001*, Lucas's ships wouldn't slowly roll and rumble to a Strauss waltz; they tumbled and whizzed to John Williams's blaring trumpets. Lucas's direction to his actors, *faster and more intense*, would apply to the editing as well: there would be no lingering or loitering; necessity had forced Marcia to cut shots in quickly, letting the entire Death Star sequence throb at a breathtaking pace all its own. Even more remarkably, under Marcia's careful editorial eye, it is always easy to tell what is going on; in several places she made editorial decisions to clarify the story and speed things up even more, such as reducing the number of X-wing pilots seen on-screen to keep the focus on Luke, and paring down the trench run so that Luke made only one attempt to take the fatal shot instead of the two Lucas had specified in his script.

With Marcia immersed in the Death Star sequence, Lucas brought in Richard Chew—his first choice for editor before Fox had imposed Jympson on him—to take apart Jympson's problematic rough cut and start over again. And then, once he'd reassembled the first hour of the film, Chew was to move on to the dogfight that followed the escape from the Death Star. Chew sat down at the editing table at Parkhouse in August; Lucas wanted a rough cut ready to look at by Thanksgiving—but with nearly 340,000 feet of live action film footage to sort through, it was a task that required yet another set of skilled eyes and hands. At the suggestion of Brian De Palma, Lucas hired a third editor, Paul Hirsch, who had edited both *Phantom of the Paradise* and *Carrie* for De Palma. But even his experience cutting those quirky films hadn't prepared him for the gigantic task that was *Star Wars*. "I've never worked on anything this complicated before," Hirsch told Lucas.

"That's all right," Lucas said matter-of-factly. "Nobody has."[74]

Lucas spent most of the autumn of 1976 sprinting back and forth between Parkhouse in San Anselmo and ILM in Los Angeles, trying desperately to keep his finger in the dam. He and Dykstra were butting heads more and more now, even as Mather and Kurtz tried to run interference between the two. Lucas was growing tired of Dykstra's having to explain why certain shots weren't working, while Dykstra, for his part, simply felt he was trying to manage Lucas's expectations. "Directors and special effects directors disagree incredibly," said Dykstra, "because [the director] conceptualizes one thing, but *I* know what is capable of being produced.... It's hard to explain that a concept won't work because of some technological thing, and this becomes a bone of contention."[75] But Lucas wasn't interested in excuses. "I was interested in the shots," he said flatly. "I didn't care how we got the shots; I just wanted the composition and the lighting to be good, and I wanted them to get it done on time."[76] Even the mild-mannered Kurtz began to share Lucas's annoyance. "John [Dykstra] has a tendency to talk everything to death," said Kurtz. "Both George and I were rather frustrated about that. John assembled a lot of talent, but it was never run properly. It was like organized anarchy."[77] But it was also working. On October 11, 1976, Lucas approved the first ILM special effects shot, initialing it with a small cursive *GL*. "They'd spent a year and a million dollars and had one shot—a cannon going *boom, boom, boom*," recalled Lucas. "I said, 'Okay, at least we're on our way.'"[78]

As Lucas had hoped, a rough cut of the film was ready by early November. It was admittedly ragged; most of the special effects shots were missing, sound effects were incomplete, none of the voices had been dubbed—Vader still spoke in Prowse's working-class English accent—and there was no music, but Lucas was ready to start showing it around, anxious to get feedback on the film, especially now that it was finally starting to resemble the version he had seen in his head for so long. "For me, it was a very rewarding thing to show it to people, even though it was in bad shape," said Lucas.[79]

Lucas's first audience was the editing team. He and his three editors watched the movie in the screening room at Parkhouse—and then watched it again and again, talking each scene through and looking for places where things could be cut or improved. Over Marcia's objections, Lucas knocked out an early scene on Tatooine in which Luke discussed the rebellion with several other young friends. Lucas thought it seemed too much like a scene from *American Graffiti*, and structurally, he didn't like the idea of introducing Luke so early in the story—so out it went. The other problematic scene, however—a conversation between Harrison Ford as Han Solo and actor Declan Mulholland, playing Jabba the Hutt—was going to require a little more work to correct.

Lucas had hoped to matte in a stop-motion Jabba over Mulholland, but that was going to take time he didn't have and more money than Fox was willing to provide. The scene could be cut, but Lucas would need some new dialogue to explain Solo's predicament. The solution, then, was to shoot additional cantina footage with Greedo—and, he hoped, insert a few shots featuring new monsters, since he had never been happy with the footage he had shot at Elstree with Freeborn's background creatures. But re-shooting was still going to require going back to Fox for more money—and with the film approaching budget overages of nearly $2 million now, all Ladd could pry out of the studio was a miserly $20,000.

It would have to do. With Freeborn still unavailable, Lucas hired twenty-five-year-old makeup artist Rick Baker and gave him six weeks to build as many creatures as he could. In January, Lucas would spend two days shooting new footage in a studio on La Brea in Hollywood, where Baker had indeed given him an impressive new array of monsters, including the cantina's memorable swing band. But Lucas was still disappointed with the final result. "I really wanted to have horrible, crazy, really staggering monsters," he told *Rolling Stone* later. "I guess we got some, but we didn't come off as well as I had hoped."[80] Audiences loved it—but Lucas would remain unhappy with the scene for nearly twenty years, until evolving digital technology would finally permit him to insert what he considered much more acceptable monsters.

Near Christmas, Marcia left for Los Angeles to work on *New York, New York* after an impassioned phone call from Martin Scorsese, whose editor had died before the movie could be completed. It was a move that irritated Lucas, who still disapproved of Scorsese and his drugs and multiple girlfriends. "For George, the whole thing was that Marcia was going off to this den of iniquity," said Willard Huyck. "George was a family homebody. He couldn't believe the stories that Marcia told him.

George would fume because Marcia was running with these people. She loved being with Marty." Indeed, Marcia could never say no to Scorsese, who made the kinds of films she wished her own husband would make. Paul Hirsch, listening from his editing table to the debate between the Lucases, thought he understood. "Marcia respected Marty above all directors, and didn't believe in *Star Wars* very much," said Hirsch. "It was not her thing."[81] Marcia left for Los Angeles and Scorsese's serious, artistic film, handing her editing duties over to Hirsch. Lucas waved good-bye, his mouth a tight white line.

At the same time he was looking over Hirsch's shoulder, Lucas was also working with Ben Burtt to improve the way the film sounded—always one of Lucas's major concerns. Until Williams could deliver the music, Lucas had cut in a temporary score of classical music, including bits of Holst's *The Planets* and Dvořák's *New World* symphony. Meanwhile, Burtt had set up an office in Parkhouse and had been working over the past year to find a sound for...well, just about everything, since Lucas insisted that every sound heard in the movie had to be created. "When a door slammed, we didn't use the sound of a door slamming on Earth," said Lucas.[82] While Burtt had found just the right sounds for laser blasts and food processors and whirring robot motors, he and Lucas still had to deal with three key voices: R2-D2, C-3PO, and Darth Vader.

For Burtt, Artoo was probably the toughest. "We had to decide his mentality and his personality," said Burtt. "We decided he was intelligent but, emotionally, a five-year-old kid. Frightened but brave."[83] The trick, then, to getting the "organic sound" Lucas wanted was for him and Burtt to record themselves cooing, beeping, and whistling into a tape recorder, which Burtt then ran through a synthesizer, tweaking pitch and speed, until he found just the right voice for any situation. "I knew I had succeeded," recalled Burtt, "because the film editors began to cut to Artoo for a reaction."[84]

When it came to Threepio, the voice Lucas had in mind was that of a slick used-car salesman, with a whiff of the Bronx about him. During filming, however, Anthony Daniels had delivered his lines in the manner of a fussy English butler, which he thought better fit the character. Lucas worried that Daniels's voice was "strongly British....I didn't want that even though everybody else liked it." But after auditioning several voice actors—including Stan Freberg—Lucas had to concede that Daniels's voice "had the most character."[85] It would stay.

Not so the voice of Darth Vader. While Vader's signature breathing had been provided by Burtt recording himself huffing into a scuba mouthpiece, Burtt had no idea how the character's speaking voice would actually sound. Lucas wanted a commanding voice for Vader, and originally considered Orson Welles before deciding he might be too recognizable. Instead, he approached actor James Earl Jones, a 1970 Oscar nominee for *The Great White Hope,* whose voice was a natural and intimidating bass. "He picked a voice that was born in Mississippi, raised in Michigan, and was a stutterer," said Jones.[86] It was also pitch perfect, though Jones asked that his name be kept out of the credits, insisting that he was "just special effects."[87]

In early January 1977, Lucas hosted another showing of the rough cut, this time for composer John Williams. Over the course of two days, Williams would watch the film several times, taking careful notes, and looking for places in the film where he could lay in musical cues. "I came back to my little room and started working on themes," said Williams. "I spent the months of January and February writing the score."[88]

Later that month, Lucas brought in Ladd and several other executives from Fox so they could finally see for themselves the project on which Ladd had been staking his reputation. Gareth Wigan, one of the few Fox executives who had steadfastly backed Ladd and Lucas over the past year, was so moved by the film that he wept with joy in his seat next to Lucas, who could only squirm uncomfortably. "I couldn't believe it," said Lucas. "I thought, 'This is *really* weird.'"[89] But even in the film's primitive state, Wigan knew he had seen something remarkable. Returning home that night, he told his wife, "The most extraordinary day of my life has just taken place."[90]

Still, Wigan's emotional response couldn't prepare Lucas for perhaps his toughest audience of all. In late February, George and Marcia invited to Parkhouse a small group of friends—including Spielberg, De Palma, the Huycks, John Milius, Hal Barwood, and Matthew Robbins—for a look at the most recent cut. "I show them all of my footage, and they give me precious opinions that I count on," Lucas explained later. "When you don't know people well, they either give you dishonest compliments or tell you how they would shoot it. And that's not what you're asking them for."[91] With this group, however, honesty wouldn't be a problem. "The reaction," said Spielberg frankly, "was not a good one."[92]

When the lights went up, Marcia—who hadn't seen the film since the first cut—burst into tears, certain it was a disaster. Huyck muttered that he found the opening crawl "jiggly, and it went on forever."[93] Barwood tried to be supportive, reassuring Lucas that there was still enough time to fix everything if they could shoot some extra footage. De Palma, however, was blistering in his criticism, carping about everything from Leia's hair to Vader's nondramatic entrance in the opening scene. "What's all the Force shit?" De Palma thundered. "Where's the blood when they shoot people?" De Palma would continue to rail at Lucas over dinner at a Chinese restaurant "like a crazed dog," recalled Gloria Katz.[94] "Brian kind of went over the top in terms of his honesty," agreed Spielberg.[95] Still, Lucas refused to back down. "You should talk," Lucas told De Palma snarkily. "None of your films have made a dime."[96] To the surprise of most onlookers, De Palma agreed to help Lucas rewrite and re-shoot the opening crawl.

Still, there was one person in the room who was impressed. "I loved it because I loved the story and the characters," said Spielberg. "I was probably the only one who liked it, and I told George how much I loved it."[97] That evening, Ladd called Spielberg on the sly to ask what he thought about what he'd seen. Spielberg told the executive he thought he had a hit on his hands—one that would eventually make about $50 or $60 million. "Wow, were we wrong!" laughed Spielberg.[98]

On March 5, 1977, Lucas settled into a seat in the control booth at Anvil Studios in the little English village of Denham. He was exhausted; only four days earlier he'd been at Goldwyn Studios in Los Angeles to spend the day recording James Earl Jones's dialogue for Darth Vader, and now he was at Anvil to oversee a week of recording sessions for John Williams's score. On the other side of the soundproof glass, Williams was, for the first time in his career, conducting the London Symphony Orchestra. As the opening moments of the film were projected overhead onto a thirty-four-foot screen and the orchestra erupted into Williams's heroic fanfare, Lucas was visibly moved. "To hear Johnny play the music for the first time was a thrill beyond anything I can describe," said Lucas, who knew he had something special in Williams's score and the immediately recognizable themes he had provided for key characters.[99] "A lot of the emotional content is carried through the music as much as through the scenes themselves," Lucas said.[100]

It was no surprise that Lucas would insist on serving as producer for Williams's recording sessions. As post-production kicked into overdrive during the spring, Lucas was still overseeing as many of the details himself as he possibly could, even acting out each of the holographic monsters that would fight one another on the *Falcon*'s chessboard. Still, he was visiting ILM less and less now, leaving Kurtz to send detailed reports back to Fox even as effects shots continued into April—and Lucas admitted that he "was happy with a lot of the special effects toward the end. The operation got very good."[101] Still, he remained annoyed with the accountants at Fox who had nickel-and-dimed him every step of the way. "The fact is that we didn't have the money, and the key to special effects is time and money," he said angrily. "I had to cut corners like crazy.... The film is about 25 percent of what I wanted it to be."[102] Those cut corners would grate on Lucas for years—part of the reason he would continue tinkering with the film for the next four decades, trying to get the effects to look the way he had always imagined them.

At the end of March, another group of Fox executives—this time the sales team, tasked with booking the film in theaters—filed into the screening room at Parkhouse to watch the latest cut of *Star Wars*. Ladd sat by the phone in his Hollywood office, waiting for bad news.

The call never came. Instead, the sales reps were ecstatic. "Extraordinary," one said succinctly, while another shouted to Ladd over the phone, "I don't believe what I've seen!"[103] And yet the enthusiasm of the sales team still couldn't overcome the skepticism of dubious Fox higher-ups, who remained uncertain that *Star Wars* could compete in an aggressive summer movie market; they were particularly worried about William Friedkin's thriller *Sorcerer*. Hoping to cut its losses, then, Fox had opted to move the release date back from summer to spring—to May 25, the Wednesday before Memorial Day, when it might have a chance to recover some of its costs before being washed away in the deluge of summer films. Lucas later claimed that it was actually *he* who had talked the studio into a May release, arguing that kids would see the movie, then spread the word back at school. Regardless, fewer than forty theaters agreed to show it.

Lucas spent the months and weeks prior to the film's release trying to manage expectations. "Making a movie is a terribly painful experience," he told the *New York Times*—and he swore that with *Star Wars*, he had gotten big-budget films out of his system, never to return, whether the movie succeeded or not. "I'm much more of a filmmaker than a film director," he insisted, drawing what he thought was an important distinction between artist and *auteur*. "So I really want to retire and do a lot of experimental work with film that will probably never be seen by anybody."[104] To the French periodical *Ecran*, he reiterated that he had taken on *Star Wars* simply because "I wanted to know if I could do it.... But now that it's done, there's no need to do it again. I want to go back to more experimental films."[105] It was an empty vow, but one that he would make repeatedly throughout his career, swearing he wanted nothing more than to abandon mainstream filmmaking and return to the kinds of eclectic, arty films he had made as a student.

And yet, even as Lucas downplayed it, the film was gaining a quiet underground momentum. Marcia had once remarked that George knew who his audience was—but so did the man Lucas and Kurtz had tapped as The Star Wars Corporation's vice president of advertising, publicity, promotion, and merchandising: Charles Lippincott. The savvy Lippincott understood that science fiction and comic book fans, even in their respective loosely organized mid-1970s states, were the natural audience for *Star Wars*. "Why not tailor a campaign and build off of that?" Lippincott asked. "Do a novelization and comic book adaptation early."[106] So two years earlier, in November 1975, Lippincott had approached Ballantine Books about publishing a novelization of Lucas's script, ghostwritten by Alan Dean Foster, an up-and-coming science fiction writer who had a knack for TV and film adaptations. Judy-Lynn del Rey, Ballantine's science fiction editor, had seen the potential in *Star Wars* immediately. "I said…we'd make millions, but everybody kept saying, 'Yeah sure, now go away.'"[107] The novel had been released in November 1976, just ahead of the first makeshift movie trailer, and by February 1977 had sold out of its first print run of 125,000, with the movie still three months away.

Lippincott had also worked hard to ink a deal with Marvel Comics for a six-issue comic book adaptation. After being stiff-armed by an uninterested Stan Lee, Lippincott had used Ed Summer, co-owner of Lucas's Supersnipe comic book store, to wangle an introduction to comics writer Roy Thomas in early 1976. With Thomas and artist Howard Chaykin on board, Lippincott went back to the still skeptical Lee to finish the deal. Lee insisted that Marvel wouldn't pay Lucasfilm a cent until the comic had sold at least 100,000 copies—terms Lippincott agreed to, on the condition that at least two issues of the series had to be published *before* the May 25 release date for the film. "I got the deal through and went back to 20th [Century Fox] and they said I was stupid," recalled Lippincott. "They didn't care about the money issue. They just thought I was wasting my time on a comic book deal."[108] Like the novel, the comics, too, would quickly blow through their initial print runs.

Lippincott also relied on fandom to spread the word about the film, hosting one of the first-ever movie-related sessions at the San Diego Comic-Con in July 1976, where he, Thomas, and Chaykin answered questions and sold posters designed by Chaykin. Several weeks later, at Worldcon in Kansas City, Lippincott made an even bigger splash when he put up a display featuring full-sized reproductions of Darth Vader, Threepio, and Artoo, as well as stills, McQuarrie's concept art, and prop blasters and lightsabers. With the aid of Gary Kurtz and the always game Mark Hamill, Lippincott hosted an hour-long slide show presentation that had the entire convention buzzing with excitement.

The next several months saw well-timed articles in several sci-fi and film trade magazines — *American Film, Sight and Sound, Fantascene* — as well as a trailer that revealed just enough of the film's spectacular effects (though Lucas was shocked when audiences laughed at the shot of a Jawa-stunned Artoo falling over) and enigmatic lobby posters that simply blared COMING TO YOUR GALAXY THIS SUMMER in gigantic letters. There were a few mainstream articles, though most got nearly everything wrong. Stormtroopers were referred to as robots. Vader was a Black Knight. Chewbacca was an apeman. It didn't seem to matter much among fandom, who could tell that this movie with the bashed-up spaceships and oily robots didn't look like anything else. By the spring of 1977, enthusiasm for *Star Wars* was like a pot rolling to a slow boil — and the lid was about to blow off.

The premiere of *Star Wars* was held on Sunday, May 1, at San Francisco's Northpoint Theater — the very same theater where *American Graffiti* had made its successful debut four years earlier. Lucas sat with Marcia, on a break from editing *New York, New York,* and braced himself for the worst; he'd warned editor Paul Hirsch that they'd likely have to recut the entire movie. Marcia had given him a good gauge of the film's success: "If the audience doesn't cheer when Han Solo comes in at the last second in the *Millennium Falcon* to help Luke when he's being chased by Vader," she told him, "the picture doesn't work."[109] As the lights went down, Lucas locked eyes momentarily with Alan Ladd, whose reputation was as wrapped up in the film as his own. The picture *had* to work.

Did it ever.

The moment the enormous Star Destroyer rumbled overhead in the film's opening shot, the audience roared with an excitement that thundered louder and louder as the movie continued. McQuarrie remembered lots of "hollering and cheering."[110] And—sure enough— the place exploded with excitement when the *Falcon* came to the rescue in the final reel. At the end of the film, the applause tidal-waved. "It kept going on, it wasn't stopping," said Ladd, "and I just never had experienced that kind of reaction to any movie *ever*. Finally, when it was over, I had to get up and walk outside because of the tears." Outside the theater, Lucas's father was proudly shaking hands with anyone and everyone. "Thank you," he would say, beaming. "Thank you very much for helping out George!"[111] Hirsch sidled up to Lucas as he left the screening, trying to gauge his reaction.

"Well," Lucas told the editor thoughtfully, "I guess we won't have to change anything after all."[112]

Still, Lucas was trying not to get *too* confident. At another showing for Fox executives several days later at the Metro Theater, the response wasn't quite as enthusiastic. Gareth Wigan, the executive who had openly wept at the private showing months earlier, remembered that three execs loved it, three liked it, two fell asleep, and the rest "really didn't get it at all and were very distressed, indeed, very worried about how they were going to get their money back."[113] Ladd could only sit with his head in his hands, insisting, "You should have seen the Northpoint!"[114]

Fox had handpicked the thirty-seven theaters in the markets where *Star Wars* would be opening, most of which were equipped only with monaural sound systems, not stereo. It was an important distinction, because that wasn't the way Lucas wanted *Star Wars* to sound; he wanted the audience to become completely immersed in the film, which meant he wanted the sound track crystal clear, in stereo, with no background hiss—and that meant he wanted the film in Dolby stereo. Film sound tended to become distorted once the movie got into the theater; a film in Dolby would actually sound the way it did as Lucas was mixing it.

Unfortunately, there weren't a lot of theaters in 1977 equipped to show films with Dolby stereo sound tracks — and those that were often had problems with speakers blowing. Lucas insisted: he wanted the film in stereo and he wanted it sounding great — at least in those theaters equipped for Dolby — and so he had overseen the stereo mix himself in April. Now in May, he was personally editing the mono mix as well, working all night at Goldwyn Studios in Hollywood — the same studio, in fact, where Marcia was working all day finishing edits for *New York, New York.*

Early on the afternoon of Wednesday, May 25, Lucas emerged bleary-eyed from yet another all-night work session at Goldwyn. As he was leaving, Marcia was just arriving, and the two of them decided to have a late lunch together, heading for the Hamburger Hamlet on Hollywood Boulevard, just across from Grauman's Chinese Theatre. From their table in the back, he and Marcia could see out the front window onto the street, which was becoming more and more crowded with people. "It was like a mob scene," Lucas recalled. "One lane of traffic was blocked off. There were police there.... There were lines, eight or nine people wide, going both ways around the block."[115] He and Marcia finished their lunch, then stepped out into the street to see what all the fuss was about. "I thought someone must be premiering a movie," Lucas said later.[116]

Someone was. Emblazoned in huge letters on the marquee on both sides of the entrance above the loud, teeming crowd were two words:

STAR WARS

8

Striking Back

1977–1979

The telephone rang back in the studio at Goldwyn, where Lucas and several sound engineers were still assembling the mono cut of *Star Wars*. It was Ladd calling with good news; *Star Wars* was selling out at each of the thirty-two theaters in which it was playing, and lines were snaking around the block even for the approaching midnight shows. As Ladd read through the numbers, Lucas held his hand over the mouthpiece and repeated them back to the engineers. The engineers were stunned—here they were, putting the final touches on a certified blockbuster!—but Lucas was having none of it; while he had seen the crowds mobbing the entrance at Grauman's only a few hours earlier, he wasn't convinced he had a hit on his hands. "I felt like it was some kind of aberration," he said later, and warned Ladd that science fiction movies tended to perform strongly in their opening days before dropping off sharply.[1] "It doesn't mean anything," he told Ladd. "I don't want to count my chickens before they're hatched....I expect it all to fall apart next week."[2]

It didn't. And it never would.

At the Avco Center Cinema in Los Angeles, lines began forming before 8 a.m., with many patrons queuing up with their morning coffee still in their hands. All one thousand seats were sold out for all seven shows, including one that started well after midnight. Another five thousand couldn't get tickets at all. "I have never seen anything like this," said the theater manager, who begged for additional help in the newspaper. "This isn't a snowball, it's an avalanche."[3] In Washington, D.C., lines at the Uptown Theater wound into surrounding neighborhoods, angering residents who found the air thick with pot smoke and their yards strewn with beer cans. ("It's an invasion!" howled one neighbor.)[4] In San Francisco, a frustrated gas station owner locked his bathrooms to keep them from being overrun by moviegoers, while a nearby tavern created a "Star Wars Special" for those who grew tired of waiting in line and opted for the bar instead.[5] At Grauman's — where the limos Lucas had seen were dropping off Hugh Hefner and an entourage of Playboy Bunnies, all of whom sat through several showings of the film — the staff barely had time to sweep away the enormous piles of empty cups and popcorn boxes between shows. "We expected it to be big," said one manager incredulously, "but nobody knew it would do this much business."[6]

It was a sentiment echoed by Lucas, who took it all in with stunned disbelief. "I had no idea of what was going to happen," Lucas said later. "I mean, I had *no idea*."[7] Gary Kurtz, too, knew that he and Lucas had something special on their hands when he was doing radio promotion on opening day and callers told him they had already seen the movie several times. "We had hoped and expected the picture would be popular. But we thought it would take a while," Kurtz told one reporter. "We didn't expect this."[8]

Multiple viewings and long waits in line quickly became part of the overall *Star Wars* experience, the great unifier, regardless of status; even celebrity senator Ted Kennedy waited in line, just like everyone else. (President Carter, however, was permitted a private screening at Camp David.) "Our research has found that in each market when people stand in line, they seem to enjoy the film more," gloated one Fox executive,[9] though humorist Erma Bombeck joked that the wait at her local theater had been so long that one young girl had to pay the adult admission by the time she reached the front of the line.[10] Fans bragged about how many times they'd seen the movie, quoting dialogue to one another as they stood in line for the fifth, tenth, twentieth time. By fall, one theater estimated that 80 percent of its *Star Wars* audience was made up of repeat viewers. To keep up with demand, some theaters ran the movie nearly nonstop for weeks, eventually wearing out the film. Fox was happy to replace any worn-out prints for $700.[11]

Critical enthusiasm, too, was immediate and practically infectious. "*Star Wars* is a magnificent film," proclaimed *Variety* on opening day.[12] *Los Angeles Times* critic Charles Champlin, who had visited Lucas during the making of the film a year earlier, was positively effusive, calling it "the year's most razzle-dazzling family movie." To Lucas's likely delight, Champlin even took a shot at the studio mentality, noting that *Star Wars* proved "there is no corporate substitute for the creative passion of the individual filmmaker."[13] A *Time* magazine cover hailed *Star Wars* as "The Year's Best Movie" in its first week, while inside the magazine, critic Jay Cocks — another Lucas fan — praised the film as "a remarkable confection: A subliminal history of the movies, wrapped in a riveting tale of suspense and adventure, ornamented with some of the most ingenious effects ever contrived for film."[14]

Accolades from Champlin and Cocks might be expected; these were Lucas groupies after all. But it quickly became clear that Lucas had run the table with *Star Wars,* winning over one critic after another. Gary Arnold in the *Washington Post* clearly picked up on Lucas's nod to his source materials, calling *Star Wars* a "witty and exhilarating synthesis of themes and clichés from the *Flash Gordon* and *Buck Rogers* comics and serials" and acknowledging that Lucas was in "superlative command of his own movie-nurtured fantasy life."[15] Meanwhile, although Vincent Canby, the much-feared reviewer for the *New York Times,* found *Star Wars* devoid of any real depth, he applauded it for being "fun and funny."[16] Gene Siskel, writing in the *Chicago Tribune,* tried to sound crotchety, grousing that Vader looked like "a black vinyl-coated frog," but admitted that he had been taken in by Lucas's zap-bang sensibility. "It simply is a fun picture," wrote Siskel. "What places it a sizable cut above the routine is its spectacular visual effects."[17]

Still, there were a few dissenters, mostly critics who sensed that Lucas had created something brand-new—the kind of pure cinematic fun that many would later call "a popcorn flick"—and weren't quite sure what to make of it. A reviewer at United Press International said he had watched "in desperate boredom, not caring a mite what happened to any of the two dimensional characters," and lamented that Lucas's film was "a $9.5 million star trek that amounts to naught."[18] Most negative reviews, however, accused Lucas of dumbing down film and pandering to the lowest common denominator. Joy Gould Boyum in the *Wall Street Journal* lamented that it was "depressing" that Lucas had wasted his time, money, and special effects wizardry "on such puerile materials"—a criticism that must have stung, as Marcia had leveled a similar complaint at her husband, urging him to make deeper, artier films.[19] Meanwhile, over in the pages of the *New York Post*, journalist Pete Hamill called *Star Wars* "the truest indication that we have moved into another Era of Wonderful Nonsense," though he conceded that while *Star Wars* was "a Big Dumb Flick," it was at least "a good one."[20]

Other critics suggested that Lucas's movie was as simple as black and white—and not in a good way. "The blockbuster, bestselling movie *Star Wars* is one of the most racist movies ever produced," wrote Walter Bremond under the headline "*Star Wars* and Blacks" in the African American newspaper *New Journal and Guide*. "The force of evil in *Star Wars* is dressed in all black and has the voice of a black man.... That character reinforces the old stereotype that black is evil."[21] Another black journalist pointed out that the two droids acted, and were treated, like slaves, all the way down to being sold to a young white man they called "Master."[22] Actor Raymond St. Jacques was particularly blistering in his condemnation. "The terrifying realization," said St. Jacques, "[is] that black people...shall not exist in the galactic space empires of the future."[23]

Lucas was flummoxed—and slightly hurt—by the accusations, especially since he had very nearly cast a black actor as Han Solo. Charles Lippincott rushed to his employer's defense in the press. "We have barely dug into this galaxy and what it's like," he told the *Washington Post*.[24] As the debate spilled over onto letters pages across the country, *Star Wars* fans rushed to its defense, pointing out in the *Los Angeles Times* that there were plenty of species living in harmony in Lucas's universe.[25]

Elsewhere, when *Star Wars* wasn't being picked apart for racism, it was being pored over for allegory or religious overtones. One columnist attributed the film's success to its channeling of the Bible, with Obi-Wan as the savior whose disciples become more powerful after his death.[26] Kurtz, with typical Zen calm, cautioned against reading too much of any particular theology into the movie. "The whole point is that almost anyone can see certain elements that fit into their lives," he told the *Los Angeles Times*.[27] Columnist Ellen Goodman struck perhaps closer to the mark when she read into *Star Wars* Lucas's own views of humanity wrestling with machines and technology—a theme Lucas had been exploring since Peter Brock wrestled with his sports car in *1:42:08*. "We want a computer age with room for feelings. We want machines, but not the kind that run us," wrote Goodman. "We want technology, but we want to be in charge of it."[28] Still others picked up on Lucas's Vietnam allegory, though Lucas, wary of politics, publicly disavowed any and all sociopolitical theories and quashed speculation on the deeper meaning of his film.

For Lucas, it was enough that *Star Wars* could be merely entertaining—and entirely the point. Only a year or so earlier, moviegoers had flocked to films like *Taxi Driver, All the President's Men, Network,* and *The Enforcer*—movies that embraced antiheroes and reinforced American filmgoers' increasing disillusionment with the media, law, and politics. Lucas found such world-weariness depressing; he worried about its effect on a generation raised in the shadow of Watergate and Vietnam, and weaned on movies about criminals and conspiracies. *Star Wars,* then, was his response to cynicism, a shot of optimism in the arm of the American psyche. "It's fun—that's the word for this movie," Lucas explained. "It's for young people.... Young people don't have a fantasy life any more.... All they've got is Kojak and Dirty Harry. There's all these kids running around wanting to be killer cops because the films they see are movies of disasters and insecurity and realistic violence."[29]

With *Star Wars,* Lucas offered no moral ambiguity; in his universe, there was little doubt who were the good guys and who were the bad guys. Lucas liked it that way—and so did audiences. The happy ending of *Star Wars,* noted *Time,* was "a rarity these days," and even Gene Siskel was inclined to agree that the film's success had sent a clear message: Americans were ready to have fun at the movies again. "Give us old-fashioned, escapist movies with upbeat endings," wrote Siskel.[30] A critic at the *Boston Globe* would put it even more concisely: "Go—and enjoy."[31]

George Lucas was gone.

By the time Lucas completed the *Star Wars* mono mix in the early morning of Thursday, May 26, his film had been out only a little more than twenty-four hours. Already it had broken attendance records in every theater in which it was playing, and set the record for the highest-ever midweek opening by any film.[32] By afternoon, the phones would be ringing off the hook at Parkhouse with reporters trying to reach Lucas for comment. They wouldn't get one. "I left for Hawaii," recalled Lucas. "I was done."[33]

Lucas had headed for the islands with Marcia, to get away from the crowds and the critics and the chatter about *Star Wars*—or so he hoped. But even in Hawaii *Star Wars* was impossible to avoid: Walter Cronkite, whose newscast Lucas had watched every evening while slaving over the early drafts of *The Adventures of Luke Starkiller,* mentioned the long lines on the evening news. Lucas raised his eyebrows. "Well, this is pretty weird."[34] Several hours later, Johnny Carson joked about the lines in his *Tonight Show* monologue. And then there was Ladd, who kept the phone in Lucas's room at the Mauna Kea Hotel ringing regularly with updates on the numbers. "Brace yourself," he would tell Lucas—and then read off the figures from yet another record-breaking day.

It wasn't until the weekend that Lucas would permit himself to believe his own press. Steven Spielberg, with girlfriend Amy Irving in tow, joined George and Marcia in Hawaii and found Lucas "in a state of euphoria."[35] At last Lucas could begin to relax, confident that he had a hit on his hands that would last longer than the weekend. In fact, the accountants at Fox were already predicting that, on its current trajectory, *Star Wars* would likely overtake *Jaws* as the highest-grossing movie of all time. Almost as if he were sizing up his competition, it was perhaps little wonder, then, that as the two of them lolled on the beach and began scooping and packing sand to form a castle, Lucas casually asked Spielberg, "What do you want to do next?"[36]

Spielberg, who had only just wrapped *Close Encounters of the Third Kind*, didn't even blink; he'd had his eye on James Bond for years. United Artists, however, which owned the Bond franchise, had politely but firmly refused to hand over the suave spy. And then, recalled Spielberg, "George said he had a film that was even better than a James Bond."[37]

Lucas began describing the character he'd come up with in the midst of slogging through the script for *Star Wars:* a dashing and wily college archaeology professor and part-time treasure hunter named Indiana Smith. Lucas had actually tried to get Indiana Smith off the ground in 1974 by handing him off to arty filmmaker Philip Kaufman, prowling for a project after completing *The White Dawn*. Lucas had enthusiastically described the character to Kaufman but admitted he didn't know what sort of treasure Indiana would be searching for. Kaufman told Lucas a story he'd heard from his dentist back in Chicago, all about the Lost Ark of the Covenant—and Kaufman and Lucas began kicking the idea around until Kaufman suddenly left, hired away by Clint Eastwood to direct *The Outlaw Josey Wales*.[38] But thanks to Kaufman, Lucas now had both his MacGuffin and his title: *Raiders of the Lost Ark*.

As Lucas explained the project to Spielberg, he also mentioned that the adventures of Indiana Smith, like *Star Wars*, would be a nod to the old weekly movie serials—particularly *Don Winslow of the Navy*—and that he envisioned Smith as wearing a fedora and carrying a bullwhip, looking something like Humphrey Bogart's grizzled gold digger in *Treasure of the Sierra Madre*. Spielberg, who spoke the same filmic language as Lucas, saw the possibilities immediately and was "completely hooked."

"Are you interested?" Lucas asked.

"I want to direct it," said Spielberg.

That was fine with Lucas. Directing *Star Wars* had been exhausting and not very much fun. Better, then, to serve as a producer—which really *would* give him a great deal of control—and turn the day-to-day drudgery of directing over to someone else.

"It's yours," Lucas said.[39]

But not yet. Lucas and Spielberg headed back to the mainland, going their separate ways—Spielberg to begin work on the wartime comedy *1941* and Lucas to prepare the sequel to *Star Wars*. Publicly, however, Lucas gave the impression of a man taking his time. "I can enjoy the success of the film, a nice office to work in, and restoring my house, going on vacations," he told one reporter. "I've decided to set a year or so aside to enjoy those distractions. Plus, I'm setting up a company and getting the sequels off on the right track."[40] Even Marcia seemed to believe that her husband was at last ready to begin a new phase in their lives, with a priority other than George's movies driving the agenda: "Getting our private life together and having a baby," she told *People* magazine. "That is the project for the rest of this year."[41]

Except it wasn't. Lucas, despite his sensitive words, was already focused elsewhere. Embedded in his contract for *Star Wars* was a ticking clock—a clause stipulating that if Lucas didn't have his sequel under way within two years, the rights would revert to Fox for the studio to do as it pleased. For a moment, Lucas considered letting them take over. "At first I was contemplating selling the whole thing to Fox to do whatever they wanted with it. I'd just take my percentage and go home and never think about *Star Wars* again," Lucas told an interviewer in 1979. But he'd also seen Spielberg decline the opportunity to involve himself in the sequel to *Jaws*—the project was proceeding without him in the summer of 1977—and Lucas blanched at the idea of anyone other than himself controlling the *Star Wars* sequels. "The truth of it is, I got captivated by the thing," said Lucas. "It's in me now."[42] So Lucas was going to make his sequel. Starting a family would have to wait. Again.

Lucas was going to do the next movie his way, on his terms. "I expected more out of *Star Wars* than was humanly possible," Lucas lamented. "I had this dream, and it's only a shadow of [that] dream."[43] For the sequel, then, he would try to realize as much of his dream as possible—and that meant *controlling* as much of it as possible, starting with perhaps the most vital component in filmmaking: the funding. While *Star Wars* was setting records and making lots of money, it galled Lucas that Fox got to pocket 60 percent of the profits for doing what he saw as absolutely nothing. In fact, *Star Wars* made Fox so much money so quickly that its stock became one of the most actively traded on Wall Street, doubling in value, and making Fox—and CEO Dennis Stanfill—a force to be reckoned with.

The last thing Lucas wanted to do was line the pockets of executives and make studios even *more* powerful. He remained as contemptuous as ever of studios and the studio mentality. "They're rather sleazy, unscrupulous people," he groused to *Rolling Stone* about studio execs. "They don't care about people. It is incredible the way they treat filmmakers, because they have no idea what making a movie is about."[44] As he began negotiations with Ladd that summer, Lucas made it clear that he intended to hold on to as much of his own film as possible—after all, he told Ladd, he was the one doing all the work. "I had fifty percent [*sic*] of the net profits because my company was going out and making the movie," Lucas explained forty years later, still bristling at the memory of his negotiations with Fox. "And I said, 'I know what I'm doing for my fifty percent. I put my heart and soul in this, my whole career is at stake, I have to actually go out and make the movie....What are you doing for your fifty percent?' [Alan Ladd] said, 'Well, I provide the money.' I said, 'You don't provide the money! You go to a bank with a letter of credit and they supply the money, so you're not doing anything! And you get fifty percent of the movie!'"[45]

Willard Huyck had heard Lucas make similar complaints in the past. "What was upsetting him was the fact that he felt he should be getting more of the movie," said Huyck. "George looked at it like a businessman, saying, 'Wait a minute. The studios borrowed money, took a 35 percent distribution fee off the top....This is crazy. Why don't we borrow the money ourselves?' So some of the bravest and/or [most] reckless acts were not aesthetic, but financial."[46]

For the sequel, then, Lucas matter-of-factly informed Ladd that he would be financing the film himself, using his profits from *Star Wars* as collateral for a bank loan, while Fox would be tasked with distribution. "It changed the whole nature of the deal—nobody had expected that," said Lucas,[47] noting with some glee that "when the tables got turned and the same system worked against them, they felt betrayed and cheated."[48] Fox also agreed to give Lucas final cut, promised not to meddle with production, and handed over all merchandising and television rights. With this hands-off approach, the studio would receive a decreasing share of the profits as the film made more money, eventually bottoming out at a 22.5 percent share to Lucasfilm's whopping 77.5 percent.

Ladd really had little choice. There were plenty of other studios that would have taken a similar deal or worse to get their hands on *Star Wars;* at least it would still be the 20th Century Fox logo that was seen before the opening credits. Spielberg wasn't at all surprised by Lucas's hardball tactics. "If you're an executive, suddenly you realize that if you're going to go into business with George Lucas, you are no longer in the 20th Century-Fox business, you are in the George Lucas business," said Spielberg, "and George is going to call every shot."[49]

Lucas had hit Fox hard, but only because—in his view—the studio had played little role in making *Star Wars* a success. To those whose contributions he valued, however, Lucas could be a most gracious benefactor. As they had done with the profits from *American Graffiti*, both Lucas and Kurtz shared much of their percentage with collaborators, doling out points—and pieces of points—to the Huycks, John Williams, Ben Burtt, the law firm of Pollock, Rigrod, and Bloom, casting director Fred Roos, and the actors. "I got a quarter of a percentage of 'Star Wars,'" Mark Hamill excitedly told the *Chicago Tribune*. "I'll make a pile of money on that picture."[50] Hamill wouldn't be the only one; Steven Spielberg, too, would win a piece of *Star Wars*, the result of an impromptu bet with Lucas over which film—*Close Encounters* or *Star Wars*—would be more successful. "[George] said, 'All right, I'll tell you what. I'll trade some points with you.... I'll give you 2.5% of *Star Wars* if you give me 2.5% of *Close Encounters*,'" recalled Spielberg. "So I said, 'Sure, I'll gamble with that. Great.'"[51] It was a good bet, one that would earn Spielberg more than $40 million over the next four decades.

That fall, Lucas set up a new organization, The Chapter II Company, to oversee production and funding of the still unnamed sequel. That would take care of the administrative side of things for Lucasfilm; but there was still the matter of ILM, which had been all but dissolved after finishing work on *Star Wars*. Lucas was determined to reboot the company, but this time he wanted his effects wizards in northern California, closer to his home base at Parkhouse. "Moving the effects back north really came out of the Zoetrope idea," Lucas explained, "which was we'd make our own movies with the support of our own facilities. And if we had the best facilities, we could make better movies and we'd pay it off with the movies. It's the philosophy I'm trying to continue."[52] What Lucas didn't have to say was that having ILM up north also made it easier for him to involve himself in production. During work on *Star Wars*, he'd left ILM on its own in Los Angeles, where— in his view—Dykstra had dawdled and delayed and burned through too much of the budget developing a camera with his own name on it. Lucas wasn't going to let that happen again.

For one thing, he wouldn't be bringing Dykstra north. While the official story would be that Dykstra had declined to join ILM so he could remain behind and set up his own company, the truth was "I wasn't invited," as Dykstra put it plainly.[53] Things had become personal between Lucas and Dykstra. While Lucas had distributed a few percentage points and gifts to some key staff at ILM, Dykstra wasn't one of them: Lucas saw him merely as work for hire, not a team player. Furious, and in need of a job, Dykstra formed his own company and rented ILM's equipment to begin producing effects for the ABC television show *Battlestar Galactica*. It was a deliberate thumb in the eye to Lucas, who had already accused *Galactica* creator Glen Larson of ripping off *Star Wars*, a squabble that would continue until practically the moment of the show's premiere, and with good reason: when the show debuted, critics noted that Dykstra's effects for *Galactica* looked strikingly similar to, and sometimes better than, those in *Star Wars*. "Maybe I feel guilty about that," Dykstra remarked coyly.[54]

Instead of Dykstra, Lucas tapped ILM workhorse Dennis Muren, along with Brian Johnson, a veteran of *Space: 1999*, to lead the effects team. Lucas was particularly pleased to pick up Johnson, who had a reputation for working quickly and cheaply. If *faster and more intense* had been Lucas's mantra-like direction for his actors on *Star Wars*, for its sequel the buzzwords would be *cheaper and quicker*. And to house the company, Lucas purchased a warehouse on Kerner Boulevard in San Rafael, formerly owned by Kerner Optical, less than six miles from his own home in San Anselmo — close enough for him to drop in unannounced at any time of day. Lucas also left the Kerner Optical signs on the door to throw off prying eyes and snooping fans; several models from *Star Wars* had been stolen from the ILM warehouse in Los Angeles, and eager fans were already pawing through the trash behind the building, looking for discarded bits of TIE fighters. Ensconced in their unmarked building in San Rafael, Muren and Johnson would slowly begin setting up the new workshop and hiring staff for a film that didn't yet exist, not even on paper.

Keeping ILM running — especially once production began on the sequel — was going to be expensive, and profits from the movie alone weren't going to be enough. As it turned out, Lucas would finance the sequel one action figure at a time, tapping into not only the substantial profits from the films themselves but also the revenues from an almost endless stream of *Star Wars* merchandise. Lucas had envisioned *Star Wars* merchandise of some sort almost from the very beginning, imagining R2-D2 cookie jars, wind-up toys, and zap guns. "I have a particular affection for games and toys; there's no doubting that I haven't grown up," he told the French magazine *Ecran* in 1977. "All of this was part of the film, the intention of launching toys in supermarkets, creating books and stuff."[55] But even he had no inkling of the juggernaut he was creating; stock prices for toymakers Mattel and Ideal spiked on the mere rumor that the companies might acquire the rights for *Star Wars* toys.

When approached by Lippincott, neither Mattel nor Ideal had expressed sufficient interest in making *Star Wars* toys. Film-based toys, so the common thinking went, had a limited shelf life, with sales sputtering out shortly after the film faded from theater screens. But Bernard Loomis, the head of Kenner, had struck gold with toys based on the *Six Million Dollar Man* television show; the bionic man's accessories and enemies lent themselves well to what Loomis called a "toyetic" quality—and he thought he detected a similar quality in *Star Wars*. Loomis contacted the head of Fox licensing and quickly closed the deal in a May meeting at the Century Plaza Hotel in Los Angeles. (The company's press release cheekily announced that the agreement was good "galaxywide.")[56] The deal, recalled Loomis, had been made on one condition imposed by Lucas himself in a fit of competitive pique: if Kenner made the toys for *Star Wars*, it couldn't also make them for *Close Encounters of the Third Kind*, or any other science fiction film. "When someone tells me I can't have something," said Loomis, "I want to know why." Shortly after signing the contract in Los Angeles, Loomis met Spielberg on the Columbia lot to learn more about the film he had just been denied rights to. Spielberg enthusiastically described *Close Encounters*, and Loomis admitted that while it sounded like a great movie, it didn't seem *toyetic*.

"Well," sighed Spielberg, "it's not *Star Wars*."[57]

It wasn't. *Nothing* was—and Kenner would quickly find itself trying to meet a tidal wave of demands for toys. Although Kenner had secured its licensing contract in May, it had had time to release only a few items, mainly puzzles and board games, by summer. The *real* toys—the action figures and vehicles—were rushed into development but, to the disappointment of Loomis and millions of kids, wouldn't be ready in time for Christmas 1977. Scrambling, Kenner announced an "Early Bird Certificate Package" (the "infamous empty box campaign," Kurtz called it) in which parents could pay $14 for an envelope with a cardboard display stand, a few stickers, and a certificate that could be mailed in to reserve the first four action figures—Luke, Leia, Artoo, and Chewbacca—which would be delivered to your doorstep the moment they were released. Kenner introduced the package at a fall 1977 toy show and sold out almost immediately, but competitors and retailers openly mocked and guffawed. "We sell toys, not promises," sniffed one retailer, who refused to sell the Early Bird kit,[58] while another insisted that "children don't really care whether they get an officially licensed product or not. A robot is a robot."[59] But Loomis was patient—"Kids will want the real 'Star Wars' item," he contended, "even if they have to wait"—and he was right.[60] Kenner would sell 40 million *Star Wars* figures in 1978.

Another major licensee, Image Factory, had also seen the potential in *Star Wars* early and offered Lucas $100,000 up front for the exclusive rights to market posters, buttons, and iron-on decals. It was an offer that shocked even the profit-conscious Lippincott. "We figured they either really knew what they were doing or they were crazy," said Lippincott.[61] Until *Star Wars*, Image Factory had manufactured belt buckles for record companies, and T-shirts featuring rock bands, pulling respectable but not lofty numbers. By the end of the year, Image Factory's poster of a lightsaber-wielding Darth Vader would outsell posters of a red-swimsuit-clad Farrah Fawcett-Majors—returning to the company nearly $750,000 on its $100,000 investment.

"*Star Wars* could be a type of *Davy Crockett* phenomenon," Lucas suggested, referring to the 1950s television show that had started a marketing fad. "I don't know whether I've done it. I don't know."[62] But he had, and where the Crockett craze had had its coonskin hats, *Star Wars* had...well, everything. There were Halloween costumes, lunch boxes, and bubble gum cards. Coca-Cola would market plastic *Star Wars* cups. Burger Chef would sell posters. A twenty-page souvenir program sold 300,000 copies. The double-LP sound track of Williams's music sold more than 650,000 copies by mid-July—one of the first, and in some cases only, albums of symphonic music many people would own. Meanwhile, a trombonist turned record producer who called himself Meco would release a disco remix of Williams's main theme that would sell 2 million copies and sit atop the Billboard charts for two weeks. Ken Films released an eight-minute Super 8 version of the film while the movie was still in the theaters, a practice unheard of at the time. Marvel Comics, rescued from its own perilous financial situation by the success of *Star Wars* comics, would continue to create new *Star Wars* stories over the next decade, spanning 107 issues. And Lucas would finally have his R2-D2 cookie jar.[63]

Not that Lucas would license just anything. That summer he had set up within Lucasfilm yet another company—this one called Black Falcon, a name borrowed from the *Blackhawk* serials—to oversee all merchandising. It was the only way, he explained, "to control things. I didn't want the market flooded with junk....If it bore the *Star Wars* name, it had to meet our standards."[64] That Lucas would ever reject a licensing offer—he turned down junk jewelry and toilet seat covers—stunned the marketing division at Fox, which had rarely seen a deal it didn't like. But Lucas didn't care what Fox thought, and he was irritated by the fact that the studio automatically received half of all merchandising profits for doing nothing but administering the contracts. In his contract for the sequel, then, Lucas made it clear that he would continue to split the merchandising profits evenly with Fox only until July 1, 1978, at which point Black Falcon would receive 80 percent to Fox's 20. It was yet another lopsided contract clause that Ladd had agreed to in order to keep Lucas and *Star Wars* on the Fox reservation, but Fox executives were growing increasingly weary with Ladd and what they saw as his inclination to give Lucas nearly everything he wanted.

But what Ladd appreciated, and Fox didn't—at least not yet—was that Lucas had given the studio more than just a successful movie; he had created a modern mythology that was quickly embedding itself in American popular culture—and Fox's logo, with its distinctive fanfare, was at the head of it. In August, Threepio, Artoo, and Darth Vader would place their feet in the concrete in front of Grauman's, where *Star Wars* was still showing. In the fall, the Los Angeles Philharmonic performed a concert of *Star Wars* music at the Hollywood Bowl. Critics held their noses, but audiences went wild for it, prompting a repeat performance the next spring. John Milius, with his typical clarity, thought he understood why *Star Wars* had struck such a nerve with audiences. "What my generation has done is bring back a certain innocence," explained Milius. "It's easy to be cynical. It's hard to be corny."[65]

But Milius also understood that innocence had consequences, and that Lucas had changed the very landscape of cinema with his accessible, *toyetic,* lightweight fun—and not necessarily for the better. In June 1977, George and Marcia had traveled to New York for the premiere of Scorsese's *New York, New York,* the kind of serious, arty film that Marcia had continued to hold up to her husband as the brass ring of filmmaking. But Scorsese's film tanked badly, barely breaking even, a flop that sent its director spiraling into drugs and depression. "*Star Wars* was in.... We were finished," said Scorsese bitterly. "*Star Wars* swept all the chips off the table," agreed director William Friedkin, who had seen his own arty entry for 1977, *Sorcerer,* booted from Grauman's in favor of Lucas's space opera. "What happened with *Star Wars* was like when McDonald's got a foothold; the taste for good food just disappeared."[66]

Perhaps there was the "dumbing down" of movies that Canby had bemoaned, or the "infantilization" of film that critic Pauline Kael had condemned in the pages of *The New Yorker*—but that wasn't necessarily all Lucas's fault. True, *Star Wars* had been the biggest film of 1977, but the second-highest-grossing film that year was the Burt Reynolds car chase romp *Smokey and the Bandit.* "Popcorn pictures have always ruled," Lucas said later. "Why do people go see these popcorn pictures when they're not good? Why is the public so stupid?" he asked rhetorically. "That's not my fault. I just understand what people liked to see."[67]

And it wasn't just American audiences that liked seeing *Star Wars;* its timeless themes, straightforward story, and breathtaking special effects played just as well to foreign audiences. Excitement over the film was running high in the weeks leading up to its December release in England; the Super 8 version of the film sold out in two days, merchandise was selling strongly, and fans in nearly every British town called their local cinemas, asking, begging them to show the film. "We've never seen anything quite like it," said one theater manager.[68] When the film opened internationally at the end of the year, it immediately set attendance records in Geneva, Sydney, and Melbourne, and sold out regularly in Rome and Milan. The film was very briefly prohibited for children in Brussels—largely because of the lopped-off arm—then reclassified as "for all" when the appropriate edit was made.[69] It was even shown at the U.S. embassy in Moscow, to an audience composed of Americans, a few Britons, and a smattering of Russians. Perhaps sensing a Cold War metaphor, several audience members hissed at the destruction of the peaceful Alderaan by the Imperial Death Star. "What a wretched trick!" muttered one viewer diplomatically.[70]

To no one's surprise, in December 1977, *Star Wars* officially became the highest-grossing film of all time, earning $120 million in revenues for Fox, and leapfrogging over *Jaws*—with $115 million in revenues for Universal—for the top position. Spielberg took it all in good-natured stride and publicly bowed to Lucas with a full-page ad in *Variety,* showing Artoo snagging a shark with a fishing pole. "Congratulations to the Cantina crowd," wrote Spielberg, "and all the forces of your imagination that made 'Star Wars' so worthy of the throne. Wear it well."[71]

"*Star Wars* is about 25% of what I wanted it to be," Lucas told *Rolling Stone* in the fall of 1977. "I think the sequels will be much, much better."[72] Kurtz, too, made it clear that he didn't want to do a sequel unless it was at least as good as the first film. The story, then, would be critical. As early as June 1977, Lucas and Kurtz casually mentioned to the *Chicago Tribune* that they were already developing a "sequel novel"—actually Alan Dean Foster's Luke-and-Leia novel *Splinter of the Mind's Eye*—"and if the story works out," said Kurtz, "we're seriously considering doing a second picture."[73] By July, Ladd—who had read through multiple drafts and pitches for *Star Wars* over the previous four years—was assuring the *Wall Street Journal* that Lucas had plenty of material on hand to write a second film.[74]

He didn't. What he *did* have, however, were plenty of ideas, which he'd typed up into a nine-page sequel treatment he had titled *The Empire Strikes Back*. It was more sophisticated than his messy first treatment for *Star Wars*, largely because Lucas had recently read Joseph Campbell's book on comparative mythology *The Hero with a Thousand Faces* and was determined to trace Luke's heroic journey more deliberately. "Intimate that a rewarding, good life is within one's reach despite adversity," Lucas jotted in his notes, "but only if one does not shy away from the hazardous struggles without which one can never achieve true identity."[75] Much of the basic structure for what would eventually become *Empire* was in place in the first treatment, and Lucas had several scenes in mind that would survive all the way through to the final draft. There would be a gambler from Han's past who would invite Han, Leia, and Chewie to dinner, "and they come into the room and there is Vader."[76] He knew Luke would study the Force under an old Jedi master, have a long fight with Vader, and end up hanging off the bottom of a city in the sky. He wanted to play up the Luke-Leia-Han triangle, and include a moment when Threepio would be destroyed. He had also decided Luke had a twin sister, though at this early stage, it wasn't clear whether that twin was Leia. Perhaps, Lucas suggested, she was on the other side of the galaxy and Luke could go look for her.

Other details were even murkier. The fate of Han Solo had yet to be decided, largely because Harrison Ford hadn't yet committed to doing three films. Lucas needed to leave himself enough room in the story to write out Solo if Ford opted out, so he ended his treatment with Han leaving the group to take on a mission to locate a high-powered financier—who was probably his stepfather—to bankroll the rebellion. Darth Vader was another question mark too, as Lucas was still trying to decide who or what Vader really was. The real conflict, as Lucas currently saw it, wasn't whether Vader would be redeemed by returning to the good side of the Force, but whether Vader would persuade Luke to give in to the Dark Side. And finally, there was perhaps his most ambitious idea, mainly because he had no idea how to pull it off: a tiny wizened Jedi master named Minch Yoda, who Lucas thought might be "the one who trained Ben [Kenobi]."[77]

After the misery of writing *Star Wars*, however, Lucas was determined to turn the task of writing the screenplay over to someone else. In late November 1977 he called in Leigh Brackett, a science fiction novelist who'd written for the pulps—exactly Lucas's sensibilities— and who had also written screenplays for *The Big Sleep*, *Hatari!*, and *Rio Lobo*, all films Lucas admired. For several days in late November and early December, Lucas and Brackett discussed Lucas's treatment and brainstormed additional plot details. On December 2, Brackett—who would be paid a flat fee of $50,000—took Lucas's notes and went off to write her first draft. Meanwhile, McQuarrie was already at work on a new series of paintings—including one of a castle for Vader on a volcano planet—and Kurtz was scouting other productions for potential crew members.

At the same time that he was working on *Empire*, Lucas began work on an empire of another sort, hiring new employees and purchasing the facilities needed to turn Lucasfilm into a real company. At the moment the company was little more than Lucas, Kurtz, Lippincott, and a couple of others working out of Parkhouse in San Anselmo, with a few trailers on a vacant lot across the street from Universal, and ILM as an outlier. "It was basically a tiny mom-and-pop company with huge potential resources," said Charlie Weber, Lucasfilm's first CEO—a former real estate executive Lucas had found by taking out an ad in the newspaper. But having Lucasfilm in northern California when most of the company's business was being done in Los Angeles was impeding

Lucas's ability to control production. Every time Lucas left Los Angeles for San Anselmo, said McQuarrie, "a great many things are left hanging until he comes back."[78] As much as Lucas hated to admit it, he knew he needed a more permanent office in southern California.

With money from merchandise beginning to trickle in that winter, Lucas had the resources to purchase a building on Lankershim Boulevard in Los Angeles, directly across from Universal Studios. The building was a former egg company, and so, just as he had with ILM's home in the Kerner Optical building in northern California, Lucas would refer to his southern California headquarters by the name of its former owner, dubbing it The Egg Company. Lucasfilm was officially in Hollywood, whether Lucas liked it or not. "Everything has mushroomed," he said with some frustration. "Before, I had these modest dreams. Now I'm sitting on top of a corporation that is taking up a lot of my time. I've had to hire people and start new hierarchies, new bureaucracies, new everything to make the whole thing work."[79]

Not that anyone could accuse Lucas himself of "going Hollywood." By the end of 1977, Lucas's personal share in *Star Wars* had earned him about $12 million after taxes, but he still dressed like a film student, wearing well-worn jeans and sneakers and flannel shirts. While there was now a Ferrari parked in his garage in San Anselmo, Lucas still preferred to drive his old Camaro. The rest of the money was going back into his company and into production on *The Empire Strikes Back*. But he was burning through his capital quickly. As Lucas studied the bottom line with Richard Tong, Lucasfilm's new accountant, one thing was becoming clear: "*Star Wars* licensing and merchandising was going to have to provide the financial base to sustain the company until *Empire* was released," said Tong.[80]

Among the first business conducted at The Egg Company was the approval of the deal memo for *Raiders of the Lost Ark*. In the spirit of the old Saturday morning serials, Lucas wanted to do the project cheaply — the budget was set at $6 million — and as quickly as possible. Spielberg asked for final cut — a director after Lucas's own heart — and also brought to Lucas's attention another collaborator he thought was perfect for the project, a twenty-eight-year-old advertising copywriter turned screenwriter named Lawrence Kasdan. Spielberg had been impressed with a romantic comedy Kasdan had written called *Continental Divide,* and Lucas, after reading it, thought Kasdan could write just the kind of screenplay they were looking for: tightly plotted, character driven, with lots of snappy dialogue.

As he had done with Brackett, Lucas brought in Kasdan for several days of brainstorming, zinging ideas around with him and Spielberg as they worked off Lucas's twenty-three-page handwritten story treatment. Even in these early sessions, Lucas was already revealing exactly what kind of executive producer he was going to be: while he always boasted of his ability to run with the best idea in the room, no matter whose it was, Lucas was generally all but certain the best ideas in the room were his. At times Spielberg would push back, and Lucas would simply shrug, a look of resignation on his face. "Okay, Steven," Lucas would say, "it's your movie."[81]

Kasdan left with Lucas's treatment and reams of notes from his discussions with Lucas and Spielberg, promising to bring a first draft back soon. With Lucas involved in story conferences, it fell to Kurtz to do most of the legwork on finding the right director for *Empire.* Briefly, Lucas had considered turning *Star Wars* into an ongoing series directed by his friends — Spielberg, Milius, perhaps even Coppola — treating it almost like one of those college film festivals in which each one tried to outdo the others' films. "I'm hoping if I get friends of mine they will want to do a much better film, like 'I'll show that George that I can do a film twice that good,'" Lucas told *Rolling Stone.* "And I think they can, but then I want to do the last one, so I can do one twice as good as everybody else."[82]

Kurtz, however, simply went hunting for good directors, sorting through a long list of potential candidates, looking seriously at John Badham, who had just completed *Saturday Night Fever,* and Englishman Alan Parker, fresh off the all-kid musical gangster film *Bugsy Malone.* After further consideration, however, Kurtz decided to have Lucas meet with only one person: Irvin Kershner — *Kersh,* as nearly everyone called him—a former USC instructor who had only just completed work on the thriller *Eyes of Laura Mars*.

Kersh remembered a number of Lucas's student films at USC, and had been especially impressed with *6-18-67*, which he thought "incredibly beautiful."[83] Kersh was close enough to being USC Mafia for Lucas to be comfortable with him—and besides, he had cut his teeth on television, leading Lucas to believe he could work quickly and cheaply. (Both assumptions would be incorrect.) More than anything else, Lucas wanted "somebody who has a vast experience in films and likes to deal with people and characters."[84] That was Kersh.

Tall and lanky, bald with a neatly trimmed gray beard, the fifty-four-year-old Kershner was also a painter, a violinist, and a Zen Buddhist who saw filmmaking as contributing to the greater good. Kersh was serious, though never brooding, and he liked people and actors—which is probably why he was so good with character. He also liked Lucas, but understood his quirks, and insisted that Lucas not meddle in production or hover over his shoulder on the set. Lucas promised he wouldn't. "If I do a sequel, I'll be a sort of executive producer," Lucas had told *People* magazine. "I'll approve the rough cut and I'll say, 'you're doing great,' and all that kind of stuff."[85] But as Kersh and others would learn, it was a vow Lucas wasn't equipped to keep.

Leigh Brackett delivered her first draft of *The Empire Strikes Back* on February 21. Lucas was disappointed; while Brackett had largely followed his story outline, her script—in a sentiment a Jedi master might appreciate—just *felt* wrong. The dialogue was clumsy—at one point Vader called someone an "incompetent idiot"—and Brackett had the characters quarreling, with Han at one point angrily telling off Luke. Lucas took it personally; he admitted that *Star Wars* was "in me now, and I can't help but get upset or excited when something isn't the way it's supposed to be."[86] Lucas flipped through the pages, first making notes and then eventually just scrawling *NO* over particularly problematic sections, such as Ben having Luke take a solemn vow "to the cause of freedom and justice."[87] Lucas invited Brackett to meet with him to go over script revisions and was stunned to learn she was in the hospital. On March 18, three weeks after turning in her first draft, Brackett died of cancer at age sixty-two.

Still in shock, Lucas and Marcia took a long-planned vacation to Mexico with director Michael Ritchie and his wife. If Marcia hoped this trip would be another relaxing retreat when they might hope to conceive a child, she would once again be frustrated; Lucas shut himself in the hotel room for most of the vacation to write a new script for *The Empire Strikes Back*. Producing sequels, not heirs, would be his main priority through the spring and summer of 1978.

The writing, while always hard, came quicker this time—Lucas said he found the process "almost enjoyable"—and he completed his own first draft in only three weeks, a blink of an eye compared with the year he'd spent on the first draft of *Star Wars*.[88] In April he sent the script over to Ladd, scrawling across the front, "Here's a rough idea of the film—May the Force be with us!"

Lucas had remodeled Brackett's script in his own image, cutting problematic scenes, moving things around, and creating new characters. Some of the dialogue was still clunky—Solo always seemed to be reciting an endless stream of technobabble—but Lucas was getting a better handle on Vader now (though he scrapped all scenes featuring Vader's volcano castle). And on page 128 of his handwritten script, as Luke battled Vader, Lucas had inserted a key line of dialogue for the villain that he was certain would define the character of Vader even as it shocked the audience to its core: *"I am your father."* Lucas was determined to keep the Luke-Vader connection a secret, even going so far as to remove the page with the revelatory dialogue on it from every copy of the script for fear it would be leaked.

Lucas also introduced the enigmatic bounty hunter Boba Fett in this early draft, modeling the character on Clint Eastwood's Man with No Name from the westerns of Sergio Leone. Lucas wanted Fett designed quickly, as he had committed the character to a holiday special he'd agreed to do for CBS that winter, and Kenner was begging for a character from *Empire* that it could market in advance of the movie. As designed by McQuarrie and ILMer Joe Johnston, Boba Fett, with his cool costume and assortment of gear, was clearly an ideal action figure. Lucas had no idea that he had almost too casually just created an icon; he would give him only four short lines of dialogue.

While Lucas had his script—and still had plenty of ideas he wasn't sure how to develop, such as a planet of Wookiees—what he didn't have was a screenwriter. Brackett's untimely death had caught him flat-footed, and no real prospects were presenting themselves. When Lawrence Kasdan came in to deliver his first draft of the screenplay for *Raiders of the Lost Ark* later that summer, Lucas was still complaining about the difficulties of moving forward with the *Empire* screenplay, a conversation that continued over lunch. Mid-discussion, Lucas suddenly had an epiphany: Would Kasdan consider being the screenwriter for *The Empire Strikes Back?*

The young writer was stunned. "Don't you think you should read *Raiders* first?" he asked Lucas.

Lucas smiled wryly. "Well, if I hate *Raiders*, I'll renege [on] this offer tomorrow."[89]

But Lucas knew he wouldn't hate it; both he and Spielberg had confidence in Kasdan to deliver the goods for *Empire*, though Lucas admitted it was something of a crapshoot. "I was desperate," he said later. "I didn't have anybody else."[90] Kasdan fretted about splitting his time between the two scripts, but Lucas told him to shelve *Raiders* and concentrate on *Empire*, as Spielberg's priority at the moment was the comedy *1941.*

Meanwhile, Lucas had managed to corral the entirety of his *Star Wars* cast for *Empire*, though Ford still wouldn't commit to a *third* film. Hamill, however, was delighted, all but convinced after the experience of shooting the first *Star Wars* that Lucas would never want to make a another one. "He told me once that he didn't want to make features any more, that he wanted to go back and make student movies," said Hamill, pledging, "I'll do those, too."[91] The budget was set at a little over $15 million, which exceeded the total of Lucas's own *Star Wars* profits. "The money I have doesn't amount to anything," he confessed.

"I couldn't direct enough films fast enough to pay for all those people. So I had to develop a company. The truth of it is that I'm very overextended right now."[92] As Tong had predicted, merchandising was going to have to keep paying off if *Empire* was going to fly.

On April 3, 1978, Lucas took Marcia with him to Hollywood to attend the fiftieth Academy Awards, where *Star Wars* was nominated in ten categories, including Best Picture, Best Director, and Best Screenplay. Lucas put up a neutral front—"he never felt it was important to have an Oscar to be happy or successful or fulfilled or anything," said Marcia—and Lucas claimed only half-jokingly that he was attending only because Marcia was nominated as well.[93] But as the evening wore on, and *Star Wars* began to sweep up nearly every technical award—John Barry and Roger Christian for art direction, John Mollo for costumes, John Williams for music—Lucas grew visibly excited, at one point looking over at Kurtz with his eyebrows raised in anticipation. Dykstra and a small team from ILM took home the Oscar for visual effects—a glorious moment for the spurned FX master—and Marcia, Paul Hirsch, and Richard Chew received the award for Best Editing, with Hirsch graciously acknowledging in his acceptance speech Lucas's own formidable skills as an editor. But Lucas was shut out in the writing and directing categories, and *Star Wars* would ultimately lose the award for Best Picture to Woody Allen's *Annie Hall.*

Lucas would always maintain that awards meant nothing to him, but there may have been just a tinge of frustration in knowing that for *Star Wars,* necessity had forced him to cede his true filmmaking passion—the editing—to others, who had then won the Oscar for their efforts, while he had gone home empty-handed. Even Coppola thought the disappointment might spur Lucas on. "Good," remarked Coppola the morning after Lucas lost the Oscar. "Now George will be back with another picture. He won't retire into moguldom. He likes to win too much."[94]

Star Wars did even better among the sci-fi crowd—the Science Fiction Writers of America presented it with a special award for the popular attention it brought to the genre—but the science fiction writers were a bit wary of Lucas's pop culture phenomenon. They wanted to be thought of as working in the more serious tradition of Ted Sturgeon and Isaac Asimov, not George Lucas and his space opera. "Those of us who work in the science fiction field professionally look for something more than Saturday afternoon shoot-em-ups," said writer Ben Bova derisively. "I had expected more of Lucas."[95] Lucas had little patience with that sort of snootiness. "I think science fiction still has a tendency to make itself so pious and serious," he shot back, "which is what I tried to knock out."[96]

Still, Lucas didn't need awards to seal his reputation as the most influential filmmaker of the moment. By mid-1978, in fact, the USC Mafia—and Spielberg—were seen as Hollywood's most successful filmmaking rebels, doing everything their own way, making pictures that aligned with their own unique visions, swapping points with one another, and doing it outside the studio system. The moguls may have built the system, said Milius, and they may have been distributing the movies, but it was the fiercely independent mavericks from Chaplin and Welles to Lucas and Coppola who always made the movies interesting and successful—and they had big plans. "We were complaining about how bad things were in Hollywood," Milius told the *New York Times*. "So Francis said, 'Okay, let's change things. George and I will take over everything in the valley and you take everything else.'"[97]

But beyond Spielberg and Lucas, most of their crew wouldn't take over much of anything. The Huycks sputtered with *French Postcards*, while Milius crashed with his surfing homage *Big Wednesday*. "Everybody wants to help each other," insisted Willard Huyck. "Everybody wants the others to be successful."[98] And yet there were cracks of resentment appearing in the normally tight-knit façade of the USC crew. Lucas, for one, though often generous, could sometimes be stingy and downright vindictive with his *Star Wars* points. Coppola didn't receive any. "Why should he?" said Lucas. "He had no connection to the movie."[99] And Milius, who had received a point from *Star Wars* in exchange for one in *Big Wednesday*, was asked to return his point to Lucas after *Big Wednesday* tanked. Milius would never forget it. "These guys got too good for everyone," said Milius. "Everybody got very, very distant. George has his entourage around him. Could do no wrong. Everything was for George."[100]

That was probably a fair assessment—and that was the way Lucas wanted it. Lately, Lucas had dismissed several employees who couldn't or wouldn't fall in line with his own view of the universe. "You must agree with George, and if you don't agree with George, then George doesn't like you," said one ILMer.[101] Even Jeff Berg, the agent who had so diligently shopped the messy fledgling *Star Wars* script, was dismissed; Lucas, through his team of shrewd attorneys, would take over his duties from this point forward. "I just didn't need him anymore," said Lucas without a shred of regret.[102]

What Lucas really needed was complete independence. "I had to become self-sufficient," he explained later. "I had to build an empire simply to make the movies the way I wanted to make them. I wanted to make my own future and not have to beg, borrow and steal to get the money to make my movies. I didn't want to have to listen to the studios and make the films on their terms and, fortunately, *Star Wars* gave me the opportunity to become independent of the studio system."[103]

Exactly what that empire would become Lucas wasn't yet certain. Initially he envisioned going into business with Coppola again, and excitedly called on his old mentor. "I'm gonna have all this money, we can do all the dreams we always wanted to," Lucas told Coppola, "and I want to do it with you." Briefly the two of them considered purchasing the Mann theater chain, or even buying 20th Century Fox. "But now I was clearly in the subordinate position," said Coppola, "and then about six months later there was less of that talk, and then there was a period of falling out. I never understood what it was about."[104] Most likely, Lucas was growing wary of Coppola's unpredictable, profligate ways. Several years earlier, when Coppola was flush with money, he had purchased a building in San Francisco, a Learjet, a theater, even a newspaper—all of which he mortgaged to the hilt the moment *Apoca-*

lypse Now ran into financial trouble. Lucas couldn't fathom shouldering that sort of debt. "I have never been like Francis and some of my other friends who are building giant empires and are constantly in debt and have to keep working to keep up their empires," said Lucas.[105]

Lucas and Coppola were simply different kinds of idealists. Coppola wanted to be a mogul; Lucas wanted to be an artist. "I prefer playing with camera film over becoming the entrepreneur behind a gigantic operation," said Lucas, who blanched at the very idea of ordering people around, attending meetings, and approving projects. "I want to get away from all of that," he insisted. "Whereas Francis... wants more and more power, I don't....I accept the power to do whatever I like with my camera. But I refuse the power to command other people."[106] Instead of a corporate headquarters, then, or a building in San Francisco, Lucas still envisioned working with his friends in a ranch house "in the middle of nowhere," similar to the one he'd grown up in. "I wanted a place full of the most advanced technology, where we could sit, see the trees and think about things."[107]

For Lucas, the middle of nowhere turned out to be the tiny village of Nicasio, about twelve miles northwest of Lucasfilm's headquarters at Parkhouse in San Anselmo, and close—though not *too* close—to San Francisco, about fifty-five miles to the south. Lucas had scouted out an isolated piece of property known as Bulltail Ranch, about 1,700 acres on the serendipitously named Lucas Valley Road, named for nineteenth-century settler John Lucas, who had received much of the surrounding land as a wedding gift in 1882. Nearly a hundred years later, George Lucas walked the property, rolling and shaded, and saw miles and miles of peace and possibility. This was where he would build his ranch. *Skywalker Ranch.*

"Okay," he told his accountants, "this is it. I'm buying."[108]

By midsummer Kasdan had completed about twenty-five pages of screenplay for *The Empire Strikes Back,* which he and Lucas and Kersh now began poring over, figuring out which ideas were worth pursuing and how they might be realized on-screen. As the creator of his fictional universe, Lucas kept the *Star Wars* encyclopedia entirely in his head, and he alone would do most of the decision making. It took Kasdan a while to grasp Lucas's particular brand of passive-aggressive communication. "Actually, the way George works is that he never tells you what he likes, just what he doesn't," said Kasdan. "Silence was its own reward."[109]

The toughest question still involved the character of Yoda. "Let's make him small," Lucas suggested. "Maybe he's slightly froglike." But no one was exactly sure how to make a small, froglike character work convincingly on film. For a moment they considered using a monkey in a costume and a mask—a suggestion that test footage revealed as unconvincing, and the monkey was nearly impossible to manage. Lucas thought he had a better solution. During filming of *Star Wars* at Elstree, Muppet maestro Jim Henson had been taping *The Muppet Show* directly across the street in the television facilities. He and Lucas had similar artistic tendencies—both were almost defiantly independent—and vowed to find a way to work together. This might be that opportunity: perhaps Yoda would work as a Muppet of some sort. "It would have the personality of a Muppet, only it would be realistic," Lucas decided.[110] He made a note to give Henson a call.

With *Empire* beginning to gel on the page, Lucas began to step up production. Profits from merchandising were flowing regularly into Black Falcon, which would immediately turn around and loan the money to Chapter II, ILM, and a new division Lucas had recently created for Ben Burtt: Sprocket Systems, devoted entirely to sound. Kersh and McQuarrie were dispatched to London, where offices for Chapter II had been opened at Elstree, while more than $1 million was poured into ILM for equipment and employees. But even after that injection of cash, keeping ILM operational was going to run about $400,000 every month, while Chapter II was going to need nearly $2 million per month to cover the costs of production and personnel. Lucas was investing everything he had in *The Empire Strikes Back*—and already his resources were being stretched precariously thin.

While it seemed there was no detail too small for Lucas to involve himself in—he was still handpicking his staff and approving merchandise—there was one project he had ceded almost entirely to others: a *Star Wars* holiday special, which CBS planned to air the week before Thanksgiving. Lucas had engaged with the project early, sitting down with television writer Bruce Vilanch to go over a story treatment that provided only some very vague but ambitious basics: it would take place on Chewbacca's home planet of Kashyyyk, the Wookiee family would overcome Imperials on their way to celebrating the holiday Life Day, and much of the special would involve Wookiees speaking to one another in their own language of grunts and roars—without the help of subtitles.

Vilanch listened carefully, then exhaled slowly. "You've chosen to build a story around these characters who don't speak," he told Lucas incredulously. "The only sound they make is like fat people having an orgasm." Lucas glared back, unamused, and Vilanch threw up his hands in surrender. Lucas, said Vilanch, "had what a director needs to have, which is this insane belief in their personal vision, and he was somehow going to make it work."[111]

It didn't. Lucas, preoccupied with making *Empire* and building his company, put the special entirely in the hands of its veteran producers, Dwight Hemion and Gary Smith, and opted instead to view video footage of the work as it was completed. But as he watched his characters woven into painfully unfunny comedy bits featuring Harvey Korman with musical interludes by Jefferson Starship, Lucas could see that he had a problem. Even Ford, Hamill, and Fisher, gamely reprising their film roles, couldn't transcend the material; all three looked miserable, though Fisher was thrilled at the chance to sing a Life Day song set to the tune of Williams's *Star Wars* theme—yet another cringe-inducing moment. The only segment that sparked any interest from Lucas was an eleven-minute animated feature by the Canadian company Nelvana Ltd., which would give audiences their first look at Boba Fett. With the wheels coming off, all Lucas could do was let it go—and take his name off the show.

Heavily promoted by CBS, and eagerly awaited by fans—this was *Star Wars* on TV, after all—*The Star Wars Holiday Special* aired on November 17, 1978, and was an unmitigated disaster. Producer Dwight Hemion called it "the worst piece of crap I've ever done"; Lucas called it a "travesty."[112] He had given up control, and *Star Wars* had ended up looking stupid. It was a mistake he was determined not to make again.

For now, the holiday special would be written off as a creative casualty of Lucas's laser-like focus on *The Empire Strikes Back*, which seemed to be straining at its own bottom line before a frame of film had been shot. By December, Lucasfilm number crunchers had estimated *Empire's* budget at a whopping $21 million. Lucas, his resources dwindling, loaned his company $20 million of his own money as collateral for a bank loan. Out at Elstree, set construction was proceeding at a cost of $3.5 million. Additionally, he and Kurtz had spent another $2 million to construct a permanent soundstage large enough to accommodate a full-sized *Millennium Falcon;* there would be no sawing his model in half this time.

Even those who knew Lucas well were aghast at his bullheaded determination to finance the entire film himself. Independence was one thing; bankruptcy was another. But those people were missing the point: Lucas wasn't paying for a movie; he was buying his own creative freedom. "This was the perfect opportunity to become independent of the Hollywood system," he said. There would be no bean counters nickel-and-diming him, denying him the money he needed to get a shot just right—and even better, there would be no studio executives staring over his shoulder in the editing room, forcing him to make what he saw as arbitrary changes. "That's the part I wanted to avoid."[113]

But even a completely Hollywood-free *Empire Strikes Back* was still just a means to a greater end. Lucas's true creative freedom lay in Skywalker Ranch. Already he was scribbling designs for buildings in notebooks and on scraps of paper, much the same way he had doodled cars in high school. The walls at Parkhouse, in fact, were covered with blueprints and concept drawings, and Lucas delighted in showing them off and enthusing about the ranch to anyone who would listen—

and that included Irvin Kershner, who visited Parkhouse to talk *Empire* and ended up talking more about Lucas's empire. "It was really an extraordinary dream," said Kershner. "All the billions of dollars ever made in the film business, and no one has ever plowed it back into a library, research, bringing directors together, creating an environment where the love of films could create new dimensions."[114]

But as he scanned the drawings and blueprints, Kershner also came to understand the truly unenviable position Lucas had put him in: *Empire* was about more than just making a sequel strong enough to keep the *Star Wars* franchise chugging along. "This," said Lucas, fanning his hand at the drawings of the ranch pinned to the walls, "is why we're making the second [film]. If it works, I'll build this. If it doesn't work, it's over."[115]

9

Darkening Skies

1979–1983

Lucas was having serious problems with his sequel. One of his actors—arguably the breakout star of the first film—had made it clear he was not coming back for the second film without a significant increase in salary. The script was weak—"it's one of those stories that shouldn't have a sequel, really," said Gary Kurtz—and Lucas, despite his promises to the contrary, couldn't stop meddling in the production.[1] When he wasn't hovering over his handpicked director's every move, Lucas simply went around him, directing several sequences himself and taking over in the editing room.

The sequel was *More American Graffiti,* and Lucas had practically been badgered into doing it. "I'm not ashamed I made it," Lucas would say later, but that didn't mean he was happy about it.[2]

Trying to cash in on Lucas's name in the midst of the *Star Wars* tsunami, Universal had re-released *American Graffiti* in May 1978 to considerable success—"even sweeter the second time around," swooned Gary Arnold in the *Washington Post*—and Ned Tanen had not too subtly reminded Lucas that he still owed Universal at least one more film.[3] To Tanen, a sequel to *American Graffiti* seemed natural—but Lucas, who was already developing the *Star Wars* sequel, balked at the idea of going back to that particular well again. Shrewdly, Tanen threatened to produce the sequel without Lucas's involvement, the very idea of which he knew Lucas would find unacceptable. Reluctantly, Lucas gave in—*this* was exactly why he had insisted on all sequel rights in his *Star Wars* contract—and agreed to deliver a follow-up to his first big hit.

It was probably doomed from the start. Lucas had already boxed himself in with the ending of *American Graffiti,* in which end cards had revealed the fates of each of the four main characters. But he developed a rough story outline anyway and began wooing his cast from the first film, landing most without ever having to show them a story outline or script. Richard Dreyfuss, however, who had played Curt, had gone on to a star-making turn in *Jaws* in 1975, followed by an Oscar-winning performance in *The Goodbye Girl* in 1977—and with the parsimonious budget provided by Universal, Lucas never stood a chance of landing him. "Not enough money," Dreyfuss huffed to the *Los Angeles Times.* "They offered me one-tenth my [usual] salary and I said no....I still get along with Lucas, he just won't be telling the story of Curt Henderson."[4]

Lucas turned over the task of finding a screenwriter to another old USC friend, Howard Kazanjian, whom Lucas had recruited to serve as the line producer for *More American Graffiti*—a throwaway title, indicative of Lucas's already flagging interest in the project. Kazanjian brought in B. W. L. "Bill" Norton, a classmate of Gloria Katz's from UCLA who met most of the criteria Lucas was looking for in his scriptwriter: he was a Californian, close to Lucas's age—and with one bomb, the 1972 drug drama *Cisco Pike,* on his short list of credits, he was also looking for an opportunity to write and direct again. "George didn't want to direct it himself," said Kurtz, "but he wanted someone he could control."[5] Norton was his man.

Norton was ferried up to Parkhouse to discuss the story lines Lucas had plotted out for his four main characters, some of which "George had already worked out in detail," remembered Norton, while "others needed fixing."[6] Lucas had devised four parallel stories, taking place over a series of New Year's Eves, following John Milner, Steve and Laurie, Terry the Toad, and—with Dreyfuss out of the picture— Toad's accidental girlfriend from the first movie, the earnest Debbie Dunham. Lucas also envisioned shooting each character's story in four distinct styles, with Debbie's hippie adventure filmed in a psychedelic split-screen style, for example, while Toad's exploits in Vietnam would be shot in black and white on scratchy 16 mm film, looking very much the way Lucas had envisioned shooting *Apocalypse Now*. Lucas stressed to Norton, in fact, that he expected him to work fast, getting the film written, shot, edited, and released before mid-August 1979, when Coppola's version of *Apocalypse Now* was due in theaters. When John Milius learned what Lucas was up to, he could only shake his head in disbelief. "He wants to steal Francis's thunder, you know?"[7]

Norton wrote quickly, though Lucas had Kazanjian looking over his shoulder, discouraging Norton from creating new characters or straying too far from Lucas's story.

"The script wasn't all that wonderful," said Kurtz, who was likely glad to be free of the project—but the script hardly mattered to Caleb Deschanel, another USC friend whom Lucas had selected as his director of photography. Shooting in multiple formats, Deschanel said later, was "a crazy idea, but we had a great deal of fun. It was really a continuation of the atmosphere at USC."[8]

Lucas gave Norton a mere forty-four days to complete principal photography—still an eternity when compared with *American Graffiti*'s twenty-eight-day shoot back in 1972. Filming began at a California drag strip, the stands crammed with extras lured in by Lucas's promise of free *Star Wars* toys. Lucas showed up on the first day, and vowed to leave Norton alone, but found he couldn't keep his hands off. He would direct nearly all of the Vietnam sequences himself, shooting several military helicopters near Stockton, California, then take over the editing process, further marginalizing Norton. Lucas knew he had

Youth Survives Crash

Just what part in saving his life the roll bar, arrow, and a safety belt played is not known but George W. Lucas, Jr., survived this crash yesterday. The high way patrol said the safety belt snapped and Lucas was thrown from the car which was slammed into the tree by another vehicle in the collision.

Lucas was a week away from barely graduating high school when he was in an automobile accident serious enough that it made the front page of the local newspaper. He was thrown free of the car just before impact. Surviving the crash changed Lucas's outlook on life and persuaded him to pursue studies in anthropology at Modesto Junior College and, later, film at the University of Southern California. (Courtesy of the *Modesto Bee*)

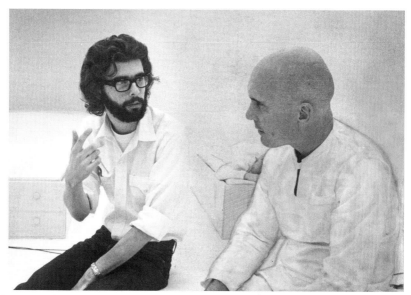

Lucas with actor Robert Duvall on the set of Lucas's 1971 science-fiction film *THX 1138*. Artfully filmed and brimming with interesting ideas, *THX 1138* fascinated critics but bewildered audiences. Its failure spelled the end of Francis Ford Coppola's Zoetrope dream, and very nearly ended Lucas's filmmaking career. (Moviestore Collection, Ltd. / Alamy)

American Graffiti (1973) was Lucas's rock-and-roll ode to his high school days cruising Tenth Street in Modesto. Lucas raged when executives at Universal lost faith in the film and cut four minutes from the final movie—a slight that further fired his longing to break away from the Hollywood system entirely. The studios, he growled, were filled with "sleazy, unscrupulous people." (Silver Screen Collection / Getty Images)

Gary Kurtz (left) served as Lucas's producer on *American Graffiti, Star Wars,* and *The Empire Strikes Back*, arguing budgets with executives and trying to keep Lucas's vision intact. Lucas grew increasingly disenchanted with Kurtz over cost overruns on *Empire*, and their relationship fractured for good over a disagreement on the story for *Return of the Jedi*. (Michael Ochs Archives / Getty Images)

"Making a movie is a terribly painful experience," said Lucas, shown here on the set of *Star Wars* with (from left) Peter Cushing, Carrie Fisher, and Dave Prowse, sans his Darth Vader helmet. *Star Wars* baffled Fox executives, who refused to provide Lucas the money he requested to finish the movie to his liking. Lucas never forgot it, and vowed he wouldn't go begging for money for one of his own movies again. (AF Archive / Alamy)

Lucas personally tapped John Dykstra to create and oversee the special effects for *Star Wars*, and to establish the workshop that would become Industrial Light & Magic. Brilliant and fiercely independent, Dykstra constantly frustrated Lucas, who accused the FX wizard of being more interested in creating the new technology than in producing the actual effects. Dykstra's groundbreaking special effects would win one of *Star Wars*'s seven Oscars. (ABC Photo Archives / Getty Images)

Marcia Lucas was a talented and highly respected film editor, who many considered to be Lucas's secret weapon. Tasked by her overextended husband with editing many of *Star Wars*'s frenetic battle sequences, Marcia brought to the film her instincts for storytelling and an intuitive sense of what excited audiences. "If the audience doesn't cheer when Han Solo comes in at the last second in the *Millennium Falcon* to help Luke when he's being chased by Vader," she told Lucas, "the picture doesn't work." Marcia would win an Academy Award for her editing on *Star Wars*. Lucas, to this day, has yet to win an Oscar. (Julian Wasser / Getty Images)

Movies—and movie fandom—changed forever on May 25, 1977, when *Star Wars* opened in fewer than forty theaters nationwide and sold out every show in nearly every theater, including Loews in New York City. Fans waited for hours for a showing, queues stretched for blocks, and standing in line became part of the *Star Wars* experience. Lucas was stunned by the film's immediate success. "I had no idea of what was going to happen," said Lucas. "I mean, I had *no idea*." (Paul Slade / Getty Images)

Francis Ford Coppola joins a beardless Lucas at the premiere of *Captain EO* at Disneyland in 1986. Closer than brothers, Lucas and Coppola would squabble and reconcile constantly for two decades while working together on project after project. "I think Francis always looked at George as sort of his upstart assistant who had an opinion," said Steven Spielberg. "An assistant with an opinion, nothing more dangerous than that, right?" (Kevin Winter / Getty Images)

Willow (1988) was a labor of love for Lucas, who handpicked both Ron Howard (left) to direct and Warwick Davis (right) to star in the Lucas-penned, Tolkien-tinged fairy tale about an abandoned baby returned to her people by the titular hero. While the film featured one of ILM's most dazzling effects to date — the "morphing" of one creature into another — critics were generally unimpressed and criticized Lucas for recycling fairy-tale clichés. "The Great Regurgitator," sniffed one detractor harshly. (MGM Studios / Getty Images)

Lucas with Steven Spielberg on the set of *Indiana Jones and the Last Crusade*. After the deliberate darkness of *Temple of Doom*—"a chaotic period in both their lives," said writer Lawrence Kasdan—*Last Crusade* was a return to the more rollicking fun of *Raiders of the Lost Ark*. (Murray Close / Getty Images)

Lucas and Steven Spielberg met at a student film festival in 1968, marking the beginning of one of film's warmest personal and professional friendships. My "valiant colleague, and great and loyal friend," Spielberg called Lucas, who in turn referred to Spielberg as "my partner, my pal, my inspiration, my challenger." (Valerie Macon / Getty Images)

Producer Rick McCallum (left) helped Lucas usher in the era of digital film-making during their television work on *The Young Indiana Jones Chronicles* in the early 1990s, proving that backgrounds, actors, and sets could be manipulated digitally. After being tasked with overseeing the new digital footage inserted into the original *Star Wars* trilogy, McCallum served as Lucas's producer on Episodes I, II, and III, quietly permitting Lucas to indulge his love of digital technology, often to the detriment of storytelling. (Francois Guillot / Getty Images)

The sixty-one-year-old Lucas met the thirty-seven-year-old Mellody Hobson in 2005 and was smitten immediately. "If you're more beautiful than I am and smarter than I am and you'll put up with me, that's all it takes," said Lucas. The two were married in 2013 at Skywalker Ranch. (Frederick M. Brown / Getty Images)

Lucas, who raised his children (left to right) Jett, Katie, and Amanda as a single parent, often cited being a father as his proudest achievement. "There was a point there where I lived only for movies," Lucas said in 2005, "[but] children are the key to life." (Gregg DeGuire / Getty Images)

Lucas with Bob Iger, chairman and CEO of the Walt Disney Company, who orchestrated Disney's $4 billion acquisition of Lucasfilm in 2012. Lucas believed the deal required Disney to use his treatments for Episodes VII through IX, and was disappointed when Episode VII was made largely without his input. "I will go my way," Lucas finally conceded, "and I'll let them go their way." (Image Group LA / Getty Images)

Longtime friend, collaborator, and *Indiana Jones* producer Kathleen Kennedy was Lucas's handpicked successor to serve as president of Lucasfilm after its sale to Disney. The first *Star Wars* film with Kennedy at the helm, *The Force Awakens,* would earn more than $2 billion in ticket sales worldwide and successfully relaunch the franchise. (Jeffrey Mayer / Getty Images)

Lucas at peace — mostly — at Skywalker Ranch. "I hope I'll be remembered as one of the pioneers of digital cinema," he said. "[Though] they might remember me as the maker of some of those esoteric twentieth-century science fiction movies." (Jean-Louis Atlan / Getty Images)

run roughshod over his director, and admitted later that their conflicting approaches to the film hadn't worked. "My whole idea for a style for *More American Graffiti* was ultimately unsuccessful, I guess," Lucas admitted. "Bill's a more conservative kind of storyteller, and I think I forced him to do things that in his heart he wasn't comfortable with."[9]

The artistic conflict was apparent on-screen as well; on its release in August 1979, *More American Graffiti* bombed with both audiences and critics, though it was Norton who took most of the heat for Lucas's decisions regarding the look of the film. The *Washington Post* called it a "blithe mockery" of the original, suffering "from a terminal case of the cutes."[10] Meanwhile, in a *New York Times* review, Janet Maslin slammed the film as "grotesquely misconceived" and—in a bit of criticism that must have stung Lucas to the core—compared its Vietnam sequences unfavorably to Coppola's *Apocalypse Now.*[11]

Kazanjian was perplexed by the criticism, but Lucas merely shrugged. "There are things I don't like. There are things I do like," he said enigmatically.[12] But he had to be concerned; regardless of his distaste for the project, his first attempt at a sequel had tanked badly. Now he was in the middle of making another sequel, with every dollar he'd earned at stake, and the experience with *More American Graffiti* had spooked him. "Everything I own, everything I ever earned, is wrapped up in *Empire* [*Strikes Back*]," he said nervously.[13] "We don't really know whether *Empire* is going to turn out to be another *More American Graffiti.... If it should be a [flop], I will lose everything."[14]

And things weren't going well with the sequel.

Screenwriter Lawrence Kasdan had been reworking the *Empire Strikes Back* script until almost the last moment before filming was to begin, doing his best to color inside the lines provided by Lucas and the late Leigh Brackett. Lucas had made it clear that out of respect for Brackett, he intended to give her a story credit—and that was fine with Kasdan, who, as he pounded the script into shape, sometimes debated whether he wanted his own name in the credits. "There were sections in the script," recalled Kasdan, "which, when I read them, made me say to myself, 'I can't believe that George wrote this scene. It's terrible.'"[15]

So was the weather. As director Irvin Kershner began filming in Finse, Norway, in March 1979, a blizzard that was massive even by Norwegian standards battered the production, with whiteout conditions making it impossible to see more than a few feet. (Improvising, Kershner simply pointed a camera out the door of his hotel room to film Hamill staggering around in the snow.) Lucas arrived at Elstree in late March to find the massive soundstage he and Kurtz had fronted with their own money—which would always be called the *Star Wars* Stage—still under construction, its insides exposed to the spring rains, and a Stage 4 that had been ravaged by fire. Furthermore, the dollar was growing increasingly weak against the British pound, pushing costs upward with each passing day. Lucas's budget, initially set at $18 million, was now inching toward $22 million; by July, it would slide up to $25 million. It was money Lucas didn't have.

Lucas swore repeatedly that he was done directing—"I think I can be more effective as an executive producer," he insisted—but he would never be entirely comfortable delegating the directing duties to someone else.[16] "It's very difficult to look over another director's shoulder," observed Kurtz.[17] And yet anytime Lucas was on the set, he would stand watching—arms folded, mouth tight—itching to look through the eyepiece. "I don't have a strong feeling of wishing it were being done another way," he declared, then backtracked immediately. "Well, perhaps once in a while," he continued. "But I much prefer that somebody else do the work." Kasdan marveled at Lucas's ability to get his own way, "trying to guide [everyone] into exactly what [he] wanted," and being "very good and funny and charming in the George-ian manner."[18] Or as Kershner noted diplomatically, "I've caught him looking through the camera only twice so far."[19] As filming went on, things would not change.

Away from Elstree, Lucas had taken it upon himself to personally oversee as much of the special effects work as possible at ILM.

"I have control over the special effects, so I feel confident that we're not going to be in trouble there," he told one journalist. "The only problem I have now is the speed of the production."[20] Lucas had tangled with Dykstra during the making of *Star Wars* over the glacial pace of creating the necessary technology. He now found that the painstakingly constructed equipment used for *Star Wars* already needed updating to handle the more sophisticated effects for *Empire*. Some shots—like the pursuit of the *Millennium Falcon* through an asteroid field—required the compositing of more than two hundred pieces of film, which in turn required ILM to build a new optical printer. Lucas's confidence in the effects was one thing; controlling the costs was another. The special effects, like everything else associated with *Empire*, it seemed, were burning through his money faster than expected.

As spring turned to summer, the situation went from bad to worse. Kershner, who had been hired for his finesse with actors, was lingering longer and longer over each scene, rehearsing and rewriting dialogue and encouraging the actors to give their input on dialogue or staging. Most of the time his devotion to the actors paid off—a long discussion with Ford and Fisher ended with Ford's Han Solo responding to Leia's declaration of love with the memorable ad-lib "I know"—but the deliberate pace was slowing production and angering Lucas.[21] The few times Kurtz stepped between Lucas and his director, he tended to take Kershner's side—and to Lucas's further annoyance, even Marcia defended Kershner's vision for the film. "Marcia and I agreed a lot," said Kershner. "We thought the [*Star Wars*] movies could hold more character and more complexity. George thought they should be simple in another way. It was a serious philosophical difference. For me, it wasn't an emotional issue. I felt it was his movie and I was working for him."[22]

Another domino tumbled over ominously in June, when Alan Ladd announced his resignation after a loud argument with Fox executives, leaving Lucas without his strongest advocate at the prickly and unpredictable studio. Ladd's departure, in fact, had been triggered largely by his devotion to Lucas, which—argued studio bean counters—had resulted in the lopsided contract for *Empire* that tilted largely in Lucas's favor. Ladd wouldn't be leaving the studio until winter, but the announcement sent Kurtz scrambling to ensure that all their contracts were signed and deals were in place.

Then, on June 5, John Barry—Lucas's talented Oscar-winning set designer turned second-unit director—collapsed at Elstree and died hours later of meningitis at age forty-three. The death sent shock waves throughout the company. Kurtz assumed second-unit responsibilities, while Lucas flew to London to try to get a handle on the fraying production. At nearly the same moment, the Bank of America, nervously eyeing the ballooning budget with a weekly payroll of close to a million dollars, suddenly threatened to pull Lucas's loan and shut down the operation. Lucas was furious and laid the blame for the budget busting squarely at the feet of Gary Kurtz, who, in Lucas's opinion, had coddled Kershner in his leisurely pace and failed to keep production on a tight leash. "George got really concerned about how long we were taking," Kurtz said flatly, "and he banged me for the cost overruns on *Empire*."[23]

As Lucasfilm's lawyers begged for patience, Lucas scrounged for funding, steering $525,000 from Black Falcon over to Chapter II, and stretched what little cash he had left by moving to a biweekly pay schedule—anything to avoid going to Fox on bended knee and asking for the money he needed to finish the movie. Lucas would never give them that satisfaction. "All the money I had made from *Star Wars* was committed to this film, plus more, but I didn't want to go to Fox and give them the movie because I'd have to give all the rights back," said Lucas. "I had to keep the picture going, somehow get people to work without pay...hope to hell that whatever they asked for didn't involve me having to go back and renegotiate big time with Fox."[24] As always with Lucas, it was a question of control: "I wanted my independence so badly." Eventually he agreed to give a few points to Fox in order to have the studio guarantee a new loan from the First National Bank of Boston—a compromise both parties found agreeable. "I think Fox was just as concerned as we were that the movie get finished," said Lucas.[25] Still, Lucasfilm remained the ultimate guarantor of the loan; if *Empire* didn't turn a profit, Lucasfilm was very likely done.

With so much at stake, Lucas felt he had no other option but to hover over Kershner for the remainder of the film. "I had to be there every day, and I had to be helping Kershner," Lucas said later, "which developed into a lot of work."[26] When asked directly whether he could get the job done more quickly than Kershner, Lucas responded matter-of-factly, "I think I could."[27] He also inserted himself into the editing process, weaving a second edit from Paul Hirsch's first cut of the film nearly as quickly as Hirsch could assemble it. Even with Lucas more directly involved, there were still some problems that were beyond his control: several reels of film were ruined in the development process, while others came in with the picture too muddy to use, forcing Lucas to abandon a number of sequences in the interests of time.

The most important scenes remaining to be filmed were those involving Yoda, whose development Lucas had put largely in the hands of Muppet creator Jim Henson, in collaboration with Stuart Freeborn and the wizards at ILM. Lucas liked Henson immensely; both were fiercely independent, presiding over their own scrappy companies, free of Hollywood interference, and each was a self-proclaimed gadget freak, committed to developing the technology needed to bring their visions vibrantly to life on-screen. Yoda, then, was an important project for both. Lucas needed a lifelike puppet and a talented puppeteer to perform him, while Henson was eager to apply the lessons learned from ILM—mostly about using smaller, remote-controlled mechanisms to move puppet eyes and ears and cheeks—to the film he then had in development, *The Dark Crystal*.

Yet while Henson oversaw much of Yoda's construction, to Lucas's surprise he had chosen not to operate the puppet himself, recommending instead that the character be put in the hands of his longtime associate Frank Oz. The versatile Oz, who performed such characters as *The Muppet Show*'s Miss Piggy and Fozzie Bear, was admired for his ability to create characters nearly at will—he considered himself an actor, not just a puppeteer—and over the past few months had immersed himself in the character of Yoda, devising his own back-story for the character, giving the diminutive Jedi master both gravitas and a subtle sense of humor, as well as a distinctive way of speaking.

Lucas did have some doubts about giving such a pivotal role to a rubber puppet, no matter how talented the puppeteer. "That was a real leap," said Lucas, "because if that puppet had not worked, the whole film would have been down the tubes."[28] He needn't have worried; not only was Yoda carefully built—with small motors and rotors to open his eyes, wiggle his ears, and pull back his cheeks—but also he was brilliantly performed by Oz, with a team of two and sometimes three other puppeteers in support. The moment filming began with Oz and Yoda in early August, it was clear the character was going to work spectacularly well. Oz was so convincing in his performance, in fact, that Kershner often found himself offering direction straight to Yoda rather than addressing his comments to Oz, crouched uncomfortably out of sight just below the set. Even Lucas could get caught up in the moment, sitting cross-legged in Yoda's home, completely wrapped up in conversation with the puppet, even with Oz in plain sight.

With Yoda literally in good hands, Lucas applied himself personally to wooing the film's other Jedi master, as well as the last holdout from his original cast. Over lunch, Lucas successfully lured Sir Alec Guinness back with the promise of one-third of a point for less than a day's work. With the final piece of the cast puzzle locked into place, Lucas headed back to San Rafael at the end of August to oversee ILM, warily leaving things in London to Kershner—but not under the supervision of Gary Kurtz. With the shoot now more than fifty days over schedule, the budget still creeping upward, and the bank nervous, Lucas decided he'd had enough of Kurtz and his indulgence of Kershner and put Howard Kazanjian, his producer from *More American*

Graffiti, in charge instead. "I had to get the film made," Lucas said without a whiff of sentimentality, "and that was all I really cared about at that point."[29]

Under the eye of Kazanjian, Kershner completed principal photography on *The Empire Strikes Back* on September 24, 1979. Lucas was relieved; now he could *really* put his hands on the film by working with editor Paul Hirsch, first out of Parkhouse and then in a rented space at 321 San Anselmo Avenue. Lucas was dissatisfied with Hirsch's first complete cut and reassembled the film to give it a quicker pace, much closer to his own preferred style. But the result was a disaster—scenes went by too fast, making it impossible to invest in any story line—and Lucas squabbled with Kershner, Hirsch, and Kurtz, all of whom eventually prevailed on him to revert to the slower, more deliberate pace of Hirsch's edit.

In the meantime, the reliable Ben Burtt would continue to edit in sound effects, and Lucas still had several key voices to dub in as well. James Earl Jones would be brought in again to perform Vader's voice, including the delivery of a key piece of dialogue—"No. *I* am your father"—that only Hamill, Kershner, and a few others had known about during filming. (Obscured by the Vader mask, Dave Prowse had delivered the line as "Obi-Wan killed your father," and wouldn't know the real plot twist until he saw the movie in the theater.) For his part, as Jones recorded Vader's dialogue in the winter of 1980, he remained convinced that Vader was lying.

The other important voice belonged to Yoda. Even as he watched Oz perform the character on the Elstree soundstage, Lucas still wasn't certain he wanted Oz speaking as the Jedi master. "George didn't want my voice," said Oz matter-of-factly. "I gave him the [voice] tape; he said, 'No thank you.'"[30] But as Lucas sat through one voice audition after another, he came to appreciate that "in terms of puppetry, the person who is actually acting the role is really into it,"[31] and that Oz— like Anthony Daniels with the voice for C-3PO—had been the natural choice all along.

Most days, however, Lucas spent at Kerner, watching Dennis

Muren, Richard Edlund, and the ILM team slowly but steadily assemble the special effects. To make the projected May 1980 release of *Empire,* the effects had to be completed no later than March. Apart from utilizing the same motion control technology pioneered in *Star Wars,* ILM would also use old-school stop-motion effects for the armored, snow-walking AT-ATs as well as for the agile tauntauns used by riders in the film's opening scenes. As the number of needed effects inched higher and higher, keeping track of each shot became more than the film librarians could handle with pencil and paper. For the first time, then, Lucas and his team invested in a new tool to help them log and locate every single frame of film: sitting on a table at ILM was a brand-new Apple computer.

Lucas, always a gadget freak, was intrigued by the filmmaking possibilities presented by computers. The computer-controlled camera at ILM and the desktop Apple filing system were all very well, but Lucas envisioned a day when computers would make film entirely obsolete. "Anybody who's worked with film realizes what a stupid 19th century idea it is," argued Lucas.[32] And that was because, with traditional film, every single element in a shot—actors, special effects, lightsaber glows, laser beams—had to be assembled individually, then put together on the optical compositor, a process that was a time-consuming headache, created considerable room for error, and often left the film scratched or faded. For someone who coveted control, then—especially someone who built his movies in the editing process—digital filmmaking, in which all the elements could be manipulated directly on a computer screen with no image degradation, seemed ideal. The only real problem was that Lucas had no idea how it would work. The technology he envisioned didn't exist yet, not even on paper.

In short, it was a perfect sort of research and development project to take on at Skywalker Ranch.

Not that there were actually any facilities yet. At the moment, the ranch was still mostly a series of drawings pinned to the walls at Parkhouse, though Lucas was slowly beginning to hire vice presidents and division directors he could install in offices the moment they were built. The computer division was one of his first priorities, and Lucas was determined to hire only the smartest, most visionary computer designers, programmers, and engineers available. His first employee was a brilliant computer scientist and physicist named Ed Catmull, then serving as the director of the New York Institute of Technology, housed in a converted chauffeur's quarters and garage on Long Island. He and Lucas hit it off almost immediately, and Catmull was quickly installed on the top floor of a building Lucas was renting in San Anselmo, with an office adjoining Marcia's. Over the next year, Catmull would bring in his former colleagues at NYIT one by one, slyly poaching his old partner Alvy Ray Smith and others to ensure the Lucasfilm computer division had the smartest staff available, just like Lucas wanted.

For Catmull and his staff—all science fiction geeks, blown away by *Star Wars*—working for Lucas was a dream job. "In all of Hollywood, George was the only person to actually invest in filmmaking technology in a serious way," said Catmull. "The big studios were too risk averse, but George understood the value of technical change. He was the one that provided the support when nobody else did."[33] Lucas put them to work developing a digital filmmaking workshop, complete with a digital editing system, a digital audio system, and a digital printer, where the images would be combined and manipulated.

Catmull, who admired Walt Disney nearly as much as he admired Albert Einstein, was hoping to persuade Lucas to let him devote some time to computer animation as well; Lucas, however, considered that scope creep. He wanted Catmull developing tools to make digital movies, not wasting his time on what Lucas regarded as high-tech cartoons. Catmull did his best to follow orders, though he continued to hire the kind of staff *he* wanted, even when that sometimes meant doing it on the sly; when Catmull hired a young former Disney animator named John Lasseter, he finagled the approval of Lucasfilm executives by giving Lasseter the title "interface designer."

The computer division would work diligently, though slowly, over the next few years to create the digital tools Lucas envisioned—and while Catmull and his team may have differed with Lucas over the ultimate objectives for the new equipment, they *did* share his knack for thinking up snappy names for their project. Over dinner one evening, one designer had suggested they name their new digital compositing computer the "Picture Maker." Alvy Ray Smith suggested they come up with something just a bit cooler—perhaps referencing the laser the computer used for most of its scanning—and proposed the name Pixer. After a bit more discussion, they decided to tweak the word slightly, giving it a name they all liked just a bit better.

Pixar.

The Empire Strikes Back opened on Wednesday, May 21, 1980, in 126 theaters, and broke attendance records in 125 of them. No other studio opened a movie against it. Once again, fans waited in line—many camping out overnight, some standing in pouring rain—while countless parents wrote notes excusing their kids from school, then stood in line alongside them. That same week, *Time* magazine put Darth Vader on its cover and hailed the movie as "a better film than *Star Wars*."[34] The following week, President Carter invited the visiting vice premier of China, Geng Biao, to watch the movie with him and the First Family at the White House. "Geng Biao was on the edge of his seat all the way through the movie," reported Carter. "Fortunately, he did not ask me for any of the weapons he saw in the movie."[35]

Reviews were generally positive; Lucas had won over critics at *Time* and the *Los Angeles Times,* and—in a real coup—even the highly opinionated Pauline Kael at *The New Yorker* proclaimed, "There is no sense that this ebullient, youthful saga is running thin in imagination." But many reviewers were put off by the film's intentionally darker, more grown-up tone. Janet Maslin argued in the *New York Times* that "the present film is just as polished and technically proficient [as *Star Wars*], but seldom as lighthearted and seldom as much fun."[36] Meanwhile, Maslin's colleague Vincent Canby found it positively "bland," dismissing it as "a big, expensive, time-consuming, essentially mechanical operation," and adding, "It looks like a movie that was directed at a distance."[37]

Lucas had also confused critics — and fans — by adding before the opening crawl that audiences were about to see EPISODE V — THE EMPIRE STRIKES BACK. Those paying attention pointed out that Lucas had tipped his hand on a re-release of *Star Wars*, with a new header on the crawl reading EPISODE IV — A NEW HOPE. From here on, Lucas would always claim that he had taken his enormous first draft of *Star Wars*, divided it into thirds, then decided to film the middle third first, with *A New Hope* as the fourth installment of a nine-part saga.

Kurtz could only shake his head. "That's not true," he said later. "There were a lot of little bits and pieces that were reasonably good ideas and that ended up being in the final draft [of *Star Wars*]," but "there wasn't enough material to do other movies."[38] Lucas, however, would maintain he'd had a galaxy-spanning epic mythology in mind all along, though he would sometimes waffle on whether he had intended it to be six parts or nine. Regardless, at least one critic bristled at Lucas's nerve in teasing fans with the promise of even more *Star Wars*. "George Lucas has revealed that the two pictures are actually parts four and five of a nine-part saga," huffed Judith Martin in the *Washington Post*, "as if audiences will some day receive the total the way devotees now go to Seattle for a week of immersion in Wagner's complete Ring Cycle" — a concept she dismissed as "nonsense."[39]

In the weeks leading up to the release of *The Empire Strikes Back*, Lucas remained uncertain whether he had a hit on his hands. "I think it stands just as much chance of being a hit as not being one," he said. "I guess I'm the biggest pessimist around here — after all, I said the very same thing about the first one."[40] He was also concerned about the math; after prints, advertising, and distribution costs, *Empire* was going to have to make $57 million just for Lucas to break even. And to build Skywalker Ranch into the kind of complex he envisioned, *Empire* was going to have to do much more than merely break even.

He needn't have worried. Within five weeks, the film had made $64 million; by September, it would surpass $160 million. *Empire* would close out 1980 as the year's biggest movie, and by the end of its first run, it would gross nearly $210 million, making it the third-most-successful movie of all time, trailing only *Star Wars* and *Jaws*. Lucasfilm would pocket more than $100 million in profits.

Lucas had literally bet the ranch — Skywalker Ranch — on *Empire* and won.

With *Empire* behind them, Marcia may have hoped that she and her husband could at last have a little downtime together. "My wife likes to have vacations," Lucas told *Starlog* magazine. "She doesn't like not to be able to go anywhere, year in and year out. She'd like to be able to say, 'Look, let's take off for two or three weeks and just cool out.' . . . It always comes down to saying [to her], 'Next week. Just let me get past this thing.' By the time you get past this thing, there's always something else. And you can't leave."[41]

This time, the something else was *Raiders of the Lost Ark*. Once again, Marcia would have to wait.

Lucas had actually shopped *Raiders* all over Hollywood for the better part of a year, sending Kasdan's first draft around to Universal, Warners, Orion, and Paramount — along with a list of terms. In a deal reminiscent of the one he had cut with Fox for *Empire*, Lucas was offering to finance *Raiders* himself to the tune of $20 million, and would then permit a studio to distribute the completed film in exchange for a percentage of the profits.

Warners, still trying to make amends to Lucas after his bitter experience with the studio on *THX 1138*, expressed interest early but then dragged their feet for so long that they were outmaneuvered by Paramount and its aggressive, forward-thinking president, Michael Eisner. "George came over to my house," recalled Eisner, "and he said, 'Let's make the best deal they've ever made in Hollywood.'"[42] On November 7, 1979, Paramount announced an agreement with Lucasfilm and The Raiders Company, in which the studio had given Lucas nearly everything he'd asked for. The film's profits would be split 60–40 in favor of the studio, until the film broke even, at which point profits would be shared equally. Not a bad deal, but Warner executives warned Paramount that giving a filmmaker what he wanted meant the end of the film industry—a criticism that had already cost Ladd his job at Fox. But Eisner wasn't a bit worried. "If we got shafted on this arrangement, we would like to be shafted two or three times a year in this way," he said.[43]

Even as Kasdan continued with his script through 1979 and into 1980, there had been a moment of clarity from Lucas regarding the name of their main character. Spielberg continued to insist he didn't like the name Indiana Smith, which put him in mind of the 1966 Steve McQueen western *Nevada Smith*. For Lucas, who simply wanted the main character to have a quintessentially American name, it was no problem to change the name to Indiana Jones.

The name was easy; casting, however, proved more difficult. As he usually did, Lucas had thrown a wide net, bringing in lots of actors and actresses for the lead roles of Indy and Marion—Christopher Guest, Debra Winger, David Hasselhoff, Jane Seymour, Sam Elliott, Karen Allen—and then videotaping various combinations to see if sparks flew. He was impressed with Tom Selleck, who had done mostly commercials and small television parts, but he had recently landed the lead role in the CBS television series *Magnum, P.I.* The network, however, sensing their actor's rising star, locked Selleck in to his contract, making him unavailable.

Lucas admitted to Spielberg that he personally thought Harrison Ford would make an ideal Indiana Jones; he had even described him in one treatment as being played by "someone like Harrison Ford."[44] But Lucas had used Ford in every movie he'd directed or produced since *American Graffiti* and didn't want to be seen as relying on a "stable" of actors, in the same way Scorsese repeatedly utilized actor Robert De Niro or Coppola had used James Caan. Still, Lucas and Spielberg met with Ford anyway and immediately knew they'd found their Dr. Jones. Ford's contract was signed in June 1980, only a few weeks before principal filming was scheduled to begin in France.

There were some inside Paramount who were still skeptical of

Spielberg's ability to bring in a film on time and on budget—and Spielberg, despite the success of *Jaws* and *Close Encounters,* was coming off the bomb *1941.* For Spielberg, then, "*Raiders* was a film to clean out my system," as he described it later, "[to] blow the saliva out of my mouthpiece."[45] Lucas advised Spielberg to approach the film almost as if he were directing an old movie serial, shooting, said Lucas, "quick and dirty."[46] In a clever bit of misdirection, Lucas also advised Paramount that the film would be shot in eighty-eight days, while he and Spielberg had privately agreed it could probably be finished more quickly than that. This way, if Paramount asked, Lucas could always tell the studio they were ahead of schedule and would be left alone.

Lucas had also supplied Spielberg with a first-rate supporting staff, utilizing much of the same crew at Elstree that Lucas had used on *The Empire Strikes Back,* installing Howard Kazanjian as an executive producer and putting ILM entirely at his disposal for special effects. (Spielberg would be permitted to hire an associate producer of his choice as well, bringing in Frank Marshall, a veteran of several films for Peter Bogdanovich.) "What I learned on *Raiders* is that you set the whole thing up," said Lucas. "Get the script pretty much the way you want it. Then, if you hire the right person whom you agree with, you go with their vision. . . . But the truth is, we agreed completely on the vision."[47] Or almost. Lucas and Spielberg still disagreed over the nature of Indy's character: Lucas saw him as a slick playboy who used treasure hunting to support a posh lifestyle, all traits that Spielberg—who saw Indy as more noble than that—tried to downplay. And ultimately, as he had done with Han Solo, Harrison Ford managed to incorporate a bit of his own personality into the character, giving Indy just the right combination of vitality and vulnerability.

Filming began on June 23, 1980, and for the most part Lucas left Spielberg alone—one of the few directors he wouldn't hover over or pick at. "You're the director," he would tell Spielberg. "This is your movie." Spielberg, who saw himself as mostly a hired gun, was having none of it. "Wait a minute, you're the producer," Spielberg would shoot back. "This is YOUR movie."[48] For the most part, Lucas was content mainly to solve problems and keep an eye on the bottom line. When the costs of building a four-engine flying wing threatened to send production over budget, for example, Lucas simply broke two engines off the concept model and told the crew to build it that way. The plane came in under budget. There were still times, however, when he found himself itching to look through the camera—and with Spielberg's indulgence, he would direct a second-unit crew. "It's great to see George running around with his director's hat on, chasing a second unit around, setting up shots and shooting them," said Spielberg.[49] At one point Kasdan asked Lucas why he hadn't directed *Raiders* himself. "Because then I'd never get to see it," Lucas responded matter-of-factly.[50]

At the moment, however, he was actually subject to a technicality that would have prevented him from directing—or at least receiving a director's credit—even if he'd wanted to. On the theatrical release of *Empire,* Lucas had placed all the film's credits at the end of the movie—just as he had done with *Star Wars*—which meant director Irvin Kershner didn't receive his director's credit at the beginning of the movie, as mandated by the writers' and directors' guilds.[51] While the guilds had looked the other way on *Star Wars*—the Lucasfilm logo, they decided, counted as the director's and writer's name—this time they threatened to have the film pulled from theaters unless Lucas recut the movie with the credits at the beginning, and fined director Irvin Kershner $25,000 for Lucas's defiance. To Lucas, it was a preposterous requirement. Why bore an audience with credits when you could jump right into the action? He refused to recut, paid Kershner's penalty himself ("I consider it extortion," Lucas seethed), then resigned from both guilds.[52] The credits would stay at the end—where most films have put them ever since—and Lucas would remain as disdainful of guilds and unions as ever.

George and Marcia trailed along after Spielberg as he moved from Elstree to Tunisia—where Spielberg filmed in many of the same locations Lucas had used in *Star Wars*—and finally to Hawaii, where the opening moments of the movie would be shot during the final week of production. Spielberg completed filming on the seventy-third day—right on the schedule he and Lucas had privately concocted but fifteen days ahead of the one they'd submitted to Paramount. They celebrated Marcia's birthday at the wrap party, where Lucas dared producer Frank Marshall to jump into her birthday cake. He did.

While principal photography had been completed quickly, Lucas was disappointed to find ILM was lagging behind, struggling mostly with the effects needed for the sequence with the opening of the Ark. ILM had been given free rein—the only direction provided in the script was "They open the box and all hell breaks loose"—but everyone, from Lucas on down to the last animator, was unhappy with the sequence.[53] With six months to finish the scene, the suggestion was made to hand off the effects to an outside company. Lucas was out of patience. "I'd done *Star Wars,* for God's sakes," he exploded. "I knew what real worry was."[54] ILM would finish the effects on time, and in spectacular fashion, but they would do so with Lucas practically straddling their shoulders.

Lucas had promised Spielberg final cut—but that didn't mean he wasn't going to involve himself in the editing process. Spielberg had insisted on using his own editor, Michael Kahn, whom he'd worked with on *Close Encounters,* and Lucas sat with Kahn to review the first pass on the movie. Spielberg wasn't concerned about what Lucas might do. "I get to change it all back if I don't like what George is doing to the picture," he said, "but I have never not liked what George has done."[55] As it turned out, Lucas asked for very few changes, for example, the removal of a joke that he thought fell flat. But there was one sequence, in which Indy shoots a scimitar-spinning swordsman dead rather than face a prolonged fight, which Lucas was still uncertain of. Spielberg had filmed the scene both with and without the fight, and Lucas actually preferred the longer version. But Spielberg, exercising the power of final cut, insisted on the shortened version—and Lucas, when he saw the reaction from a test audience, had to agree. "Well, I guess that works," he admitted to Spielberg.[56]

There was one last editorial opinion that mattered. After watching the final cut, Marcia Lucas pointed out that the audience hadn't seen what happened to Marion after she and Indy survived the ordeal with the Ark. There was a collective slapping of foreheads, and Harrison Ford and Karen Allen returned to film a brief scene on the steps of San Francisco City Hall, in which Marion and Indy walk away arm in arm, in what Allen called their "*Casablanca* moment."[57] George might have intuitively known when a film didn't work logically, but Marcia could always tell when he'd shortchanged the audience emotionally.

As 1980 drew to a close, *The Empire Strikes Back* and *Raiders of the Lost Ark* weren't the only projects Lucas had had his hands on over the past year. In November, Lucas donated nearly $5 million to the University of Southern California to underwrite the costs of constructing a fifteen-thousand-square-foot post-production facility, with state-of-the-art equipment for—what else?—editing, sound recording, and animation, three of Lucas's passions. "It's logical and appropriate for me to support the place that provided me with the means to get going into film," Lucas said.[58] A year later, Marcia would participate in the groundbreaking ceremony, and the $14 million project would be completed by November 1984. Gone were the rickety buildings and worn-looking central patio; in their place were the George Lucas Instructional Building, the Steven Spielberg Music Scoring Stage, the Marcia Lucas Post-Production Building, and the Gary Kurtz Patio.

Another project had come at the request of Coppola, who asked Lucas to help one of their idols, seventy-year-old director Akira Kurosawa, find the funding he needed to complete his samurai drama *Kagemusha,* which had been left in the lurch by Japan's Toho studios. "It was a tragedy," said Lucas. "It was like telling Michelangelo, 'All right, you're 70 and we're not letting you paint anymore.'"[59] With the heft of *Star Wars* behind him, Lucas went to Ladd, who secured funding from Fox just as he was being hustled out the door. On its release in 1980, *Kagemusha* went on to win the Palme d'Or at the Cannes Film Festival, vindication for the venerable filmmaker, as well as for Lucas, who saw it as practically a moral obligation to assist fellow filmmakers in need, "either young directors who haven't yet had a shot at it," Lucas said, "or older directors who've been passed by but still have creative ideas."[60]

As for a young director who hadn't yet had a shot, in 1980 that was Lucas's scribe of choice, Lawrence Kasdan, who was looking to direct one of his own screenplays, the steamy thriller *Body Heat*. Ladd was interested in producing it at his own production outfit, The Ladd Company, but informed Kasdan—in a move reminiscent of Lucas's experience on *American Graffiti*—that he had to find a "name" producer who could step in if the film ran into trouble. Lucas thought the idea of Kasdan needing an overseer was "ridiculous," but he threw the weight of his name behind the project anyway, and assured Ladd that he would be happy to defer his fee to cover the cost of any overages. Publicly, however, Lucas maintained a low profile, keeping his name off the credits ("there would have been a giant controversy about *me* making this picture," he sighed), and making sure all credit for the film's success went to Kasdan.[61] *Body Heat* opened to strong reviews in 1981 and turned a healthy profit; Lucas's faith in Kasdan to pull it off had never wavered. Kasdan would go on to write and direct hits like *The Big Chill* and *Silverado*, and would come back to write both *Return of the Jedi* and, more than thirty years later, *The Force Awakens*.

Less successfully, Lucas had also helped find funding for a project by another old friend. John Korty—who, perhaps more than anybody else, had inspired American Zoetrope with his northern California beachfront film studio—had been experimenting with a new kind of animation he called "lumage," in which an image was cut out and then lit from below the animation stand instead of above. Lucas, always intrigued by animation, arranged for Korty to meet with Ladd, who agreed to finance Korty's *Twice Upon a Time* for The Ladd Company. The film would open in 1982, and quietly sink out of sight. "Nobody knew quite how to sell it," sighed Korty.[62]

Lucas, however, would have no problem selling another movie he already had in pre-production in 1980. On May 14—one week before the premiere of *The Empire Strikes Back*—he had announced at a press conference that he already had a title for his next film: *Revenge of the Jedi.*

George Lucas was finally done with Hollywood.

While work on *The Empire Strikes Back* had required him to maintain offices in southern California, with that film wrapped—and before production could kick in on *Jedi*—Lucas closed down The Egg Company and brought everything north. The move would take several months, and Lucas couldn't get away fast enough. "Hollywood is like a grandiose high school as far as I'm concerned," he said derisively— and to his disappointment, employees at The Egg Company hadn't behaved much better.[63] "It was a bunch of spoiled people," said Lucasfilm chief of operations Robert Greber.[64] Assistant Bunny Alsup lamented that "our delightful, casual Lucasfilm was fading into a big-deal corporation."[65] Lucas also clashed with his own handpicked president, Charlie Weber. "George was focused on building the ranch, making *Jedi,* creating this kind of filmmaker's community," said one Lucasfilm insider, "while Charlie was looking at diversifying into other businesses to invest George's money. But George had no interest in diversifying."[66] Lucas dismissed Weber and promoted Greber. The Egg Company was gone; Lucasfilm would now reside entirely in northern California, much of it at the ranch once it was completed.

At the moment, Lucas was concentrating mainly on building what he referred to as the "farm group," a small cluster of buildings that would eventually house the ranch manager and caretaker, with the main ranch house further up a curving road beyond a man-made lake. Lucas wanted everything to be interesting and well designed; the Victorian-influenced buildings would be octagonal, with casement windows and stained glass, tongue-and-groove paneling, cupolas, and fireplaces—modern, with state-of-the-art equipment, yet looking as if they'd been sitting in the hills for generations. "[George] set out to bring the vision we shared [for Zoetrope] into reality—the way *he* saw it," said Coppola, who, flush with the success of *Apocalypse Now,* was trying to get back in the empire-building business himself. Looking for a new headquarters for Zoetrope, he was angling to purchase a property he couldn't afford at Hollywood General Studios. "Lucas has a bank called *Star Wars*," said Spielberg coyly. "Coppola doesn't have a bank—only courage and fortitude."[67]

The courageous Coppola approached Lucas and Spielberg for funding and was turned down by both. Coppola was irked, but Lucas was even madder at what he saw as Coppola's colossal gall at trying to one-up him. "Francis helped me and gave me a chance, but at the same time he made a lot of money off me," Lucas said later. "Francis has a tendency to see the parade marching down the street and to run in front of it with a flag and become the leader." What annoyed Lucas more than anything else was the very idea that Coppola would abandon northern California in favor of the pestilence of Hollywood. "I thought Francis was betraying all of us in San Francisco who had been struggling to make this community a viable film alternative."[68] Coppola would raise the money and head south anyway—and true to form, he would lose the studio three years later, hard on the heels of his musical flop *One from the Heart*.

That was typical Coppola—and typical Lucas. Sitting together for an interview years later, both were asked what they would do if suddenly given $2 billion to do anything they wished. Where Coppola replied with his usual bombast—"I'd borrow another $2 billion and build a city!"—Lucas's response was straight out of Modesto: "I'd invest a billion of it," he said, "and use the other billion to build a town."[69] With Skywalker Ranch, that's exactly what he was doing. No detail was too small for Lucas to obsess over. Visitors to Parkhouse would find one room filled with fabric swatches, blueprints, and furniture samples, as if Lucas wanted everyone to understand just how seriously he was taking this ranch endeavor. Within a year he would proudly be walking the property with a reporter from the *New York Times*, showing off the nearly completed main house, swimming pool, and tennis courts. The three-acre lake—which Lucas would later dub Lake Ewok—would be stocked with trout, while an electronic deer fence lined the perimeter, much to the annoyance of the neighbors. Beneath their feet, a series of tunnels connected the buildings, and closed circuit television cameras swept the complex, looking for invaders or the merely nosy. "It's a totally controlled environment," Lucas said proudly.[70] *Totally controlled.* Just the way he liked it.

With the company's shift north, the other major task was to ensure that ILM—still working out of the Kerner Building—stayed in business permanently. Up until now, as one ILM model maker described it, "a kind of lifestyle had been established where everybody worked on one film and, when it was done, everything came to an end."[71] Lucas wanted that to change. While Weber had boasted that ILM could become a "first-class entity" by continuing to create effects for Lucas-produced films, Lucas wasn't actually involved with enough films at any given moment to keep ILM open full-time.[72] Instead, he let it be known that ILM could be hired to produce effects for anyone. "We were trying to bring in outside projects so that we can keep everyone here working," said Lucas.[73]

The first non-Lucas project to come through the door would be the Paramount-Disney film *Dragonslayer,* though even it had a touch of family about it, as it was written, produced, and directed by two members of the USC Mafia, Hal Barwood and Matthew Robbins. Over the next three years, ILM would take on a dozen more projects on its way to becoming the preeminent special effects shop; over a fifteen-year period, from 1980 to 1995, ILM would win the Academy Award for Best Visual Effects thirteen times, often competing with itself in the same category.

There was one particular special effect that would turn out to have far-reaching impact, though the film in which it appeared, *Star Trek II: The Wrath of Khan,* wouldn't even be in contention for the Academy Award. The remarkable sequence—a computer-generated flyover of the creation of a planet, with volcanoes bursting and clouds forming— was actually the result of frustration on the part of Ed Catmull, who had spent the previous two years trying to convince Lucas that his computer division could do more than just build digital editing and mixing equipment. Determined to prove the point, Catmull and his team put together the computer-animated footage that would become *Star Trek II*'s "Genesis Effect" sequence. Catmull called it "a sixty second commercial to George Lucas" to prove they could create realistic animation with the computer, and hoped for the best. It was groundbreaking work—the first fully computer-animated sequence to appear in any film—and wowed everyone but Lucas, who watched from a doorway, congratulated the team on one of the camera shots, then disappeared.[74]

Still, Lucas was pragmatic enough to appreciate it as the kind of work ILM needed. When Mark Hamill—understandably protective of the *Star Wars* franchise—heard that the computer division was doing a computer animation for the rival *Star Trek* franchise, he whirled on Lucas in mock protest. "You traitors!" Hamill roared. "George, how could you do that?"

"It's business, kid," said Lucas.[75]

Lucas had no idea what was going to happen in *Revenge of the Jedi*. Beyond the title, he had little more than some notes scribbled on yellow pads. Harrison Ford, tiring of Han Solo, had urged Lucas to kill his character off—but Lucas had hedged his bets in *Empire*, merely deep-freezing Solo in carbonite. His fate, it seemed, hinged on whether Ford would sign on for the third movie—but now that Lucas had slid a third *Star Wars* clause into Ford's contract for multiple Indiana Jones films, Solo seemed safe.

Gary Kurtz still wasn't so sure. At one point, Kurtz and Lucas had sat down to discuss the plot of the final film, which Kurtz—who had loved *Empire*'s more serious, grown-up feel—wanted to end on a more poignant, almost downbeat note. "The original idea was that they would recover Han Solo in the early part of the story," recalled Kurtz, "and that he would die in the middle part of the film in a raid on an Imperial base."[76] That would have left Leia alone to assume her new duties as queen of the upstart Alliance, "with Luke riding off into the sunset, metaphorically, on his own. And that would have been a bittersweet ending," said Kurtz, "but I think it would have been dramatically stronger."[77]

Lucas wouldn't even consider it—and Kurtz thought he knew why. During production on *Empire,* Kurtz had spent a fair amount of time ferrying representatives from the Kenner toy company around the set. Lucas was clearly keeping an eye on the "toyetic" qualities of his franchise—and "George then decided he didn't want any of the principals killed," said Kurtz.[78] Or, as Ford put it more sardonically, "George didn't think there was any future in dead Han toys."[79] "It's a shame," said Kurtz later. "They make three times as much on toys as they do on films. It's natural to make decisions that protect the toy business, but that's not the best thing for making quality films."[80]

The Lucas-Kurtz partnership—which had produced three of the most successful films in history in less than a decade—was on increasingly thin ice. Lucas was still smarting over Kurtz's budget busting on *Empire,* while Kurtz was wary of the growing influence of merchandising. But as Lucas worked his way through his first story treatment for *Jedi*—disregarding Kurtz's ideas for a bittersweet ending—one plot element finally cracked the ice for good: Lucas had made an assault on the Death Star a pivotal part of his story. "It sounds redundant," he confessed, "but we'll do it again."[81]

Kurtz wasn't going to do it again. "We had a kind of mutual parting of the ways, because I just didn't want to do another attack on the Death Star," he told an interviewer.[82] "So we agreed that I should probably leave."[83] Lucas tapped Howard Kazanjian, who had already stepped in at the tail end of *Empire* and had served as his producer on *Raiders,* to fill the same role on *Jedi.* Kurtz, meanwhile, left to work with Jim Henson on his ambitious film *The Dark Crystal.* "It wasn't acrimonious," Kurtz said of his departure. "It was just that [Lucas] felt he would probably be more comfortable with someone else handling the production on *Jedi,* and I felt that I would prefer a different kind of challenge, that wasn't kind of repeating something I had already done."[84] While Kurtz would always refer to his relationship with Lucas as "professional," the two of them would not work together again.

With a new producer in place, Lucas turned next to the important matter of his director. Briefly, he considered Kershner; although he could be slow, Lucas liked him, but Kershner dismissed the idea immediately. "I didn't want to become simply another Lucas employee," said Kershner. "I love George, but I wanted to go my own way."[85] In the meantime, Lucas had Kazanjian scouting for potential directors, though with Lucas's present persona non grata status with the Directors Guild, Kazanjian had to be picky—for the sake of both Lucas and his director. A DGA director could be blacklisted for working with Lucas, or the guild could force the director to walk off the film mid-project—and fine him if he refused.

Lucas was looking seriously at experienced directors like Richard Donner, up-and-comers like Joe Dante, and several quirky *artistes* like David Cronenberg and David Lynch. It was Lynch, in fact, who intrigued Lucas the most; at the suggestion of Stanley Kubrick, Lucas had screened a copy of Lynch's darkly disturbing *Eraserhead* and found it "bizarre...but interesting."[86] It was the kind of highly personal filmmaking Lucas admired. Unfortunately, said Lynch, "I had next to zero interest, but I always admired George. He's a guy who does what he loves. And I do what I love." Lynch went to visit with Lucas at the ranch, where Lucas took him for a ride in his Ferrari and then to lunch at a salad bar. Lynch came down with a mean migraine headache and by his own recollection "crawled into a phone booth" to call his agent. "No way I can do this," he moaned into the phone. "No way!" The reason was simple. "Lynch decided he didn't want to do a George Lucas movie," said Mark Hamill. "He felt he couldn't be constantly answering to another producer. George didn't want to restrict someone that original." Lucas could only agree with Hamill's assessment. "I think I may have gone a bridge too far on that one."[87]

Rather than a visionary, Lucas decided he was better off with a workhorse—preferably one who had worked in television, where it was generally accepted that the director was subservient to the executive producer. In early 1981 Lucas screened the thriller *Eye of the Needle* by the Welsh director Richard Marquand, who had spent much of his career directing television movies, including the 1979 biopic *Birth of the Beatles*. Like Lynch, Marquand, too, was invited to the ranch, and spent the entire day with Lucas and Marcia, eating dinner, then talking late into the evening. "[Lucas] thought Richard was a director he would feel comfortable with," said one insider, "one who could understand that essentially it'd be George's movie."[88] That was fine with Marquand. "I was bowled over by *Star Wars*," he said. "What made me hesitate about directing *Jedi* was the fact that anybody would consider *me* for such a picture."[89] Furthermore, Lucas liked that Marquand respected the need to bring in a project on time and on budget—but mostly he liked that the soft-spoken Marquand was willing to adhere as closely as possible to Lucas's vision for the movie. Said Marquand later, "I always had the feeling that possibly I'd find myself in a situation where I was a horse dragging this thing along, with George holding the reins."[90] He had no idea.

The last missing piece to be found was the screenwriter. For *Jedi*, Lucas wanted to write an entire script himself first, rather than just handing off a story treatment to a screenwriter, as he had done with *Empire*. But the writing was a chore, as usual, and Lucas found himself leaving blank the final pages of a revised draft, knowing full well they could be fixed when he handed the script off to his screenwriter of choice, Lawrence Kasdan. Lucas hadn't been entirely sure whether Kasdan would take the job, now that *Body Heat* had put him on the map as a successful writer-director, but it turned out that all Lucas had to do was ask. "I was surprised to find myself writing *Jedi*, because I was already a director and I had no intention of writing for anyone ever again," said Kasdan. "But George asked me as a favor, and he'd already been so helpful to me."[91]

In early summer 1981, Lucas called Kasdan, Kazanjian, and Marquand out to Parkhouse for a story meeting to work out details of the plot. There were several elements Lucas knew he needed. He wanted to feature Jabba the Hutt, now that he finally had the resources to build the character he had envisioned, then scrapped, in *Star Wars*. He wanted Luke to have a twin sister, though he *still* wasn't certain it was

Leia. And he wanted a primitive society aiding the rebels, another idea he'd lifted from the early drafts of *Star Wars* in which he'd brought a planet of Wookiees to the aid of the heroes. At the same time, he also had McQuarrie and Joe Johnston at ILM sketching ships and creatures, with little idea where or how any of them fit into the movie—"a free-for-all," as one ILM artist described it. "The process was the same for *Jedi* as [for] *Empire*," recalled Kasdan. "There were designs and pictures of things before I even started writing."[92]

The toughest part of the script was ensuring they gave every character something memorable to do—and Kasdan, looking for dramatic impact, suggested killing someone off, arguing that it would give the movie "more emotional weight if someone you love is lost along the way." But Lucas dismissed such suggestions outright. "You don't have to kill people," he told Kasdan with just a hint of annoyance. "You're a product of the 1980s. You don't go around killing people. It's not nice."[93] Still, Lucas wasn't above teasing Kasdan about his desire to inject a little angst into the script. As he described Luke dragging the mortally wounded Vader to safety near the conclusion of the film, Lucas, with a straight face, suggested "the ultimate twist": "Luke takes [Vader's] mask off...and then Luke puts it on and says, 'Now I am Vader.' Surprise!...'Now I will go and kill the fleet and I will rule the universe.'"

Kasdan could barely contain his enthusiasm. "That's what I think should happen," he told Lucas.

"No, no, no," Lucas shot back, slightly exasperated. "Come on, this is for kids."[94]

Star Wars had been born of Lucas's own love of comic books, fairy tales, and Saturday morning serials—his way, as he had said at the time, of giving a new generation its own mythology. There would be no bittersweet endings, no killing off of central characters, no heroes turning evil. "The whole point of the film...is for you to be real uplifted, emotionally and spiritually, and feel absolutely good about life," Lucas explained to Kasdan. "That is the greatest thing that we could possibly ever do."[95]

Not everyone shared Lucas's optimism. "George has a predisposition for happy endings," sighed Harrison Ford.[96] Even Hamill, the comic book fan who was nearly always inclined to give the story the benefit of the doubt, admitted to being somewhat disappointed in *Jedi*'s lack of heft, complaining to Lucas that it "all seemed so pat."

Lucas smiled. "So are fairy tales."[97]

As Kasdan went on his way to write the next draft of the script, Lucas had his legal team working to wrap up the legal and financial negotiations with Fox, which had been dragging on for nearly two years. With Ladd now out of the picture, Lucas wasn't inclined to negotiate nicely, and discussions hadn't gone well, with Fox griping that the percentage of the profits Lucas was offering was so low that the studio wouldn't have much incentive to promote the film. Lucas had little sympathy for their complaints, and little patience; once again, he was going to be putting all of his own money on the line. But after tying up nearly all of his *Empire* profits in the ranch, Lucas didn't have enough on hand to cover the $30 million he thought it would take to make *Jedi*. That gave Fox some much-desired leverage—financing in exchange for profits—but Lucas wasn't going to make it easy on them. And when negotiations between Lucasfilm and Fox began to falter—with Greber playing with relish the role of the bad cop—Lucas finally gave Fox an ultimatum: reach an agreement within thirty days, or he would take his movie to another studio.

Fox, now under the leadership of CEO Marvin Davis—a former oilman and an amiable enough blowhard—did its best to stand firm. The studio was still willing to take a lopsided deal on the gross receipts, though it was pushing for its piece of the pie to actually *increase* as the film earned more and more money, rather than bottoming out, as it had with *Empire*. Lucas eventually agreed that in exchange for a loan of $20 million, Fox's share in the profits would increase incrementally as the film made money, topping out at 40 percent once the film cleared $105 million. There were other sticky details to work out involving television, cable, and video rights—"Fox was greedy," complained

Greber—but the deal still tilted heavily in Lucasfilm's favor. After inking the 224-page final contract, the six-foot-four Davis draped an enormous arm over Lucas's shoulder. "Georgie boy," drawled Davis, "you're going to make me rich with movies."[98]

Lucas was doing just fine in that regard without Davis. In June 1981, *Raiders of the Lost Ark* had premiered to near-unanimous raves from audiences and critics. "One of the most deliriously funny, ingenious, and stylish American adventure movies ever made," wrote Vincent Canby in the *New York Times*, applauding Lucas and Spielberg as a "happy collaboration."[99] In the pages of *Time*, Richard Schickel hailed the film as "surely the best two hours of pure entertainment anyone is going to find" and compared it favorably to "the kind of movie Walt Disney might have made had he lived into the 1980s."[100] In the *Chicago Sun-Times*, Roger Ebert reviewed the film almost feverishly, cheering *Raiders* as "an out-of-body experience, a movie of glorious imagination and breakneck speed that grabs you in the first shot, hurtles you through a series of incredible adventures, and deposits you back in reality two hours later—breathless, dizzy, wrung-out, and with a silly grin on your face."[101]

Not everyone was as enthusiastic. While Pauline Kael had been won over by the more adult-themed *Empire Strikes Back*, she was disappointed in both Lucas and Spielberg for reverting to what she regarded as childish entertainment. "There's no exhilaration in this dumb, motor excitement," lamented Kael. "If Lucas...weren't hooked on the crap of his childhood—if he brought his resources to bear on some projects with human beings in them—there's no imagining the result.... [E]ssentially, George Lucas is in the toy business."[102] It was a punch that Kael couldn't land; Lucas *liked* being in the toy business. Those looking for *art*, he insisted, needed to look elsewhere. "I don't take it that seriously," Lucas said. "My films are closer to amusement park rides than to a play or novel. You get in line for a second ride."[103] Roger Ebert put it best by putting it succinctly: "[*Raiders*] wants only to entertain. It succeeds."[104]

It succeeded spectacularly, albeit slowly. The first weekend grosses, totaling a little more than $8 million, were somewhat disappointing, though perhaps unsurprising as the film had been released with little hype or promotion. Even the movie poster played up the collaboration of Lucas and Spielberg more than the film itself. Once again, Lucas and Spielberg kept an eye on things from a beach in Hawaii, building their usual good luck sand castle as the numbers came in. "I thought we had failed," Spielberg said, "[except] this time, the sand castle lasted a long time. It didn't get washed away right away, which is always our way of guessing if the film has legs. We have this weird superstition."[105] *Raiders of the Lost Ark* would earn more than $160 million before the end of 1981, making it the year's highest-grossing movie. By April 1982, it would be the fourth-highest-grossing film of all time, sitting behind *Star Wars, Jaws,* and *The Empire Strikes Back.* Superstition indeed.

George and Marcia Lucas arrived in London on January 7, 1982, four days before filming on *Revenge of the Jedi* was scheduled to begin at Elstree. They didn't arrive alone; five months earlier, after years of trying unsuccessfully to conceive, the Lucases had adopted a newborn baby girl they named Amanda. Lucas had held her in his hands only hours after she was born, and immediately felt himself a changed man—"just like a bolt of lightning hit me," he said. "The challenge is always trying to do something that's all-consuming while having a private life," he explained later. "I had made the decision, after *Star Wars,* that I had certain goals in my private life. One was to be independent of Hollywood, the other was to have a family. When you have kids, you have a priority in your life."[106] Lucas may have meant it, but as work progressed on *Jedi,* he'd find it harder and harder to make his family his priority. And by the time work on the film was complete, his private life would be in shambles.

Lucas had hired Richard Marquand largely because he sensed Marquand would stay closest to his own vision for the film—there would be no comic ad-libs or artsy restaging of shots that had already been storyboarded—and once Lucas arrived in London, he all but took over the film. "George came and he never left," said producer Robert Watts. "Richard couldn't grasp it and George was concerned, so he never left." Lucas had hovered over Kershner during *Empire*, but Kershner had been an older, more seasoned director who was still willing to push back at his producer. Not so the low-key Marquand. "He was intimidated by George," said production designer Norman Reynolds.[107] Marquand compared his job to "trying to direct *King Lear*—with Shakespeare in the next room."[108]

Lucas knew he was in Marquand's way—but he didn't care. Marquand was "essentially doing a movie that's been established, [and] ultimately I'll have the final say," said Lucas.[109] Cast and crew tended to look to Lucas for direction or guidance, even with Marquand standing nearby. Marquand, scrambling for control of the film, tried to put the best face on things, insisting that he really did want Lucas on the set, providing input. "If I am going to do this properly, you've got to give me your time," he told Lucas. "I like my producer around. And you're more than the producer—you wrote this goddamn thing, so let's get it right."[110] But Lucas did more than just provide suggestions or direct second unit; "George harassed Richard Marquand into more or less doing what he wanted," said Kurtz.[111] Most mornings, Lucas would ask to see Marquand's shot list for the day—an intensely private list most directors guard like a diary. To ensure he got the shots he wanted, Lucas insisted that Marquand film in the "documentary" style Lucas had used on *Star Wars*, with multiple cameras catching the action from various angles, and then choosing the best shot in editing. Marquand found it all exasperating. "I imposed my will a little bit, as I have a tendency to do," Lucas admitted.[112] "I hadn't realized that ultimately it's probably easier for me to do these things than to farm them out."[113] Marquand could only stand by, said Watts, and "take in what George said, and make it sound like it was his idea as well."[114]

That didn't mean all of Lucas's ideas were popular. Both cast and crew alike found his new heroes, the Ewoks, somewhat grating. Lucas had sent the characters back through design again and again, finally settling on a cuddly teddy bear–like look. ("Dare to be cute," Lucas told *Rolling Stone* later. "The worst we could do is get criticized for it.")[115] Ralph McQuarrie had thrown up his hands in resignation over the creatures. "There was a feeling that it was maybe too obvious a marketing idea," said one designer. "I think Ralph didn't like that too much." But Lucas loved them, instructing second-unit director Roger Christian to get lots of footage of Ewoks dancing and celebrating for *Jedi*'s final scene. "So I started doing that, and George fell in love with it, but I said, 'Please get me off this,'" said Christian. The fact was "George loved them. Nobody else did."[116] Lucas was so enchanted by one of the young actors inside the costumes, eleven-year-old Warwick Davis, playing the feisty Ewok Wicket, that he signed him to another film that was still just a wisp of an idea, a fairy tale with a little person as the hero that would eventually become *Willow*.

The final weeks on *Jedi* were spent on location, with the desert around Yuma, Arizona, standing in for Tatooine, and the redwoods of Crescent City, California, doing duty as the forest moon of Endor. To keep the production a secret, Lucas, Kazanjian, and Lucasfilm's marketing department had hats, clipboards, and film cans labeled with the name of a fictitious horror movie called *Blue Harvest*. The façade quickly fell away in Yuma, however, when dune buggy enthusiasts caught a glimpse of Harrison Ford on Jabba the Hutt's enormous skiff and surmised what was really going on. As he had in London, Lucas shadowed Marquand around the Arizona desert, doing more than just advising as Marquand shot the elaborate fights and stunts. "Richard would set a lot of the shots up, but George was always there kind of like [an] advisor," said co-producer Jim Bloom diplomatically. Lucas was particularly frustrated with the mouth of the sarlacc, visible at the bottom of an enormous pit dug into the desert sand. Lucas debated whether the monster should even be seen at all, and bickered with Kazanjian over the cost. The final creature—a large round mouth lined with rows of teeth—was horrifying, though it bore enough of a resemblance to a certain body part that Carrie Fisher took to referring to it as "the sand vagina."[117] Lucas could only sigh with irritation.

By the time he reached Crescent City, his nerves were fraying, and his patience with Marquand—and pretty much everyone else—was nearly exhausted. "I'm not having fun," he told one reporter testily. "No matter how much I think everybody knows about *Star Wars* now, they don't. I've given Richard the answers to a million questions over the last year, filled everybody in on everything I can think of, and yet when we get here the crew comes up with a thousand questions a day—I'm not exaggerating—that only I can answer....I'm only doing this because I started it and now I have to finish it. The next trilogy will be all someone else's vision."[118]

Principal photography on *Jedi* wrapped in mid-May 1982; Marquand had brought the film in on time and on budget. Crew members remarked that Marquand looked pale and ill—and truth be told, Lucas didn't look great either. He'd lost twenty pounds over the past five months, which most attributed to exhaustion. What only very few people knew was that Lucas's private life was coming unraveled. Even as Lucas settled into ILM to oversee *Jedi*'s effects, Ken Ralston, an ILM team member since *Star Wars*, noticed a definite change in his boss. "We were wondering what had happened to George," said Ralston. "*Jedi* wasn't the same experience we'd had before.... [T]here was a definite lack of involvement with him directly; we weren't getting the kind of feedback and information that we got before and you could feel something wasn't right."[119]

What wasn't right was that George and Marcia's thirteen-year marriage was quickly imploding, largely because of Lucas's own neglect. He knew he could be difficult to live with. "It's been very hard on Marcia, living with somebody who is constantly in agony, uptight and worried, off in never-never land," Lucas told *Rolling Stone*.[120] Charles Lippincott, Lucasfilm's master of marketing, wasn't entirely surprised; he was one of the few in whom Marcia had confided, complaining to Lippincott that George just couldn't leave the stresses of filmmaking in the editing room. "George would take problems to bed with him," said Lippincott, "and [Marcia] said this caused a lot of problems."[121] But it went deeper even than that; for George Lucas, movies would always be *the other woman*. As devoted to Marcia as he might be, there was forever one more movie, one more project, demanding the time and attention he couldn't or wouldn't give to his wife. And for all of his talk about making family a priority, Marcia was the one who had put her career on hold while he pursued one project after another, moving from *Star Wars* to *More American Graffiti* to *Empire* to *Raiders* to *Jedi* with scarcely any downtime.

Marcia had finally had enough. "For me, the bottom line was just that he was all work and no play," she explained later. "I felt that we paid our dues, fought our battles, worked eight days a week, twenty-five hours a day. I wanted to stop and smell the flowers. I wanted joy in my life. And George just didn't. He was very emotionally blocked, incapable of sharing feelings. He wanted to stay on that workaholic track. The empire builder. The dynamo. And I couldn't see myself living that way for the rest of my life."[122] Lucas insisted that part of that empire was for her; if he could equip Skywalker with a state-of-the-art editing and mixing system, she could essentially edit from home. "If a director wants her to edit, it will be much easier to convince him to do it up here," Lucas said. "The whole reason for the ranch actually—it's just a giant facility to allow my wife to cut film in Marin County."[123]

It was too little, too late—for once the marriage had gone cold, Marcia began to look elsewhere for the warmth she craved from Lucas, finding it in the company of Tom Rodrigues, an artist nine years younger than herself, who had been hired to create the ornate stained-glass windows in the library dome at Skywalker Ranch. Marcia insisted she hadn't actually been unfaithful to her husband—at least not yet—and had suggested marriage counseling, hoping to salvage the relationship in therapy. But Lucas refused; as far as he was concerned, therapists and psychiatrists were nearly as untrustworthy as Hollywood executives. Marcia next suggested a trial separation; Lucas dismissed that option as well. Hoping to head off the argument in a less confrontational way, he had recently granted journalist Dale Pollock the access he needed to write an authorized biography, hoping that Marcia would be reminded of how much fun they used to have and how much they still loved each other. The two of them even attended George's twentieth high school reunion together, where Lucas, in an effort to throw off the press, showed a sillier side by switching name tags with a similarly bearded classmate.

None of it mattered. Marcia finally asked for a divorce, and all Lucas could do was beg her not to go public with the decision until after the release of *Jedi*, about a year away. But that wasn't going to make it easy on anyone. After sitting out *Empire*, Marcia was determined to help edit *Jedi*, along with Duwayne Dunham and Marquand's editor of choice, Sean Barton, who had cut *Eye of the Needle*. At that point, she and her husband were barely speaking; when Kazanjian asked Lucas whether Marcia was going to help edit *Jedi*, Lucas shrugged off the question with "You're gonna have to ask her."[124] Marcia would mostly handle what Lucas mockingly called "the dying and crying" sequences, though as the most experienced editor of the three, she would usually get the last look at any cut before it went to Lucas.[125] Kazanjian, who had double-dated with George and Marcia years earlier, now sadly watched them go their separate ways each evening. "George would go home," said Kazanjian, "and Marcia would stay in the editing room."[126]

Despite their best efforts to keep things civil, the two of them sometimes bickered in front of the crew. Barton remembered sitting hunched over his editing table one afternoon when Marcia mentioned to George that she wanted to recut a scene Barton had just completed. "You can make it different," Lucas snapped, "but you're not going to make it better."[127] Marcia was tiring quickly of that kind of disparagement. "I felt I had something to bring to the table," she said later. "I was the more emotional person who came from the heart and George was the more intellectual and visual, and I thought I provided a nice balance. But George would never acknowledge that to me. I think he resented my criticisms, felt that all I ever did was put him down. In his mind, I always stayed the stupid Valley girl. He never felt I had any talent, he never felt I was very smart, he never gave me much credit."[128]

Marcia wasn't the only one Lucas squabbled with; other crew members found him touchy, with a hair-trigger temper. One evening

Lucas became particularly annoyed with Dunham for pointing out that the current cut of the movie made the fate of Vader unclear. "We just left him there [on the Death Star] and we don't see him again," Dunham told Lucas. "Did he blow up in the Death Star or did Luke take him or what happened to him?" Kazanjian added that he too was concerned that audiences would be uncertain whether Vader was actually dead. "George got pretty heated," recalled Dunham. "It's rare to see George like that, but obviously that hit a nerve. I said, 'Okay, sorry I asked.'"[129] But Lucas knew that Dunham and Kazanjian were right; Mark Hamill and a second-unit crew were quickly dispatched to Skywalker Ranch to film Luke setting fire to Vader's funeral pyre.

Looking back later, Lucas knew he'd been touchy and gloomy. "I was trying to finish the movie, but now I was also going through a divorce," he said. "I tried to hold myself together emotionally and still do the movie, but it was very, very hard. It was an act of great energy just to get up and go to work. I was so, so depressed."[130] On a day in late November 1982 that came to be known around ILM as "Black Friday," Lucas reordered or discarded nearly a hundred special effects shots. "All of this stuff, all this material, was just tossed out," moaned Ken Ralston, "and we couldn't even use them on other shots. It was bad." Lucas just rolled his eyes; he had no time for crybabies. "When they start screaming," he remarked, "you can tell whether it's a real scream or just kind of whiny."[131]

ILM, then, was going to have to hustle to get all the needed effects completed by February 1983—a task that seemed nearly impossible. Marcia, still editing the film next door at Sprocket, was so concerned about the ILM staff that she pulled aside ILM manager Tom Smith in tears. "She worried we weren't aware of how serious the deadline was," recalled Smith, "and said it was keeping her awake at night." Lucas wasn't buying it. "If she was breaking into tears, it probably had nothing to do with the movie," he said dismissively.[132]

Still, ILM added extra shifts to keep production running nearly around the clock, and Lucas would come in every morning at 8:45 to check on things personally. He would watch footage in the cozy screening room—his reserved seat was second-row center—noting his approval or disapproval, then would run over to Sprocket to supervise Ben Burtt dubbing in sound, or loiter behind Dunham as he cut in effects shots. But the looming deadline was affecting both the special effects and the editing; at ILM, Lucas found himself approving effects that he knew weren't up to their usual standards, while at Sprocket he was gnashing his teeth in frustration over the problematic battle at the sarlacc pit, a sequence that contained more edits than any other scene in the movie. Lucas had grown particularly annoyed with the character of Boba Fett. "I don't know whether it was the way it was shot, but Boba didn't measure up to some standard George had," said Dunham. Lucas had finally had enough. In the name of time, and no small bit of frustration, Boba Fett would be given one of the most anticlimactic demises in film history.

"Just throw him in the pit," sighed Lucas.[133]

As production continued on *Jedi* throughout 1982, it probably came as little surprise to Marcia that her husband—despite his repeated promises that family was his new priority—had already started work on yet another film, falling this time into the waiting arms of Indiana Jones. With the enormous success of *Raiders of the Lost Ark* had come talk of the inevitable sequel, and Lucas had taken it on himself to write a treatment called *Indiana Jones and the Temple of Death*, completing the twenty-page draft at the end of May 1982, just as *Jedi* was wrapping in London.

The relics being pursued this time were holy Sankara stones (Lucas admitted later, "I couldn't think of another MacGuffin that I thought would work"), which Indy has to retrieve from an Indian temple, saving the enslaved children of a nearby village in the process. The story was darker, the humor as black as Lucas's own disposition as his marriage crumbled. "I wasn't in a good mood," Lucas admitted.[134] Spielberg, too, was under a black cloud, the result of a recent accident on the set of the Spielberg-produced *Twilight Zone: The Movie* that had killed actor Vic Morrow and two children. Spielberg was never charged or investigated in the incident, which had resulted in indictments of several crew members, including director John Landis,[135] but the entire experience had rocked and depressed the normally upbeat Spielberg. Their respective moods scared off writer Lawrence Kasdan, whom Lucas approached about turning his notes into a script. "I didn't want to be associated with *Temple of Doom*," said Kasdan later. "I just thought it was horrible. It's so mean. There's nothing pleasant about it. I think *Temple of Doom* represents a chaotic period in both their lives, and the movie is very ugly and mean-spirited."[136]

Instead, Lucas would hand his treatment off to Willard Huyck and Gloria Katz, his collaborators on *American Graffiti*, instructing them to write quickly so they could get a full script over to an ambivalent and increasingly busy Spielberg. "I'm afraid we might lose him," Lucas told the Huycks, "so you guys better get this done fast."[137] The Huycks, long used to working from Lucas's story treatments, had a first draft script in front of Spielberg in August. There were plenty of in-jokes (continuing a habit of naming characters after pets, the character Short Round was named for the Huycks' own dog), and the Huycks had infused the script with some of their own love of Indian culture and films like *Gunga Din*, but the somber, and sometimes frightening, tone Lucas had set in his story treatment remained intact. Some Lucasfilm staffers also worried that the film might be too violent—a concern that would plague the film right up until the moment of its release.

Huyck and Katz would continue to tinker with the script on into 1983, completing the shooting script—now called *Indiana Jones and the Temple of Doom*—on April 10, less than two weeks before shooting was scheduled to begin. Lucas, looking for any distractions before the premiere of *Jedi* in May, joined Spielberg and the *Temple of Doom* crew on location in Sri Lanka in late April, finally touching down in a helicopter near the Kandy River, where the film crew had constructed a long rope bridge over a ravine. Six days later, Lucas took a second-unit crew to film the sequence in which Indiana Jones cuts the bridge's supporting ropes with a machete, sending a number of villains tumbling into the river below. As Lucas rolled camera, the supporting cables were blown with a small explosion, the bridge—now split in half—collapsed against opposite sides of the cliff, and fourteen dummies plummeted into the ravine below, mechanical arms flailing. Lucas loved it. He lingered in Sri Lanka for several more days, engaging in squirt gun fights with Spielberg, and watching romantic sparks fly between Spielberg and the film's leading lady, Kate Capshaw. Most thought Lucas appeared tired. When Lucas sat down for an extended interview with *Rolling Stone* later that month, the interviewer noted that he looked "so gloomy, so unhappy, so downright miserable."[138] Ken Ralston at ILM thought Lucas seemed "totally fried."[139]

Fried or not, there was still *Jedi* to attend to—and on May 7, Lucas screened a special preview of the film for Lucasfilm employees at San Francisco's Coronet Theatre. For the most part, he was pleased with the final film, though he still regretted that he'd been unable to get the Ewoks to blink. (He would fix that decades later through digital technology.) He'd also renamed the film at practically the last minute, rightly deciding that *revenge* was a trait unbecoming in a Jedi knight, and substituted the word *return* instead. The change required the recall of movie posters that had already been printed with the old title. Lucas would make them available for sale exclusively to members of the *Star Wars* Fan Club.

The opening of *Return of the Jedi* on Wednesday, May 25, 1983, was officially an Event. The cliff-hangers from *Empire* had audiences lining up for a day in advance, counting down the hours, minutes, and seconds until the premiere of the film in which they'd see how everything was resolved. Fans debated the fate of Han Solo and bickered over the identity of the "other" Yoda had mentioned. People skipped out of work—many of those who didn't would take their school-age children to the midnight showing—threw parties, celebrated birthdays, even held screenings of the first two movies while waiting in line. One fan even tried to steal the film at gunpoint.

As always, *Star Wars* was all about the experience of seeing it. *Return of the Jedi* opened in 820 theaters across the United States and

Canada—quite a step up from the 126 in which *Empire* had debuted three years earlier—and shattered records for the largest opening day gross, with ticket sales of $6.1 million. Just as they had when *The Empire Strikes Back* premiered, most studios didn't bother to open a movie against *Jedi,* holding back big releases like *Superman II* and the latest James Bond film, *Octopussy. Jedi* was going to have to earn $115 million to break even—but from day one, its success seemed inevitable. "After doing about $46 million in the first week, we knew that we would make our money back shortly," said Kazanjian. It would do so in less than five weeks—and by the end of 1983, when the film was still playing after thirty-two weeks in release, *Return of the Jedi* was closing in fast on the $250 million mark.

Critics were split, and even those who gave it positive reviews often found reasons to hedge their bets. Gary Arnold at the *Washington Post* called it "a triumph," though he thought Harrison Ford looked tired.[140] *Time* magazine, which had gambled correctly on the success of the film by putting Lucas on the cover, hailed *Jedi* as "a brilliant, imaginative piece of filmmaking," but cautioned Lucas and other filmmakers against relying too much on special effects and creatures—a criticism that would be leveled against him and his three *Star Wars* prequels twenty years later. ILM artist Joe Johnston, discussing *Jedi* with journalist Gerald Clarke, said perhaps too truthfully, "We were never sure whether the movie was a vehicle for the effects or for the story."[141] A few even figured out that Lucas had finally made his Vietnam movie. "You can look at *Jedi* and see the Vietnam War there," said Kazanjian. "You can see the Ewok guerrillas hiding in the jungles, taking on this improper force of mechanized bullies—and winning."[142]

Most of the negative criticism leveled at the film tended to train its fire on either the acting or Marquand's directing. One of the film's harshest critics, John Simon at *National Review,* took to the television news show *Nightline* to lament that *Jedi* was "dehumanizing" and, cryptically, that it made children "dumber than they needed to be." An amused Gene Siskel and Roger Ebert, appearing on the same show to refute Simon, flatly told the critic he needed to lighten up.[143]

Lucas heard none of it; as usual, four days before the film's release, he had left for Hawaii, this time spending two weeks in Honolulu, waiting for the phone calls that would bring him the box office numbers. He was relieved to be done with it—not just *Jedi* but *Star Wars* as a whole. "That dumb screenplay I first wrote ten years ago is at least finished," he told *Rolling Stone*. "It's all in a movie now. It's been ten years since I started this.... [T]here hasn't been a day in my life where I haven't gotten up in the morning and said, 'Gee, I've got to worry about this movie.' Literally. Not one single day."[144] To *Time* magazine, he compared the making of the *Star Wars* trilogy to pushing a train slowly up a hill, then holding on for dear life as it careened down the other side. "I'm burned out," he admitted wearily. "In fact, I was burned out a couple of years ago, and I've been going on momentum ever since. *Star Wars* has grabbed my life and taken it over against my will. Now I've got to get my life back again—before it's too late."[145]

Getting his life back meant moving forward without Marcia. On Monday, June 13, Lucas called an all-hands meeting at Skywalker Ranch. Staff gathered to find George and Marcia holding hands as they tearfully announced they were getting divorced. The staff was stunned; they'd had no idea. "They were a team," said Sprocket manager Jim Kessler. "If he was black, she was white, and vice versa. It was a well-balanced thing. Independently, they were kind of like balls with unweighted sides, so they spun out in goofy ways."[146] Marcia would relocate immediately to Los Angeles; their daughter Amanda, now two years old, would remain largely in George's custody—one of the few conditions of the divorce that Lucas truly embraced. "I've got a daughter now and she's growing up around me and she's not going to wait," said Lucas. "I don't want her to grow up to be eighteen and have her say, 'Hey Dad, where have you been all my life?'"[147]

The ranch would remain his work in progress, but with the exception of *Indiana Jones and the Temple of Doom*, which was still in production in London, he was done with movies, at least for a while; he was taking at least a two-year sabbatical from filmmaking, he told *Time*. "[Family] became my first priority," he said later. "I didn't think it was going to be, because before that, making films [was] my first priority.... But then I realized that this was my life. And then...I was divorced, and it really *was* my life. So I just simply said, 'Okay, I'm retiring.' I put my companies and the making of movies and everything on the side."[148]

Steven Spielberg wasn't so sure Lucas could ever retire; he had heard it all before. "Every time George is making a film, he talks about retiring and never working again," said Spielberg. "But the minute it is finished, he is already thinking up his next opus. I can see him running Lucasfilm, making three to five pictures a year, and then some day returning to directing, which is where I think he belongs. I believe his destiny is behind the camera."[149]

But Lucas insisted he meant it—especially when it came to *Star Wars*. "I look upon the three *Star Wars* films as chapters in one book. Now the book is finished, and I have put it on the shelf."[150] As far as he was concerned, he was never taking that particular book down off the shelf again. *Not ever.*

PART III

RETURN

1983–2016

10

Empty Flash

1983-1994

The skies were dark and gray when Lucas arrived in northern London in late June 1983—weather that perfectly suited his own state of mind as he returned to Elstree Studios, where production was continuing on *Indiana Jones and the Temple of Doom*. Since announcing his divorce a month earlier, Lucas felt both physically and emotionally drained. Partly, he admitted later, he'd collapsed under the weight of his own success, which had made him neglectful of his personal life. "Success...is a very difficult emotional experience to go through," he said. "It's a very devastating experience when it happens. Some people can deal with [it], some people can't. I thought in the beginning it was a piece of cake. I had a little bit of success with [*American*] *Graffiti,* and a lot of success with *Star Wars,* but the full impact didn't hit me for a few years after that."[1] It was the beginning, he said, of "a several-year tailspin."[2]

At Elstree, Lucas would step in from time to time to helm a few second units, mostly overseeing the mass fistfight in the movie's opening scene at Club Obi Wan—which, while complicated, didn't involve dealing with any real acting, making it just the kind of sequence Lucas normally would enjoy. But it was no fun for him, and Lucas even *looked* miserable. His beard, while never unkempt, was as thick as it had ever been, dark with flecks of white at the chin. Between takes, he would often lean against the wall and stare blankly, hands thrust deep into his pockets, stroking his beard absently.

While Lucas would always claim Spielberg took considerable relish in directing some of the film's gorier or more disturbing scenes — whether it was eating bugs and brains or having Indy strike a child — Spielberg too would look back on *Temple of Doom* as an unhappy experience. "It was too dark, too subterranean, and much too horrific," he reflected — strong words, considering he had only just finished serving as the writer and producer of the 1982 haunted house movie *Poltergeist*. But Spielberg thought it even "out-poltered *Poltergeist*. There's not an ounce of my own personal feeling in *Temple of Doom*."[3]

For Lucas, however, there was one moment that perfectly summed up his own feelings: as the evil priest Mola Ram prepares to lower a human sacrifice down into the temple's fiery pit, he slowly and deliberately reaches out and rips the victim's still-beating heart out of his chest — as literal a metaphor for Lucas's own heartbreak as he would ever put on-screen. "I was going through a divorce," Lucas reminded one journalist later, "and I was in a really bad mood." Frank Marshall, one of *Temple*'s producers, thought the film was probably somewhat cathartic for the morose Lucas. "As I think you can see in the movie," he said later, "there's a lot of darkness being worked out."[4]

Principal photography on *Temple of Doom* wrapped on August 26, 1983. With that, Lucas shut down his production offices at Elstree — and now, for the first time in more than a decade, Lucasfilm had no movies in production. As he had promised, and whether Spielberg believed it or not, George Lucas was retiring from filmmaking. For someone who loved film as much as Lucas did, it felt odd to have no projects of his own to tinker with. But completing the *Star Wars* trilogy had sapped his creative energy — "[and] then," recalled Lucas, still wincing at the memory, "the divorce. Divorce is a very difficult thing financially and emotionally."[5]

"Difficult" was putting it mildly, especially when it came to the terms of the divorce settlement. While Marcia was entitled to half of everything under California law, Lucas was not inclined to settle graciously; as far as he was concerned, *he* was the aggrieved party. "He was very bitter and vindictive," recalled Marcia.[6] At the time of their separation, Lucasfilm, including the still uncompleted ranch, was worth between $50 and $100 million—and Lucas made it clear that he had no intention of giving Marcia a single square inch of Skywalker Ranch; nor did he want to pay spousal support in perpetuity. To be done with it all, he'd pay her off with nearly all the cash he had on hand—about $50 million—and keep the ranch.

Lucas refused to be magnanimous about it. While they would see each other only as long as it took to make decisions about raising Amanda together, Lucas would chip away at their mutual friends to make certain Marcia was never again invited to parties and holiday celebrations. "That really hurt," said Marcia later. "It's not enough that I'm erased from his life, he wants to blackball me too, with people who were my friends."[7] But the anger went beyond the personal; while Lucasfilm would have to acknowledge Marcia's editing Oscar as one of the seven Academy Awards won by *Star Wars,* her contributions to Lucas's films and to the company would be all but erased from most Lucasfilm-sanctioned histories.[8] One noteworthy relationship improved in the shadow of the divorce, however. "George came to me and wanted to be my friend," said Francis Ford Coppola, still suffering from the humiliation of bankruptcy after losing his most recent version of Zoetrope.[9] "Francis had lost everything financially," observed one friend. "George had lost everything emotionally."[10] The two were reconciled. Again.

With no movies in production, it wasn't a great time for Lucasfilm to be paying out a large cash settlement. Fortunately, money continued to pour in to the licensing division. *Return of the Jedi* had turned into a merchandising juggernaut, with more than fifty licensees for everything from cream rinse to vases to the reliable Kenner toy line. For the moment, then, Lucas could continue to build Skywalker Ranch on action figures and soda. "I'll still spend a minimal amount of time at the company, but it won't be very much time," Lucas explained. "I've sort of got the company to the point where it can operate by itself."[11] He assured reporters that he wasn't really doing much more than "pok[ing] my head into some doors."[12]

But of course he was doing more than that. To get Lucasfilm and Skywalker Ranch to the point where they really could operate by themselves, Lucas envisioned his organization as a one-stop, full-service company for other filmmakers. For screenwriters, the ranch offered an idyllic retreat where they could work on screenplays in comfort and quiet; for film editors, there would be access to the finest editing equipment available. And for special effects, ILM still offered its services as the gold standard against which all others were judged. At the moment, ILM was juggling several outside projects—including *Star Trek III* and *Starman*—but its main priority was completing the effects for *Indiana Jones and the Temple of Doom*. "Because it was George and Steven's project, there wasn't an option to say no, or *How about next year?*" said model shop supervisor Lorne Peterson.[13]

Apart from ILM, Lucas was still fiddling with a couple of other divisions he was planning to house permanently on the property. A year earlier he had directed Ed Catmull at the computer division to find the right person to head up a new computer gaming group. Lucas would never be the video game junkie that Spielberg or Howard Kazanjian was, but he was fascinated with the idea of interactive storytelling, in which the decisions a player makes directly affect the outcome of the story, making every trip through a game unique. (There was also a matter of financial practicality: reinvesting in his own company allowed Lucas to reduce his tax burden.) Catmull wooed Peter Langston, a Unix Jedi master if ever there was one, and Lucas finally lured him in with an offer he couldn't refuse: Lucasfilm's COO Roger Faxon had cut a deal with the video game king Atari, which had offered Lucasfilm $1 million to do nothing more, as Langston put it, than "see what you can make."[14] With that, the Lucasfilm Games Group was up and running.

Lucas wasn't ready to hand the keys to the *Star Wars* universe over to the games division just yet; games would have to be stand-alone, without any references to either *Star Wars* or Indiana Jones—but apart from telling the team what they *couldn't* do, Lucas left his programmers alone. Taking the lessons the computer division had learned from creating the Genesis Effect for *Star Trek II,* Langston and his team figured out how to create fractal technology—in which images become clearer and more detailed as the player moves closer to an object—for less powerful home computers like the eight-bit Atari 800, a task many programmers had considered impossible. Lucasfilm programmers poured their efforts into two games: a futuristic basketball-soccer hybrid called *Ballblazer,* and a science fiction search-and-rescue game called *Rescue on Fractalus!,* in which the player maneuvered a star fighter through an alien landscape to rescue downed pilots. (The working title had been *Rebel Rescue,* a connection to the *Star Wars* universe Langston and his team couldn't resist.)

Lucas played a few of the early demos, and even in video games, his sense for what an audience might experience was as keen as ever. After piloting his ship around the landscape in an early version of *Fractalus,* Lucas grew impatient simply flying around, landing, and picking up pilots, and asked why there was nothing to shoot at. When told the game had been designed without the use of the FIRE button, Lucas looked up quizzically. "Was that a game design," he asked, "or a moral choice?" The design team shifted nervously. Lucas nodded. "Principle, uh huh," he said. "It's not going to work."[15] A FIRE button was added, as were on-screen antiaircraft cannons for the player to destroy.

Unfortunately, while the games division had broken new ground with its first two games, the Atari company was sinking fast, largely because of a $25 million investment in the rights to *E.T.: The Extra-Terrestrial,* then hastily assembling a terrible game that no one bought. There were endless delays and discussions—Lucas even jumped into the fray at one point to negotiate the logo—until Lucasfilm finally cut its relations with Atari (but kept its million dollars) and reached a deal with the upstart Epyx company, which put the two games on shelves in 1986. Both sold well enough, and Lucas was willing to continue bankrolling the division, permitting it to become an independent business entity within Lucasfilm, while keeping his hands largely off it. The only real direction he would give Langston and his team was an oft-repeated mantra: "Stay small. Be the best. Don't lose any money." Hal Barwood, a longtime friend and later a project leader in the games division, compared Lucas's involvement to that of a rich uncle: "He paid the tuition fees to get you through college, but never knew what your major was."[16]

Lucas would be a bit more invested in another Lucasfilm start-up, this one spun out of Sprocket Systems, where soundman Tom Holman had been hard at work designing a new auditorium at Sprocket's C Building. Kazanjian remarked that the new theater had "the best sound system in the world."[17] That was because Holman, after taking into account the acoustics in the room, the placement of the speakers, the ambient noise in the theater, and plenty of other small details, had developed a precise set of specifications that provided the audience with an immersive, chest-rattling sound experience. Holman referred to it as simply a crossover network, in which the treble and the bass were divided electronically, rather than just being split into two different speakers, and the configuration soon came to be called the "Tom Holman Crossover." Others called it the "Tom Holman Experiment"—but either way, it was eventually referred to as the THX sound system, a serendipitous nod to Lucas's feature *THX 1138*.

Temple of Doom was being mixed at Sprocket specifically so it would sound great in a theater with the THX system; but the problem was, once the movie went into theaters with a sound system that *wasn't* configured to Holman's specifications, it was going to sound terrible. At the urging of Sprocket's manager Jim Kessler, "we came to the conclusion [that it would be] great if we could get theaters that the public goes to... to sound this good," said Lucas. "Because then what we hear here [in the sound editing room] is the same thing they would hear there [in the theater]. And that really started the whole THX program."[18] For Lucas, this was a big deal. He took seriously the way his movies sounded—having Ben Burtt's sounds and John Williams's music already made his films sound like no one else's—and he resented having his movies sound great in the editing room, then terrible once they were inside a theater. "Sound is half the experience in seeing a film," Lucas explained later—an obvious, if underappreciated, point, particularly to audiences who looked for the Dolby logo as an indication of a movie's sound quality.[19] But Dolby stereo alone couldn't ensure that a movie would sound great once it left the sound editing room; THX had more to do with the *theater* in which a film was shown—a part of the movie experience Lucas couldn't control. Until now.

Unlike most sound systems, THX didn't—and still doesn't—require theaters to purchase any particular set of equipment or speakers. It does, however, involve a theater's reconfiguring its speaker arrangement, altering acoustics, and in some cases even changing the film's illumination to meet very precise specifications. On March 1, 1983, Lucasfilm issued to theaters notice of its "Theater Alignment Program" (TAP), providing specifications that theaters could adapt to make movies sound as good as they possibly could. Nearly a hundred theaters participated in the program, leasing new equipment from Lucasfilm and paying to have their theaters reconfigured or retrofitted to reflect THX's acoustical requirements. "THX became a kind of quality control process for the…exhibition of the film," Lucas said proudly.[20]

In the coming decades, more than four thousand theaters around the world would undergo Lucas's quality control process on their way to becoming "THX Certified Cinemas"; audiences, too, would come to recognize the metallic THX logo shown just before a film—accompanied by its "deep note," which slowly builds in volume as it swirls through the sound system and eventually makes the entire theater rumble—as the definitive mark of great movie sound. Lucas had controlled the way his movies were filmed, edited, financed, and merchandised. Now he would control the way they sounded in the theaters as well—and get paid to do it, no less.

And then there was Pixar. Lucas still wasn't sure what to do with Ed Catmull and his team in the graphics group within the computer division, who were still more interested in making movies with their Pixar computer than they were in building the digital editing system Lucas had asked them for. "I think Ed's greatest fear was that at some point somebody higher up—George in particular—was going to say, 'Wait a minute, the stuff you were supposed to build, you haven't built,'" said Bob Doris, one of Catmull's co-directors. "And it was becoming pretty clear that this was a problem."[21] Still, Catmull and his team *were* working; in addition to the Pixar Image Computer, they would have a digital picture editor they called EditDroid, as well as a digital sound editor called SoundDroid, ready to show by 1984. But Catmull's heart wasn't in it; instead, he and John Lasseter were planning an animated short they intended to unveil at the 1984 SIGGRAPH conference, an annual gathering of scientists, engineers, and devotees of computer graphics. That was when they'd show Lucas what they really could do. Lucas would be impressed. Catmull was sure of it.

For now, however, Lucas was much more interested in raising two-year-old Amanda, and in "fun and sun and skiing and boogeying and reading and pleasure writing."[22] He was even taking dance and guitar lessons, and racing cars again—a hobby he'd given up shortly after the birth of Amanda. He was trying to learn to loosen up—one of Marcia's main complaints about him was that he was too tightly wound—and in December 1983, he would even start dating again, after being introduced to singer Linda Ronstadt backstage at one of her four concerts at Concord Pavilion that October.[23]

On the face of it, it was an odd pairing; Lucas was quiet and introspective and—another gripe of Marcia's—not terribly adventurous in bed. Ronstadt, by contrast, was a heartbreaker and a man-eater, known for high-profile romances with celebrities like musician J. D. Souther, journalist Pete Hamill, and California governor Jerry Brown. And yet she also clearly had a penchant for creative types—she'd briefly dated Steve Martin and had just ended a relationship with Jim Carrey—and liked that Lucas was so protective of their privacy, being careful to ensure they were never photographed together. Lucas was so low-key, in fact, that as he trailed along after Ronstadt in a San Anselmo drugstore, the proprietor thought he was her houseboy. "George is lucky to be with her," said one friend. "He will have more fun than he's ever had in his life. Then she will break his heart into thousands of pieces and go on to someone else."[24] Lucas would defy the odds; he and Ronstadt would date for five years. Neither would ever discuss the details of their relationship publicly.

Besides, reporters were much more interested in asking Lucas about the future of *Star Wars*. Would there be more movies? In 1983 Lucas would say only that he was reading books on mythology and scrawling vague notes with themes and ideas for the next two trilogies. The first trilogy, he explained, would be melodramatic, showing the politics that put the Empire in place. The final three, he continued, would be all about "moral choices, and the wisdom needed to distinguish right from wrong."[25] More than that, however, he couldn't, or wouldn't, say.

For staff at Skywalker Ranch, Lucas's so-called retirement meant he was more involved in the day-to-day operations than ever before. He no longer needed the weekly updates from CEO Robert Greber, or Sprocket manager Jim Kessler; instead, he would simply show up at ILM to watch the effects team at work, or sit behind Ben Burtt as he edited sound effects for *Temple of Doom*, making employees feel as if the school principal were sitting in their classroom. For Greber, it was clear there were now one too many CEOs inside the organization. Lucas agreed. "The only problem," Greber said later, "was that we agreed [the CEO] should be him, and not me."[26] Lucas became simply the boss—without a formal title, but clearly in control. Greber, meanwhile, slid over to a seat on the four-member board of directors—a board that could meet and advise but remained accountable to the company's lone shareholder: George Lucas. For Lucas, Lucasfilm was a family business, just like his father's stationery store. Family businesses didn't need stockholders.

Family businesses probably didn't have as much land as Lucas had, either. As construction on the ranch continued—the enormous Victorian-style Main House was nearly complete, and work was under way on the gigantic Tech Building, which would house the post-production facilities—Lucas continued to quietly purchase land adjacent to the ranch, scooping up the Grady Ranch and Big Rock Ranch on Lucas Valley Road. He envisioned using part of the acquired land for the second phase of the ranch, where he would build a new head-quarters for ILM and the rest of the digital production facilities,[27] most of which were currently working several miles away at the Kerner building and a collection of surrounding warehouses. But Lucas played the politics of the situation poorly, once again carrying out the purchase of the properties in the name of his accountant—and once again, area residents accused Lucas of having something to hide, this time berating Marin County planners for permitting him to establish "an industrial beachhead." Lucas, his hackles up, pointed out that he was going to leave most of the land undeveloped and argued that having Lucasfilm own and develop the property kept out more undesirable developers. Neighbors were having none of it and sarcastically suggested that Marin County planners would next be issuing zoning exemptions for Union Carbide.[28] Lucas could only roll his eyes. The argument would roil for nearly a decade. Meanwhile, ILM would remain stranded at Kerner.

The spring of 1984 brought Lucas another controversy of his own making, this time involving *Indiana Jones and the Temple of Doom*. After submitting the movie to the Motion Picture Association of America, which would determine the film's rating, Lucas was informed that because of the film's graphic violence, the MPAA was leaning toward assigning the film an R rating—a disaster for a franchise that was trying to appeal to all ages. "[*Temple of Doom*] was too gross to be

PG," admitted Lucas, but "it wasn't quite gross enough to be an R."[29] Lucas and Spielberg's intentionally disturbing film would nevertheless have a far-reaching effect on movie ratings. While the MPAA eventually relented and approved the more desirable PG rating for *Temple of Doom,* shortly thereafter the MPAA created the PG-13 rating, meaning parents were "strongly cautioned" that some material could be inappropriate for children under age thirteen.

Even as the May 23 release date for *Temple of Doom* approached, some newspaper ads still cautioned parents that the film might be "too intense" for children. The warning did nothing to scare parents or their children away; on its opening day, *Temple of Doom* set a one-day record by taking in more than $9 million — "Jones' Builds a Temple of Gold," screamed the front page of *Variety.* By the end of its international run, it would take in $333 million. And all from Lucas's budget of a little under $29 million.

While audiences made it the biggest movie of 1984, reviews for *Temple of Doom* ran from merely unimpressed to hugely disappointed. "Dark" was the word reviewers used most often to describe it, though the *Washington Post* critic pulled out all the stops in calling it "mean spirited and corrupt at its core."[30] Lucas admitted that "we went darker than any of us really wanted to go" but thought he and Spielberg should be given credit for "mak[ing] a different movie from *Raiders*. We didn't want to just do the same movie over again."[31] Looking back on the film nearly thirty years later, Lucas was still favorably disposed toward it, even as it seemed to sum up on-screen both his and Spielberg's own personal winters of discontent. "I like *Temple of Doom,*" Lucas insisted, "[but] is it fun to think back about that stuff emotionally for us?" He shook his head sadly and slowly answered, "Nooooo."[32]

Each year, at a Fourth of July bash held at Skywalker Ranch, Lucas would give away what he called the Lucasfilm Yearbook, outlining the accomplishments of Lucasfilm and each division over the past year, complete with yearbook-style photos and brief bios of every staff member. In 1984, among photos of Indiana Jones and Luke Skywalker, the yearbook noted that the Pixar computer would soon be moved over to ILM for use in special effects. But ILM didn't want it—and despite the fact that the computer division was right next door to ILM in the Kerner building, ILM wasn't all that interested in working with Ed Catmull and his graphics group either. "We got treated as a sideshow," said computer animator Tom Porter. "Not disrespected, but certainly not embraced."[33]

Since creating the Genesis Effect for *Star Trek II*, Catmull and his graphics team had used their computers only one other time, providing the briefing sequence in *Return of the Jedi* in which a computerized image of a force field projects out from Endor to surround the Death Star—hardly the earth-shattering stuff Catmull knew they were capable of. "The effect wasn't so groundbreaking as the tools used to do it," said programmer Tom Duff. ILM wasn't all that impressed by it—and neither was Lucas. "We kept waiting for George to come around and ask us to be in the movies," said Alvy Ray Smith, "but he never came."[34]

For months, Catmull and Bob Doris had been trying to figure out a way to prove that the graphics group and its Pixar computer were worth Lucas's time and investment. This was especially critical now that much of the digital editing equipment Lucas had asked for had recently been completed, at least in prototype, and unveiled in April at the National Association of Broadcasters convention in Las Vegas. The video editing console, called EditDroid, had impressed convention-goers with its sleek console, multiple video screens, and trackball controller; some thought it looked like it belonged on the Death Star. It didn't always work—it had a tendency to lock up—but every demonstration still drew an enormous crowd, especially as team leader Ralph Guggenheim had smartly managed to snag a snippet of footage from *Return of the Jedi* to exhibit the machine's editing capabilities. "People weren't even looking at the editing system," said one attendee. "They just wanted to see *Star Wars*."[35] Meanwhile, the SoundDroid digital sound editing machine sat in the basement of Sprocket's Building C. SoundDroid was less flashy than EditDroid but much more functional;

director Miloš Forman had already put it to use to improve the sound quality for *Amadeus*.

Lucas now had the editing hardware he had asked for—or at least a start on it—but Catmull was still determined to prove that the value of the graphics group and the Pixar computer lay in filmmaking, not simply in hardware. In the weeks leading up to the 1984 SIGGRAPH conference in Minneapolis, Catmull, Alvy Ray Smith, and their team had all five of Lucasfilm's state-of-the-art computers—as well as a borrowed Cray computer in Minnesota—running round the clock, doing the work needed to render a two-minute animated film called *The Adventures of Andre and Wally B.* The film was mainly a showpiece for the capability of the Pixar, in which the cartoonish main character Andre is pursued by a bee through a fully realized environment of fields, forests, mountains, rocks, and roads. But with character designs by John Lasseter, both Andre and Wally B had real personalities, a trait that would make the film a pleasant rarity at SIGGRAPH.

Lucas would be in the SIGGRAPH audience for the premiere of *Andre and Wally B*—but only by happenstance; he was actually in Minneapolis to accommodate Linda Ronstadt, who was performing in the city that same week as part of the tour for her *What's New* album. Smith swallowed his pride; he was just happy the boss would be there to see the film in person—and to see the audience's response. As the lights went down at the Minneapolis Auditorium, Lucas and Ronstadt were quietly seated with Catmull and Smith, among a sea of thousands of SIGGRAPH attendees. It went better than Smith had hoped; the audience started roaring with the opening shot of computer-animated trees and continued right on through the closing credits. "People there *know* when they're seeing something new and great," said Smith. "I was of course thrilled, because I was the director of this piece and because George Lucas was there. He was finally seeing what he had."[36]

Lucas had indeed seen what he had—and he didn't like it. Failing to grasp the possibilities in what he'd just watched, Lucas instead complained that the characters were primitive and that the story was awful.

"He couldn't make the leap from the crudeness of it then to what it could be," said Smith. "He took it literally for what it was, and assumed that's all we could do."[37] Lucas had had enough of Catmull and his movies. Catmull was frustrated, but so was Lucas; the computer division was becoming an expensive hole down which he was pouring his money and getting very little in return. He wanted them concentrating on his editing system, not making cartoons. Catmull and his Pixar group were living on borrowed time, and knew it. As far as Lucas was concerned, the only person inside Lucasfilm who had any business making movies was George Lucas.

Though Lucas had retired from the movie business, television was another matter. During the filming of *Return of the Jedi,* Lucas had become so enamored of the cute, cuddly Ewoks—and was convinced that kids would want to see more of them—that he began tossing around an idea for a live-action TV film. Still smarting from the disastrous *Star Wars Holiday Special* of 1978, however, Lucas was not inclined to cede control to outsiders; this time he would handpick his creative team. Still, one had to wonder just how serious Lucas was about the project. To serve as producer, Lucas hired Tom Smith, who had just stepped down as the manager of ILM and was looking for opportunities to produce or direct. The writing duties he handed to his own nanny, a young man named Bob Carrau, who had no experience as a writer—which suited Lucas fine, as he planned on dictating most of the story to Carrau anyway.

To hold it all together, however, he had hired as director his old friend John Korty—who, despite the failure of the Lucas-produced *Twice Upon a Time,* was still directing successful made-for-TV movies. "I couldn't figure out if I was doing George a favor or he was doing me a favor," Korty said later. "It's not a film I would have chosen to do on my own." And yet, even with the experienced Korty at the helm, Lucas couldn't leave things alone, rewriting scenes and trying to manage Korty from afar. "As the shooting went on, George—his big thing is 'Let's have more conflict, let's have more fights, let's have more explosions,'" recalled Korty. "I was probably trying to deal with the relationships more, and at one point late in the shooting I got a memo from him or something about 'We need another fight, and why don't we do this to the monster and drop a bomb on him or something,' and I wrote back and I said, 'George, if we do any more to this monster, the audience is going to have more sympathy for the monster than for the heroes!'"[38]

The Ewok Adventure aired on ABC on November 25, 1984, and was successful enough that Lucas immediately began production on a sequel, *The Battle for Endor,* hiring filmmaking brothers Ken and Jim Wheat to write and direct. Producer Tom Smith, having learned his lessons from *The Ewok Adventure,* included in the overall budget a line item for what he called the "George Factor," to cover the costs of shooting any new scenes envisioned by Lucas during filming and editing. Lucas kept largely out of the Wheats' way, though ILMer Joe Johnston had gleefully provided Lucas with a set of three rubber stamps—reading GREAT, CBB (for "could be better"), and 86 (for "try again")—that Lucas could use to stamp his comments on scripts and character designs. "He was like a kid with a new toy when he saw those," Ken Wheat said later. "There was no way anybody could ever be confused about his choices."[39] Lucas, who apparently never seemed content with a sequel unless it was darker than its forebear, had also told the Wheats, "I want this to be all about death."[40] The resulting film, then, *The Battle for Endor,* would air on November 24, 1985, with a disclaimer advising "parents' discretion," since the Wheats had opened the film with a sequence in which a little girl's family are killed by Marauders.

While not as successful as *The Ewok Adventure, The Battle for Endor* would still pull in respectable enough numbers that Lucas briefly considered another sequel before finally shelving the project indefinitely. Their success also encouraged him to invest in two Saturday morning cartoons for ABC, *Droids* and *Ewoks,* produced by the animators at Nelvana—the same company that had provided the Boba Fett cartoon for the *Star Wars Holiday Special.* Lucas publicly professed to having high hopes for the two cartoons, but when Police drummer Stewart Copeland, who had been hired by Lucas to write music for

Droids, met with Lucas to discuss the series, he thought Lucas's real motivations were obvious. "On his desk," recalled Copeland, "he had rows of toys, and that was what the music was for. 'This is the product, here are the toys.'"[41] Any toy-related largesse wouldn't last long; *Ewoks* would be canceled after two seasons, *Droids* after only one, pummeled in their time slots by *The Smurfs.*

By January 1985, Lucas had been running Lucasfilm himself, without a true president, for a little more than a year. While he liked running things his way, the company, with its various projects and disparate revenue sources, had grown to a point where Lucas couldn't keep his fingers in everything. It was time to bring in a president who could serve as a project manager, preferably someone with a background in finance and, ideally, someone who could be a tough administrator and would put the interests of the company before his own popularity. But he refused to consider hiring anyone who had been affiliated with a studio, to give the keys to Lucasfilm to a Hollywood insider. "Down there," as he would always call Hollywood, "for every honest, true filmmaker, trying to get his film off the ground, there are a hundred sleazy used car dealers trying to con you out of your money."[42]

Lucas found his candidate sitting on his own board of directors in Doug Norby, a Harvard-educated former CFO of Itel, a company that had made, then lost, millions of dollars in underhanded deals involving the purchase and leasing of IBM equipment. When the bottom dropped out of the company, Norby cooperated with financial investigators to figure out what had happened — and on the basis of his findings, several of his Itel partners went to jail. Norby didn't, and when he was brought on board at Lucasfilm, some staffers saw him as rather slick and quick to protect his own interests. But Lucas trusted him and liked his up-front, somewhat aggressive style. "Do what you have to do," he told Norby, "and I'm just going to stay out of it."[43]

Norby's hiring was announced in February at an all-hands meeting held on the ILM soundstage. Norby made a better showing than

Lucas that morning, sounding confident and enthusiastic as he outlined the hard tasks in the coming year. Lucas, by contrast, came off as a scold, grousing that it was time for staff to start acting as if they worked for a company, rather than like uninvited guests in his home who ate all his food and spent all his money.[44] Norby, regaining the floor, diplomatically stated that it was simply time for Lucasfilm to start earning its keep. The company had to do more than just make money off licensing and merchandising, or wait for Lucas to make another movie. Lucas had supported the company out of his own pocket long enough. Lucasfilm had to start turning a profit. Every division was going to have to change.

That included even ILM. At the moment, ILM was working almost exclusively on films by Lucas and his friends, as well as the *Star Trek* movies, the one reliable outside franchise. But Norby wanted them to take on even *more* outside work, and issued a press release announcing that ILM was now open for business from anyone. Accountants at ILM were asked to develop a flat rate for the company's services—generally about $25 million per film—as well as to determine more reliable costs for work such as model making or painting mattes so ILM could bid on contracts for those particular jobs. It was a major change in mentality for ILM, and some balked at the idea of doing work for hire, essentially going to studios hat in hand for commissions. "A lot of people were resisting the rendezvous with reality," said Norby.[45]

Working with Lucasfilm's new CFO Doug Johnson (staff would refer to Norby and Johnson derisively as "The Dougs"), Norby even trained his eye on Lucas's pet project of the moment, Skywalker Ranch, where work was continuing at what Norby thought was an intentionally glacial pace that permitted some of the contractors to play fast and loose with billable hours. Until he and Johnson had a better handle on the finances, Norby ordered all non-construction-related workers—essentially artists, glassworkers, and landscapers—to pack up and go home. Lucas may have raised his eyebrows in surprise, but he liked that The Dougs had no problem being the bad guys, taking care of the one big task that Lucas dreaded: dealing with people.

Cash flow continued to be a problem. Not only had the divorce settlement depleted most of Lucas's cash reserves, but also one of the most dependable sources of revenue—toy money from Kenner—was starting to evaporate. In 1985, Kenner was in a state of flux, in a manner very similar to what was going on at Lucasfilm, as the company worked to separate itself from General Mills. In an effort to improve its finances, Kenner had saturated the market with a glut of *Star Wars* toys. But with no new movies on the horizon, the frenetic demand for all things *Star Wars* was more than just waning; as one toy sales expert told the *Wall Street Journal,* "It's gone."[46] In 1985, sales of *Star Wars* toys plummeted to about $35 million, down from $135 million the year before. Doing the math, Norby calculated that Lucasfilm would run out of cash in about five months. Norby was willing to look anywhere to increase the company's cash flow, even persuading Marcia—now married to Rodrigues, and with a new daughter—to permit Lucas to spread out payments for the divorce settlement over ten years. (Lucas would end up paying it off in five.) He even dared to broach the subject of more *Star Wars* films with Lucas—a surefire way to refill Lucasfilm's coffers—but Lucas begged off, saying he was exhausted.

It was inevitable, then, that Norby had to begin laying off employees. That was fine with Lucas, who thought his company had grown fat with nonessential personnel. "I'd go off and make movies and come back two years later and find everybody had hired an assistant," he told the *New York Times* in a display of public pique.[47] Inside the organization, however, staff were convinced that Norby and Johnson were running roughshod over Lucas—that Lucas, if he really knew what was going on, would *never* permit something as coldhearted as layoffs. It was that perception among staff that Lucas could do no wrong, said Bob Doris, that showed Lucas's true strength as an administrator. "It's a George thing," said Doris. "He's successful at creating a myth for himself. I'm sure The Dougs weren't doing anything more or less than George wanted them to do."[48] In truth, Lucas had always been a somewhat aloof administrator anyway; when Lucas was around, staff operated under an unwritten protocol they jokingly called "Queen's rules":

Do not approach George.

Do not chat up George.

Should George start a conversation, keep to work-related topics.

"It seemed to me the company was carefully designed to protect [Lucas], to keep the rest of the world away so he could do what he wanted," said Pixar's Malcolm Blanchard. "That's his personality, a shy guy who likes to makes films."[49]

And it was filmmaking, ultimately, that Lucas wanted his company to be about. Anything else—apart from the games division, which was one of the few arms of the company that were making any money—was considered scope creep. "This company has gotten too diversified," Lucas complained to staff. "We're going to concentrate on movies."[50] The graphics group was trying; the team had recently created another jaw-dropping special effect, this time for the Spielberg-produced *Young Sherlock Holmes,* which had featured a stained-glass knight—the first fully computer-generated character on a movie screen. The effect was credited to ILM, but the work had been done by the Pixar computer, based on a character design by John Lasseter. At this point, however, none of it seemed to matter; anything that wasn't devoted to filmmaking was to be bundled up, repackaged, reorganized, or sold off.

That included the digital editing equipment. With EditDroid and SoundDroid, Lucas now had his digital editing system—or at least the beginnings of one. But both machines were buggy, and the technology, which relied heavily on videodiscs, was expensive. "George wanted to license all the cool technology that they had developed," said Bob Doris, "but he had no interest in being the manufacturer."[51]

EditDroid and SoundDroid, then, were spun off into a new division called The Droid Works, which entered into a joint venture with the editing equipment company Convergence, now also tasked with selling and marketing the editing equipment. Lucas would monitor the company at arm's length, keeping an eye on the progress of the digital editing technology he had done much to establish—and waiting until it finally progressed to the point where it worked well enough to use for a movie.

That left only the graphics group and their Pixar image computer. "We can't afford to fund this stuff," Norby told Lucas, as he turned his eye toward Catmull and his division. "It was clear Lucas had to let us go," said Alvy Ray Smith.[52] For a moment, Catmull thought Lucas might dismantle the group altogether and sell the Pixar computer to the highest bidder, but Lucas was hoping to do for the graphics division what he had for The Droid Works: hook it up with a venture capitalist who might appreciate the potential of the technology. Lucas actually had noble hopes for the Pixar; he thought it might be useful in medical imaging or for scientific simulations, and there were serious discussions with Siemens and Philips, which saw its potential for high-resolution CAT scans. Neither discussion went anywhere. Most thought Lucas's asking price of $35 million was too high, though they weren't just getting the Pixar; they were getting Catmull and his entire graphics division as well. As discussions dragged on into late 1984, Alvy Ray Smith asked a friend of his, Alan Kay, if he knew of any potential investors—ideally someone with a bit of computer expertise who could appreciate what he'd be getting with the Pixar, and might also understand that getting Catmull and his team in the deal was worth the entire cost of the transaction. Kay thought he knew exactly the right person, and called on an old friend of his who happened to be both computer savvy and a multimillionaire: Apple co-founder Steve Jobs.

At once charming and volatile, Jobs—who at that moment was waging a war with the board of directors at Apple that he would ultimately lose—met with Catmull, Smith, and Lucasfilm accountants to discuss the Pixar and look at the numbers. When it came to the hardware, Jobs liked what he saw. "It was one of those sort of apocalyptic moments," he said later. "I remember within ten minutes of seeing the graphical user interface stuff, just knowing that every computer would work this way someday; it was obvious once you saw it." But Jobs, like others, thought the price tag was too high—"I'm more in the $10 to $15 million range," he told them—and opted to bide his time to see if the price would drop.[53]

It did. In November 1985, after a complicated deal involving Philips Electronics and General Motors fell through at the very last minute, Jobs phoned Norby and found him eager to dispose of Pixar at a fire-sale price. While it would later be misreported that Jobs purchased Pixar from Lucasfilm outright, the truth was slightly more complicated. Jobs actually capitalized Pixar with $10 million, $5 million of which Pixar then paid to buy exclusive rights to the Pixar technology— though Lucas made certain that Lucasfilm would continue to be able to use the technology it had pioneered. The other $5 million was used to run the company, with Ed Catmull installed as president and Alvy Smith as vice president.[54] The company, then, had actually been purchased by both Jobs *and* the forty employees of Pixar. The only real sticking point for the deal was where to sign it. Jobs wanted Lucas to come to Woodside, about seventy miles south of Skywalker Ranch; Lucas wanted Jobs to come to him. They settled on meeting in San Francisco, at the offices of Lucas's attorneys, about halfway between both of them, completing the deal in February 1986.

To many, Pixar seems like "the one that got away" from Lucas. Under Jobs, it would eventually become a $7 billion company, responsible for successful family-oriented films whose profits surely had accountants at Lucasfilm wringing their hands over the missed opportunity. And certainly, Pixar was one of those rare instances where Lucas either misread or misunderstood the enormous potential of his own technology. But it was a shortsightedness born of Lucas's own kind of intense focus and drive. Giving up Pixar hadn't cost him anything creatively—he'd still be able to use the computer, after all—and it hadn't required him to compromise his own conception of films or filmmaking. For Lucas, getting rid of the company had simply been the right business decision made at the right time. "Once that [Pixar computer] was developed, then we didn't need a company that manufactured computer hardware," said Lucas plainly. "I didn't particularly want to be in hardware manufacturing. So we sold that off."[55]

"Entertainment is good ideas, not technology," Lucas said later. "The truth is, I'm not that enamored with new technology; I just acknowledge its existence."[56]

Skywalker Ranch was complete. The dream of Zoetrope—that glittering do-it-yourself film empire, far from the prying eyes and interfering hands of Hollywood—had finally been realized. But not by Coppola. And not completely.

The first phase—mainly the so-called Farm Group of administrative buildings, the Main House, and several outbuildings—was finished. But like Thomas Jefferson with Monticello, Lucas would never be truly done building Skywalker Ranch. Still, in the summer of 1985, things were in good enough shape that he could declare the ranch officially open for business. Lucas intended the ranch to be "like a big home, a big fraternity where filmmakers could work together and create together...create stories, and you need a place to finish the movie, to do the postproduction, sound and editing."[57] There were no soundstages, a throwback to the early days of Zoetrope, when he and Coppola had enjoyed shooting their films, guerrilla style, out on location. "Lucasfilm is not a production company," Lucas stressed. "We don't have a studio, we don't have production heads. We have a producer who produces a movie....The rest of Lucasfilm is really a series of companies [like ILM or Sprocket]....And now they're service organizations for other people who make movies."[58] Almost any pre- or post-production work could be done on-site, far away from the prying eyes and interference of Hollywood suits. "They have no idea what making a movie is about," Lucas said scornfully. "To them, the deal is the movie. They have no idea of the suffering, the hard work. They're not filmmakers. I don't want to have anything to do with them."[59]

The showpiece, of course, was the Main House, a fifty-thousand-square-foot Victorian mansion, all picturesque gables and square turrets, wrapped in a surprisingly cozy veranda. At the back, under an enormous stained-glass dome, was Skywalker's research library—Lucas would continually stock the library by purchasing abandoned collections from other studios like Paramount—with a gleaming redwood spiral staircase made of materials salvaged from a collapsed bridge. Lucas was so proud of the library, in fact, that his own private office was accessible only from the upper balcony level of the library. At the moment, Lucas had decorated the walls with old movie posters—he was a stealth collector of memorabilia—as well as paintings and original art from comic book artists like Carl Barks and Alex Raymond. (Eventually the walls would be hung with original works by Norman Rockwell, one of Lucas's key investments.) Many of the opulent furnishings—the stained glass, the antiques, the Victorian furniture—had been selected by Marcia in her last unhappy years of their marriage, serving as Skywalker's decorator.

In scattered locations on the grounds surrounding the Main House—and Lucas had been careful to lay out the property so no structure was visible from any other—were the Carriage House (housing theater operations and licensing), the Stable (for production, publicity, and the gaming division), the Gate House (animation, business affairs, and finance), and the Brook House (more of the games division). Still under construction was the Tech Building, built to resemble a brick winery, where Lucas intended to put Sprocket, which he'd rename (what else?) Skywalker Sound. All in all, more than a hundred employees would make the move from rented offices in Marin County to report to work on the ranch. Rumors to the contrary, Lucas would never live at the ranch—he would make his home in the renovated Parkhouse in San Anselmo, now that the company was at Skywalker—which meant that the only thing really missing from the ranch was ILM, which was still working out of warehouses at Kerner, about fifteen miles away, much to Lucas's continued annoyance.

Always a stickler for details, Lucas had concocted an elaborate backstory for Skywalker Ranch to explain the amalgamation of architectural styles he had fused into the Main House and other buildings at the ranch. According to Lucas, the Main House was built in 1869 by a retired sea captain, whose children then added on to the ranch at various times, embracing the architectural styles of the moment. The Brook House, for example, had been executed in the Craftsman style, which became popular in southern California in the early 1900s, while the Tech Building was being built to reflect the Art Moderne style of the 1930s. "It's my biggest movie," Lucas said of Skywalker Ranch. "I've always been a frustrated architect."[60]

If the ranch was a movie, then Lucas was producing, directing, and editing it with his usual penchant for control. Even nature was controlled to a certain extent: the lake on the property was man-made, ostensibly to provide water for his own private fire department, though birds had taken up residence in the flora on its shores, turning Lucas's water supply into a perfectly crafted bird sanctuary. And to make it seem as if the ranch really had been sitting in the hills near Nicasio since 1869, Lucas brought down from Oregon more than two thousand full-grown trees. The effect worked: the mature trees gave the brand-new facility a timeless ambience—a special effect worthy of ILM. Like Walt Disney, who had created Disneyland as a manufactured reality in the orange groves of Anaheim, Lucas had his own perfectly controlled environment tucked away in the hills of Nicasio. Lucas, however, did his world-building in private.

"I've loved creating the ranch—I find business exciting and challenging," Lucas told a Gannett news reporter visiting Skywalker Ranch that autumn. "There have been exciting parts to it. But I prefer making movies."[61]

For 1985, however, Lucas had put his efforts mostly into rescuing the films of old friends, often without credit, rather than directly involving himself in the production of movies. "On the one hand, I'm [known for] doing these huge productions, and at the same time I'm helping on these little productions for my friends," said Lucas. "But in most of the interviews with me, they're passed right over as though they never existed. But those movies may be closer to what I am than *Star Wars.*"[62] That could certainly be said of *Latino,* a gritty and politically charged film about the conflict between the Sandinista government of Nicaragua and the U.S.-backed Contras, written and directed by Lucas's old friend Haskell Wexler. Given its contentious, though relevant, topic — Nicaragua would turn into a political quagmire for Ronald Reagan's administration by 1987 — Wexler was having difficulties getting the film distributed and called on Lucas for help. "George Lucas helps his friends with whatever they're doing," said producer Tom Luddy, a friend to both Lucas and Wexler. "He's the kind of person who is loyal to his friends. And Haskell Wexler is one of his oldest friends."[63]

Lucas had also stepped in to help another old friend who had run into trouble: Walter Murch, who had just been unceremoniously fired from his directorial debut, Disney's *Return to Oz,* which was filming in London. When Lucas heard the news, he called the film's producer in his hotel room in London, waking him up at 3:30 a.m. "You're making a mistake," Lucas said matter-of-factly. The producer was unimpressed. "I'm head of the studio," he snapped, then hung up and went back to sleep. Lucas flew to London anyway and managed to salvage Murch's reputation with Disney, which permitted him to finish the film without further incident. Lucas even hosted a preview showing for Disney executives in the screening room at his house in San Anselmo. "That was Big Brother's arm around Walter," said Murch's wife, Aggie. "George was saying, 'You'd better not hurt my little brother.'"[64]

Disney didn't, but the critics did. Lucas thought there was only one thing that might have made the reviews even worse. "The critics came crashing down on the picture anyway," he remarked at the time, "but they didn't come down nearly as hard as they would have if my name had been on it."[65] It was a complaint he would continue to make throughout his career. As for Murch, he was rattled enough by the experience that he'd never direct another film again.

And then there was Coppola. This time Coppola had gotten involved with a film by another mutual friend, Paul Schrader, who'd written both *Taxi Driver* and *Raging Bull* for Martin Scorsese, and had also recently directed *American Gigolo* and *Cat People*. Schrader was writing and directing a project close to his own heart called *Mishima*, an arty biopic based on the life of Yukio Mishima, the Japanese author, poet, and playwright who had committed ritual suicide in 1970 at age forty-five. Coppola had offered to finance the film himself, but when his latest Zoetrope endeavor collapsed, Coppola had to appeal to Lucas for money. Lucas said yes almost immediately; Schrader was making the kind of deliberately artistic film Lucas admired, shooting each of the film's three narratives in a different style—the approach Lucas had experimented with in *More American Graffiti*. Lucas eventually talked Warner Bros. into financing half the film, and even flew to Japan to check on Schrader's progress as he completed the movie. *Mishima* would be released as a co-production of Lucasfilm and American Zoetrope and, on its release in October 1985, would be little seen but highly regarded.

Lucas spent the end of 1985 in court. And it was all President Ronald Reagan's fault.

In March 1983, President Reagan had proposed a missile defense system that would rely in part on space-based launching systems to knock any incoming enemy nuclear missiles out of the sky. While Reagan called his system the Strategic Defense Initiative (SDI), its opponents—starting with Senator Ted Kennedy—had derisively dubbed it "Star Wars." The term had picked up traction in the media to the point where the terms "Star Wars" and "SDI" were used interchangeably, much to Lucas's increasing annoyance. When dueling activist organizations began using the term "Star Wars" in competing television commercials in the weeks leading up to a summit between Reagan and Soviet leader Mikhail Gorbachev, Lucas finally went to court, arguing that affiliating the term "Star Wars" with SDI was an infringement on his trademark, and that he didn't want his film associated with "a noxious subject, particularly nuclear holocaust."[66]

Lucasfilm lawyers finally had their day in court on November 25.

Things didn't go well. Judge Gerhard A. Gesell (the same judge who had presided at the 1974 trials of the Watergate defendants) quickly ruled against Lucas, citing "non-trade use" of the term "Star Wars." "When politicians, newspapers, and the public generally use the phrase Star Wars for their convenience," wrote Gesell in his opinion, "[the] plaintiff has no rights as owner of the trade-mark to prevent this use of Star Wars."[67] It wasn't the last time Lucas would go to court to protect *Star Wars;* in 1990 he would sue rapper Luther Campbell of 2 Live Crew for calling himself Luke Skyywalker, slapping the performer with a $300 million lawsuit. This time Lucas would have better luck; Campbell would eventually settle, paying Lucas $300,000, and agreeing to stop using the name.[68] But Campbell would never forget it. Spotting posters for *Star Wars: The Force Awakens* in New York twenty-five years later, Campbell would get angry all over again. "Every time I see a trailer, or an ad, for that movie," seethed Campbell, "all I can think is I want that motherfucker George Lucas to give me my money back."[69]

And still the question dogged him: Would he be doing any more *Star Wars*? "I don't know," Lucas told a reporter in late 1985. "I probably won't do any more personally." He had rough plots in his head, he promised, but "they're not written down like stories."[70] For now, he said, "I want to produce other directors' films, to be just the executive producer and to shoot some films of my own that will be experimental instead of commercial," adding, "I want to try to do some films that no one has ever done, [regardless of] whether they're watched, whether they're successful."[71]

It's unlikely, however, that he intended for that to be the fate of *Howard the Duck*.

After nearly two years of keeping a low profile, Lucas was ready to enter the public spotlight again in 1986. As Lucasfilm CEO Doug Norby continued paring away at employees and reorganizing divisions inside the company—and with overhead rumored to be approaching $20 million per year—the media and business analysts wondered aloud whether Lucas was getting back into films because he needed the money. "The appeal of Mr. Lucas's principal stock in trade, the 'Star Wars' saga, appears to be waning," wrote Michael Cieply in the *Wall Street Journal.*[72] *Star Wars* fans, it was argued, had moved on. Toy sales continued to plunge, and even Marvel Comics was preparing to wrap up its monthly *Star Wars* comic after nine years.

Norby's pruning and rearranging, while unpopular, had actually done much to steady Lucasfilm. With merchandising receipts down, however, ILM would have to step up as the most reliable source of revenue. Over the past year, the effects shop had indeed taken on more and more outside work, producing effects for *The Goonies, Explorers, Back to the Future,* and even the opening credits sequence for *Out of Africa.* At the Academy Awards in March, ILM would win yet another Oscar, this time for the special effects for *American Graffiti* actor, now director, Ron Howard's *Cocoon.* And yet, even as ILM expanded its work, Lucas would gripe about the company's becoming complacent. "A lot of wild, rebellious enthusiasm seems to be paling a bit, for better and for worse," Lucas told *Time.* "While it's reassuring to see the company becoming more stable and professional, it's a challenge to keep things fresh."[73]

Inside Lucasfilm, everyone seemed certain Lucas had another big project in development, another game-changing franchise like *Star Wars* or the Indiana Jones films. "I think George will search his instincts for something new," said one employee,[74] while another noted proudly that Lucas "has this terrific instinct for popular taste. I'm sure he's got something completely different up his sleeve."[75]

He didn't. But what he did have was plenty of old friends whose work he respected, whose company he enjoyed, and for whom he was more than happy to act as a producer—and for Lucas, that was usually more than enough. The resulting films would meet with only varying degrees of critical and popular enthusiasm—one would even be considered among the worst films of all time—but Lucas never regretted making any of them, or putting them out under the Lucasfilm imprint. "The company is designed so I don't have to make commercially profitable movies," Lucas explained patiently. "Your bottom-line assumption has to be that every movie loses money. They don't, of course, but you go on that assumption. It's like baseball. You don't always get into the World Series, but you go on playing."[76]

One collaborator Lucas liked a great deal was Jim Henson, with whom he had remained friendly since working together with him to develop Yoda for *The Empire Strikes Back*. Following the lukewarm reception of his groundbreaking 1982 film *The Dark Crystal*, Henson was looking for a big-name producer for his next film, the fantasy-fairy tale *Labyrinth*. "Jim and I both wanted to work with each other, and that was a movie nobody wanted," Lucas said later.[77] While the vision for the film was entirely Henson's, the script remained problematic, with several writers—including Dennis Lee, Laura Phillips, Terry Jones, Elaine May, and Henson himself—unable to crack the structure of the story. Lucas offered to tinker with it too. "I'm strong with script and editing," Lucas remarked. "One contribution I could make to *Labyrinth* was to keep the script focused. It's a real trick to keep a script focused."[78]

After Lucas sat through two days of story meetings at Parkhouse with Henson and his creative consultant Larry Mirkin, one had to wonder how much help he really was. Mirkin recalled Lucas taking out a clipboard and drawing three or four concentric circles and tracing a line through them as he explained the main character's journey through the labyrinth. Lucas was "a really lovely, unassuming guy," said Mirkin, "but I don't remember it leading to anything very helpful to the writer."[79] More memorable—at least to Mirkin's mind—was their lunch at a local restaurant, where Lucas was joined by Linda Ronstadt, who turned every head as she entered the dining area.

Lucas enjoyed working with Henson, and took great pleasure in arranging for Darth Vader to show up on the first day of filming at Elstree to present Jim with a good luck card. Both he and Lucas would need it; *Labyrinth* bombed with audiences almost immediately upon its release in June 1986, earning only $12 million off its budget of $25 million. Henson took it hard; Lucas didn't. "It's disappointing when something doesn't work, but it's part of the game," he told the *Los Angeles Times*. "You win some, you lose some."[80]

Lucas's next production, which opened a mere six weeks later, would fare just as badly.

At first blush, *Howard the Duck* seemed like an ideal project for Lucas. It was based on a comic book he loved, and Howard's co-creator, writer Steve Gerber, was just the kind of defiantly independent artist Lucas admired. Shortly after completing *American Graffiti*, in fact, Lucas had pressed issues of the *Howard the Duck* comic into the hands of Willard Huyck and Gloria Katz, telling them they were "very funny" and might be worth turning into a movie.[81] Huyck and Katz had eventually produced a script that they then shopped around Hollywood for nearly a decade, with no takers except Universal, which promised to back it on the condition they bring in Lucas as executive producer. Once again, Lucas would permit his name to be used as a favor to friends. And once again, it would cost him.

Production of *Howard the Duck* was a disaster from the beginning — and the biggest problem was Howard himself. After Huyck and Katz had unsuccessfully pushed for an animated version of the film, Lucas suggested instead that they handle Howard as a special effect, and put him in the hands of ILM. Unfortunately, ILM treated Howard as little more than a complicated duck costume, cramming one of seven actors inside the suit — usually the three-foot-four Ed Gale, who could barely see, fell over constantly, and had to be carried from set to set.

The experience was a bad one, too, for Huyck and Katz, both of whom felt they'd been marginalized on their own film. Borrowing a page from Lucas's playbook, they left for Hawaii the week their film opened in August 1986 — which meant they weren't around to see the disastrous reviews. The headlines practically wrote themselves: "'Howard the Duck' Lays an Egg," snickered the *Washington Post*, while the *New York Times* called the film "A Fowl Brew." And those were the *kind* reviews. Lucas thought the film had never been given a chance; the movie's promotional materials had prominently played up his involvement — his name was above the title on the first movie posters —

which Lucas believed had caused critics to judge it unfairly. Still, Lucas tried to remain upbeat. "If I had to do it over, I'd do it again," he said a year later. "Look—making movies is like a sporting event. Playing the game is the best part. You put all your effort into it, and sometimes you'll be successful, sometimes the public won't connect."[82] Executives at Universal weren't nearly as understanding; two production heads nearly came to blows in a heated argument over who was to blame for green-lighting the film.

Interestingly, Lucas's most successful film for the year was one that didn't play in traditional movie theaters at all—and came out of a job offer that Lucas never even accepted. In 1984 the Walt Disney Company, on the hunt for fresh blood to reenergize its brand, had approached Lucas about taking over as head of production. Lucas, a lifelong Disney fan, was flattered but refused; he had his own company to manage, after all, and wasn't looking for the kinds of headaches and drama currently rocking Disney's board of directors, which had barely managed to survive a hostile takeover by financier Saul Steinberg. Still, Lucas had advised Disney's new majority stockholder, the billionaire Bass family of Texas, on their purchase of 25 percent of the company, and strongly endorsed the selection of Michael Eisner, his go-getter ally at Paramount, as an ideal CEO. Once Eisner was in place, he immediately reached out to Lucas and Spielberg about developing attractions, based on either *Star Wars* or Indiana Jones, for the Disney theme parks. Spielberg declined, preferring to concentrate on more adult film content—he currently had *The Color Purple* and *Empire of the Sun* in the pipeline—but Lucas was thrilled at the idea of having the opportunity to play in the Disney kingdom, which had so inspired him as a boy. While always skeptical of studios, for Disney he would make an exception.

In February 1985, at a Disney shareholder meeting in Anaheim with six thousand excited shareholders in attendance, Disney and Lucasfilm formally announced an agreement under which Lucasfilm would develop several attractions for the Disney parks, including a new ride based on *Star Wars*.[83] The ride, called Star Tours, would use military-grade flight simulators to give riders the sensation of flying through the *Star Wars* universe, even putting them in the middle of an ILM-produced dogfight with TIE fighters and an assault on the Death Star. At four and a half minutes long, it was ILM's longest visual effects sequence to date. When the ride opened in January 1987, Lucas was at Disneyland with Eisner to cut the ribbon, both of them waving enthusiastically at record crowds that would keep the ride running at capacity for the next sixty hours straight. "I've always felt that there's only one first-class amusement park operation, and this is it," said Lucas appreciatively. "When I did something, I've always wanted to make sure it was done right.... [T]his is the only place in the world like that."[84]

While the ride was the high-profile attraction, Lucas and Eisner were trying to keep under wraps their other ambitious project for the parks: a 3-D movie called *Captain EO*, which would feature another A-lister Disney had recently signed, pop megastar Michael Jackson, still enjoying his post-*Thriller* glow of invincibility. Disney, looking to add some zip to its lineup of in-park films, pitched Lucas and Jackson several ideas during a Valentine's Day meeting with Disney Imagineers in 1985. "We were asked to come up with some concepts to go with three elements," said Imagineer Rick Rothschild. "The elements were George Lucas, Michael Jackson, and 3-D."[85] Both Lucas and Jackson preferred a story treatment called *The Intergalactic Music Man*, in which Jackson's character would arrive on a cold and passionless planet, where he would convince an evil queen—through song and dance—that things are better with warmth and color. But while Lucas had agreed to serve as executive producer for the film, he had no intention of taking on the day-to-day chores of directing it. Jackson was hoping Lucas could persuade Steven Spielberg to take the job, but with Spielberg booked, Lucas brought in an old acquaintance he promised Jackson and Eisner they'd be happy with: Francis Ford Coppola.

Coppola's first directive: change the title to *Captain EO*, an allusion to Eos, the Greek goddess of dawn or light—a decision that met with no objection from Lucas, Jackson, or Disney's handpicked line producer and screenwriter for the project, Rusty Lemorande. Coppola began filming at Laird Studios in Culver City in June 1985 and completed work in August — a quick shoot, certainly, but not as hassle-free as Lucas had promised. Coppola, while fascinated with the much-improved 3-D process — which involved two cameras filming simultaneously at slightly different angles — had often struggled to figure out just the right lighting. Jackson held his song-and-dance routines close to the vest, refusing to show Coppola what he'd be doing until practically the day the sequence was shot. And Lucas didn't make things any easier, dropping in unannounced and insisting on changes that were either technically difficult or expensive to shoot, even scrapping all the footage that had already been shot using the model spaceships. Harrison Ellenshaw, Disney's special effects supervisor, thought Lucas was somewhat distracted by other projects — namely, completion of Skywalker Ranch — "so he could never give *Captain EO* or any of the other things full attention," said Ellenshaw. "So it's kind of like having Michelangelo come by every other day for half an hour and telling you, 'If I had the time, I'd do the Sistine Chapel, but since I don't, let me tell you what you need to do.' And then he'd wait two days, and then he comes by and says, 'You didn't do it right, do this, do that.' Everything was constantly in flux."[86]

Captain EO premiered at Disneyland and Walt Disney World in September 1986. Lucas attended the Disneyland premiere, cutting the ribbon in front of nearly two thousand invited guests. Both parks had rebuilt or refitted existing theaters to accommodate the film and all its incorporated special effects; the theater itself, as Lucas would always argue, was a critical part of the experience. At Disneyland, the film played in the seven-hundred-seat Magic Eye Theater, which had been equipped with flashing lights, fog machines, and concussive audio that pulsed and huffed and throbbed in perfect sync with the action on-screen, making the movie immersive entertainment. (Lemorande would remark that the film wasn't a movie, it was a "feelie.")[87] Clocking in at a fast-paced seventeen minutes, the film boasted a price tag of more than $20 million — nearly twice what Lucas had spent on *Star*

Wars—making it one of the most expensive films, on a per-minute basis, ever produced.

Disney was delighted with the film. It would play for more than a decade (and then, after Jackson's death in 2009, return for another five-year run) to tens of millions of park-goers, making it one of Lucas's most widely seen films. Movie critics may have tried to argue that *Captain EO* wasn't a great film—"[It's] only the fourth best film at EPCOT," insisted Richard Corliss—but Disney patrons didn't care;[88] most would pay it at least one obligatory visit during a trip to the park, while hard-core fans would sit through it repeatedly. Still, critic Charles Solomon, writing in the *Los Angeles Times*, lamented that, given the caliber of the talent involved, audiences were entitled to something more than "the most elaborate rock video in history." Of course, "no one expects an amusement-park diversion to be *Gone With the Wind*," wrote Solomon wearily, "but given that list of credits and the film's lavish budget... audiences have a right to expect more than empty flash."[89]

Speaking of films, would there be more installments of *Star Wars*? It was a question that would continue to be lobbed at Lucas wherever he went, shouted at him across hotel lobbies or tacked on to the end of even the briefest of interviews. This was particularly true in 1987, as fans and media alike marked the tenth anniversary of the release of the first *Star Wars*. Lucas was surprised by the fuss. While all three *Star Wars* films had taken in $1.4 billion at the box office, and another $2.6 billion in merchandising, the blush was clearly off the rose. Sales of *Star Wars*–related merchandise had virtually petered out. The *Droids* and *Ewoks* cartoons had already faded from Saturday morning television. Although all three films had fared well on videocassette, the premiere of *Star Wars* on network TV in 1984 didn't even win its time slot, losing out to the trashy miniseries *Lace* on ABC.

Lucas was surprised, then, when the science fiction magazine *Starlog* asked to work with Lucasfilm to host the first-ever *Star Wars* convention at the Stouffer Concourse Hotel in Los Angeles in May

1987. More than nine thousand fans, many dressed in character, thronged the hotel, paying $18 for three days of events and the opportunity to buy merchandise and memorabilia, greeting one another with "May the Force be with you." Lucas stunned the crowd by making an appearance on the stage in the Grand Ballroom on the last evening of the convention, strolling out to John Williams's music and thunderous applause. "Oh, I thought there were only seven of you here," he joked, as he prepared to take questions from the audience.[90]

And to the inevitable question, Lucas would only deflect cryptically, giving different answers to different interviewers. "I'm kicking it around in my head," he told the *New York Times*. "I keep milling the story around to make it more interesting to myself."[91] In the *Los Angeles Times*, he struck a less optimistic tone, saying, "I haven't really thought about *Star Wars*. I mean, I think about it from time to time, but it will take a lot of ruminating before I can come up with the energy to do three more."[92] But in the *Wall Street Journal*, Lucas was more encouraging. "Right now, there are too many other things I'm more interested in," he said. "But there will be more; it's just a matter of when."[93]

Among those "other things" was his continuing relationship with Linda Ronstadt. While he and Ronstadt still managed to keep from being photographed together in public, she continued to visit Lucas regularly at his home in San Anselmo or at the ranch. Friends were surprised the relationship had lasted this long; "Linda does have a roving eye," said music producer Peter Asher, "and she does not want to settle down."[94] And yet Ronstadt was genuinely smitten; she had recently rented property in northern California so she could be closer to Lucas, and playfully carried around an *Empire Strikes Back* lunchbox.[95] Lucas, too, seemed willing to become more adventurous for her; in addition to the dance and guitar lessons, he had even tried—for a couple of months, anyway—to develop a hipper look by ditching his glasses for contacts and shaving off his trademark beard.

Even as Lucas groused to the press that he had to "work hard at having a private life," rumors continued to fly about their relationship status; there was even speculation in the gossip magazines that the two of them had gotten married.[96] They hadn't. But they *had* quietly gotten engaged—"ring on the finger and all," as Ronstadt put it.[97] More and more, Ronstadt could be found spending time at Skywalker Ranch, riding horses across the pristine countryside—and when the time came to record her 1987 album of traditional Mexican folk songs, *Canciones de Mi Padre*, she chose to use Skywalker Sound's facilities. Lucas had even dreamily suggested building them a honeymoon cottage on the Grady Ranch property adjacent to the Skywalker compound,[98] a proposal that eventually bogged down in the continuing zoning disputes with Marin County neighbors.

More publicly, Lucas had two films in production, both of which were much closer to his heart and to his own interests than any of the movies he'd produced over the past two years. During production on *Captain EO*, Coppola had mentioned to Lucas that he was still hoping to make a film he'd had on the back burner for years, a biopic about automobile designer and businessman Preston Tucker. Coppola—whose own father had invested in Tucker's car company in the 1940s—had purchased the rights to Tucker's story in 1976, and envisioned filming it as "a sort of Brechtian musical in which Tucker would be the main story," but would also incorporate the lives of Henry Ford and Thomas Edison as part of a larger American fable. Coppola had even managed to get Leonard Bernstein to agree to write the music, when—the source of Coppola's continued heartache—the bottom had dropped out of Zoetrope.

Coppola, looking for a backer, said he was "embarrassed and shy" about approaching Lucas for support. "It was a role reversal, like going to a very successful and busy younger brother," said Coppola. "I didn't want George to feel I was intruding, trying to capitalize on his success."[99] But Lucas reassured his old mentor that the request "wasn't a big drama," reminding him that he had relied on Coppola's financial support for *American Graffiti*. Plus, Lucas loved the story, calling it "the best project Francis had ever been involved with."[100] Indeed, in

addition to its being about cars—always a subject Lucas loved—
Lucas could relate to Tucker's story, in which a maverick designer
bucks the system to create a new kind of car in line with his own
unique vision. "[It's] about how you take a dream and carry it through
to reality, and what you're up against," explained Lucas. "The people
in it come up with interesting, creative ideas that are important and
relevant to the world we live in—but they're not listened to and the
ideas are stifled from the top. That sounds likes the business both
Francis and I are in."[101] But Tucker's downfall, in which he lost nearly
everything, more closely paralleled Coppola's own adventures in moviemaking. It was no wonder both Lucas and Coppola were taking the
project so personally.

Lucas agreed to put up the $24 million budget, and even managed
to squeeze additional funding and a distribution agreement out of Paramount, leveraging the studio's desire to lock down Coppola for a
third *Godfather* film. But to Coppola's quiet disappointment, Lucas,
invoking his rights as producer, took over much of the project.
"George's fortunes were rising just as mine were falling," said Coppola.
"So it created a dramatic situation in that the person that had always
been the sponsor of things was no longer able to do so."[102] To write the
screenplay, Lucas brought in Arnold Schulman, a respected film writer
who had recently delivered the screenplay for the film adaptation of
A Chorus Line. Schulman nearly resisted the offer, telling Lucas he
didn't want to write a movie about cars. "This film is not about cars,"
Lucas told him. "It's about Francis."[103] Lucas directed Schulman to
write a script that was upbeat and entertaining, not intellectual and
messagey. "I wanted to make it an uplifting experience that showed
some of the problems in corporate America, and Francis didn't resist,"
said Lucas. "Francis can get so esoteric it can be hard for an audience
to relate to him."[104]

Tucker: The Man and His Dream opened in August 1988 to generally
positive reviews ("the best thing Mr. Coppola has done in years," wrote
Janet Maslin)[105] but a tepid audience response, earning a little less than
its $24 million budget, which made it officially a flop. Holding court with

reporters in the weeks leading up to the film's release, Coppola carelessly went into pre-release damage control mode, telling a *New York Times* reporter that he had forfeited control of the movie to Lucas. "I think it's a good movie," Coppola conceded. "It's eccentric, a little wacky, like the Tucker car, but it's not the movie I would have made at the height of my power."[106] Lucas couldn't believe Coppola's colossal gall, and immediately went on the record with a San Francisco reporter to set things straight, at least as he saw it. "The truth of it is: Francis and I worked on the movie together, and he made the movie he wanted to make....Who knows what it'd have been if he made the movie on his own?" said Lucas—then, in his parting shot, took a scathing swipe at Coppola: "And who knows what it would have been if he'd made it at the height of his powers—which was five or six years ago."[107] It was yet one more bump in their always tumultuous, complicated fraternal relationship.

Although his friendship with Coppola was unlike any between Lucas and his other fellow filmmakers, he would have a genuinely warm—and decidedly non-fractious—relationship with Ron Howard, for instance, his handpicked director for the other film he had in production in 1987: the Tolkien-tinged fairy tale *Willow,* a project Lucas had been mulling over since the earliest drafts of *Star Wars.* Howard, on a hot streak following the hits *Splash* and *Cocoon,* had sealed his deal for *Willow* on a handshake with Lucas in 1985, when the film was still scarcely more than a few pages in Lucas's notebooks. "Let's just both commit to this," Lucas said earnestly. At Howard's suggestion, Lucas hired Bob Dolman, who had written an unsuccessful TV pilot for Howard but had also penned episodes of *SCTV* and *WKRP in Cincinnati,* which Lucas admired. Dolman was dispatched to Skywalker Ranch to spend several days with Lucas and Howard in story conferences, always one of Lucas's favorite parts of the process, as he could talk through plots and characters, then hand them off to a screenwriter without ever having to bleed on the page himself.

With his story for *Willow,* Lucas had distilled all the elements he loved best from fairy tales, movies, and folklore—there's a bit of Moses, a dash of *Lord of the Rings,* a nod to *The Wizard of Oz*—to tell the story of Willow Ufgood, a farmer from a race of small people who finds a full-sized baby and must return her to her own people, whom she is destined to rule as their princess. Along the way, Willow picks up a warrior sidekick, encounters fairies and trolls, and battles an evil queen and dragons. Lucas dug deep into his own work for inspiration as well—he was determined, for example, finally to make a movie with little people as heroes, an idea he had flirted with but then abandoned in *Star Wars*—and at its heart was a theme Lucas loved: "Mr. Average Man rises to the occasion."[108] Dolman worked his way through seven drafts before he, Howard, and Lucas were finally happy with it.

Securing the funding was just as tough; even with Lucas and Howard attached to the project, fantasy films hadn't fared well over the last few years. Lucas could attest to that, as *Labyrinth* had been one of those failures. Furthermore, the film had no real stars; it was going to rely on some expensive special effects; and its main character would be a little person, played by Warwick Davis, who had charmed Lucas as Wicket the Ewok. Suffice it to say, wallets weren't exactly flying open at the studios. Lucas's savior—once again—was Alan Ladd, now the CEO of MGM, who agreed to provide half the film's $35 million budget in exchange for theatrical and TV rights. Lucas would provide the other half, and retain cable and home video rights.

Principal photography on *Willow* began in New Zealand in April 1987, then circled back through Wales to Elstree, where Lucas had a number of enormous sets sprawled across several soundstages. While Lucas tried to linger unobtrusively on the set, Howard knew that he was being watched closely. *Willow* was the first original story Lucas had written since *Indiana Jones and the Temple of Doom*, and Howard understood that he was expected to take good care of the project. "I know he was disappointed in the outcome of *Labyrinth* and *Howard the Duck*," recalled Howard. "But those movies weren't his ideas, and the thing he really enjoys most is kind of cooking up his own ideas and really following it through."[109] Howard was trying hard not to blow it.

One of *Willow*'s most memorable moments, however, wasn't made on a soundstage but rather came out of the workrooms of ILM. One sequence in the film called for Willow, an aspiring wizard, to attempt to turn an enchanted goat back into a woman—but the spell goes slightly awry, and the goat changes into an ostrich, then into a tortoise and a tiger, before finally reverting to human form. Supervisor Dennis Muren pondered ways of doing the effect with props and models, then thought better of it and turned the effects over to the computer department. Starting with establishing shots of each creature, the computer was used to transition seamlessly from one animal to the next in a single shot. It was the first use of computer morphing (or "morfing," as Lucas would always spell it), and that wondrous effect alone would be enough to earn ILM yet another Oscar nomination for Best Visual Effects. It would lose to itself, again, for its work on the groundbreaking *Who Framed Roger Rabbit?*

In the months leading up to the release of *Willow*, there was speculation that Lucas might have another big franchise on his hands—that Willow Ufgood might become the next Luke Skywalker or Indiana Jones. And for a moment, it seemed that Lucas might have done it; on its release on May 20, 1988, *Willow* opened at number one at the box office. But reviews were unkind—and in some cases brutal—and audiences never really connected with *Willow* as Lucas had hoped. Janet Maslin, writing in the *New York Times*, applauded Lucas for trying to stage another "high, ambitious fantasy," remarking that the effort "has a certain nobility, even when the film itself does not."[110] But many reviewers felt that Lucas was not only recycling fairy-tale clichés but also blatantly ripping off *himself,* using old tricks and tropes, but not nearly as well as before. "A 'Star Wars' without star quality," declared *Time,* while *Newsweek*'s David Ansen called Lucas "The Great Regurgitator."[111] That one stung, and Lucas accused reviewers of trying too hard to be clever. "They tell you a little about what a movie is about, and come up with some spiffy little remark. I really don't give them much concern."[112] That, however, would never be entirely true; Lucas had rather cathartically made a point of naming one of *Willow*'s villains General Kael, after one of his most thoughtful but often harshest critics, Pauline Kael.

* * *

On March 3, 1988, Lucas and Spielberg sat side by side at a table in front of the U.S. Senate Judiciary Committee, looking vaguely uncomfortable in their suits, like schoolboys who had been forced to dress up for company. The issue at hand was a seemingly mundane one—the Senate, as part of its constitutionally mandated "advise and consent" role for treaties, was in the midst of considering the Berne Convention, part of an international agreement regarding copyright. But for Lucas, this was no small matter; the treaty formally guaranteed artists the right to claim authorship of their work and—key to Lucas—the ability to object formally to defacement of their work. "The practical issue is colorization," Lucas stated in his testimony, referring to the recent move by cable magnate Ted Turner to add color to the old black-and-white movies shown on his cable networks. But Lucas, who stood at the cutting edge of digital technology, thought the problem went beyond mere colorizing. "Current and future technology," he warned, "will alter, mutilate and destroy" films and other works of art for future generations. "Tomorrow more advanced technologies will be able to replace actors," Lucas continued, "or alter dialogue and change the movement of the actors' lips to match."[113]

Ironically, in less than a decade Lucas would be doing much the same to his own work, as he began tinkering with the first three *Star Wars* films, amping up special effects, adding dialogue, and slightly modifying a number of key scenes. But Lucas would argue that, as the creator of the movies, he and he alone was entitled to make any changes he deemed fit to his own work. "Who better, than the person whose hard labor and unique talent created the art, to determine what is an appropriate alteration?" he argued. The Senate would approve the treaty a year later, providing Lucas and other artists with the protections he sought—but embedded in Lucas's testimony was a charge that could likely be leveled against Lucas by irritated *Star Wars* fans: "People who alter or destroy works of art and our cultural heritage for profit, or as an exercise of power, are barbarians."[114]

* * *

But would there be more *Star Wars?* During a lengthy interview with film critic Charles Champlin in the spring of 1988, Lucas mentioned that he had ideas and notes enough not for just three trilogies but for *four.* "I'm not sure how I could get to all of them in my lifetime," he added, before moving on to other topics. Lucas, who had just turned forty-four, was reflective and generally upbeat that spring. At the moment, the fates of *Willow* and *Tucker* were still unknown. He was thrilled with everything that was happening with the ranch—a small vineyard had recently been planted near the Tech Building, lending further veracity to its fictitious backstory as an old winery—but he remained frustrated with the continued local opposition to his proposal to move ILM there. Lucas had recently tried to make nice to a group of about forty neighbors by inviting them over for sandwiches and a tour of the property, but there was still much hand-wringing in the community about the thought of a 300,000-square-foot building going up in the hills, larger than any existing building in the county. "I don't have anything against George Lucas," said one Lucas Valley neighbor. "He's a nice man.... Hey, I liked Walt Disney, too, but that doesn't mean I want to live next to Disneyland."[115]

In some press accounts Skywalker Ranch was compared unfavorably with Xanadu, the castle-like retreat in *Citizen Kane,* and Lucas to the hermit-like Charles Foster Kane. Lucas argued that he wasn't a recluse—he still enjoyed getting out and doing things—but he *did* value privacy. In 1988, in fact, he and Linda Ronstadt would amicably end their relationship, doing it so quietly that the news didn't even make it into the gossip magazines. Post-breakup, Lucas adopted another daughter, Katie, and in 1993 would adopt a son, Jett.[116] "My main focus was really raising my kids," Lucas said later. "I knew I couldn't direct and raise these kids at the same time. A director...isn't free to go to parent-teacher conferences. So I said, 'Well, I'll be a producer. I can take days off when I need them, and basically focus on raising my kids.'"[117] Coppola felt that being a father and a family man had changed Lucas for the better. "He raised those kids as a mother, really," said Coppola. "He wanted to have a family.... He saw what my kids meant to me. He realized that that was really, in the end, all you have."[118]

The privacy and secrecy surrounding Skywalker continued to intrigue, and slightly baffle, the media, critics, and even some friends. John Milius thought that Lucas was wasting his energy by focusing on the ranch instead of on filmmaking. "Francis really tried to do things with his power," said Milius. "He made movies with [German filmmaker] Wim Wenders, produced *The Black Stallion*, produced George Lucas. George built Lucasland up there, his own private little duchy — which was producing what? A bunch of pap."[119] Strong words coming from the writer-director of *Conan the Barbarian*, and not entirely fair; while Lucas *had* produced several mainstream duds, he'd also helped out — often without credit — arty, underappreciated films like *Mishima* and, in 1988, *Powaqqatsi*, an experimental documentary by filmmaker Godfrey Reggio that throbbed to a score by composer Philip Glass. It was the kind of film that some part of Lucas still aspired to make; like his student films *Herbie* and the first *THX 1138*, *Powaqqatsi* was something of a "tone poem," with images and sound evoking emotional responses from the viewer. Lucas and Coppola served as executive producers, and Lucas helped negotiate a distribution deal with Cannon films.

On the flip side of *Powaqqatsi* was Don Bluth's animated dinosaur film *The Land Before Time*, executive produced by both Lucas and Spielberg. It had been Spielberg's idea, explained Lucas, for a *Bambi*-type adventure "about baby dinosaurs, and he wanted me to executive produce it with him."[120] Lucas had initially wanted to do the film without dialogue, similar to the *Rite of Spring* segment in the Disney film *Fantasia*, but had lost that argument: this was a kids' movie, not a tone poem. Lucas also involved himself in the editing process, where he and Spielberg suggested that Bluth tone down some of the film's scarier sequences — this from the two who had delighted in human sacrifice and brain eating in *Temple of Doom*, an irony that was not lost on Bluth. *The Land Before Time* would be a smash with audiences and critics, spawning several sequels and a cable television cartoon.

The most successful film Lucas had in production in the spring of 1988, however, was a third Indiana Jones film, which both he and Spielberg were hoping would be a return to form after the misfire of the grisly, gloomy *Temple of Doom*. Lucas had actually finished a treatment for the third film as early as September 1984, while *Temple of Doom* was still in the theaters, writing an eight-page story outline called *Indiana Jones and the Monkey King*. This time, Lucas put Indy on the trail of the Fountain of Youth, which brought him in contact with a magical spider monkey who possesses eternal life. It was an odd quest, but Lucas's preferred MacGuffin, the Holy Grail, had been vetoed by Spielberg early on. "Steven didn't like it," remembered Lucas. "He said, 'I just don't get it.'"[121] But Lucas hadn't been terribly happy with the *Monkey King* treatment either, and brought in up-and-comer Chris Columbus, who'd written *Young Sherlock Holmes* and *Gremlins*—and who would later go on to direct *Home Alone* and *Harry Potter and the Chamber of Secrets*—to adapt his story treatment into a screenplay. That script, too, Lucas would shelve.

In January 1986 Lucas tried again, this time bringing in writer Menno Meyjes, who had written the screenplay for *The Color Purple* for Spielberg. There would be no monkey king in this attempt; Spielberg had figured out the hook needed to make a Grail quest work. "The search for the father is the search for the Holy Grail," he told Lucas.[122] If Lucas and Meyjes could figure out a story in which a Grail quest worked as a metaphor for Indy's own relationship with his father, Spielberg would be happy. But Meyjes's final script wasn't quite right either; it would take one more writer, *Lethal Weapon*'s Jeffrey Boam, to put the script into its final shape—and even Boam's screenplay would be punched up by playwright Tom Stoppard, under the credit "Barry Watson."

While writing the story, Lucas had envisioned Indy's father as "more of a professor...[a] Laurence Olivier type, an Obi-Wan Kenobi type." But Spielberg had something different in mind. Indiana Jones had been spawned partly by Spielberg's thwarted desire to direct a James Bond film—so in a way, that made James Bond the father of

Indiana Jones. It only made sense to Spielberg, then, that Sean Connery—the first, and to his mind *best*, James Bond—should play Indy's father, Henry. Lucas wasn't so sure—he worried Connery might "want to take over a little bit"—but left it to Spielberg to corral and manage Connery. He needn't have worried; as it turned out, Lucas found working with Connery to be a "fun experience."[123]

That could be said for most of the shoot as well. In contrast to their experience on *Temple of Doom*, both Lucas and Spielberg generally enjoyed the time they spent on *Indiana Jones and the Last Crusade*. Much of the film was shot at Elstree, which to Lucas now felt practically like home. "We couldn't imagine *not* shooting at Elstree," said Frank Marshall, who was producing *Last Crusade* along with his wife, Kathleen Kennedy. In the late 1980s, however, Elstree, along with most of the English economy, was in a fragile state, and was in danger of being sold for scrap by its owners, Thorn-EMI Screen Entertainment. Spielberg made an appearance before Parliament to make the case for the studio's worth, and Lucas tried to purchase the studio himself, but was stiff-armed by Thorn. Their efforts saved half of it— about three stages—while the rest was torn down to make way for a Tesco grocery store. Even the *Star Wars* stage Lucas and Kurtz had built for *The Empire Strikes Back* was dismantled and carted off to rival studio Shepperton.

The final weeks of shooting were spent back in the United States, primarily in Colorado, where Spielberg would shoot the opening sequence of the film, a 1912 adventure of a Boy Scout–aged Indiana Jones, played by eighteen-year-old River Phoenix. Like the selection of Connery, casting Phoenix—who'd played Ford's son in *The Mosquito Coast* three years earlier—was a pitch-perfect choice, with the young actor perfectly aping Ford's mannerisms and vocal inflections as he was chased over and through a circus train. The sequence was something akin to a comic book "secret origins" story for the wily archaeologist, explaining his whip, his hat, his fear of snakes, even his chin scar. It also better defined the character to Spielberg's and Ford's liking; while Lucas continued to argue that Indy should be a morally ambiguous soldier of fortune who sold artifacts to finance an exotic lifestyle, *Last Crusade*'s opening sequence at last showed Indy to be a historical activist at heart, committed to preserving relics in a museum, where they belonged. Lucas could only shake his head in quiet objection. The argument was lost for good.

Indiana Jones and the Last Crusade opened on May 24, 1989, and would sprint to the $100 million mark in a record nineteen days, on its way to $450 million worldwide by March of 1990. Critics were mostly impressed, as well as largely relieved that Lucas and Spielberg had abandoned the dimness of *Temple of Doom* for the effervescence of *Last Crusade*. Peter Travers in *Rolling Stone* thought the movie worked nearly perfectly, calling it "the wildest and wittiest Indy of them all."[124] Roger Ebert gave it what he felt was an almost obligatory thumbs-up, while the Associated Press thought it was "certain to restore the luster of [Lucas's] golden touch."[125]

While Spielberg had tried to end the film on a conclusive note, showing Indy and his father riding off on horseback into the sunset (yes, yes, Sallah and Brody were there, too)—a shot that looked an awful lot like the final moments of *THX 1138*—critics and fans were already asking if this was really the last they'd see of Indiana Jones. "Probably," Lucas said, "unless I come up with some completely inspired idea. Three, I think, is a pretty nice number." The next question, of course, was whether there would be more *Star Wars*. "It's still sitting on the shelf," Lucas told a reporter for the Associated Press. "It'll be a few years before I get back to it. That's the way those things work. I've got to get motivated by ideas and themes and that sort of thing before I can go back and do it."[126]

At the moment, however, Lucas wasn't motivated by *Star Wars* at all. In the two years since its release, *Indiana Jones and the Last Crusade*, in which Indy and his estranged father had come to an understanding and reconciliation, seemed to be taking on a special resonance. Since the early 1980s, George Lucas Sr. had been struggling with Alzheimer's disease, needing near-constant care and attention. Lucas had seen to it that his father was placed in one of the best nursing homes in northern California—and when Lucas's mother, Dorothy, passed away in March 1989 at age seventy-five, only two months before the premiere of *Last Crusade,* Lucas and his sisters tended more and more to their father's needs. While George Jr. and George Sr. had never been entirely at odds, they had long put any differences aside—and with *Indiana Jones and the Last Crusade,* Lucas had seemed to almost subconsciously offer his father both farewells and forgiveness (as film-goers discovered in *Last Crusade's* final moments, Indiana Jones, like Lucas, had been named after his own father). When George Sr. passed away in December 1991, Lucas must surely have at last known that he had made his father proud. His sister Kate was sure of it. "When my brother made it so big, that was a real thrill for him, of course," she recalled. "It was nice he lived to see that."[127]

Such personal associations aside, *Indiana Jones and the Last Crusade* had gotten him interested in Indiana Jones again, though not, as fans might have hoped, in doing another movie. After watching Jones as a teenager in the opening sequence of *Last Crusade,* Lucas had been struck by the endless storytelling possibilities provided by a young Indy having adventures in the era of Teddy Roosevelt, Amelia Earhart, and Pancho Villa. Recalling how little interest he'd had in his own schooling, Lucas wondered if he might use Indy to make learning fun and engaging. What if he could expand on the prologue from *Last Crusade,* showing Indy's adventures from childhood on into his early twenties, and have him encounter famous figures from history? It would be a real opportunity, he thought, to educate and inspire—to correct some of the problems of the educational system he believed had failed him as a student.

Already Lucas was exploring methods of interactive learning, teaming up with Apple and National Geographic to create an interactive videodisc called *GTV: A Geographic Perspective on American History,* which contained forty videos about historic events. The association with MTV was deliberate; GTV's videos were part music video, part *Schoolhouse Rock,* part sketch comedy. Also included in the package was a program called Showmaker—"like a junior video editing system," declared Lucas happily—with which students could make their own short films using the images and video from the disc.[128] Working with educators, Lucas had been careful to ensure that the content actually reflected approved curriculum—and by March 1990, eighteen of San Francisco's middle schools were using GTV in their classrooms.

Lucas found the work inspiring. In 1991 he would establish the George Lucas Educational Foundation (GLEF) in an effort to reignite what he saw as a docile and uninspiring education system—"a morass," he called it derisively—by providing it with new and exciting technological tools for teaching. Suddenly, the young man who had been bored with school was trying hard to improve them—a paternal instinct that George Lucas Sr. would have approved of. "Occasionally, in school, you stumble across a teacher that lights your fire and gets you going and it becomes one of those great moments. It happens once or twice in your life," said Lucas. "And I keep thinking, why can't education be as exciting all the time?"[129] He would oversee the creation of two more interactive multimedia programs for use in high schools and junior colleges—*Life Story: The Race for the Double Helix,* created in association with Apple and the Smithsonian, and the environmentally themed *Mystery of the Disappearing Ducks,* made with the cooperation of Apple and the National Audubon Society. By 1992, nearly 2,300 schools would be using the programs—but Lucas acknowledged that both the hardware and the videodiscs were expensive enough to make the program cost-prohibitive for many schools. As he had with Edit-Droid and Pixar, Lucas quickly abandoned the idea of being a manufacturer of the technology; instead, GLEF would eventually spin off two companies: Edutopia, an online clearinghouse for education knowledge and best practices, and, in 2013, Lucas Education Research.

Lucas's most ambitious educational project, however, would be *The Young Indiana Jones Chronicles,* which he would pour much of himself into for nearly three years, and which would revive his enthusiasm for filmmaking. From the beginning, it was always Lucas's intention that *Young Indiana Jones* would end up as another interactive educational tool, with each episode ported over to videodisc, where viewers could access hours of additional information at the click of a mouse. When Indiana Jones meets Teddy Roosevelt on a safari, for example, Lucas envisioned the viewer being able to click on any animal seen on-screen, which would then access articles on the animal's environment, maps of its habitat, and hours of video footage. "[*Young Indiana*] started out as a project to teach turn-of-the-century history in the eighth grade for an interactive prototype that I'm developing," Lucas explained to the *Los Angeles Times*.[130]

In 1990 Lucas sat down with Rick McCallum, a German-born producer he'd met several years earlier in London while poking around the sets of the film *Dreamchild*. Lucas laid out for McCallum not only his lofty ambitions for the television series—he wanted a show that would both educate and entertain—but also his unorthodox approach to writing, shooting, editing, and producing it. Lucas would write all the basic stories—and he had plenty of historical figures in mind for Indiana Jones to meet, from Louis Armstrong to Albert Schweitzer—but rather than set up a shooting schedule for each individual episode, Lucas wanted McCallum using a stable of talented directors, including Nicolas Roeg and Terry Jones, who would shoot film constantly. The footage would then be shipped to Lucas back at Skywalker Ranch, where he would begin assembling the episodes using, for the first time, EditDroid. If there were places where he thought an additional scene was necessary, he would ask McCallum to have his director shoot the desired footage, even in the midst of filming another episode. Lucas was essentially treating the series as one long extended film—and for this reason, *Young Indiana Jones* was almost constantly in production for nearly two years, moving from one exotic location to another while Lucas edited furiously back at Skywalker. It was a seat-of-the-pants approach to filmmaking, almost a return to the guerrilla style he had used in film school. Lucas loved it.

Young Indiana Jones was more than just an educational initiative; for Lucas it was also something of an experiment in digital filmmaking. While he had, over the past decade, developed and then deployed digital filmmaking technology for others, he had yet to use it at any real length on a project of his own. When the questions inevitably arose about more *Star Wars,* Lucas would often point out that those films relied heavily on special effects, which made them very expensive; on top of that, to create the worlds Lucas envisioned in his head often far exceeded the capabilities of any soundstage in Hollywood or Elstree. But what if he could create those special effects and those sets digitally? With *Young Indiana Jones,* he'd start experimenting with the digital technology he had on hand, using the computer to fill out crowd scenes by turning ten actors into an expensive-looking throng of two hundred, or creating digital backgrounds rather than using a more time-consuming matte painting.

The mere idea of having Lucas involved with an Indiana Jones television series was enough to persuade ABC to provide the bulk of the funding for the project; even with Lucas's computer technology keeping costs down, each episode would run about $1.6 million. But while Lucas had managed to negotiate an aggressive deal, he didn't have control over everything. For one thing, it would be up to ABC to oversee the promotion of the show—and the network would never seem to know quite what to do with it, promoting it as "a big action thing," Lucas complained.[131]

After nearly two years of writing, filming, editing, and post-production, the pilot episode finally premiered in March 1992, to mostly polite reviews. Critics applauded its noble goals, even as they found it all just a bit boring. Writing in the *New York Times,* the respected critic John J. O'Connor lauded it as a "perfectly admirable idea" but thought the execution was "clunky" and heavy-handed. "Every time a bit of information is plopped into the script," wrote O'Connor, "the sound of Mr. Lucas picking up a teacher's blackboard pointer can almost be heard in the background."[132] Still, ABC was happy enough with the pilot to grant Lucas a full season—and then seemed uncertain what to do with the episodes Lucas gave them, cutting the first season short after only six episodes. While disappointed with ABC's handling of the project, Lucas was having the time of his life, rarely complaining about the fifty hours he was putting in each week between the writing, editing, and supervision of the digital effects. "I'm only doing this because I want to do it," he insisted. "It gives me a huge advantage, because I could[n't] care less if [the networks] don't like it. I've given up my paying job as a movie producer to do this. So I'm doing it out of love."[133] It was the happiest, and most engaged, he'd been with a project since college.

Unfortunately, the labor of love never turned into a ratings bonanza for ABC. Trying to jump-start viewership late in the second season, Lucas brought in Harrison Ford to take up the hat and fedora again to play a fifty-year-old Indy telling a story of solving a murder alongside Sidney Bechet and Ernest Hemingway as a young man in 1920s Chicago. Ford, looking somewhat the worse for wear under the beard he had grown for shooting *The Fugitive,* filmed his part in less than a day at his own ranch — and Lucas was intrigued by seeing Ford as a middle-aged Indy living in the 1950s. It was an interesting premise, Lucas thought, for another Indiana Jones movie.

This time, however, even Harrison Ford couldn't rescue Indiana Jones. After two seasons and twenty-four episodes, *Young Indiana Jones* quietly faded from TV screens.[134] Still, it had been worth the effort. The show had superb production values — it had multiple Emmy Awards in editing, art direction, and visual effects to prove it — and most critics agreed it was a well-intentioned, good-looking dud. But if *Young Indiana Jones* was a failed experiment as far as creating a television series with a higher calling went, it had been an unqualified success when it came to exploring the possibilities of digital filmmaking. The digital tricks he had learned on *Young Indiana Jones* might, Lucas hinted, even make it possible to do another *Star Wars.*

It had been more than a decade since the Great Credits Fiasco of 1980, when Lucas had quit the Motion Picture Academy in disgust during the squabble over the placement of Irvin Kershner's director's credit. But in 1992 the Academy, perhaps acknowledging that the prodigal son was responsible for some of the biggest movies in film history, was ready to make amends. The board of directors voted to award him the

Irving G. Thalberg Memorial Award, reserved for "creative producers, whose bodies of work reflect a consistently high quality of motion picture production." It was a distinguished and well-intentioned olive branch from the Academy, and one that Lucas would accept, even if he *still* refused to become a member of the Academy.

On March 30, Spielberg took the stage at the Dorothy Chandler Pavilion to present the award personally, introducing Lucas as his "valiant colleague, and great and loyal friend."[135] Lucas strolled out on stage in a black tuxedo, and in heartfelt prepared remarks reminded Hollywood that filmmaking was about more than business deals and executives:

> I'd like to thank the Academy members and the Board of Governors for this tremendous honor, not only for myself, but for the thousands of talented men and women, robots and aliens and others with whom I've been lucky enough to share the creative experience in the last few years. Movies are not made in isolation; it's a group activity. And it's only because of the work, the very hard work, of many actors, writers, directors, producers, creative technicians, thousands of assistants of all kinds, and projectionists, that I'm able to stand here and accept this award. I'm very, very grateful to them all.[136]

The award—a heavy bust of Thalberg mounted on a wooden block—was the only Academy Award George Lucas had ever won. ("I'm too popular for that," Lucas would grumble in 2015. "They don't give Academy Awards for popular films.")[137] Still, the Thalberg Award was an appropriate honor for Lucas to receive; while introducing Lucas that evening, Spielberg—who had received the Thalberg Award in 1987, and would finally win an Oscar for Best Director in 1994 for *Schindler's List*—pointed out that Lucas had "changed the look and the sound of not only his movies, but everybody else's movies."[138]

By 1992 that was certainly the case. Knowing that Lucasfilm could no longer rely on *Star Wars* merchandising, Lucasfilm president Doug

Norby had rolled all the bread-and-butter divisions of the company—
THX, ILM, Lucasfilms Games, and a few others—into a new division called LucasArts Entertainment Company. And it was LucasArts
that was truly changing the look and sound of everyone else's movies.
Lucas's THX sound system was rapidly becoming the gold standard in
movie sound—and not just in theaters. Electronics companies like
Technics were now producing home versions of the system too, giving
every home theater owner the opportunity to watch videocassettes
with window-rattling sound. "It's just a desire to present a film as the
filmmakers intended it to be seen, heard and experienced," Lucas
explained.[139]

But the real advances were being made over at ILM, which seemed
to be producing one game-changing effect after another, year after
year. In 1989 ILM had created the morphing water pseudopod—a
writhing tube of water that could make human faces—for James
Cameron's film *The Abyss,* an effect so spectacular that it practically
won the Oscar on its own. Still, competition was ramping up; there
were more and more effects companies setting up shop, including
some led by former ILMers, like Richard Edlund's Boss Films. That
sort of competition had convinced ILM manager Steve Ross that he
had to turn ILM into a brand name all its own, and he thought he
might have done it with the effects for *Terminator 2,* with its
computer-generated morphing liquid metal Terminator. "I believe
people will become interested in seeing an ILM movie as much as they
would an Arnold Schwarzenegger movie," said Ross.[140] And sure
enough, at the 1992 Oscars—the same ceremony where Lucas received
the Thalberg Award—ILM films received all three nominations in
the Best Visual Effects category, with *Terminator 2* beating out *Hook*
and *Backdraft.*

And then came *Jurassic Park.*

After acquiring Michael Crichton's bestseller about a dinosaur-
themed amusement park gone wrong, Spielberg had pondered the best
way to create convincing on-screen dinosaurs. Initially, he pushed
ILM to consider using a combination of stop motion, animation, and

animatronics, skeptical that computer-generated imagery (CGI) had advanced to the point where it would be convincing. But Dennis Muren, ILM's special effects supervisor, thought they could make it work. "Prove it," said Spielberg.[141]

Lucas would never forget the day they did. "We did a test for Steven, and when we put [the dinosaurs] up on the screen, everyone had tears in their eyes," recalled Lucas. "It was like one of those moments in history, like the invention of the lightbulb or the first telephone call. A major gap had been crossed and things were never going to be the same."[142] With their completely convincing dinosaurs, Muren and his team had fundamentally changed the role of the computer in special effects. It had gone from simply being *a* tool in filmmaking to being *the* tool. Spielberg, eyes wide with amazement, could only agree. "There we were, watching our future unfold," he said.[143] Muren, while impressed, was more contemplative. "I don't know where the end of this stuff is," said Muren. "I mean, how real is real?"[144]

When Lucas strolled across the stage to collect his Thalberg Award, the in-house orchestra at the Chandler Pavilion had struck up the theme from *Raiders of the Lost Ark,* not the march from *Star Wars*—an indication of the trilogy's faded reputation by the early 1990s. It had been nearly a decade since *Return of the Jedi,* and while Lucas would always be asked if more was coming, the original films were starting to be regarded—if they were regarded at all—through a warm haze of nostalgia reserved for movies like *The Wizard of Oz, Gone With the Wind,* or even *American Graffiti:* all terrific movies with their own loyal followers, but none with a pervasive pop culture saturation. *Star Wars* had gone from a sensation to a pleasant, though distant, memory.

Or so it seemed.

In 1988 Lou Aronica, the head of mass-market publishing for Bantam Books, had written Lucas a letter that was part business proposal, part fan letter. Aronica had heard Lucas hem and haw about future *Star Wars* films and thought it would be a shame if no one ever learned what happened to Luke, Han, and Leia after *Return of the*

Jedi—and he suggested that Bantam could produce a series of books continuing the story where Lucas had left off. "This body of work is too important to popular culture to end with these three movies," wrote Aronica. It had taken a year for Lucas to get back to him—and his response, while encouraging, was unenthusiastic: "No one is going to buy this," Lucas said.[145] But he gave Aronica the licensing and his blessing anyway, as well as a few conditions: namely, the books had to be post-*Jedi*—there could be no talk of prequels, since Lucas planned to carve that space out for himself—and there would be no killing off of the existing characters, nor could they bring back any who were already dead. Aronica quickly hired Hugo Award–winning author Timothy Zahn—who was already a huge *Star Wars* fan—and in 1991 Zahn's first *Star Wars* novel, *Heir to the Empire*, slowly but steadily climbed its way to the number one spot on the *New York Times* bestseller list.

Zahn followed *Heir to the Empire* with two equally successful *Star Wars* novels in 1992 and 1993. Meanwhile, Dark Horse Comics, flexing its muscles with a Lucasfilm license of its own, produced the six-issue bimonthly series *Dark Empire*, which was so successful it would spawn two sequels. Clearly, *Star Wars* still had a pulse. LucasArts had felt it too, finally releasing several *Star Wars*–based video games in 1993, the first time Lucas had agreed to let his programmers play in the *Star Wars* universe. There were *Star Wars* games for Nintendo and Super Nintendo, new trading cards, and bendable figures. Even the Lucasfilm Fan Club magazine, which had been launched quietly in 1987, was renamed *Star Wars Insider*.

So would there be more *Star Wars*, then? For Lucas it now seemed to be a matter of having the digital technology available to make the movie look on-screen the way he envisioned it in his head—but that could be costly, and Lucas, even after the success of *Jurassic Park*, still wasn't sure that CGI technology was where he wanted it. "If I were to do them [the prequels] the way I'd done the other *Star Wars* films, they would be astronomically expensive, over $100 million," he told the *Wall Street Journal*. "So we have to sort of reinvent the wheel…and be able to accomplish them with a reasonable amount of money. It's all sort of dependent on how fast the new technology falls into place, but it's coming along pretty fast now."[146]

As to just *how* fast, Lucas intended to put the technology to the test in a film he'd been trying to make since the early 1970s called *Radioland Murders*. Conceived at roughly the same time as *American Graffiti*—it was one of the films he'd dangled before Universal during his initial deal—*Radioland* would, Lucas hoped, tap in to the same kind of nostalgia for old radio shows that *Graffiti* had for cruising. But Lucas wanted it played in much broader gestures than *Graffiti*, citing his own fondness for the Abbott and Costello film *Who Done It?*, in which the comic duo investigated a murder at a radio station. Lucas had passed his story treatment on to Willard Huyck and Gloria Katz, and their script had enough traction at Universal for the studio to feel comfortable announcing that the film was in production, with Lucas directing and Kurtz producing. But things fell apart after that, and the project sat in a development dead zone for the next decade.

When Lucas finally dusted it off again, he promised Universal that he could shoot the movie inexpensively—he thought for about $10 million—because he intended to use CGI to finish the tops of partially completed sets and to create digital background mattes that would negate the need for elaborate, and expensive, 1940s-era sets constructed on a soundstage. Universal, while skeptical, agreed, on the condition that Lucas rewrite the script to give it a faster, more modern feel. Ron Howard recommended the team of Jeff Reno and Ron Osborn, who had written and produced the quirky TV series *Moonlighting*—but even with Reno and Osborn's chatty script in hand, Lucas would pick apart what he considered the best bits from all the varying treatments and push and pull them together into the final script. It was not a good start.

Looking for a director with an intentionally comedic touch, Lucas hired English comedian Mel Smith, a veteran of the English TV comedy sketch show *Not the Nine O'Clock News*, and whose only directing experience had been the 1989 dud *The Tall Guy*. But Lucas had liked that film's slapstick style ("We're more in Benny Hill territory here," complained one critic) and liked Smith personally.[147] Smith would have his work cut out for him from the moment he arrived at Carolco Studios in North Carolina; most of the sets were only partially finished, with the rest to be filled in later via digital compositing. Smith would squint through the eyepiece of the camera, then ask drily, "Now, tell me what I'm seeing?"[148]

Radioland Murders bombed on its release in October 1994, with attendance falling off by a staggering 78 percent in the second week, and earning back only $1.3 million of its $15 million budget. Reviews were scathing—most criticized its too-fast pacing, and overreliance on slapstick and sight gags, both of which had been intentional on Lucas's part. But Lucas brushed off the criticism. "It came out almost exactly or even better than I hoped it would come out," he told reporters defiantly.[149] "I like my movies, and I'm always surprised if they do very well or do terribly. But *Radioland Murders* was inexpensive and we learned quite a bit."[150]

What Lucas had learned was that it was possible to build a world convincingly in the computer: sets could be completed or constructed entirely, backgrounds could be dropped in, skies could even be darkened. "I think we may have reached a level here where we have actually created reality," said Lucas, "which, of course, is what we were trying to do all along."[151]

So would there be more *Star Wars* then? This time, Lucas had a definitive answer: "I plan to start work on the screenplays soon."[152]

11

A Digital Universe

1994–1999

George Lucas began the morning of Tuesday, November 1, 1994, as he did most weekday mornings, coming downstairs to the kitchen of his house in San Anselmo—still called Parkhouse or Park Way by those who remembered—to have breakfast with his children. He was exhausted; he'd been up all night tending to thirteen-year-old Amanda, who was nursing a cold, and the morning had come too soon. Still, being a father would always be Lucas's proudest achievement; in 2015 he would note that he wanted his epitaph to read "I was a great dad."[1] Spending the mornings with the kids just before school was one of his favorite parts of the day, a time when he could be at his silliest, whether he was throwing one of them over his shoulder or arguing playfully about the day's schedule. After breakfast, he drove Amanda and six-year-old Katie to school, just as he always did—only today, instead of continuing out to the ranch, Lucas returned home to Parkhouse, climbed the stairs to his office, sat down at his desk, and prepared to start writing the script for the next *Star Wars* film.

Lucas knew this was a big deal; before he had even written a word, he took a moment to be interviewed on camera, looking confident and remarkably unfazed by the task he had before him. "I'm all set," he told his off-camera interviewer as he sank into his chair. "Now all I need is an idea." Even though Lucas was now fifty years old, his preferred attire had changed little in the past three decades: today's outfit consisted of jeans, tennis shoes, and a blue-and-green-plaid shirt, open at the collar. His beard had gone mostly white. His hair—Lucas had always been blessed with good hair—was swept back and up into a towering salt-and-pepper pompadour. The voice was still reedy, but there was new fire in his eyes as he chatted casually with the interviewer about his writing process ("It takes a great deal of concentration") and his hopes that the digital technology at his disposal would finally allow him to bring any world he might summon on the page directly to the screen. "I didn't want to go back and write one of these movies unless I had the technology available to really tell the kind of story I was interested in telling," he explained later. "I wanted to be able to explore the world I'd created to its fullest. So I waited until I had the technological means to do that."[2]

But technology wasn't going to make the actual writing any easier. In that department, Lucas remained almost defiantly analog, writing his treatment out in longhand on lined notebook paper, just as he had back in 1972. As he sat down at his desk that November, his plan was to write all three movies at once—an ambitious goal, particularly for someone who agonized over writing as much as Lucas did. But he promised there was a method in this particular brand of madness: "I'll take a year to write them, a year to prepare them, and a year to shoot them," he explained. "And I'll shoot them all at once." The one thing he *wasn't* planning to do, however, was direct them, suggesting only that he would "decide after [he got] the films prepared."[3] But there was, he thought, little chance of his being in the director's chair; as miserable as writing made him, directing was the one part of the filmmaking process he dreaded the most, now largely because it required him to be away from his children for long stretches at a time.

Coppola had always affectionately referred to Lucas as "a single mother," but it was a label Lucas wore with pride. "There's no one I admire more than single mothers," he told the *New York Times*, "because they are the real heroes."[4] Indeed, the policies Lucas had put in place in his company were family friendly enough that *Working Mother* magazine had named Lucas a Family Champion in 1994, a designation given to CEOs who oversaw a workplace supportive of the needs of working parents. The same magazine had listed Lucasfilm among the best companies for working mothers, citing the ranch's two child care centers, flexible work schedules, and progressive policies that provided paid leave for employees to attend to sick family members, as well as insurance coverage for domestic partners and their dependents. "We've discovered that quality of life is a much greater asset in securing people than high salaries," Lucas said. "[We're] just doing what one should be doing." He also pointed out that he, too, was a single parent of three. "I guess I qualify as a working mother," he added, to Coppola's likely delight.[5]

"It's through me that the organization hopefully tries to take a more compassionate view of its employees and what we do," Lucas told *Time* magazine on another occasion. "I rule at the will of the people who work for me."[6] He didn't, however, rule alongside Doug Norby, who had unceremoniously resigned as Lucasfilm's president and CEO in 1992 to return to the board of directors. At that time, Lucas had issued a tight-lipped statement wishing Norby well, then quietly promoted his vice president for business affairs, Gordon Radley, to the post of president and chief operating officer, a position he would hold for nearly a decade, largely owing to his ability to stay out of Lucas's way. The shake-up had raised eyebrows on Wall Street, with some analysts wondering aloud whether Lucas intended to take his company public. But Lucas, as the company's sole stockholder, had no intention of giving up that kind of control.

Lucas's form of benevolent dictatorship was obviously working; morale was generally up and turnover was low. "I find myself with this little country," Lucas observed. "It's got about 2,000 citizens and they are very complex. Some are very loyal and some of them are very dissatisfied.... [Y]ou have to try to make things work. And it's not that easy. But you try to keep people from being used and abused and listen to their grievance and try to do what is fair."[7] Consequently, Lucasfilm employees could choose from a wide range of services and benefits, especially at Skywalker Ranch, where they could enjoy three restaurants and enroll in a variety of classes, including yoga, ballet, and tai chi.

And Lucas was still working to both expand and consolidate his empire. Over the past few years, he had continued to acquire land adjacent to the ranch—and was still doing so in his accountant's name—eventually increasing Skywalker to nearly five thousand acres. While Lucas would finally win approval to build three new administrative office buildings on the nearby Big Rock Ranch, ILM would remain stranded in the warehouses in San Rafael, a casualty of continued pushback by Marin County residents who refused to be swayed by Lucas's promises of new jobs and protected open space.

Even as Lucas grumbled about its absence from Skywalker Ranch, ILM continued on its streak of Oscar-winning visual effects. After the razzle-dazzle of *Jurassic Park* in 1993, ILM had awed audiences the next year with more subtle and even more convincing effects for Robert Zemeckis's *Forrest Gump,* superimposing actor Tom Hanks into historical footage of President Kennedy, creating crowds at a rally in Washington, D.C., and digitally compositing the feather that floated over the opening credits. With ILM in his corner, Lucas was regarded as the sage of digital filmmaking, with everyone else trying to catch up. Steven Spielberg, now with an Oscar to his name following the success of *Schindler's List,* looked on with admiration. "ILM has no peer and there is no one even close," said Spielberg, who had just founded his own DreamWorks production company in partnership with music magnate David Geffen and former Disney executive Jeffrey Katzenberg. Journalists, sniffing for a story about strife between Lucas and Spielberg, suggested that DreamWorks might eventually eclipse Lucasfilm in the realm of digital effects—but Lucas shrugged it all off as nonsense. "I want to see Steven succeed. I don't think him succeeding...is going to hurt me," he told the *Los Angeles Times,* adding, "We have an agreement not to overtly hurt each other."[8]

Still, the larger and more successful Lucasfilm became, the more Lucas raged and railed against the Hollywood machine. Even as the head of a billion-dollar company, Lucas still saw himself as the misunderstood little guy. His company, he insisted, was just "a little mud hut outside the castle."[9] The studio system was dead, he proclaimed. "It died...when the corporations took over. The studio heads suddenly became agents and lawyers and accountants,"[10] people who were "more interested in stock options than making good movies."[11] Like Luke Skywalker and the rebels defying the odds to beat the Empire, he was the leader of a small group of revolutionaries who had squared off against the faceless, soulless Hollywood machine. "They see us as outcasts, as those wacky guys up there who cause trouble because we want creative freedom," Lucas told the *New York Times.*[12] "Up here, we don't have stockholders or dividends. Everything I make goes back into making something else. If we make a mistake, we die." Ultimately, said Lucas, adopting the tones of the radical hippie many supposed him to be, "we learned one rule that came out of the '60s: Acquire the means of production."[13]

It all sounded positively revolutionary, but Carrie Fisher knew better. "Skywalker [Ranch]," observed Fisher drolly, "is where George gets to make up the rules."[14]

Days before sitting down in his office to begin handwriting his treatment for Episode I, Lucas had already sent Rick McCallum, his producer from *Young Indiana Jones,* out to scout locations, billing all travel to the production company Lucas had set up for the new trilogy, JAK Productions—named for his children, Jett, Amanda, and Katie. At the same time, ILM artist Doug Chiang was hired to serve as the art director for the prequels, stepping into the role filled by Ralph McQuarrie on the first *Star Wars* trilogy. "Even though I'd just started writing," said Lucas, "I already knew certain things that needed to be designed," such as spaceships and planets. Meanwhile, other artists at ILM had been tasked with working on character designs that were still little more than a few brief phrases on the page, with Lucas giving his artists vague descriptions—"This character is cowardly and insecure"—and letting them take it from there.[15] That included the conceptual design for the amphibious Jar Jar Binks, a character Lucas had high hopes for, who would go through nearly eighteen months of design.

After more than twenty rewrites and revisions, Lucas would have the first rough draft for Episode I—at this point called simply *The Beginning*—completed on January 13, 1995. The script would never be entirely finished; building off the strategy he'd used on *Young Indiana Jones,* he would revise the script during filming and even during post-production. But he was comfortable enough with certain elements of the story to ask effects supervisor David Dozoretz and Ben Burtt—who was becoming one of Lucas's most deft editors—to cut together a number of low-resolution, roughly animated storyboard sequences, called "animatics," to guide the computer animators in much the same way Lucas had used his World War II dogfight footage to inspire the visual effects team on the original *Star Wars.* "The only way you can evaluate the effects shots you're going to need is to cut in temporary action scenes," said Lucas. "With Episode I, it was the first time I was able to use computerized animatics to pre-visualize the entire film before I even started shooting."[16] The first sequence Burtt and Dozoretz were instructed to assemble, then, was the podracing scene, the high-tech drag race Lucas envisioned as young Anakin Skywalker's ticket to freedom. Fast cars had always been one of Lucas's favorite means of escape, whether it was the car in *THX,* John Milner's deuce coupe in *American Graffiti,* or even the *Millennium Falcon.* It was little surprise that Lucas had included it in the script from the very beginning.

While Lucas was keeping the development of Episode I a tightly guarded secret, just the knowledge that he was at work on the next film seemed enough to excite *Star Wars* fans. "Part of the reason for doing this is that it's the first question I get asked," said Lucas. "I think a lot of people want to see it."[17] That certainly seemed to be the case, to judge by the reemergence of *Star Wars* in popular culture—on television, the Energizer Bunny could be seen battling Darth Vader in a commercial for batteries—and the revived interest in *Star Wars*–related merchandise. In August 1995, Lucas re-released the *Star Wars* trilogy on home video, this time issuing the three films with THX sound and a digitally remastered picture. To Lucas's shock and delight, more than 28 million cassettes were sold, generating a profit to Lucasfilm of more than $100 million.

The same year, Hasbro—which had soaked up Kenner years earlier—reactivated its option to produce action figures and issued a new line of *Star Wars* toys under the imprint "The Power of the Force." A manager at FAO Schwarz in New York was surprised to see that there were more adults than children buying the new line of toys—a singularity that made the new figures some of the bestselling toys of the year. Marketing directors everywhere would make a note. Toys weren't just for kids anymore. Especially *Star Wars* toys.

In fact, Lucas had shrewdly convened a "*Star Wars* Summit" at Skywalker Ranch for licensees and international agents, where he briefed them on his plans for the future of the *Star Wars* franchise. Over the course of two days of presentations, Lucas reinforced the need for him to maintain quality control, especially in the areas of publishing, where some characters—such as Luke Skywalker, who'd been given a love interest in a fiery smuggler named Mara Jade—were living lives far beyond the ones he had written for them in the original trilogy. At a second summit in April 1995, Lucas—who showed up bleary-eyed, joking that he'd been dragged away from writing the script—tantalized the room by hinting that he was considering directing the first of the three prequels himself.

As Lucas continued slowly to ramp up pre-production—by early 1996 he would have his art department putting together storyboards for a film that didn't yet have a workable script—he was becoming more and more convinced that digital technology would help him make Episode I both quickly and cheaply. "The techniques that we pioneered in the [*Young Indiana Jones*] TV series that we're now using in features are going to be one of the major differences about the way movies are made," Lucas proclaimed.[18] Perhaps the most critical of those techniques involved "blurring the line" between production and post-production, so new scenes could be added or old scenes could be re-shot or re-staged, even during the editing process. "It's not an assembly line. I don't write first, then design, then shoot. I'm doing everything together," he told a reporter.[19] And because he planned to use the computer to create or fill in most of the sets, Lucas was predicting big savings in the expense of making his films. "I don't think it's going to cost much relative to the top end that I would ever make a movie for," he predicted. "I would never go above the $50 million range."[20]

That wouldn't even be close. When all was said and done, Episode I would cost nearly $115 million. And almost all of it would come out of Lucas's own pocket.

In the meantime, producer Rick McCallum—who'd spent nearly a year scouting suitable locations and facilities to shoot Lucas's still unfinished script—had found a home base for the production. Briefly, Elstree Studios in London had been considered, though that was mostly for sentimental reasons; every *Star Wars* movie had been filmed there from 1976 on. Since the fire sale of the facility in the late 1980s, however, the studio was a shell of its former self, and hardly large enough for a production of the scope Lucas was envisioning, even with many of the sets being built in the computer. Instead, McCallum would find what Lucas needed a little less than ten miles northwest of Elstree at the Leavesden Aerodrome—a gigantic former Rolls-Royce factory that had recently been converted to film production for the James Bond picture *GoldenEye*.

In the summer of 1996, then, Lucas had McCallum reserve the entire studio—including its one-hundred-acre back lot—for two and a half years, which would leave the studio at his disposal, as needed, until practically the day the film was to be released. Immediately,

Lucas dispatched a team from the art department, led by production designer Gavin Bocquet, to begin constructing sets across Leavesden's nine soundstages. Even at this early date, coordination with ILM was critical, as the art department and construction team had to know exactly what parts of the set to build and what to leave for the computer to construct digitally. Most sets would end up being a hybrid of partially constructed pieces — a platform, a bit of wall, a door, and a table — surrounded by blue- or greenscreen onto which the rest of the set could be superimposed digitally later. Lucas and others would come to refer to this amalgamation of high and low tech as a "digital back lot." By December, nearly sixty sets would be scattered across the Leavesden soundstages, taking up about 800,000 square feet of space.

As he fielded regular reports from London and continued to revise his script, Lucas found — quite to his surprise — that he was enjoying playing in his *Star Wars* sandbox again. He was especially intrigued by the nearly infinite possibilities that digital filmmaking put into his hands, and he had one more test subject in mind over which to wave his digital wand before unleashing its full power on Episode I. A movie so terrible, said Lucas, that "every time I saw it, I'd think, 'Oh God, that's so awful, I can't watch this.'"[21]

Star Wars.

"The original *Star Wars* was a joke, technically," Lucas insisted.[22] "We did a lot of work, but there is nothing that I would like to do more than go back and redo all the special effects, have a little more time."[23] While he didn't intend to go quite so far as to redo *all* the special effects, he did hope "to go back and fix some of the things that have bugged me forever," as he told a reporter. "There were things I had to compromise on that weren't the way I really wanted them to be."[24]

Lucas had started plotting his digital changes to *Star Wars* several years earlier, at a 1993 meeting with McCallum and a team from ILM led by Dennis Muren. At that time, Lucas had complained most loudly about the cantina sequence, which he was still unhappy with nearly twenty years later, laying the blame squarely on tightfisted Fox executives who'd refused his requests for money to finish several creatures. With digital technology at his disposal, he hoped to excise some of the rubber-masked monsters dictated by his minuscule budget and fill the cantina instead with the kinds of exotic creatures he'd envisioned from day one. He also still regretted being unable to include Han Solo's conversation with Jabba the Hutt at Docking Bay 94, and hoped now to incorporate a digital Jabba into the discarded scene. Muren nodded, and further suggested that ILM take the opportunity to clean up or even redo some of the other effects shots, making tweaks to a few of the dogfights and inserting better explosions. Lucas okayed those suggestions as well—and then suggested they go even further than that, eagerly proposing they insert new digital footage into both *Empire* and *Jedi*. He hoped the alterations could be made quickly enough to release the new edition of the trilogy in time for the twentieth anniversary of *Star Wars* in 1997.

It would be more difficult than he hoped—for when the films were removed from storage in 1994, Lucas discovered to his dismay that the negatives had severely deteriorated over the past fifteen years. *Star Wars*, in particular, was a mess, grubby with dirt, deeply scratched, its colors faded. Lucas groaned; before any work could be done on new footage, the original negative would need to be restored. It would take ILM more than a year to clean up the negative, often using the computer to digitally fill in scratches and match colors frame by frame.[25] The new digital effects were then integrated into the film, sometimes cut directly into the original negative. "We called it an experiment in learning new technology, and hoped that the theatrical release would pay for the work we had done," said Lucas. "It was basically a way to take this thorn out of my side and have the thing finished the way I originally wanted it to be finished."[26] The effort had cost nearly $5 million for the restoration and a little more than four and a half minutes of new or reworked material.

For many fans of the original *Star Wars*, it was four and a half minutes too much. Lucas released *Star Wars: The Special Edition* in theaters in January 1997—special editions of *Empire* and *Jedi* would follow in

February and March, respectively—to enormous hype and impressive numbers, racking up $35 million in its first four days of release. But many fans, who had grown up with the movies in their original state, were furious with Lucas for tampering with them. In addition to the revised cantina sequence, ILM had digitally added characters and creatures to other scenes, sending more stormtroopers chasing after Han Solo on the Death Star, and inserting droids, dewbacks, Jawas, and other creatures in the streets of Mos Eisley with almost too much relish. Such digital clutter was distracting, and inconsequential to the story. The same could probably be said for the new sequence with Han and Jabba, which added a bit more backstory to their antagonistic relationship but ultimately left the two characters unchanged.

That wasn't the case, however, with an alteration Lucas saw as little more than a minor tweak, but one that fans would come to regard as an unforgivable reinventing of one of the trilogy's most popular characters. At Lucas's request, ILM had altered the cantina confrontation between Han Solo and the bounty hunter Greedo—which had ended with Han gunning the hapless Greedo down—to instead show Greedo squeezing off a shot first, thus turning Han's previously aggressive blast into what Lucas saw as simply self-defense.

Fans were apoplectic. To many, that single shot from Greedo had immediately changed the very nature of Han Solo's character, denying him an evolution from selfish, morally ambiguous pirate to self-sacrificing hero. HAN SHOT FIRST! they insisted, a rallying cry that would soon be emblazoned across T-shirts, stickers, and, eventually, much of the Internet as a defiant reminder of the perils of meddling with a mythology.

At first, Lucas insisted lamely that Greedo had *always* shot first, and that muddy editing had made the true nature of the confrontation unclear. "What I did was try to clean up the confusion," Lucas explained patiently. "It had been done in all close-ups and it was confusing about who did what to whom. I put a little wider shot in there that made it clear that Greedo is the one who shot first, but everyone wanted to think that Han shot first, because they wanted to think that he actually just gunned him down."[27]

And yet this was more of Lucas's retroactive continuity—for his own shooting script for *Star Wars*, dated May 15, 1976, clearly never gave Greedo a chance to squeeze off a shot:

> Suddenly the slimy alien disappears in a blinding flash of light. Han pulls his smoking gun from beneath the table as the other patrons look on in bemused amazement.
>
> *HAN:... but it will take a lot more than the likes of you to finish me off...*
>
> Han gets up and starts out of the cantina, flipping the bartender some coins as he leaves.
>
> *HAN: Sorry for the mess.*[28]

But Lucas was determined to stick to his long-running narrative that he'd had all of the details of the entire *Star Wars* saga planned out from the start. "Han Solo was going to marry Leia," he insisted, "and you look back and say, 'Should he be a cold-blooded killer?' Because I was thinking mythologically—should he be a cowboy, should he be John Wayne? And I said, 'Yeah, he should be John Wayne.' And when you're John Wayne, you don't shoot people [first]—you let them have the first shot. It's a mythological reality that we hope our society pays attention to."[29]

Another good try, but fans weren't buying it, and never would. While Lucas would never regret the alteration—and never quite understand the objections—he would also never live it down, deflecting question after question about it for the next two decades. "The special edition, that's the one I wanted out there," he would state in 2004, throwing up his hands in annoyance. "This is the movie I wanted it to be, and I'm sorry you saw half a completed film and fell in love with it."[30] It wasn't just fans who were annoyed, however; Gary Kurtz, who had produced both *Star Wars* and *Empire*, argued that the digital changes were "probably a wrong philosophy.... It's not the way it was in the first place. The way it was in the first place was the way we released it."[31] Lucas dismissed such razzing; as far as he was concerned, as the creator of the art, he and he alone had the right to do with it as he pleased—though for all his talk, one wonders how he might have reacted to, say, Kurosawa digitally altering even one frame of *The Hidden Fortress*. Still, he wasn't above acknowledging the controversy to the fans, even wearing a T-shirt reading HAN SHOT FIRST as he directed *Revenge of the Sith*.[32]

Such controversies aside, the special editions had proven to him that he "could actually pull off the things that [he] wanted to pull off."[33] And the generally enthusiastic reception from fans old and new had further shown that audiences were still eager to see *Star Wars* in the theater—"a celebration of the theatrical experience," Lucas called it.[34] He stoked additional excitement that winter by publicly announcing a decision he'd actually made some time earlier: after twenty happy years out of the director's chair, he was going to direct all three *Star Wars* prequels.

It wasn't a decision he'd made easily. "[Lucas] didn't necessarily want to direct them," said Ron Howard. And, in fact, Lucas had approached Howard, Spielberg, and Robert Zemeckis about taking the reins of one or more of the prequels, only to receive the same retort from each of them: "George, *you* should do it." "I don't think anybody wanted to follow-up that act at the time," said Howard. "It was an honor, but it would've been too daunting."[35] Still, not everyone was as encouraging. Coppola—who'd seen his own career defined and consumed by *The Godfather*—believed that Lucas's devotion to *Star Wars* had sidetracked him from making the small, arty films that were his passion. "I think *Star Wars*, it's a pity," said Coppola, "because George Lucas was a very experimental crazy guy, and he got lost in this big production and never got out of it."[36] Marcia Lucas likened the decision to focusing on a pea at the bottom of the inverted Lucasfilm pyramid, the seed from which a colossal and choking vine had sprung. For Lucas, though, it was a matter of control. "We were going to be attempting new things; and in truth, I didn't quite know how we were going to do them," he said. "So I figured I needed to be there at all times."[37]

There was also just a touch of fatalism involved as well. "It took a long time for me to adjust to *Star Wars*," confessed Lucas. "I finally did, and I'm going back to it. *Star Wars* is my destiny."[38]

Lucas had taken a different approach to the casting for Episode I, handing off much of the work to casting director Robin Gurland, who spent two years compiling lists, collecting photos, meeting with actors and agents, and winnowing the roster of candidates down to a manageable size before handing it off to Lucas. There was still no script to speak of, but most of the actors were willing to meet with Lucas anyway, excited by the idea of appearing in a *Star Wars* movie. That was certainly the case with Samuel L. Jackson, who had made a very public appeal to Lucas on the British talk show *TFI Friday* in December 1996, begging to be considered for any role. "I got invited to the Ranch to see if I was serious about that," Jackson said later. "[I said], 'Yeah, sure! You can make me a stormtrooper if you want, I don't care—as long as I know I'm in the movie, I don't care if anybody else knows or not.'"[39] Jackson would ultimately be a very visible presence in the role of Jedi master Mace Windu, a name Lucas salvaged from the opening line of his 1973 first draft of *Journal of the Whills*.

While Lucas had in the past expressed an aversion to working with name actors—"I don't think George is interested in collaboration with an actor," said Ron Howard; "he's not a 'kick-it-around' guy"—he had no such qualms when it came to Episode I.[40] Besides Jackson, Lucas brought in Irish actor Liam Neeson, who'd rocketed to A-list prominence as the star of Steven Spielberg's Oscar-winning *Schindler's List*, and spent most of his first meeting with Lucas swapping stories about their families. Lucas liked Neeson immediately— he thought he would lend Episode I the same kind of gravitas that Alec Guinness had brought to the original *Star Wars*—and hired him to anchor the film as the astute Jedi master Qui-Gon Jinn.

Very briefly, Lucas had considered an even bigger name than Neeson, indulging a phone call from Michael Jackson, who wanted to play the role of Jar Jar Binks in full makeup and prosthetics, rather than as the CGI creation Lucas preferred. Lucas gently refused the superstar—and dancer Ahmed Best, who would eventually land the role, thought he knew why. "My guess is ultimately Michael Jackson would have been bigger than the movie," said Best, "and I don't think [Lucas] wanted that."[41] Instead, the part went to Best, who would stand in for Jar Jar during filming, wearing a headpiece with the character's eyes so actors could match sightlines, and a costume with bits that resembled gills, so computer animators could mimic the way the light played off him. Lucas also liked the way Best moved and sounded, and permitted Best to endow Binks with a voice—which Best played as a kind of West Indian patois—and a loping, hand-flapping stride, which would be digitized over Best later. "George told me that we were really going out on a limb," said Best. That would be putting it mildly.[42]

Principal photography on Episode I—still titled *The Beginning*—would start on June 26, 1997, at Leavesden. Security was tight; the script—which Lucas hadn't finished until practically the last minute—would remain strictly guarded, and even Lucas would be required to wear a name tag on set, though his would read YODA. While Lucas hadn't directed in nearly two decades, he found "it wasn't a hard thing" to get back into the familiar rhythms. "As soon as Liam Neeson walked on the set, dressed as a Jedi, I said to myself, 'I guess I'm back,'" said Lucas. "It was as if those twenty years had never elapsed."[43]

Still, there were some marked differences between 1977 and 1997. In contrast to the year he had spent making the original *Star Wars*, when he would come in each morning and walk the sets, mapping out camera angles between his fingers and running his hands over still-wet paint, in 1997 most of his sets were barren—usually just a platform, a flight of stairs, or a piece of sculpture, set against a gigantic blue screen. "We built as little as we could get away with, and then put up bluescreens," said producer Rick McCallum.[44] That still didn't stop Lucas from touring all of the production departments each day, picking up and poking at masks, examining costumes, and fiddling with props. For the first time since 1982, a new Yoda puppet had been built, completely redesigned not only to look younger but also to be much lighter on the arm of Frank Oz, who had complained about the original Yoda being "really fuckin' heavy."[45] There were also several new R2 units that ran much more smoothly and reliably than the malfunctioning droids from the original trilogy. Threepio — a bare-wired skeletal version of himself in Episode I — would be a life-size rod puppet, manipulated by a puppeteer who would later be removed digitally. The reliable Anthony Daniels, however, would continue to provide his voice.

There were other things, too, that would never change: Lucas was still as bad with actors as ever. Despite working this time with several big-name actors, Lucas wasn't about to indulge any deep drills into character or ponderous method acting. "It isn't about trying to find the motivation for every moment," he insisted. "I'm not like some directors who will sit for days and analyze what is going on." And it didn't seem to matter to Lucas that digital filmmaking was a new experience not just for him but for his actors as well, who were being asked to work with incomplete sets and react to characters that didn't exist. "It took about ten days or two weeks before everyone felt really comfortable with the bluescreen," recalled McCallum, but even then, Lucas remained unresponsive to the needs of his performers.[46] "Sometimes I say cut," he said with a shrug, "[and] sometimes I forget."[47]

While Lucas had initially intended to shoot the film digitally, the available technology, to his disappointment, wasn't yet advanced enough for him to film the entire movie in an acceptable widescreen format. Lucas would shoot a few scenes digitally anyway as a kind of test run, recording some sequences on digital high-definition tape, which would then need to be recorded back to film to be shown in theaters. Watching the footage later, Lucas was convinced he would never shoot on film again. Nevertheless, despite his earlier boast that his digital back lot would make it possible to shoot the movie for around $50 million, costs had escalated rapidly throughout pre-production and continued to climb right on through filming. But Lucas, who in the past had begged studio executives for the money he needed to finish a film, vowed not to scrimp when it came to financing his own movie, no matter the cost. Consequently, he was now pouring all of his money down a funnel labeled Episode I, risking everything, just as he had done with *The Empire Strikes Back*. "When you're making a $100,000,000 movie and it's your money—pretty much all the money you've got—there's a huge risk," said Lucas. "Studios can take that risk and then write it off onto something else. I didn't have anything else.... I was gambling everything again."[48] Episode I was fast becoming the most expensive independent film in history—and it was all being paid for by one person.

Lucas surrounded himself with much of the same crew he had used on *Young Indiana Jones,* from costumers to his director of photography, who were familiar with his working style and "knew the kinds of tricks we would be using on this movie." Beyond that, "there was a language that had been developed in the course of doing [the *Star Wars*] series," said Lucas, "[and] I wanted to continue it on this film, without having to train a whole new group of people."[49] He relied particularly heavily on McCallum, who saw his job as "enabl[ing] a director to achieve everything that he can."[50] But even McCallum was a subordinate, not a collaborator. "The great thing about Rick is that he never says no," said Lucas—and that was part of the problem.[51] Unlike the first trilogy, when Lucas had often been subjected to pushback from Gary Kurtz, Irvin Kershner, Lawrence Kasdan, and Marcia Lucas—who offered differing opinions regarding production, directing, writing, and editing—the prequels would be entirely Lucas's vision, without compromise. His control was complete.

Not that he could control everything. While they were shooting on location in Tunisia, doubling again for the desert planet Tatooine, a massive storm blew through the region, destroying most of the crew's carefully constructed sets. It was 1976 all over again, when a rare rainstorm had washed out most of the sets for *Star Wars*. "It was as if the storm had hidden away for twenty years, just waiting to come back," remarked Lucas, who continued filming on what sets remained intact as the crew, along with military assistance provided by the governor of Tozeur, cleaned up and reconstructed everything.[52]

Lucas would wrap things up back at Leavesden, completing principal photography on September 30. He had maintained a brisk pace over the past three months, personally overseeing more than 2,500 shots, but now the post-production work was going to continue at an accelerated pace that ILM supervisor Dennis Muren wasn't sure they could maintain. "George wanted us to produce 2,200 shots in a year and a half," said Muren. "And you just think, there's no way you can do it. And then he says, as he usually does, 'Well, just think about it,' and he walks out."[53]

As Muren and his team at ILM began assembling digital effects, Lucas was working with editors Paul Martin Smith—another alumnus of *Young Indiana Jones*—and Ben Burtt on a first cut of the film, laying in the animatics until the corresponding digital effects were complete. Editing was still Lucas's favorite part of the filmmaking process, and now he had complete control over nearly every aspect of the film, from the placement of actors and props to the color of draperies or a cloak. "Because of the technology we used to edit the film, we were able to manipulate everything in the frame," said Burtt. "We could immediately interpret what George wanted to see." And as he had done while making *Young Indiana Jones,* Lucas could immediately note where there might be any holes in the story he could fill, or whether additional pickup footage was required for clarity. Several times, in fact, he would return to Leavesden—where his sets were still in place—to film needed scenes, including a brief sequence in which Anakin says good-bye to Padmé's handmaiden, who had disappeared without explanation in the first cut. Over the next eighteen months, Lucas, Burtt, and Smith would continue to tighten and refine the story, which Lucas would see as still in flux right up until the end. "The script is just a rough sketch of what I'm going to do," he explained, "and the filming is just gathering the materials—but the editing is how I create the final draft."[54]

The rest of the movie was still being processed at ILM. Most Tuesdays, Lucas would drive down to ILM—still working out of the Kerner warehouses in San Rafael—to review the shots that had been completed during the past week. There was more computer programming than model making going on at ILM these days; the sound of circular saws and the smell of glue had largely given way to the hum of servers and occasional whiffs of ozone. While some sequences would utilize both old and new technologies, integrating both digital and model spaceships into a few dogfights, most effects would be entirely digital. "Of course, you don't want to fall into the trap of technology driving your vision," warned graphics supervisor John Berton, but Lucas was reveling in the new technology, asking ILM to fill the screen with a dazzling number of spaceships and battle droids.[55] Creating virtual sets and gigantic crowds was becoming old hat to the ILM crew; more and more now they were being asked to create believable characters who wore believable clothing and carried believable props and weapons. If Lucas thought a character didn't look convincing, or moved in an unrealistic way, he'd scrap the shot and ask ILM to try again. "[Lucas] always said that he only directed half of the movie during principal photography," said ILM supervisor John Knoll. "The rest he directed afterward, here at ILM."[56]

Lucas, however, had more than just his movie to attend to during post-production. There were licensing deals to finalize, and Lucas found that toy companies were falling over themselves to grab a piece of the new *Star Wars* universe. Both Hasbro and Galoob announced gigantic deals to market toys and action figures, with the companies giving Lucasfilm stock valued at more than $225 million. The Lego Group waded into the licensing waters for the first time, earning the right to produce the enormously popular *Star Wars*–themed Lego sets that would, by 2012, help make Lego the world's most valuable toy company. There would also be the usual fast food and candy deals, with Episode I Happy Meals, Jar Jar Binks Pez dispensers, and a billion-dollar arrangement to put nearly every major character on Pepsi cans.

Distribution was another prize up for grabs. Because Lucasfilm had paid for the movie itself, however, distribution would be largely a matter of bragging rights. Most of the major studios began wooing Lucas. ("He ain't easy to woo," said one studio executive. "He's not easy to get to.") The rights eventually went to Fox, which paid $80 million without seeing a single frame of the movie.[57] The deal made sense—after all, Fox had distributed the original trilogy—but Lucas had taken the opportunity to gouge an additional pound of flesh out of the studio, demanding it transfer all remaining rights to the original *Star Wars* back to Lucasfilm, which already held the rights to *Empire* and *Jedi*. And like that, Lucas owned all of *Star Wars* outright. The circle, as Vader had said, was now complete.

Even with Fox on board, Lucas would maintain total control over the promotion and distribution of the film; any course of action, any decision, would need his approval. Deftly gauging fan excitement—and shrewdly utilizing the newly ascendant Internet to spread the word—Lucas was dribbling out information in parsimonious thimblefuls on the new starwars.com website. In September 1998 came the announcement that the official name of the upcoming film was not *Shadows of the Empire*, as fans had speculated, but rather *Star Wars: Episode I—The Phantom Menace*, a title that sent Internet chat rooms into frenzies of debate and conjecture.[58]

Then, in late November 1998—exactly six months to the day before the film's release date—Lucas deftly released a two-minute, ten-second trailer in only twenty-six cities, creating, according to the *New York Times*, "a film event that had no precedent."[59] Showings of *Meet Joe Black* and *The Waterboy* were suddenly sold out, the tickets scooped up by fans who paid full admission just to catch the trailer for *The Phantom Menace*, applauded and cheered for three minutes, then left as soon as the main feature began. Several days later the trailer went up on starwars.com, where it was downloaded more than 10 million times, in an era when fans still relied on agonizingly slow dial-up connections to surf the Web. A second trailer went up in March 1999, with eager fans grabbing it up so quickly—there were nearly 340 downloads each second—that the website crashed. Undeterred, enthu-siasts dissected each trailer shot by shot, trying to guess at plot ele-ments.[60] Still other devotees reported weeping openly while watching the trailers. *Star Wars* was coming back—and fans were certain it was going to be better than ever.

"What can I say?" said one admirer after watching the trailer. "George Lucas must be a superior form of life!"[61]

Lucas was feeling good about *The Phantom Menace*. For the first time ever, he felt he'd been able to make a movie look on the screen exactly the way it had looked in his head. Final touches—John Williams's score, Ben Burtt's sound effects—were still going in as late as March 1999, but Lucas felt happy enough about what he was seeing to wrap his arms around ILM supervisor Chrissie England, who'd been with him since the Parkhouse days, and thank her for her hard work. "[He] gave me a big hug," recalled England, "and said, 'You really did a great job. I'm really proud of you'"—words he had never once spoken to Marcia.[62]

Still, in the weeks leading up to the release of *The Phantom Men-ace*, Lucas was doing his best to manage expectations. "For every per-son who loves Episode I, there will be two or three who hate it," he said. "All I can do now is throw it out there in the real world—and wait to see what everyone thinks."[63] Still, Steven Spielberg's very pub-lic assessment—"Oh my God. Your jaw will hang open for a week"—had only served to further spike expectations upward, and fans were waiting in line for tickets more than a month in advance.[64]

With that swell of anticipation behind it, it was no surprise that *The Phantom Menace* would premiere to enormous business. Its May 19, 1999, opening day take of $28.5 million broke all records, as did its $132.4 million opening week. By the end of the year, it would make more than $926 million worldwide, most of it going right back into the coffers of Lucasfilm.

While success at the box office was probably inevitable—even the most casual of *Star Wars* fans was going to check this one out—most critics were unimpressed. "The movie is a disappointment. A big one," wrote David Ansen in *Newsweek*. "[Lucas's] rhythm is off....He doesn't seem to care about building a character."[65] Ansen admitted to being impressed with the design and digital effects, a feeling that was shared by Roger Ebert, who hailed *The Phantom Menace* as "a visionary breakthrough."[66] But while fans had initially jumped to the film's defense— this was the church of *Star Wars* critics were burning down!—they too would eventually concede that Episode I had been underwhelming, with too much backstory and talk about trade and taxes, and that the overreliance on digital effects—"endless scenes of computer-generated talking frogs fighting computer-generated robots"—left the film looking sterile and lacking in any real heart.[67] Even Ewan McGregor, starring as a younger Obi-Wan, would eventually concede that the film was "disappointing" and "flat."[68]

Lucas had gambled and lost badly with the character of Jar Jar Binks. Despite all efforts to make the character a breakout star—he was even on the cover of *Rolling Stone* beside the headline "JAR JAR SUPERSTAR"—fans immediately found him annoying rather than endearing. Worse, with Binks's pidgin English and comically lazy demeanor, there were immediate accusations of negative stereotypes and racism; Lucas took a particular beating from Joe Morgenstern in the *Wall Street Journal*, who called Jar Jar "a Rastafarian Stepin Fetchit on platform hoofs, crossed annoyingly with Butterfly McQueen."[69] While Lucasfilm spokesperson Lynne Hale would dismiss such accusations as "absurd," the charge stung actor Ahmed Best, who had played and voiced Jar Jar, and also happened to be African American.[70] "Even though you play characters, you put a lot of your own personality into it, you get emotionally and personally invested in the work that you do, it's your work and you take pride in it," said Best. "So when your work is criticized negatively, you feel a hit."[71]

Worse, Lucas had made a tweak to the *Star Wars* mythos that many would consider as unforgivable as Greedo shooting first: a biological explanation for the Force. To explain Anakin's unique status as "the Chosen One" who would bring balance to the Force, Lucas had introduced the concept of midi-chlorians, intelligent microscopic forms that exist symbiotically in the cells of living beings and help tune them in to the power of the Force. It was an ill-advised explanation that drained the Force of its mystery and awe, making it a mere biological attribute like blue eyes. Gary Kurtz, whose own spiritual views had helped shape the concept of the Force two decades earlier, called the idea "the destruction of the spiritual center of the force, turning [it] into DNA and blood." Kurtz was also quick to note, however, that "George has a very clear idea of what he wants. And whether you agree with that or not, he goes about getting that."[72]

Lucas's relationship with his audience was changing in the movie's aftermath. The film was a monster hit, but *Star Wars* true believers were losing faith both in the franchise and in Lucas—and with the rise of the Internet, those same fans could make their opinions widely and loudly known in a way that hadn't existed even fifteen years earlier, when *Jedi* had been released to some muted grumbling about Ewoks. While Lucas had cleverly used the Internet to co-opt fandom for the promotion of the film, he was unprepared for the way the same technology, and the same fans, could just as quickly turn on him after the movie was released. While Lucas would always insist that online carping never bothered him, chalking it up to "one person typing out their opinion," the sniping and snarking clearly irritated him—a flashback to the studio executives who complained about his movies and demanded they be recut. When fans groused about midi-chlorians or griped about Anakin building C-3PO, Lucas—unwisely rising to the bait—dismissed them as "nitpicky." "I'm sorry if they don't like it," he said with palpable annoyance. "They should go back and see *The Matrix* or something."[73]

Clearly, the criticism had gotten under his skin, to the point where he dreaded doing one more promotion or sitting for one more interview. Eventually, he would abandon the Internet altogether. "I want people to like what I do. Everybody wants to be accepted at least by somebody," he insisted. "But we live in a world now where you're forced to become part of this larger corporate entity called the media....

Since I'm doing the films myself, I don't have quite that obligation. I'd just as soon let my own films die than have to go out and sell them on a circuit. And I do as little as I have to, to feel responsible."[74]

That sort of apathetic attitude, however, wasn't going to sit well with the licensees who had paid a fortune for the rights to *Star Wars* merchandise, saturated the market with goods, and expected Lucas to deliver. Hasbro, which paid $650 million for the toy rights to all three prequels, suddenly saw its stock tumble by 25 percent on countless bins of unsold action figures and spaceships. Privately, Lucasfilm executives conceded that the movie had likely been too aggressively marketed — did anyone *really* want a necktie with Qui-Gon Jinn on it? — and further admitted to Hasbro and others that the movie "did not live up to expectations."[75]

By this point, however, Lucas was already looking ahead to Episode II — and also had his eye on a spectacular vista near the base of San Francisco's Golden Gate Bridge.

In 1776 the Spanish established a garrison — their northernmost outpost in the Americas, in fact — at the tip of the San Francisco peninsula, guarding the mouth of San Francisco Bay. By 1822 that fort, in a state of disrepair, passed into Mexican hands, where it remained until 1846, when it was captured by a small group of American soldiers as part of the Bear Flag Revolt. The U.S. Army promptly took over, setting up a permanent post on the site though maintaining the fort's original Spanish designation, the Presidio. The army occupied the Presidio for the next 148 years, erecting hospitals and housing, until the base was finally shuttered by the federal Base Reduction and Closure Commission, which deemed the facility no longer of use for military purposes. With the departure of the army, the Presidio site — 1,500 acres of prime waterfront territory, quite literally in the shadow of the Golden Gate Bridge — was turned over to the administration of the National Park Service in 1994.

Maintaining the site under public stewardship, however, would prove expensive. In 1996, then, Congress created a new federal agency, the Presidio Trust, to preserve and maintain the park and—in a directive unique among national parks—work to attract non-federal resources that would eventually support and maintain the park without the need for annual federal funding. The direction came with an ultimatum: if the Presidio failed to become self-sufficient by 2013, it would be sold off as excess property. With that sort of shadow hanging over its head, it was little wonder, then, that the Presidio Trust was actively seeking bids for private use of the property.

Lucas was interested. After more than a decade of trying to bring ILM onto Skywalker Ranch, Lucas had changed his mind—and changed his plans. Instead, he'd create a stand-alone digital arts complex—housing ILM, THX, LucasArts, and the main offices of Lucasfilm—and he'd do it in plain sight, in the Presidio compound on the site of the decommissioned Letterman Army Medical Center. Or that, at least, was the plan. While Lucasfilm was perhaps one of the most widely recognized and most successful companies in the world, as Lucas had learned in his dealings with his Marin County neighbors, not everyone wanted to live or work next door to him or his company. Several years earlier in Modesto, there had even been some objections to a proposed statue in Lucas's honor, with some city officials cloaking their objections behind an argument against the use of city funds to erect a statue honoring *anyone*—even the town's most famous resident. Money would be raised privately instead to erect a sculpture of two teenagers leaning on a '57 Chevy, a tip of the hat both to Lucas's days cruising Modesto's streets and to *American Graffiti*. The dustup had been minor, but the message was clear: not everyone loved George Lucas.

Lucas had submitted the proposal for his digital complex to the Presidio Trust in 1998, bidding against several local developers, including the powerful Shorenstein Company. Lucasfilm CEO Gordon Radley was lobbying hard for the project, assuring skeptics that "this isn't about *Star Wars* at all" and comparing the proposed site to an artists' commune. While Lucas planned to keep the footprint small and build everything in as environmentally sensitive a manner as possible, many locals weren't so sure. "I don't believe the public interest is served by having Lucas as a tenant," argued one critic, though he admitted that "it will be nicer to have Lucas than a bunch of venture capitalists."[76]

Such objections, however vocal, were in the minority. On June 14, 1999, the Presidio Trust approved Lucas's plans to turn the Letterman site into a digital arts complex. Here, at the base of the Golden Gate Bridge—not far from the warehouse where Lucas and Coppola had established American Zoetrope forty years earlier—Lucas would construct the rest of his cinematic empire.

At last, he said, he would "create an organization to make the kind of movies [he] wanted to make."[77]

But first, he had more *Star Wars* to attend to.

12

Cynical Optimism

1999–2005

At the time of the release of Episode I in May 1999, Lucas had been writing the script for Episode II for nearly a year. He was struggling with this one more than others, mainly because the second film would largely be a love story, driven by character and dialogue, neither of which was Lucas's strong suit. By his own estimate, it would take fourteen or fifteen drafts before he was comfortable enough with it to pass his handwritten pages over to his assistant to type. At the center of the title page, dated March 13, 2000, Lucas had scrawled

EPISODE II
JAR JAR'S GREAT ADVENTURE

The title was a joke, Lucas's way of making the point that he had taken to heart one of the key criticisms of *The Phantom Menace*. For Episode II, Binks would be relegated to a minor supporting role, and any larger plans Lucas had had for the loping Gungan were shelved.

Lucas would always defend the much-loathed character; he would even suggest at a Disney Expo in 2015 that Binks had been inspired in part by the look and mannerisms of Goofy. ("I know that you will look at him differently now," Lucas said with a grin. "I love Goofy and I love Jar Jar.") Fans delighted in theorizing that Lucas's abandoned storyline would have revealed the bumbling comic relief to be a cold-blooded Sith Lord.[1] Lucas would offer only coy silence in response.

He had also decided he was indeed done using film, and publicly announced that Episode II would be filmed entirely digitally. After careful review of the small bit of digital footage he had shot during *The Phantom Menace*—about six minutes' worth of lightsaber duels—Lucas was convinced that digital footage would be just as clear and stable as film. In some cases, in fact, it was even *clearer,* requiring digitally shot footage to be lit differently in order to soften hard edges between objects in the foreground and the background. Making everything look right and work properly required special cameras and lenses, which Sony and Panavision obligingly delivered.[2] There was some hand-wringing in the industry—mostly from those "down there" in Hollywood—who fretted for the future of filmmaking. One reporter wondered aloud if movies would even be called *films* anymore. Lucas thought that was taking things too literally. "It will be called *cinema,*" he said reassuringly.[3]

There would be still another significant change in the way Lucas made Episode II: for the first time, production for a *Star Wars* film wouldn't be based in London, though Lucas still intended to film a few sequences at Elstree. Instead, he had established offices for JAK Productions in Australia at the newly opened Fox Studios in Sydney—so newly opened, in fact, that Episode II would be the first major film to shoot there. Once again, Lucas had taken out an extended lease on the entire facility, which would permit him to leave his sets in place during post-production for any additional pickups or new footage.

Also, as he had done with *The Phantom Menace,* Lucas had put nearly every element of pre-production in motion without the benefit of a completed script. Doug Chiang and his crew of artists began working on designs for new buildings, spaceships, and planets for Episode II, based only on Lucas's own enthusiastic descriptions. Lucas would show up at Chiang's offices in the main house at Skywalker Ranch to review concepts and models, approving some, rejecting others, and asking for still more ships and cities for any sequences he happened to be writing that particular week. If he liked a drawing's basic concept but thought it needed work, he would stamp OK on it; if he loved a drawing just as it was, he would stamp FABULOUSO [*sic*] on it. (Over the next eighteen months, only four drawings would ever receive a FABULOUSO.)

Meanwhile, casting had begun in November 1999, with casting director Robin Gurland searching for actors to play characters who still weren't fleshed out much beyond brief descriptions on the page. And over in Sydney, Gavin Bocquet and his crew were busily constructing seventy sets or partial sets, even more than had been required for *The Phantom Menace*. "George had always told us that Episode II was going to be much smaller [than *Phantom Menace*]," said Bocquet, "but it didn't turn out that way."[4] Everything about Episode II, in fact, from its budget and sets to its cameras and special effects, would be bigger, fancier, and more high-tech than Episode I.

With shooting scheduled to start in May or June of 2000, Lucas was beginning to feel the pinch of his deadline as 1999 came to an end. He was spending more and more time in his writing room, less with Doug Chiang reviewing designs. "Later, when the crunch came, I worked on Saturdays as well, writing four days a week," said Lucas. "But even so, I had to work awfully hard and fast to get all the drafts finished in the amount of time I had."[5] By April 2000, with only a little more than two months to go before filming was to begin, Lucas finally called for help, bringing in screenwriter Jonathan Hales—yet another graduate of *Young Indiana Jones*—and huddling with him out at the ranch to talk through script changes, a process that mostly involved Lucas talking while Hales scribbled notes madly. As Hales went home to London to rewrite the script, Lucas headed for Long Beach to drive in the annual Toyota Pro/Celebrity Race. After he had picked the habit up again over the past decade, he hadn't let go.

Hales would cut things close, delivering his revised script to Lucas on June 23, just as Lucas was leaving for Sydney to begin principal photography. Though cast and crew were already setting up, preparing to start filming, no one yet had a complete copy of the script. With cameras practically ready to roll, Lucas gave Hales's draft a final read, then called the writer in London. "Some of this is brilliant, some of it is not so brilliant," he told Hales with typical candor. "We'll talk about what's not brilliant."[6] It was a brusque but effective tactic that had worked with Lawrence Kasdan in the 1980s and would work with Hales now; Hales would deliver his final revisions to Sydney shortly thereafter, even as Lucas already had the cameras rolling.

Lucas began principal photography on Monday, June 26, 2000, filming actor Ian McDiarmid, as the duplicitous Supreme Chancellor Palpatine, on Fox's Stage 6, which contained only a podium and an elevated pod. The rest of the soundstage was wrapped entirely in bluescreen, onto which ILM would later matte digitally created footage of the enormous Galactic Senate chambers. McDiarmid found it all slightly disorienting. "The script had just arrived at the last minute," recalled McDiarmid. "I was in midair on this pod, there was a camera pointing right at me, and I was addressing crosses and markers rather than real actors." The first appearance of a very real R2-D2, however, had the crew buzzing with excitement. "Everyone goes a bit silly [over Artoo]," said Ewan McGregor.[7]

There would be similarly deferential excitement for fifty-four-year-old Anthony Daniels, who hadn't worn the full C-3PO costume since completing *Return of the Jedi* nearly twenty years earlier. On the first day of filming, Daniels snapped on the droid's golden suit — dingy and nearly gray for Episode II — then slowly shuffled his way across the soundstage toward Lucas. Crew members parted respectfully before him, gaping in awe, some smiling, others waving and calling out, "Hello, Threepio!" Finally, Daniels delicately sauntered up alongside Lucas. "Hello, I am See-Threepio," he said in the familiar voice, muffled only slightly by the mask, then extended his hand. "And you are?"

"I am...astonished," said Lucas with genuine warmth. "Astonished that you can still get into that suit!"[8]

Lucas loved shooting in the digital high-definition format. With footage going to digital videotape that could then be directly uploaded into a computer for editing, he could see what he'd shot immediately at the end of each day, without having to worry about bad negatives, torn sprocket holes, or underdeveloped film—annoyances that had plagued him on the first *Star Wars* trilogy. Furthermore, since digital cameras didn't need to be stopped and reloaded with film—which then required more color balance and focus checks—Lucas could essentially point his cameras and shoot, which not only made directing less stressful but also allowed him to complete more shots each day than with a traditional film camera. "It was vastly superior in every way, and it was cheaper," Lucas said matter-of-factly. "You'd have to be nuts *not* to shoot this way."[9]

The more Lucas played with his digital technology, the more he loved it. Even as he squinted at his sets through the eyepiece of the camera, in fact, he wondered if it might be possible to get by without building any sets *at all*, shooting his actors solely against bluescreen and inserting all the sets digitally later. ILM group supervisor John Knoll talked Lucas off that particular ledge, explaining that it was too difficult at the moment for computer animators to fake the kinds of shadows and reflections created by tangible objects—an argument Lucas accepted, though barely. But director of photography David Tattersall didn't like the technique much either. "Bluescreen is a necessary, essential part of shooting *Star Wars*, but it isn't my favorite part," said Tattersall. "George is the only one who seems to like it....There's no artistry in lighting bluescreen; it is just a technical process."[10]

Lucas, however, continued to argue that high-definition filmmaking was more than just a technical trick; in his opinion, it actually forced filmmakers to up their game. Because high definition by its very nature often revealed imperfections in sets or makeup—even the smallest blemish or brushstroke would show up on camera—Lucas thought it pushed everyone to work that much harder to make sets, makeup, and costumes convincing. For a perfectionist like Lucas, who agonized over every detail in every frame of film, it was yet another means of ensuring that everything on-screen would look exactly the way he wanted it. You couldn't cheat or take shortcuts; the high-def camera would give you away.

Lucas's director of photography wasn't the only one tiring of bluescreen, however; Lucas's actors, too, were finding it continually bewildering to work with no tangible sets and few real characters. "It's a bit like playing chess... and I'm not very good at chess," said McGregor. "You do your reactions and you just hope that the computer-generating-guy matches his actions to what you're doing. It's a weird process."[11] Nineteen-year-old Hayden Christensen, who'd been cast as Anakin Skywalker after a year-long search that had included a momentary look at Leonardo DiCaprio, also found bluescreen a bit overwhelming at times. "Usually we were just in a sea of blue, not really knowing what we were supposed to be looking at," said Christensen.[12] Yet seventy-eight-year-old English actor Christopher Lee, who'd done his time in Hammer horror cheapies in the 1960s, had no problem playing against invisible monsters, and leaped into his lightsaber battle against a computer-generated Yoda with relish, hacking and slashing away dramatically at the diminutive Jedi master, who wouldn't be added to the scene for at least another six months.

The digital Yoda, in fact, was something of a dream come true for Lucas, who'd been frustrated by Yoda's lack of mobility ever since *The Empire Strikes Back*. With the digital technology now at Lucas's disposal, Yoda was no longer limited to shuffling slowly along the floor at the end of Frank Oz's arm, or being carried on Mark Hamill's back to disguise the fact that Yoda was a puppet. While Oz would still provide Yoda's distinctive voice, he was no longer needed to do the actual performing. Instead, Lucas planned to create Yoda entirely in the computer during post-production, giving him the ability to move around the screen freely.

Despite their low-level anxiety about bluescreen, Lucas's actors would spend most of the Australian winter—June, July, and August— eagerly chasing one another around empty bluescreened soundstages, leaping into the cockpits of half-completed spaceships, and walking under archways deep in conversation with characters that weren't there. As a director, Lucas was becoming much warmer toward his actors, offering them encouragement and advice beyond simply "faster" and "more intense." Lucas was genuinely fond of—as well as a bit protective of—Natalie Portman, who had quietly done much of the heavy lifting on *The Phantom Menace* as Padmé Amidala, the young queen who would eventually give birth to the twins Luke and Leia. Portman had grown up in the years since wrapping *The Phantom Menace* and was completing her first year at Harvard as production work began on *Attack of the Clones*. Exhausted from final exams, she fell asleep during her first costume fittings. Lucas was also pleased with his choice of Christensen for the young Anakin/Darth Vader, agreeing entirely with McCallum's assessment of the young man: "There is something about him that makes you think, 'Yeah, this guy could lose it.'"[13]

Early July saw a visit from an old friend, Francis Ford Coppola, who'd come all the way to Australia mainly just to check on Lucas. The two of them went to dinner together in town, talking movies and families like the old friends they were. And yet, even with more than thirty years of friendship behind them—and by this point, Lucas was clearly the more successful of the two—it didn't take long for the pair of them to fall almost unconsciously into the old familiar roles again, with Lucas playing the padawan to Coppola's Jedi master. A crew photo taken of Coppola on the set shows Coppola standing at the center of the shot, beaming in a brightly patterned shirt with his arms folded confidently behind his back, while Lucas stands deferentially off to one side, hands shoved in his pockets. The body language was telling. Old habits tended to die hard, even thirty years later.

After filming on the Fox soundstages for several months, Lucas headed for Italy in late August for the first of several location shoots. Normally, location shooting took place *before* any filming on soundstages so that the lighting could be matched between exteriors and interiors; with digital filming and editing, however, the lighting could easily be tweaked in the computer to ensure a match. That still didn't make other things easier; local officials at the Palace of Caserta demanded that Lucas keep all equipment and lighting away from walls and ceilings, making it nearly impossible to provide the needed lighting. After huddling with Tattersall, Lucas opted for a low-tech solution to his high-tech problem by hanging lights from large helium balloons that then floated lazily overhead, giving everything a soft, almost dreamlike glow. Later, as cameras were set up at the Plaza de España in Seville, the one crew member who was mobbed the most for autographs was Lucas himself, who obligingly signed scraps of paper passed to him through the fence surrounding the gigantic Spanish plaza.

The last several weeks of shooting would be a sentimental journey for Lucas. In the second week of September, he returned to Tunisia to film on several of the locations where sets constructed for *The Phantom Menace* were still standing—and, in fact, were being well maintained by the Tunisian tourist board, which rightly saw the sets as a boon to tourism. But after completing a few scenes on the Mos Espa sets, Lucas pushed farther out into the surrounding desert, to the very site where he had constructed the Lars homestead for the original *Star Wars*. Here he discovered that construction crews had unearthed and cleaned up several original sets and props that had lain buried in the Tunisian sand since 1976; other sites, such as the Lars dining room, were intact and occupied by locals, but still remained remarkably unaltered. Lucas looked around in awe. The *Star Wars* trilogy—and, truth be told, George Lucas and his filmic empire—had been born here in the desert twenty-five years earlier. "It was a very nostalgic experience," he admitted.[14]

Lucas would wrap up principal photography on September 20 at another nostalgic location: Elstree Studios in London. Each of the first three *Star Wars* movies had been filmed here beginning in 1976, but Lucas hadn't been back since completing *Indiana Jones and the Last Crusade* in 1988. Here on Elstree's familiar soundstage, he would film Ewan McGregor clinging to a flying assassin droid as a wind machine whipped at him furiously. And with that, filming was over; Lucas had completed principal photography in sixty days, a day and a half ahead of schedule. He immediately headed for Skywalker Ranch, where Ben Burtt was already waiting with a rough cut of the movie—and Lucas could hardly wait to get his hands on it. "My heart is actually in the editing room," he said.[15] For Lucas, the fun part was about to begin.

"I never thought I'd do the *Star Wars* prequels, because there was no real way I could get Yoda to fight," Lucas said later. "But once you had digital, there was no end to what you could do."[16] That way of thinking was actually somewhat worrisome to the crew at ILM, who knew that Lucas expected them to keep pushing the boundaries of eye-popping digital effects. Lucas, in fact, had spooked visual effects supervisor John Knoll by informing him that he had "held back" on the number of special effects he wanted to do in *The Phantom Menace* "because I wasn't sure you guys [at ILM] could do it." Knoll assured Lucas that ILM would get the job done, but privately conceded, "That was a scary thing to hear," especially considering that *Phantom Menace* had required more than two thousand effects shots.[17]

No other digital effect was more important, perhaps, than creating a convincing Yoda. It fell to animator Rob Coleman to oversee the team that would spark to digital life one of *Star Wars'* most beloved characters, who many fans thought was already lifelike enough in the hands of Frank Oz and shouldn't be messed with. Coleman understood exactly what was at stake. "On Episode Two, I was stressing about living up to what Frank [Oz] had created," Coleman reflected later. "I went back and studied what Frank Oz had done frame by frame."[18] Even then, once Lucas had decided that Yoda would engage in a high-energy lightsaber duel—indicated in the script only with the stage direction "YODA ATTACKS!"—both he and Coleman knew it was important not to make the diminutive Jedi look silly. "It was one of those situations where we set ourselves an impossible task and then just hoped we could accomplish it," said Lucas.[19] Coleman would end up creating a physical yet graceful Yoda, who swooped and darted deftly as he battled Count Dooku in what would become one of the movie's most memorable and talked-about sequences.

Lucas also had ILM working on a chase through the skies of Coruscant, with Anakin speeding through the city in what was essentially a flying hot rod with an exposed engine in the front, much like Lucas's old Fiat Bianchina. It was even yellow—yet another in a long line of yellow Lucas race cars. This sequence, too, would be created almost entirely in the computer, closely adhering to the animatics that Burtt and ILM effects supervisor David Dozoretz had cut into the first rough edit. Most of the stormtroopers would also be entirely digital, finally giving Lucas the battalions of armored fighters that his limited number of stormtrooper costumes would never have permitted him to include in the original trilogy. Even better from Lucas's perspective, digital technology continued to give him complete control over every element on the screen, permitting him to remove actors from one scene and insert them into another, or to change the background setting of an entire sequence with the click of a mouse. And because both the movie and the special effects had all been created digitally, there was no need to transfer special effects over to film before cutting them into the movie itself, resulting in a loss of image quality. Effects in the finished movie would look almost exactly the way ILM had produced them with the computer.

Lucas and Burtt screened their first full cut of the movie in February 2001, assessing where cuts could be made to pick up the pace—the first edit was nearly three hours long—and to eliminate scenes that were redundant or unnecessary, or simply didn't work. Just as important, Lucas could also see where pieces of his story might be missing, where a new scene might be needed to fill in a hole in the plot, or new conversations were needed to convey necessary information to the audience. Several times throughout 2001, Lucas went back and wrote new scenes, calling his actors back to the studio to complete a series of pickups. While Lucas had maintained his sets at Fox Sydney, he saw no need at this point ever to shoot on a set again; instead, he would shoot all of the new footage at Ealing Studios in West London, on a small soundstage swathed entirely in bluescreen. Everything else could be added later. *Star Wars* had become a truly digital universe.

There were nearly 400,000 Jedi knights in England.

That, at least, would be the official word from the census office of the United Kingdom, following the results of the country's 2001 census, in which just over 390,000 of 52 million residents of England and Wales wrote "Jedi" in the blank on their census form asking for their religion. An online campaign claimed that if enough residents wrote in *Jedi*, it would be formally recognized as a religion by the British government—and while that wasn't actually true, census officials credited a boost in returned forms from younger residents to their desire to see Jedi receive an official government designation. In the end, enough fans had written in *Jedi* to make it the fourth-largest religion in the United Kingdom—a phenomenon the census office recognized in a press release under a cheeky headline mimicking Yoda's distinctive speaking pattern: "390,000 JEDI THERE ARE."[20]

As for Lucas, his own religious views had both mellowed and sharpened with age. "I'm a cynical optimist," he told *Time* magazine, laughing. "I'm a cynic who has hope for the human race."[21]

There were times when it would be easier to be more cynical than hopeful. In August 2001, Lucas revealed on starwars.com that the title of Episode II would be *Attack of the Clones*—an announcement that met with near-audible groans and laughter from critics and fans. The official line from Lucasfilm was that the title "harken[ed] back to the sense of pure fun, imagination, and excitement" of the pulpy serials that had inspired *Star Wars*.[22] Critics were having none of it. "When you're managing a multibillion dollar toy franchise," jeered *Entertainment Weekly*, "maybe you don't have time to come up with cool titles."[23]

Things would improve in October, with the release of *The Phantom Menace* on DVD—the first *Star Wars* movie to be released in the new digital format. Lucas had pulled out all the stops for the double-disc set, instructing ILM to complete the special effects on deleted scenes and package them as part of the disc's many bonus features.

The DVD would take in a record-setting $45 million in its first week of release. Despite the thrashing the film had taken from fans and critics, everyone still wanted to take it home.

Still, for *Attack of the Clones*, Lucas was going to scale back the merchandising significantly. Lucasfilm's marketing executives conceded that Episode I had been "over-licensed, over-shipped...[and] over-saturated," and announced they were cutting merchandising by nearly two-thirds. There would be no neckties, no fast food tie-ins, and—to the likely relief of Pepsi, which had circulated nearly 8 *billion* cans of soda featuring Episode I characters with little to show for it— no official soft drink. As he had done with Episode I, Lucas would tightly, and dramatically, coordinate the promotion for Episode II, hiding one trailer on the starwars.com website that could be accessed only by inserting a *Phantom Menace* DVD into a home computer. Lucas would also debut a full-length trailer in November, in front of the highly anticipated *Harry Potter and the Sorcerer's Stone*. Lucas had deliberately played up the love story between Anakin and Padmé, a decision that left some fans cold. Furthermore, after all the hype and excitement that had surrounded the trailers for Episode I—and then the relative disappointment of the film itself—many fans were refusing to get fooled again.

Lucas attempted some damage control by inviting webmasters of *Star Wars* websites—especially those who oversaw sites where he had taken a beating on Episode I—out to Skywalker Ranch, ostensibly to discuss the release of Episode I on DVD, but actually to win them over well in advance of the release of Episode II. The webmasters were given a tour of the ranch, autographed copies of the Episode I DVD, and twenty minutes to pepper Lucas with questions. But goodwill would go only so far. This time, fan excitement would be tinged with skepticism. Lucas had turned his own fans into cynical optimists.

As the May 2002 release date approached for *Attack of the Clones*, Lucas was spending more time at ILM, screening dailies twice a week now instead of only once. Lucas would sit in the same place every time he entered the ILM theater, still always taking the center seat in the second row. In one corner of the theater stood a full-sized R2-D2 next to a totem pole listing all of the films for which ILM had received an Oscar nomination for Best Visual Effects. With more effects companies embracing the digital technology ILM had pioneered, competition was getting tighter each year, and ILM hadn't produced an Oscar winner since taking home the trophy in 1995 for *Forrest Gump*. Since then, they'd continued to receive a nomination each year — *Mighty Joe Young* in 1999, *The Phantom Menace* in 2000 (it had lost to the game-changing, time-stopping effects in *The Matrix*), and the most recent film on the pole, *The Perfect Storm*, which would lose the Oscar in 2001 to *Gladiator*.

Lucas would continue to edit the film even from his seat in the second row, asking that characters be moved from one scene to another, blending together different takes of the same scene, or zooming in on a particular section of the frame. On April 8, 2002 — only a little more than a month before *Attack of the Clones* would open — Lucas signed off on the final effects shot. Days later, he met with the art department again to ask them to start thinking about designs for Episode III, once more without benefit of a script or even any notes. Really, the only set he could describe at the moment was the volcano world where Anakin Skywalker would be cut down and Darth Vader would rise from the ashes. Lucas had loved the concept drawings of Vader's castle on a sea of lava that Ralph McQuarrie had done for him more than two decades earlier, during pre-production on *The Empire Strikes Back*. He wanted to see *that* in the next film — or at least something like it. "We never truly know what George is doing," lamented McCallum.[24]

Ben Burtt put a final edit of *Attack of the Clones* in Lucas's hands on April 10, and Lucas would host a special preview for staff and crew at Skywalker Ranch's three-hundred-seat Stag Theater. But there would be no film spooled onto enormous reels and placed on a projector; because the entire movie had been put together digitally, *Attack of the Clones* could be stored on a DVD and shown with a digital projector. That, at least, was the ideal scenario. At the moment, most theaters still relied on film projectors, so for the majority of theaters showing Episode II, Lucas would have to scan the digital version of his movie back onto film—an expensive process that would also result in a loss of picture quality. Nevertheless, just as he had encouraged cinema owners in the mid-1980s to install new speakers and reconfigure their theaters for THX by promising them *Return of the Jedi*, now he would spur them toward digital technology simply by assuring them that such technology was the wave of the future. They could evolve—and show films like *Attack of the Clones*—or slowly go extinct.

Most chose to evolve. Studios and cinemas alike would follow Lucas's lead; studios would begin distributing movies both digitally and on film, while theaters would begin slowly converting to digital projection systems. As Lucas prepared to release *Attack of the Clones* in 2002, only about thirty theaters in the *world* could accommodate digital films. The technology was expensive: digital projection systems would cost a theater about $100,000, ten times more than the traditional 35 mm projectors. But studios like Paramount—which, by 2014, would be the first to distribute its films entirely in a digital format—worked with theaters to finance the conversion to digital systems, and by 2014, 92 percent of the 40,045 screens in the United States would have digital capability.[25] And Lucas had led the charge, clenching a DVD of *Attack of the Clones* in his upraised fist.

Attack of the Clones was released on May 16, 2002, in 3,161 theaters. It would reap $110.2 million in its first four days, on its way to a worldwide gross of $649 million by the end of the year—a staggering number, to be sure, but well short of *Phantom Menace,* and only enough to make it the *fourth*-highest-grossing film of the year.[26] The film may not have set a record, but it was wildly profitable, a box office success that was not merely inevitable, thought *New York Times* critic A. O. Scott, but downright predictable; after all, *everyone* was going to see *Star Wars.* "Like weary Brezhnev-era Muscovites, the American moviegoing public will line up out of habit and compulsion," wrote Scott, "ruefully hoping that this episode will at least be a little better than the last one."[27]

And indeed, some critics *were* kinder to Episode II, with *Rolling Stone* applauding it for being "crammed with action, grand digital design and a dark side Lucas hasn't flaunted since 1980's *The Empire Strikes Back*."[28] Nearly every review praised the digital effects, though Episode II would ultimately lose the Oscar to director Peter Jackson's *Lord of the Rings: The Two Towers*, the middle part of another epic trilogy that was unfurling on movie screens at the same time as Lucas's prequels. Roger Ebert spent a lot of time on the digital technology in his review for the *Chicago Sun-Times*, complaining that the images were often "indistinct," which he blamed — to Lucas's likely delight — on the fact that his local theater lacked the digital projection system that Lucas favored.

But beyond the special effects, most critics found the film unremarkable, even boring — a trait Ebert blamed on Lucas's dialogue-heavy script. "They talk and talk and talk," Ebert complained,[29] a gripe that Peter Travers seconded, adding snarkily, "Lucas still can't write dialogue that doesn't induce projectile vomiting."[30] David Ansen, writing in *Newsweek* under a headline reading "Attack of the Groans," complained bitterly about nearly everything, from the script to the digital effects to the wooden acting — which Ansen also blamed on Lucas's screenwriting. "Yes, it's better than *The Phantom Menace*," Ansen conceded. "No, it's not great."[31]

Lucas was typically dismissive of the criticism. Anything the critics didn't like — clunky dialogue, over-the-top extended battle sequences — Lucas claimed had been done intentionally. And what about those eye-rolling love scenes that the *New York Times* had called "the most embarrassing romantic avowals in recent screen history"?[32] "I was very happy with the way it turned out in the script and in the performances, but I knew people might not buy it," he said defiantly. "It is presented very honestly, it isn't tongue in cheek at all, and it's really played to the hilt....[T]his film is even more of a melodrama than the others."[33] He had done it all on purpose, he claimed.

One critic at the *Los Angeles Times* wasn't buying it. In a scathing article headlined "SECLUSION HAS LEFT LUCAS OUT OF TOUCH," critic

Patrick Goldstein argued that one of Lucas's biggest problems as a filmmaker was that there was no one in his organization who would tell him that intentional melodrama was a bad idea. "No one seems to deliver bad news," wrote Goldstein. "Lucas's best work was made with strong collaborators.... [His] talents are probably better suited as a conceptual thinker and producer than director."[34]

Lucas bristled at the very suggestion that he needed collaborators rather than subordinates. "That's one of the problems of a democracy. You get these individual voices that are very loud, and very dysfunctional," he sighed. "And if you cater to those voices, you end up with a very dysfunctional society."[35]

The solution: Create. Oversee. *Control everything.*

The cramped attic space of Skywalker Ranch's Main House had been converted into a makeshift art department. Artists' tables butted up against one another, and piles of art books and journals teetered on low tables. Space was tight: artists worked practically elbow to elbow, and some wore earphones to listen to music privately as they sketched; some of the more gadget-savvy even had the new Apple iPod on their table, white earbuds dangling. It was here under the eaves that Lucas had installed his concept artists to begin work on designs for Episode III. Lucas would stroll the room—stepping past a bathroom door with a sign reading DOOKU'S THRONE ROOM hanging on it—peering over shoulders or spreading drawings out on the side tables. As usual, the artists were flying without a net. It was June 2002, a month after the release of *Attack of the Clones,* and Lucas hadn't written a word of the new screenplay yet. McCallum, once more tasked with watching the bottom line, grimly compared Lucas's creative process to "building backward, designing a twenty-five-floor skyscraper without foundations," then sighed gustily. "Do you know what it's like to budget a film without a script?"[36]

But Lucas wasn't going to be rushed. The script for Episode III would be critical; not only did he have to finish telling the story of Anakin Skywalker's descent into the Dark Side, but also he had to make sure that Episode III logically led back to the original *Star Wars*. "I've painted myself into a corner," he said, using a metaphor his artists could understand. "I have to get from there to here, and I have to connect these two things [the original trilogy and the prequels] in a very precise way....Writing is a lot of puzzle-solving." But even as pencils flew and McCallum fretted, Lucas left for Canada with his children for a vacation. While on vacation, he'd jot down ideas for Episode III, as well as for another film he was hoping to put into production soon, and which as yet had only a working title: *Indiana Jones IV.*

It would take Lucas a long time to really begin writing Episode III — and with each passing day, artists and designers became more and more anxious. In a November 1 meeting with McCallum and Rob Coleman, who would again be animating Yoda, Lucas casually mentioned that he'd start writing "when reality hits." McCallum was stunned. "You said you've *been* writing," he said gently. Lucas waved him off. "I've been *thinking* about it," said Lucas. Three weeks later, Lucas met with designers to review drawings of planets and a few characters. "Keep up the good work. The stuff was great, guys," he told them as he left the room. "I just have to figure out a movie to go with it."[37]

By mid-December, he'd finally forced himself to sit at the desk in his office for four days a week, trying to get anything at all down on the page. McCallum would beg Lucas for tidbits of information about sets, any information he could convey to the crew at Fox Studios in Sydney, where carpenters anxiously hung on any word from Lucas about what a particular set should look like. Lucas continued writing through the Christmas and New Year's holidays, scrawling his draft in pencil on lined paper, as always. "This is all subject to change," he insisted as he reviewed with designer Gavin Bocquet a list of sets and characters — including a ten-year-old Han Solo, whom Lucas envisioned working with Yoda to track down the villainous General Grievous.

Lucas finally completed his fifty-five-page rough draft — already titled *Revenge of the Sith*, a nod to his abandoned title for *Return of the*

Jedi—on January 31, 2003. Even then, only McCallum was given the completed draft; rather than hand over a script to the design crew, Lucas preferred to describe the look of the sets personally to Bocquet and his team, "so they know what's going on and can plan," he told McCallum, "but not enough information so they lock something down—because everything is going to change."[38] And then back he went into his writing room to work on the next draft. McCallum, more amused now than annoyed, left for Sydney to confer with production heads about the sets and props they would begin building, based on a script they still weren't permitted to read.

It's likely, too, that Lucas's focus was elsewhere, at least in the early part of 2003. On Saturday, February 8, with San Francisco mayor Willie Brown and Congresswoman Nancy Pelosi beside him, Lucas presided over the official groundbreaking for his Digital Arts Center on the grounds of the Presidio. It had taken longer than he had hoped for the day to arrive; the official agreement with the Presidio Trust hadn't been signed until August 2001, nearly two years after the deal was announced. Even then, work had stalled for yet another two years, but Lucas was determined that the $300 million project would now proceed quickly and smoothly, shooting for a grand opening sometime in 2005.

But this time, work would proceed without him. While Lucas had presided over nearly every element of the design and construction of Skywalker Ranch, Lucasfilm CFO Micheline Chau—who was on her way to replacing Gordon Radley as president and COO—politely but firmly informed Lucas that he couldn't visit the Presidio site unless he was invited. As Chau delicately put it, "George and I had a conversation about freedom and letting go."[39] Over the next year and a half, Lucas would be invited to the site only three times, which was just long enough for him to obsessively review twenty different window designs and more than a hundred fabric swatches for the walls of the movie theater.

Chau's directive probably kept work on *Revenge of the Sith* on track. With the Presidio facility unavailable to him, Lucas had to go back to his desk each day, writing from 8:30 a.m. until 6 p.m. Even after forty years of writing scripts, it hadn't gotten any easier. "I can be chained to my desk and I still can't write it. [But] I do it, you know," he added proudly. "I do get it done." On April 10, a group of designers came into his office to find him sitting at his desk, pencil down, head bowed. "I just finished the first full draft," he told them.[40] He would start the second draft immediately; filming at Fox Sydney was scheduled to begin in two months.

On the morning of May 1, Lucas walked into the art department and threw the recently completed script down on a table. Even at 10:00 in the morning, he already looked tired. "Next week...I'm bringing in a guest director so I don't have to do this anymore," he told his artists calmly. "I've done pretty much everything I can do....The director's coming in on Thursday, so I want to go through all this"—and here he gestured to all the art plastered on the walls and scattered across the tables—"and show him everything that's here."[41] Nervous glances were exchanged; concept design supervisor Ryan Church remembered wondering if he would need to move back to Hollywood to look for work. For the next week, the ranch was buzzing with excitement and nervousness, everyone speculating on the identity of the mysterious director. On Thursday, May 8, Lucas introduced his guest director to the crew: Steven Spielberg.

Spielberg, however, wasn't coming on board to direct the film; instead, Lucas had invited him to participate in the editing of some of the extensive animatics Ben Burtt had prepared for a number of key sequences. "I said [to Steven], 'We'll give you a laptop and we'll give you the program, and I'll give you some scenes,'" said Lucas, "'and you can direct the scenes while you're just sitting by the pool.' He loves to do that." Spielberg would tinker mostly with the climactic lightsaber duel between Anakin and Obi-Wan on the volcano planet Mustafar. "I want these guys pouring, dripping sweat," Spielberg told Lucas excitedly. "Their hair at some point should be smoking." Lucas loved it. "We have very, very similar sensibilities," he said.[42]

With filming scheduled to begin at Fox Studios in Sydney at the end of June, Lucas arrived in Australia on June 15, bringing along the third draft of his script, which he was still revising. He also brought his children; *Revenge of the Sith* would be something of a family affair for the Lucases, with all three kids — and Lucas too — making cameo appearances in the film. Lucas would make his screen debut as the blue-faced Baron Papanoida, walking outside a theater box at the opera house, with fifteen-year-old Katie — also in blue face — as his daughter. Amanda, now twenty-two, would be seen huddling with senators, while ten-year-old Jett — who had played a Jedi youngling named Zett Jukassa in *Attack of the Clones* — reprised the role for Episode III, doing some very minor stunts as he flipped and battled stormtroopers with a lightsaber and, to his delight, would even get to die heroically on-screen.

Lucas completed the fourth and final draft of *Revenge of the Sith* in Sydney on June 26; four days later, he began filming on Stage 2 at Fox Studios. Bocquet and his team had constructed seventy-one sets this time — about as many as he had for Episode II — in an attempt to help Lucas keep his promise that Episode III would be smaller and less expensive than the film before it. It was — though just barely: Lucas would top out his budget for *Revenge of the Sith* at $113 million, compared to the $120 million he'd spent on *Attack of the Clones*.

He was shooting entirely digitally again, which gave him the ability to review a shot instantly on the numerous high-def plasma screens he'd set up in what came to be called the "video village," a small camp of folding chairs, video monitors, and equipment set up on the soundstage. Here Lucas could see every camera angle at once, displayed across the various monitors, then select the shots he wanted and transmit them immediately to Burtt at Skywalker Ranch for editing. Lucas also used the village as a kind of home base, holding court as he reviewed the shooting schedule each morning, tweaked the script, huddled with actors, or oversaw a costume adjustment. While Lucas consulted regularly with McCallum and other crew members, the final decision on anything was his and his alone. McCallum understood perfectly. "Film is a director's medium. Television is a producer's medium," said McCallum. "Working with George is a George medium." Lucas didn't disagree.

"I guess I've been accused of being a micromanager, but as far as I'm concerned, that's what making a movie is all about," he said. "I'm really responsible for every single detail on the picture."[43]

On July 2, Anthony Daniels, once again reprising his role as Threepio, made his first appearance on set, picking his way around cables in his gleaming gold costume. Lucas shook his hand warmly, calling out loudly, "*Star Wars* has arrived!" The same could probably have been said of the amiable Peter Mayhew, whose appearance in the full Chewbacca costume was met with audible gasps as he loped his way across the soundstage. Actor Ewan McGregor admitted to being starstruck, even getting a bit emotional as he shot a final scene with R2-D2 in August. "I find myself quite choked up about it, about this little robot, you know."[44]

Lucas was continuing to improve in his interactions with his actors, more often telling them when takes were good, and giving them actual directions on the delivery of lines or the pacing of a scene. And yet, some habits were hard to break; during one particularly difficult scene requiring multiple takes, even as his actors asked for a moment to collect themselves, Lucas could be heard muttering, "Oh, I just want to get through it."[45] Still, it was better than the days of "Faster, and more intense."

If asked, Lucas would probably admit that he had mellowed a bit over the past thirty years. Partly it had to do with age. His beard was white now, though it would always be meticulously trimmed. His hair, by contrast, could sometimes get long, and he would comb it back a bit into his pompadour, now wavy and white. The intensity and stubbornness were still there too, but Lucas found he could relax more on the set, a change he attributed mostly to the presence of his children, who ensured that he never took himself too seriously. (Children, and teenagers in particular, he joked, were "the key to a nervous breakdown.")[46] By the time principal photography was completed on September 17 — five days ahead of schedule — Lucas would even call *Revenge of the Sith* "the most fun film I've ever worked on."[47]

Still, he wasn't going to get too sentimental. As some crew members hugged or dabbed at their eyes as they bade one another good-bye, Lucas remained remarkably unemotional; fleeting friendships were simply part of moviemaking. "You're all friends, you know each other," he explained. "But I have a tendency to not let my private life and my professional life mix—and once the movie finishes, everybody goes their own way. When you're together, you're together, and when you're not, you're not." And besides, for Lucas, it was still far too early to celebrate; *Revenge of the Sith* wasn't even close to being finished. As crew members passed around congratulatory drinks, Lucas pulled aside ILM's John Knoll, who would oversee much of the post-production work. "I've been working on it for eighteen months," he told Knoll, "and I have exactly eighteen months to go."[48]

Special effects work at ILM was proceeding at a slower pace than Lucas hoped, so he enacted the only solution he understood: he hovered over people, dropping in daily to review footage while he ate his lunch—a sandwich and a soda in a to-go box, prepared by the downstairs kitchen. Other times, Lucas would plant himself at an animation station, watching as the computer animator moved elements in and out of the frame and offering suggestions on different angles from which to "film" the sequence. In December, Lucas invited Coppola to the ranch to observe firsthand how the digital process worked; after Coppola's earlier failed experiments with technology, Lucas wanted his mentor to see how it could be done right. Coppola, looking dapper in a gray suit, watched with fascination as Lucas demonstrated his ability to direct the movie digitally, moving characters out of one scene and into another, raising a character's arm, even inserting a blink. Typically, Coppola was concerned about the impact such spontaneous editing might have on the story. "Are you changing the script much," he asked Lucas, "or is it holding up pretty well?"

Lucas considered for a moment. "It's holding up."

Coppola nodded, then looked around the editing room approvingly. "You're doing what you like to do most," he told Lucas warmly. "Having fun."[49]

As Lucas continued the editing, he made notes for several pickup shots and additional footage. While the script *was* holding up, there were places where clarification was needed, and Lucas had scheduled time for additional filming at Shepperton in London for late August 2004, his first time back at the studio since filming the throne room ceremony for the first *Star Wars* film twenty-five years earlier. It was here Lucas would film a final shot of Anthony Daniels dressed as Threepio. Even with the improvements built in to the costume over the past two decades, it was still difficult for Daniels to hear much, and Lucas stood by patiently for several takes until Daniels finally got his lines right and hit his marks. Lucas called "Cut!" and flashed a thumbs-up to Daniels, who felt as if he had been repeatedly and patiently incarcerated inside Threepio's shell for decades.

"It's only been twenty-five years," Lucas told Daniels kindly.

"And we're still not getting it right," teased Daniels.

"Thank you," Lucas said, as the two men shook hands. "Thank you for everything."[50]

Lucas had plenty of other nooks and crannies of the *Star Wars* universe to attend to in the months leading up to the release of *Revenge of the Sith*. In September 2004 he'd released the original trilogy on DVD for the first time — and typically couldn't keep his hands off it, inserting several new tweaks to the films he'd already modified. During filming on Episode III, he'd taken the opportunity to record Ian McDiarmid reading the Emperor's dialogue from *The Empire Strikes Back*—which had been made several years before McDiarmid had even been cast in the role — and dubbed his voice over the original dialogue, thus ensuring consistency with the prequels. Curiously, he also digitally removed actor Sebastian Shaw from the final scene in *Jedi*—where the redeemed Anakin materializes to join Yoda and Ben Kenobi at Luke's side — and replaced him with Hayden Christensen. (He had been only half-joking when he suggested to ILM that they insert Liam Neeson's Qui-Gon Jinn into the scene as well.) While fans would continue to gripe about Lucas's changes—and the HAN SHOT FIRST movement would rumble back to life again, especially as many home viewers were seeing all of Lucas's tweaks to their beloved films for the first time—they would still buy anything *Star Wars,* spending more than $100 million for the DVDs on their first day of their release.

A year earlier, starting in November 2003, he'd also begun managing at arm's length a successful animated "micro-series"—twenty-five episodes, running from three to twelve minutes each—called *Star Wars: Clone Wars,* which followed Obi-Wan and Anakin on adventures occurring between Episodes II and III. It was Lucas's intention to use the cartoon to "bridge the gap" between the two movies, and he had provided director and animator Genndy Tartakovsky, the creator of *Dexter's Laboratory* and *Samurai Jack,* with a story line and ground rules, then left him largely alone. Lucas had been so pleased with the resulting cartoons—which were fast, witty, and exciting—that he permitted Tartakovsky to introduce one of *Revenge of the Sith*'s villains, General Grievous, in a March 2005 episode, two months before the premiere of Episode III.

By the time the episode aired on the Cartoon Network on March 25, fans were already lining up for *Revenge of the Sith.* In Seattle, one young fan had set up an elaborate camp with a powder-blue couch at its center. From here he would post daily live updates to his blog until he was evicted by the mayor for camping on public property. (He was later relocated to a private sidewalk outside another theater.) In Los Angeles, *Star Wars* lovers lined up outside a theater where the movie wouldn't even be playing, hoping to persuade Fox to premiere the film at Grauman's Chinese Theater. The ploy didn't work, but fans had a great time anyway, staging lightsaber fights, raising money for charity, and maintaining a genial party atmosphere. "Nerdy Gras," one fan called it.[51]

Lucas and McCallum attended the May 16 premiere of *Revenge of the Sith* at the UCI Empire Theatre in London, which showed the movie as the final installment of a six-film *Star Wars* marathon. Lucas had been concerned that people might find the movie too downbeat; the violence, in fact, had earned *Revenge of the Sith* the first PG-13 rating for a *Star*

Wars film. "It's not a happy movie by any stretch of the imagination," Lucas admitted. "It's a tragedy....It will probably be the least successful of the *Star Wars* movies—but I know that."[52]

He was wrong; *Revenge of the Sith* set a single-day record of $50 million, on its way to an opening weekend of $108 million and a worldwide gross of $848 million. Furthermore, the movie's darker themes didn't seem to turn off fans or critics at all; in fact, many thought Lucas had returned to form. A. O. Scott, who had eviscerated Episodes I and II in the *New York Times*, thought Episode III was not only the best of the prequels but also even better than the original *Star Wars*. The critic for *Variety*, too, thought Lucas had redeemed himself after the disappointment of the first two movies, declaring that "despite fans' varying degrees of loss of faith that set in with *Menace* and *Clones*, most will be inspired enough to believe again."[53]

Over at *Newsweek*, David Ansen compared the film favorably with *The Empire Strikes Back* and applauded Lucas himself for his artistic consistency. "For all the technological changes Lucas has embraced, his wide-eyed, childlike approach to storytelling...has remained the same," wrote Ansen. "You can argue whether it's for better or worse. What you can't argue with is that he's stayed true to his vision, and that that vision has changed the cultural landscape irrevocably."[54] Still, even Ansen and Scott noted they had also had to put up with Lucas's usual bad dialogue, as well as the complete lack of chemistry between the two romantic leads, and way too much digital showing off— though everyone, as always, loved Yoda, a testament to the animation skills of Rob Coleman.

Lucas was delighted with the response to *Revenge of the Sith*—but he was even more thrilled to finally cut the ribbon at the grand opening of his digital arts center at the Presidio in June. The compound was officially designated the Letterman Digital Arts Center, for the Letterman army hospital that had stood on the site since 1898; architects had even designed some of the buildings to use the recycled remains of the hospital, blending the Presidio's unique history into the center's very DNA. The twenty-three-acre campus featured four five-story buildings made of brick and terra-cotta, totaling about 850,000 square feet—and all of it financed solely by Lucasfilm to the tune of $350 million. Here, among Japanese maples and weeping willow trees, and with views of the Golden Gate Bridge and the Palace of Fine Arts, Lucas would relocate ILM, THX, Lucas Arts, the George Lucas Educational Foundation, and the headquarters of Lucasfilm— about 2,500 employees in total.

While Lucas hadn't gotten ILM to the ranch, he *had* finally brought the ILMers into the fold, not only providing them with the best equipment and a state-of-the-art facility, but also putting them where they could easily interact and collaborate with their counterparts at THX and LucasArts, two of the company's most profitable subsidiaries. As he had done by hiding ILM in plain sight at the Kerner building, Lucas would give little indication at the Letterman compound of what was really going on inside each of the four rather prim-looking buildings; the only giveaway was a bronze statue of Yoda near the front entrance. After twenty-five years of gawking at Skywalker Ranch in the hills of Nicasio and aching to get in, the public, for the first time, was welcome to take a look inside a Lucasfilm compound, even if it was just the smallest of peeks. Visitors would be permitted into the lobby of Building B, where they could see *Star Wars* props and other memorabilia, including life-size replicas of Darth Vader and Boba Fett. And proving once and for all that Lucas wasn't above poking a little fun at himself, there stood off to one side an immense "carbonite" block encasing not an anguished Han Solo but rather a tongue-lolling Jar Jar Binks.

Lucasfilm president Micheline Chau thought the company's very public presence in the San Francisco community was good for Lucasfilm, and good for the region—especially since declining revenues had recently forced both Coppola and producer Saul Zaentz to shutter their own studios in the area. "We spent a lot of years hidden away, and I'm not sure it was good for the company as a whole," said Chau. "The world has changed. To be the epicenter of the digital revolution, we have to be out here, evangelizing the cause."[55] There was also speculation that the company's higher profile meant that Lucas was preparing to take the company public—a rumor Chau quashed immediately. There would only ever be one stockholder at Lucasfilm: George Lucas.

On the evening of June 9, 2005, Lucas donned a rare tuxedo to receive the American Film Institute's Life Achievement Award, given annually to an individual whose career "has contributed to the enrichment of American culture."[56] In the eyes of many, it was a long time coming; Harrison Ford had received the same award in 2000, and Spielberg had been a recipient in 1995. Whether one enjoyed Lucas's films or not, it was impossible to deny that he'd enriched American culture; over the past three decades, he'd practically *created* it, whether via major technological and merchandising innovations or just the characters and stories of his movies themselves.

While Lucas was generally disdainful of awards, he seemed genuinely touched by the pomp and circumstance surrounding this one. After a heartfelt introduction by Spielberg—"You have done more for the collective consciousness of this planet than you will ever know"— Lucas took the stage to a thunderous standing ovation, then hoisted the award victoriously over his head for a moment. He thanked the crowd warmly—"I halfway expected to have a room full of stormtroopers and Princess Leias," he joked, getting his first of many laughs—and bowed to Spielberg as "my partner, my pal, my inspiration, [and] my challenger." He gave high praise to Coppola for giving him his start. "He never gave up on me," Lucas said fondly; "he took me from not being able to write a word to being the king of wooden dialogue," a line at which Harrison Ford laughed harder than anyone else. His biggest thanks, however, were reserved for his children, "who have made my life extra special." Amanda and Katie, seated next to Spielberg, wept openly.[57]

"I love cinema," Lucas concluded. "All kinds...no matter how big, no matter how small. I love to watch them. I love to make them. But if I didn't have anyone to enjoy them or appreciate them, there wouldn't be any point. So, thank you all for going to the movies," he said warmly, "especially *mine!*"[58]

And they would keep going to the movies—especially his—all summer long. *Revenge of the Sith* would finish the year as the highest-grossing film in the United States for 2005, and the third-highest-grossing of the six *Star Wars* films. It was also the culmination of two trilogies that had taken up more than thirty years of Lucas's life. He was "happy and relieved" to be done with the series, he told a local reporter, and now that it was over—especially now that he had the new digital playground out at the Presidio at his disposal—he was ready to move on. "I'm going to do other types of projects," he told *American Cinematographer,* "things that I've wanted to do for a long time, definitely a very different kind of filmmaking than what I've been engaged in."[59]

There would be esoteric art films, he said, and maybe even another Indiana Jones movie. But of one thing he was certain: there would be no more *Star Wars.* "*Star Wars* is finished," Lucas said. "I do have a lot of other movies that I want to make....I don't have to answer to anybody....That's what I've earned: to be able to do what I want to do."[60]

13

Letting Go

2005-2016

George Lucas was in love.

It happened—as love so often does—unexpectedly. At the age of sixty-one, Lucas was concentrating mostly on being a father. As corny as it sounded, he would always call it the job that made him the happiest. "There was a point there where I lived only for movies," he said, "but now I know the truth: Children are the key to life, the key to joy, the key to happiness."[1] Still, he admitted, "there's a lonely part to having kids alone....Without two [parents], the emotional need is always there. You don't have that level of sharing. But also, you don't have to compromise. But let's face it," he added somewhat wistfully, "I'd rather be married. But I'm not. As you grow up, you understand that there is no such thing as a perfect life."[2]

When asked about his love life in 2005 on *60 Minutes*, Lucas laughed out loud. "What love life?" he said. "It hasn't changed much....I'd love to get married again, but I'm not gonna get married unless it's the right person." He admitted that at his age, he was set in

436

his ways and could be "difficult," but thought that "whomever I'd be interested in now is also the same way."[3] Coppola, interviewed for a *60 Minutes* piece on Lucas several years earlier, thought the problem was that Lucas had "very high standards. I mean, he wants Queen Noor or Grace Kelly or someone," said Coppola. "She can't be too tall, she has to be wonderful with kids." But Lucas immediately dismissed the accusation that he was too picky. "I speak for those who are the single ones, to say, 'I am not picky,'" he insisted. "But I want someone who's right. And I'm not gonna walk into anything, because marriage is a serious thing."[4]

Lightning would strike where Lucas least expected it: at one of the endless conferences and fund-raisers he attended with mind-numbing regularity. At one crowded function, friends introduced him to thirty-seven-year-old Mellody Hobson, president of the Chicago financial firm Ariel Investments, one of the nation's largest African American–owned money management companies. The Princeton-educated Hobson was smart and charismatic, with an admiring circle of powerful friends, including Oprah Winfrey, Jeffrey Katzenberg, Warren Buffett, and former senator Bill Bradley. The Reverend Al Sharpton called her "black America's business princess."[5] Princess or not, Lucas was immediately smitten. By early 2006, the two of them were quietly dating.

For a while they kept their relationship private, succeeding so well that few of their friends realized they were an item. When Hobson casually mentioned to Arianna Huffington that she was having dinner with Lucas, Huffington recoiled in shock. "I said, 'You can't go,'" recalled Huffington. "I thought he was a ladies man"—an allegation that would likely have horrified Lucas.[6] Eventually, he and Hobson would be seen at high-powered events together, showing up at a 2006 White House reception where Spielberg was being feted as a Kennedy Center honoree, and the 2007 Oscars, where Oprah gaped at the television screen in delighted disbelief as she watched her friend laughing in the audience, seated next to Lucas.

For those observing them together, it was clear this was no casual fling. Lucas and Hobson would arrange their busy schedules to ensure they saw each other every weekend—and when they were together, they seemed to hold hands constantly. "I've known George a long time and I've never seen him this happy," said David Geffen.[7] Matthew Robbins, who'd known Lucas longer than most, was delighted for the couple. "They're very much in love," he said.[8]

The difference in age and race didn't matter to their friends—or to either of them. "[Our relationship] works because we are extraordinarily open-minded people," Hobson told Winfrey. "And we're open to what the universe brings us. I think we didn't have preconceived ideas about what a partner should be, and so we allowed ourselves to discover something that was unexpected."[9] Lucas, too, knew they were an unlikely couple. "I'm a 60s, West Coast, liberal, radical, artsy, dyed in the wool 99 percenter before there was such a thing. And she's an East Coast, Princeton grad, Wall Street fund manager....You would never think that we would get together, have anything in common," Lucas explained. "But when we did...we realized we have *everything* in common....I was attracted to her because she's *really, really* smart.... If you're more beautiful than I am and smarter than I am and you'll put up with me, that's all it takes. I'm there."[10]

As Anakin Skywalker had said in Lucas's script for *Attack of the Clones,* "Unconditional love is essential to a Jedi's life." They were words he had written in 2002, and four years later, George Lucas had found it.

At Lucasfilm, there was one question on everyone's mind: *Now what?*

Lucas had gotten Episodes I, II, and III out of the way—but would there be a VII, VIII, and IX? Lucas threw cold water on expectations; he insisted that he was finished with *Star Wars* for good. "I get asked all the time, 'What happens after *Return of the Jedi*?' and there really is no answer for that," he told a reporter patiently. "The movies were the story of Anakin Skywalker and Luke Skywalker, and when Luke saves the galaxy and redeems his father, that's where that story ends."[11] What that meant for Lucasfilm, however, was turning off what had been a very profitable spigot; the prequels alone had gener-

ated $2.4 billion at the box office, with much of the profits going right
back into the company.

With no new *Star Wars* films on the horizon, then, Lucasfilm
would be "a widget-driven" company, said Lucas, not entirely kidding.
There would be books and video games and music and special
effects—but with the exception of another Indiana Jones film, there
would be no more movies. "I have no intention of running a film company. That is the last thing in the world I'd do," Lucas told the *New
York Times*. "I'm trying to get back to that place [where] the company
functions without me and *Star Wars*, where they don't need some
genius at the head to run the company. What I am doing is so I don't
need to be a visionary."[12]

At the moment, Lucasfilm was in an enviable position; the company had virtually no debt ("I don't believe in debt," Lucas had growled
years earlier, and he still meant it), and Lucas wanted as much of the
company as possible to be self-sufficient. ILM, THX, and Skywalker
Sound were doing the most to earn their keep, generating the bulk of
their revenue from non–*Star Wars* projects. But ILM was now just one
of many digital effects companies that offered their services for hire—
the grand old man with the coolest car, perhaps, but still just one
among many. *Revenge of the Sith*, in fact, marked the first time ILM
failed to receive an Oscar nomination for its effects in a *Star Wars* film.
Chrissie England, the new president of ILM, was committed to making the company even more deft and flexible by lending its people out
to other effects outfits or consulting with directors.

LucasArts, however, was more problematic; an aggressive internal
review of the organization by vice president Jim Ward hadn't gone well.
"I walked into quite a mess," remembered Ward.[13] The division had
misjudged the rising popularity of console game systems like PlaySta-
tion and Xbox, and was still aiming its games largely at the PC market.
Furthermore, both Ward and Lucas were frustrated by LucasArts'
inability to come up with original game concepts; most of its games
were now deeply rooted in the *Star Wars* universe, a habit Lucas was
hoping to break. Trying to cut costs and refocus, the division slashed

staffing and recalled a number of games in progress, but would continue to struggle for several more years.

One Lucasfilm vice president wondered aloud whether "George's challenge is coming up with the next creative generation." Lucas dismissed that suggestion outright. "It's not like we have to come up with a movie every year. I don't want to be Pixar," he said with just a touch of derision. "I'm not depending on these people to take the company into a megahit reality. I'm trying to build a company where we don't make miracles, but we do a good job."[14] But the Pixar comparison was apt—and probably stung a bit. After selling the company to Steve Jobs in the mid-1980s, Lucas had watched his rival produce one animated blockbuster after another. He'd learned his lesson. After dismissing computer animation for fifteen years, Lucas was determined to get into the game now himself, and had recently established Lucasfilm Animation, with offices at nearby Big Rock Ranch and in a sandcrawler-shaped building he was constructing in Singapore, officially giving Lucasfilm an international presence.

With *Star Wars* films phased out, Lucas was now putting all of his efforts into developing a number of series for television. Partly it was a matter of cost; for the same $200 million he might spend on a movie, he explained, he could make fifty two-hour movies for television. "In the future market, that's where it's going to land, because it's going to be all pay-per-view and downloadable," he predicted—a remarkably prescient statement, essentially anticipating on-demand and streaming services for television and film ten years before such technology was widely available.[15] But then this was the same George Lucas who, in a 1994 interview with the *Wall Street Journal,* had foretold that people "will really go for" computer-based home shopping services, "to order up things at home and not have to go out," practically defining the appeal and convenience of Amazon.com a year before the company publicly announced its existence. In the same interview, he predicted the popularity of what he called "party-line" video games, which would be played "with two or three other people, you can see them all as you play," accurately describing the complex multiplayer functionality of today's video games at a time when Internet service still required a hardwired telephone.[16]

Despite his *No More Star Wars* decree, Lucas excited *Star Wars* fans by announcing he had in production two *Star Wars*–related television series. One was a live-action series eventually called *Star Wars: Underworld,* following criminals and gangs (McCallum would later compare it to *Deadwood* in space) and set in the era between Episodes III and IV of the *Star Wars* franchise. (It would languish in development hell, and never be produced.) The other was a computer-animated series called *Clone Wars,* a follow-up to Genndy Tartakovsky's similarly named micro-series for Cartoon Network, which had charted the adventures of Obi-Wan and Anakin in the Clone Wars. Tartakovsky, however, thought it was a terrible idea, and accused Lucas of going back to the well one too many times. "I think it's the easiest thing to do, because he doesn't need to come up with a whole new thing," said Tartakovsky. "There's so much more he could explore."[17]

"It's not a matter of trying to prove anything to anybody," Lucas insisted. "I don't have to."[18]

And still Lucas—who called himself "semi-retired"[19] at this point—was determined "to go off and make my own feature films, which are more about exploring the aesthetics and conventions of cinema…[the] kind of moviemaking I haven't done since I was in college, so I'm looking forward to getting back to the basics of cinema."[20] Lucasfilm CEO Micheline Chau had heard it all before. Lucas could pursue his great art all he wanted; her concern was to "think about what life is like after *Star Wars,* and after George."[21]

Except *Star Wars,* it seemed, wasn't really going *anywhere. Star Wars* merchandising had surged and would be enough to keep Lucasfilm in the black for years, if not decades, to come. Episode III merchandise alone brought in more than $3 billion worldwide, and Hasbro saw its own profits jump by 15 percent on the coattails of *Star Wars* toys.[22] At this point, fans would buy nearly any figures based on the *Star Wars* universe, no matter how obscure or brief their screen time— Major Bren Derlin!—or, in some cases, whether they'd even appeared in the movie at all. There were figures of Threepio and Artoo based on Ralph McQuarrie's original concept paintings and—one of the more popular though hard-to-get figures—a stormtrooper with a removable helmet that revealed the face of George Lucas underneath (and for those who wanted Lucas fighting for the Alliance, he was also available as an X-wing pilot named Jorg Sacul—"Lucas" spelled backward).

There may have been no more *Star Wars* movies on the horizon, but under their Lucasfilm licensing agreements, there were plenty of comics and novels in which fans could follow their heroes—and villains—and which added so many new characters, planets, ships, and aliens to the *Star Wars* universe that they would be officially classified as the *Star Wars* Expanded Universe. The galaxy grew so large, in fact, that Lucasfilm eventually hired its own staff to keep tabs on and catalog everything, though it was Lucas, and Lucas alone, who would ultimately decide what was considered to be "canon"—that is, officially part of the *Star Wars* universe.

Still, in the grand scheme of things, his was a tenuous hold on the mythology he'd created—for *Star Wars* no longer belonged to Lucasfilm, or even to George Lucas; it belonged to everybody. And there was no better time to drive that point home than in 2007, the thirtieth anniversary of the release of *Star Wars*. On the first day of the year, Lucas served as the grand marshal of the Tournament of Roses Parade in Pasadena, accompanied by hundreds of fans dressed as stormtroopers, Jedi knights, Sand People, and Imperial officers. For the rest of the year, *Star Wars* would be celebrated around the world. The U.S. Postal Service issued commemorative postage stamps, and painted four hundred mailboxes across the country to resemble R2-D2. In May, Celebration IV would draw 35,000 people, making it one of the largest *Star Wars* conventions—and two months later, 30,000 European fans filled the ExCel Centre in London as part of Celebration Europe, the first Lucasfilm-sanctioned *Star Wars* convention outside the United States. In Paris, the Official *Star Wars* Fan Club of France would host a showing of all six movies at its Reunion II convention at the Grand Rex, the largest single-screen theater in Europe.

Lucas himself would even get into the act, presiding over a showing and panel discussion of the film on its official birthday, May 25, at the Samuel Goldwyn Theater in Los Angeles, where he would crack wise about wanting to go back and tinker with it again. ("It's a *JOKE*, people!" he said as he pirouetted away from the crowd.)[23] More and more now, Lucas was willing to make himself the butt of the joke — a mood shift that could likely be traced directly back to the influence of Mellody Hobson — and had even cooperated with the creators of the sketch comedy series *Robot Chicken* and with *Family Guy* creator Seth MacFarlane for affectionate, and often biting, parodies of both *Star Wars* and himself. For *Robot Chicken*, in fact, Lucas would lend his own voice to the stop-action version of himself, muttering a pitch-perfect "Oh, dear God..." as he stepped off an elevator in front of hundreds of adoring fans — a moment likely rooted in personal experience.

For most filmmakers, getting mobbed by the eager fans of one iconic film franchise would be more than enough. But Lucas had one other brand name to attend to that summer. In June, he and Spielberg would travel to rural New Mexico to begin principal photography on a film they were disguising with the code name *Genre*, but which Lucas would usually refer to by a more casual title: *Indiana Jones IV.*

Perhaps appropriately, getting Indiana Jones to the big screen again had been an adventure twenty years in the making, leaving multiple wounded writers in its path and generating some friction between old friends.

For a long time, things hadn't looked good for the wily archaeologist, starting with perhaps the most important element of any Indiana Jones movie after Indy himself: namely, what object would Dr. Jones be looking for? Lucas thought he had found his answer as early as 1992, only a few years after the release of *Indiana Jones and the Last Crusade*. After working with Harrison Ford on the 1950s-era *Young*

Indiana Jones episode, Lucas was convinced the next film should be set in the atomic age. "[I thought] if I did it in the '50s, maybe we could change [it] into a '50s movie," said Lucas, "[and] I thought, *Hey, that could be fun*...so I thought, *That's the MacGuffin: aliens.* For God's sake, it can't miss."[24]

Except it did. Both Ford and Spielberg vetoed the idea, with Spielberg standing particularly firm in his objections. "I had done *E.T.,* I had done *Close Encounters;* I'd had my fill of extraterrestrials," said Spielberg, "so I resisted that [idea] for many years." But Lucas, stubborn as ever, eventually persuaded Spielberg to let him take a crack at a story treatment, and brought in screenwriter Jeb Stuart—hot off Ford's hit *The Fugitive*—to lend a hand with the writing. He and Lucas completed their first draft, called *Indiana Jones and the Saucermen from Mars,* in May 1994. "It was a lot about Indiana Jones being involved in Roswell," said Lucas—and, as promised, "the alien was the MacGuffin."[25] Lucas would continue to revise the script over the next year, first with Stuart and then with Jeff Boam, who'd written *Indiana Jones and the Last Crusade.* By 1996, both Lucas and Spielberg were pleased enough with the script to think about moving into pre-production by summer.

And then came *Independence Day,* the sci-fi blockbuster of 1996, most of which involved aliens and flying saucers. Spielberg suddenly lost his nerve. "We're not doing a flying saucer movie," he told Lucas flatly, "and that's it." The script went into Lucas's desk drawer, and there it sat until February 2000, when Harrison Ford's tribute at the American Film Institute brought Lucas, Ford, Spielberg, and *Indiana Jones* producers Frank Marshall and Kathleen Kennedy together again. As the group drank and talked backstage, Ford casually asked, "How is *Indy IV* coming?" Two months later, Ford, Lucas, and Spielberg huddled to discuss possible stories for the next Indiana Jones adventure. Lucas's only requirement: "I won't do it without aliens. That's the only thing that's going to work." Spielberg finally conceded. "Working with George is still the same," he reported affectionately. "We still argue, we still compromise, and we still deal with each other like the brothers that we are."[26]

Over the next two years Lucas would keep rewriting and revising, even while working nearly full-time on *Attack of the Clones*. Despite continued grumbling from Ford and Spielberg, he was sticking with aliens, and he'd recently come up with a new MacGuffin. "We'd actually written an [unproduced] episode of *Young Indiana Jones* about a crystal skull, which was found in Guatemala," said Lucas. "I thought it was kind of cool, because it's a supernatural object. So we started to say, 'Well, what if it was an alien skull?'" Spielberg agreed it was an object worthy of being pursued by Indiana Jones, and he and Lucas brought in Frank Darabont, the talented writer-director of *The Shawshank Redemption* and *The Green Mile*, to work on a new script. It was the beginning of what Darabont would later describe as a "wasted year or more of my life."[27]

With Lucas spending most of 2002 working on *Revenge of the Sith*, Darabont consulted regularly with Spielberg instead, embedding Spielberg's sensibilities and preferences, rather than Lucas's, into the script. Little wonder, then, that when Darabont turned in his script, titled *Indiana Jones and the City of the Gods*, in May 2003, "Steven was ecstatic," according to Darabont. "We both were. It was going to be his next film. He told me it was the best script he'd read since *Raiders of the Lost Ark.* . . . As a screenwriter, you dream of making a guy like Steven Spielberg happy and excited." But Lucas was neither happy nor excited. "George Lucas read it, didn't like it, and threw ice water on the whole thing," said Darabont with a touch of bitterness. "The project went down in flames. . . . It was just such an awful surprise, after all my hopes and effort. I really felt I'd nailed it, and so did Steven."[28]

Lucas and Spielberg sat on the project for another year, with Lucas picking at Darabont's script before finally bringing in another writer, Jeff Nathanson, who'd written *Catch Me If You Can* for Spielberg. Lucas, who admitted that the writer "was kind of caught between Steven and me," also rejected Nathanson's revision, called *Indiana Jones and the Atomic Ants.* In stepped writer David Koepp, no stranger to franchises, as he'd penned two *Jurassic Park* movies and the first *Mission: Impossible.* Koepp worked mostly with Spielberg, though he found Lucas to be "a fountain of ideas," and in July 2006 turned in a script with a suitably dramatic atomic age title, *Indiana Jones and the Destroyer of Worlds.* Lucas *still* wasn't entirely pleased—he was determined to keep flying saucers in the story—but after a few more revisions and tweaks, he was finally happy by Christmas 2006, nearly fourteen years after coming up with his "can't miss" concept. Even with the script complete, naming the movie would be a point of contention. Lucas wanted it to be *Indiana Jones and the Kingdom of the Crystal Skulls,* while Spielberg wanted it to be a single *Crystal Skull*—a debate Spielberg would win. "Steven and I have both gotten more curmudgeonly as we've grown older," sighed Lucas. According to Spielberg, Lucas had finally thrown up his hands in mock surrender. "I don't care what you call it," Lucas told him. "Just get the word *kingdom* in there somewhere."[29]

Indiana Jones and the Kingdom of the Crystal Skull went into pre-production with most of the familiar cast and crew returning. While Spielberg was unsuccessful in coaxing Sean Connery out of retirement, both Ford and Karen Allen were back, as were producers Frank Marshall and Kathleen Kennedy, who had continued to produce one powerhouse movie after another over the past thirty years. But there was a big change, at least for Lucas: before one minute of film had been shot, Spielberg made it clear to Lucas that he wanted to use as few digital effects as possible. "Steven said, 'I don't want to do that. I want to do the real deal,'" said Lucas. "And we're doing it." There were few complaints. "I love being on a physical set," said Harrison Ford, who, at the age of sixty-five, would be doing most of his own stunt work with only minimal digital assistance. "I don't so much love being in front of a blue screen."[30]

Filming would take place at the same rapid pace Lucas had established for every *Indiana Jones* movie. Production bounced from New Mexico to Connecticut to Hawaii—a homecoming of sorts, as this was where Lucas and Spielberg had dreamed up Indiana Jones on a beach in 1977—then finally settled onto soundstages in Los Angeles, and all within a span of eighty days. Spielberg said that directing it was "a recreational activity"—and in truth, after directing a string of darker and more cerebral films like *Munich* and *War of the Worlds,* he was more than happy to yield to Lucas's more pulpy, pop vision and tastes...even when he didn't entirely share them.[31] "I never liked the MacGuffin," Spielberg later confessed. "George and I had big arguments about the MacGuffin. I didn't want these things to be either aliens or inter-dimensional beings. But I am loyal to my best friend," he noted with genuine warmth. "When he writes a story he believes in—even if I don't believe in it—I'm going to shoot the movie the way George envisioned it. I'll add my own touches, I'll bring my own cast in, I'll shoot the way I want to shoot it, but I will always defer to George as the storyteller of the Indy series. I will never fight him on that."[32]

With relatively few digital shots to complete, post-production on *Crystal Skull* moved along quickly. Spielberg, defying the high-tech Lucas, had edited the movie manually on film; Lucas could only shake his head in amusement, calling his friend "a sentimental sort of guy." But Lucas knew his audience was sentimental too. "There's a lot of anticipation on the part of the older audience, because they loved the previous films," he said, knowing full well he was running the very real risk of disappointing fans who had waited twenty years for another Indiana Jones movie—a frustration he'd experienced firsthand with his return to *Star Wars.*[33] "All we can do is hurt ourselves," Lucas admitted to *Time* magazine. "All it's going to do is get criticized. I mean, it's basically *Phantom Menace* we're making. No matter how you do it, no matter what you do, it won't be what the other ones were in terms of the impact or the way people remember them."[34]

It seemed at first he had reason to be concerned. Mediocre reviews of the film trickled out in advance of the May 22, 2008, premiere, though mostly on Internet fan sites, despite Lucas's attempts to control media access tightly. Most reviewers, however, took a more measured approach, with some, like Roger Ebert—under the headline "I Admit

It: I Loved 'Indy'"—feeling practically a moral obligation to defend the film. "It takes a cold heart and a weary imagination to dislike an *Indiana* film with all of its rambunctious gusto," wrote Ebert.[35] More typical were lukewarm reviews like the one in the *New York Times* that found the film pleasant enough but lacking "any sense of rediscovery," laying the blame on Spielberg, who had "just grown out of this kind of sticky kids' stuff."[36] *Newsweek,* borrowing a metaphor from *Sunset Boulevard,* provided perhaps the briefest and most cogent analysis of *Crystal Skull:* "Indy is still big; it's just that, in the new world of movie franchises, the *Crystal Skull* feels smaller."[37]

Still, the film took in $151.1 million in its first five days, an impressive though not record-breaking number, even with a major push from Paramount and Spielberg, who were promoting the movie aggressively.[38] Lucas was doing his best, too, but he would always be miserable during promotional tours, his annoyance nearly palpable.

"I love making movies; I'm not the biggest fan of selling them," he told the *New York Times* in late June. "I'm doing all my selling for two more weeks. Then I'm sold out."[39]

Lucas had vowed that once he got *Indiana Jones* out of the way, "then I'm going to go and do my own little movies—theatrical movies, but I'm not sure if they'll get shown anywhere."[40] Coppola, meanwhile, had done exactly that, writing, directing, and producing *Youth Without Youth* on a budget of $5 million. The film had been released in December 2007 in only eighteen theaters and, perhaps predictably, had quickly sunk out of sight. Coppola offered no apologies for pursuing his art. "We make films for ourselves," Coppola said. "If no one wants to see them, what can we do?"[41] But Lucas, despite his art-for-art's-sake posturing, found he had little patience with that kind of martyred artist mentality. "If you're making a work of art or a film and nobody sees it, I don't see where it does anybody any good," Lucas argued.[42] At any rate, his own esoteric films would have to wait once again. "You get sidetracked easily," he admitted. "I do, anyway."[43] Especially when it came to *Star Wars,* "a sandbox I love to play in."[44]

This time it was *The Clone Wars*, the computer-animated series Lucas was moving ahead with, producing it with the critical assistance of director, writer, and animator Dave Filoni, who'd impressed Lucas with his work on Nickelodeon's animated hit *Avatar: The Last Airbender*. Filoni was a good "get"; besides his experience and talent as a director and animator, he was a *Star Wars* fan who could talk Imperial politics as easily as Lucas. Together they plumbed early drafts of *Star Wars* for abandoned ideas they could weave through a new cartoon series, writing scripts out at Big Rock Ranch with a team of equally devoted *Star Wars* fans, which would eventually include Lucas's daughter Katie.

Lucas took the same approach to selling an animated series that he had with *Young Indiana Jones*, waiting several years for animators to produce at least twenty-two episodes of the series before he began making the rounds of the networks, looking for takers. Typically, he had no intention of negotiating; he was the one financing the series—each episode cost him between $750,000 and $1 million—and was asking the networks to pay only the licensing fee to distribute and broadcast the show. As he saw it, networks should be falling over themselves at the very idea of having an officially sanctioned *Star Wars* program in their lineup. Furthermore, there would be no cherry-picking the series; a network had to take all twenty-two episodes or lose out altogether. "It's much easier for me to just do the show I want, [then] say, 'Here it is, do you wish to license it or not?'" Lucas said with only a hint of exasperation. "That's it. There's no notes, no comments. I don't care what your opinion is. You either put it on the air or you don't."[45]

Most passed. Even Cartoon Network, which had run the *Clone Wars* micro-series in 2003, was only lukewarm toward the new one. But once Lucas promised Time Warner he would combine several episodes to make a theatrically released *Clone Wars* movie, the studio—smelling future *Star Wars*–related projects if it got involved with Lucas—agreed to distribute the film and strongly encouraged its corporate cousins at Cartoon Network to take another look at Lucas's remaining episodes. This time, Cartoon Network agreed to pick up the series, promising to debut it in the autumn of 2008, following the summer release of the *Clone Wars* movie in August.

Unfortunately, the movie was a dud. Some viewers were put off by the character designs, in which the heads appeared to be made of carved wood—a look Lucas said was deliberately inspired by the 1960s television marionette series *Thunderbirds*. Others found they didn't like having to root for Anakin, knowing he would soon become Darth Vader. Whatever it was, *The Clone Wars* hadn't worked. While it would easily recover its $8 million budget on its way to earnings of $65 million, ticket sales dropped off so sharply between the first and second weeks that critics rushed to brand it the first true *Star Wars–*related flop. The *New York Times* seemed to take particular glee in pointing out the film's dismal financials, practically cackling under a headline reading "The Empire Goes Slack."[46]

Still, a deal was a deal. On the evening of Friday, October 3, Cartoon Network debuted the first episode of the *Clone Wars* series, and hoped for the best. Four million viewers tuned in, making it the most watched series premiere in the history of the channel.[47] Lucas had also shrewdly promoted the series across media, offering exclusive content online, including games and episodes with commentary. The *New York Times*, eating crow, conceded that while *Clone Wars* hadn't worked as a feature-length film, it made for an entertaining half hour on television. Cartoon Network would air twenty-two episodes in the first season, then renew the show annually for another five seasons. More important, Lucas had successfully moved *Star Wars* into yet another medium. *Star Wars* truly was always on now, and on everywhere.

Lucas was enjoying his respite from filmmaking. As he had hoped, the company was doing fine in what he still referred to as "the widget business," though in truth, much of its revenue was still coming in from *Star Wars–*related merchandising and licensing. LucasArts, recently unshackled from Lucas's initial *No Star Wars* directive, had returned to developing games set in the *Star Wars* universe, providing endless opportunities for fans to play as Jedi knights, bounty hunters, storm-troopers, and X-wing pilots, or even take the controls of the *Millennium Falcon*. It would strike pay dirt with its *Battlefront* series, permitting players to direct armies fighting for the Rebel Alliance or the Empire, and its hugely successful *Lego Star Wars* games, allowing players to play through the six movies using Lego vehicles and minifigures.

Out at the Letterman complex, ILM was still working hard for others, and had become the effects shop of preference for a number of hugely successful film franchises, including the *Iron Man, Harry Potter,* and *Pirates of the Caribbean* series. ILM would also contribute effects to what would become not just the biggest film of 2010 but the most successful of all time: James Cameron's ambitious and almost entirely digital blockbuster *Avatar.* Cameron intended for *Avatar* to be the first film in a trilogy, and Lucas—who knew a thing or two about the challenges, perils, and expectations that came with wrapping one-self up in a franchise—publicly wished Cameron well. "Creating a universe is daunting," Lucas told *The New Yorker.* "I'm glad Jim is doing it—there are only a few people in the world who are nuts enough to. I did it with *Star Wars,* and now he's trying to challenge that. It's a lot of work."[48]

Skywalker Sound, meanwhile, was handling the sound duties for nearly forty films and television shows at a time, and its scenic location—nestled inside the Tech Building on Skywalker Ranch—had made it a destination of choice for a number of filmmakers, including Kevin Smith and documentarian Michael Moore, who had made extensive use of the ranch's facilities. Lucas, in fact, had built an inn where visiting filmmakers could stay, with twenty-six themed guest rooms named for artistic icons like John Ford, Winsor McCay, and George Gershwin. There was a Skywalker Ranch fire brigade, which responded to calls both on the ranch and in the Marin County region, in fire engines painted in USC cardinal red. "There's a little film community up here, and we have a different way of looking at things," Lucas said. "We're actually more interested in making movies than making money."[49] Except Lucasfilm really *was* making money.

He and Hobson were still seeing each other regularly, with Hobson flying to San Francisco to stay with him at the ranch, or Lucas jetting to Chicago to spend the weekend with her. Lucas, liberal though never overtly political, began to take a more active interest in politics with the encouragement of the politically savvy and plugged-in Hobson. A friend of hers from Chicago, Senator Barack Obama, could often be found working out of Hobson's offices at Ariel while setting up more permanent headquarters for his campaign for president of the United States. Hobson was actively involved in raising money for Obama, and Lucas, too, quickly became a fan, calling him "a hero in the making."[50] He would find himself at the White House Correspondents' Dinner in 2009, Hobson at his side, buttoned up to the neck in yet another suffocating tuxedo shirt.

There were times, too, when Lucas seemed to be looking for things to do. In early 2010 he showed up on *The Daily Show with Jon Stewart*—one of the few television shows, along with *Law and Order*, that he regularly watched—ostensibly to promote a book he hadn't even written.[51] Instead, he talked about *Clone Wars* and let Stewart tease him about *Star Wars* minutiae and the general awfulness of *The Phantom Menace*. "My son says his favorite movie is *The Phantom Menace*," Stewart deadpanned. "And I explained to him: *No, it's not.*" Striking a more serious tone, Stewart asked Lucas how he reacted to both the love and anger he generated in his devoted, passionate, and sometimes irrational fan base. Lucas smiled wryly. "It's a work of fiction. It's a metaphor. It's not real," he said matter-of-factly. "And therefore you can either like it or not like it. Whatever."[52]

And yet, as dismissive as he might have been, Lucas seemed determined to keep picking fights with his fans, going in yet again to make minor changes to the original *Star Wars* trilogy for its release on Blu-ray in 2011. There was more fiddling with the Han-Greedo showdown—Lucas couldn't ever seem to leave it alone—and Ewoks at last were given eye blinks. But the latest heresy, fans thought, was giving Vader an anguished "Noooooooo!" as he lifted the Emperor off Luke and threw him over the railing to his death at the end of *Return of the Jedi. Star Wars* fans were apoplectic all over again, and took to social media to complain loudly. "George Lucas hates *Star Wars* fans," tweeted one of them, "and happens to find himself in the best position to hurt them."[53] But as usual, even the angriest of fans still had to have *Star Wars* in the newest format; the Blu-ray release of the complete saga would sell nearly 3 million copies, grossing $258 million. Whatever, indeed.

In May 2011, Lucas headed for Walt Disney World to attend the celebration marking the reopening of Star Tours, the attraction Lucas had created for the parks back in 1987. The ride had aged relatively well, but with all that had been achieved in special effects over the intervening two decades, Star Tours had been closed for some time for a thorough reconfiguring. With digital technology and improved mechanics, ILM and Disney Imagineers had since created a new and more convincing experience for the ride, in which the riders would have the opportunity to visit several different planets. Lucas had been checking in on the project twice a month for two years; he especially liked the Disney Imagineers, who didn't seem to know the word *no,* and he was fond of Disney CEO Bob Iger. The feeling was mutual.

On the morning of Lucas's visit, Iger invited him to breakfast at the Hollywood Brown Derby restaurant. The restaurant was normally closed at that early hour, so Lucas and Iger had the place to themselves — a deliberate choice by Iger, who wanted to speak to Lucas in confidence. As Lucas picked at an omelet and Iger, fresh from a workout, downed a yogurt parfait, Iger casually posed the question he'd been dying to ask Lucas for a while now: *Would you consider selling Lucasfilm to Disney?*

Lucas chewed quietly for a moment as he mulled it over. He *was* thinking about retiring, he told Iger; he was sixty-seven years old now, and the restructuring of Lucasfilm over the past few years had been part of his effort to make the company less dependent on his leadership and vision. But he still had projects to attend to — *The Clone Wars* was entering its fourth season, and the live-action *Star Wars* was on the drawing table — and he had ideas for a number of movies he might put into production.

The answer, for the moment, was a qualified no. "I'm not ready to pursue that now," he told Iger. "But when I am, I'd love to talk."

Iger, a deal maker who'd recently brought Pixar and Marvel Entertainment into the Disney fold, was prepared to wait Lucas out. "Call me when you're ready," he said.[54]

Lucas was hoping to make another trilogy.

It was one he'd had in mind for a long time—since the late 1980s, in fact, when he'd been in conversation with George Hall, a respected photographer of military aircraft. At that time Hall, a Vietnam veteran and student of military history, told Lucas the story of the Tuskegee Airmen, a group of African American military pilots who overcame racism, segregation, and prejudice to become one of the most highly respected bands of fighters in World War II. It was a story well suited to Lucas's sensibilities, with a small group of individuals triumphing over enormous odds—exactly the way he still saw himself and Lucasfilm in his never-ending tangle with mainstream Hollywood. "Like *Tucker*, it's a story too good to be true," said Lucas.[55] It was just the kind of story he adored. He was determined to bring it to the screen.

But it was a *big* story—too big, he thought, to tell in a single film. "The question is, how do you make it small and personal and deal with it in a thematic way?"[56] His answer: turn it into a trilogy. In the first one, he would tell the story of the pilots and their training in segregated Alabama; in the second, he'd trace their successes in World War II in their dogfights over Europe; and in the third, he'd follow them back into civilian life, where they would fight to overcome ongoing racism and segregation. "I see the movie less as a race picture than as an aerial action adventure," he told the *Los Angeles Times* in 1990. "I've always been drawn to underdogs and intrigued by the relationship between man, machine, and excellence."[57] For Lucas, that made the middle part of the trilogy—with the World War II dogfighting sequences—the obvious place to start.

Lucas regarded the film as something of a social and moral crusade, one that he would wage for more than twenty years. For those who cynically thought Lucas's commitment to racial equity had begun with his relationship with Mellody Hobson, Lucas could, if asked, point to the development of what would eventually become *Red Tails*. From the beginning, it had been critical to him to hire a black writer for the screenplay and a black director to sit at the helm. "I thought, 'This is the proper way to do this,'" Lucas said later.[58]

Initially, Lucas had brought in writer Kevin Sullivan and director Thomas Carter to help develop the project, but after several false starts had backburnered the project in favor of the *Star Wars* prequels. In 2007 he tried again, this time hiring John Ridley, a novelist and screenwriter who'd written for *Martin* and *The Fresh Prince of Bel-Air*, to write a script that focused more closely on the middle part of the trilogy. For his director, Lucas chose Anthony Hemingway, a veteran of the TV show *The Wire*, but a rookie film director. Hemingway had been all but certain he wouldn't be the man hired for the job; after his interview at the ranch, his parting words to Lucas had been *May the Force be with you.* "Oh my God, I walked out of that meeting after I said that and completely wanted to jump off the fifteenth floor," said Hemingway, still wincing at the memory.[59] On the drive home, he received a call from Lucas on his cell phone telling him he had the job. Hemingway pulled over and cried.

Red Tails—named for the distinctive tails on the Tuskegee pilots' aircraft—finally began principal photography in April 2009. The film was being shot digitally, and with more than an hour of aerial dogfighting to be inserted digitally by ILM in post-production, much of the movie was shot with actors in cockpits in front of greenscreen. As was his working style now, Lucas assembled a full edit of the film, eyeballed places where additional footage was needed, then had Hemingway go back to shoot again. When Hemingway was pulled away in early 2010 to begin work on the HBO series *Treme,* Lucas stepped behind the camera himself to supervise a series of re-shoots. Lucas also called in cartoonist Aaron McGruder, the creator of the *Boondocks* comic strip, to help write new dialogue for some of the new footage. McGruder, who had taken shots at both Jar Jar Binks and Lucas in his comic strip over the years, was both thrilled and nervous to be asked, and "was really happy" to find he and Lucas got along fine.[60] Jar Jar Binks never even came up. "Not at all," said McGruder. "Not even close."[61]

After two years of post-production Lucas did something he was loath to do: he made the rounds in Hollywood, looking for a studio to distribute the film. He found few takers; one studio's executives didn't even show up for the screening, a snub Lucas found particularly galling. "Isn't this their job?" he exploded. "Isn't their job at least to *see* movies?"[62] It was typical Hollywood, thought Lucas: afraid to take a chance on any movie that didn't look like most others. "It's because it's an all-black movie," he told Jon Stewart somewhat ruefully. "I showed it to all of them and they said, *Nooo, we don't know how to market a movie like this.*"[63] Lucas finally persuaded Fox to distribute the film, though the studio balked at paying any of the associated costs. Lucas would end up paying for everything out of his own pocket, investing $35 million in distribution—which even covered the costs of making prints—in addition to the $58 million he'd already spent making the film. No one could say Lucas didn't put his money where his mouth was.

The first previews in Atlanta seemed encouraging, with young people sounding especially enthusiastic. Lucas was pleased. "I'm making it for black teenagers," he told the *New York Times*. "They have a right to their history just like anybody else does. And they have a right to have it kind of Hollywoodized and aggrandized and made corny and wonderful just like anybody else does."[64] Ultimately, Lucas's corny approach would be seen as part of the problem. Reviews were brutal. "The movie is devoid of visceral thrills, drained of emotional energy, and head-scratchingly awful throughout," wrote a critic for *Mother Jones*. "[*Red Tails* is] one of the most appallingly bad war movies of recent memory." If Lucas cried racism, *Mother Jones* countered that the only bias Lucas was challenging was "the one against vapid filmmaking."[65] That one hurt.

Many critics applauded Lucas for having the temerity to openly address important themes and subject matter, but lamented that he had addressed them so *badly*. "Filled with clichés [and] one-dimensional characters," sniffed one English reviewer,[66] while the *New York Times* compared the film to a well-intentioned classroom lesson, the kind of pseudo-documentary Lucas had made for *Young Indiana Jones*. Even ILM was called out by several reviewers for producing overly digitized, unconvincing special effects that had elicited audible laughter from audiences during the dogfighting scenes.

Lucas was hurt and frustrated. He was also worried that the failure of his film might scare studios away from backing major motion pictures by black filmmakers—or featuring black characters—perpetually consigning them instead to low-budget productions. "I'm saying, if this doesn't work, there's a good chance you'll stay where you are quite a while," Lucas said, referring to African American filmmakers. "It'll be harder for you guys to break out of that [low-budget] mold."[67] While slightly condescending, it was an earnest and not entirely baseless concern. Lucas had intuitively tapped into a growing movement demanding greater diversity in film and pop culture. To his likely delight, two years after the premiere of *Red Tails*, a film written, produced, and directed by African Americans—and featuring a nearly all-black cast—would win the Academy Award for Best Picture. That film, *12 Years a Slave*, would also win an Oscar for Best Adapted Screenplay for John Ridley, who had written *Red Tails* for Lucas.

For now, however, the entire *Red Tails* experience had left Lucas bitter and angry. He'd dealt with Hollywood's insensitivity to artists before, watching helplessly as his own movies were hacked up by studio suits—but this was something seamier, a streak of racism in the system that left a bad taste in his mouth. "My girlfriend is black," he told *USA Today*, "and I've learned a lot about racism, including the fact that it hasn't gone away, especially in American business."[68] He'd made up his mind. "I'm retiring," he told the *New York Times* wearily. "I'm moving away from the business, from the company, from all this kind of stuff."[69]

Several weeks after the disastrous opening of *Red Tails*, Lucas picked up the phone and called Kathleen Kennedy, the old friend who'd produced all four *Indiana Jones* films among a thirty-year run of blockbusters. Apart from the *Indiana Jones* movies and the other films she'd produced for Spielberg—*E.T., Jurassic Park, Schindler's List, War of the Worlds*—there were also the features she and her husband, Frank Marshall, had produced with Spielberg as part of their Amblin Entertainment production company, including *Gremlins, Who Framed Roger Rabbit?,* and *Back to the Future.* Kennedy had great instincts for film, and an even keener business sense, but Lucas counted her among his inner circle of friends as well. He knew she was in New York putting the final touches on *Lincoln* for Spielberg, he told her, and he wanted to meet her in the city for lunch.

Kennedy assumed that Lucas merely wanted to catch up. But over lunch, Lucas wanted to talk business—namely his. "I suppose you've heard that I'm moving forward fairly aggressively to retire," he told her matter-of-factly.

Kennedy was stunned. "Actually, no," she said.

"I was surprised by that," Kennedy said later. "And part of me didn't really quite believe him." She listened patiently as Lucas explained that while he intended to maintain the title of chief executive and serve as co-chairman for at least one more year, he wanted someone to co-chair the company with him, with the ultimate goal of making that person the head of Lucasfilm. Kennedy started rolling though her Rolodex in her head, ticking off for Lucas the names of potential candidates to take over the company.

"No, no, no," Lucas said sharply. "I'm thinking about *you* doing this."

Kennedy never even blinked. "You know, George, I actually might really be interested in that."[70]

On June 1, Kennedy formally stepped in as the co-chair of Lucasfilm. It had been an easy decision to make. "I wanted to do this for him as well as myself," Kennedy said later, "because I knew how important it was to him."[71] Lucas would admit as much, announcing, "I've spent my life building Lucasfilm—and as I shift my focus into other directions, I wanted to make sure it was in the hands of someone equipped to carry my vision into the future."[72] One of their first mutual objectives, he told Kennedy, would be to "build this company up so it functions without me"—and to do that, he continued, "we need to do something to make it attractive." There was no more obvious way to make Lucasfilm attractive—and keep it functioning beyond Lucas's involvement—than to take advantage of the company's most visible and valuable commodity: *Star Wars*. While Lucas had insisted the story he had set out to tell was finished with *Return of the Jedi*, he admitted now he might have a few ideas for Episodes VII, VIII, and IX in a drawer in his office. "So I said [to Kennedy], 'Well, let's just do these movies.'"[73]

Lucas and Kennedy brought in Michael Arndt, the Oscar-winning writer of *Little Miss Sunshine*, to take a crack at writing Episode VII, based on Lucas's story ideas—really just a "brief synopsis," as Kennedy remembered, but enough to start. To provide Arndt with support and guidance on the *Star Wars* universe, they also brought in Lawrence Kasdan, who understood Lucas's rhythms and sensibilities perhaps better than any other screenwriter, to consult with Arndt as needed.

In August, Lucas made a trip to Orlando on the pretext of making a surprise appearance at a panel at *Star Wars* Celebration VI, but with another even more secret agenda in mind. Lucas took the stage at his panel to earsplitting applause, without giving the slightest indication that the gears of *Star Wars* were slowly turning again. Then, while in Orlando, Lucas took to lunch two other Celebration attendees—Mark Hamill and Carrie Fisher—to try to persuade them to reprise their roles in future *Star Wars* movies. Hamill was shocked. "The idea that he would say, 'We want to do VII, VIII, IX' was the farthest thing from my mind," said Hamill.[74] But he and Fisher both agreed to reprise their roles—and, after considerable discussion, so did Harrison Ford, largely on promises of a meaningful story arc that would close the book on Han Solo once and for all.

Kennedy was still settling into her new position when Lucas surprised her as well—by casually bringing up the idea of selling the company to Disney. "He started to lay out what he was thinking," said Kennedy, but he was intentionally vague: "It was a kind of, 'Down the road, this is something I've been thinking of.'"[75]

Only it wasn't down the road; a little more than a year since their breakfast conversation at the Brown Derby restaurant, Lucas was back in discussion with Iger about what a sale to Disney might look like. Lucas pointed out that he and *Star Wars* would always be indelibly linked, regardless of whether or not he still owned the company; his obituary, he told Iger irreverently, would inevitably begin with "*Star Wars* creator George Lucas..." Lucas, then, was determined to have it both ways, proposing to hand the entire company over to Iger and Disney while still maintaining complete control over *Star Wars*. He and his team had been taking care of the franchise for a long time, Lucas argued, and therefore knew better than anyone else how to market, license, and produce *Star Wars* films. "I think it would be wise to keep some of this [structure] intact," he told Iger firmly. "We need a few people to oversee the property, you know, who are just dedicated to doing that, so we're sure we get this right."[76]

But Iger wasn't biting. He was happy to offer Lucasfilm the same kind of limited autonomy he'd given to Marvel and Pixar, in which the company would remain essentially intact. But he wanted Lucas to understand in no uncertain terms that if Disney owned the company, it would be Disney—and not Lucasfilm—that would have final say over all things *Star Wars*. For the deal to succeed, it was Lucas, not Disney, who would have to pay the highest price: he was going to have to relinquish control. For Lucas—the rebel who had bucked the Hollywood system and fought for the right to control his own destiny—it was an almost unbearable price to pay.

After further discussion with Iger, Lucas eventually agreed to sell the company, but not before securing a small compromise: as part of the deal, Disney had to agree to take his story treatments and use them as the basis for any future films. It wasn't the full control he wanted, but at least it gave him some residual influence over the franchise he had created. But even that concession at times seemed more than Lucas could stomach; every time Iger asked Lucas for his story treatments, Lucas snappishly refused to hand them over until the deal was done. "Ultimately, you have to say, 'Look, I know what I'm doing.

Buying my stories is part of what the deal is,'" said Lucas. "I mean, I could've said, 'Fine, well, I'll just sell the company to somebody else.'" Iger was just going to have to trust him.

As talks continued, Kennedy could see the conflict openly in Lucas's face. Before she headed out the door each Friday to fly back home to Los Angeles, Kennedy would stick her head into Lucas's office to see how he was doing. Some days, he seemed content and ready to move on; other days, he seemed uncertain. "I'm sure he paused periodically to question whether he was really ready to walk away," said Kennedy. Still, Lucas thought the partnership with Disney made sense and, in a way, brought his own life full circle; he had, after all, been at Disneyland on its opening day in 1955, and in the 1980s had proudly brought *Star Wars* into the Disney parks with the opening of the Star Tours attraction. At that time he had praised Disney for its commitment to quality, saying, "When I did something, I've always wanted to make sure it was done right and it was maintained right, operated correctly...and this is the only place in the world like that."[77] Only Disney truly appreciated, as Lucas did, the benefits of being in complete control of a universe.

By fall, Iger finally provided Lucas with a broad description of the terms of the deal—which included the use of Lucas's story outlines. Lucas, protective to the very end, would hand them over only after Iger signed an agreement limiting the number of people at Disney who could read them. Iger was delighted with what Lucas gave him—or so he said publicly. "From a storytelling perspective, they had a lot of potential," Iger said enigmatically. It wouldn't be the last time Lucas would squabble with Disney over his *Star Wars* story treatments.

On October 30, 2012, with cameras rolling to capture the occasion, George Lucas and Walt Disney Company president Bob Iger signed the agreement selling Lucasfilm to Disney for a staggering $4.05 billion—half in cash, the other half in nearly 40 million shares of Disney stock. That massive amount of money would go to Lucasfilm's sole stockholder: George Lucas. With the stroke of a pen, Lucas became one of Disney's biggest shareholders, owning 2 percent of

Disney's current shares; only the Steven P. Jobs Trust, which had sold the company Pixar—"my company," Lucas still calls it—owns more.

Lucas's hand had been steady as he signed the papers, but it had been an emotional moment. "He was saying goodbye," said Iger. Lucas promptly flew back to San Francisco to say his farewells to the staff—now Kennedy's staff—at Lucasfilm, then issued a carefully worded statement to the media. "It is now time for me to pass *Star Wars* on to a new generation of filmmakers," Lucas said. "I'm confident that with Lucasfilm under the leadership of Kathleen Kennedy, and having a new home within the Disney organization, *Star Wars* will certainly live on and flourish for many generations to come."[78]

That was a certainty. At the same time it had announced its acquisition of Lucasfilm, Disney had also promised the world another *Star Wars* movie by Christmas of 2015. They could thank George Lucas for that. With all the pieces Lucas had put in place, Kennedy immediately put Episode VII into pre-production, bringing in J. J. Abrams to direct, and assigning script duties entirely to Lawrence Kasdan. And in a way, things almost seemed the same, as Lucas would still sit in on the story sessions with Kasdan and his writing team at Disney, trying to explain the rules of the universe he'd created.

For the most part, though, Lucasfilm and *Star Wars* were moving on without Lucas. With his business affairs in order, Lucasfilm in Kathleen Kennedy's capable hands, and no more movies to make, Lucas was prepared to move on to the next major milestone, this one in his personal life. After dating her for seven years, Lucas had proposed to Hobson in January 2013. They were ready to spend the rest of their lives together, and were making plans to have a family; already, a surrogate was carrying a child for them, due in August. The wedding was arranged to take place a couple of months before that.

On Saturday, June 22, Lucas—looking very much like a man without a worry in the world—wed Mellody Hobson at Skywalker Ranch, under one of those impossibly blue and warm California skies. Hobson was walked down the aisle by one of her mentors, former senator Bill Bradley, while Lucas waited, beaming, with his twenty-year-old son, Jett, at his side, serving as his best man. Amanda and Katie stood off to the other side, serving as bridesmaids. Journalist Bill Moyers, a former Baptist minister, officiated the ceremony. "It takes only one person to have met the love of your life," Moyers said touchingly.[79] Eyes were dabbed all around.

It was a power wedding in every sense of the word. Among the two hundred guests in attendance were Harrison Ford, Steven Spielberg, Oprah Winfrey, Jeffrey Katzenberg, Robert De Niro, Samuel L. Jackson, Ron Howard, and Quincy Jones—with music provided by Van Morrison and Janelle Monáe. There were affectionate jokes that Hobson was one of the lower-profile people at her own wedding. A week later, however, at a second reception in Hobson's hometown of Chicago, it was Lucas who could be said to have had one of the lower profiles, as the event—at Chicago's Promontory Point, jutting out into Lake Michigan—bustled with the political elite: a former congressman, a mayor and a former mayor, a university president, even a U.S. secretary of commerce. And only Hobson could have arranged for a twenty-two-piece wedding band with rock star Prince as the front man.

Yet, despite the heavy hitters in their widening circle of friends, Lucas remained as unaffected as usual. He would wear a tuxedo for Hobson, who regularly brought him to receptions and conferences and other formal social events, but left on his own, he would return to the comfortable jeans, button-up shirt, and well-worn white tennis shoes. There would be expensive restaurants, certainly, but Lucas still liked picking up drive-thru from Taco Bell, or sitting down at Sizzler. "George says to me, 'We are normal,'" said Hobson. "And we are. We go to movies every weekend. He likes to have the same experience that others do, so we don't watch in a screening room closed off to the world. We go to the local theater in whatever city we are in."[80]

And he was about to experience parenting a young one again, too. On August 9, 2013—almost seven weeks after their wedding—Lucas and Hobson's surrogate delivered a baby girl they named Everest

Hobson Lucas, after the son of a close friend. It was Lucas's first biological child. At age sixty-nine, he was a father again.

While Lucas had long been one of the world's most successful filmmakers, with the sale of Lucasfilm he had also become very, very rich.
By 2015, *Forbes* would list him at number ninety-four on its list of the
four hundred wealthiest Americans, with an estimated worth of $5
billion.[81] Lucas found it all just a bit embarrassing. "I've never been
that much of a money guy," Lucas told *Businessweek*. "I'm more of a
film guy, and most of the money I've made is in defense of trying to
keep creative control of my movies."[82]

Lucas vowed to donate the bulk of his wealth to charity; in 2010
he had signed the Giving Pledge, an effort by billionaires Warren Buffett and Bill Gates to encourage wealthy Americans "to commit to giving the majority of their wealth to the philanthropic causes and
charitable organizations of their choice." For Lucas, his cause of choice
would always be education. "I am donating the majority of my wealth
to improving education," he promised. "It is the key to the survival of
the human race."[83]

Already Lucas had made significant donations to the USC School
of Cinematic Arts, donating $175 million in 2006 for a complete over-
haul of the campus buildings he'd built or improved with an earlier
contribution in the 1980s. In 2014 he would endow three chairs in the
department, and in 2015 he and Hobson would donate another $10
million to the school to create the George Lucas Foundation Endowed
Student Support Fund for Diversity, providing financial support for
black and Hispanic students attending film school. Another $25 mil-
lion would go to the University of Chicago Laboratory Schools to
develop and build a new arts hall, which Lucas required be named for
the influential black photographer and filmmaker Gordon Parks. And
in 2014 Lucas would donate $500,000 to the Norman Rockwell
Museum in Stockbridge, Massachusetts, to help the museum develop
interactive online tools.

They could probably have started by digitizing Lucas's own collection; Lucas owned more than fifty Rockwell paintings, hanging them on the walls at Skywalker and lending them to museums. In 2010, in fact, he and Spielberg had lent the Smithsonian American Art Museum nearly sixty of their own Rockwell paintings for what became an enormously popular exhibit. It was his Rockwell paintings, in part, that had inspired what Lucas hoped would be one of his legacy projects: a museum in which he could show and share all the art, animation cels, comic pages, movie posters, props, memorabilia — including most of his *Star Wars* collection — and countless other works of art and artifacts he'd collected over the past five decades. "I don't have enough walls," he explained, "which is why I want to build a museum."[84]

He thought he knew exactly where to put it. On the grounds of the Presidio near Crissy Field, stood an abandoned 93,000-square-foot former commissary that had briefly been occupied by a sporting goods store but now stood vacant. The Presidio Trust, the same board that had granted Lucas permission to develop his Letterman Digital Center onsite, was now accepting proposals for use of the commissary. Lucas submitted a proposal to spend $700 million to develop eight acres at Crissy Field, including turning the abandoned commissary into the George Lucas Museum of Narrative Art. Lucas and Hobson had assembled a powerful slate of backers that included U.S. senator Dianne Feinstein, House minority leader Nancy Pelosi, California governor Jerry Brown, and the cofounders of Twitter and YouTube. Its approval seemed inevitable.

It wasn't. In February 2014, Lucas was stunned to learn that the Presidio Trust had rejected his proposal outright. Some thought the Presidio Trust had it in for Lucas, with whispered accusations that he was either too rich or too liberal or too successful to prevail with the politically charged trust — a campaign that continued to escalate until the National Park Service stepped in to explain coolly that "the museum does not merit one of the most important sites in the entire Presidio."[85] The trust offered to work with Lucas to find a more suitable site. Lucas agreed, and the conversation dragged on for another eight weeks or so — just long enough for Hobson to grow tired of the "doodling around." If the trust wasn't able to locate the museum in Lucas's hometown, then why not hers? Hobson, a longtime friend of Chicago mayor Rahm Emanuel, offered to make a phone call. "Don't worry," she told her husband. "I'll talk to the mayor. I'm sure he'll love it."[86]

Emanuel was definitely interested. After putting together a task force to look for suitable locations, Emanuel thought he'd found Lucas the ideal site: a seventeen-acre parking lot on the lakefront between Soldier Field and McCormick Place, and practically within the shadow of the planetarium. Furthermore, if Lucas would stick with his pledge to pay for all costs associated with the museum, Emanuel offered to rent the site to Lucas for one dollar a year. Lucas agreed that the site was ideal and hired the Chinese architect Ma Yansong to begin working on concept drawings for the museum, including paintings showing what it would look like sitting on the lakefront site. Yansong came up with a futuristic design that looked to some like a giant amoeba oozing out onto the lakeshore; others thought it looked like Jabba the Hutt. Whatever it was, it wasn't helping Lucas make his case with the Chicago community. Politics, too, were starting to creep into the discussion — this was Chicago, after all — with some alleging that the land was Emanuel's payback to Hobson for donating money to his mayoral campaign, an accusation both parties ignored.[87]

Back in San Francisco, mayor Ed Lee was scouring *his* waterfront for an alternative site to offer Lucas, hoping to woo him back to his hometown. But Lucas had vowed to stick with Emanuel and Chicago for the long haul. The Chicago City Council's zoning committee okayed the project, and Lucas was ready to move forward, when the nonprofit Friends of the Parks — arguing that a museum was an inappropriate use of lakefront property — filed a complaint in federal court formally objecting to the project. The proposal ground to a halt, and Emanuel went scouting for other more expensive sites, which also bogged down in mudslinging. Lucas, while refusing to back down, threw up his hands in frustration. It was mind-boggling. He couldn't give away a museum. "Doing this museum, I've realized that most cities don't want museums, they don't really care about them," Lucas said during an interview with the *Washington Post*. "You know, it's too esoteric for most people, and they don't see them as educational institutions."[88] In May 2016, Hobson, once again tired of the foot-dragging, issued a blistering press release in which she accused Friends of the Parks of hijacking the process "in order to preserve a parking lot," and warned that she and Lucas were "now seriously pursuing locations outside of Chicago."[89]

By late June, Lucas decided he was done fighting. "No one benefits from [Friends of the Parks'] seemingly unending litigation to preserve a parking lot," he echoed wearily.[90]

He will take his museum elsewhere, preferably back to San Francisco, where Mayor Lee has offered a prime piece of waterfront property—an island, actually—directly between San Francisco and Oakland. If it's not located there, Los Angeles mayor Eric Garcetti has also enthusiastically offered the museum a home in southern California. Whether that is just a bit too close to Hollywood for Lucas's tastes remains to be seen. As of July 2016, he has yet to make a decision.

In January 2015, Lucas surprised everyone by releasing, through the Disney distribution machine, the computer-animated musical fantasy *Strange Magic*. The movie, Lucas's take on Shakespeare's *Midsummer Night's Dream*, was for his daughters, he said, and one he'd been trying to make for years. With a classic rock and roll sound track behind it— the title was lifted from an ELO song—it was essentially *American Graffiti* with fairies and bog creatures and a fairy-tale lesson about not judging others by how they look. Released with little fanfare—though with a poster reminding audiences that it was "FROM THE MIND OF GEORGE LUCAS"—*Strange Magic* opened to mixed reviews and tanked within two weeks.

Lucas scarcely seemed to care. He was much more interested in being a doting father than in promoting films at this point, wheeling Everest around dutifully in a stroller or taking her to Disneyland. "By the time she's five, she'll have her own career going and being in school and talking about her friends and her homework," Lucas said. "The fun, goofy time will fall into place in reality, as opposed to right now, [when] she doesn't have much else to do but hang out with her father."[91]

Meanwhile, anticipation was running high for Episode VII. So far, Iger, Kennedy, and Abrams had shown that they too knew a thing or two about promoting *Star Wars*. When the title of the film was announced in November 2014 as *Star Wars: The Force Awakens*, fans parsed it with the same obsessive care with which they'd analyzed the titles *The Phantom Menace* and *Revenge of the Jedi*. Abrams and Kennedy carefully doled out only the smallest, most tantalizing nuggets of information, sparking fan interest into a frenzy as the film's December 2015 release date approached. As usual, it seemed everyone was excited about *Star Wars*.

Lucas wasn't one of them. Publicly he put up a good front, telling *USA Today* that he was looking forward to seeing a *Star Wars* film in a movie theater with an audience, without knowing what was going to happen first. Lucas wouldn't ever quite get the full crowd experience; he would end up seeing the film at a private viewing with Kennedy and others in early December. He didn't immediately make his views on the movie known; it was left to Kennedy to inform reporters afterward that Lucas had seen the movie and "he really liked it"—a tepid response to be sure.[92] When he was asked to clarify, Lucas's reply was deliberately narrow. "I think the fans are going to love it," he said. "It's very much the kind of movie they've been looking for."[93] But it clearly wasn't the kind of movie George Lucas had been looking for.

Much to Lucas's irritation, Disney had disregarded the story treatments he had given them in 2012—the ones that Iger had claimed "had a lot of potential"—and had gone instead in their own direction, using a script with story elements by Kasdan, Arndt, and Abrams, but none by Lucas. "They decided they didn't want to use those stories, they decided they were gonna go do their own thing," Lucas complained to journalist Charlie Rose in an interview that ran on Christmas Day 2015.[94] Furthermore, apart from those few early story sessions in 2012, Lucas hadn't been involved in *The Force Awakens* at all. Kennedy, caught between her old boss and her new masters at Disney, did her best to be understanding. "If there's one thing I've learned about [George] it's that he's never ever held back," she said. "Having him 100 percent on board is up to him and he can't do that unless he's running everything."[95]

It's telling that Lucas would compare tearing himself away from *Star Wars* with divorce; his 1983 divorce from Marcia, and its aftermath, had been one of the most miserable experiences of his life, mentally, physically, and emotionally. Watching *The Force Awakens*, he said, was "an awkward reality," like attending the wedding of your grown child after you've been divorced. "I gotta go to the wedding," Lucas said. "My ex will be there, my new wife will be there, but I'm going to have to take a very deep breath and be a good person and sit through it and just enjoy the moment, because it is what it is and it's a conscious decision that I made."[96]

Lucas would always resent that Disney had permitted Abrams to make a movie "for the fans." "They wanted to do a retro movie," said Lucas. "I don't like that." To him, that was just as bad as knuckling under to bullying from studio executives who didn't know a thing about film but still demanded arbitrary cuts to reduce a movie's running time. Regardless of what people thought of the prequels, they could never say Lucas hadn't been faithful to his own vision for *Star Wars*. It was no wonder, said Lucas, that the people at Disney "weren't that keen to have me involved....If I get in there, I'm just going to cause trouble, because they're not going to do what I want them to do. And I don't have the control to do that anymore, and all I would do is muck everything up. And so I said, 'Okay, I will go my way, and I'll let them go their way.'"[97]

And so George Lucas had given up control. But that didn't mean he was ever going to be happy about it.

At age seventy-two, George Lucas is retired, enjoying life, and especially enjoying being a husband and a father. He still makes his home

at the house on Park Way, and despite the rumors, he still owns
Skywalker Ranch—all 6,100 acres of it now—as well as Skywalker
Sound, which he's happy to make available to Disney, or any other
studio, to use for a fee. He still dresses in the familiar jeans and flan-
nel shirts, with white running shoes; the suits come out only for special events. He's a devoted husband, remains a proud father to his
three grown children, and is happy spending most of his day trailing
along after Everest. While he stays off social media—the venomous
online comments and trolling in the wake of the release of *The Phantom Menace* convinced him to abandon the Internet for good—he's
hardly a recluse: he travels widely, attends charity events, and has no
problem obliging autograph requests.

Still, he's looking for things to do. He still hopes to build his
museum in San Francisco or Oakland or Los Angeles, or wherever
anyone who values such things will have it. If and when the museum is
ever built, you can bet Lucas will be intimately involved in its layout,
design, color scheme, and lighting. As with his movies, Lucas will
never be entirely happy with a building project unless he can put his
hands on as much of it as possible.

Like any good parent, Lucas finally saw *Star Wars* leave the house
without him; *The Force Awakens* shattered nearly every box office
record on its release in December 2015, steadily climbing its way past
$2 billion in worldwide revenues. Episode VIII—still unnamed in
mid-2016—was scheduled for 2017, with Episode IX to follow in
2019. In the meantime, Disney also announced a number of spin-offs,
including *Rogue One,* set just before Episode IV, and movies featuring
Han Solo and Boba Fett. The *Star Wars* universe, born of Lucas's sweat
and frustration and scrawled onto his remarkably low-tech notepads in
pencil, seemed poised to exist in perpetuity, passed down from generation to generation into the hands of new writers and filmmakers for
them to embrace and then make their own. *Star Wars* remained as
timeless as the imagination, a mythology permanently woven into the
culture.

Lucas's involvement with his other beloved franchise, however, seems secure—at least for now. With Disney willingly in his corner, Steven Spielberg announced he wanted to bring back Indiana Jones for a fifth time—and that he intended to bring along not only Harrison Ford but also George Lucas for Dr. Jones's next adventure. "George is going to be an executive producer on it with me," said Spielberg during the promotion of *The BFG*—and then, in a not-so-subtle dig at Disney, explained that "I would never make an Indiana Jones film without George Lucas. That'd be insane."[98] Take that, *Force Awakens*.

Lucas still hoped, too, to return to making the kinds of small, personal, arty films he'd been promising to make his entire career—documentaries, tone poems, avant-garde ramblings, "whatever I want to do," said Lucas, "regardless of whether it has any commercial potential or not."[99] His personal films are his "real gift," said Coppola affectionately.[100] "I still hope that he made so much money out of [*Star Wars*] that he will just make some little movies. He promises me that he will."[101] Added Steven Spielberg, "We're still waiting, George!"[102]

Lucas in his early seventies was reflective, though good-natured, about his legacy as a filmmaker—and as a human being. He hoped to be remembered first and foremost as a great dad. After that? "I'll probably be forgotten completely," he said, only half-joking. "I hope I'll be remembered as one of the pioneers of digital cinema. In the long run, that's probably all it will come down to." Then, with a twinkle, he added, "They might remember me as the maker of some of those esoteric twentieth-century science fiction movies."[103]

More likely he would be remembered as the fiercely independent creator of some of cinema's most memorable and profitable films, as well as some of pop culture's most iconic characters. Lucas changed the way audiences watched—and rewatched—movies; he demolished then reinvented the way movies were made, marketed, and merchandised. He changed the way fans embraced and *adored* not just movies and characters and actors but directors, producers, and composers—all of whom Lucas made active and visible collaborators on his films. He redefined the way movie studios financed, distributed, and controlled—and then, ultimately, *didn't* control—the art of filmmaking.

Lucas also unapologetically invested in what he believed in the most: himself. As a result, the film empire he created would empower not just him but other, similar-minded filmmakers to produce movies exactly as they envisioned them, without a studio imposing its own priorities, grousing about budgets, or micromanaging the process. George Lucas—the small-town son of the owner of a stationery store—had said no to the family business then built a cinematic empire based on his own uncompromising vision of the film industry not as it was, but as he thought it *should* be. Much of that vision lay in the possibilities presented by new technology—technologies Lucas developed with his own money—an inherent ability to hire the right people, and a preternatural knack for asking the right questions. "I can't help feeling that George Lucas has never been fully appreciated by the industry for his remarkable innovations," said director Peter Jackson. "He is the Thomas Edison of the modern film industry."[104]

Lucas, mellowed with age, easily dismissed such sentiments. He knew what he'd done. He knew his place, and he seemed comfortable with it. When asked by interviewer Charlie Rose in December 2015 what he thought the first line of his obituary might say, Lucas gave perhaps the best summation of his lengthy career, or at least the kind of response one could expect from someone at once so modest and audacious, in two single-syllable words.

"I *tried*," he said, laughing.

Acknowledgments

While writing, almost by definition, is a lonely craft—ultimately, it's just you and the page and a closed door—biographers, simply by the nature of our work, still rely on the assistance and generosity of others. As I researched, wrote, and worked on this project over the last three years, it was my pleasure to speak with, spend time with, and get to know many wonderful people. This book is all the better for it, as am I.

The unauthorized nature of this project made it very difficult to get family, friends, coworkers, and collaborators to sit for an interview, so I'm especially grateful to those who took the time to speak with me. My thanks, then, to Randal Kleiser, John Korty, Gary Kurtz, Paul Golding, and Larry Mirkin, who were willing to go on the record, and to Justin Bozung and Mani Perezcarro, who helped me coordinate several of those interviews. The fearless Ken Plume was very helpful as well, and I valued his guidance and conversation highly.

Anyone who writes history or biography understands how invaluable archivists and librarians are to our work—and this project was no exception. My thanks to the countless librarians and archivists at the Library of Congress, the Montgomery County Public Library, the Stanislaus County Library, the Margaret Herrick Library at the Academy of Motion Picture Arts and Sciences, Warner and Universal Studios, and the University of Southern California. Special thanks go to Barbara

Alexander and Claude Zachary for their help with researching Modesto and the USC film department, respectively, and to blogger-journalist Leo Adam Biga for his research on *American Graffiti*.

At Little, Brown, I couldn't have asked for a better or more patient editor than John Parsley, whose excitement for this project was infectious and, frankly, uplifting as the piles of research materials to slog through got deeper and deeper on my desk. His keen ear for clunkers and sharp red pencil always made this book better — and usually made me slap my forehead and exclaim, "Of course! Why didn't *I* think of saying it that way?" His quiet manner of speaking also masked a loud enthusiasm for All Things George Lucas — and I'm so pleased that he was always happy to indulge me in long debates about what Imperial engineers could *possibly* have been thinking when they came up with AT-ATs.

I'm also grateful to the equally patient Reagan Arthur at Little, Brown, who helped keep everything on track and on time, even when I made things exciting for her. I also appreciate the support and enthusiasm of Malin von Euler-Hogan, Karen Landry, and Amanda Heller, the world's most impressive copyeditor, who not only had to deal with my pet phrases and keep all my endnotes in order but also had to deal with terms such as *Kashyyyk* and *sarlacc*. If you spot any further errors, they're mine, not hers.

My agent, Jonathan Lyons, has been at my side — and had my back — for the better part of a decade now, and was this project's biggest supporter, and loudest cheerleader, when it was still little more than a long email between the two of us. There were times I made him work harder than I meant to, but his response was always the same: "Don't worry about it." He's smart, kind, and promptly responds to my weird emails and even weirder phone calls — and I thank his wife, Cameron, and his boys, Roan, Ilan, and Finn, for sharing him with me.

As always, I am grateful for the many family members, friends, and colleagues who always took the time to ask how the project was going, offered their support and excitement, and were understanding when dinners were missed or invitations were refused. My thanks, in particular, to James McGrath Morris, Kitty Kelley, Scott Phillips, Marron and Mike Nelson, Mike and Cassie Knapp, Marc and Kathy Nelligan, Jack and Mindy Shaw, Raice and Liselle McLeod, and Bill and Terrie Crawley. This project would also not have been possible without the support and patience of Sidney Katz, Lisa Mandel-Trupp, Lindsay Hoffman, and Jackie Hawksford. I could also always count on the love and support of my parents, Larry Jones and Elaine and Wayne Miller, and of my brother, Cris, who always let me be Han when we played with our Kenner *Star Wars* figures, even though he's still cooler than me to this day.

Finally, none of what you've got in your hands today would have happened without the support, love, and enthusiasm of my wife, Barb, and our daughter, Madi, who spent the last three years rooting for me and urging me on. If there's anyone who's worked as hard or harder on this project, it's Barb—the *real* Dr. Jones—who let me spread out my mess across our dining room table for more than two years; went to dinners and walked our dog, Grayson, by herself; and always came to check on me at two in the morning. She's the real hero of this project. And she did it all without a lightsaber.

—*Damascus, Maryland, July 2016*

Notes

Prologue: Out of Control

1. "'Star Wars' Star Is on Cloud Nine," *Independent* (Long Beach, Calif.), June 10, 1977.
2. J. W. Rinzler, *The Making of Star Wars: The Definitive Story Behind the Original Film* (New York: Del Rey, 2007), 160 (hereafter *MOSW*).
3. *MOSW*, 146.
4. *MOSW*, 143.
5. Kerry O'Quinn, "The George Lucas Saga," *Starlog*, reprinted in Sally Kline, ed., *George Lucas: Interviews* (Jackson: University Press of Mississippi, 1999), 104 (hereafter Kline, *GL Interviews*).
6. *GL Interviews*, xiv.
7. Robert Watts, quoted in *MOSW*, 151.
8. *MOSW*, 160.

Chapter 1: Scrawny Little Devil

1. Joanne Williams, "Inside George Lucas: Success Allows 'Little Movie' Freedom," *Modesto Bee*, June 1, 1980.
2. Jean Vallely, "'The Empire Strikes Back' and So Does George Lucas," *Rolling Stone*, June 12, 1980.
3. Williams, "Inside George Lucas."
4. *Biography: George Lucas: Creating an Empire*, A&E Television, 2002 (hereafter *Creating an Empire*).
5. "The Modesto Arch," Historic Modesto website, http://www.historicmodesto.com/thearch.html.
6. See Fifteenth Census of the United States, 1930, for Modesto City, Calif., sheet 7B.

7. "George Lucas Sr. Story Rivals Son's Film Saga," *Modesto Bee,* January 30, 1976.

8. "Play Presented by High School Class to Capacity House," *Modesto Bee and News-Herald,* December 8, 1930.

9. "Dorothy Bomberger and George Lucas Marry at Methodist Church," *Modesto Bee and News-Herald,* August 4, 1933.

10. "George Lucas Sr. Story Rivals Son's Film Saga."

11. Karyn Hunt, "Business Leader G. W. Lucas Dies," *Modesto Bee,* December 19, 1991.

12. "Dorothy Bomberger and George Lucas Marry at Methodist Church." See also "Dorothy Bomberger and George Lucas to Wed: Invitations in Mails," *Modesto Bee and News-Herald,* July 23, 1933; and "Plan Wedding," *Modesto Bee and News-Herald,* July 24, 1933.

13. See "Club's Speaker Lauds Roosevelt," *Fresno Bee,* December 19, 1933.

14. See "Dorothy B. Lucas Dead at 75," *Modesto Bee,* March 12, 1989.

15. "Two Stationery Stores Change Hands Here," *Modesto Bee and News-Herald,* January 26, 1949.

16. "George Lucas Sr. Story Rivals Son's Film Saga."

17. L. M. Morris advertisement, *Modesto Bee and News-Herald,* November 30, 1934.

18. See "Morris Rites Will Be Tomorrow," *Modesto Bee and News-Herald,* February 4, 1949.

19. Dale Pollock, *Skywalking: The Life and Films of George Lucas,* updated ed. (New York: Da Capo Press, 1999), 13.

20. "George Lucas Sr. Story Rivals Son's Film Saga."

21. Pollock, *Skywalking,* 14.

22. Ibid.

23. Ibid.

24. *Omnibus Special Edition: George Lucas: Flying Solo,* BBC Television, 1997 (hereafter *Flying Solo*).

25. Pollock, *Skywalking,* 15.

26. Gerald Clarke, "I've Got to Get My Life Back Again," *Time,* May 23, 1983.

27. *Creating an Empire.*

28. *Flying Solo.*

29. Pollock, *Skywalking,* 15.

30. "Two Stationery Stores Change Hands Here"; "Morris Rites Will Be Tomorrow."

31. "George Lucas Sr. Story Rivals Son's Film Saga."

32. Williams, "Inside George Lucas."

33. *Creating an Empire.*

34. Ibid.

35. Pollock, *Skywalking,* 37.

36. Ibid., 19.

37. Denise Worrell, *Icons: Intimate Portraits* (New York: Atlantic Monthly Press, 1989), 286.

38. *Flying Solo.*
39. Pollock, *Skywalking,* 16.
40. *Creating an Empire.*
41. Alan Arnold, *Once Upon a Galaxy: A Journal of the Making of The Empire Strikes Back* (New York: Ballantine, 1980), 219.
42. "George Lucas: A Life Making Movies," Academy of Achievement interview, June 19, 1999, http://www.achievement.org/autodoc/page/luc0int-1 (hereafter "GL: A Life Making Movies").
43. Pollock, *Skywalking,* 15.
44. Clarke, "I've Got to Get My Life Back Again."
45. Pollock, *Skywalking,* 37, 39.
46. Ibid., 11. For a variation on this story, see Peter Biskind, *Easy Riders, Raging Bulls: How the Sex-Drugs-and-Rock 'n' Roll Generation Saved Hollywood* (New York: Simon & Schuster, 1998), 37.
47. *Creating an Empire.*
48. Arnold, *Once Upon a Galaxy,* 189.
49. Pollock, *Skywalking,* 20.
50. Arnold, *Once Upon a Galaxy,* 189–90.
51. Pollock, *Skywalking,* 20.
52. Arnold, *Once Upon a Galaxy,* 189–90.
53. Jess Cagle, "Director: So, What's the Deal with Leia's Hair?" *Time,* April 29, 2002.
54. Pollock, *Skywalking,* 22.
55. *Creating an Empire.*
56. Pollock, *Skywalking,* 22.
57. "GL: A Life Making Movies."
58. Arnold, *Once Upon a Galaxy,* 220.
59. Pollock, *Skywalking,* 18.
60. *Creating an Empire.*
61. Clarke, "I've Got to Get My Life Back Again."
62. Arnold, *Once Upon a Galaxy,* 221.
63. Pollock, *Skywalking,* 18.
64. Arnold, *Once Upon a Galaxy,* 220.
65. *Creating an Empire.*
66. Donald Ault, ed., *Carl Barks: Conversations* (Jackson: University Press of Mississippi, 2003), 130.
67. Arnold, *Once Upon a Galaxy,* 221.
68. Virginia Mecklenberg and Todd McCarthy, *Telling Stories: Norman Rockwell, from the Collections of George Lucas and Steven Spielberg* (New York: Abrams, 2010), 20.
69. Ibid., 18.
70. Marcus Hearn, *The Cinema of George Lucas* (New York: Abrams, 2005), 10–11 (hereafter *COGL*).
71. John Baxter, *George Lucas: A Biography* (London: HarperCollins Entertainment, 1999), 24–25.

72. Worrel, *Icons,* 286.

73. Clarke, "I've Got to Get My Life Back Again."

74. Lucas has often said that the only channel available in Modesto was KRON, an NBC affiliate from San Francisco. *Have Gun, Will Travel,* however, was on CBS, not NBC. To watch *Have Gun, Will Travel*—as Lucas remembers doing—he would have been tuned to KPIX, a CBS affiliate broadcasting out of San Francisco.

75. While Lucas recalls seeing the Flash Gordon serials on a show called *Adventure Theater,* which he and countless other sources have reported as airing on KRON each evening at 6 p.m., there may be some confusion. *Adventure Theater* didn't premiere on KRON until 1960—and even then, it aired at 2:30 in the afternoon. (At 6 p.m., KRON was broadcasting *Fireman Frank.*) Lucas certainly *could* have seen Flash on *Adventure Theater* in 1960; in 1955, however, a better bet is probably KTVU from Stockton, which was broadcasting a show called *Super Serial* each evening at 6. He may also be confusing *Adventure Theater* with *Science Fiction Theater,* which aired nightly at 7 p.m. on KRON in 1955. Also adding to the possible confusion: in 1956, NBC aired its own *Adventure Theater,* a new thirteen-part police anthology series. Regardless, the Flash Gordon serials were broadcast on a channel available in Modesto, and Lucas watched them.

76. Arnold, *Once Upon a Galaxy,* 220.

77. Ibid., 220–21.

78. "GL: A Life Making Movies."

79. *COGL,* 61.

80. Worrell, *Icons,* 285.

81. *COGL,* 11.

82. Pollock, *Skywalking,* 21.

83. "Newspaper for Juniors Is Published by Two Boys," *Modesto Bee and News-Herald,* August 18, 1955.

84. Ibid.

85. Ibid.

86. Ibid.

87. Pollock, *Skywalking,* 20.

88. Clarke, "I've Got to Get My Life Back Again."

89. Pollock, *Skywalking,* 37.

90. Ibid., 23.

91. *Creating an Empire.*

92. While Pollock (*Skywalking*) says that Lucas attended an Elvis concert in San Francisco "right after" the *Sullivan* appearance, Presley wasn't scheduled to be in northern California until nearly a year later.

93. Stephen Farber, "George Lucas: The Stinky Kid Hits the Big Time," *Film Quarterly* 27, no. 3 (Spring 1974): 2–9.

94. *Creating an Empire.*

95. *COGL,* 12.

96. "GL: A Life Making Movies."

97. "An Interview with George Lucas," Milken Institute Global Conference, April 30, 2012, http://www.milkeninstitute.org/events/conferences/global-conference/2012/panel-detail/3586 (hereafter Milken).
98. *COGL*, 12.
99. *Flying Solo.*
100. Pollock, *Skywalking*, 24.
101. *Flying Solo.*
102. Worrell, *Icons*, 285–86.
103. *COGL*, 12.
104. Worrell, *Icons*, 285–86.
105. *COGL*, 12.
106. Pollock, *Skywalking*, 27.
107. "Faros Car Club Members Talk About *American Graffiti* and Cruising," *Modesto News* video, June 7, 2014, http://www.youtube.com/watch?v=rrQiJ3RYODM.
108. Pollock, *Skywalking*, 27.
109. *Creating an Empire.*
110. Milken.
111. *Creating an Empire.*
112. Pollock, *Skywalking*, 29.
113. Ibid.
114. "George Lucas Talks to the *Bee*'s Marijke Rowland," video, *Modesto Bee*, June 7, 2013, http://www.modbee.com/welcome_page/?shf=/2013/06/07/2752579_video-george-lucas-talks-to-the.html.
115. Pollock, *Skywalking*, 25.
116. Richard Heseltine, "The Real American Graffiti Artist," *Motor Sport*, June 2009.
117. "George Lucas–Allen Grant," Modesto CruiseRoute, YouTube video, July 13, 2012, http://www.youtube.com/watch?v=KMxhdiVQv0w.
118. As reported faithfully in the *Modesto Bee* throughout 1961 and 1962. See, for example, "Modesto Sports Car Club Wins Contest," *Modesto Bee and News-Herald*, March 20, 1961.
119. Pollock, *Skywalking*, 24.
120. Ibid., 46.
121. "History and Today," Canyon Cinema website, http://www.canyoncinema.com/about/history.
122. *COGL*, 16.
123. Pollock, *Skywalking*, 27.
124. Jason Walsh, "Episode III: A New Hack," *Pacific Sun*, February 12–18, 2010.
125. *COGL*, 13.
126. Pollock, *Skywalking*, 38.
127. John Seabrook, "Why the Force Is Still with Us," *The New Yorker*, January 6, 1997.
128. All accounts of the accident are vague and, at times, conflicting, especially as the story has been spun, misreported, and made more dramatic in the fifty

years since the incident. See "DHS Student Is Injured Seriously in Car Crash," *Modesto Bee and News-Herald,* June 13, 1962; Pollock, *Skywalking,* xiii–xvi; and Baxter, *George Lucas,* 38; as well as a seriously retconned version of events in Mark Cotta Vaz and Shinji Hata, *From Star Wars to Indiana Jones: The Best of the Lucasfilm Archives* (San Francisco: Chronicle, 1994).

Chapter 2: Geeks and Nerds

1. *Creating an Empire.*
2. Pollock, *Skywalking,* xv.
3. *Creating an Empire.*
4. Williams, "Inside George Lucas."
5. "GL: A Life Making Movies."
6. *Creating an Empire.*
7. *COGL,* 13.
8. Arnold, *Once Upon a Galaxy,* 187.
9. Ibid.
10. "GL: A Life Making Movies."
11. Williams, "Inside George Lucas."
12. Pollock, *Skywalking,* 34–35.
13. *Creating an Empire.*
14. *COGL,* 13.
15. George Lucas interviewed on *CBS This Morning,* July 2013.
16. Arnold, *Once Upon a Galaxy,* 188.
17. *COGL,* 14; "GL: A Life Making Movies."
18. *COGL,* 14.
19. Heseltine, "The Real American Graffiti Artist."
20. Michael Rubin, *Droidmaker: George Lucas and the Digital Revolution* (Gainesville: Triad, 2006), 8.
21. "An AFI Interview with Haskell Wexler," AFI, September 18, 2010, available at https://site.douban.com/106789/widget/notes/127384/note/91565727.
22. Williams, "Inside George Lucas."
23. *COGL,* 16.
24. See USC School of Cinematic Arts documentary, 2009, available at http://cinema.usc.edu/about/history/index.cfm.
25. Pollock, *Skywalking,* 43.
26. *George Lucas: Maker of Films,* television documentary, KCET, 1971.
27. Susan King, "Remastered Classic: Now That's a Birthday Gift," *Los Angeles Times,* March 27, 2009.
28. "A Legacy of Filmmakers: The Early Years of American Zoetrope," *THX 1138: The George Lucas Director's Cut,* special ed. DVD, Warner Home Video, 2004.
29. "GL: A Life Making Movies."
30. Ibid.; Kline, *GL Interviews,* 35.
31. Terence M. Green, "USC Cinema-Television School Has Close-Knit Ambi-

ance of Mini-Studio: Facility Is Replacement for Old Bungalows," *Los Angeles Times*, March 24, 1985.

32. "A Legacy of Filmmakers."
33. Kline, *GL Interviews*, 35.
34. "A Legacy of Filmmakers."
35. Green, "USC Cinema-Television School."
36. Pollock, *Skywalking*, 50.
37. *Creating an Empire.*
38. *COGL*, 16.
39. Pollock, *Skywalking*, 49.
40. "A Legacy of Filmmakers."
41. Trevor Hogg, "Assembly Required: A Walter Murch Profile," Flickering Myth website, July 21, 2010, http://www.flickeringmyth.com/2010/07/assembly -required-walter-murch-profile.html.
42. *COGL*, 16.
43. Kline, *GL Interviews*, 35.
44. Baxter, *George Lucas*, 49.
45. Ibid., 50.
46. *Creating an Empire.*
47. *COGL*, 16.
48. "A Legacy of Filmmakers."
49. Ibid.
50. *COGL*, 16.
51. "GL: A Life Making Movies."
52. Ibid.
53. *COGL*, 17–18.
54. *COGL*, 18.
55. Rubin, *Droidmaker*, 11.
56. *Creating an Empire.*
57. Pollock, *Skywalking*, 56.
58. *Creating an Empire.*
59. Baxter, *George Lucas*, 57.
60. Pollock, *Skywalking*, 50.
61. *Creating an Empire.* Years later, Lucas would deny that it was "star troopers" he was drawing, saying that it was probably cars instead.
62. Pollock, *Skywalking*, 47.
63. Biskind, *Easy Riders*, 317–18.
64. *COGL*, 16, 18.
65. Arnold, *Once Upon a Galaxy*, 188.
66. *Creating an Empire.*
67. Arnold, *Once Upon a Galaxy*, 186.
68. Pollock, *Skywalking*, 57.
69. "Lucas, Coppola, and Kurosawa," *Kagemusha: The Criterion Collection*, DVD, Criterion Studio, 2009.

70. Ibid.
71. *COGL,* 21.
72. Pollock, *Skywalking,* 51.
73. See "Writer-Director Paul Golding on Giving *Pulse* Life," Video Junkie website, May 10, 2014, http://originalvidjunkie.blogspot.com/2014/05/writer -director-paul-golding-on-giving.html?zx=4c515a2976ba414c.
74. *Creating an Empire.*
75. *Flying Solo.*
76. *COGL,* 19.
77. Don Glut, *I Was a Teenage Movie Maker* (Jefferson, N.C.: McFarland & Co., 2007), 166.
78. *COGL,* 20.
79. Pollock, *Skywalking,* 44.
80. *COGL,* 19.
81. Baxter, *George Lucas,* 62.
82. William Keck, "USC Grads Honor Film School; Lucas, Zemeckis, Ferrell Reminisce," *USA Today,* September 28, 2004.
83. *COGL,* 20.
84. Baxter, *George Lucas,* 61.
85. *COGL,* 20.
86. Pollock, *Skywalking,* 57.
87. *COGL,* 20.
88. Glut, *I Was a Teenage Movie Maker,* 158.
89. Stuart Silverstein, "Lucas Seeks to Produce Respect for Filmmaking: 'Star Wars' Creator Speaks at a Ceremony at USC Honoring the $175 Million He Has Pledged to Its Film School," *Los Angeles Times,* October 5, 2006.
90. Barry Koltnow, "End of the Beginning: A Contented George Lucas Looks Back at the Six Parts of His 'Star Wars' Film Epic," *Orange County Register,* May 15, 2005.
91. Baxter, *George Lucas,* 55–56.
92. Pollock, *Skywalking,* 56, 59–60.
93. *COGL,* 22.
94. *COGL,* 22.

Chapter 3: The Right Horse

1. Baxter, *George Lucas,* 71.
2. Gerald Peary, interview with Verna Fields, *The Real Paper* (Boston), October 23, 1980.
3. Kline, *GL Interviews,* 5.
4. Ibid.
5. *Creating an Empire.*
6. Pollock, *Skywalking,* 65, 61.
7. Ibid., 63.
8. Ibid., 64.
9. Ibid., 62.

10. *COGL,* 22.
11. *COGL,* 21–22.
12. *COGL,* 23.
13. Pollock, *Skywalking,* 67.
14. Ibid., 47.
15. Steve Silberman, "Life after Darth," *Wired,* May 2005.
16. Karina Longworth, *Masters of Cinema: George Lucas* (New York: Phaidon, 2012), 11.
17. Silberman, "Life after Darth."
18. Pollock, *Skywalking,* 47.
19. Kline, *GL Interviews,* 6.
20. *COGL,* 20.
21. Sheerly Avni, *Cinema by the Bay* (Nicasio, Calif.: George Lucas Books, 2006), 36.
22. *COGL,* 24.
23. Hogg, "Assembly Required."
24. Pollock, *Skywalking,* 46.
25. Ibid., 63.
26. Ibid., 62, 63, 66.
27. Baxter, *George Lucas,* 70.
28. Pollock, *Skywalking,* 65.
29. Paul Golding, author interview, November 1, 2014.
30. *COGL,* 25.
31. Pollock, *Skywalking,* 58.
32. Justin Bozung, "Watch the Amazing George Lucas Film *The Emperor* and Read about How It Was Made," *TV Store Online,* April 1, 2014, http://blog .tvstoreonline.com/2014/04/watch-george-lucas-brilliant-student.html.
33. Ibid.
34. *COGL,* 25.
35. Bozung, "Watch the Amazing George Lucas."
36. Ibid.
37. Ken Plume, "An Interview with John Milius, IGN website, May 7, 2003, http://www.ign.com/articles/2003/05/07/an-interview-with-john-milius.
38. Bozung, "Watch the Amazing George Lucas."
39. Pollock, *Skywalking,* 66, 65.
40. Ibid., 68.
41. *Flying Solo.*
42. *COGL,* 17–18.
43. Pollock, *Skywalking,* 59.
44. Ibid., 70.
45. Ibid.
46. Ibid.
47. *COGL,* 26, 27.
48. *COGL,* 27.
49. *COGL,* 27.

50. Charles Champlin, *George Lucas: The Creative Impulse: Lucasfilm's First Twenty Years* (New York: Abrams), 9.

Chapter 4: Radicals and Hippies

1. *George Lucas on Working with Francis Ford Coppola,* American Film Institute video, http://www.youtube.com/watch?v=kNcdS8L9pcA.
2. *Creating an Empire.*
3. Peter Cowie, *Coppola: A Biography,* rev. ed. (New York: Da Capo Press, 1994), 15.
4. Biskind, *Easy Riders,* 149.
5. Cowie, *Coppola,* 20, 22.
6. Biskind, *Easy Riders,* 36.
7. *Creating an Empire.*
8. Biskind, *Easy Riders,* 37.
9. Lester D. Friedman and Brent Notbohm, eds., *Steven Spielberg: Interviews* (Jackson: University Press of Mississippi, 2010), 38.
10. *Creating an Empire.*
11. *COGL,* 27.
12. *COGL,* 27.
13. *Creating an Empire.*
14. Ibid.
15. Quick review, *Finian's Rainbow, DVD Journal,* http://www.dvdjournal.com/quickreviews/f/finiansrainbow.q.shtml.
16. *Lucas on Working with Coppola.*
17. "Show Beat," *Danville Register* (Va.), July 30, 1967.
18. *Flying Solo.*
19. Baxter, *George Lucas,* 84.
20. *Flying Solo.*
21. *Lucas on Working with Coppola.*
22. *COGL,* 28.
23. *Lucas on Working with Coppola.*
24. Audie Bock, "Zoetrope and *Apocalypse Now,*" *American Film,* September 1979.
25. Pollock, *Skywalking,* 68.
26. Thomas Kevin, "'A' Grades for Film Festival Students," *Los Angeles Times,* January 22, 1968.
27. Charles Champlin, "US Student Film Series Will Open at Fairfax," *Los Angeles Times,* February 21, 1968.
28. J. W. Rinzler and Laurent Bouzereau, *The Making of Indiana Jones: The Definitive Story Behind All Four Films* (New York: Del Rey, 2008), 12 (hereafter *MOIJ*).
29. *Creating an Empire.*
30. Ibid.
31. *MOIJ,* 12.
32. George Lucas, acceptance speech for the AFI Life Achievement Award, 2005.

33. Leo Janos, "Steven Spielberg: *L'Enfant Directeur*," *Cosmopolitan*, June 1980.
34. Joseph McBride, *Steven Spielberg: A Biography*, 2nd ed. (Jackson: University Press of Mississippi, 2010), 62, 66.
35. Ibid., 137–38.
36. Pollock, *Skywalking*, 62, 63.
37. *Creating an Empire*.
38. Pollock, *Skywalking*, 65.
39. Ibid., 65, 63.
40. Gene D. Phillips and Rodney Hill, eds., *Francis Ford Coppola: Interviews* (Jackson: University Press of Mississippi, 2004), 13.
41. Biskind, *Easy Riders*, 94.
42. *Flying Solo*.
43. Baxter, *George Lucas*, 84–85.
44. *COGL*, 31.
45. See George Lucas, *Filmmaker*, Zoetrope/Lucasfilm, 1968.
46. *COGL*, 28.
47. Michael Goodwin and Naomi Wise, *On the Edge: The Life and Times of Francis Coppola* (New York: William Morrow and Company, 1989), 87.
48. Cowie, *Coppola*, 53.
49. Biskind, *Easy Riders*, 208.
50. Baxter, *George Lucas*, 87–88.
51. John F. Kearney, "For Film Director Hollywood Out, Stinson Beach Is In," *Daily Independent Journal* (San Rafael, Calif.), February 14, 1967.
52. John Korty, author interview.
53. Kearney, "For Film Director."
54. *COGL*, 31.
55. Cowie, *Coppola*, 55.
56. *COGL*, 31.
57. Cowie, *Coppola*, 39.
58. Pollock, *Skywalking*, 88.
59. *COGL*, 34–35.
60. Francis Ford Coppola, interview of John Milius, April 8, 2010, https://www.youtube.com/watch?v=JZswrVALi2M.
61. Phillips and Hill, *Francis Ford Coppola*, 95.
62. "A Brief History of Zoetrope Films," Zoetrope.com, http://www.zoetrope.com/zoe_films.cgi?page=history.
63. Phillips and Hill, *Francis Ford Coppola*, 15.
64. Cowie, *Coppola*, 45.
65. Peter Hartlaub, "In a Valley Not Far, Far Away," *San Francisco Chronicle*, April 27, 2007.
66. Pollock, *Skywalking*, 83.
67. *Creating an Empire*.
68. Cowie, *Coppola*, 56.
69. Louise Sweeney, "A Coppola Objective: An 'All-Consuming' Film," *Christian Science Monitor*, August 30, 1969.

70. Biskind, *Easy Riders,* 92.
71. Hartlaub, "In a Valley Not Far, Far Away."
72. Hogg, "Assembly Required."
73. Sweeney, "A Coppola Objective."
74. Biskind, *Easy Riders,* 258.
75. Phillips and Hill, *Francis Ford Coppola,* 16.
76. "A Legacy of Filmmakers," bonus disc, *THX 1138.*
77. Mel Gussow, "Movies Leaving 'Hollywood' Behind: Studio System Passé; Film Forges Ahead," *New York Times,* May 27, 1970.
78. John Patterson, "American Zoetrope: In a Galaxy Not from Hollywood...," *The Guardian,* November 17, 2011.
79. "Indies—Francis Ford Coppola and George Lucas on Set of *Rain People,*" King Rose Archives, ca. 1968, http://www.youtube.com/watch?v=JhfY4LVpevI.
80. *Creating an Empire.*
81. Biskind, *Easy Riders,* 98.
82. "A Legacy of Filmmakers."
83. See Biskind, *Easy Riders,* 92; Goodwin and Wise, *On the Edge,* 96; and Cowie, *Coppola,* 56.
84. Pollock, *Skywalking,* 89.
85. Gerald Nachman, "Coppola of Zoetrope—Older, Wiser and Poorer," *Los Angeles Times,* November 7, 1971.
86. "A Legacy of Filmmakers." See also *COGL,* 36.
87. *COGL,* 36.
88. Gussow, "Movies Leaving 'Hollywood' Behind."
89. John Leighty, "Hippie Capitalist Makes Films in SF," *Fresno Bee,* April 10, 1970.
90. Sweeney, "A Coppola Objective."
91. Nachman, "Coppola of Zoetrope."
92. Cowie, *Coppola,* 57; Gussow, "Movies Leaving 'Hollywood' Behind."
93. Cowie, *Coppola,* 57.
94. Nachman, "Coppola of Zoetrope."
95. "A Legacy of Filmmakers."
96. Kline, *GL Interviews,* 7.
97. Sweeney, "A Coppola Objective."
98. Gussow, "Movies Leaving 'Hollywood' Behind."
99. Leighty, "Hippie Capitalist Makes Films in SF."
100. Trevor Hogg, "Hot Rods & Droids: A George Lucas Profile," Flickering Myth website, June 8, 2011, http://www.flickeringmyth.com/2011/06/hot-rods-droids-george-lucas-profile.html.
101. Kline, *GL Interviews,* 146.
102. Sweeney, "A Coppola Objective."
103. "Movies Leaving 'Hollywood' Behind."
104. *COGL,* 38.

105. George Lucas, commentary track for *THX 1138*.
106. Christine Richert, "Modestan's Movie Will Open," *Modesto Bee and News-Herald*, June 1, 1971.
107. Kline, *GL Interviews*, 4.
108. George Lucas, commentary track for *THX 1138*.
109. "THX 1138—Made in San Francisco," *American Cinematographer*, October 1971.
110. Kline, *GL Interviews*, 12.
111. George Lucas, commentary track for *THX 1138*.
112. Pollock, *Skywalking*, 90.
113. Kline, *GL Interviews*, 12.
114. George Lucas, commentary track for *THX 1138*.
115. *COGL*, 37.
116. *COGL*, 36.
117. "Hollywood," *The Times* (San Mateo, Calif.), January 24, 1970.
118. Pollock, *Skywalking*, 92.
119. "A Legacy of Filmmakers."
120. Kline, *GL Interviews*, 12.
121. Leighty, "Hippie Capitalist Makes Films in SF."
122. "A Legacy of Filmmakers."
123. Ibid.
124. Ibid.
125. Ibid.
126. Biskind, *Easy Riders*, 235.
127. Goodwin and Wise, *On the Edge*, 106.
128. Biskind, *Easy Riders*, 98–99.
129. Ibid., 98.
130. "A Legacy of Filmmakers."
131. George Lucas, commentary track, *THX 1138*.
132. *Creating an Empire*.
133. Biskind, *Easy Riders*, 100.
134. Ibid., 99.
135. *COGL*, 46.
136. *Creating an Empire*.
137. Francis Ford Coppola interviewed on *The Howard Stern Show*, June 8, 2009.
138. Biskind, *Easy Riders*, 93.
139. "A Legacy of Filmmakers." There is a great deal of confusion among nearly everyone involved regarding the timeline relevant to screenings of *THX*, the demise of Zoetrope, and Coppola's involvement with *The Godfather*. Most versions of the story have Coppola agreeing to direct *The Godfather* only after the events of "Black Thursday." That meeting happened in November, however, while Coppola accepted the directing job in September. Some versions of events move Black Thursday to May or June; but Lucas insists the meeting took place in November. Most versions of the story also recall Lucas editing

THX when Coppola received the call, which could not have happened after Black Thursday, as the film had been taken away from him. Deferring to Lucas's memory, then, means Coppola accepted *The Godfather* two months *before* the events of Black Thursday, depriving most storytellers of the triumphant exclamation point to the story.

140. Biskind, *Easy Riders*, 101.
141. "A Legacy of Filmmakers."
142. Kline, *GL Interviews*, 4.
143. Nachman, "Coppola of Zoetrope."
144. Biskind, *Easy Riders*, 101.
145. *Creating an Empire.*
146. *George Lucas: Maker of Films*, 1971.
147. "Airport 'Junk' — Lancaster," *The Gazette* (Montreal), March 8, 1971.
148. Nachman, "Coppola of Zoetrope."
149. *George Lucas: Maker of Films.*
150. Kline, *GL Interviews*, 37.
151. *Creating an Empire.*
152. "A Legacy of Filmmakers."
153. Biskind, *Easy Riders*, 99.
154. "A Legacy of Filmmakers."
155. Kline, *GL Interviews*, 6.
156. "A Legacy of Filmmakers."
157. Cowie, *Coppola*, 61.
158. "A Legacy of Filmmakers."
159. Biskind, *Easy Riders*, 102.
160. "George Lucas at 70: The Star Wars Creator on Filmmaking," *The Telegraph* (London), http://www.telegraph.co.uk/culture/star-wars/10828279/George-Lucas-at-70-the-Star-Wars-creator-on-filmmaking.html.
161. "A Legacy of Filmmakers."
162. Pollock, *Skywalking*, 100.
163. Biskind, *Easy Riders*, 102.
164. "A Legacy of Filmmakers."
165. Biskind, *Easy Riders*, 102.
166. Kenneth Turan, "Film: THX 1138," *Washington Post*, April 17, 1971.
167. Roger Ebert, review of *THX 1138*, 1971, http://www.rogerebert.com/reviews/thx-1138-2004.
168. Roger Greenspun, "Film: Lucas's 'THX 1138': Love Is Punishable Crime in Future," *New York Times*, March 12, 1971.
169. Vincent Canby, "Wanda's a Wow, So's THX," *New York Times*, March 21, 1971.
170. "Review: 'THX 1138,'" *Variety*, March 16, 1971.
171. Pollock, *Skywalking*, 96.
172. Biskind, *Easy Riders*, 235.
173. "A Legacy of Filmmakers."
174. Biskind, *Easy Riders*, 235.
175. Ibid.

Chapter 5: American Graffiti

1. Garry Jenkins, *Empire Building: The Remarkable Real Life Story of Star Wars* (Secaucus, N.J.: Citadel, 1999), 24.
2. Ibid., 25.
3. Ibid., 22, 26.
4. Gary Arnold, "Chalking 'Graffiti' Up to Experience," *Washington Post*, May 26, 1974.
5. David Sheff, "George Lucas," *Rolling Stone*, November 5–December 10, 1987.
6. Kline, *GL Interviews*, 42.
7. Jenkins, *Empire Building*, 28.
8. Chris Taylor, "'Star Wars' Producer Blasts 'Star Wars' Myths," Mashable.com, September 27, 2014, http://mashable.com/2014/09/27/star-wars-myths-gary -kurtz/.
9. Ken Plume, "An Interview with Gary Kurtz," IGN, November 11, 2002, http://www.ign.com/articles/2002/11/11/an-interview-with-gary-kurtz.
10. Kline, *GL Interviews*, 38.
11. Biskind, *Easy Riders*, 235.
12. *Empire of Dreams: The Story of the Star Wars Trilogy*, directed by Kevin Burns, bonus disc, *The Star Wars Trilogy*, DVD boxed set (Nicasio, Calif.: Lucasfilm, 2004).
13. Kline, *GL Interviews*, 38.
14. Chris Murphy and Ken White, "George Lucas Interviewed," *Modesto View*, June 1, 2012.
15. *MOSW*, 4.
16. American Film Institute video, "George Lucas on *American Graffiti*," October 30, 2009, https://www.youtube.com/watch?v=WvmFpj2Bgyc.
17. "GL: A Life Making Movies."
18. George Stevens Jr., *Conversations at the American Film Institute with the Great Moviemakers: The Next Generation, from the 1950s to Hollywood Today* (New York: Vintage, 2014), 301.
19. Pollock, *Skywalking*, 102.
20. Ibid.
21. Philip Horne, "'The Godfather': 'Nobody Enjoyed One Day of It,'" *The Telegraph* (London), September 22, 2009.
22. *MOSW*, 5.
23. Susy Vader, "Charlie Chaplin Stole the Show at the 1971 Cannes Film Festival," *Australian Women's Weekly*, June 23, 1971. It has often been reported that Lucas served as a cameraman on *Gimme Shelter* for filmmakers Albert and David Maysles—and even filmed the fatal stabbing of Meredith Hunter. Lucas, with typical aplomb, says he simply doesn't remember shooting anything for the film.
24. Pollock, *Skywalking*, 103.
25. *MOSW*, 5.

26. Baxter, *George Lucas,* 117.
27. Ibid., 116, 117.
28. Stevens, *Conversations with the Great Moviemakers,* 301.
29. Ibid.
30. *Creating an Empire.*
31. Jenkins, *Empire Building,* 31.
32. "GL: A Life Making Movies."
33. Ibid.
34. Kline, *GL Interviews,* 26.
35. "GL: A Life Making Movies."
36. Paul Scanlon, "The Force behind George Lucas," *Rolling Stone,* August 25, 1977.
37. Pollock, *Skywalking,* 31.
38. Biskind, *Easy Riders,* 236.
39. Ibid.
40. Gary Arnold, "Cruising through 'American Graffiti': Hot Rods, Good Times and Longings," *Washington Post,* August 31, 1973.
41. The percentage of net varies from story to story. Ultimately, Lucas and Coppola both recall having to split forty points between them.
42. Pollock, *Skywalking,* 107.
43. *COGL,* 54.
44. Pat Perry, "San Rafael Is Site for Movie of 1962 Teens," *Daily Independent Journal* (San Rafael, Calif.), June 14, 1972.
45. Pollock, *Skywalking,* 108.
46. *Creating an Empire.*
47. Judy Klemesrud, "'Graffiti' Is the Story of His Life," *New York Times,* October 7, 1973.
48. *COGL,* 56.
49. *Creating an Empire.*
50. Ibid.
51. Baxter, *George Lucas,* 32.
52. Ibid.
53. "Cindy Williams Interview: Film-Television Star to Appear at Nov. 2 Screening of 'American Graffiti' in Omaha," Leo Adam Biga's blog, October 25, 2012, http://leoadambiga.com/2012/10/25/cindy-williams-interview-film-television-star-to-appear-at-nov-2-screening-of-american-graffiti-in-omaha/. Used with permission of author-journalist-blogger Leo Adam Biga.
54. *COGL,* 6.
55. *MOIJ,* 14.
56. The story, however, wasn't Spielberg's; it was by science fiction writer Philip Wylie.
57. *MOIJ,* 14.
58. *MOIJ,* 14.
59. Kline, *GL Interviews,* 18.

60. George Lucas on *American Graffiti,* American Film Institute video, http://www.youtube.com/watch?v=WvmFpj2Bgyc.
61. Klemesrud, "'Graffiti' Is the Story of His Life."
62. Ibid.
63. *Creating an Empire.*
64. *COGL,* 62.
65. Baxter, *George Lucas,* 127.
66. Kline, *GL Interviews,* 16.
67. *Creating an Empire.*
68. Kline, *GL Interviews,* 16.
69. Klemesrud, "'Graffiti' Is the Story of His Life."
70. Arnold, *Once Upon a Galaxy.*
71. Kline, *GL Interviews,* 16, 41.
72. Biskind, *Easy Riders,* 237.
73. *Creating an Empire.*
74. *COGL,* 64.
75. "George Lucas: A Galaxy Far, Far Away," *Easy Riders, Raging Bulls,* mini-documentary, Shout Factory, 2004.
76. *COGL,* 64.
77. See "Shooting Schedule, American Graffiti as Shot," *COGL,* 74–75.
78. Paul Rowlands, "Candy Clark Talks about *American Graffiti,*" Money Into Light website, April 28, 2012, http://www.money-into-light.com/2012/04/candy-clark-talks-to-paul-rowlands.html.
79. *MOSW,* 7.
80. Biskind, *Easy Riders,* 237.
81. Biographical information from David M. Herszenhorn, "Wolfman Jack, Raspy Voice of the Radio, Is Dead at 57," *New York Times,* July 2, 1995; Richard Harrington, "Leader of the Pack: Deejay Wolfman Jack, the Voice of a Generation," *Washington Post,* July 3, 1995; and XERB1090 website, http://www.xerbradio.com.
82. Kline, *GL Interviews,* 29, 39.
83. Ibid., 22–23.
84. Klemesrud, "'Graffiti' Is the Story of His Life."
85. Baxter, *George Lucas,* 128.
86. *COGL,* 66.
87. Hogg, "Assembly Required."
88. Kline, *GL Interviews,* 21.
89. Ibid., 29.
90. *COGL,* 69.
91. *COGL,* 69.
92. Pollock, *Skywalking,* 118.
93. Biskind, *Easy Riders,* 243.
94. *COGL,* 6, 70.
95. Biskind, *Easy Riders,* 243.

96. *Creating an Empire.*

97. Biskind, *Easy Riders,* 243.

98. Ibid., 244.

99. See Lillian Ross, "Some Figures on a Fantasy," *The New Yorker,* November 8, 1982.

100. Biskind, *Easy Riders,* 244.

101. *COGL,* 71.

102. Biskind, *Easy Riders,* 244.

103. Pollock, *Skywalking,* 120.

104. Kline, *GL Interviews,* 43.

105. "A Legacy of Filmmakers."

106. Kline, *GL Interviews,* 77.

107. "Wendy Lucas Comments on *American Graffiti,* the State Theatre, Modesto, May 31, 2008," http://www.youtube.com/watch?v=yvEwUOR0kkE.

108. Kline, *GL Interviews,* 77–78.

109. Ibid., 77.

110. Pollock, *Skywalking,* 123.

111. Jay Cocks, "Cinema: Fabulous '50s," *Time,* August 20, 1973.

112. Gary Arnold, "Cruising through 'American Graffiti': Hot Rods, Good Times and Longings," *Washington Post,* August 31, 1973.

113. Charles Champlin, "A New Generation Looks Back in 'Graffiti,'" *Los Angeles Times,* July 29, 1973.

114. Stephen Farber, "'Graffiti' Ranks with 'Bonnie and Clyde,'" *New York Times,* August 5, 1973.

115. Kline, *GL Interviews,* 21.

116. Peter Hartlaub, "The Chronicle Panned It: 'American Graffiti,'" *SF Gate,* February 4, 2015.

117. Ibid.

118. See Gene Siskel, "Graffiti—How Many Golden Oldies Can You Handle?" *Chicago Tribune,* August 24, 1973.

119. Farber, "'Graffiti' Ranks with 'Bonnie and Clyde'"; Klemesrud, "'Graffiti' Is the Story of His Life."

120. Cocks, "Cinema: Fabulous '50s."

121. Arnold, *Once Upon a Galaxy.*

122. Klemesrud, "'Graffiti' Is the Story of His Life."

123. Ibid.

124. Ibid.; Paul Gardner, "'Graffiti' Reflects Its Director's Youth," *New York Times,* September 19, 1973.

125. *Creating an Empire.*

126. While negotiating for clearance rights for the film, Lucas had tried to get Universal to include money to clear the songs for a sound track album at the same time. Had Universal secured the sound track rights at that time, it would have saved the studio the millions it later paid to secure sound track rights after the movie was a success.

127. Biskind, *Easy Riders,* 237.

128. Ibid., 320.
129. Pollock, *Skywalking*, 128.
130. Biskind, *Easy Riders*, 319.
131. *Creating an Empire*.
132. *COGL*, 82.
133. See *MOSW*, 14.
134. Kline, *GL Interviews*, 32.

Chapter 6: Bleeding on the Page

1. Larry Sturhahn, "The Making of *American Graffiti*," *Filmmakers Newsletter*, March 1974.
2. *MOSW*, 14.
3. *MOSW*, 26.
4. Biskind, *Easy Riders*, 322.
5. *COGL*, 78.
6. Biskind, *Easy Riders*, 322.
7. Vallely, "*The Empire Strikes Back* and So Does George Lucas."
8. *MOSW*, 7.
9. Stephen Zito, "George Lucas Goes Far Out," *American Film*, April 1977.
10. See *MOSW*, 8–11.
11. *MOSW*, 9.
12. *MOSW*, 15.
13. *MOSW*, 50.
14. *MOSW*, 9–11.
15. *Empire of Dreams*.
16. Kline, *GL Interviews*, 44.
17. Vallely, "*The Empire Strikes Back* and So Does George Lucas."
18. Pollock, *Skywalking*, 126.
19. Bob Thomas, "Lucas Fortune Changes," *Baltimore Sun*, August 28, 1973.
20. *MOSW*, 12.
21. Jenkins, *Empire Building*, 43.
22. Paul Rosenfield, "Lucas: Film-Maker with the Force," *Los Angeles Times*, June 5, 1977.
23. See Gene Siskel, "A Day with the 'Smartest' Film Mogul," *Chicago Tribune*, April 9, 1978.
24. Farber, "George Lucas: The Stinky Kid Hits the Big Time."
25. Jenkins, *Empire Building*, 46.
26. Ibid., 39.
27. *MOSW*, 13.
28. Paul Scanlon, "George Lucas Wants to Play Guitar as 'Star Wars' Takes a Vacation," *Rolling Stone*, July 21, 1983.
29. *MOSW*, 12–13.
30. *MOSW*, 12.
31. Kline, *GL Interviews*, 81.
32. Jenkins, *Empire Building*, 47.

33. *Empire of Dreams.*
34. Biskind, *Easy Riders,* 320.
35. Vallely, *"The Empire Strikes Back* and So Does George Lucas."
36. Mary Murphy, "Radioland by Graffiti Team," *Los Angeles Times,* September 27, 1973.
37. *MOSW,* 14.
38. *MOSW,* 14.
39. Biskind, *Easy Riders,* 253.
40. Klemesrud, "'Graffiti' Is the Story of His Life."
41. Kline, *GL Interviews,* 80.
42. *MOSW,* 8; and see page 17 for Lucas's handwritten notes.
43. Charles Lippincott, quoted in Jim Hoagland, "The Politics of Star Wars," *Washington Post,* December 11, 1977.
44. Spellings are consistent with those in Lucas's first rough draft, May 1974. See *MOSW,* 19–22.
45. *MOSW,* 24.
46. Laurent Bouzereau, *Star Wars: The Annotated Screenplays* (New York: Ballantine, 1997), 10.
47. Lee Grant, "Lucas: Feet on Ground, Head in the Stars," *Los Angeles Times,* December 10, 1977.
48. *MOIJ,* 16–17.
49. Pollock, *Skywalking,* 142, 147.
50. *Flying Solo.*
51. Farber, "George Lucas: The Stinky Kid Hits the Big Time."
52. Biskind, *Easy Riders,* 255–56.
53. *MOSW,* 25.
54. *Empire of Dreams.*
55. *Flying Solo.*
56. Cowie, *Coppola,* 121.
57. Vallely, *"The Empire Strikes Back* and So Does George Lucas."
58. Scanlon, "George Lucas Wants to Play Guitar."
59. Zito, "George Lucas Goes Far Out."
60. Vallely, *"The Empire Strikes Back* and So Does George Lucas."
61. Kline, *GL Interviews,* 80.
62. *Empire of Dreams.*
63. Biskind, *Easy Riders,* 320–21.
64. Aljean Harmetz, "And It Almost Didn't Get to the Screen," *New York Times,* May 26, 1977.
65. Kline, *GL Interviews.*
66. *Empire of Dreams.*
67. Arnold, "Chalking 'Graffiti' Up to Experience."
68. *MOSW,* 36.
69. Jason DeBord, "World Exclusive Interview with Colin Cantwell," Original Prop blog, November 13, 2013, http://www.originalprop.com/blog/

2014/11/13/colin-cantwell-video-interviews-star-wars-prototype-models
-nasa/.

70. *Empire of Dreams.*
71. Angela Watercutter, "*Star Wars* Conceptual Artist Ralph McQuarrie Dies at 82," *Wired*, March 4, 2012.
72. *MOSW,* 32.
73. *Empire of Dreams.*
74. Ibid.
75. *Flying Solo.*
76. See *Adventures of the Starkiller* summary in *MOSW,* 27–30.
77. *MOSW,* 42.
78. Jenkins, *Empire Building,* 62–63.
79. "George Lucas Was More Than a Director for *Star Wars,*" *Baltimore Sun,* July 7, 1977.
80. Jenkins, *Empire Building,* 63.
81. "Exclusive Star Wars Interview with John Dykstra," *Fantasy Film Journal* 1, no. 1 (Winter 1977). Reproduced at http://originaltrilogy.com/topic/John -Dykstra-Interview-Circa-July-1977/id/12285.
82. Ibid.
83. *MOSW,* 50.
84. *MOSW,* 51.
85. "Exclusive Star Wars Interview with John Dykstra."
86. Alex French and Howie Kahn, "Inside the Magic Factory: The Definitive Oral History of ILM, the Special Effects Powerhouse that Revolutionized Moviemaking and Changed Entertainment Forever," *Wired,* June 2015.
87. *Empire of Dreams.*
88. French and Kahn, "Inside the Magic Factory."
89. "Exclusive Star Wars Interview with John Dykstra."
90. *Empire of Dreams.*
91. *MOSW,* 80.
92. *MOSW,* 51.
93. *MOSW,* 53.
94. *MOSW,* 51.
95. French and Kahn, "Inside the Magic Factory."
96. *COGL,* 6.
97. Biskind, *Easy Riders,* 278.
98. *MOSW,* 49.
99. *MOSW,* 59.
100. *MOSW,* 94.
101. Biskind, *Easy Riders,* 324.
102. Ibid.
103. *MOSW,* 67.
104. *Empire of Dreams.*
105. *MOSW,* 67.

106. Pollock, *Skywalking,* 151.
107. Ibid., 150.
108. Ibid., 151.
109. It was a practice that would cause some controversy for Nunn—and others—several years later, when she appeared in *Penthouse* magazine at age sixteen.
110. Jenkins, *Empire Building,* 79.
111. *MOSW,* 101.
112. Jenkins, *Empire Building,* 80.
113. *MOSW,* 102.
114. *Flying Solo.*
115. Hamill's screen test—as well as Fisher's and Ford's—can be seen at various sites online and are well worth watching.
116. *MOSW,* 103.
117. *MOSW,* 104.
118. *Flying Solo.*
119. *MOSW,* 95, 124.
120. *Empire of Dreams.*
121. *MOSW,* 95.
122. Pollock, *Skywalking,* 152.
123. *Empire of Dreams.*
124. Piers Paul Read, *Alec Guinness: The Authorised Biography* (New York: Simon and Schuster, 2003).
125. Arnold, *Once Upon a Galaxy,* 229.
126. Read, *Alec Guinness,* 503.
127. Ibid., 504.
128. Pollock, *Skywalking,* 153.
129. Jeremy Skinger, "The Man Who Literally Built Star Wars," Esquire.com, May 4, 2014.
130. *MOSW,* 54.
131. Alexis C. Madrigal, "The Remarkable Way Chewbacca Got a Voice," The Atlantic.com, August 7, 2014.
132. *MOSW,* 56.
133. J. W. Rinzler, *The Sounds of Star Wars* (San Francisco: Chronicle, 2010), 9.
134. "*Star Wars:* The Hit Film and How It Was Put Together," *Colorado Springs Gazette-Telegraph,* August 27, 1977.
135. *MOSW,* 54.
136. See Lucas's acceptance speech, AFI Tribute to George Lucas, June 9, 2005.
137. *Empire of Dreams.*
138. *MOSW,* 124.
139. Pollock, *Skywalking,* 154.
140. Rosenfield, "Lucas: Film-Maker with the Force."
141. *MOSW,* 82.
142. See Jenkins, *Empire Building,* 39–40.
143. Vallely, "*The Empire Strikes Back* and So Does George Lucas."
144. *MOSW,* 85.

145. *MOSW,* 89.
146. *MOSW,* 124.
147. *MOSW,* 124.
148. Jenkins, *Empire Building,* 74.
149. *MOSW,* 94.
150. *COGL,* 98.
151. *MOSW,* 107.
152. *MOSW,* 111.
153. *MOSW,* 132.
154. *MOSW,* 84.

Chapter 7: *"I Have a Bad Feeling About This"*

1. Paul Scanlon, "The Wizard of Star Wars," *Rolling Stone,* August 25, 1977.
2. Pollock, *Skywalking,* 160.
3. *Creating an Empire.*
4. Read, *Alec Guinness,* 505.
5. *MOSW,* 166.
6. Ibid.
7. Read, *Alec Guinness,* 504.
8. Quoted in *MOSW,* 174.
9. Scanlon, "The Wizard of Star Wars."
10. Pollock, *Skywalking,* 168.
11. Alex French and Howie Kahn, "Inside the Magic Factory," *Wired,* June 2015.
12. Claire Clouzot, "The Morning of the Magician: George Lucas and *Star Wars*," *Ecran,* September 15, 1977.
13. Zito, "George Lucas Goes Far Out."
14. Kline, *GL Interviews,* 81.
15. *MOSW,* 141.
16. *MOSW,* 143.
17. Clouzot, "The Morning of the Magician."
18. *MOSW,* 160, 164.
19. Pollock, *Skywalking,* 162.
20. *Creating an Empire.*
21. *MOSW,* 174.
22. Zito, "George Lucas Goes Far Out."
23. O'Quinn, "The George Lucas Saga."
24. *Creating an Empire.*
25. John Seabrook, "Letter from Skywalker Ranch: Why Is the Force Still with Us?" *The New Yorker,* January 6, 1997.
26. Robert L. Rose, "Career Comes on Silver Platter for Mark Hamill," *Salt Lake City Tribune,* June 12, 1977.
27. *MOSW,* 148.
28. Pollock, *Skywalking,* 165.
29. Jenkins, *Empire Building,* 116.
30. *MOSW,* 188.

31. *MOSW,* 188.
32. *Empire of Dreams.*
33. Arnold, *Once Upon a Galaxy,* 231.
34. Chris Hastings, "Anxious He Was...Revealed: Why George Lucas Was Convinced His Star Wars Dream Would Be a Flop," MailOnline (London), May 17, 2014.
35. Arnold, *Once Upon a Galaxy,* 127.
36. *Empire of Dreams.*
37. *MOSW,* 177.
38. "George Lucas: Heroes, Myths, and Magic," *American Masters,* PBS, March 17, 1993.
39. Zito, "George Lucas Goes Far Out."
40. Scanlon, "The Wizard of Star Wars."
41. Arnold, *Once Upon a Galaxy,* 183.
42. *Empire of Dreams.*
43. *MOSW,* 185.
44. Clouzot, "The Morning of the Magician."
45. *MOSW,* 182.
46. John Dykstra, "VFX Then and Now," CreativeCow.net, 2013, https://library.creativecow.net/kaufman_debra/VFX_John-Dykstra/1.
47. *MOSW,* 189.
48. Pollock, *Skywalking,* 169.
49. *MOSW,* 190.
50. *MOSW,* 146.
51. *Creating an Empire.*
52. Pollock, *Skywalking,* 168.
53. Zito, "George Lucas Goes Far Out."
54. Pollock, *Skywalking,* 168.
55. Biskind, *Easy Riders,* 327.
56. *MOSW,* 196.
57. Scanlon, "The Wizard of Star Wars."
58. *MOSW,* 208.
59. *Empire of Dreams.*
60. Ibid.
61. Biskind, *Easy Riders,* 329–30.
62. O'Quinn, "The George Lucas Saga."
63. *MOSW,* 218.
64. French and Kahn, "Inside the Magic Factory"; *Creating an Empire.*
65. Pollock, *Skywalking,* 173.
66. Zito, "George Lucas Goes Far Out."
67. *MOSW,* 223.
68. Dykstra, "VFX Then and Now."
69. Robbie Blalack, quoted in *MOSW,* 228.
70. French and Kahn, "Inside the Magic Factory."

71. *MOSW,* 97.
72. *Creating an Empire.*
73. Scanlon, "The Wizard of Star Wars."
74. Arnold, *Once Upon a Galaxy,* 94.
75. Zito, "George Lucas Goes Far Out."
76. Scanlon, "The Wizard of Star Wars."
77. *MOSW,* 255.
78. French and Kahn, "Inside the Magic Factory."
79. *Empire of Dreams.*
80. Scanlon, "The Wizard of Star Wars."
81. Biskind, *Easy Riders,* 330.
82. Aljean Harmetz, "Star Wars Robots Gaining Stardom," *Des Moines Register,* June 15, 1977.
83. Ibid.
84. Aljean Harmetz, "Inside C3PO and His Sidekick R2D2," *Chicago Tribune,* June 24, 1977.
85. Ibid.
86. *Empire of Dreams.*
87. Frank Lovece, "Fast Chat: James Earl Jones," *Newsday,* March 12, 2008. His name would appear in the credits starting with *The Empire Strikes Back.*
88. *MOSW,* 246.
89. *MOSW,* 247.
90. *Empire of Dreams.*
91. Clouzot, "The Morning of the Magician."
92. *Empire of Dreams.*
93. *Flying Solo.*
94. Biskind, *Easy Riders,* 334.
95. *MOSW,* 256.
96. Biskind, *Easy Riders,* 334.
97. *MOSW,* 256.
98. *Creating an Empire.*
99. *Empire of Dreams.*
100. Jon Burlingame, "Spielberg and Lucas on Williams," Film Music Society, February 8, 2012, http://www.filmmusicsociety.org/news_events/features/2012/020812.html.
101. Scanlon, "The Wizard of Star Wars."
102. Kline, *GL Interviews,* 82.
103. *MOSW,* 272.
104. Donald Goddard, "From 'American Graffiti' to Outer Space," *New York Times,* September 12, 1976.
105. Clouzot, "The Morning of the Magician."
106. Ed Gross, "Retrovision Exclusive: The Selling of Star Wars, Part 1," Comic BookMovie.com, September 11, 2011.

107. "When Movie Becomes a Hit, It Can Make Book Best Seller," *Lincoln Star* (Neb.), July 10, 1977.

108. Gross, "Retrovision Exclusive."

109. Biskind, *Easy Riders,* 335.

110. *Empire of Dreams.*

111. *MOSW,* 288, 289.

112. Arnold, *Once Upon a Galaxy,* 95.

113. *COGL,* 110.

114. *MOSW,* 290.

115. *COGL,* 110.

116. *MOSW,* 293.

Chapter 8: Striking Back

1. Pollock, *Skywalking,* 185.

2. *MOSW,* 293–94.

3. Lee Grant, "'Star Wars' Out of This World," *Los Angeles Times,* June 4, 1977.

4. Karen de Witt, "The Movie That Ate Cleveland Park," *Washington Post,* June 23, 1977.

5. "Queues for Star Wars Are Creating Havoc in the Street," *Los Angeles Times,* July 30, 1977.

6. Greg Conroy, "Moviegoers Are 'Spacy' over 'Star Wars,'" *Bloomington Pantagraph* (Ill.), November 27, 1977.

7. Pollock, *Skywalking,* 182.

8. "Star Wars Sends Audiences Wild," *Waukesha Daily Freeman* (Wis.), June 6, 1977.

9. Bob Thomas, "Star Wars: New Force in Films," *Los Angeles Times,* August 12, 1977.

10. See Erma Bombeck, "At Wit's End: 'Star Wars' Line Inspires Heroism," *Baltimore Sun,* September 18, 1977.

11. Conroy, "Moviegoers Are 'Spacy' over 'Star Wars.'"

12. A. D. Murphy, "Review: 'Star Wars,'" *Variety,* May 25, 1977.

13. Charles Champlin, "'Star Wars' Hails the Once and Future Space Western," *Los Angeles Times,* May 22, 1977.

14. Jay Cocks, "Cinema: 'Star Wars': The Year's Best Movie," *Time,* May 30, 1977.

15. Gary Arnold, "Star Wars: A Spectacular Intergalactic Joyride," *Washington Post,* May 25, 1977.

16. Vincent Canby, "'Star Wars'—A Trip to a Far Galaxy That's Fun and Funny," *New York Times,* May 26, 1977.

17. Gene Siskel, "'Star Wars' Flashes with Space Wizardry," *Chicago Tribune,* May 27, 1977.

18. "Director George Lucas Lost to the Stars," *Playground Daily News* (Fort Walton Beach, Fla.), May 29, 1977.

19. Joy Gould Boyum, "The Triumph of Camp," *Wall Street Journal,* June 6, 1977.

20. See Pete Hamill, "Star Wars: Dumb Good Times Here Again?" *Chicago Tribune,* June 8, 1977.

21. Walter Bremond, "Star Wars and Blacks," *New Journal and Guide,* October 1, 1977.

22. Bernard E. Garnett, "Racism Mars 'Star Wars' Brilliance: Slave-Like Robots Call Owner 'Master' & Accept Discrimination," *Afro-American,* June 25, 1977.

23. Quoted in Dorothy Gilliam, "The Black Heavies: What Do Today's Most Notorious Bad Guys Have in Common?" *Washington Post,* September 11, 1977.

24. Ibid.

25. See "More 'Star Wars' Skirmishes," *Los Angeles Times,* July 31, 1977.

26. See, for example, James Robison, "'Star Wars' Called a Biblical Remake," *Chicago Tribune,* September 24, 1977.

27. John Dart, "Star Wars: Religious Impact in Parable Form," *Los Angeles Times,* May 1, 1978.

28. Ellen Goodman, "A Star Wars Fantasy Fulfillment," *Washington Post,* July 30, 1977.

29. "In 'Star Wars'…George Lucas Brings Space Fantasy to Life," *Kentucky New Era,* July 5, 1977.

30. Siskel, "'Star Wars' Flashes with Space Wizardry."

31. Bruce McCabe, "Star Wars Is a Blockbuster," *Boston Globe,* May 26, 1977.

32. "Fox's 'Star Wars' Heads for Hyper Space: First Day B.O., 255G; House Records Tumble," *Variety,* May 26, 1977.

33. *MOSW,* 295.

34. *MOSW,* 295.

35. Champlin, *George Lucas,* 79.

36. *MOIJ,* 19.

37. Champlin, *George Lucas,* 79.

38. Kaufman, who bickered with leading man Clint Eastwood, would lose this job almost immediately when he was removed from the director's chair by Eastwood, who opted to direct the movie himself.

39. Champlin, *George Lucas,* 79.

40. *MOSW,* 306.

41. "The *Star Wars* Phenomenon," *People,* July 18, 1977.

42. Arnold, *Once Upon a Galaxy,* 183.

43. Scanlon, "The Wizard of Star Wars"; Lee Grant, "Lucas: Feet on Ground, Head in the Stars," *Los Angeles Times,* December 10, 1977.

44. Vallely, "*The Empire Strikes Back* and So Does George Lucas."

45. George Lucas and Robert Redford, *The Power of Story: Visions of Independence at 2015 Sundance Film Festival,* January 29, 2015, https://www.youtube.com/watch?v=YX-9QCkwHiI.

46. Biskind, *Easy Riders,* 321.

47. J. W. Rinzler, *The Making of Star Wars: The Empire Strikes Back* (New York: Del Rey, 2010), 10 (hereafter *MOESB*).

48. Pollock, *Skywalking*, 199.

49. Biskind, *Easy Riders*, 341.

50. Robert Kerwin, "A Down-to-Earth Mark Hamill," *Chicago Tribune*, December 18, 1977.

51. Eric Dodds, "George Lucas Lost a $40 Million Bet to Steven Spielberg over *Star Wars*," Time.com, March 31, 2014.

52. *MOESB*, 52.

53. French and Kahn, "Inside the Magic Factory."

54. Pollock, *Skywalking*, 198.

55. Clouzot, "The Morning of the Magician."

56. "General Mills Wins Battle to Make 'Star Wars' Toys," *Wall Street Journal*, June 8, 1977.

57. D. Martin Myatt, "An Interview with Bernard Loomis," Rebelscum.com, http://www.rebelscum.com/loomis.asp.

58. Pamela G. Hollie, "Santa Brings I.O.U's for 'Star Wars' Toys," *New York Times*, December 15, 1977.

59. "Caught Short on Production: Star Wars Toys Lost in Time Warp," *Los Angeles Times*, September 30, 1977.

60. Pam Luecke, "'Star Wars' Toys Top Market, but 'Force' Needed to Find Them," *Hartford Courant*, December 21, 1977.

61. William K. Knoedelseder Jr., "Stairway to the 'Star Wars,'" *Los Angeles Times*, July 4, 1977.

62. *MOSW*, 224.

63. Bill Knoedelseder, "Merchandise Galaxy," *Los Angeles Times*, July 4, 1977.

64. Arnold, *Once Upon a Galaxy*, 198.

65. Robert Lindsey, "The New New Wave of Film Makers," *New York Times*, May 28, 1978.

66. Biskind, *Easy Riders*, 344.

67. Ibid.

68. "Coming December 27: English Barmy for 'Star Wars,'" *Los Angeles Times*, November 18, 1977.

69. See David Sterrit, "'Star Wars' Creating Worldwide Heroes,' *Christian Science Monitor*, December 14, 1977.

70. Kevin Klose, "'Star Wars' in Moscow," *Washington Post*, November 22, 1977.

71. The ad appeared in *Variety*, December 2, 1977.

72. Scanlon, "The Wizard of Star Wars."

73. Robert Kerwin, "Technical Wizardry Wins the 'Star Wars,'" *Chicago Tribune*, June 19, 1977.

74. See Earl C. Gottschalk, "'Star Wars' Sequels Waiting in the Wings," *Pocono Record* (Stroudsburg, Pa.), July 21, 1977.

75. *MOESB*, 12.

76. *MOESB*, 20.

77. *MOESB*, 22.

78. *MOESB*, 32.

79. *MOESB*, 21.

80. *MOESB*, 32.
81. *MOIJ*, 23.
82. Scanlon, "The Wizard of Star Wars."
83. *MOESB*, 36.
84. Ibid.
85. "The Star Wars Phenomenon."
86. *MOESB*, 39
87. *MOESB*, 40.
88. *MOESB*, 43.
89. *MOIJ*, 25.
90. Pollock, *Skywalking*, 207.
91. *MOSW*, 249.
92. *MOESB*, 54.
93. Pollock, *Skywalking*, 187.
94. Ibid., 191.
95. Ben Bova, "Letters," *Time*, June 20, 1977.
96. *MOSW*, 306.
97. Robert Lindsey, "The New Wave of Filmmakers," *New York Times*, May 28, 1978.
98. Robert Lindsey, "The 'New-Boy' Network Strikes Hollywood," *Chicago Tribune*, July 2, 1978.
99. Pollock, *Skywalking*, 197.
100. Biskind, *Easy Riders*, 340.
101. Baxter, *George Lucas*, 251.
102. Pollock, *Skywalking*, 200.
103. Stevens, *Conversations with the Great Moviemakers*, 321.
104. Biskind, *Easy Riders*, 340.
105. Scanlon, "The Wizard of Star Wars."
106. Clouzot, "The Morning of the Magician."
107. Stevens, *Conversations with the Great Moviemakers*, 315.
108. *COGL*, 125.
109. *MOESB*, 64.
110. *MOESB*, 22.
111. Frank DiGiacomo, "The Han Solo Comedy Hour!" *Vanity Fair*, December 2008.
112. Ibid.
113. *Empire of Dreams*.
114. Pollock, *Skywalking*, 208.
115. Champlin, *George Lucas*, 64.

Chapter 9: Darkening Skies

1. Baxter, *George Lucas*, 279.
2. *COGL*, 129.
3. Gary Arnold, "American Graffiti II: The Whole Gang's Made Good," *Washington Post*, May 27, 1978.

4. Gregg Kilday, "Lucasfilm Drafts Flicker for 'Murders,'" *Los Angeles Times,* December 16, 1978.
5. Baxter, *George Lucas,* 279.
6. Champlin, *George Lucas,* 59.
7. Baxter, *George Lucas,* 261.
8. *COGL,* 129.
9. Champlin, *George Lucas,* 60.
10. Gary Arnold, "'More American Graffiti': Not Necessarily," *Washington Post,* August 3, 1979.
11. Janet Maslin, "Screen: 'More American Graffiti' Covers '64 to '67," *New York Times,* August 17, 1979.
12. *COGL,* 129.
13. Arnold, *Once Upon a Galaxy,* 178.
14. *MOESB,* 219–23.
15. Baxter, *George Lucas,* 271.
16. Scanlon, "The Wizard of Star Wars."
17. David Lewin, "Can the Makers of Star Wars Do It Again?" *New York Times,* December 2, 1979.
18. *MOESB,* 131, 132.
19. Arnold, *Once Upon a Galaxy,* 162.
20. Ibid., 179.
21. To read the transcript of this fascinating conversation, see Arnold, *Once Upon a Galaxy,* 136–40.
22. Baxter, *George Lucas,* 274.
23. Chris Gore, "Gary Kurtz Interview: The Original Star Wars Producer Speaks," FilmThreat.com, March 5, 2000, transcribed at http://nightly.net/topic/1248-excerpts-from-gary-kurtz-interview.
24. *MOESB,* 206.
25. *COGL,* 127.
26. *MOESB,* 206.
27. Arnold, *Once Upon a Galaxy,* 176.
28. *COGL,* 125.
29. *MOESB,* 236.
30. "In Confidence: An Interview with Frank Oz," 2015, https://www.youtube.com/watch?v=0BN-l4r2eIA.
31. *MOESB,* 308.
32. Ryder Windham, Daniel Wallace, and Pablo Hidalgo, *Star Wars Year by Year: A Visual Chronicle* (New York: DK Publishing, 2012), 119.
33. Karen Paik, *To Infinity and Beyond! The Story of Pixar Animation Studios* (San Francisco: Chronicle, 2007), 19.
34. Gerald Clark, "The Empire Strikes Back!," *Time,* May 19, 1980.
35. Hugh Sidey, "The Presidency: To Dare Mighty Things," *Time,* June 9, 1980.
36. Janet Maslin, "Film: Robots Return in 'Empire Strikes,'" *New York Times,* May 21, 1980.

37. Vincent Canby, "'The Empire Strikes Back' Strikes a Bland Note," *New York Times,* June 15, 1980.
38. Taylor, "'Star Wars' Producer Blasts Star Wars Myths."
39. Judith Martin, "The Empire Strikes Back," *Washington Post,* May 23, 1980.
40. *MOESB,* 314.
41. O'Quinn, "The George Lucas Saga."
42. *MOIJ,* 28.
43. *MOIJ,* 36.
44. *MOIJ,* 26.
45. *COGL,* 133–34.
46. *MOIJ,* 33.
47. Champlin, *George Lucas,* 80.
48. *MOIJ,* 16.
49. *MOIJ,* 71.
50. *MOIJ,* 23.
51. There was also a debate over whether having the title "Lucasfilm" at the opening of the film constituted the producer inserting his name before the director's, another violation of guild policy.
52. Aljean Harmetz, "Burden of Dreams: George Lucas," *American Film,* June 1983.
53. *MOIJ,* 54.
54. *MOIJ,* 112.
55. *MOIJ,* 115.
56. *MOIJ,* 124.
57. *MOIJ,* 116.
58. Aljean Harmetz, "Lucas Gives $5 Million to U.S.C. Cinema," *New York Times,* November 20, 1980.
59. Diana Waggoner, "In Homage to the Master, George Lucas and Francis Coppola Unleash Their Clout for Kurosawa," *People,* October 27, 1980.
60. Champlin, *George Lucas,* 76.
61. Ibid., 88.
62. Ibid., 90.
63. Arnold, *Once Upon a Galaxy,* 208.
64. J. W. Rinzler, *The Making of Star Wars: Return of the Jedi* (New York: Ballantine, 2013), 19 (hereafter *MOROTJ*).
65. *MOESB,* 250.
66. *MOROTJ,* 19.
67. Richard Corliss, "Cinema: The New Hollywood: Dead or Alive?" *Time,* March 30, 1981.
68. Biskind, *Easy Riders,* 417.
69. Champlin, *George Lucas,* 83.
70. Aljean Harmetz, "But Can Hollywood Live Without George Lucas?" *New York Times,* July 13, 1981.
71. *MOROTJ,* 5.

72. *MOROTJ*, 4
73. *MOROTJ*, 5.
74. David A. Price, *The Pixar Touch: The Making of a Company* (New York: Vintage, 2009), 41.
75. *MOROTJ*, 118.
76. Geoffrey Boucher, "Did 'Star Wars' Become a Toy Story? Producer Gary Kurtz Looks Back," *Los Angeles Times*, August 12, 2010.
77. Taylor, "Star Wars Producer Blasts Star Wars Myths."
78. Boucher, "Did 'Star Wars' Become a Toy Story?"
79. Geoffrey Boucher, "'Star Wars' Sequel: Harrison Ford Open to Idea of Han Solo Role," *Entertainment Weekly*, November 5, 2012.
80. Boucher, "Did 'Star Wars' Become a Toy Story?"
81. *MOROTJ*, 11.
82. Taylor, "Star Wars Producer Blasts Star Wars Myths."
83. Boucher, "Did 'Star Wars' Become a Toy Story?"
84. Gore, "Gary Kurtz Interview."
85. *MOROTJ*, 9.
86. *MOESB*, 207.
87. *MOROTJ*, 42.
88. *MOROTJ*, 36.
89. Jon Phillip Peecher, ed., *The Making of The Return of the Jedi* (New York: Ballantine, 1983), 69.
90. *MOROTJ*, 46.
91. *MOROTJ*, 46.
92. *MOROTJ*, 16, 59.
93. *MOROTJ*, 64.
94. For a longer excerpt of the *Jedi* story conference, see *MOROTJ*, 62–77.
95. *MOROTJ*, 65.
96. Gerald Clarke, "Great Galloping Galaxies!" *Time*, May 23, 1983.
97. *MOROTJ*, 133.
98. *MOROTJ*, 115.
99. Vincent Canby, "Movie Review: 'Raiders of the Lost Ark,'" *New York Times*, June 12, 1981.
100. Richard Schickel, "Cinema: Slam! Bang! A Movie Movie," *Time*, June 15, 1981.
101. Roger Ebert, "Movie Review: 'Raiders of the Lost Ark,'" rogerebert.com.
102. Pauline Kael, "Whipped," *The New Yorker*, June 15, 1981.
103. Schickel, "Cinema: Slam! Bang! A Movie Movie."
104. Ebert, "Movie Review: 'Raiders of the Lost Ark.'"
105. *MOIJ*, 126.
106. "George Lucas" segment, *60 Minutes*, CBS, March 25, 1999.
107. *MOROTJ*, 151.
108. Peecher, *Making of The Return of the Jedi*, 38.
109. Scanlon, "George Lucas Wants to Play Guitar."
110. *MOROTJ*, 120.

111. Baxter, *George Lucas,* 332.
112. *MOROTJ,* 153.
113. *COGL,* 140.
114. *MOROTJ,* 152.
115. Scanlon, "George Lucas Wants to Play Guitar."
116. *MOROTJ,* 44, 138.
117. *MOROTJ,* 191.
118. *MOROTJ,* 201.
119. *MOROTJ,* 233.
120. Scanlon, "George Lucas Wants to Play Guitar."
121. Jenkins, *Empire Building,* 254.
122. Biskind, *Easy Riders,* 422.
123. Mitch Tuchman and Anne Thompson, "Lucas, Spielberg, and 'Raiders,'" *Film Comment,* July–August 1981.
124. Baxter, *George Lucas,* 333.
125. Clarke, "I've Got to Get My Life Back Again."
126. Jenkins, *Empire Building,* 253.
127. *MOROTJ,* 238
128. Biskind, *Easy Riders,* 422.
129. *MOROTJ,* 259.
130. *MOROTJ,* 233.
131. *MOROTJ,* 259, 260.
132. *MOROTJ,* 261.
133. *MOROTJ,* 264.
134. *MOIJ,* 130.
135. An investigation found that under-the-table payments had been made to skirt the laws on working with underage performers. All were acquitted or paid fines.
136. Baxter, *George Lucas,* 336–37.
137. Champlin, *George Lucas,* 100.
138. Scanlon, "George Lucas Wants to Play Guitar."
139. *MOROTJ,* 322.
140. Gary Arnold, "Return of the Jedi: Both Magical and Monstrous, the Star Wars Finale Is a Triumph," *Washington Post,* May 22, 1983.
141. Clarke, "Great Galloping Galaxies!"
142. Champlin, *George Lucas,* 96.
143. See *Nightline,* ABC, undated clip from 1983, archived at http://abcnews .go.com/Nightline/video/critics-spar-over-star-wars-trilogy-on-1983 -nightline-episode-18344732.
144. Scanlon, "George Lucas Wants to Play Guitar."
145. Clarke, "I've Got to Get My Life Back Again."
146. Rubin, *Droidmaker,* 317.
147. "George Lucas Getting a Divorce," *Baltimore Sun,* June 16, 1983.
148. "George Lucas" segment, *60 Minutes,* March 25, 1999.

149. Clarke, "I've Got to Get My Life Back Again."
150. Clarke, "Great Galloping Galaxies!"

Chapter 10: Empty Flash

1. Beth Ashley, "Success Took Toll on Lucas, but Studio Still Thrived," *San Bernardino County Sun,* October 6, 1985.
2. Aljean Harmetz, "'Star Wars' Is 10, and Lucas Reflects," *New York Times,* May 21, 1987.
3. McBride, *Steven Spielberg,* 355.
4. Bryan Curtis, "Temple of Gloom," *Grantland,* August 21, 2012.
5. Harmetz, "'Star Wars' Is 10, and Lucas Reflects."
6. Biskind, *Easy Riders,* 423.
7. Ibid.
8. The notable exceptions are the volumes in J. R. Rinzler's *Making of Star Wars* series, which, while sanctioned by Lucasfilm, struggle mightily, and for the most part successfully, to ensure that Marcia receives credit for her contributions to *Star Wars, Raiders of the Lost Ark,* and *Return of the Jedi.*
9. Biskind, *Easy Riders,* 423.
10. Aljean Harmetz, "Filming a Japanese Writer's Dramatic Life and Death," *New York Times,* December 30, 1984.
11. Gene Siskel, "And After 10 Years, Lucas Is Taking Break," *Chicago Tribune,* May 15, 1984.
12. Dale Pollock, "George Lucas Comes Back to Earth," *Los Angeles Times,* May 29, 1983.
13. *MOIJ,* 168.
14. Rob Smith, *Rogue Leaders: The Story of LucasArts* (New York: Chronicle, 2008), 12.
15. Steve Bloom, "The Empire Strikes Paydirt: Lucasfilm: How They Created the Incredible Ballblazer and Rescue on Fractalus," *Computer Games,* 1984.
16. Smith, *Rogue Leaders,* 25.
17. *MOROTJ,* 306.
18. "George Lucas on the THX Sound System," American Film Institute, November 20, 2009, https://www.youtube.com/watch?v=1RxI7Dqq1b8.
19. Hans Fantel, "In the Action with 'Star Wars' Sound," *New York Times,* May 3, 1992.
20. "George Lucas on the THX Sound System."
21. Rubin, *Droidmaker,* 317.
22. Pollock, "George Lucas Comes Back to Earth."
23. See Jon D. Hull, "Linda Ronstadt: New Album, New Look," *San Francisco,* April 1984.
24. "What's New with Linda Ronstadt? She's Singing Her Love Songs to Star Wars Czar George Lucas," *People,* March 26, 1984.
25. Clarke, "I've Got to Get My Life Back Again."
26. Rubin, *Droidmaker,* 335.

27. Letter to Maury Stompe, PEP Housing, from Jeremy Tejirian, Planning Manager, Marin County, June 23, 2015.
28. Michael Cieply, "Turning Point: George Lucas Moves to Produce TV Shows, Movies in Volume," *Wall Street Journal*, January 22, 1986.
29. *MOIJ*, 181.
30. Anita Kempley, "'Indiana Jones': No Fun on the Killing Ground," *Washington Post*, May 25, 1984.
31. *MOIJ*, 182.
32. Curtis, "Temple of Gloom."
33. Rubin, *Droidmaker*, 241.
34. Ibid., 241, 278.
35. Ibid., 338.
36. Ibid., 373.
37. Price, *The Pixar Touch*, 59.
38. John Korty, author interview.
39. Owen Williams, "Endor's Game: The Story of the Ewok Spinoff," *Empire*, September 2015.
40. Frank Megarelli, "PTS Presents Director's Chair with the Wheat Brothers," podcast, October 19, 2015.
41. Craig Hunter Ross, "Exclusive Interview: The Police's Stewart Copeland," *On Tour Monthly*, April 2014.
42. Harmetz, "But Can Hollywood Live without George Lucas?"
43. Rubin, *Droidmaker*, 394.
44. Ibid., 391–92.
45. Ibid., 395.
46. Cieply, "Turning Point."
47. Aljean Harmetz, "A Pained Lucas Ponders Attacks on 'Willow,'" *New York Times*, June 9, 1988.
48. Rubin, *Droidmaker*, 396.
49. Ibid., 261.
50. Ibid., 391.
51. Ibid., 336.
52. Ibid., 394, 398.
53. Rubin, *Droidmaker*, 410.
54. It chafes Alvy Ray Smith to this day that Jobs is generally perceived as having "bought" Pixar from Lucas. "The implication of 'buy' is to 'own and run,'" Smith says. "The implication of 'invest' is to own an interest in and let managers (ultimately responsible to the board) run [the company]. Pixar was of the second type. Use of the term 'buy' is a marketing ploy to make it seem that Steve was the single inspired genius who had all the ideas of Pixar and made it work. That's not how it worked. Not even close." While ownership of Pixar was initially split 70–30 between Jobs and Pixar employees, by 1994 Jobs would own the company outright. See "Pixar Myth No. 1: Steve Jobs Bought Pixar from Lucasfilm," http://alvyray.com/Pixar/Pixar Myth1.htm.

55. Lisa Vincenzi, "A Short Time Ago, on a Ranch Not So Far Away...," *Millimeter*, April 1990.
56. Denise Abbott, "George Lucas: His First Love Is Editing," *American Cinemeditor*, Spring 1991.
57. Charles Champlin, "The Last Maverick: Inside George Lucas's Empire," *Los Angeles Times*, May 15, 1988.
58. *COGL*, 147.
59. Kline, *GL Interviews*, 93.
60. Champlin, "The Last Maverick."
61. Beth Ashley, "George Lucas Is Ready to Roll Again with Films," *San Bernardino County Sun*, October 6, 1985.
62. Champlin, "The Last Maverick," 117.
63. Deirdre English, "A Conversation about rhe Movies: Dinner with Luddy," *Mother Jones*, December 1984.
64. Aljean Harmetz, "After 46 Years, Hollywood Revisits Oz," *New York Times*, June 16, 1985.
65. Champlin, "The Last Maverick," 112.
66. "Judge Asked to Bar 'Star Wars' in TV Ads," *Logansport Pharos-Tribune* (Ind.), November 26, 1985.
67. See opinion *Lucasfilm Ltd. v. High Frontier*, U.S. District Court for the District of Columbia, November 26, 1985.
68. See Chuck Philips, "Campbell Pays $300,000 in Skywalker Settlement," *Los Angeles Times*, September 26, 1990.
69. Matt Giles, "Why George Lucas Once Sued 2 Live Crew Front Man Luther Campbell," Vulture.com, January 3, 2016.
70. Ashley, "George Lucas Is Ready to Roll Again with Films."
71. Clouzot, "The Morning of the Magician."
72. Cieply, "Turning Point."
73. Richard Zoglin, "Cinema: Lights! Camera! Special Effects!" *Time*, June 16, 1986.
74. Cieply, "Turning Point."
75. William Scobie, "Lucas Strikes Back with His Secret Film Empire," *The Observer*, July 20, 1986.
76. Pat H. Broeske, "The Willow in the Wind," *Los Angeles Times*, May 15, 1988.
77. *COGL*, 150.
78. Aljean Harmetz, "'Star Wars' and Muppet Wizards Team Up in 'Labyrinth,'" *New York Times*, September 15, 1985.
79. Larry Mirkin, author interview.
80. Sue Martin, "'Star Wars,' Lucas Still a Force," *Los Angeles Times*, May 26, 1987.
81. "A Look Back at Howard the Duck," *Howard the Duck*, DVD (extra), 2009.
82. Bob Thomas, "Studios Say No to George Lucas," *St. Petersburg Times*, February 4, 1987.

83. See Thomas C. Hayes, "Disney, Lucasfilm Team Up: Holder Told of '85 Plans," *New York Times,* February 7, 1985.
84. *COGL,* 152.
85. Jack Mathews, "'Captain EO' Is Latest from Lucas; Film to Be Shown at Disney Parks," *Hartford Courant,* September 12, 1986.
86. Jordan Zakarin, "The Making of 'Captain EO': Lucas, Coppola, and Michael Jackson's Messy, Miraculous Disney Space Adventure," Yahoo Movies, December 9, 2015, https://www.yahoo.com/movies/the-making-of -captain-eo-lucas-coppola-and-162110246.html.
87. Richard Corliss, "Let's Go to the Feelies," *Time,* September 22, 1986.
88. Ibid.
89. Charles Solomon, "Movie Review: A Cosmic Journey in 'Born of Stars,'" *Los Angeles Times,* October 9, 1986.
90. Martin, "'Star Wars,' Lucas Still a Force."
91. Harmetz, "'Star Wars' Is 10, and Lucas Reflects."
92. Martin, "'Star Wars,' Lucas Still a Force."
93. Stephen J. Sansweet, "Lucas Speaks: 'Star Wars' Is a Rose Is a Rose...," *Wall Street Journal,* May 22, 1987.
94. "What's New with Linda Ronstadt?"
95. See Stu Schreiber, "Linda Ronstadt, to the Beat of a Different Drum," *USA Weekend,* November 28–30, 1986.
96. Sansweet, "Lucas Speaks: 'Star Wars' Is a Rose Is a Rose..."
97. Jonathan Schwartz, "The US Interview: Linda Ronstadt—Checking in with the Ex–Flower Child at Home in Tucson," *US Weekly,* December 25, 2000.
98. Pat H. Broeske, "But Meanwhile, 'Zone Wars' Go On," *Los Angeles Times,* May 15, 1988.
99. Donna Rosenthal, "The Dream and Its Men: Francis Ford Coppola and George Lucas Immortalize a Legendary Car and Its Own Inventor," *Sun-Sentinel* (Broward County, Fla.), August 14, 1988.
100. Robert Lindsey, "Francis Ford Coppola: Promises to Keep," *New York Times,* July 24, 1988.
101. Sansweet, "Lucas Speaks: 'Star Wars' Is a Rose Is a Rose..."
102. *COGL,* 158.
103. *COGL,* 159.
104. Lindsey, "Francis Ford Coppola: Promises to Keep."
105. Janet Maslin, "Glimpsing the Soul of an Old Machine," *New York Times,* August 12, 1988.
106. Lindsey, "Francis Ford Coppola: Promises to Keep."
107. Goodwin and Wise, *On the Edge,* 457.
108. Champlin, "The Last Maverick."
109. Malcolm L. Johnson, "Howard Fulfilling Fantasies with Extravagant 'Willow,'" *Hartford Courant,* May 20, 1988.
110. Janet Maslin, "Willow; A George Lucas Production," *New York Times,* May 20, 1988.
111. See Pat Broeske, "Weeping over 'Willow,'" *Los Angeles Times,* May 22, 1988.

112. Michael Cieply, "Lucas Hits Critics: Applause Greets 'Willow' at Cannes," *Los Angeles Times*, May 24, 1988.

113. "Statement of George Lucas, Chairman of the Board, Lucasfilm, Ltd.," *The Berne Convention*, U.S. Senate Subcommittee on Patents, Copyrights and Trademarks, February 18 and March 3, 1988.

114. See Lucas's testimony submitted for the record, ibid., 482–90.

115. Broeske, "But Meanwhile, 'Zone Wars' Go On."

116. Jett was named after James Dean's character, Jett Rink, in *Giant*.

117. Stevens, *Conversations with the Great Moviemakers*, 320–21.

118. "George Lucas" segment, *60 Minutes*, March 25, 1999.

119. Biskind, *Easy Riders*, 424.

120. Windham, Wallace, and Hidalgo, *Star Wars Year by Year*, 141.

121. *MOIJ*, 184.

122. *MOIJ*, 186.

123. *MOIJ*, 190, 209.

124. Peter Travers, "Indiana Jones and the Last Crusade," *Rolling Stone*, May 24, 1989.

125. Bob Thomas, "Lucas Brings Back His Golden Touch Again," *Indiana Gazette* (Pa.), May 27, 1989.

126. Ibid.

127. Karyn Hunt, "Business Leader G. W. Lucas Dies," *Modesto Bee*, December 19, 1991.

128. Vincenzi, "A Short Time Ago, on a Ranch Not So Far Away."

129. Bernard Weinraub, "Software: Rescuing Children from Boredom," *New York Times*, August 1, 1993.

130. Daniel Cerone, "Interactive 'Jones': George Lucas Dreams of Multimedia Adventures for 'Young Indiana Jones,'" *Los Angeles Times*, March 4, 1993.

131. Daniel Cerone, "Rethinking Indiana Jones: Lucas Picks Up Where Indy Began, Breaking TV's Rules in the Process," *Los Angeles Times*, March 1, 1992.

132. John J. O'Connor, "Meeting Indiana Jones as a Boy and a Teen-Ager," *New York Times*, March 4, 1992.

133. Cerone, "Rethinking Indiana Jones."

134. Four more episodes would be shown on ABC's Family Channel.

135. See "George Lucas Receiving the Irving G. Thalberg Memorial Award," Oscars YouTube page, uploaded November 24, 2009, at https://www.youtube.com/watch?v=USJNgbfnpQE.

136. George Lucas, acceptance speech on receiving the Irving G. Thalberg Memorial Award, March 30, 1992.

137. George Lucas interview, *Charlie Rose*, CBS, December 25, 2015.

138. "George Lucas Receiving the Irving G. Thalberg Memorial Award."

139. Charles Champlin, "The Home Audience Is Listening: Technology: George Lucas's THX Sound System Has Made Its Way from Movie Theaters to Living Rooms. Cheap It's Not," *Los Angeles Times*, May 30, 1990.

140. Andrew Pollack, "Computer Images Stake Out New Territory," *New York Times*, July 24, 1991.

141. McBride, *Steven Spielberg,* 420.
142. Thomas R. King, "Lucasvision: George Lucas, Creator of 'Star Wars,' Talks about the Convergence of Entertainment and Technology," *Wall Street Journal,* March 21, 1994.
143. McBride, *Steven Spielberg,* 420.
144. Richard Corliss, "They Put the ILM in Film," *Time,* April 13, 1992.
145. Chris Taylor, *How Star Wars Conquered the Universe: The Past, Present, and Future of a Multibillion Dollar Franchise* (New York: Basic Books, 2014), 288.
146. King, "Lucasvision."
147. Chris Hicks, "Film Review: 'The Tall Guy,'" *Deseret News* (Salt Lake City), December 7, 1990.
148. *COGL,* 182.
149. *Radioland Murders* press conference, Pasadena, California, October 8, 1994.
150. *COGL,* 182.
151. King, "Lucasvision."
152. Ibid.

Chapter 11: A Digital Universe

1. Lucas interview with Charlie Rose.
2. Laurent Bouzereau and Jody Duncan, *Star Wars: The Making of Episode I— The Phantom Menace* (New York: Ballantine, 1999), 105 (hereafter *MOE1*).
3. Bob Thomas, "Return to 'Star Wars': Filmmaker George Lucas Planning to Write, Prepare and Shoot Three Films at Once," *Santa Cruz Sentinel,* November 13, 1994.
4. Orville Schell, "A Galaxy of Myth, Money, and Kids," *New York Times,* March 21, 1999.
5. "Commitment to Women Earns Nod from Magazine," *Santa Cruz Sentinel,* September 14, 1994.
6. Orville Schell, "Film: 'I'm a Cynic Who Has Hope for the Human Race,'" *Time,* March 21, 1999.
7. Schell, "A Galaxy of Myth, Money, and Kids."
8. Martha Groves, "George Lucas and Film's Tech Revolution," *Los Angeles Times,* June 4, 1995.
9. Patrick Goldstein, "The Force Never Left Him," *Los Angeles Times,* February 2, 1997.
10. Pollock, *Skywalking,* 246.
11. Bernard Weinraub, "The Ultimate Hollywoodian Lives an Anti-Hollywood Life," *New York Times,* October 20, 1994.
12. Goldstein, "The Force Never Left Him."
13. Schell, "A Galaxy of Myth, Money, and Kids."
14. Goldstein, "The Force Never Left Him."
15. *MOE1,* 12, 18.
16. *MOE1,* 38.
17. Press conference for *Radioland Murders.*
18. Ibid.

19. David A. Kaplan, "The Force Is Still with Him," *Newsweek,* May 12, 1996.
20. Press conference for *Radioland Murders.*
21. Bruce Handy, "Cinema: The Force Is Back," *Time,* February 10, 1997.
22. Jody Duncan, *Mythmaking: Behind the Scenes of Attack of the Clones* (New York: Ballantine, 2002), 218 (hereafter *Mythmaking*).
23. Scanlon, "George Lucas Wants to Play Guitar."
24. Goldstein, "The Force Never Left Him."
25. The most recent remastered VHS release had been made from an interpositive of the film—essentially a print—rather than from the negative.
26. *COGL,* 183.
27. Alex Ben Block, "5 Questions with George Lucas: Controversial 'Star Wars' Changes, SOPA, and 'Indiana Jones 5,'" *Hollywood Reporter,* February 9, 2012.
28. *Star Wars* shooting script, May 15, 1976. Peter Mayhew, with considerable relish, posted the original pages of his *Star Wars* script on his Twitter feed in early 2015.
29. Hank Stuever, "George Lucas: To Feel the True Force of Star Wars, He Had to Learn to Let It Go," *Washington Post,* December 5, 2015.
30. Associated Press, "Lucas Talks as Star Wars Trilogy Returns," September 15, 2004.
31. Ken Plume, "An Interview with Gary Kurtz," IGN.com, November 11, 2002.
32. On November 30, 2015, while discussing *The Force Awakens* at a SiriusXM radio town hall meeting, director J. J. Abrams was asked whether *he* believed Han had shot first. His enthusiastic response: "Oh, hell yes."
33. *MOE1,* 105.
34. Claudia Puig, "'Star Wars' Appeal Is a Surprise Even to Creator Lucas," *Los Angeles Times,* February 4, 1997.
35. Jonathan McAloon, "Steven Spielberg Refused to Direct Star Wars Prequels," *The Telegraph,* November 26, 2015.
36. Wendy Ide, "Francis Ford Coppola: 'I May Only Make One More Film,'" *Screen Daily,* December 8, 2015.
37. *MOE1,* 75.
38. Biskind, *Easy Riders,* 424.
39. "A Jedi Trio," *Star Wars Insider,* October–November 1999.
40. Goldstein, "The Force Never Left Him."
41. Nicola Agius, "Michael Jackson Asked George Lucas to Cast Him as Jar Jar Binks in Star Wars," *Mirror* (UK), July 26, 2015.
42. *MOE1,* 51.
43. *MOE1,* 75.
44. *MOE1,* 78.
45. Brian Jay Jones, *Jim Henson: The Biography* (New York: Ballantine, 2013), 308.
46. *MOE1,* 88, 83.

47. See the documentary *The Beginning: Making Star Wars—Episode I*, Lucas-film, 2001.
48. *COGL*, 197.
49. *MOE1*, 77.
50. *COGL*, 201.
51. *MOE1*, 77.
52. *MOE1*, 93.
53. French and Kahn, "Inside the Magic Factory."
54. *MOE1*, 136.
55. Mark Cotta Vaz and Patricia Rose Duignan, *Industrial Light & Magic: Into the Digital Realm* (New York: Del Rey, 1996), 294.
56. *MOE1*, 134.
57. Kim Masters, "The Lucas Wars," *Time*, September 30, 1996.
58. See J. C. Herz, "Game Theory: 'Star Wars' World with a Sense of Humor," *New York Times*, October 29, 1998.
59. Bernard Weinraub, "Now Playing: Two New Minutes of 'Star Wars,'" *New York Times*, November 23, 1998.
60. See Adam Rogers, "The Phantom Media Blitz," *Newsweek*, November 14, 2001.
61. Weinraub, "Now Playing."
62. *COGL*, 207.
63. *MOE1*, 149.
64. Devin Gordon, "Waiting for Star Wars," *Newsweek*, February 28, 1999.
65. David Ansen, "Star Wars: The Phantom Movie," *Newsweek*, May 16, 1999.
66. Roger Ebert, "Star Wars—Episode I: The Phantom Menace," May 17, 1999, reprinted on rogerebert.com.
67. Adam Rogers, "The Phantom Media Blitz," *Newsweek*, November 14, 2001.
68. "Lucas Admits Star Wars 'Let Down,'" BBC News website, April 23, 2002, http://news.bbc.co.uk/2/hi/entertainment/1945447.stm.
69. Joe Morgenstern, "Our Inner Child Meets Young Darth Vader," *Wall Street Journal*, May 19, 1999.
70. Eric Harrison, "A Galaxy Far, Far Off Racial Mark?" *Los Angeles Times*, May 26, 1999.
71. Ross McDonagh, "'I've Done My Damage': Jar Jar Binks Actor Ahmed Best Confirms He Will Never Return to Star Wars," *Daily Mail*, January 12, 2016.
72. Plume, "Interview with Gary Kurtz."
73. Ian Freer, "George Lucas Interview," *Empire*, September 1999.
74. Schell, "I'm a Cynic Who Has Hope for the Human Race."
75. John Horn, "The Empire Bounces Back," *Newsweek*, April 28, 2002.
76. Drummond Pike, quoted in Patricia Leigh Brown, "Design Notebook: A Force in Film Meets a Force of Nature," *New York Times*, March 30, 2000.
77. Freer, "George Lucas Interview."

Chapter 12: Cynical Optimism

1. See George Lucas's remarks at Disney Legends ceremony, D23 Expo, Anaheim, California, August 14, 2015.
2. For those who need to know: Episode II would be shot with a Sony HDW-F900 24-P digital camera.
3. *COGL*, 233.
4. *Mythmaking*, 23.
5. *Mythmaking*, 17.
6. *COGL*, 216.
7. *Mythmaking*, 35, 50.
8. *Mythmaking*, 27.
9. *Mythmaking*, 36.
10. *Mythmaking*, 34.
11. *COGL*, 226.
12. *Mythmaking*, 64.
13. *COGL*, 221.
14. *Mythmaking*, 126.
15. *Mythmaking*, 204.
16. French and Kahn, "Inside the Magic Factory."
17. *COGL*, 227.
18. "The Chosen One," *Star Wars: Revenge of the Sith*, bonus featurette, DVD, 2005.
19. *COGL*, 231.
20. See "Census 2001 Summary Theme Figures and Rankings: 390,000 Jedi There Are," Office for National Statistics, United Kingdom, February 13, 2003. Also see "Jedi Knights Demand Britain's Fourth Largest 'Religion' Receives Recognition," *Daily Mail* (UK), November 16, 2006.
21. Schell, "I'm a Cynic Who Has Hope for the Human Race."
22. "Lucas Announces Episode II Title," abcnews.com, August 6, 2001.
23. Adam B. Vary, "Lucas Names 'Episode II,'" *Entertainment Weekly*, August 20, 2001.
24. J. W. Rinzler, *The Making of Star Wars: Revenge of the Sith* (New York: Ballantine, 2005), 15 (hereafter *MOE3*).
25. See Richard Verrier, "Paramount Stops Releasing Major Movies on Film," *Los Angeles Times*, January 18, 2014.
26. The three top-grossing films of 2002 were *The Lord of the Rings: The Two Towers*, grossing $936 million worldwide; *Harry Potter and the Chamber of Secrets*, grossing $878 million; and *Spider-Man*, earning $821 million.
27. A. O. Scott, "Film Festival Review: Kicking Up Cosmic Dust," *New York Times*, May 10, 2002.
28. Peter Travers, "Star Wars: Episode II: Attack of the Clones," *Rolling Stone*, May 16, 2002.
29. Roger Ebert, "Star Wars—Episode II: Attack of the Clones," May 10, 2002, rogerebert.com.

30. Travers, "Star Wars: Episode II: Attack of the Clones."
31. David Ansen, "Attack of the Groans," *Newsweek,* May 19, 2002.
32. Scott, "Film Festival Review: Kicking Up Cosmic Dust."
33. *Mythmaking,* 89, 91.
34. Patrick Goldstein, "Seclusion Has Left Lucas Out of Touch," *Los Angeles Times,* May 21, 2002.
35. Schell, "I'm a Cynic Who Has Hope for the Human Race."
36. *MOE3,* 27.
37. *MOE3,* 31, 35.
38. *MOE3,* 40.
39. Laura Holson, "Is There Life After Star Wars for Lucasfilm?," *New York Times,* May 1, 2005.
40. *MOE3,* 48, 51.
41. *MOE3,* 54–55.
42. *MOE3,* 57, 128.
43. *MOE3,* 19, 78.
44. *MOE3,* 74, 128.
45. *MOE3,* 82.
46. "George Lucas Accepts the AFI Life Achievement Award in 2005," American Film Institute, June 9, 2005, https://www.youtube.com/watch?v=lHvOSZi 3t14.
47. *MOE3,* 151.
48. *MOE3,* 151, 149.
49. *MOE3,* 165.
50. *MOE3,* 209.
51. Brian Braiker, "Putting the Hype in Hyperspace," *Newsweek,* April 7, 2005.
52. Ian Freer, "George Lucas Interview," *Empire,* September 1999.
53. Todd McCarthy, "Review: Star Wars: Episode III—Revenge of the Sith," *Variety,* May 5, 2005.
54. David Ansen, "The End of the Empire," *Newsweek,* May 15, 2005.
55. Sharon Wasman, "Lucas's New Headquarters Give Bay Area Film a Lift," *New York Times,* July 20, 2005.
56. "The AFI Life Achievement Award," http://afi.com/LAA/.
57. "George Lucas Accepts the AFI Life Achievement Award."
58. Ibid.
59. Ron Magid, "George Lucas Discusses His Ongoing Effort to Shape the Future of Digital Cinema," *Amerian Cinematographer,* September 2002.
60. Silberman, "Life after Darth."

Chapter 13: Letting Go

1. "George Lucas Accepts the AFI Life Achievement Award."
2. Schell, "A Galaxy of Myth, Money, and Kids."
3. George Lucas, interview with Lesley Stahl, *60 Minutes,* CBS, March 10, 2005.

4. *60 Minutes,* March 28, 1999.

5. Bryan Curtis, "George Lucas Is Ready to Roll the Credits," *New York Times Magazine,* January 17, 2012.

6. Bethany McLean, "Why Sheryl Sandberg, Bill Bradley, and Oprah Love Mellody Hobson," *Vanity Fair,* March 30, 2015.

7. Ibid.

8. Curtis, "George Lucas Is Ready to Roll the Credits."

9. "First Look: George Lucas Opens Up about His Relationship," oprah.com, January 2012.

10. Curtis, "George Lucas Is Ready to Roll the Credits."

11. Geoff Boucher, "George Lucas: 'Star Wars' Won't Go beyond Darth Vader," *Los Angeles Times,* May 7, 2008.

12. Holson, "Is There Life After 'Star Wars' for Lucasfilm?"

13. Smith, *Rogue Leaders,* 176.

14. Holson, "Is There Life After 'Star Wars' for Lucasfilm?"

15. Ibid.

16. Thomas R. King, "Lucasvision,"*Wall Street Journal,* March 21, 1994.

17. Dave Itzkoff, "Free to Follow His Heart Right Back to 'Star Wars,'" *New York Times,* June 29, 2008.

18. Ibid.

19. "Is the Force Still with Him?" *Variety,* February 13, 2005.

20. Ty Burr, "George Lucas Interview," *Boston Globe,* October 2005.

21. "Darth Vader's New Offices," *Newsweek,* June 26, 2005.

22. Associated Press, "Hasbro's Profit Gets a Lift from Sale of 'Star Wars' Toys," *New York Times,* February 7, 2006.

23. "The Month-Long Party Begins: Happy Birthday, *Star Wars,*" *Wired,* May 25, 2007.

24. *MOIJ,* 230.

25. *MOIJ,* 231.

26. *MOIJ,* 233.

27. "Interview with Frank Darabont," Lilja's Library: The World of Stephen King website, February 6, 2007, http://www.liljas-library.com/showinterview.php?id=38.

28. Ibid.

29. *MOIJ,* 236, 237, 283.

30. *MOIJ,* 244.

31. Terrence Rafferty, "Indiana Jones and the Savior of a Lost Art," *New York Times,* May 4, 2008.

32. Helen O'Hara, "Spielberg: More Indy & Jurassic Park," Empireonline.com, October 26, 2011.

33. *MOIJ,* 289, 292.

34. Richard Corliss, "A Conversation with George Lucas," *Time,* March 14, 2006.

35. Roger Ebert, "I Admit It: I Loved 'Indy,'" *Chicago Sun-Times,* May 19, 2008.

36. Manohla Dargis, "The Further Adventures of the Fedora and the Whip," *New York Times*, May 22, 2008.
37. Jennie Yabroff, "Culture: Indiana Jones 'Crystal Skull' Movie Review," *Newsweek*, May 18, 2008.
38. The five-day record at that point was held by Lucas, with *Revenge of the Sith* and its five-day take of $172.8 million.
39. Itzkoff, "Free to Follow His Heart Right Back to 'Star Wars.'"
40. Hartlaub, "In a Valley Not Far, Far Away."
41. Itzkoff, "Free to Follow His Heart Right Back to 'Star Wars.'"
42. Lucas interview with Charlie Rose.
43. Itzkoff, "Free to Follow His Heart Right Back to 'Star Wars.'"
44. Ibid.
45. Ibid.
46. Chris Suellentrop, "The Empire Goes Slack," *New York Times*, August 15, 2008.
47. Kimberly Nordyke, "'Star Wars' a Force for Cartoon Network," *Hollywood Reporter*, October 6, 2008.
48. Dana Goodyear, "Man of Extremes," *The New Yorker*, October 26, 2009.
49. Hartlaub, "In a Valley Not Far, Far Away."
50. Windham, Wallace, and Hidalgo, *Star Wars Year by Year: A Visual Chronicle*, 292.
51. The book was Alex Ben Block and Lucy Autrey Wilson's *George Lucas's Blockbusting: A Decade-by-Decade Survey of Timeless Movies Including Untold Secrets of Their Financial and Cultural Success*, which pretty much locks up the award for Longest Book Title of All Time.
52. *The Daily Show with Jon Stewart*, Comedy Central, January 5, 2010.
53. See Brian Gilmore, "The Best Internet Reactions to the Star Wars Blu-Ray Changes," Ranker.com, September 2011.
54. Devin Leonard, "How Disney Bought Lucasfilm—and Its Plans for 'Star Wars,'" *Bloomberg Businessweek*, March 7, 2013.
55. Elaine Dutka, "Lucas' Next Movie: Tuskegee Airmen," *Los Angeles Times*, August 11, 1990.
56. Weinraub, "The Ultimate Hollywoodian Lives an Anti-Hollywood Life."
57. Dutka, "Lucas' Next Movie: Tuskegee Airmen."
58. Curtis, "George Lucas Is Ready to Roll the Credits."
59. Ibid.
60. Eric Larnick, "Aaron McGruder of 'Boondocks' on Working with George Lucas and His Future in Comics," *Comics Alliance*, January 20, 2012.
61. Curtis, "George Lucas Is Ready to Roll the Credits."
62. Ibid.
63. *The Daily Show with Jon Stewart*, January 9, 2012.
64. Curtis, "George Lucas Is Ready to Roll the Credits."
65. Asawin Suebsaeng, "Airmen Deserved a Movie That's Not Completely Unwatchable," *Mother Jones*, January 21, 2012.
66. John Patterson, "Red Tails Offers the Best—and Worst—of George Lucas," *The Guardian*, June 1, 2012.

67. Curtis, "George Lucas Is Ready to Roll the Credits."

68. "Red Tails Salutes Tuskegee Airmen," *USA Today,* January 4, 2012.

69. Curtis, "George Lucas Is Ready to Roll the Credits."

70. See Sarah Ellison, "Meet the Most Powerful Woman in Hollywood," *Vanity Fair,* February 8, 2016; and Leonard, "How Disney Bought Lucasfilm."

71. Ellison, "Meet the Most Powerful Woman in Hollywood."

72. Richard Verrier and Ben Fritz, "Kathleen Kennedy to Helm Lucasfilm as George Lucas Phases Out," *Los Angeles Times,* June 2, 2012.

73. Leonard, "How Disney Bought Lucasfilm."

74. Dewayne Bevil, "Mark Hamill's Role in New 'Star Wars' Movie Began with Lunch in Orlando," *Orlando Sentinel,* May 16, 2014.

75. Ellison, "Meet the Most Powerful Woman in Hollywood."

76. Unless otherwise noted, information in this section is drawn from Devin Leonard, "How Disney Bought Lucasfilm — and Its Plans for 'Star Wars,'" *Bloomberg Businessweek,* March 7, 2013.

77. Windham, Wallace, and Hidalgo, *Star Wars Year by Year: A Visual Chronicle,* 134.

78. "Disney to Acquire Lucasfilm Ltd.," Walt Disney Company press release, October 30, 2012, https://thewaltdisneycompany.com/disney-to-acquire -lucasfilm-ltd/.

79. Zach Johnson, "George Lucas Marries Mellody Hobson: See Their Romantic Wedding Picture!" *Us Weekly,* June 25, 2013.

80. Ellison, "Meet the Most Powerful Woman in Hollywood."

81. Kerry A. Dolan and Luisa Kroll, eds., "Forbes 400," September 29, 2015, http://www.forbes.com/forbes-400/.

82. Leonard, "How Disney Bought Lucasfilm."

83. George Lucas to Giving Pledge, July 16, 2010, givingpledge.org.

84. John King, "Saying No Thanks to George," *Metropolis Magazine,* April 2014.

85. Ibid.

86. Associated Press, "George Lucas Fills in Details on Chicago Museum," October 18, 2014.

87. Chrisopher Zara, "Star Wars Museum: Rahm Emanuel Got Campaign Cash from Disney, George Lucas' Wife, before Pushing to Donate City Land," *International Business Times,* November 20, 2014.

88. Stuever, "George Lucas: To Feel the True Force of 'Star Wars,' He Had to Learn to Let It Go."

89. Mellody Hobson, "Statement: We Are Now Seriously Pursuing Locations Outside of Chicago," press release, May 3, 2016.

90. Jason Keyser, "Lucas Abandons Plan to Build Museum in Chicago After Lawsuit," Associated Press, June 24, 2016.

91. Brian Truitt, "Lucas' 'Magic' Lives On, at Home and On Screen," *USA Today,* January 12, 2015.

92. Austin Siegemund, "George Lucas to Attend 'Star Wars: The Force Awakens'

Premiere: 'He Really Liked It' (Exclusive)," *Hollywood Reporter*, December 4, 2015.

93. Jen Chaney, "George Lucas Delivered His Verdict on 'The Force Awakens,'" Vulture.com, December 7, 2015.

94. Lucas interview with Charlie Rose.

95. Siegemund, "George Lucas to Attend 'Star Wars: The Force Awakens.'"

96. Stuever, "George Lucas: To Feel the True Force of 'Star Wars,' He Had to Learn to Let It Go."

97. Lucas interview with Charlie Rose.

98. See Matt Kranis, "Steven Spielberg Reveals George Lucas's Role in 'Indiana Jones 5,'" MoviePilot.com, June 20, 2016, http://moviepilot.com/posts/3973492.

99. Stuart Silverstein, "Lucas Seeks to Produce Respect for Filmmaking," *Los Angeles Times*, October 5, 2006.

100. Curtis, "George Lucas Is Ready to Roll the Credits."

101. Ide, "Francis Ford Coppola: 'I May Only Make One More Film.'"

102. Sean Smith, "The King of the Worlds," *Newsweek*, June 26, 2005.

103. *COGL*, 251.

104. Mike Fleming Jr., "Star Wars' Legacy I: Five Iconic Directors Recall When George Lucas Changed Everything," *Deadline Hollywood*, December 18, 2015.

Select Bibliography

Books

Alinger, Brandon. *Star Wars Costumes*. New York: Chronicle, 2014.

Anderson, Kevin J., and Ralph McQuarrie. *The Illustrated Star Wars Universe*. New York: Bantam, 1995.

Arnold, Alan. *Once Upon a Galaxy: A Journal of the Making of The Empire Strikes Back*. New York: Ballantine, 1980.

Avni, Sheerly. *Cinema by the Bay*. Nicasio, Calif.: George Lucas Books, 2006.

Avni, Sheerly, and Steve Emerson. *Letterman Digital Arts Center*. Commemorative program. June 25, 2005.

Baxter, John. *George Lucas: A Biography*. London: HarperCollins Entertainment, 1999.

Biskind, Peter. *Easy Riders, Raging Bulls: How the Sex-Drugs-and-Rock 'n' Roll Generation Saved Hollywood*. New York: Simon & Schuster, 1998.

Bouzereau, Laurent. *Star Wars: The Annotated Screenplays*. New York: Ballantine, 1997.

Bouzereau, Laurent, and Jody Duncan. *Star Wars: The Making of Episode I—The Phantom Menace*. New York: Ballantine, 1999.

Champlin, Charles. *George Lucas: The Creative Impulse: Lucasfilm's First Twenty Years*. New York: Abrams, 1992.

Chen, Milton, ed. *Edutopia: Success Stories for Learning in the Digital Age*. San Francisco: Jossey-Bass, 2012.

Cowie, Peter. *Coppola: A Biography*. Revised edition. New York: Da Capo Press, 1994.

Davis, Warwick. *Size Matters Not: The Extraordinary Life and Career of Warwick Davis*. Hoboken: Wiley & Sons, 2011.

Duncan, Jody. *Mythmaking: Behind the Scenes of Attack of the Clones*. New York: Ballantine, 2002.

Friedman, Lester D., and Brent Notbohm, eds. *Steven Spielberg: Interviews.* Jackson: University Press of Mississippi, 2010.

Galbraith, Stuart, IV. *The Emperor and the Wolf: The Lives and Films of Akira Kurosawa and Toshiro Mifune.* New York: Faber & Faber, 2002.

Glintenkamp, Pamela. *Industrial Light & Magic: The Art of Innovation.* New York: Abrams, 2011.

Goodwin, Michael, and Naomi Wise. *On the Edge: The Life and Times of Francis Coppola.* New York: William Morrow and Company, 1989.

Hayes, David, and Jonathan Bing. *Open Wide: How Hollywood Box Office Became a National Obsession.* New York: Hyperion, 2004.

Hearn, Marcus. *The Cinema of George Lucas.* New York: Abrams, 2005.

Jenkins, Garry. *Empire Building: The Remarkable Real Life Story of Star Wars.* Secaucus, N.J.: Citadel, 1999.

Kaminski, Michael. *The Secret History of Star Wars.* Kingston, Ont.: Legacy, 2008.

Kenny, Glenn, ed. *A Galaxy Not So Far Away: Writers and Artists on Twenty-Five Years of Star Wars.* New York: Henry Holt, 2002.

Kline, Sally, ed. *George Lucas: Interviews.* Jackson: University Press of Mississippi, 1999.

Longworth, Karina. *Masters of Cinema: George Lucas.* New York: Phaidon, 2012.

McBride, Joseph. *Steven Spielberg: A Biography.* 2nd edition. Jackson: University Press of Mississippi, 2010.

Mecklenberg, Virginia, and Todd McCarthy. *Telling Stories: Norman Rockwell, from the Collections of George Lucas and Steven Spielberg.* New York: Abrams, 2010.

Paik, Karen. *To Infinity and Beyond! The Story of Pixar Animation Studios.* San Francisco: Chronicle, 2007.

Peecher, Jon Phillip, ed. *The Making of The Return of the Jedi.* New York: Ballantine, 1983.

Phillips, Gene D., and Rodney Hill, eds. *Francis Ford Coppola: Interviews.* Jackson: University Press of Mississippi, 2004.

Pollock, Dale. *Skywalking: The Life and Films of George Lucas.* Updated edition. New York: Da Capo Press, 1999.

Price, David A. *The Pixar Touch: The Making of a Company.* New York: Vintage, 2009.

Read, Piers Paul. *Alec Guinness: The Authorized Biography.* London: Simon & Schuster, 2003.

Rinzler, J. W. *The Making of Star Wars: The Definitive Story behind the Original Film.* New York: Del Rey, 2007.

_____. *The Making of Star Wars: The Empire Strikes Back.* New York: Del Rey, 2010.

_____. *The Making of Star Wars: Return of the Jedi.* New York: Ballantine, 2013.

_____. *The Making of Star Wars: Revenge of the Sith.* New York: Ballantine, 2005.

Rinzler, J. W., and Laurent Bouzereau. *The Making of Indiana Jones: The Definitive Story Behind All Four Films*. New York: Del Rey, 2008.

Rubin, Michael. *Droidmaker: George Lucas and the Digital Revolution*. Gainesville: Triad, 2006.

Salewicz, Chris. *George Lucas*. New York: Thunder's Mouth Press, 1999.

Schickel, Richard. *Spielberg: A Retrospective*. New York: Sterling, 2012.

Smith, Rob. *Rogue Leaders: The Story of LucasArts*. New York: Chronicle, 2008.

Smith, Thomas G. *Industrial Light & Magic: The Art of Special Effects*. New York: Ballantine, 1987.

Stevens, George, Jr. *Conversations at the American Film Institute with the Great Moviemakers: The Next Generation, from the 1950s to Hollywood Today*. New York: Vintage, 2014.

Taylor, Chris. *How Star Wars Conquered the Universe: The Past, Present, and Future of a Multibillion Dollar Franchise*. New York: Basic Books, 2014.

Vaz, Mark Cotta, and Patricia Rose Duignan. *Industrial Light & Magic: Into the Digital Realm*. New York: Del Rey, 1996.

Vaz, Mark Cotta, and Shinji Hata. *From Star Wars to Indiana Jones: The Best of the Lucasfilm Archives*. San Francisco: Chronicle, 1994.

Windham, Ryder, Daniel Wallace, and Pablo Hidalgo. *Star Wars Year by Year: A Visual Chronicle*. New York: DK Publishing, 2012.

Worrell, Denise. *Icons: Intimate Portraits*. New York: Atlantic Monthly Press, 1989.

Documentaries

American Masters: George Lucas: Heroes, Myths, and Magic. Directed by Jane Paley and Larry Price. PBS Television, 1993.

Biography: George Lucas: Creating an Empire. A&E Television, 2002.

Empire of Dreams: The Story of the Star Wars Trilogy. Directed by Kevin Burns. Bonus disc, *The Star Wars Trilogy*. DVD boxed set. Nicasio, Calif.: Lucasfilm, 2004.

Omnibus Special Edition: George Lucas: Flying Solo. BBC Television, 1997.

Movies on DVD

American Graffiti: Special Edition. Directed by George Lucas. Universal City: Universal Studios, 2011.

Howard the Duck: Special Edition. Directed by Willard Huyck. Universal City: Universal Studios, 2008.

Indiana Jones and the Kingdom of the Crystal Skull. Directed by Steven Spielberg. Hollywood: Paramount Home Entertainment, 2008.

Indiana Jones and the Last Crusade. Directed by Steven Spielberg. Hollywood: Paramount Home Entertainment, 2008.

Indiana Jones and the Temple of Doom. Directed by Steven Spielberg. Hollywood: Paramount Home Entertainment, 2008.

Labyrinth: Anniversary Edition. Directed by Jim Henson. Culver City: Sony Home Pictures Entertainment, 2007.

More American Graffiti. Directed by Bill Norton. Universal City: Universal Studios, 2003.

Raiders of the Lost Ark. Directed by Steven Spielberg. Hollywood: Paramount Home Entertainment, 2003.

Radioland Murders. Directed by Mel Smith. Universal City: Universal Studios, 2006.

Star Wars: Episode I—The Phantom Menace. Directed by George Lucas. Beverly Hills: 20th Century Fox, 2013.

Star Wars: Episode II—Attack of the Clones. Directed by George Lucas. Beverly Hills: 20th Century Fox, 2013.

Star Wars: Episode III—Revenge of the Sith. Directed by George Lucas. Beverly Hills: 20th Century Fox, 2013.

Star Wars: Episode IV—A New Hope. Directed by George Lucas. Beverly Hills: Fox Home Entertainment, 2006.

Star Wars: Episode V—The Empire Strikes Back. Directed by Irvin Kirshner. Beverly Hills: Fox Home Entertainment, 2006.

Star Wars: Episode VI—The Return of the Jedi. Directed by Richard Marquand. Beverly Hills: Fox Home Entertainment, 2006.

THX 1138: The George Lucas Director's Cut. Special edition. DVD. Directed by George Lucas. Burbank: Warner Home Video, 2004.

Tucker: The Man and His Dream. Directed by Francis Ford Coppola. Hollywood: Paramount Home Video, 2000.

Willow: Special Edition. Directed by Ron Howard. Beverly Hills: 20th Century Fox, 2003.

Index

About the Author

BRIAN JAY JONES is the author of the *New York Times* bestseller *Jim Henson: The Biography*. He worked for nearly two decades as a public policy analyst and speechwriter, and has a degree in English from the University of New Mexico. He lives in Maryland with his wife. He continues to believe that Han shot first.